ion:

8/10/-

Physical Properties of Molecular Crystals, Liquids, and Glasses

WILEY SERIES ON
THE SCIENCE AND TECHNOLOGY OF MATERIALS

Advisory Editors:
J. H. Hollomon, J. E. Burke, B. Chalmers, James A. Krumhansl

PHYSICAL PROPERTIES OF MOLECULAR CRYSTALS, LIQUIDS, AND GLASSES
  A. Bondi
FRACTURE OF STRUCTURAL MATERIALS
  A. S. Tetelman and A. J. McEvily, Jr.
ORGANIC SEMICONDUCTORS
  F. Gutmann and L. E. Lyons
INTERMETALLIC COMPOUNDS
  J. H. Westbrook, editor
THE PHYSICAL PRINCIPLES OF MAGNETISM
  Allan H. Morrish
FRICTION AND WEAR OF MATERIALS
  Ernest Rabinowicz
HANDBOOK OF ELECTRON BEAM WELDING
  R. Bakish and S. S. White
PHYSICS OF MAGNETISM
  Sōshin Chikazumi
PHYSICS OF III-V COMPOUNDS
  Otfried Madelung (translation by D. Meyerhofer)
PRINCIPLES OF SOLIDIFICATION
  Bruce Chalmers
APPLIED SUPERCONDUCTIVITY
  Vernon L. Newhouse
THE MECHANICAL PROPERTIES OF MATTER
  A. H. Cottrell
THE ART AND SCIENCE OF GROWING CRYSTALS
  J. J. Gilman, editor
SELECTED VALUES OF THERMODYNAMIC PROPERTIES OF METALS AND ALLOYS
  Ralph Hultgren, Raymond L. Orr, Philip D. Anderson and Kenneth K. Kelly
PROCESSES OF CREEP AND FATIGUE IN METALS
  A. J. Kennedy
COLUMBIUM AND TANTALUM
  Frank T. Sisco and Edward Epremian, editors
MECHANICAL PROPERTIES OF METALS
  D. McLean
THE METALLURGY OF WELDING
  D. Séférian (translation by E. Bishop)
THERMODYNAMICS OF SOLIDS
  Richard A. Swalin
TRANSMISSION ELECTRON MICROSCOPY OF METALS
  Gareth Thomas
PLASTICITY AND CREEP OF METALS
  J. D. Lubahn and R. P. Felgar
INTRODUCTION TO CERAMICS
  W. D. Kingery
PROPERTIES AND STRUCTURE OF POLYMERS
  Arthur V. Tobolsky
PHYSICAL METALLURGY
  Bruce Chalmers
FERRITES
  J. Smit and H. P. J. Wijn
ZONE MELTING, SECOND EDITION
  William G. Pfann
THE METALLURGY OF VANADIUM
  William Rostoker

Physical Properties of Molecular Crystals, Liquids, and Glasses

A. BONDI

Shell Development Company

John Wiley & Sons, Inc., New York · London · Sydney

Library of Congress Catalog Card Number: 67-26225
GB 471 O8766X
Printed in the United States of America

To my wife Edith who took on the family's communal responsibilities and thus let me commune with the molecules

Preface

The primary purpose of this book is the development of a methodology that should enable chemists and chemical engineers to relate certain physical properties of condensed phases to molecular structure—the chemist in order to guide the synthesis of compounds with specific physical properties and the chemical engineer in order to estimate property data required for process calculations on new substances. My ultimate purpose might have been the presentation of calculating schemes that would permit precise prediction of physical properties from molecular structure data alone. The physics of molecular condensed phases are not now and may never be known sufficiently well to allow attainment of that goal by tractable theoretical formulations.

Hence two paths were open for the present enterprise: one, the expansion of precision data of given compounds to produce high-precision tables of property data of their derivatives by the laborious, if strictly empirical, procedures used for the liquid phase data of hydrocarbons by API-Research Project 44; the other, to produce easily usable methods that yield less precise information rapidly but are based on sufficiently transparent physical reasoning to produce improvements of the order of approximation warranted by the needs. In this context it may be well to remember that some physical properties are more cheaply determined experimentally than they can be calculated, once the compound has been synthesized.

The second path has been selected as the more useful for the purposes outlined earlier. The method adopted is also one of extrapolation from known data, but it is based on the principle of similarity analysis. Available theory is used first to obtain experimentally accessible measures of the important properties, geometrical, force, and so on, of individual molecules. In the second step these molecular parameters are used under guidance of theory to make the physical properties and the state variables of interest dimensionless. The resulting plots of experimental data, an application of similarity analysis to molecular physics, form the basis of most of the correlations presented in this book.

The states of matter treated are molecular crystals, liquids, and glasses. The physical properties are the p-v-T and related thermal properties and those transport properties that yielded to the method of treatment chosen. Surface tension and adsorption (at the liquid/liquid and liquid/solid interfaces) and mass diffusion in the liquid state were not ready for inclusion in the present edition but should be ready for the second edition of this book.

Although, to my knowledge, no parallel summary of the properties of molecular crystals and glasses is available at present, there is a certain amount of overlap between the section on the properties of liquids and the excellent book *Physical Properties of Liquids and Gases* by R. C. Reid and T. K. Sherwood.[1] The extent of overlap is quite small, however, because the property correlations in the Reid–Sherwood book are largely restricted to those substances that can be characterized by T_c, p_c, or V_c, that is, to substances of comparatively low molecular weight. Instead the energy of vaporization and the van der Waals dimensions are used here as reducing parameters because of our primary interest in substances of higher molecular weight, the critical constants of which are experimentally inaccessible. Just enough overlap has been maintained between the two books, especially in the method catalog in Chapter 14, to permit a smooth switch from one to the other.

Molar refractivity (or polarizability) and dipole moment data are contained in Chapter 14 as means to estimate molar interaction energies, that is, as tools, but are not discussed separately because they are not properties of direct technological interest. Sections on optical and electrical properties have been omitted for the same reason. Only the dielectric loss has been touched on in the chapters on rotational diffusion. Future editions may contain a more detailed treatment of dielectric loss and of dc conductivity in all three condensed phases.

In spite of their obvious technological interest, phase nucleation and growth rate, as well as the closely related problems of material strength and fracture, have been omitted as falling outside the scope of the present book. They warrant, and have received, full-length presentation in separate monographs.

The structure of this book is obvious from the table of contents. Just enough background material has been presented in each chapter to establish contact with the generally available lore of the given area. In the sections on molecular crystals and glasses a more elaborate background was required because of the paucity of textbook information. The temptation to write a

---

[1] McGraw-Hill, New York, 1966 (2nd ed.).

new physical chemistry textbook has been carefully avoided. Therefore physical chemistry texts should be used with this book in course work.

I should be grateful for advice on any improvements required, especially for teaching purposes.

I am indebted to many past and present colleagues at the Emeryville Research Center of the Shell Development Company for the fruitful discussions that led to this work. Without the patient help of my secretaries, especially Mrs. Florence Jorgensen, the whole effort would have remained a pious wish.

A. BONDI

Emeryville, California
September 1967

ACKNOWLEDGMENTS

The following publishers and individual investigators kindly consented to the reproduction of illustrative material and, in the case of my own papers, to extensive text quotations: Academic Press, Inc., New York; the American Chemical Society; the American Institute of Chemical Engineers; the American Institute of Physics; the American Petroleum Institute; the Chemical Institute of Canada; Consultants Bureau, New York; Elsevier Publishing Company, Amsterdam; the Faraday Society; Harvard University Press, Cambridge, Massachusetts; Carl Hanser Zeitschriften Verlag, Munich; Dr. Th. Holleman, Amsterdam; Dr. R. W. Keyes, Pittsburgh, Pennsylvania; La Chimica e L'Industria, Milan; Dr. David McCall, Bell Telephone Laboratories, Murray Hill, New Jersey; Pergamon Press, Inc., New York; Physica, Leiden; the Physical Society of Japan, Tokyo; the Physical Society, London; Dr. W. Reese, Monterey, California; Dietrich Steinkopff Verlag, Darmstadt; D. Van Nostrand Company, Princeton, New Jersey; Professor Y. Wada, Tokyo; John Wiley and Sons, Inc., New York.

A. B.

Instructions for the User

I have foreseen at least three groups of users: chemical engineers, who want to estimate physical properties for process calculations; chemists, who want to guide product development work by an understanding of why (and how) the numerical magnitude of a given physical property depends on the details of molecular structure; and physical chemists, who want to establish the fit of a newly determined physical property datum into the existing scheme of nature.

For the assistance of the first two groups most correlations described in the text have been restated as estimating methods at the end of each major section. Because these methods have been used less widely than those based on the conventional corresponding states correlations, their reliability has not been tested as extensively. A quantitative statement of the likely error range of a given method would therefore have been misleading and has been omitted in most cases. (Advice on such experience by users will be gratefully received so that an improved second edition can be produced.) Section 15 should be consulted (before using this book for the first time) in regard to the suitability of the methods in the case at hand.

Because the same basic energy and molecular geometry information is required for nearly all methods given, the requisite molecular structure increments have been collected in Tables 14.1 to 14.16.

Substantial computational simplifications can be achieved when the properties of liquid mixtures have to be calculated by following the scheme outlined in Section 15.3 and the associated Table 15.2 of mixing rules for the molecular energy and geometry parameters. The properties of the entire plant stream should then be estimated like those of a pure compound with the calculated average molecular parameters.

The third type of user, the physical chemist, in search of rationalization of experimental data, is best advised to enter his data into the appropriate correlation in dimensionless form. Small deviations from the average curve are probably of little significance because of the approximate nature of all such correlations. Certain types of large deviation may have theoretically obvious reasons. If there is no obvious explanation for a large deviation, however, the investigator will be confronted with the alternative of re-examining the accuracy of the experimental data or believing that he has made a new discovery. Hopefully it is the latter.

If the property at hand is an equilibrium property, it—or its change with state variables—can be checked for internal consistency with other equilibrium properties of the same compound by the rules of thermodynamics. Some of these internal consistency checks are discussed in Section 15.4.

Transport property data of condensed phases, by contrast, cannot be subjected to any (rigorous) internal consistency check, so that the external consistency check represented by the fit to a generalized property correlation stands by itself.

All three groups of users should recognize that generalized correlations of the type attempted here at best reflect the understanding of the day they were printed. The only long-range value of the present work is therefore the demonstration of the efficacy of similarity in an otherwise almost intractable area of molecular physics. For compounds differing substantially in molecular structure from those used for the preparation of a given correlation curve the user would be well advised to develop a correlation curve specifically valid for—at least the closest analogs of—his own compound series.

Nearly all the methods in this book consist of simple arithmetical expressions that are easily incorporated into computer programs. No useful purpose seemed to be served by increasing the bulk of the book by inclusion of pathway graphs, flow diagrams, or FORTRAN statements of the recommended equations or equation sequences. The availability of standard formats for physical property computation subroutines in the APPES program obviates the need for any elaboration of that subject (see Ref. 1 of Chapter 15).

Contents

Physical Properties of Molecular Crystals, Liquids, and Glasses

I

Properties of Molecules

The following section deals exclusively with those features of molecules that are reflected in the physical properties enumerated in the Contents. With one exception (the first ionization potential), only ground-state properties of molecules determine the macroscopic properties of condensed phases. Transient excited species, such as free radicals, although of importance for the rate and direction of chemical reactions, are present in such minute concentrations that their effect on the bulk physical properties of the system can be ignored, particularly since there is no reason to believe that their physical properties are very different from those of their unexcited parent molecules.[1]

Those physical properties of condensed phases that are treated in this book are ultimately the manifestations of but three characteristic features of molecules: their size and shape; the forces acting between molecules; and, when the molecule is polyatomic, the internal rotational motions of the molecule. Bond stretching and bending vibrations affect condensed-phase properties in too few circumstances to justify their consideration in this introductory chapter.

1.1 SIZE AND SHAPE OF MOLECULES

The spatial extent of molecules is related to the electron density distribution on their outside. As this distribution trails off exponentially with the distance from the atom nucleus, the size of an atom or a molecule is not a definite magnitude but depends strongly on the forces involved. Interpenetration of electron clouds of molecules in contact is resisted by the Pauli exclusion principle; it is assisted by the attractive forces between the molecules and by

---

[1] Recent work by Czekella, et al., [7] suggests that the dipole moment of certain polar species may be much higher in the excited than in the ground state. This would, of course, change their volatility relative to their environment.

Table 1.1   van der Waals Radii of Light Elements as Function of
Their Chemical Combination (All in Å)

	H	F	Cl
Free atom (from gas-phase properties)	1.5		
Diatomic molecule X_2 (from gas-phase properties)	1.25	1.5	1.75
Attached to aliphatic carbon atom (x-ray diffraction)	1.2	1.40[a]	1.73[a]
Attached to aromatic carbon atom[b] (x-ray diffraction)	1.0	1.47	1.77
Negative ion	1.54	1.33	1.81

[a] From liquid-density correlation for n-alkyl monohalides.
[b] And in aliphatic perhalides.

the kinetic energy that the molecules possessed at the time of impact, hence depends on the temperature. In condensed phases we can neglect the last-named effect. Because of this delicate balance between electron density and intermolecular forces, the van der Waals radius (r_w) of light atoms is not an absolute property but depends on the bonding state in which it is held in a molecule, as shown by the examples in Table 1.1. Fortunately, these are extreme cases, and for most atoms r_w is nearly independent of the molecular environment. The relation between the electronic properties of atoms and their van der Waals radii is apparent qualitatively from the relation of r_w to the atom's position in the periodic table (Table 1.2) and has been expressed quantitatively through its relation to the first ionization potential [5].

The dependence of r_w on external forces is most clearly demonstrated by the data in Table 1.3, which gives the comparatively small value of nonbonded contact radii that occur within molecules in which the strong chemical forces and stiff chemical bonds squeeze neighboring nonbonded atoms into closer proximity than the weak intermolecular forces are able to do. The decrements in V_w caused by such crowding effects are listed in Table 14.17.

Table 1.2   Mean van der Waals Radii (in Å)[a]

Element					H	He
r_w					1.20	1.40
Element	B	C	N	O	F	Ne
r_w	...	1.70	1.55	1.50	1.47	1.54
Element	Al	Si	P	S	Cl	A
r_w	...	2.10	1.80	1.80	1.75	1.88
Element	Ga	Ge	As	Se	Br	Kr
r_w	...	...	1.85	1.90	1.85	2.02
Element	In	Sn	Sb	Te	I	Xe
r_w	...	...	...	2.06	1.98	2.16

[a] Only the most frequently used values for single-bonded forms of the elements are quoted here.

Table 1.3 Nonbonded Contact Radii Within Molecules[a]

Atom	H	C	N	O	F	Cl
Contact radius (r_c), Å	0.92	1.25	1.14	1.13	1.08	1.44
$r_c - b^{b}$, Å	0.62	0.48	0.47	0.47	0.44	0.45

[a] From L. S. Bartell, *J. Chem. Phys.* **32**, 827 (1960).
[b] b is the covalent-bond radius. Except for hydrogen, this difference suggests that on the average $r_c = b + 0.46 \simeq r_w - 0.30$ Å.

The electron exchange in covalently bound structures leads to the familiar shapes of molecules indicated by the schematic drawing in Figure 14.1, which shows the mode of calculation of molecule volumes and surface areas from bond distances, bond angles, and van der Waals radii. A collection of bond distances and van der Waals radii is presented in Tables 14.1 and 14.2. The van der Waals volume increment of a given atom is therefore a function of the atom(s) to which it is bonded, even if its radius were completely invariant. For convenience, the van der Waals volumes (V_w) and areas (A_w) of various atoms have been assembled in Table 14.1 for the important case of bonding to carbon. Nonbonded contact distances in x-ray crystallography yield only limiting values for r_w. Those values of r_w and V_w that were found compatible with observed density of the crystal at $0°K$, the liquid at the critical point, and the Lennard-Jones force constants of the gas have been adopted [5]. They are thus subject to further improvement or adjustment.

1.2 FORCES IN AND BETWEEN MOLECULES

The forces between molecules are largely determined by two kinds of interaction: the London dispersion forces and the forces between permanent electric dipoles. The London dispersion energy E_L, which results from the mutual attraction of correlated electrons in neighboring molecules, is most conveniently related to molecular properties in its original form or by the Slater-Kirkwood forms [16]:

$$E_L = -\frac{3}{4} U \frac{\alpha^2}{d^6} \quad \text{for like molecules,}$$

$$E_L = -\frac{3}{2} \frac{U_1 U_2}{U_1 + U_2} \frac{\alpha_1 \alpha_2}{d_{12}^6} \quad \text{for unlike molecules,}$$

$$E_L = -\frac{3e\hbar}{4m_e^{1/2}} \frac{\alpha^{3/2} N^{1/2}}{d^6} \quad \text{for like molecules,}$$ (1.1)

$$E_L = -\frac{3e\hbar}{2m_e^{1/2}} \frac{\alpha_A \alpha_B}{d^6 (\alpha_A/N_A)^{1/2} \times (\alpha_B/N_B)^{1/2}} \quad \text{for unlike molecules,}$$

where U is generally taken as the first ionization potential of the molecules, α is their polarizability, N is the number of valence electrons, and d is the distance between interacting atoms. In polyatomic molecules E_L is the sum of the contribution of all individual interactions of the neighboring molecules' constituent atoms. The polarizability α, in turn, depends directly on the electronic structure of the molecule because

$$\alpha_v \sim \sum \frac{A_i}{\nu_i^2 - \nu^2},$$

where A_i is the oscillator strength of the ith oscillator with absorption frequency ν_i. Thus the magnitude of U depends on the tightness with which the loosest electron of a molecule is bound to its orbital. Typical values of polarizability increments are given as refractivity in Table 14.1. Inspection of these data shows that there is a close relation between the forces that hold a molecule together and those acting between molecules. Combined with the van der Waals radii to give the closest distance of approach r_0, this information can be used to acquire a feel for trends in E_L with molecular structure, as shown by examples in Table 1.4, but the approximations made in the derivation of the equations are, as Pitzer has shown [16], too drastic to permit exact estimation of intermolecular force fields.

Table 1.4 Comparison of Experimental and Theoretical Heat of Sublimation of Various Simple Substances at 0°K (in kcal/mole)

Substance	L^0 (exp)[a]	L^0 (calc)[a,b]
Neon	0.45[c]	0.47
Argon	1.85[c]	1.92
Krypton	2.59[c]	3.17
Nitrogen (N_2)	1.78[d]	1.64
Oxygen (O_2)	2.20[d]	1.69
Methane	2.19[e]	2.42
Chlorine (Cl_2)	7.05[f]	7.18

[a] $L_0 = \Delta H_s$ at 0°K.
[b] Calculation from simple dispersion theory: F. London, *Trans. Faraday Soc.* **33**, 8 (1937).
[c] E. R. Dobbs and G. O. Jones, *Progr. Phys.* **20**, 516 (1957).
[d] Calculation from data in *Cryogenic Engineering*, R. B. Scott, New York (1959).
[e] E. Whalley, *Phys. Fluids* **2**, 335 (1959).
[f] Gmelin, *Handbuch der Anorganischen Chemie, Band Chlor.* Verlag Chemie, Berlin, 1927.

In dealing with the dispersion forces between larger polyfunctional molecules, we should remember that (because of the geometrical averaging of dispersion force interactions) the interactions between like groups are always somewhat larger than those between unlike groups. Such molecules can therefore never be expected to be packed in random arrangement even in the liquid state [12].

An important feature of dispersion forces between polyatomic molecules is their strong dependence on the angle between the axes of neighboring molecules if the polarizability of the intramolecular bonds is anisotropic. Detailed calculation by means of London's relations [10] shows that the intermolecular attraction in specific orientations of typically anisotropic polarizability ellipsoids can be as much as 1.8 times larger and some others much smaller than their average attractive interaction.[1] The consequences of this phenomenon for various condensed-phase properties have so far been explored only sketchily, in part because of the cumbersome calculations and in part because of the paucity of reliable polarizability anisotropy data. The quantitative effect of polarizability anisotropy on the barrier to internal rotation and on the energy of rotational isomerization in the liquid compared with gaseous state might be important but have so far been estimated only crudely in a single case. More work is clearly needed here.

The directionality of the orientation interaction of permanent electrical dipoles is primarily reflected in the magnitude (and sign) of factor B in the dipole energy (E_D) relation

$$E_D = -\frac{B\mu^2}{d^3} \quad \text{at closed Distances, and}$$

$$E_D = -\frac{B\mu^4}{d^6 kT} \quad \text{at larger Distances,}$$

(1.2)

where μ is the dipole moment of the interacting group or molecule. For the average attractive configuration of molecules in liquids (or dense gases) $B = \frac{2}{3}$; for chain arrangement in attractive configurations $B = 2$; in repulsive configuration, $B = -2$.

The macroscopic dipole moment of a polyfunctional molecule is the resultant of the vectorial addition of all the group moments in the molecule. Hence in bulk electrical properties a symmetrical molecule, such as p-dichlorobenzene, exhibits a zero dipole moment, whereas the corresponding o-isomer has a high dipole moment. On molecular scale, however, the individual dipoles interact. Most physical properties depend on such local interaction. The macroscopic dipole moment of a molecule is therefore a poor

[1] Calculations of this orientation effect in J. Chem. Phys. 14, 591 (1946), Figure 1, should not be used because they are marred by an arithmetic error.

Table 1.5 Comparison of Standard Energy of Vaporization Increment of Electrostatically Repulsive Tightly Covered "Percompounds" with that of Ordinary Compounds (all in kcal/mole)

Group	E_V° of "Percompounds"	Ordinary Nonpolar[a]		Polar Compounds[a]	
—F	0.60	(F_2)	0.80	(R—F)	2.4
—Cl	2.05	(Cl_2)	2.6	(R—Cl)	3.5
—Br	2.80	(Br_2)	3.7	(R—Br)	4.0
—I	4.60	(I_2)	4.9	(R—I)	5.4
—NO_2	2.41	$(NO_2)_2$	4.57	(R—NO_2)	6.1
—C≡N	(3.)[b]	(C≡N)$_2$	3.26	(R—C≡N)	5.2

[a] Comparison compound in parentheses.
[b] Rough estimate from sublimation data.

guide to physical properties. This was first illustrated by Hildebrand's solubility experiments with the three isomeric dichlorobenzenes, all of which exhibit the same activity coefficients in solution irrespective of the large differences in macroscopic dipole moment [9].

Interactions between molecules of the type CX_4 or C_nX_{2n+2} with large permanent electric dipole moments in the C—X bonds differ from those between other types of molecules because electrostatic repulsion reduces the London force attraction during the frequent C—X $\cdots$ X—C contacts. Hence in such compounds the energy of vaporization contribution per —X group is low (Table 1.5). A systematic analysis of the manifestations of this repulsion effect in physical properties has yet to be made.

Molecular structure thus affects the magnitude of dipolar interaction energy in three ways: by its effect on the magnitude of the dipole moment [20], the steric arrangements that may or may not permit mutual orientation of the interacting dipoles at optimum angles, and the size of the van der Waals radii of the interacting atoms, for they determine the minimum possible distance of approach. The last factor is probably the most important one because of the high inverse power with which the distance enters the dipole-energy relations. The large diameter of the higher halide atoms thus precludes a significant contribution of the dipole energy to the total interaction energy of organic halides in spite of their high dipole moments. The special case in which dipoles can interact over very short distances (namely, when one end of the polar group is a hydrogen atom) is discussed under the heading "Hydrogen Bonds."

Approach of a permanent electrical dipole to a nonpolar molecule causes a small distortion of the latter's electron cloud and thereby induces a temporary dipole in the nonpolar molecule. The interaction with this induced dipole is also attractive but generally very small and can be neglected in approximate calculations.

The equations given for E_L above are first-order approximations for spherical molecules; the higher order terms in r^{-8} and r^{-10}, representative of quadrupole and octupole interactions, have been omitted. The total interaction energy also contains a repulsion term that is proportional to the degree of charge density interpenetration

$$E_r = A \exp\left(\frac{-bd}{d_w}\right)$$

for the constants A and b of which numerous data are now available [18]; b is generally ≈ 13.5. A fortunate accident of nature has provided that at the usual intermolecular distances in liquids the repulsion term is often nearly equal but opposite in sign to the contribution of the neglected higher order attraction terms. Hence for crude estimates of the effect of changes in molecular structure on molecular interaction energies, $E_L + E_D$ is often a sufficiently good approximation. Typical values of E_L and E_D are given in the discussions of the energies of sublimation and vaporization.

The *hydrogen bond* is the rather specific type of interaction between certain groups A—H $\cdots$ B. Its contribution to the cohesive energy of condensed systems is usually larger than predicted by the dipole orientation energy (Table 1.6). At present its magnitude cannot be predicted accurately from a priori reasoning, primarily because its nature is only beginning to be understood. Considering the vast amount of work on this subject, excellently reviewed by Pimentel and McClelland [15], this is rather disheartening. The amount of information available, however, is sufficient to furnish a large catalog of correlatable information, which is referred to in every section of this book. The chemical conditions for the formation of hydrogen bonds can be stated empirically: atom A, of A—H $\cdots$ B, the proton donor, can be an atom such as O or N, with a set of paired electrons, one substantially more electronegative than hydrogen, or even a carbon atom with sharply reduced electron density, as in X_3CH, N$\equiv$C—H, —C$\equiv$C—H groups, where X = halogen atoms. Atom B, the proton acceptor, is most often O or N. When these hydrogen bonds occur within rather than between molecules, their effect on physical properties is usually nil, that is, the molecule has the same properties as if the group A—H $\cdots$ B where just two (methyl or) methylene groups [3]. Any tendency to form such intramolecular hydrogen bonds even part of the time sharply reduces the effect of hydrogen bonding on most physical properties.

In keeping with the chemical nature of the phenomenon, a correlation is obtained if the hydrogen-bond contribution to the heat of sublimation of group AH is plotted against the electronegativity of A, as shown on Figure 1.1.

Table 1.6 Dipole Interaction Energy of Hydrogen-Bonded Substances [4]

Substance	μ^a (D)	$d_w,^b$ (Å)	$\dfrac{2}{3}\dfrac{\mu^{2\,c}}{d_w^{3}}$ (kcal/mole)	$2\dfrac{\mu^{2\,d}}{d_w^{3}}$ (kcal/mole)	X	$H_s(X)$ (kcal/mole)	$\delta_s(X)^e$ (kcal/mole)
Me_2NH	1.02	2.75	0.48	1.06	NH	4.56	2.65
		3.05					
$MeNH_2$	1.23	2.75	0.69		NH_2	6.40	3.95
		3.05		1.52			
Phenyl NH_2	1.48	2.75	1.01		NH_2		
		3.05		2.22			
MeOH	1.80	2.75	$\cdots$	3.60	OH	8.20	5.75
Phenols					OH	6.4–7.2	4.0–4.6

[a] Dipole moments from C. P. Smyth, [20].
[b] The distance 2.75 Å corresponds to parallel alignment of two adjacent NH groups, whereas the 3.05 Å is the well-established minimum distance in (chainlike) hydrogen bonding configuration (see J. M. Robertson, *Organic Crystals*, Cornell University Press Ithaca, New York, 1957).
[c] Parallel alignment of dipoles.
[d] Chain alignment of dipoles.
[e] Here and elsewhere $\delta_s(X) = \Delta H_s(\text{polar cpd}) - \Delta H_s(\text{nonpolar homomorph})$.

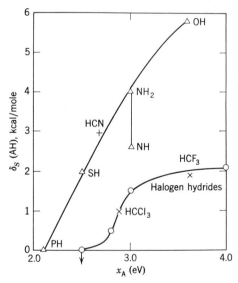

Figure 1.1 Hydrogen bond contribution $\delta_S(AH)$ to the heat of sublimation as function of the electronegativity (x_A) of atom A.

1.3 MOLECULAR INTERACTIONS IN INORGANIC SYSTEMS

Inorganic substances form molecular crystals and liquids instead of continuous ionic networks only if the following conditions are met:

1. All coordination sites of the metal ion are occupied by monovalent ions, functional groups, or a polydentate ligand.

2. If condition 1 is not met entirely, continuous ion-network formation can still be inhibited by steric effects; that is, by an umbrella-shaped ligand.

3. At least 80% of the van der Waals area of the metal ion must be covered by the ligand atoms, that is, the shielding ratio $A_r > 0.8$, if

$$A_r = \frac{N_x}{4}\left(1 - \frac{m^2}{r^2}\right) \quad \text{if} \quad r_2 > l, \tag{1.3}$$

or

$$A_r = \frac{N_x}{4}\left(\frac{r_1}{r_2}\right)^2 \quad \text{if} \quad l \geq r_2, \tag{1.4}$$

where N_x is the number of halogen atoms per molecule; r_1, r_2 are the van der Waals radii of halogen and central atoms, respectively, l is the bond distance between halogen and central atom, and $m = (r_2^2 - r_1^2 + l^2)/2l$. As suggested in Chapter 14 the van der Waals radius of metal atoms may be approximated as $r_2 \sim 0.735 \times 10^{-8} [R]_\infty^{1/3}$, where $[R]_\infty$ is the refractivity increment of the metal shown in Table 14.4.

The fact that condition 3 is insufficient is demonstrated by the following example: planar or nearly planar coordination of the stoichiometric number of halogen atoms, as in the tetra(chlorides, bromides, and iodides) of the lanthanide or actinide metals, leaves enough coordination sites for continuous (ionic) association although $A_r > 0.8$.

Hence the structure of the inorganic compound must be known before we can assume that it forms a molecular crystal or liquid. The detailed structure of the compound in the condensed phase must be known before the appropriate physical property correlations can be applied. These correlations are applicable only if the structure is independent of temperature, that is, does not dissociate in the temperature range under consideration. Specifically, the correlation has to be used for Al_2Br_6, not $AlBr_3$, or $Al_4(OEt)_{12}$, not $Al(OEt)_3[6]$, etc. Because of the paucity of data, little experience has been gained so far in the use of physical property correlations for inorganic molecular crystals and liquids. In the few cases tried they have worked.

1.4 RELATION OF MEASURABLE ENERGY QUANTITIES TO INTERMOLECULAR FORCES

Two energy quantities are of primary importance in this book: the heat of sublimation $\Delta H_s'$ (at the lowest first-order solid phase transition), a measure of the lattice energy of solids, and the standard energy of vaporization $E°$ (at the temperature at which $V^* = 1.70$). Because of the steepness of the force–distance relations, only the closest intermolecular contact distances are important. In crystals these distances are, almost by definition, the van der Waals, $d_w(AB) = r_w(A) + r_w(B)$. In liquids these distances are far less clearly defined. In nonpolar liquids we may set $d_w(AB) \approx r_w(A) + r_w(B) + (V_w/A_w)(V^* - 1)$ and find surprisingly close agreement between $(\Delta H_s/E°)$ (observed) and $[d_w \text{ (liq)}/d_w \text{ (solid)}^6]$. In polar liquids we may assume that closest approach distances between polar groups are the same as in the solid, an assumption that is supported by the comparatively small fractional differences between $H_s(X)$ and $E°(X)$.

To convert the pairwise interactions E_L and E_D into the heat of sublimation we must sum over all relevant distances in the crystal. Such a summing procedure would be far too cumbersome for the semiquantitative correlation of heat of sublimation increments with molecular constants and, for the inverse procedure, the rough estimate of such increments from molecular

Table 1.7 Approximate Contribution of Dispersion Energy and Dipole Orientation Energy to the Standard Heat of Sublimation Increments of Organic Halides [4]

Halide	Radical	$E_L{}^a$ (kcal/mole)	$E_L{}^b$ (kcal/mole)	$E_D + E_L$ (kcal/mole)	$H_L(X)$, (kcal/mole)
F	1-n-Alkyl	0.92	1.78	2.70	2.73[c]
	Phenyl (mono)	0.82	1.07	1.89	1.90
	n-Alkyl perfluoride	0.68	0 to −1.2	<0.68	$0.74 + \dfrac{1.70}{N_F}$
Cl	1-n-Alkyl	2.16	1.50	3.66	4.22[c]
	Vinyl	2.05	0.73	2.78	3.1[d]
	Phenyl	2.03	0.94	2.97	3.5
Br	1-n-Alkyl	2.76	1.31	4.07	4.93[c]
	Phenyl	2.33	0.87	3.20	4.28
	Perbromides	2.10	0 to −1.0	<2.10	3.3
I	1-n-Alkyl	3.67[e]	1.12	4.79	6.52[e]
	Phenyl	3.40[e]	0.72	4.13	5.03
	Periodides	>2.6			4.6

[a] Following the recommendation by K. S. Pitzer [*Adv. Chem. Phys.* **2**, 59 (1959)], the dispersion energy was calculated by means of the London formula using the polarizability data and the affective ionization potentials recommended by Pitzer. The sum of the van der Waals radii was taken as the closest approach distance in the solid state.

[b] In the absence of sufficient crystal structure information regarding the exact relative position of the C—X dipoles, the dipole orientation energy was taken simple as $E_D \approx \mu^2/d_w{}^3$. The group moment for ethyl groups was used for μ of alkyl halides.

[c] This is $H_s(X)$ for the ethyl halides.

[d] This is $H_s(Cl)$ for vinylidene chloride, no other datum being available.

[e] Used the polarizability recommended by Ketelaar = 5.61×10^{-24} cm^3/molecule.

Table 1.8 Dipole Interaction Energy E_p and Dispersion Energy Contribution E_{disp} to the Heat of Sublimation Increment of Ethers and Carbonyl Compounds [4]

Substance	μ (D)	d_w (Å)	E_D (kcal/mole)	E_L[a] (kcal/mole)	$E_D + E_L$ (kcal/mole)	$H_s(X)$ (kcal/mole)	$\delta_s(X)$ (kcal/mole)
Aliphatic ether							
(Me)	1.30	3.32	0.45	2.4	2.9	2.7	
(Et)	1.22		0.40		2.8	2.2	
Diphenyl ether	1.14	3.29	0.35	2.3	2.7[b]	2.0	
			−0.35	1.8	1.4[b]		
Ethylene oxide	1.88	3.32	0.95	2.4	3.4	4.1	
Furan	0.69	3.29	0.13	2.3	2.4[b]	1.6	
			−0.13	1.8	1.7[b]		
Acetaldehyde	2.72	3.20[c]	2.33			6.40	2.3
Propionaldehyde	2.73	3.20[c]	2.35			...	...
Benzaldehyde	3.10	3.20[c]	3.02			7.1	2.8
Acetone	2.84	3.20[c]	2.53			5.63	2.2
Methyl ethyl ketone	2.78	3.20[c]	2.43			5.17	1.7
Acetophenone	3.00	3.20[c]	2.84				

[a] The dispersion energy has been estimated from the attractive terms only by means of the relation

$$\frac{u(O/CH_2)}{u(CH_2/CH_2)} \cdot H_s(CH_2) = E_L,$$

when $u(a/b) = \alpha_a \cdot \alpha_b / d_w [(\alpha_a/N_a)^{1/2} + (\alpha_b/N_b)^{1/2}]$.
[b] The upper line is based on attractive configuration of the dipoles in adjacent layers, the lower line is for the repulsive configuration

```
    R   R
    |   |
    O   O
    |   |
    R   R.
```

[c] Corresponds to parallel alignment of carbonyl dipoles in attraction configuration.

constants. Instead we assume that for a given group (or molecule) the ratio $\Delta H_s(X)/E_L(X)$ is the same as the ratio $H_s(Y)/E_L(Y)$ for the equistructural hydrocarbon or hydrocarbon fragment. The constants α_i are readily available from molecular refractivity data, N_i are known, and for d_{AB} we use the sum of the appropriate van der Waals radii.

The magnitude of the dipole contribution $E_D = N_A B \mu^2 / d_{AB}^3$ is estimated for the known orientation (if x-ray diffraction data are available) or for the most probable orientation as judged from packing molecular models or from scale drawings. Comparison of results obtained by calculation for several dipole orientations with observed heats of sublimation often suggests the most probable magnitude of the dipole effects in a given class of compounds.

For molecules with permanent dipoles attached to different carbon atoms E_D is calculated separately for each dipole by using the group dipoles given by Smyth [20] and is never calculated by using macroscopically observed vector sums of the various dipoles in the molecule. The underlying assumption is that dipoles interact as point dipoles at the close range prevailing in crystals. This assumption is put to a severe test when we consider such extended

Table 1.9 Sum of Dispersion and Dipole Contributions to the Heat of Sublimation Increments of Sulfides [4]

Substance	μ (D)	d_w (Å)	E_D (kcal/mole)	E_L (kcal/mole)	$E_D + E_L$ (kcal/mole)	$H_s(\cdot S\cdot)$ (kcal/mole)
Aliphatic thioethers	1.40	3.8[a]	0.35	4.2	4.5	4.5–5.1
Aliphatic disulfides	1.40[b]	3.8[a]	~0[c]	5.9[d]	5.9	3.2–4.0
		3.8	−0.4[e]	7.7[e]	7.3	
Thiophene	0.50	3.60	0.06	5.4[f]	5.5	3.9

[a] Assuming $r_w = 2.0$ for the methylene group.

[b] This is the C—S bond moment. The macroscopic dipole moment of alkyl disulfides is 1.96 D (see L. M. Vivshan, G. Gorin, and C. P. Smyth, *J. Am. Chem. Soc.* **72**, 477 (1950).

[c] In staggered configuration there is no dipole–dipole interaction possible, only dipole–polarizability interaction, which is negligible in magnitude compared with the dispersion energy.

[d] This is the average of S $\cdots$ S and S $\cdots$ CH$_2$ attraction.

[e] In nonstaggered configuration the dipoles repel each other and the sulfur atoms interact primarily with each other.

[f] The large discrepancy between this figure and $H_s(S)$ may be due to a somewhat greater separation of molecules in the crystal from 3.6 Å.

Table 1.10 Dipole Interaction Energy of the Cyano Group in Crystalline Cyanides [4]

Substance	μ[a] (D)	d_w, (Å)	$\dfrac{2}{3}\dfrac{\mu^2}{d_w{}^3}$ (kcal/mole)	$H_s^\circ(\cdot C\equiv N)$ (kcal/mole)	$\delta_s^\circ(\cdot C\equiv N)$ (kcal/mole)
Me—C≡N	3.40	3.30	3.09	8.37	3.6
Et—C≡N	3.57	3.30	3.40	7.23	2.4
Phenyl—C≡N	4.39	3.30	5.15	—	—

[a] Dipolements from C. P. Smyth, [20].

Table 1.11 Dipole Interaction Energy of the Nitro and Nitroxo Dipoles in Solids [4]

Substance	μ[a] (D)	d_w (Å)[b]	$\dfrac{2}{3}\dfrac{\mu^2}{d_w{}^3}$ (kcal/mole)	$H_s(X)$ (kcal/mole)	$\delta_s(X)$ (kcal/mole)
Nitro methane	3.50	3.05	4.13	9.66	3.73
Nitro ethane	3.68	3.05	4.58	—	—
Nitro benzene	4.21	3.05	6.00	6.82	1.72
Methyl nitrate	2.85	3.05	2.74	9.62	1.83

[a] C. P. Smyth, [20].

[b] The distance 3.05 Å corresponds to parallel alignment of N=O dipoles in attraction configuration.

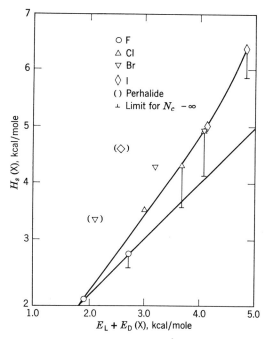

Figure 1.2   Plot of $H_s(X)$ versus the sum of dispersion and orientation energy per halide atom in the molecule. The straight (45°) line represents perfect agreement.

dipole systems as those of the nitro groups, carboxylate esters, or ethylene carbonate.

The data collected in Tables 1.7 through 1.11 suggest that these primitive calculations give at least a semiquantitative relation between the heat of sublimation and molecular properties. Particularly noteworthy is the parallelism between the dipole moment and group increment, as we change from aliphatic to aromatic compounds. Although there is no systematic trend of the deviations from calculated results with the oxygen compounds, a plot of the halide data (Fig. 1.2) shows a regular growth of the deviation with increasing magnitude of $H_s(X)$. The magnitude of the deviation varies inversely as the size of the hydrocarbon group to which it is attached, being almost negligible for $N_c \to \infty$.

1.5   MOTIONS IN MOLECULES

The internal stretching and bending vibrations of small molecules affect the properties of condensed phases, such as their vapor pressure, only through their effect on the zero-point energy and their comparatively small contribution to the dispersion energy. The practical importance of these two contributions is that they account for the effect of isotopic substitution on the vapor pressure and other physical properties.

Gross physical properties of condensed phases, however, are affected by the low-frequency torsional oscillations and internal rotations of chain molecules as well as the ring puckering and conformation changes of alicyclic ring structures. These internal motions of comparatively large groups of atoms within a molecule affect the heat capacity and the density (especially of liquids) and, through the density, almost all other physical properties of the system.

The extent of the freedom of rotation is commonly expressed as the height of the potential energy barrier ($V°$) to internal rotation or equivalent conformation changes. The magnitude of $V°$ ranges from zero or near zero for electrostatic bonds, as in ionic compounds, and for 180° bonds as in methyl acetylene, to very large values (>15 kcal/mole) for single bonds with large

$$O$$
$$\|$$

amounts of double-bond character, such as the amide—N—C-bond. Needless to say, the double and triple bonds have barriers to rotation in excess of 40 kcal/mole. The nature of the barriers to rotation around single bonds is still somewhat obscure in the case of hydrides, such as ethane [13], [21], in which the distance between the interacting hydrogens is larger than their repulsion envelopes. In many other cases in which internal rotation requires passage through repulsion envelopes, as in the 2,2', etc., substituted diphenyls [11], calculation of the barrier from E_r-versus-distance relations seems to be straightforward. A fairly extensive collection of barrier data has been included in Table 14.29.

Although the height of the barrier determines rate of passage over it, the multiplicity and geometry of the barriers around a given bond determine the existence and concentration of the molecule in more than one conformation. If all barrier wells around a bond are of equal depth, all "conformers" or "rotamers" are present in equal concentration; but, if the depth of the multiple barriers differs, one conformation is more stable than any of the others. The existence of especially favorable conformations is important for many physical properties, especially of larger molecules, and the barrier-well difference, the energy of rotational isomerization ΔE_{iso} is being recognized as an increasingly important physical property, especially of polymer molecules. Because the experimental determination of ΔE_{iso} is difficult, there are not many data. Moreover, its magnitude and even its size depend on the environment. Gas-phase ΔE_{iso} data *cannot* be transferred to the calculation of liquid-state properties. A few typical data have also been included in Table 14.29.

Whenever $V° > 3RT$, passage across the barrier becomes rare enough that it is more realistic to speak of (large-amplitude) torsional oscillations around the bond under consideration. The frequency of this torsional oscillation is

$$v_r = \frac{\sigma}{2\pi}\left(\frac{V^0}{2I_{red}}\right)^{\frac{1}{2}}, \tag{1.5}$$

where σ is the symmetry number and I_{red} is the reduced moment of inertia of the rotor.

The amplitudes of all intramolecular vibrations can be observed in high-resolution electron and x-ray diffraction experiments on molecules in the gas phase [1]. These amplitudes are of the order of 0.02 to 0.1 Å, hence of the same order of magnitude as the amplitudes of lattice vibrations in molecular crystals. Intramolecular motions make on important contribution to those properties that are functions of lattice-vibration amplitudes.

REFERENCES

[1] Bartell, L. S. and D. A. Kohl, *J. Chem. Phys.* **39**, 3097 (1963).

[2] Bondi, A., *J. Phys. Chem.* **58**, 929 (1954).

[3] Bondi, A. and D. J. Simkin, *A.I.Ch.E.J.* **3**, 473 (1957).

[4] Bondi, A., *Proc. Intl. Conf. Condensation and Evaporation of Solids*, Gordon and Breach, New York, 1964, p. 181.

[5] Bondi, A., *J. Phys. Chem.* **68**, 441 (1964).

[6] Bradley, D. C., *Prog. Inorg. Chem.* **2**, 303 (1960).

[7] Czekalla, J., *Z. Elektrochem.* **64**, 1221 (1960). [See also the recent review article on this subject by W. Liptay in *Modern Quantum Chemistry*, O. Sinanğolu, ed., Academic, New York, 1965, Part III, p. 45.]

[8] Eliel, E. L. et al., *Conformational Analysis*, Wiley, New York, 1965.

[9] Hildebrand, J. H. and R. L. Scott, *Solubility of Non-Electrolytes*, Reinhold, New York, 1951.

[10] Hirschfelder, J. O., R. B. Bird, and C. F. Curtis, *Molecular Theory of Gases and Liquids*, Wiley, New York, 1958.

[11] Howlett, K. E., *J. Chem. Soc.* **1960**, 1055.

[12] Jehle, H., *Proc. Natl. Acad. Sci.* **50**, 516, 738 (1963); *Adv. Quant. Chem.* **2**, 195 (1965).

[13] Lowe, J. P. and R. G. Parr, *J. Chem. Phys.* **44**, 3001 (1966).

[14] Mizushima, S., *Structure of Molecules and Internal Rotation*, Academic, New York, 1954.

[15] Pimentel, G. C. and A. L. McClelland, *TheHydrogen Bond*, Freeman, San Francisco, 1960.

[16] Pitzer, K. S., *Adv. Chem. Phys.* **2**, 59 (1959).

[17] Pitzer, K. S. and W. E. Donath, *J. Am. Chem. Soc.* **81**, 3213 (1959).

[18] Rowlinson, J. S., *Chem. Soc. Ann. Rept.* **56**, 22 (1959).

[19] Rowlinson, J. S., *Liquids and Liquid Mixtures*, Academic, New York, 1959.

[20] Smyth, C. P., *Electric Dipole Moments and Molecular Structures*, McGraw-Hill, New York, 1955.

[21] Wilson, E. B., *Adv. Chem. Phys.* **2**, 367 (1959).

GENERAL READING

E. A. Moelwyn-Hughes, *Physical Chemistry* Macmillan, New York, 1964, 2nd ed., Sections VII and XIII.

A. I. Kitaigorodskii and K. V. Mirskaya, *Soviet Phys.—Crystallographia* **6**, 408 (1962), present a method to estimate ΔH_s from the contact distance data of x-ray crystallography by using a combination R^{-6} attraction and exponential repulsion term. This method has been widely used by x-ray crystallographers even though ΔH_s (calc) $< \Delta H_s$ (observed) because of the omission of higher order attraction terms.

"Intermolecular Forces," *Discussions Faraday Soc.*, No. 40 (1966) is an excellent source of basic background information on the subject matter of this chapter.

2

Corresponding-States Principle

The theories of the physical properties of (technically important) substances in condensed phases are almost always too complicated and in many cases too inaccurate to be useful for the direct calculation of the desired property datum. This difficulty can be circumvented by arrangement of the dependent and of the independent variables occurring in the basic differential equations in the form of dimensionless variables. Substitution of the available experimental data into the dimensionless groups and plotting the resulting numbers in effect lets nature do the calculation that theory might have supplied. The first successful attempt to use this method of property representation goes back to van der Waals, who divided each of the p-v-T properties of a variety of substances by the value of the property at the critical point. When expressed in this coordinate system, the properties of many substances are represented by equations that contain only universal constants. Such substances were said to be in corresponding states when they were at the same "reduced" temperature ($T_R = T/T_c$), pressure ($P_R = P/P_c$), or density ($\rho_R = \rho/\rho_c$).

In this first example the dimensionless groups are the result of a strictly empirical combination of experimental data rather than a combination of macroscopic and molecular properties. Restatement of van der Waals' reduced equation of state in terms of molecular force and dimension parameters came 50 years later. In line with the purpose of the present work to emphasize relations to molecular structure, such molecular reducing parameters are used throughout. There is no implication that the classical corresponding-states representation is in any way inferior to that preferred here. The many well-established engineering calculations based on the use of the critical constants are evidently useful and have been thoroughly covered by Reid and Sherwood (loc. cit). They are restricted to substances, however, the critical constants of which can be measured, at least in principle. In the present work the emphasis is on those substances for which this measurement is impossible, even in principle. Relations between the two methods of property representation are given wherever there is an overlap.

One of the advantages of guidance by theory, however imperfect, is its assistance in the choice of reducing parameters; for instance, there is, a strong temptation to use the absolute melting point (T_m) for the physical properties of solids. Short contemplation of the mechanics of melting suggests that only those solids that gain the same number of degrees of freedom on melting can be in corresponding states at a given value of T/T_m. In practical terms this means that T/T_m is a corresponding temperature only for solids of similar crystal structure with identical entropy of fusion.[1]

2.1 CORRESPONDING-STATES PRINCIPLE FOR SIMPLE SYSTEMS

The number of molecular parameters (or physical properties) required to define corresponding states can be stated without reference to any particular model of the condensed phase. The simplest case, that of the perfect liquid, was defined by Pitzer [9] as one that meets the following conditions:

1. The translational partition function is classical.
2. All internal degrees of freedom are identical in gas and condensed phase.
3. The intermolecular potential energy depends only on intermolecular distances (not on directions, etc.)
4. The potential function for a pair of molecules can be written in the form $\phi(r) = \epsilon f(r/\sigma)$, where ϵ and σ are characteristic constants and $f(r/\sigma)$ is a universal function.

These four conditions hold even approximately only for systems composed of truly spherical molecules, such as the rare gases. For all other substances meeting conditions 1 and 2, a third constant at least would be required to adjust for deviations from spherical symmetry of the molecules.

One of the consequences of meeting all four conditions is the universality of the critical constants when expressed in terms of the molecular parameters ϵ and σ, which can be determined from a priori calculations (mentioned in Chapter 1), from crystal properties as well as from gas properties. The reduced critical constants $\tilde{T}_c = kT_c/\epsilon$, $\tilde{P}_c = P\sigma^3/\epsilon$, and $\tilde{v}_c = v_c/\sigma^3$ are compared in Table 2.1. The extent of "imperfection" of the various substances can be measured as deviation from the constants of the rare gases. This imperfection due to lack of spherical symmetry is the subject of the next chapter.

Another imperfection is associated with deviation from condition 1 "classical" behavior. As shown by de Boer [4], this quantum imperfection is best represented by the reduced de Broglie wavelengths of the relative motion

---

[1] Note the additional restriction on the use of T/T_m as generalized temperature scale in Section 3.1.

**Table 2.1   Generalized Critical Constants
of Various Substances[a,b]**

Substance	$\tilde{T}_c$	$\tilde{v}_c$	$\tilde{P}_c$
He	0.52	5.75	0.027
Ne	1.25	3.33	0.111
Ar	1.26	3.16	0.116
Xe	1.30	2.90	0.132
H_2	1.12	4.30	0.064
N_2	1.37	2.96	0.131
CH_4	1.34	2.96	0.126
C_2H_6	1.33	2.85	0.129
C_6H_6	1.28	2.92	0.119
CO_2	1.43	2.95	0.165
CS_2	1.13	3.10	0.103

[a] From data in *Molecular Theory of Gases and Liquids*, J. O. Hirschfelder, C. F. Curtis, and R. B. Bird, Wiley, New York, 1959; and the *American Institute of Physics Handbook*, McGraw-Hill, New York, 1957.
[b] L. I. Stiel and G. Thodos, *J. Chem. Eng. Data* 7, 234 (1962) suggest the following general relations: $(\tilde{T}_c)^{-1} \simeq 0.705\tilde{v}_c$; $(\tilde{T}_c)^{-1} \simeq 65.3 Z_c^{0.815}$, and $\tilde{v}_c \simeq 154\ Z_c^{0.815}$, where $Z_c \equiv P_c v_c / RT_c$.

of the molecules,

$$\tilde{\Lambda} = \frac{2^{1/2} h}{\sigma \sqrt{m\epsilon}}.$$

Quantum effects can be disregarded when $\tilde{\Lambda} < 0.2$. The fact is often overlooked that not only hydrogen, helium, and neon, but also the lowest members of the hydrocarbon series, should exhibit quantum effect deviations from chemical behavior, as shown by the data in Table 2.2. The extent of these effects has yet to be studied in detail.

The correction of corresponding-states correlations to allow for deviations from molecule sphericity, and introduction of polar interactions and of intramolecular flexibility will be treated in Chapter 7. In the present introductory Chapter several more general questions need be considered.

**Table 2.2   Values of the Quantum-Mechanical Parameter $\tilde{\Lambda}$
for Various Substances**

Substance	He^4	Ne	Ar	Xe	H_2	N_2	CH_4	C_2H_2	C_2H_6	C_3H_8
$\tilde{\Lambda}$	2.67	0.592	0.186	0.064	1.73	0.23	0.27	0.17	0.13	0.092

2.2 APPLICATION TO SOLIDS

All the recounted principles are as applicable to the correlation of the equilibrium, including elastic properties of crystalline solids, as they are to the properties of dense gases and liquids, with the exception of the packing density, which must now be considered as a separate (independent) variable. So far just the packing density of rare-gas solids has been derived satisfactorily from a priori theory; that of all other crystals must be accepted as a basic variable, at least at 0°K. Thermal expansion from 0°K, on the other hand, is clearly related to molecular properties requiring only the lattice heat capacity as additional input information.

2.3 THE KIHARA POTENTIAL

A basic weakness of nearly all theories of the liquid and of the solid state, and therefore also of the semiempirical correlations used in this book, is the implicit or explicit assumption of central-force-field interaction between neighboring molecules. Although acceptable for many systems composed of small molecules, this assumption, when applied to larger polyatomic molecules, is too crude to yield satisfactory representation of the data. A better model is required especially when most significant interactions are between the surface atoms rather than between all atoms of neighboring molecules. This interaction between surface atoms is considered explicitly by Kihara [7], who separates a molecule into a "core" and a "mantle." The core is essentially the part of the molecule enclosed by the chemical bonds, whereas the mantle extends from the surface-atom centers over a width of the order of the van der Waals radii. These surface atoms of neighboring molecules are then allowed to interact by a conventional pair potential, such as the 6:12 potential.

Because the Kihara potential in effect adds an additional disposable parameter to the property calculation, it can be expected to yield meaningful potential and distance constants only when the additional constants can be obtained from a separate theory. A rational procedure for the calculation of Kihara constants has now been presented by Danon [3]. The next step in the refinement of the correlations of this book should probably be based on the formulation of a set of packing-density parameters that consider only (or primarily) the distance between mantle atoms reduced by means of Kihara mantle-thickness constants. The power of the Kihara method is illustrated by the accuracy with which it calculates heats of sublimation from constants derived from gas imperfection measurements, Table 2.3.

The properties of spherical polar molecules can be correlated by a corresponding-states relation amplified by a dipole-interaction parameter

$$t^* \equiv \frac{\mu^2}{\sqrt{8\varepsilon\sigma^3}}.$$

Table 2.3 Heat of Sublimation of Various Molecular Crystals Calculated from Vapor Phase Property Derived Kihara Potential Constants[a]

Substance	Kihara Constants[b]			Crystal Parameters				
	$\rho 0$ (Å)	l (Å)	U_0/k (°K)	Z —	$\Delta H_{s(calc)}$ (kcal/mole)	$\Delta H_{s(obs)}$	$d_{(calc)}$ (Å)	$d_{(obs)}$ (Å)
CH_4	3.15	0.547	226	12	3.29	2.51	4.00	4.16
N_2	3.47	1.094	124		1.99	1.65	2.83	4.00
C_2H_4	4.2	1.33	256		3.8	4.5		
Benzene	3.6	1.94	740		10.2	10.67		
CO_2	3.36	2.30	309	12 n[c]	4.72	6.44	4.19	4.16
				6 nn	5.90[d]		4.16	

[a] T. Kihara [7].
[b] ρ_0 = equilibrium intercore distance (where $U_{(\rho)} = U_0$); l = characteristic interatomic distance in the core; d = lattice parameter.
[c] n = nearest neighbors; nn = next nearest neighbors.
[d] Includes contribution of quadrupole interaction.

which is in effect the ratio of the close-range dipole-interaction energy μ^2/σ^3 to the dispersion energy ϵ.

An empirical deviation parameter has been developed by Pitzer [9] and Riedel [11] which adjusts the property estimates obtained from a classical corresponding-states treatment for the effects of asphericity and dipole interactions. These deviation factors are: Pitzer's acentric factor $\omega = \log P_r - 1.0$ at $T_R = 0.70$ and Riedel's $\alpha_c \equiv (d \ln p/d \ln T)$ at $(T = T_c) - 7.0$. Both are thus obtained from vapor-pressure data and are related by the equation $\alpha_c = 5.811 + 4.919\omega$. The relation of ω (or α_c) to the deviation from spherical symmetry of nonpolar hydrocarbon molecules is remarkably good and has been worked out in detail by Altenburg [1]. He finds that (1) for spherically symmetric molecules,

$$\alpha_c = 3.75 + 5\left(1 - \frac{6}{8 + 0.288N_e}\right);$$

(2) for isoparaffins (rather accurately),

$$\alpha_c = 6.10 + 0.85 \frac{\overline{R^2}}{a_1^2},$$

where N_e = number of valence electrons per molecule, $\overline{R^2}$ = average of the square of the molecule radius, a_1 = bond distance between carbon atoms. Recently Thompson [14] has shown that the relation of ω to the radius of gyration of nonpolar molecules is of very general applicability. An additional increment in ω is found for polar compound and can be related to the orientation energy E_D.

2.4   CORRESPONDING-STATES PRINCIPLE FOR POLYMERS

All of the above-mentioned versions of the corresponding-states correlation for gas- and liquid-phase properties are designed either explicitly or implicitly for rigid molecules. They are, therefore, not well suited for the correlation of the properties of liquids composed of flexible long-chain molecules. The standard treatment for the latter is that developed by Prigogine [10]. It is based on the following model of the polymer molecule. A chain composed of x equal-sized links is tied together by bonds varying in flexibility continuously from those permitting free rotation of each link to those that are completely stiff. However, a given chain has only one fixed degree of flexibility. The chain links interact with nonbonded neighbors by a $6:12$ (or similar) potential with force constants ϵ and σ (like those for a free molecule of the size and kind of the chain link). Each chain link is surrounded by Z nearest neighbors, two of which are the neighboring chain links; hence $Z-2$ are nonbonded. The degrees of freedom due to the rotation of the chain links are counted as part of the total number of external degrees of freedom ($3c$) per molecule. This number ($3c$) can therefore take on the following extreme values: for completely stiff chains, $3c=6$; for free rotation of the chain links, $3c=1+2x$. We obtain now for the reduced temperature $T^* \equiv ZckT/q\epsilon$, for the reduced volume $v^* \equiv v'/\sigma^3$, and for the reduced pressure $p^* = pZ\sigma^3/q\epsilon$, where $qZ = Z - 2x + 2$, $v' =$ volume (of liquid) per repeat unit. The theory of the p-v-T properties of x-mers has been worked out sufficiently well that reasonable values of σ, ϵ, and c can be obtained by calculation from the experimental data for a wide variety of long-chain hydrocarbon compounds ([6], [12], [13]).

A peculiar feature of the theory is the need for a somewhat arbitrary even if intuitively acceptable choice for the size of chain links. Although comparatively easy in the case of hydrocarbons, this choice can become difficult with many nonhydrocarbons. A more serious, yet unavoidable, weakness of the theory is that the two bonded neighbors are counted as part of the Z nearest neighbors. This assumption restricts the validity of the theory to low temperatures. Moreover, it is strictly a liquid-phase theory, hence the vapor pressure cannot be calculated from it. Its major advance over any previous theory is the introduction of an explicit quantitative measure of molecular flexibility $3c$. Particularly interesting is the effect of chain flexibility on the reduced temperature $T^* = ZckT/q\epsilon$. For a long stiff chain where $x \gg 6$, $c=2$, $c/q \to 0$. Hence $T^* \simeq 0$ at all temperatures for entirely stiff chains and $T^* \sim T$ for flexible chains, or, in general, a system composed of flexible-chain molecules is always at a higher reduced temperature than are those containing stiffer molecules.

A closely related treatment has been developed [2] which employs basically the same reduced variables as the Prigogine theory in the form of an empirical correlation. Since the theory is not used, σ and ϵ or their equivalents are obtained from extraneous data. The geometrical variable σ has been replaced by the van der Waals volume V_w (see Section 1.1 above), and the potential variable ϵ by the standard energy of vaporization $(E°)$,[1] respectively, Z has been fixed arbitrarily at 10. Then $T^* \simeq 5cRT/E°$, $\rho^* = V_w/V$, and $P^* = (P + P_i)5V_w/E°$, where P_i = internal pressure $(\partial E/\partial V)_T$ (at atmospheric pressure). This treatment avoids the need for an arbitrary choice of segment size, and makes ρ^* the packing density of the liquid. As always, this simplification or generalization was bought at a price; the inability of the system to accommodate low-molecular-weight compounds in the generalized density correlation ρ^* versus T^*, shown in Figure 2.1 in comparison with the similar

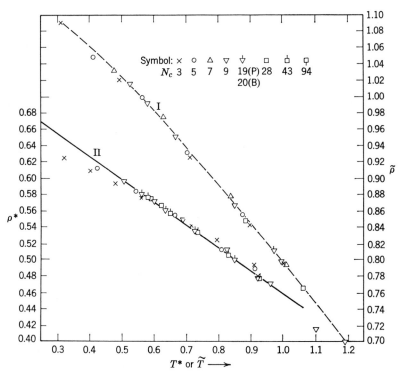

Figure 2.1 Comparison of the generalized density versus temperature relations of Prigogine ($\tilde{\rho}$ versus $\tilde{T}$ scales) curve I and Bondi (ρ^* versus T^* scales) curve II for n-paraffins. [Line II is calculated by (8.2).]

[1] $E° = \Delta H_v - RT$ at T, where $V/V_w = 1.70$.

Prigogine treatment of the same set of n-paraffin hydrocarbons. The assumption of bonded neighbors as two of the Z nearest neighbors has been carried implicitly into this new correlation, the utility of which is therefore also restricted to low temperatures ($T^* < 0.9$), which means to below the atmospheric boiling point. As a result of the extraneous introduction of E° and V_w into the correlation scheme, the constant c and therefore the number of excited external degrees of freedom is obtained by combination of these constants with a measured density, as will be set forth later on. Tables for the calculation of E° from group increments have been assembled in Chapter 14. This corresponding-states correlation appears to be valid also for most polar compounds, but not for hydrogen bonded substances. For small rigid compounds for which this has been tested, $\tilde{T} = kT/\epsilon$ and $T^* = 5cRT/E^\circ$ are numerically identical, leading to the unexpected results that often when $3c = 6$, $E^\circ \simeq 5c\epsilon \simeq 10\epsilon$.

REFERENCES

[1] Altenburg, K., *Ber. Bunsenges* **65,** 801, 805 (1961); *Kolloid-Z.*, **178,** 112 (1961); *Z. Physik. Chem.* **228,** 120 (1965); **230,** 13 (1965); **231,** 77 (1966).
[2] Bondi, A. and D. J. Simkin, *A.I.Ch.E.J.* **6,** 191 (1960).
[3] Dannon, F. and K. S. Pitzer, *J. Chem. Phys.* **36,** 425 (1962).
[4] de Boer, J., et al., *Physica* **14,** 139, 149, 520 (1948).
[5] Flory, P. J. and O. J. Vrij, *J. Am. Chem. Soc.* **86,** 3515 (1964).
[6] Hijmens, J., *Physica* **27,** 433 (1961).
[7] Kihara, T., *Adv. Chem. Phys.* **5,** 147 (1963); *Rev. Mod. Phys.* **25,** 831 (1953); **27,** 412 (1955).
[8] Pitzer, K. S., *J. Chem. Phys.* **7,** 583 (1939).
[9] Pitzer, K. S., et al ., *J. Am. Chem. Soc.* **77,** 3427, 3433 (1955); **79,** 2369 (1957).
[10] Prigogine, I., *The Molecular Theory of Solutions*, Interscience, New York, 1957.
[11] Riedel, L., *Chem. Ingr.-Tech.* **26,** 83, 259, 679 (1954); **27,** 209, 475 (1955).
[12] Simha, R. and S. T. Hadden, *J. Chem. Phys.* **25,** 702 (1956).
[13] Simha, R. and A. T. Havlik, *J. Am. Chem. Soc.* **86,** 197 (1964).
[14] Thompson, H. W., Ph.D. thesis, Pennsylvania State University, 1966.

3

Molecular Crystals Including Crystalline Polymers

The strong directionality of intermolecular force fields in crystals seems to preclude the development of useful generalizations in the manner of corresponding-states correlations. Fortunately such pessimism has proved groundless in many instances and suitable corresponding-states-type correlations could be developed. Whether a given crystal will fall into the "well-behaved" class cannot yet be predicted with certainty.

3.1 THE PACKING DENSITY AT 0°K

An obvious fundamental property of a crystal is $\rho_0^* = V_w/V_0 = \rho^*$ at $T = 0°K$, the packing density in the absence of thermal vibrations. It can vary in principle from 0.52 to 0.74 for open- and close-packed cubic structures, respectively, of spheres, and from 0.785 to 0.903 for open- and close-packed arrays, respectively, of infinitely long cylinders. The incidence of either of these cannot be predicted a priori. Moreover, the packing density of polyatomic molecules with their many "bulges" and irregular shapes is nearly unpredictable even if we could say in what array they are to crystallize. We can hardly expect, therefore, to find simple generalizations for the description of the volumetric properties of crystalline solids composed of polyatomic molecules.

The wide range of zero-point packing densities experimentally observed (mostly by Biltz [4], [5]) is illustrated by the examples in Table 3.1. Many complex organic molecules occupy the narrow range $0.70 < \rho_0^* < 0.78$, which is quite accidentally near that for closely packed spheres. This uniformity in ρ_0^* is responsible for the approximate atom increment additivity

25

Table 3.1   Packing Density of Various Molecular Crystals at $0°K$[a]

Substance	Crystal Type	ρ_0^*
F_2	—	0.56
Cl_2	orthorhombic[c] (layer structure)	0.74
Br_2	orthorhombic[c] (layer structure)	0.75
I_2	orthorhombic[c] (layer structure)	0.76
CF_4	—	0.69
CCl_4	(monoclinic)	0.69
CBr_4	monoclinic[d]	0.69
CI_4	monoclinic[d]	0.68
O_2	rhomb-bc	0.60
CO	cubic (like N_2)	0.60
N_2	fcc	0.59[b]
NO	cubic	0.73
N_2O	fcc (like CO_2)	0.70
CO_2	fcc	0.76
CS_2	—	0.69
S_8	rhombic	0.766
P_4	rhomb/monocl	0.676
CH_4	$N_c > 5$ triclinic	0.67; C_3H_8: 0.695; $n\text{-}C_5H_{12}$: 0.711; $n\text{-}C_9H_{20}$: 0.727
C_2H_6	$N_c > 4$ orthorhombic	0.68_4; $n\text{-}C_4H_{10}$: 0.725; $n\text{-}C_6H_{10}$: 0.722; $n\text{-}C_8H_{10}$: 0.735
C_2H_4	—	0.670
Benzene	orthorhombic	0.697; φMe: 0.675; 1,3,5-Me$_3\varphi$: 0.736
Naphthalene	monoclinic	0.721
Anthracene	monoclinic	0.733
MeOH		0.677; EtOH: 0.698; n-BuOH: 0.720; $n\text{-}C_{12}OH$: 0.736
Phenol	monoclinic[e]	0.690; phenethanol: 0.716
Cellulose		0.720; $(CH_2)_\infty$: 0.762

[a] From data by Biltz [4], [5], except where noted otherwise.
[b] L. H. Bolz et al., *Acta Cryst.* **12**, 247 (1959).
[c] Collin, R. C., *Acta Cryst.* **5**, 431 (1952).
[d] Sackmann, H., *Z. phys. Chem.* **208**, 235 (1958).
[e] Scheringer, C., *Z. Krist.* **119**, 273 (1963).

of the zero-point volume of many nonionic compounds [5]. Molecular crystals with $\rho_0^* < 0.6$ are rarely found, probably because of insufficient stability of open lattices.

Procedure 3.1   CALCULATING PROCEDURE: DENSITY AT $0°K$

Given. Molecular structure and thus molecular weight M.

 STEP 1: Estimate the van der Waals volume, V_w, from the increments given in Tables 14.1 through 14.17. If no increments are available, estimate V_w by means of the method outlined in Figure 14.1, using the van der Waals radius data assembled in Tables 14.1 through 14.16 and bond distance data from the literature.

STEP 2: Guess the packing density ρ_0^* by comparison with ρ_0^* data in Table 3.1 of substances surmised to have the same crystal structure as the substance under consideration. A slightly more accurate guess can be made if the crystal structure is known, because the chain of comparisons in Table 3.1 is narrowed down correspondingly.

STEP 3: Then the density at 0°K is ρ_0: $\rho_0 \simeq \rho_0^* \cdot M/V_w$. [Alternatively, $V_0 = \Sigma\, V_0(X)$ of $V_0(X)$ increments in Tables 14.1 through 14.16. Then $\rho_0 = M/V_0$.]

3.2 LATTICE COHESION

The cohesion forces that hold the crystal lattice together can be measured directly as the heat of sublimation ΔH_s at a temperature T at which the vapor pressure is sufficient for such measurement. The desired fundamental property of the crystal lattice $\Delta H_s^\circ = \Delta H_s$ at $T = 0°K$ is then given by

$$\Delta H_s^\circ = \Delta H_s(T) + \int_0^T [C_p(s) - C_p(g)]\, dT.$$

As we shall see later on, $C_p(s) - C_p(g)$ is about $2R$ at $T > \theta_D$,[1] and becomes negative at $T < \theta_D$ before becoming 0 at $T = 0°K$. Hence ΔH_s° is rarely much larger than ΔH_s^1, the heat of sublimation at the lowest first-order transition temperature, and is sometimes slightly smaller. Conversion of ΔH_s^1, for which group increments to H_s are readily available (Table 14.1 and Ref. [7]) will thus rarely be uncertain by as much as 0.5 kcal/mole, the usual experimental uncertainty of heat-of-sublimation data.

The lattice energy $U_0 = -(\Delta H_s^\circ + E_Z)$ is the zero-point energy due to intermolecular vibrations in the crystal. For many closely packed crystals of nonassociating substances $E_Z \approx (\frac{9}{8})R\theta_D$. This means that for most molecular crystals with $70 < \theta_D < 180°K$, we find $160 < E_Z < 400$ cal/mole, less than the usual uncertainty in the experimental values of ΔH_s, hence $-U_0 \approx \Delta H_s^\circ$. However, in crystals held together by hydrogen bonds, such as solid HF or H_2O, or crystals composed of larger hydrogen-bonded molecules, such as sucrose, E_Z is quite large because of the large effect of hydrogen-bond formation on molecular frequencies. According to Whalley, E_Z (ice) = 3.5 kcal/mole [30]. The lattice energy of crystals held together even partly by hydrogen bonds can therefore be substantially larger than $\Delta H_s^\circ + 0.5$ kcal/mole.

The heat of sublimation of most molecular crystals can be estimated from the group increment data in Tables 14.1 to 14.16. When group-increment data are not available, they can be estimated from dipole moments and other molecular properties by the procedure illustrated in Tables 1.6 through 1.10.

---

[1] θ_D is the Debye temperature of the crystal lattice.

Procedure 3.2 CALCULATING PROCEDURE: HEAT OF
SUBLIMATION AT 0°K.

Given: Molecular structure.

STEP 1: Break the molecular structure formula into its various functional groups.

STEP 2: Associate the appropriate H_s^1 increment and decrements (in Tables 14.1 to 14.16 as well as 1.5 to 1.10) with each functional group and add them together; the result is ΔH_s^1, the heat of sublimation at the lowest first-order transition temperature, T_1, of the crystal.

STEP 3: If T_1 is known, $\qquad \Delta H_s^\circ \approx \Delta H_s^1 + \Delta C_p(\text{s, g})(T_1 - \theta_D),$

where θ_D, the Debye temperature, has been obtained by the method of Section 3.3 and $\Delta C_p(\text{s, g})$ is taken from Figure 3.8.

STEP 4: If the crystal is not known to have a first-order phase transition at $T < T_m$, and the molecule is not spherically symmetrical, we may assume that $T_1 = T_m$.

3.3 THERMAL VIBRATIONS

Most physical properties of crystals are affected by the frequency (and amplitude) of the thermal oscillations of atoms or molecules above their equilibrium lattice positions. Thanks to modern X-ray diffraction and neutron-scattering techniques, lattice-vibration spectra can be measured directly. The thermal-vibration amplitudes of atoms and molecules in the crystal lattice are, in principle, available as "*B*-factors" from x-ray diffraction data. At present, however, only two or three groups of investigators (worldwide) estimate these factors sufficiently free from accumulated errors to be useful for conversion to lattice frequencies. The likelihood that highly automated x-ray diffraction equipment and increasing skill will broaden the availability of reliable *B*-factors, and the fact that they have been used successfully for thermodynamic property calculations [3] [10] suggest at least a short discussion of the means to exploit this information.

The oscillation amplitudes $\bar{u}$ are converted to the desired frequencies ν_D by means of the Debye–Waller theory, which yields

$$\bar{u}^2 \left(= \frac{3B}{8\pi^2} = 3.80 \times 10^{-2}B \right) = \frac{3h^2 T}{4\pi^2 m k \theta_D} = 1.425 \times 10^{-14} \frac{T}{M\theta_D{}^2},$$

$$\theta_D = 0.612 \times 10^{-6} \left(\frac{T}{MB} \right)^{1/2} {}^\circ\text{K},$$

(3.1)

for the translational vibrations. For the rotational oscillations with angular amplitude $\bar{\varphi}$, the Debye–Waller theory yields the torsional oscillation frequency ν_R:

$$\bar{\varphi}^2 = \frac{kT}{4\pi^2 I \nu_R{}^2} \quad \text{or} \quad \nu_R = 0.59 \times 10^{-9} \left[\frac{T}{(\bar{\varphi}^2)I} \right]^{1/2},$$

$$\theta_R = 2.83 \times 10^{-20} \left[\frac{T}{(\bar{\varphi}^2)I} \right]^{1/2},$$

(3.2)

where I is the appropriate moment of inertia of the molecule. All other symbols have their usual meaning; (3.1) and (3.2) are valid only if $T > \theta_D$ and θ_R, respectively, where $\theta_D = h\nu_D/k$ and $\theta_R = h\nu_R/k$. If $T < \theta_D \simeq \theta_R$, a more elaborate form of the theory must be used. Because few x-ray diffractions data are obtained at such low temperatures, the simple relations (3.1) and (3.2) generally suffice.

As slow-neutron scattering yields the lattice frequencies directly [15] there is no need to encumber this book with the required calculations. Raman and infrared spectra and the vibronic components of low-temperature electronic spectra of crystals also yield translational and, particularly, torsional lattice frequencies directly. Typical spectroscopic data are presented in Table 3.2.

Table 3.2 Typical Lattice Vibration Frequencies of Molecular Crystals (All in cm^{-1})[a]

Substance	$T_1(°K)$	Translational			Torsional		Oscillation			Ref.
Allene	95	69	79					50	111	a
Benzene	270	67					43	78	128	b
Anthracene	298	59					48	68	120	b
p-Dichlorobenzene	298	8	17	35	27.5	49	56	72	93	c
Ice	255	52	213	301				601	(800)	c
Methane	18	27	45					58	95	d

[a] J. Blanc, C. Brecher, and R. C. Halford, *J. Chem. Phys.* **36**, 2654 (1945).
[b] D. W. J. Cruickshank, *Rev. Mod. Phys.* **30**, 163 (1958).
[c] Most data are available from Landolt-Börnstein, *Zahlenwerte und Funktionen*, Vol. 1/4 (Kristalle). Quotations here are restricted to instances where data on translational and torsional oscillations were available.
[d] Stiller, H. and S. Hautecler, *Proc. AEA Conf. Inelastic Scattering of Neutrons in Solids and Liquids*, 1962, p. 281.

The rotational oscillations should be correlatable with the lattice energy and molecular structure through the simple proportionality

$$\nu_R = \frac{1}{2\pi}\left(\frac{2\Delta H_s(i)}{I_i}\right)^{1/2}, \tag{3.3}$$

where $\Delta H_s(i)$ is the appropriate component of the lattice energy and I_i the corresponding principal moment of inertia. With $\Delta H_s(i)$ generally unknown, we have to make the assumption of a uniform force field and use ΔH_s instead. The data of Table 3.3 indicate to what extent ν_R could be guessed from a knowledge of $\Delta H_s/I_i$. It is noteworthy that correlatability seems to improve with increasing molecule size, being poorest for the oscillations of small molecules around their long axis and best for oscillations around the short axis.

Table 3.3 Correlation of Torsional Lattice Vibrations[a] of Rigid Molecules in Molecular Crystals with Molecular-Structure Parameters[b]

Substance	$\dfrac{(\Delta H_s'/N_A I_A)^{1/2}}{c\omega_3}$	$\dfrac{(\Delta H_s'/N_A I_B)^{1/2}}{c\omega_2}$	$\dfrac{(\Delta H_s'/N_A I_C)^{1/2}}{c\omega_1}$	Ref.
CO_2	2.26	(3.97)		c
CS_2	2.21			a
N_2O	3.0	(4.9)		c
H_2O	3.85	(3.7)	2.95	a
C_2H_2			3.95	d
C_2H_4	4.7		3.63	d
C_2H_6	5.15		3.57	d
CH_4	6.1			j
MeCl	7.78		(2.42)	e
MeBr	9.3		(2.30)	e
MeI	10.0		(2.32)	e
$Cl–CH_2–CH_2–Cl$	5.55		2.32	f
$Br–CH_2–CH_2–Br$	11.2		2.09	f
Allene			2.08 (4.9)	g
Benzene	1.81		2.70	i
Naphthalene	2.03	1.90	2.57	i
Anthracene	1.81		1.90	i
Pyridine	2.02	2.45	2.25	f
Chlorobenzene	2.01	1.66	1.92	f
p-Dichlorobenzene	3.12	2.20	3.46	h
p-Dibromobenzene	3.24	1.78	3.27	h
p-Diiodobenzene	2.75	2.10	3.46	h

[a] Reference a of Table 3.1.

[b] The molecular structure parameters are the heat of sublimation $\Delta H_s'$ and the principle moments of inertia. If we set the force constant $= 2\,\Delta H_s$, then the theoretical value of all the ratios given on this page should be 4.44. [See Ewing, G. E. and G. C. Pimentel, *J. Chem. Phys.* **35**, 925 (1961).] ω is in cm^{-1} and $c =$ velocity of light.

[c] D. A. Dows, *Spectrochim. Acta* **13**, 308 (1959).

[d] R. G. Snyder, Shell Development Company, private communication, March 1960.

[e] W. J. Lafferty and D. W. Robinson, *J. Chem. Phys.* **36**, 83 (1962).

[f] I. Ichishima, *J. Chem. Soc. Japan* **71**, 332, 366, 443, 485, 551, 507 (1950).

[g] J. Blanc, C. Brecher, and R. C. Halford, *J. Chem. Phys.* **36**, 2564 (1962).

[h] E. Gross and A. Korshanov, *Acta Physicochim. URSS* **20**, 351 (1945).

[i] D. W. J. Cruickshank, *Rev. Mod. Phys.* **30**, 163 (1958).

[j] Reference d of Table 2.3.

In the absence of x-ray diffraction, neutron scattering, or spectroscopic data the lattice frequencies required for thermodynamic property calculations have to be estimated through indirect means.

The calculation of ν_D, the maximum translational lattice frequency from elastic constants, goes back to Debye's classical paper. Here we use the simplified method recently proposed by O. L. Anderson [1]:

$$\theta_D = \frac{h\nu}{\kappa} D = \frac{h}{k}\left(\frac{3}{4\pi}\frac{N_A}{V_s}\right)^{\frac{1}{3}} \bar{u}_m,$$ (3.4)

where all symbols have their usual meaning. The average sound velocity $\bar{u}_m$ is derived from the elastic constants of the crystal through the following calculation

$$u_m = \frac{1}{3}\left(\frac{2}{\bar{u}_T^3} + \frac{1}{\bar{u}_L^3}\right)^{-\frac{1}{3}},$$ (3.5)

where the transverse sound velocity $\bar{u}_T = (G_H/\rho)^{\frac{1}{2}}$ and the longitudinal sound velocity is given by

$$u_L = [K_H + (4/3)G_H/\rho]^{\frac{1}{2}}.$$ (3.6)

The translational and torsional oscillation frequencies are temperature dependent, and to a fair approximation

$$\theta_i(T) = \theta_1^0(1 - 5 \times 10^{-2}T),$$ (3.7)

where $\theta_i(T)$, θ_1^0 are θ_D and θ_R at $T = T$ and $T = 0°K$, respectively. The value θ_i^0 is generally obtained by extrapolation [9].

If we assume, with Lindemann, that melting occurs when the amplitude of thermal oscillation is a fixed fraction of the interatomic distance, then we obtain a direct relation between the melting temperaure T_m and θ_D:

$$\theta_D^2 = \frac{T_m}{Aa^2L},$$ (3.8)

where A = atomic (or molecular) weight, a = lattice constant, L = Lindemann constant. This relation yields for the amplitude of thermal vibrations at $T > \theta_D$:

$$\frac{(u^2)^{\frac{1}{2}}}{a} 4.36 \times 10^{-14}\left(\frac{LT}{T_m}\right)^{\frac{1}{2}}$$ (3.9)

or more generally

$$(\bar{u}^2)^{\frac{1}{2}} = gr\left(\frac{T}{T_m}\right)^{\frac{1}{2}}$$ (3.10)

if at $T_m: (\bar{u}^2)_m^{\frac{1}{2}} = gr$, where $g = 0.22$ for face-centered-cubic lattice. For most monatomic crystals $0.1 < g < 0.2$ [9]. A useful consequence of this relation is the suggestion that within a series of crystals for which g = constant, all crystal properties that depend on thermal lattice vibrations can be correlated in terms of the reduced temperature T/T_m.

The above generalizations have been derived from observations on metallic crystals. The temperature dependence of $\bar{u}^2$ in organic crystals is not as clearly, if at all, related to the dimensions of the molecule, and may instead be estimated by means of the simple formula

$$\bar{u} \approx 2.48(v_s^{\frac{1}{3}} - v_0^{\frac{1}{3}}) \tag{3.11}$$

where v_s, v_0 are the molecular volumes of the solid at the temperature of observation and at $0°K$, respectively [14]. The proportionality constant is due to the assumption of simple cubic packing, and would have to be changed to suit the crystal type at hand. However, the underlying assumption of spherical molecules is so crude that such refinement appears to be out of place.

The lattice vibrations of anisometric molecules are generally anisotropic, for instance the vibration amplitude of long-chain molecules is largest normal to their fiber axis, and that of a platelet molecule (aromatic hydrocarbon) is largest normal to the ring plane. The exact relation of the amplitude in the various directions could probably be estimated from the anisotropy of polarizability of the molecules in question, using London's appropriate formula for the calculation of intermolecular forces [21].

Superimposed on the vibrations of the center of gravity of the molecules on a lattice are the vibrations of the atoms within the molecule relative to each other. Although generally small compared with $\bar{u}$, they cannot be ignored in larger molecules where the total internal oscillation amplitude of part of a molecule relative to its center of gravity is of the same order of magnitude as $\bar{u}$. In crystals composed of long-chain molecules, especially high polymers, some or all of the lattice vibrations are virtually identical with the skeletal vibrations of the molecules.

3.4   HEAT CAPACITY, ENTHALPY, AND ENTROPY

These three properties are related directly to the thermal vibrations discussed above and can be calculated as follows:

The contributions of the translational-vibration frequencies (or the equivalent θ_D) are calculated by means of Debye's theory and the contributions of the rotational oscillation by means of Einstein's harmonic-oscillator approximation using the generally available tables. These lattice contributions (C_v^s, E^s, S^s) of the crystal must be added to the internal-vibration contribution $[C_{vibr}, E_{vibr}, S_{vibr}]$, calculated for the ideal gas.[1] The addition is straightforward for entropy and enthalpy, but in the case of heat capacity one generally wants to convert C_v to C_p.

Molecular crystals can generally be distinguished from ionic or covalent crystals by their large expansion coefficients (α_s). Because, by definition, $\alpha_s = 0$ for harmonic-oscillator crystal lattices, the common assumption that

---

[1] See Section 9.9 (Heat Capacity of Liquids) for methods to estimate the internal-vibration contributions.

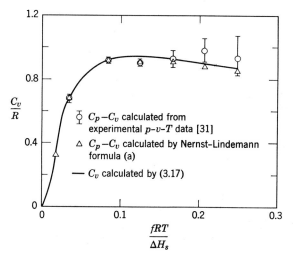

Figure 3.1   Heat capacity of solid xenon, A. C. H. Hallett in *Ar, He and the Rare Gases*, G. A. Cook, ed., Interscience, New York, 1961.

the heat capacity of molecular crystals should be that of a Debye solid, cannot be generally applicable, especially if $T_m \gg \theta_D$. Several theoretical treatments of the heat capacity of anharmonic solids are now available [12], [11], [32], [38]. With a single exception [12], all theories conclude that at $T > \theta_D$, the range where anharmonicity should matter, C_v (anharmonic) $< C_v$ (harmonic), so that C_v should go through a maximum somewhere between θ_D and T_m.

The theories can only be tested on one monatomic solid, xenon, because for argon $\theta_D \approx T_m$ [11], and no p-v-T measurements on krypton have been reported. Precision p–v–T measurements on solid rare gases are so difficult that the available xenon data [31] yield the rather unsatisfactory uncertainty band in the C_v versus T curve shown in Figure 3.1. Although not supporting such a conclusion unequivocally, the data indicate that C_v of xenon goes through a maximum, as expected from theory. The theoretical values of C_v are also seen to fall within the uncertainty band of the experimental data.

3.4.1   Applications

The theory by Leibfried and Ludwig [9] for the heat capacity of anharmonic crystals at $T > \theta_D$ can be cast into the form

$$\frac{C_v^{\,s}}{fR} = 1 + \frac{f}{2}\frac{RT}{\Delta H_s}\left(\frac{a_1 f}{3} - a_2\right), \tag{3.17}$$

and

$$\frac{C_p^{\,s}}{fR} = 1 + \frac{f}{2}\frac{RT}{\Delta H_s}\left(\frac{a_1 f}{3} + a_3\right), \tag{3.18}$$

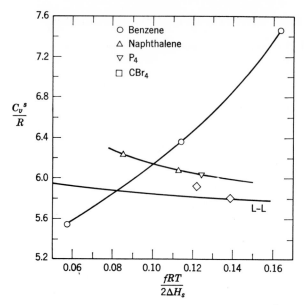

Figure 3.2   Lattice heat capacity C_v^s of molecular crystals at $T > \theta_D$, $L - L = (3.17)$ [8].

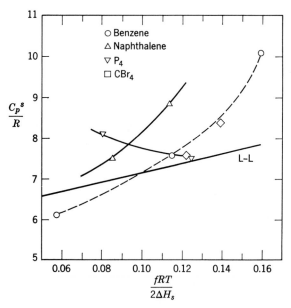

Figure 3.3   Lattice heat capacity C_p^s of molecular crystals at $T > \theta_D$, $L - L = (3.18)$ [8].

where $C_v{}^s$ and $C_p{}^s$ are the lattice contributions to C_v and C_p, respectively; f is the number of degrees of freedom per molecule in the lattice; the numerical value of the dimensionless coefficients a_i is derived from theory and depends on the choice of the potential function. For the 6:12 potential and cubic monatomic crystals $a_1 = 0.69$, $a_2 = 1.73$, $a_3 = 0.54$. If we consider the theory applicable, at least as guideline also for crystals composed of rigid polyatomic molecules, we recognize from (3.17) that $-dC_v{}^s/dT$ becomes flatter as f becomes larger. For $f = 6$, the slope is only $\frac{2}{3}$ that of $f = 3$. Conversely, according to (3.18), $dC_p{}^s/dT$ should increase rapidly with increasing f.

3.4.2 Rigid Molecules

The comparison between theory and experiment, in Figures 3.2 and 3.3, indicates rather general qualitative but poor quantitative agreement with (3.2) and—with the glaring exception of benzene—qualitative as well as fair quantitative agreement with (3.1) for several crystals composed of rigid polyatomic molecules. The large positive deviation of $C_v{}^s$ of benzene from the theory of simple anharmonic crystals could be due to two causes: a very different force law and crystal structure, or vacancy formation. The first cannot be ruled out because, as shown in Figure 3.4, $C_v{}^s$ of benzene conforms surprisingly closely to the heat-capacity curve of anharmonic crystals (at $T > \theta_D$) predicted by Eastabrook's theory [12]:

$$\frac{C_v{}^s}{fR} = 1 + q\gamma\,dT, \tag{3.19}$$

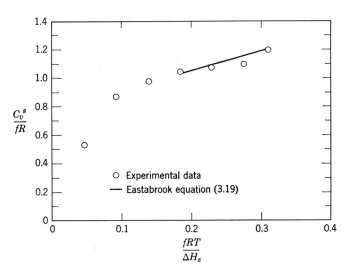

Figure 3.4   Lattice heat capacity of solid benzene [8].

where γ is the Grueneisen constant and q is a numerical constant of the order 0.9, the exact magnitude of which depends on the force law chosen. Because $(1 + \gamma \alpha T) = C_p/C_v$, this theory predicts that $C_v^s - C_v^s$ (harmonic) is of the same order as $C_p - C_v$.

The general disagreement of Eastabrook's theory with more rigorously derived theories and with experiment leads to the impression that the agreement in the case of benzene is fortuitous and that the large positive deviation of C_v^s (benzene) is due to lattice-defect formation. This increase in lattice heat capacity $(\delta_d C_v^s)$ as caused by defect formation can be formulated by following Nölting [29]:

$$\frac{\delta_d C_v^s}{R} = \frac{n_d^\circ}{2}\left(\frac{\Delta H_d}{RT}\right)^2 \exp\left(-\frac{\Delta H_d}{2RT}\right) \qquad (3.20)$$

where n_d° is the pre-exponential constant in the temperature function of the defect concentration:

$$n_d = n_d^\circ \exp -\left(\frac{\Delta H_d}{2RT}\right), \qquad (3.21)$$

and ΔH_d is the enthalpy of defect formation. At present the magnitude of ΔH_d cannot be predicted. We might guess that it must be of the order of ΔH_s. It is experimentally determined as

$$\Delta H_d = R \frac{d \ln (\delta_d C_v^s T^2)}{d(T^{-1})} \qquad (3.22)$$

Table 3.4 Comparison of $C_p - C_v$ of Molecular Crystals from p–v–T Data With That Calculated by L–L Theory[a] [8]

Substance	T (°K)	$\dfrac{T}{T_m}$	$\dfrac{fRT}{2H_s'}$	$\dfrac{C_p - C_v}{R}$ (exp)	$\dfrac{C_p - C_v}{R}$ (theor)
CBr$_4$	273	0.855[b]	0.122	1.67	2.08
	311	0.972[b]	0.139	3.09	2.38
P$_4$	293		0.124	1.52	1.65
Benzene	270	0.97	0.154	2.12	2.10
Naphthalene	298	0.845	0.105	1.81	1.44
Ethane	77	0.69	0.094	1.27	1.27
n-Octane	200	0.925	0.156[c]	4.20	4.67[c]
n-Hexadecane	280	0.962	0.183[c]	6.5	8.6[c] (6.3)[d]

[a] L–L = Leibfried and Ludwig [20] for a 6:12 potential.
[b] This is T/T_{tr}.
[c] For these flexible molecules assumed $f = 6 + (N_c - 1)$; N_c = number of carbon atoms per molecule.
[d] The value in parentheses results from the assumption $f = 3 + (N_c - 1)$.

and $\delta_d C_v^s = C_v^s$ (obs) $- C_v^s$ (theor), where C_v^s (obs) $= C_p - (C_p - C_v) - C_{\text{vibr}}$ and C_v^s (theor) is that obtained from Eq. (3.1) if $T > \theta_D$, and as a Debye solid if $T \geq \theta_D$. In the case of benzene $\Delta H_d = 5.3$ kcal/mole ($\approx \Delta H_s/2$); $n_d^o \approx 4$.

In the absence of systematic investigations of molecular crystals we may guess that defect formation will make important contributions to C_v^s when $\rho_s^*(T_m) < 0.65$. There is ample evidence that $\delta_d C_v^s \sim 0$ when $\rho_s^*(T_m) > 0.66$.

According to the Leibfried–Ludwig theory, it is obvious from (3.17) and (3.18) that

$$\frac{C_p - C_v}{R} = 1.13 f^2 \frac{RT}{\Delta H_s}. \tag{3.23}$$

This simple expression represents the available experimental data surprisingly well, as shown by the data in Table 3.4. In view of its straightforward theoretical background (3.6) appears to be a more desirable choice than the commonly used [40] mostly empirical correlation by Lord [25].

3.4.3 Flexible Molecules

Application of (3.17) and (3.18) to crystals composed of flexible molecules has been tried by reinterpretation of f to include also the degrees of freedom due to torsional oscillations of chain segments. After initial successes, this attempt has been abandoned in favor of more careful analysis. In the meantime it appears that the available data can be described by a rather simple-minded procedure.

Inspection of the data suggests division of the temperature scale into two parts. At $T > 0.9 T_m$, the most suitable temperature scale seems to be T/T_m, whereas at $T < 0.9 T_m$, the scale $RT/\Delta H_s$ appears to serve rather well. Then, for the best studied case, the n-alkanes with $N_c > 7$, including linear polyethylene, at $T < 0.9 T_m$:

$$\frac{C_v^s}{R} = 0.65 n_m + 0.85 n_c \frac{RT}{H_s(CH_2)} \tag{3.24}$$

and at $T > 0.9 T_m$:

$$\frac{C_v^s}{R} = 0.7 n_m + 0.43 n_c \left(\frac{T}{T_m}\right)^2, \tag{3.25}$$

where n_m = number of methyl groups per molecule, n_c = number of methylene groups per molecule. Equation 3.25 will not represent the polyethylene data because at $T > 0.9 T_m$ crystallite melting obscures the heat capacity of the stable crystals. In (3.24) and (3.25), C_v^s does not contain the contributions due to torsional oscillation. In many physical properties, such as the thermal expansion, these have to be added to C_v^s in order to obtain the lattice heat capacity of interest. These frequencies are now well known for n-alkanes [34], for polypropylene [35], and for polyoxymethylene [36], but a more general evaluation of the lattice-heat capacity characteristics of other crystalline high polymers has to wait for the spectral assignments required for a reliable calculation of the contribution of internal motions.

The heat capacity of crystalline polyethylene has been calculated by Wunderlich [42] using a Tarasov frequency distribution obtained from a fit to the very low temperature data, and the usual high-frequency optical-vibration data for C_i, ignoring the intermolecular lattice contribution, contained in the second term of (24). At $T < 150°K$ this neglect is fully justified. However, the discrepancy between calculation and experiment of higher temperatures is just of the order of the second term of (3.24), indicating that the lattice contribution, of the order $\sim 0.1\ C_v$ at $300°K$, should not be ignored in estimates of the heat capacity of crystalline polymers at higher temperature.

The major component of the heat capacity of polymeric solids, the contribution of internal degrees of freedom, including those due to torsional oscillation or hindered rotation of side groups as well as the backbone chain, can be estimated by the same procedures used for low-molecular-weight substances once the appropriate frequency assignments and barrier heights have been made. It is noteworthy that the barrier heights effective in the crystalline solid can be taken as essentially equal to those active in the gas phase [40], [43].

3.4.4   Calculating Procedures for Heat Capacity, Enthalpy and Entropy

This section deals only with the crystal lattice contributions to the thermodynamic properties of molecular solids. The contributions of the internal vibrations (including torsional oscillations) should be obtained, in order of preference, from frequency assignments, from the tabulated[1] ideal gas-heat capacity and enthalpy data or from the group increments tabulated in Section 9.9, Calculating Procedures.

Procedure 3.3 HARMONIC OSCILLATOR APPROXIMATION

Debye Method. Estimate the bulk modulus K_0 and the shear modulus G of the solid in question by means of the calculating procedures of Chapter 4. Then estimate the Debye temperature by means of (3.4) to (3.6) and read the harmonic oscillator contribution for the appropriate number of degrees of freedom to the lattice thermodynamic properties C_v, U, and S from the readily available tables.[2]

Einstein + Debye Method. Estimate the principal moments of inertia of the molecule (37) and its heat of sublimation $\Delta H'_s$ (using the group increments of Tables 14.1 seq. in the absence of experimental data). Then estimate the translational reference temperature

[1] American Petroleum Institute Tables, "Selected Properties of Hydrocarbons," *JANAF-Tables Thermodynamic Properties of Inorganic Compounds* and [21].
[2] For example, in Section 4 of the *American Institute of Physics Handbook*, 2nd ed., New York, 1963.

Table 3.5 (Tentative) Constants for the Approximate Estimation of $\theta_D{}^a$ and $\theta_R{}^b$ of Molecular Crystals Composed of Rigid Molecules

Types of Compounds	a_6	$a_7^{(A)}$	$a_7^{(C)}$	$a_7^{(B)}$
Monocyclic aromatic and hetero aromatic and olefinic compounds[c]	1.7	0.74	0.72	0.64
Polynuclear aromatic hydrocarbons	1.7	0.74	0.75	0.64
Aryl dihalides	1.08	0.48	0.48	0.43
Alkyl monohalides	1.7[d]	e	—	0.62
Alkyl dihalides	—	e	—	0.65
Ice	1.97	0.37	0.39	0.49

[a] From the relation

$$\theta_D = a_6 \frac{1}{c} \frac{(N_A)^{1/3}}{V_w} \frac{(\Delta H_s)^{1/2}}{M} \; ;$$

only the coefficients for the highest observed frequencies are given.
[b] From the relation

$$\theta_R = a_7 \frac{1}{c}\left(\frac{\Delta H_s}{N_A I_i}\right)^{1/2}$$

where i stands for the indices A, B, C, of the principal moments of inertia.
[c] With $N_c \geq 3$.
[d] Valid only for $M > 100$. At $M < 100$ $a_7 \simeq 0.9$.
[e] These coefficients have to be guessed from the data of Table 3.3, keeping in mind that $a_7 = 1.44 \div$ (coefficient of Table 3.3).

θ_D and the torsional reference temperature θ_R from the coefficients and equations of Table 3.5. The contributions of the three translational degrees of freedom may then be obtained from θ_D in a table of the Debye functions and the contribution of the torsional degrees of freedom from θ_R in a table of the Einstein functions. The sum of the two contributions should be the desired datum.

CALCULATING PROCEDURE FOR HEAT CAPACITY OF SOLIDS

Procedure 3.4

Given: Rigid molecule, molecular structure, heat capacity of the ideal gas.
STEP 1: Estimate $\Delta H_s'$ (Table 14.1).
STEP 2: Estimate V_w (Table 14.1).
STEP 3: Estimate $\theta_D = a_6(N_A/V_w)^{1/3}(\Delta H_s/M)^{1/2}$, where the constant a_6 is obtained from Table 3.5.
STEP 4: Calculate the principal moments of inertia I_A, I_B, I_C of the molecule (see Refs. [16], [36], and [37]).
STEP 5: Estimate $\theta_R^{(i)} = a_7(\Delta H_s/I_c)^{1/2}$, where the constant a_7 is obtained from Table 3.5.
There is insufficient information at present to make an a priori choice between the two methods if a significant discrepancy occurs between the two estimates, as at $\theta < 0.5$.

Procedure 3.5 ANHARMONICITY CORRECTIONS

If $\rho_s^* > 0.65$ and $T > 1.5\theta_D$ or θ_R, anharmonic lattice vibrations may contribute significantly to the thermodynamic properties. The lattice heat capacity and derived properties are then best estimated by means of (3.17), (3.18), and, in the case of flexible molecules, (3.24) and (3.25) and their obvious modifications for enthalpy and entropy estimates.

Procedure 3.6 CORRECTIONS DUE TO LATTICE DEFECT FORMATION

If $\rho_s^* < 0.65$ and $T > 1.5\theta_D$ or θ_R, there is a strong possibility of sufficiently extensive lattice defect formation to affect the heat capacity, etc. The concurrent loosening of the lattice is often observable by line narrowing in nmr measurements. The requisite correction of the thermodynamic properties can be substantial but is still in a somewhat uncertain state. A rough estimate of the correction could be made with (3.20) by using the guess $\Delta H_d \approx \Delta H_s/2$ and $n_d^o \approx 4$.

Procedure 3.7 HEAT CAPACITY, ETC., OF POLYMER CRYSTALS

Vibrational assignments are generally available [34], [35], [36] only for polymers for which the experimental heat capacity data are also readily available[1] [42]. In the rare event that frequency assignments are available but not the calorimetric data, the anharmonicity corrections (3.24) should be introduced at $T > 2\theta_D$ (acoustical).

3.5 THERMAL EXPANSION

The Maxwell equation of classical thermodynamics

$$\left(\frac{\partial P}{\partial T}\right)_v = \left(\frac{\partial S}{\partial V}\right)_T \tag{3.26}$$

leads to the isentropic expansion law

$$-\frac{T}{V}\left(\frac{\partial V}{\partial T}\right)_s = \frac{C_v}{V\alpha_s K_0} = \frac{1}{\gamma}, \tag{3.27}$$

more commonly defined as

$$\gamma = -\frac{d\ln\theta_D}{d\ln V},$$

where α_s is the cubic expansion coefficient, K_0 is the isothermal bulk modulus of the solid, θ_D is the Debye temperature; the heat capacity C_v should be replaced by the lattice heat capacity C_v^s when dealing with crystals composed of polyatomic molecules in order to maintain comparability of γ, the Grüneisen constant. The latter is nearly independent of temperature between $T = 0.2\theta_D$ and θ_D. In that range K_0 is also nearly independent of temperature, hence $\alpha_s \sim C_v \sim C_p$. Actually α_s increases faster than C_p at $T > \theta_D$ especially at $T > 2\theta$ because of the effect of anharmonicity, neglected in the Grüneisen

[1] F. S. Dainton et al., *Polymer* **3**, 263–321 (1962).

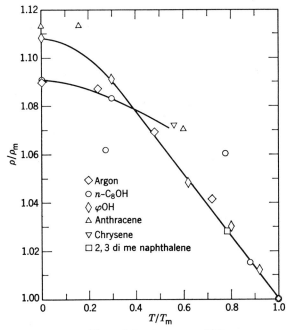

Figure 3.5 ρ/ρ_m versus T/T_m.

approximation. A rough linear approximation to the temperature dependence of α_s at $T > \theta_D$ has been derived by Cartz [9] from experimental data on cubic crystals:

$$\frac{\alpha_s}{\alpha_s(0.5T_m)} = 0.74 + 0.52 \frac{T}{T_m}, \qquad (3.28)$$

where $\alpha_s(0.5T_m)$ is α_s at $T = 0.5T_m$.

Another useful generalization is the old observation that the volume increase between $0°K$ and the melting point is about 5 to 10%. However, the curve of ρ versus T between these two temperatures differs somewhat for different substances, even in the absence of phase transitions. This is shown in Figure 3.5 in the reduced coordinates ρ/ρ_m versus T/T_m, where $\rho_m =$ density of the solid at the melting point and $T_m =$ melting point in $°K$. The slope of these expansion curves decreases with decreasing temperature as it must, since at $T \rightarrow 0°K$, $d\rho/dt \rightarrow 0$ just as $C_p = dE/dT \rightarrow 0$.

3.5.1 Effects of Molecular Structure

The relations between the expansion coefficients of (molecular) crystals and the structure of the constituent molecules exist on two levels of sophistication. On the highest level we look at single crystals only and find that thermal expansion is generally very anisotropic. The data of Table 3.6 show—in

Table 3.6   Examples for the Anisotropy of Linear Thermal Expansion of Various Molecular Crystals (from X-Ray Diffraction Data)
(In Units of 10^{-6} $°K^{-1}$)

Substance	α_1 Normal to Ring Plane	α_2 Normal to Dipole Sheet or Parallel to Long Axis	α_3 in Ring Plane	Ref.
Aromatics				
p-Dinitrobenzene	93	74	11	a
p-Nitroaniline	150	7.5	24	a
Naphthalene	225	40	115	b
Anthracene	130	30	80	b
	Normal to C–C Chain (1)	Normal to C–C Chain (2)	Parallel to C–C Chain	
Aliphatic compounds				
n-$C_{19}H_{40}$	166	102	0	b
n-$C_{24}H_{50}$	116	40	0	b
		In OH Bond Plane	Normal to OH Bond Plane	
Acetylene dicarboxylic acid	250	30	7.3	c
Pentaerythritol	131	0	0	b
Urea	76	24		

a P. J. A. McKeown et al., *Acta Cryst.* **4**, 391 (1951).
b [24].
c K. Gallagher et al., *Acta Cryst.* **8**, 561 (1955).

some typical examples—how α_s varies relative to the three axes of crystals composed of nonpolar molecules. The long-chain paraffins represent an extreme case with $\alpha_s \approx 0$ parallel to the long axis of the molecule.

3.5.2   Anisotropic Expansion of Single Crystals and Oriented Polymers

Very polar molecules, especially those forming hydrogen bonds, can give rise to similar anisotropy because there is little thermal expansion in the dipole sheets. X-ray diffraction patterns of systems, containing hydrogen bonds as well as large hydrocarbyl radicals, exhibit hardly any thermal vibration in the dipole region and substantial thermal agitation of the hydrocarbyl groups [2]. Quantitative prediction of the anisotropic thermal expansion factors is possible in principle by calculation of the local force fields from X-ray diffraction data. Such calculations are so laborious, however, that length measurements by X-ray diffraction at different temperatures are easier and more reliable. A practical consequence of anisotropic expansion of single crystals is the weakening of polycrystalline systems during temperature rises due to the development of stresses at the grain boundaries. This problem may be less serious with semicrystalline polymers because the crystallites are embedded in a viscous matrix which facilitates stress equalization.

The only oriented molecular crystals met with in technology are those occurring in oriented films and fibers. The thermal expansion of oriented films and fibers is difficult to measure because of the ever-present amorphous domains, which may be in a state of elastic extension after orientation and would snap back on heating. The lengthwise contraction on heating of oriented (stretched) fibers which is occasionally observed [17] may therefore be unrelated to changes in density. From what has been said already we may expect that the more highly oriented a fiber is, the more anisotropic its thermal expansion will be. If the degree of crystallization of the system at hand is unaffected by the orientation process, the isotropic expansion coefficient α_s stays unchanged even though the component coefficient $\alpha_\perp$ and $\alpha_\parallel$, as well as the density change during the stretching process. Then $\alpha_\parallel + 2\alpha_\perp = \alpha_s$. This relation has been verified experimentally for the case of noncrystalline (glassy) polymers at large draw ratios [13]. In general $\alpha_\parallel < \alpha_\perp$, as expected. Thermal expansion normal to the direction of orientation is of the order expected for isotropic systems (see below).

3.5.3 Isotropic Thermal Expansion

The magnitude of the cubic thermal expansion of isotropic solids, α_s, has been derived by Ludwig [26] from the theory of anharmonic vibrations of crystal lattice such that

$$\frac{\alpha_s N_A \epsilon}{C_v^{\,s}} = \tilde{\alpha}_s, \tag{3.29}$$

where $\tilde{\alpha}_s$ is a pure number, the magnitude of which should depend only on the force law [27] and on the crystal structure, and ϵ is the magnitude of the pair potential at equilibrium. For practical purposes it is more convenient to replace $N_A \epsilon$ by ΔH_s; then one obtains a dimensionless cubic expansion coefficient:

$$\alpha_s^* = \alpha_s \frac{\Delta H_s}{C_v^{\,s}}, \tag{3.30}$$

the magnitude of which should also depend on crystal structure only, and which is identical to a formulation presented by Grüeneisen 40 years ago [41].

3.5.4 Rigid Molecules

The data collection in Table 3.7 indicates the perhaps unexpected uniformity of α_s^* taken at $T > \theta_D$ for crystals composed of rigid molecules.[1] Preservation of this uniformity to $T < \theta_D$ has not yet been tested. Also shown in

[1] Here and throughout this section, α_s is taken to be the datum measured between 0.7 and $0.9 T_m$. Volume data at $T > 0.95 T_m$ may be marred by premelting.

Table 3.7   Cubic Expansion Coefficients of Crystalline Solids Composed of Rigid Nonassociating Molecules at $T/T_m \simeq 0.9$ [8]

Substance	$10^4 \alpha_s,$ $(°K^{-1})$	$\alpha_s T_m$	$\dfrac{\alpha_s \Delta H_s'}{C_v{}^s}$
A	17	0.14	0.53
Kr	11	0.13	0.44
Br_2	2.67	0.066	0.28
I_2	2.7	0.11	0.41
$P_4{}^a$	3.6	0.11_4	0.42
S_8	2.4	0.090	0.48
Al_2I_6	2.20	0.102	0.52
TiI_4	2.23	0.093	0.42
$CBr_4{}^b$	3.61	0.115	0.39
Methyl iodide	5.1	0.107	0.42
Ethylene	11.7	0.12	0.46
Ethane	9.3	0.094	0.38
Benzene	5.4	0.15	0.47
Naphthalene	2.93	0.103	0.41
Anthracene[c]	2.8	0.14	0.57
Phenanthrene	2.86	0.10_7	0.53
1,2-Benzanthracene	2.28	0.099	0.54
Triphenylene	1.51	0.071	0.35
Diphenyl	3.0	0.103	0.48
m-Terphenyl	2.35	0.085	0.48
p-Dinitrobenzene[d]	2.30	0.103	0.38
1,3,5-Tribromobenzene[d]	2.80	0.107	0.47
Average reduced coefficients	—	$0.10_5 \pm 0.02$	0.44 ± 0.05

[a] Data *above* the first-order transition temperature.
[b] Data below lowest first-order transition temperature T_1 (at $\sim 0.9 T_1$), used $\alpha_s \cdot T_1$.
[c] Literature data range from 1.9 to 3.6; hence, this line very uncertain.
[d] Extrapolated from $0.43 T_m$ by means of Cartz. Eq. (3.28). Probably low.

Table 3.7 is the product $\alpha_s T_m$, which had once been suggested by Klemm [18] and Biltz [4] as a measure of the nearly universal thermal expansion from $T = 0°K$ to $T = T_m$. This product is less uniform than α_s^*. For substances with *first-order phase* transitions at $T_1 > \theta_D$, the rule should be modified to $\alpha_s T_1 \approx 0.1$, where α_s refers to the temperaure range between θ_D and T_1.

3.5.5   Flexible Molecules

The dimensionless expansion coefficient α_s^* of crystals composed of flexible molecules naturally contains $C_v{}^s$ as estimated by (3.24). The resulting numerical values of α_s^* in Table 3.8 are of the same order as those of crystals composed of rigid molecules, but somewhat smaller. The variations noted are probably due to the variable quality of the rather difficult measurements.

Table 3.8 Cubic Expansion Coefficient of Crystalline Solids Composed of Flexible Nonassociating Molecules at $T/T_m \simeq 0.9$ [8]

Substance	$10^4 \alpha_s$, (°K^{-1})	$\alpha_s T_m$	$\dfrac{\alpha_s \Delta H_s'^a}{(5+N)R}$
p-Terphenyl	2.64	0.128	0.46
n-Octane	5.35	0.115	0.334
n-C$_{23}$H$_{48}$[b]	4.1	0.128	0.342
n-C$_{24}$H$_{50}$[b]	3.65	0.114	0.31
n-C$_{36}$H$_{62}$	3.64	0.126	0.325
n-(CH$_2$)$_\infty$	3.13	0.128	0.315
(CH$_2$–O)$_\infty$	2.4	0.108	0.29
Polyethyleneterephthalate	1.6[c]	0.086	0.25
Average			0.31 ± 0.02$_6$

[a] In the case of polymers this is $\alpha_s H_s'/nR$, where n is the number of mobile segments per repeating unit.
[b] Here α_s is taken at $\leqslant 0.9 T_{tr}$, and the item in column 3 is $\alpha_s T_{tr}$.
[c] From extrapolation to 100% crystallinity.

Hence exact calculation of C_v^s is hardly warranted and the approximations

$$\alpha_F^* = \frac{\alpha_s H_s^{\;1}}{(5+D_s)R} \quad \text{at} \quad N_s < 100, \qquad (3.31)$$

and

$$\alpha_F^* = \frac{\alpha_s H_s^{\;1}}{nR} \quad \text{at} \quad N_s > 100, \qquad (3.32)$$

when n is the number of truly mobile segments per repeating unit in the polymer, appear to be entirely adequate, and where H_s^1 and n are the heat of sublimation increment and the number of skeletal torsional oscillators (with $h\nu/k < T_m)^1$ per repeating unit in the polymer, respectively. Typical examples of α_s^* for flexible molecules are presented in Table 3.8.

The choice of examples among crystals composed of long-chain molecules is restricted because they are not only difficult to purify but small amounts of homologous impurities that stay as solid solutions in the crystal lattice cause premelting or premature loosening of the lattice far below the melting or transition points, respectively. The effect of this premelting of n-paraffins on the expansion coefficient is shown in Figure 3.6. The sharp rise in α_s shown there occurs with pure samples at $0.95T_m$ ($0.85T_{tr}$) and above. Hence most examples for Table 3.8 are restricted to $T \leq 0.85T_m$ (or $0.85T_{tr}$).

[1] The more accurate estimates by means of (3.17) to (3.25) did not seem justified for this purpose.

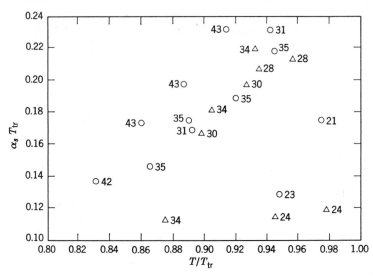

Figure 3.6   Effect of premelting on the expansion coefficient of pure n-paraffins. Numbers indicate N_c. The variables for n-$C_{43}H_{88}$ are $\alpha_s T_m$ versus T/T_m. Data by W. M. Mazee.

"Premelting" or partial melting over a wide temperature range in semi-crystalline polymers is associated with the wide size range of crystallites down to molecular dimensions, as well as the inability of the system to acquire an equilibrium (truly annealed) crystal state. As a result, constancy of the expansion coefficient of semicrystalline polymers is generally restricted to the temperature range $T_g < T < 0.85T_m$, where T_m is the so-called maximum melting point of the polymer, if there is no prior first-order phase transition. In order to relate the observed expansion coefficient of the semicrystalline polymers to the molecular structure of the crystalline component, it should be extrapolated to 100% crystallinity by making measurements on samples differing widely in crystallinity (see the mixture rule below). Direct measurement of the thermal expansion of the crystalline component is more conveniently done by X-ray diffraction measurements at several temperatures. The thermal expansion coefficient α_L of the amorphous phase can be estimated by methods given elsewhere. The large difference between α_L and α_s makes it necessary to know the crystallinity of a polymer sample at least approximately before its thermal expansion can be estimated. The presence or absence of molecular flexibility must be kept in mind when C_v^s is estimated, since the approximation $C_v^s \approx R [6 + (N_s - 1)]$ is based on the assumption that the N_s chain links are classical torsional oscillators for which $\theta_E < T$. When the joints between links are so stiff or the temperature is so low that $\theta_E > T$, the chain-link contribution to C_v^s has to be estimated from the Einstein function for the appropriate value of T/θ_E.[1] Owing to the comparatively slow change of bulk modulus with temperature, low-temperature values of α_s can be estimated from the proportionality $\alpha_s \sim C_p$ mentioned earlier. The large number of experimental low-temperature heat capacity data [21] should make this a useful extrapolation method.

Crystals composed of flexible molecules tied together by dipole sheets at intervals ≥ 20 methylene groups (at $\theta_D < T < T_1$) or by random crosslinks at intervals ≥ 40 chain links (at $T_g < T < 0.85 T_m$) exhibit cubic expansion coefficients of the same order as expected for the individual chain link.

3.5.6 Hydrogen-Bonded Species

The lattice heat capacity C_v^s of hydrogen-bonded crystals is distinctly smaller than that of ordinary van der Waals crystals because of the high libration frequency (200 to 800 cm^{-1}) [26] [30] of molecules tied to each other

Table 3.9 Lattice Frequencies Due to Hydrogen Bonds (All in cm^{-1})[a]

Crystal	Translational Vibrations	Torsional Oscillations[b]
Ice	213 to 301	601, (800)
Formic acid	170————→ 255	
Acetic acid		451
Oxalic acid · 2H$_2$O	161————→ 270	
Glucose	142, 168————→ 224	

[a] From Ref. 20.
[b] The assignment of the observed vibration frequencies is uncertain.

by hydrogen bonds. At least three, possibly all six, degrees of freedom may therefore contribute less than R to C_v^s. The appropriate magnitude of C_v^s will have to be estimated from harmonic-oscillator tables. Typical lattice-frequency data for hydrogen-bonded molecules are given on Table 3.9. An important consequence of these high lattice frequencies is that for small hydrogen-bonded molecules, $T_m \lesssim \theta_D$ or θ_R. Hence for such substances anharmonicity of lattice vibrations makes a much smaller contribution to α_s than for the usual substances, for which $T_m > 2\theta_D$ (or θ_R). As a result we find (in Table 3.10) that α_s^* and $\alpha_s T_m$ of crystals composed of small hydrogen-bonded molecules is far smaller than that of "normal" substances. Hydrogen-bonded substances of higher molecular weight, for which generally $T_m > 2\theta_D$, appear to behave essentially like nonassociated compounds. However, no

[1] As discussed on pp. 14 and 15.

Table 3.10   Cubic Expansion Coefficient of Crystalline Solids Composed of Hydrogen Bonded Molecules, at $T/T_m \simeq 0.9$

Substance	$10^4\alpha_s$, (°K^{-1})	$\alpha_s T_m$	$\dfrac{\alpha_s \Delta H'_s}{C_v^s}$	Ref. α_s	ΔH_s
Ice (H$_2$O)	1.59	0.043	0.25[a]	b	c
Ammonia	2.95	0.058	0.19$_5$	d	d
Hydrogen sulfide	5.3	0.101	0.234	e	e
Methanol	2.5	0.044	0.26[a]	f	g
Ethanol	1.6	0.025	0.23[a]	f	g
Glucose	0.84	0.035	~0.42	h	g
Phenol	3.6	0.113	0.44	f	g
Formic acid	3.01	0.092	(0.17)	f	g
Acetic acid	4.04	0.117	0.47	f	g

[a] In view of the high frequency of the torsional oscillations $C_v^s/6R \simeq 0.7$ on the average.
[b] R. W. Powell, *Proc. Roy. Soc. (London)*, **A247**, 464 (1958).
[c] [19].
[d] B. Kit and D. S. Evered, *Rocket Propellant Handbook*, Macmillan, New York, 1960.
[e] Gmelin, *Handbuch der Anorganischen Chemie*, Vol. Schwefel. Verlag Chemie 1953.
[f] W. Biltz et al., *Z. Phys. Chem.* **151**, 13 (1930).
[g] [7].
[h] G. S. Parks et al., *J. Phys. Chem.* **32**, 1366 (1928).

regularities can be found among any group of hydrogen bonded compounds for the product $\alpha_s T_m$.

3.5.7   Mixture Rules

Mixture rules for α_s can be formulated only with great caution because the crystal structure of single-phase mixtures is rarely like that of its components. When two-phase mixtures are found, however, it may be reasonable to assume that

$$\alpha_s = \sum_i \varphi_i \alpha_s(i), \qquad (3.33)$$

where φ_i is the volume fraction of the ith phase. This rule should hold particularly for suspensions of crystals in liquids that occur in semicrystalline polymers, in which validity of the rule can be expected at least at $T > T_g$. At $T < T_g$ it might hold at equilibrium, but volume relaxation times will often be too long for equilibrium to be established.

Another factor that has to be considered at $T < T_g$ is the thermoelastic effect, that is, the effect of stress due to differential expansion of the two phases on the expansion coefficient of the mixture of crystals and glassy continuum. According to Kerner [17]

$$\alpha_s(\text{suspension}) = \sum \varphi_i \alpha_i + \frac{4_G}{V_{\text{susp}}} \sum \frac{V_{\text{susp}} - K_i}{4_G + 3K_i} (\alpha_1 - \alpha_i)\varphi_i, \quad (3.34)$$

where G_1 and α_1 are the rigidity modulus and expansion coefficient, respectively, of the glassy continuum. Because the expansion coefficient of the glass is usually very close to that of the crystal, the thermoelastic effect is rarely significant.

3.6 VAPOR PRESSURE OF MOLECULAR CRYSTALS

The vapor pressure of a crystal can be estimated from the thermodynamic properties of the crystal and the vapor by the relation

$$-\ln P = \frac{H_s^\circ}{RT} + \frac{F_{\text{trans}}^\circ(g) + F_{\text{rot}}^\circ(g) - (F_D^\circ + F_{\text{tors}}^\circ)(c)}{RT} + \frac{BP}{RT} + \frac{V_s(1 - P)}{RT}$$

or in the more familiar form:

$$-\ln P = \frac{H_s^\circ}{RT} + \frac{C_p^\circ(g) - C_p(s)}{R} \ln T + \frac{S_{\text{trans}}^\circ(g) + S_{\text{rot}}^\circ(g) - S_D^\circ + S_{\text{tors}}^\circ}{R}$$

$$+ \frac{BP}{RT} + \frac{V_s(1 - P)}{RT},$$

where P is in atmospheres, the free-energy functions have the obvious meaning, and the last two terms on the right covering gas imperfections and entropy change of the solid, respectively, can be neglected unless $P > 1$ atm, which is rare with crystals. The underlying assumption is that internal molecular vibrations are unaffected by changing from the vapor to the solid phase. The free-energy functions and entropy of the gas can be obtained from [14] and [19]. Computer programs for estimating moments of inertia of complex molecules [36], [37] as well as manual calculating procedures [16] are widely available. The functions $F_D(c)$ and $F_{\text{tors}}(c)$ can be computed by the methods given in this chapter.

The accuracy of vapor pressures estimated from ΔH_s increments and from correlated crystal lattice, including libration, frequencies will hardly be better than to within an order of magnitude. It may be worthwhile to check the estimate with a calculation of the vapor pressure of the liquid at the melting point T_m by a suitable correlation scheme [6], [33]. The desired vapor pressure of the solid, $p(T)$, is then

$$\ln \left[\frac{p(T_m)}{p(T)} \right] = \frac{\Delta \bar{H}_s}{R} \left(\frac{1}{T} - \frac{1}{T_m} \right), \quad (3.37)$$

CALCULATING PROCEDURE: CUBIC THERMAL EXPANSION COEFFICIENT (α_s) OF CRYSTALS FOR THE TEMPERATURE RANGE $0.7T_m < T < 0.9T_m$, or $0.7T_{tr} < T < 0.95T_{tr}$

Procedure	Molecule Type	Available Data	Procedure and Equation	Error	Section
3.5	Rigid, nonassociated	T_m	$\alpha_s = 0.105/T_m \ [°K^{-1}]$	±20	3.5.3
					3.5.4
		Molecular structure	1. Estimate ΔH_s^1 by (15-10).		
			2. Select f (Number of external degrees of freedom per molecule).		
			3. $\alpha_s = 0.44fR/\Delta H_s^1 \ [°K^{-1}]$.	±12	3.5.4
3.6	Flexible, nonassociated	T_m	$\alpha_s = 0.120/T_m \ [°K^{-1}]$	±5	3.5.5
		Molecular structure	1. Estimate ΔH_s^1 by (15-10).		
			2. Determine N_s = Number of independently mobile segments per molecule.		
			3. $\alpha_s = 0.33(N_s + 5)R/\Delta H_s^1 \ [°K^{-1}]$.	±5	3.5.5
3.7	Polymers, nonassociated	T_m	$\alpha_s = 0.11/T_m$	±15	3.5.5
		Molecular structure	1. Estimate H_s^1 by (15-10).		
			2. Determine n_s = Number of independently mobile segments per repeating unit.		
			3. $\alpha_s = 0.28 n_s R/H_s^1$.	±10	
3.8	Hydrogen bonded	Molecular structure	1. Estimate ΔH_s^1 by (15-10).		3.4
			2. Estimate $\omega_D, \omega_R, C_D^s$ by Procedure 3.1 and Table 3.10.		3.5.6
			3. $\alpha_s = \alpha^*(C_D + C_R)/\Delta H_s^1$.	±10	
			4. When $M < 60 \ \alpha_s^* = 0.23$. When $M > 70 \ \alpha_s^* = 0.44$.	±7	
3.9	For all types	α at T and $P = 0$ (Atmospheric pressure)	Effect of Pressure:		4.3
			1. Estimate K_0 by Procedures 4.1 to 4.5.		4.4
			2. Take $K_1 = 8$ unless known otherwise.		
			$3.^a \ \ln\left[\dfrac{\alpha(P)}{\alpha(0)}\right] = \left(\dfrac{2}{K_1} - 1\right)\ln\left(1 + \dfrac{K_1 P}{K_0}\right)$.		
3.10	For all types	α at $0.7T_m < T < 0.9T_m$ From Procedure 3.5 to 3.8; Molecular structure	α at $T < 0.7T_m$:	%	
			1. Estimate ΔH_s^1 by (15-1).		
			2. Estimate moments of inertia.		
			3. Estimate ω_D, ω_R by Procedure 3.4.		
			4. Estimate C_D, C_R by Procedure 3.5.		
			5. $\alpha_s(T) = \alpha(0.87T_m) \cdot [(C_D + C_R)(T)/(C_D + C_R)(0.87T_m)]$.		

[a] I am indebted to Professor Geoffrey Gee for directing my attention to this relationship, which is probably valid to 4000 atm.

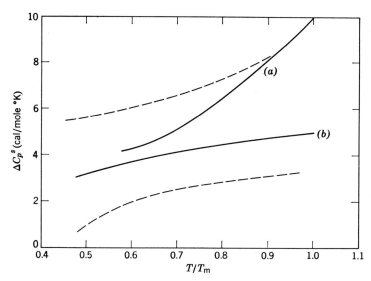

Figure 3.7   Heat capacity difference between crystalline solid and vapor as function of the reduced temperature (at $T < \theta_D$ $\Delta C_p{}^s$ becomes <0). The broken curves indicate the observed limits for the respective classes: (a) typical for hydrocarbons and slightly polar compounds with $T_m > 200°K$; (b) typical for very polar compounds and for hydrocarbons with $T_m < 180°K$.

where $\Delta \bar{H}_s = \Delta H_s(T_m) + \frac{1}{2}(T_m - T)\Delta C_p(s, g)$. Crude estimates of $\Delta C_p(s, g)$ are presented in Figure 3.7. Unless $T_m - T$ is very large, errors in $\Delta C_p(s, g)$ will not have a significant effect on the vapor-pressure calculation. Many vapor-pressure data on molecular crystals have been published in recent years. These measurements are very difficult, and small amounts of volatile impurities (which are very laborious to remove) can seriously falsify the data. The curvature of the vapor pressure versus temperature relations and the derived heat of sublimation should be checked for inernal consistency and for compatibility with data on related compounds before the experimental data are accepted (See Section 15.4).

REFERENCES

[1] Anderson, O. L., *J. Phys. Chem. Solids* **24**, 909 (1963).
[2] Bacon, G. E., *Rev. Mod. Phys.* **30**, 94 (1958).
[3] Becka, L. N. and D. W. J. Cruickshank, *Proc. Roy. Soc. (London)* **A273**, 435, 455 (1963).
[4] Biltz, W., et al., *Z. Phys. Chem.* **151**, B (1930).
[5] Biltz, W., *Raumchemie der Festen Stoffe* Leopold Voss (Leipzig, 1934).
[6] Bondi, A. and R. B. McConaughy, *Proc. Am. Petr. Inst.* **42**, (III) 40 (1962).

[7] Bondi, A., *J. Chem. Eng. Data* **8**, 371 (1963).
[8] Bondi, A., *J. Appl. Phys.* **37**, 4643 (1966).
[9] Cartz, L., *Proc. Phys. Soc.* (*London*) **B68**, 951, 957 (1955).
[10] Cruickshank, D. W. J., *Rev. Mod. Phys.* **30**, 163 (1958).
[11] Dobbs, E. R. and G. O. Jones, *Rept. Progr. Phys.* **20**, 516 (1957).
[12] Eastabrook, J. N., *Phil. Mag.* **2**, 1415 (1957).
[13] Hellwege, K. H., J. Hennig, and W. Knappe, *Kolloid Z.* **188**, 121 (1963).
[14] Hirschfelder, J. O., D. P. Stevenson, and H. Eyring, *J. Chem. Phys.* **5**, 896 (1937).
[15] *Inelastic Scattering of Neutrons in Solids and Liquids*, International Atomic Energy Agency, Vienna, 1963.
[16] Janz, G. J., *Estimation of Thermodynamic Properties of Organic Compounds*, Academic Press, New York, 1958.
[17] Kerner, E. H., *Proc. Phys. Soc.* (*London*) **B69**, 808 (1958).
[18] Klemm, W., *Z. Elektrochem.* **34**, 526 (1928).
[19] Kolobov, E. I., *Russ. J. Phys. Chem.* **34**, 339 (1960).
[20] Landolt-Börnstein, *Zahlenwerte und Funktionen*, Springer, Berlin, 1955, Vol. I/4, *Kristalle*.
[21] Landolt-Börnstein, *Zahlenwerte und Funktionen*, Springer, Berlin, 1961, Vol. II/4, *Kalorische Zustandsgrössen*.
[22] Leibfried, G. and W. Ludwig, *Solid State Phys.* **12**, 275 (1961).
[23] London, F., *J. Phys. Chem.* **46**, 305 (1942).
[24] Lonsdale, K., *Z. Krist.* **112**, 188 (1959).
[25] Lord, R. C., *J. Chem. Phys.* **9**, 700 (1941).
[26] Ludwig, W., *J. Phys. Chem. Solids* **4**, 283 (1958).
[27] MacDonald, D. K. C. and S. K. Roy, *Phys. Rev.* **97**, 673 (1955).
[28] Maslov, Y. P., *Russ. J. Phys. Chem.* **35**, 478 (1960).
[29] Nölting, J., *Ber. Bunsenges.* **68**, 939 (1964).
[30] Pimentel, G. C. and A. L. McLellan, *The Hydrogen Bond*, Freeman, San Francisco, 1960.
[31] Packard, J. R. and C. A. Swenson, *J. Phys. Chem. Solids* **24**, 1405 (1963).
[32] Pathak, K. N., *Phys. Rev.* **139**, A1569 (1965).
[33] Reid, R. C. and T. K. Sherwood, *Properties of Gases and Liquids*, McGraw-Hill, New York, 1958.
[34] Snyder, R. G. and J. H. Schachtschneider, *Spectrochim. Acta* **19**, 85, 117 (1963).
[35] Snyder, R. G. and J. H. Schachtschneider, *Spectrochim. Acta* **20**, 853 March 1964.
[36] Snyder, R. G., Shell Development Company, private communication.
[37] Tolles, W. M. and W. D. Gwinn, "Program to Obtain Moments of Inertia," University of California, Berkeley, 1961.
[38] Wallace, D. C., *Phys. Rev.* **131**, 2046 (1963).
[39] Whalley, E., *Trans. Faraday Soc.* **54**, 1613 (1958).
[40] Wulff, C. A., *J. Chem. Phys.* **39**, 1227 (1963).
[41] Zwikker, C., *Physical Properties of Solid Materials* Pergamon Press, London, 1954.

GENERAL READING

Handbuch der Physik, S. Flügge, ed., Springer, Berlin, 1955, Vol. VII/1, *Kristallphysik*.
Swalin, R. A., *Thermodynamics of Solids*, Wiley, 1962.

4

Elastic Properties
of Molecular Crystals
Including Polymer Crystals

Growing concern with semicrystalline polymers and with organic crystals as semiconductors has made it worthwhile to put at the disposal of the engineer and the chemist an organized body of information correlating the elastic properties of molecular crystals with molecular structure. Owing to the preoccupation of physicists with metallic and ionic crystals, comparatively few experimental investigations of the elastic properties of molecular crystals have been published. However, the perfection of ultrasonic and x-ray techniques now permits convenient measurements on complicated crystal structures, and the pace of publication has quickened perceptibly in recent years.

The main purpose of the present work is the extension of the few available data on very few compounds through the use of corresponding-state-type correlations, in order to permit extrapolation from single datum points over a wide range of temperature and pressure conditions and the estimation of the elastic properties of new substances from molecular-structure information alone. An incidental benefit of the latter attempt is the possibility to set upper limits for the elastic moduli that any conceivable molecular structure might yield, and thus prevent futile searches for organic compounds that might have the rigidity desired by materials engineers.

The scope of corresponding-states-type correlations of the properties of solids is far more limited than that of liquids because their packing density is determined by molecule geometry and anisotropy of force-field distribution, and only secondarily by the ratio $fRT/\Delta H_s$, the ratio of thermal kinetic to potential (lattice) energy. For liquids, on the contrary, the latter ratio is the primary factor determining packing density. Hence property correlation can be strictly valid only for a given crystal-structure type. In the absence of enough data to produce these many specialized correlations only rather crude average

53

Table 4.1 Elastic Constants of Various Molecular Crystals (All in 10^{10} dynes/cm^2; All Adiabatic)

Substance	T (°K)	C_{11}	C_{22}	C_{33}	C_{12}	C_{13}^{a}	C_{23}^{a}	C_{44}	C_{55}	C_{66}	Ref.
S$_8$ orthorhombic	293	24.0	20.5	48.3	13.3	15.9 [31]	17.1	4.3	8.7	7.6	45
Benzene	293	14.1	8.7	18.2	6.4	—	7.0	3.4	8.1	2.1	54
	170	8.02	9.26	7.88	3.85	4.80	5.08	3.18	5.53	1.95	22
	250	6.14	6.56	5.83	3.52	4.01	3.90	1.97	3.78	1.53	22
Naphthalene	~298	7.80	9.90	11.90	4.45	3.40 [31]	2.30	3.30	2.10	4.15^{b}	1
Hexamethylenetetramine	295	16.43	—	—	4.33	—	—	5.15	—	—	19
Benzil	293	11.20	—	2.95	—	−0.09	−1.46 [14]	4.16	—	5.98	11
Ice	257	13.85	—	14.99	7.07	5.81	—	3.19	—	—	27
Pentaerythritol	293	6.1	—	8.0	−2.50	0.50	0.38 [16]	3.5	—	4.6	53

^{a} Numbers in parentheses are changed indices for elastic constants.
^{b} In addition there are: C_{15}, −0.6; C_{25}, −2.7; C_{34}, +2.9; C_{46}, −0.5.

correlations could be produced, which work out rather more poorly in the case of elastic properties than had been found to be the case with thermal expansion and heat capacity (Chapter 3).

All properties and state variables will be generalized in terms of the fundamental parameters: heat of sublimation (a measure of lattice energy), van der Waals volume (a measure of molecule geometry), and the number of external degrees of freedom per molecule, including those due to internal torsional oscillation. Except for the rather similar correlation of the properties of rare-gas crystals, no rational property correlation of molecular solids has been found in the literature. Hence no informaton is being suppressed by examining the available information in this one-sided manner.

It should be noted in passing that Grüneisen's classical papers of 40 years ago anticipated the correlation of elastic properties of crystals at $0°K$ in terms of their heat of sublimation and molal volume. The only significant improvement since then is the definition of a temperature scale $zfRT/\Delta H_s$ by Leibfried and Ludwig [29] which, because of the difficulty of defining the number of nearest neighbors (z), is only of limited utility. Widespread applicability of any such scheme has been made possible by the provision of simple methods to estimate ΔH_s and V_w. (Sections 14.1 and 14.4.)

4.1 GENERAL PRINCIPLES

Most crystals are as anisotropic with respect to the elastic moduli as they are with respect to thermal expansion. The few published measurements of such elastic anisotropy of molecular single crystals have been collected in Table 4.1.

Most measurements, however, have been carried out on polycrystalline substances which were treated as effectively isotropic. The moduli of primary interest are the bulk modulus K = (applied hydrostatic pressure) $\div$ (negative dilatation); Young's modulus E = (uniaxial stress on a thin rod) $\div$ (normal strain); shear modulus G = shear stress $\div$ shear strain. These three moduli[1]

---

[1] In all of the following correlations the elastic moduli of polycrystalline systems have been calculated, where necessary, from the elastic constants C_{ij} of single crystals as Voigt averages, using the method of Hungtington [18]:

$$\bar{K} = \tfrac{1}{3}(F + 2D); \quad \bar{G}_v = \tfrac{1}{5}(F - D + 3H);$$
$$\bar{E}_v = \frac{(F - D + 3H)(F + 2D)}{2F + 3D + H}$$

where

$$F = \tfrac{1}{3}(C_{11} + C_{22} + C_{33}); \quad D = \tfrac{1}{3}(C_{12} + C_{23} + C_{13}); \quad H = \tfrac{1}{3}(C_{44} + C_{55} + C_{66}).$$

For engineering purposes it appeared unnecessary to calculate also the usually slightly lower Reuss-average moduli, and then average the Voigt and Reuss averages. Other considerations for the conversion of single-crystal properties to those of a polycrystalline aggregate can be found in a recent paper by Kneer [21].

Table 4.2   Relations Among Elastic Moduli[a]

Known	K	E	G	σ'
E, σ	$\dfrac{E}{3(1 - 2\sigma')}$	E	$\dfrac{E}{2(1 + \sigma')}$	σ'
E, K	K	E	$\dfrac{3KE}{9K - E}$	$\dfrac{1}{2} - \dfrac{E}{6K}$
E, G	$\dfrac{GE}{3(3G - E)}$	E	G	$\dfrac{E}{2G} - 1$
K, σ'	K	$3K(1 - 2\sigma')$	$\dfrac{3K(1 - 2\sigma')}{2(1 + \sigma')}$	σ'
K, G	K	$\dfrac{9KG}{6K + G}$	G	$\dfrac{3K - 2G}{6K + 2G}$
G, σ'	$\dfrac{2G(1 + \sigma')}{3(1 - 2\sigma')}$	$2G(1 + \sigma')$	G	σ'

[a] From Pearson, C. E., *Theoretical Elasticity*, Harvard University Press, Cambridge, Massachusetts, 1959.

are related to each other by the equations shown in Table 4.2. A fourth constant occurs there; Poisson's ratio $\sigma' \equiv -e_2/e_1$, where e_1 and e_2 are the strains parallel and perpendicular, respectively, to the uniaxial stress applied to a thin rod. The range $\frac{1}{4} < \sigma' < \frac{1}{2}$ is usually found, the low end generally (but not exclusively) characteristic of hard crystals, whereas $\sigma' = \frac{1}{2}$ means the substance is a "liquid," that is, $K \gg G$.

A systematic investigation of the relation between σ' and crystal structure, chemical composition, etc., is entirely lacking in the area of molecular crystals, most of the available data having been assembled in Table 4.3. Poisson's ratio seems to be roughly correlated with T/T_m and with the packing density ρ^*. Specific effects should be expected with layer lattice crystals. The curves of σ' versus temperature for benzene and for two semicrystalline polymers in Figure 4.1 show the expected trend from the value $\frac{1}{3}$, typical of hard solids, to $\frac{1}{2}$ as the melting point is approached. A correlation with the degree of crystallinity can be found for polyethylene in Ref. [63].

Unless mentioned otherwise, only the isothermal elastic moduli are discussed in this section. Adiabatic moduli will be designated by the subscript "ad."[1] In this connection it should be pointed out that, contrary to rather

[1] $K = K_{ad} \dfrac{C_v}{C_p}$; $E = E_{ad} \dfrac{2}{3}(2 - \sigma') - \dfrac{C_p}{C_v}\left(\dfrac{1 - 2\sigma'}{3}\right)$; $G = G_{ad}$.

Table 4.3 Isothermal Elastic Moduli ... Molecular Crystals (by Sonic M...od Except Where Noted Otherwise)

Substance	T (°K)	I/T_m	ρ^*	$\Delta H_{sl}/V_w$ (10^{10} dyn cm^{-2})	E^*	K_0^*	G^*	σ'	Ref.
Argon	0	0	0.74	0.425		5.60	3.32	0.25	a, b
	60	0.72	0.72			4.61	2.52	0.27	a, b
	80	0.95	0.71			3.74			a
Xenon	0	0	0.74	0.59		6.1			c
	100	0.62	0.70			3.9			c
	150	0.93	0.67			2.6			c
Ice (polycrystalline)	0	0		6.3		1.46			i
	140					1.42			i
(single crystal)	257	0.94			1.46	1.21	0.546	0.32	i, j
Benzene	170	0.609	0.50	0.886	8.02	6.05	3.22	0.29	d
(single crystal)	250	0.900	0.63		5.09	4.25	1.97	0.33	d
Naphthalene	210	0.595	0.676	0.975	13.6	8.1	5.6	0.22	c
(single crystal)	298	0.85	0.661		9.2	6.2 (6.7)	3.7	0.25	c (f)
	(298)	0.85	0.661		8.06	5.0	3.22	0.25	g
Hexamethylenetetramine	293	0.59	0.672	1.06	12.65	7.50 (7.75)	5.20	0.23	h (f)
(single crystal)									
n-triacontane	173			0.81			2.60		k
	293					(6.0)	1.25		k (f, l)

a K_0^-: J. R. Barker and E. R. Dobbs, *Phil. Mag.*, 7th Ser. **46**, 1069 (1955).
b G^-: G. O. Jones and A. R. Sparkes, *Phil. Mag.*, 8th Ser. **10**, 1053 (1964).
c [22].
e [65], from longitudinal sound velocity, using σ' from Ref. g.
f [10], (by static compression).
g [11]; the absolute level of these moduli is clearly at variance with those derived from References e and f.
h [19].
i A. J. Leadbetter, *Proc. Roy. Soc. (London)* **A287**, 403 (1965).
j [24].
k [40].
l Extrapolated from the compression data of n-$C_{28}H_{58}$ in Ref. f.

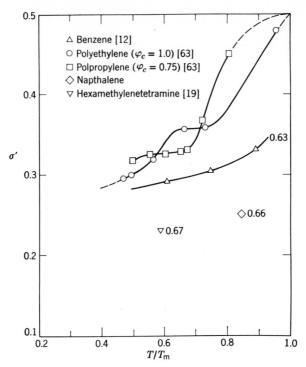

Figure 4.1   Temperature dependence of Poisson's ratio σ'; parameter by pure compound curves (points) is ρ^*.

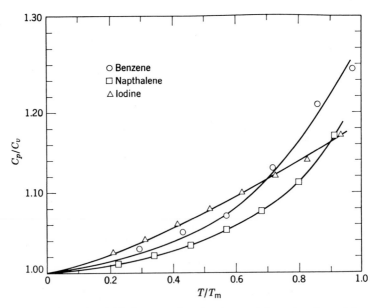

Figure 4.2   The ratio C_p/C_v for several molecular crystals as function of temperature.

frequent statements in the literature, C_p/C_v of molecular crystals is quite large and cannot be neglected. Typical experimental data, presented in Figure 4.2. show that near the melting point C_p/C_v is of the same order as it is for liquids (see Section 3.4 for calculation of C_p/C_v).

All of the conventional elastic moduli defined above assume linear relations between deformation and stress and are therefore strictly valid only for infinitely small deformation. Accepting a constancy of the elastic modulus to within $\pm 1\%$, the 6:12 or exp:6 potential, characteristic of molecular crystals, yield a strain of about 0.4% as upper limit of the approximately linear, or "small strain" regime. Finite deformations of crystalline solids can be expressed phenomenologically, as through the method of Murnaghan [34] or through a molecular theory for anharmonic motions along the contour of the potential-energy well. Large deformations of molecular crystals are generally restricted to compression and perhaps shear, because most molecular crystals break in extension at very small elongations.

The temperature coefficients of the elastic moduli M of isotropic solids have been derived from thermodynamic considerations by Anderson and Dienes [2] as follows:

$$\frac{dM}{dT} = \alpha_s V\left(\frac{\partial M}{\partial V}\right)_T + \left(\frac{\partial M}{\partial T}\right)_V = -K\alpha_s\left(\frac{\partial M}{\partial P}\right)_T + \left(\frac{\partial M}{\partial T}\right)_V, \quad (4.1)$$

$$\frac{d \ln M}{dT} = \frac{2\, d \ln \theta D}{dT} - \frac{\alpha_s}{3} + f(\sigma')\frac{d\sigma'}{dT}, \quad (4.2)$$

$$\frac{d \ln \beta_T}{dT} = \alpha_s + \frac{d \ln \alpha_s}{dT} - \frac{d \ln C_p}{dT}, \quad (4.3)$$

where $\beta_T = K_0^{-1}$. Because in general not even the magnitude of $(\partial M/\partial T)_V$ nor of the first and third terms in the second equation are known, only the last equation has a chance of being applicable in practice.

Recently Anderson [2a] and Chang [11a] showed that it is possible to derive a more convenient set of relations from equations (4.1) to (4.3) if we take the pressure coefficient of the moduli into consideration. As shown later (4.23) $K(P) = K_0 + K_1 P$ is in excellent agreement with experiment, especially at high pressures. According to Chang (loc. cit.),

$$-\frac{1}{\alpha_s}\frac{d \ln K_0}{dT} = K_1 - 1, \quad (4.4)$$

where α_s is the volumetric thermal expansion coefficient discussed in Chapter 3. More generally, then,

$$K_0(T) = K_0(0) - bT \exp\left(\frac{-\theta_D}{2T}\right), \quad (4.5)$$

where $b \approx 2C_v^s(K_1 - 1)^2/V_0$, and similarly, if $d\sigma'/dT = \text{const.} = \text{small}$,

$$E(T) = E_0 - b_1 T \exp\left(\frac{-\theta_D}{2T}\right),$$

where $b_1 \approx b$. The above definition of b uses the relation that the Grüneisen constant $\gamma = (1/2)(K_1 - 1)$.

4.2 GENERAL EFFECTS OF MOLECULAR STRUCTURE AND CRYSTAL STRUCTURE

The elastic moduli of a crystal expresses the change in energy of the system due to deformation. On a molecular scale the system's resistance to deformation depends on the curvature $(d^2\varphi/dr^2)$ of the potential-energy well near its bottom. The elastic moduli of a crystal are therefore specified as soon as the force law and the crystal symmetry have been fixed.

Specifically, Barron and Domb [4] observed that Young's modulus of close-packed-cubic crystals should be $E = 1.35a^2(d^2\varphi/dr^2)$ and their bulk modulus $K = 1.08a^2(d^2\varphi/dr^2)$, where a is the lattice parameter; their Poisson constant is $\sigma' = 0.27$. Assuming the 6:12 (Lennard-Jones–Devonshire) potential one obtains for the generalized elastic moduli C_{ij}^* of monatomic molecular crystals

$$C_{ij}^* = \frac{C_{ij}\sigma^3}{\epsilon} = (a_{ij}\rho^{*5} - b_{ij}\rho^{*3})f\left(\frac{kT}{\epsilon}\right), \tag{4.6}$$

where the force constants σ and ϵ have their usual meaning, and a_{ij} and b_{ij} are numerical constants which depend on the lattice geometry of the crystal. The explicit dependence on packing density as well as temperature should be noted.

The temperature dependence of the elastic moduli at atmospheric pressure is a function of the increase in vibrational energy with temperature. For the case of rare-gas crystals (assuming a 6:12 potential) Ludwig [30] derived the relations

$$\tilde{E} = C_{11}^* = \frac{C_{11}\sigma^3}{\epsilon} = 102.5\left(1 - 0.25\frac{U_h}{N_A\epsilon} - 0.14\frac{TC_v^h}{N_A\epsilon}\right), \tag{4.7}$$

$$\tilde{G} = C_{44}^* = 51.2\left(1 - 0.11\frac{U_h}{N_A\epsilon}\right), \tag{4.8}$$

$$\tilde{K} = \frac{C_{11}^* + 2C_{12}^*}{3} = 68.4\left(1 - 0.32\frac{U_h}{N_A\epsilon}\right), \tag{4.9}$$

where the constants σ, ϵ have their usual meaning, U_h, C_v^h are the internal energy and the heat capacity (at constant volume) of the crystal, respectively, in the harmonic-oscillator (Debye) approximation. Since $C_v^h/N_A\epsilon$ is a universal form of α_s (see Section 3.5.3), the temperature coefficient of Young's modulus and of the bulk modulus is primarily the expansion coefficient.

As in earlier treatments, we replace the force constants for spherical molecules, ϵ and σ, by the more generally applicable ΔH_s, the heat of sublimation (at the lowest first-order transition temperature as standard state) and V_w, the van der Waals volume. The reduced moduli are then defined as $K_0^* = K_0 V_w/\Delta H_s$, $E^* = E V_w/\Delta H_s$, and $G^* = G V_w/\Delta H_s$. The nonspecific force contributions of molecular structure should be eliminated by this reducing procedure. However, owing to the still implied central force law, only gross effects are taken care of in this way.

4.3 THE BULK MODULUS (AT LOW PRESSURES)

From the point of view of correlation with molecular structure, it is advantageous to separate the discussion of the bulk modulus at infinitely small compressions from that at large deformation, which will be treated later on. Moreover, quantitative correlations are proposed here only for the isotropic bulk modulus, the practically important property of polycrystalline systems A better feel for the effects of molecular structure is obtained, however, from data showing the anisotropic response of crystals to hydrostatic compression, such as those of Table 4.4. There it is apparent that crystals composed of elongated nonpolar molecules are more compressible normal than parallel to

Table 4.4 Anisotropy of Compressibility of Various Molecular Crystals (All at Room Temperature; Percent Compression between 0 and 10,000 atm of Crystal a, b, and c)

Substance	$\dfrac{\Delta V}{V}$	$\dfrac{\Delta a}{a}$	$\dfrac{\Delta b}{b}$	$\dfrac{\Delta c}{c}$	Ref.
Diphenyl	10	5.4[a]	3.0	2.2[b]	c
p-Terphenyl	9	5.4[a]	3.0	1.4[b]	c
p-p-Quaterphenyl		5.4[a]	3.0	~0	c
Graphite	2.3	~0	~0	2.3[a]	d
n-C_{34}-H_{70}	—	5.7	5.6	~0	e
$C(CH_2OH)_4$	—	1.0[f]	—	4.4[g]	a

[a] Normal to ring planes.
[b] Parallel to long axis of molecule.
[c] Kabalkina, S. S. Soviet Phys.—Solid State 4, 2288 (1963).
[d] Kabalkina, S. S. and L. F. Vereshchagin, Soviet Phys.—Doklady 5, 373 (1960).
[e] Kabalkina, S. S. and Z. V. Troitskaya, J. Struct. Chem. (USSR) 9, 22 (1961).
[f] In hydrogen-bond plane.
[g] Normal to layers of hydrogen bonds.

the long axis of the molecules in parallel alignment. Crystals of polar, especially hydrogen-bonded, molecules are 4 to 6 times more compressible normal than parallel to the plane of dipoles.

The temperature dependence of the low-pressure bulk modulus K_0 can be expressed by a simple modification of (4.9) as

$$K_0^*(T) = K_0^*(0)\left(1 - \frac{1.92U_h}{H_s} - \frac{1.26TC_v^h}{H_s}\right),$$ (4.10)

where U_h and C_v^h are the lattice contributions to the internal energy and heat capacity of the crystal in the harmonic-oscillator approximation, and can be obtained from the Debye tables for the appropriate value of the Debye temperature θ_D and number of external degrees of freedom per molecule and $K_0^*(0)$ is K_0^* at $T = 0°K$. The conversion from the pair potential $N_A\epsilon$ to ΔH_s was made with the assumption that the number of nearest neighbors, z, is 12. Where $z \neq 12$, the numerical coefficients have to be multiplied by a factor $z/12$.

The practical applicability of (4.10) is severely handicapped by the frequent impossibility of defining z. Yet the desire to define a temperature-independent value of K_0^*, such as $K_0^*(0)$ can be met to a limited extent by giving z the correct value, when known, as with Ar, H_2O, and polyethylene, and an arbitrary value which makes (4.10) reproduce the known temperature dependence of K_0^*. The $K_0^{*\prime}(0)$ so obtained should be a function of ρ^* only. Grüneisen showed that for solids following an $n:m$ force law, $K_0^*/\rho^* = m:n/9$, which yields $K_0^*/\rho^* = 8$ for the favorite $6:12$ potential, somewhat less than is actually observed (as will be seen in the next section), but of the correct order of magnitude. A completely empirical but perhaps more useful alternative correlation of $K_0^*(T) = f\rho^*$, T/T_m will be presented as part of the discussion of the effects of molecular structure.

4.3.1 Nonassociating Polar and Nonpolar Compounds [7]

The few molecular crystals with well defined z and f, the elastic moduli of which have been measured over a range of temperature, are A, $X_e(f = 3, z = 12)$, ice $(f = 6, z = 4)$ and perhaps highly crystalline polyethylene $(f = 1, z = 6)/(per CH_2 group)$. The accuracy of the representation of the best data by (4.10) suggested evaluation of the "effective" z from the temperature function of K_0. This yields $z = 8$ for benzene [22] and for CBr_4 [31].

With the exception of the higher n-paraffins (nC_{18} and nC_{28}), for which $z \approx 6$ and $f \approx 3 + (N_c - 1)$, the assumption $z = 8$ appears to be in reasonable agreement with the rather scattered data. Within that scatter one can clearly discern the expected trend of $K_0^*(0)$ with packing density. Some of the scatter is undoubtedly due to the inapplicability of a central force field assumption to polyatomic molecules, and some of the scatter is caused by the uncertain extrapolation of high pressure compression data from above 5000 atm to atmospheric pressure.

The theory underlying (4.7) through (4.10) assumes a uniform isotropic monatomic crystal lattice. Lattice defects that are likely to appear between $0.9T_m$ and T_m would lower the moduli below those predicted by the theory. Noncentral forces may be expected to invalidate the theory. The great practical importance of the theory, prediction of the elastic modulus at any temperature from a single datum or even from molecular structure information alone, calls for a quantitative assessment of its reliability.

Peculiarly, the only data for a monatomic molecular crystal, the bulk moduli of Xenon decrease far more slowly with increasing temperature than demanded by Ludwig's theory (4.7) as has also been observed by Barron and Klein [5a]. By contrast, there is excellent agreement with the theory, in form of (4.10) with the temperature dependence of the moduli data of ice,[1] up to $0.93T_m$, and with those for benzene, [27] also up to $0.9T_m$. Only the temperature coefficient of the shear modulus of benzene is very much steeper than demanded by theory. It appears in summary that Ludwig's theory contains the basic elements required for representation of the experimental modulus data but that more experience has to be gained with its use before one can point the direction of its further elaboration.

Among the empirical correlations only the relation of the zeropoint moduli to packing density is worthy of comment. There the outstanding puzzle is the contrast between the comparatively regular trend of the data for complicated substances and the sharp deviation of the argon and xenon data from the common trend, that is, their far lower zeropoint moduli than corresponds to their high packing density. The ordering parameter in the correlation of zero-point moduli may well be one that characterizes the applicable potential function.

4.3.2 Hydrogen-Bonded and Other Strongly Associated Substances

This group of compounds must be divided into three broad classes before rational correlation of elastic properties can be undertaken. One class contains substances that, like water, form a three-dimensional network of hydrogen or other strong association bonds connecting small rigid molecules. Here all deformations involve deformations of the hydrogen (or association) bonds. Consequently, at least to a close approximation, $\Delta H_s/V_w$ is an appropriate reducing parameter, as is evident from the previously noted location of ice on the general correlation curve of Figure 4.3 and 4.4. Levulose with its three primary hydroxyl groups very nearly meets this specification and hence fits very nearly into the correlations of the same figure.

The second and more highly populated class of compounds is composed of

[1] See references in Figure 4.3.

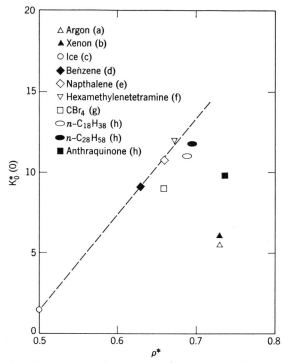

Figure 4.3   Plot of zero-point bulk modulus $K_0^*(0)$ versus packing density ρ^* [7]: [a] J. R. Barker and E. R. Dobbs, *Phil. Mag.* **46**, 1069 (1955). The authors' (extrapolated) value of $K_0(0)$ has been entered, for (4.4) does not represent the data. [b] From [14]. Here the $K_0(0)$ is from the authors' extrapolation. [c] From [11]. Here the author's value $K_0(0)$ coincides with that derived from (4.4), using $z = 4$. [d] From [10]. $K_0(0)$ obtained by means of (4.4), which represents the data excellently with $z = 8$. [e] S. S. Yum and R. T. Beyer, *J. Chem. Phys.* **40**, 2538 (1964), took Poisson's ratio $= 0.25$ from data by K. S. Alexandrov et al. *Soviet Phys.—Cryst.* **8**, 164 (1963) whose absolute value of $K_0(T)$ appears rather low; $K_0(0)$ from (4.4) with $z = 8$. [f] S. Haussühl, *Acta Cryst.* **11**, 58 (1958) and $z = 8$ and θ_R and θ_D from L. N. Becka and D. W. J. Cruickshank, *Proc. Roy. Soc. (London)* **A273**, 435, 455 (1963); $K_0(0)$ by (4.4). [g] From [13]. $K_0(0)$ by (4.4), taking $z = 8$. [h] P. W. Bridgman, *Proc. Am. Acad. Arts Sci.* **76**, 1, 55 (1948); **77**, 115 (1949).

molecules forming association chains along one or two of its molecule axes. For the first case, the reduced bulk modulus should be

$$K_0^* = K_0^* \left[\frac{2V_w(R)}{3H_s(R)} + \frac{1}{3} \frac{V_w(X)}{H_s(X)} \right] \quad \text{or} \quad K_0^* = K_0^* \left[\frac{2}{3} \frac{V_w}{H_s(h)} + \frac{1}{3} \frac{V_w(X)}{H_s(X)} \right],$$

(4.11)

where $H_s(R)$ and $V_w(R)$ are the heat of sublimation and V_w increments, respectively, of the nonpolar molecule component, $V_w = V_w$ of entire molecule, $H_s(h) = \Delta H_s$ of the hydrocarbon homomorph of the molecule and

$H_s(X)$, $V_w(X)$ are the corresponding increments for the associating functional group. For the less frequent case of association along 2-space axes:

$$K_0^* = K_0\left[\frac{1}{3}\frac{V_w(R)}{H_s(R)} + \frac{2}{3}\frac{V_w(X)}{H_s(X)}\right] \quad \text{or} \quad K_0^* = K_0\left[\frac{1}{3}\frac{V_w}{H_s(h)} + \frac{2}{3}\frac{V_w(X)}{H_s(X)}\right].$$

(4.12)

Whether the reducing parameter $H_s(R)/V_w(R)$ or $H_s(h)/V_w$ is more suitable for data representation is not entirely clear. With the few available data, $H_s(R)/V_w(R)$ appears to give a slightly more regular variation with ρ^* and T/T_m than does $H_s(h)/V_w$ (see Figure 4.5). On the other hand, for a compound like oxalic acid, only $H_s(h)/V_w$ can be used to represent the contributions in the two coordinates normal to the direction of the hydrogen-bond axis. Neither form of the reduced bulk modulus coincides entirely with the guidelines for nonassociating compounds transferred from Figure 4.4.

The third group of associating substances is exemplified by the carboxylic acids, the typical stable dimer of which acts almost like a weakly polar compound. Hence, to a good approximation, the reduced bulk modulus should

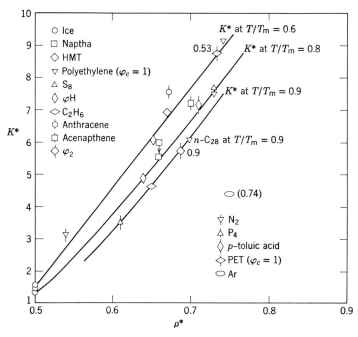

Figure 4.4 Plot of reduced bulk modulus of nonpolar and slightly polar compounds versus packing density and homologous temperature (curve parameters).

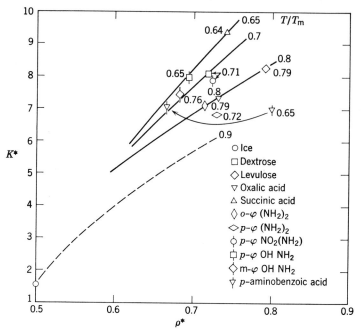

Figure 4.5 Reduced bulk modulus of hydrogen-bonded crystals versus packing density with T/T_m as parameter. The indicated adjustment of p-aminobenzoic acid takes care of the volume change due to ammonium-salt formation.

be

$$K_0^* \equiv \frac{K_0 V_w}{H_s(h)},$$

where the group

$$
\begin{array}{c}
\text{O}\cdots\text{H}\!-\!\text{O} \\
\diagup\diagdown\ \ \ \ \ \ \ \ \ \diagdown\!\!\diagup \\
\text{R}\!-\!\text{C} \qquad\qquad \text{C}\!-\!\text{R} \\
\diagdown \ \ \ \ \ \ \ \ \ \ \ \diagup \\
\text{O}\!-\!\text{H}\cdots\text{O}
\end{array}
$$

might be represented by R—⬡—R in the homomorph. The bulk modulus of the only currently available example, p-toluic acid, fits quite well onto the correlation of Figure 4.4 in this manner.

4.3.3 Polymeric Crystals

Polymeric crystals can be fitted into the scheme of simple crystals if one takes cognizance of the fact that the unit of reference, the repeating unit, always has two nearest neighbors connected by chemical bonds, that is, with a bond of high modulus E_p. The work of Asahina [2a] and Sakurada [47] provided the majority of available E_p data (Table 4.5) and the means to calculate E_p from spectroscopic force constants and molecular-structure data. The reducing parameter for the elastic moduli of isotropic high polymer crystals is therefore $(2V_w/3H_s + 1/3E_p)$, where V_w and H_s refer to the repeating unit[1]. If the polymer has side chains, the correction becomes less important

Table 4.5 Spectroscopic Elastic (Young's) Modulus E_p of Various Polymer Molecules [9]

Polymer	$E_p \times 10^{10}$(dyn/cm.^{2}) (calc.)	(obs.)
Polyethylene	182–340	260
Polytetrafluoroethylene	160	—
Poly(vinyl chloride) (syndiotactic)	160 (or 230?)	—
Poly(vinylidene chloride)	—	41.5
Polyoxymethylene	220	54
Polyisobutylene	70–84	—
Polypropylene (isotactic)	49	42
Polystyrene	—	12
Poly(vinyl alcohol)	—	255
Poly(ethylene terephthalate)	122–146	76
Nylon 66	196–157	—
Cellulose I	—	137
Cellulose II	—	90
Poly(ethylene glycol)(M $=\infty$)	4.8	—
Poly-3,3-bis(fluoromethyl)oxacyclobutane	110	—
Poly-3,3-bis(chloromethyl)oxacyclobutane	100	—
Poly-3,3-bis(bromomethyl)oxacyclobutane	92	—
Poly-3,3-bis(iodomethyl)oxacyclobutane	77	—

than for polyethylene and approaches V_w/H_s as the side chain size is increased Typical E_p data have been assembled in Table 4.5. As a rule $E_p \gg H_s/V_w$ and $K_0^*(L) \approx K_0 2V_w(u)/3H_s(u)$.

Another feature of polymer crystals is a pervasive defect structure. Part of that defectiveness is an inherent property of the lamellar crystals and is connected with the return bonds that stick out on the plane surfaces of the lamellae or platelet crystals [14]. Moreover, the difficulty of achieving perfect alignment of the large molecules out of a usually very viscous melt into the

[1] For shorter-chain compounds, such as n-paraffins, we can write

$$K_0^*(L) = K_0 \left\{ \frac{V_w}{\Delta H_s} \left[\frac{2}{3}\left(1 + \frac{1}{N_s}\right) \right] + \left[\frac{1}{3E_p}\left(1 - \frac{1}{N_s}\right) \right] \right\}, \qquad (4.13)$$

where N_s = number of skeletal atoms per molecule (= N_c in case of n-paraffins).

growing lattice causes the formation of defects inside the crystallite. Super-imposed on these peculiarities of the system is the experimental problem of degassing polymer samples completely, which would be especially trouble-some with static-compressibility measurements. Actually polymer crystals are rarely, if ever, obtained in the absence of amorphous components. Hence the recorded elastic properties of the crystals are usually the result of data extrapolation to 100% crystallinity.

The Hashin–Shtrikman theory [18] of elastic properties of a hard matrix with randomly dispersed soft inclusions (the amorphous regions) appears to be well suited for making such extrapolations even from a single datum point. It can be expressed in the convenient form

$$\frac{K - K_c}{K_c} = \frac{1 - \varphi_c}{(K_a/K_c - 1)^{-1} + \varphi_c f(\sigma_c')}, \tag{4.14}$$

where $K - K_c < 0$ and K_c, K_a are the bulk moduli of the crystalline and amorphous regions, respectively, K_a being obtainable from the correlation of Section 8.3.; φ_c is the volume fraction crystallinity; and $f(\sigma_c')$ is a slowly varying function of the Poisson's ratio σ_c' of the crystalline phase:

σ_c' :	0	0.25	0.33	0.40	0.50
$f(\sigma_c')$:	0.333	0.455	0.500	0.540	0.600.

Equation 4.14 has been derived for spherical shape of the discontinuous phase and is therefore only crude approximations for the lamellar crystals of semicrystalline polymers; yet, (4.14) represents the elastic properties of semi-crystalline polyethylene rather well.

4.4 COMPRESSION OF SOLIDS AND THEIR EQUATION OF STATE

The bulk modulus K_0 discussed so far describes only the behavior at or near zero compression. The description of finite compression requires additional information about the pressure dependence of the bulk modulus. The simplest assumption that one can make, namely, that

$$K = K_0 + K_1 P \tag{4.15}$$

has so far been the most successful. It leads to the compression isotherm

$$-\ln V_r = \frac{1}{K_1} \ln \left(1 + \frac{K_1 P}{K_0} \right), \tag{4.16}$$

which describes the available compression data of molecular solids rather satisfactorily. The constant $K_1 = 8 \pm 1$ for practically all molecular crystals for which data are available is in noteworthy agreement with Tobolsky's result of $K_1 = 7$ from LJD theory [55]. Hence for first approximations we might use the "universal" compression isotherm

$$-\ln V_r = 0.13 \ln \left(1 + \frac{8P}{K_0}\right).\tag{4.17}$$

Two additional compression isotherms have been examined in view of frequent discussion of them in the literature. In analogy to (4.15), it is sometimes assumed that the compressibility decreases linearly with pressure:

$$\beta = \beta_0 - \beta_1 P,\tag{4.18}$$

then

$$-\ln V_r = \beta_0 P - \beta_1 P^2.\tag{4.19}$$

Equation 4.28 represents the data very much less satisfactorily than does (4.16) because the underlying assumption is at variance with the facts. The constants β_0 and β_1 can be related to the force-law exponents m, n by the relation

$$\frac{2\beta_1}{\beta_0^2} = 1 + \frac{m+n+6}{3} \cdot [66]\tag{4.20}$$

However, although β_1/β_0^2 is comparatively constant, it leads to absurdly low values of the repulsion constant m if one assumes that in all molecular crystals, $n = 6$.

The other compression isotherm tried on Bridgman's data is that based on Murnaghan's finite strain theory [34]:

$$p = \tfrac{3}{2}K_0\left[\left(\frac{\rho}{\rho_0}\right)^{7/3} - \left(\frac{\rho}{\rho_0}\right)^{5/3}\right]\left\{1 - \zeta\left[\left(\frac{\rho}{\rho_0}\right)^{2/3} - 1\right]\right\} + \cdots,\tag{4.21}$$

where ζ is a new constant and subscript (0) refers to the data at atmospheric pressure. In contrast to the alkali-metal crystals, which according to Birch [6] require only the first term in brackets, compression data of molecular crystals require both terms for adequate representation. Since no simple relation of ζ to K_0 or any other crystal property could be discovered, this equation has not been pursued further.

A phenomenological equation of state for solids by Debye has the form

$$p + \frac{dU}{dV} = \frac{\gamma U_h}{V},\tag{4.22}$$

where U_h has the same meaning as in (4.7), γ is the Grüneisen ratio $VK\alpha_s/C_v^s$, and dU/dV is the so-called internal pressure (P_i) of the solid. Multiplication of both sides of (4.22) with the reducing parameter $V_w/\Delta H_s$ leads to

$$\frac{V_w}{\Delta H_s}\left(P + \frac{dU}{dV}\right) \equiv P_s^* = \gamma\rho^* \frac{U_h}{\Delta H_s},\tag{4.23}$$

which for $T > 1.5\theta_D$ (when $U_h \approx fRT$) (4.32) becomes

$$P_s^* \approx \gamma \rho^* fRT/\Delta H_s \qquad (4.24)$$

or, with $T^* \equiv fRT/\Delta H_s$, simply becomes

$$\rho^* = F\left(\frac{P_s^*}{\gamma T^*}\right). \qquad (4.25)$$

It is important to note that the reduced pressure P_s^* defined in (4.24) has the finite value P_i^* at $p = 0$. The large magnitude of P_i in solids makes this definition of P_s^* preferable for use with solids to the conventional reduced pressure for gases $\tilde{P} \equiv p\sigma^3/\epsilon$. For practical application of (4.25) one will have to redevelop this set of equations more rigorously. Another alternative is to plot ρ^* versus $P^*/\gamma T^*$ and obtain the function F empirically. The ratio γ should be essentially independent of temperature and depend only (but very slowly) on ρ^*. The magnitude of γ of molecular crystals of different structures covers too wide a range to permit any reasonable guess at present. A useful general equation of state for solids has yet to be developed.

For simple solids, such as crystalline argon, Hamann and David [16] found the Lennard-Jones and Devonshire equation of state

$$\frac{pv}{kT} = 1 + \frac{2z}{T}(A\tilde{\rho}^4 - B\tilde{\rho}^2) \qquad (4.26)$$

to represent the data quite well, indicating that it is better suited for solids than for liquids, its original target. The implicit character of (4.26) makes it rather awkward for engineering calculations. However, the authors [16] provide an extensive tabulation of pv/NkT as $F(\tilde{\rho}, \tilde{T})$ which should make the calculation easy for the compression of those simple solids for which meaningful Lennard-Jones force constants are available and for which the assumptions underlying (4.26) are tenable.

4.5   YOUNG'S MODULUS AND SHEAR MODULUS

The two moduli are discussed together because their relations to molecular structure are quite similar and, more importantly, because their relation to the practical application of molecular crystals of commerce is rather similar. Molecular crystals are generally used at temperatures so high on the T/T_m scale that they creep in extension and in shear. Hence the moduli given here are upper limits having mostly been obtained in dynamic measurements. Loss moduli will be discussed in Chapter 5.

In consonance with the third law of thermodynamics both moduli have to intercept the 0°K axis with zero slope and must become zero (under static conditions) at the melting point. However, the temperature trajectory between these two points is quite different as will be recalled from (4.7) and (4.8). They will be restated in terms of more directly useful coordinates as

$$E_T^* = E_0^* \left(1 - \frac{1.50U_h}{\Delta H_s} - \frac{0.84TC_v^h}{\Delta H_s}\right), \tag{4.27}$$

$$G_T^* = G_0^* \left(1 - \frac{0.66U_h}{\Delta H_s}\right), \tag{4.28}$$

where U_h and C_v^h are the lattice contributions to the internal energy and heat capacity of the crystal in the harmonic-oscillator approximation and can be read from Debye-function tables for the appropriate values of θ_D and the number of external degrees of freedom per molecule. Here, as earlier, z was assumed as 12 when converting from $N_A\epsilon$ to ΔH_s.

At $T > 1.5\theta_D$, the following approximations can be made:

$$E_T^* = E_0^{*\prime} \left(1 - \frac{2.34fRT}{\Delta H_s}\right), \tag{4.29}$$

$$G_T^* = G_0^{*\prime} \left(1 - \frac{0.66fRT}{\Delta H_s}\right), \tag{4.30}$$

where f is the number of external degrees of freedom per molecule and $E_0^{*\prime}$, $G_0^{*\prime}$ are not necessarily identical with the true zero-point values E_0^*, G_0^*. Both of these equations are valid only to about $0.9T_m$ (or $0.9T_{tr}$ if there is a first order solid–solid transition temperature T_{tr}). Beyond that temperature, the drop to zero is more rapid than predicted by (4.27) to (4.30). However, between these limits the validity of (4.29) is quite satisfactory, as shown by the few available examples in Figure 4.6. In contrast to the observations with bulk moduli, no changes in z (from 12) had to be made to obtain this agreement with experiment. The utility of (4.30) appears to be rather doubtful because it seems to be valid only at very low temperatures of little practical interest.

4.5.1 Rigid Nonassociating Molecules

The absolute magnitude of E^* or E_0^* or $E_0^{*\prime}$ is more difficult to fit into a general correlation than the temperature coefficient. Even the packing density ρ^* which proved to be such an excellent guide in the case of the bulk modulus just shows a trend with some rather serious deviations (Fig. 4.7). There are several sources of difficulty. Instead of correlating with the experimentally readily accessible ρ^* at $0.9T_m$, the determined or extrapolated packing density at $0°K$ might have been used. The uncertainties of extrapolation militated against this course of action, which probably would not have improved the situation significantly. Another source of complications is the arbitrariness of

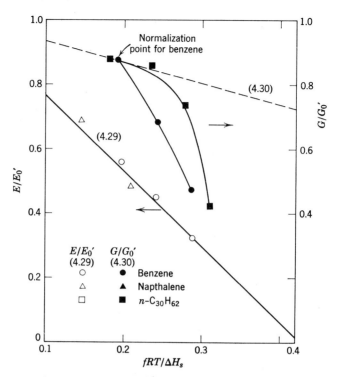

Figure 4.6 Change of elastic modulus with temperature.

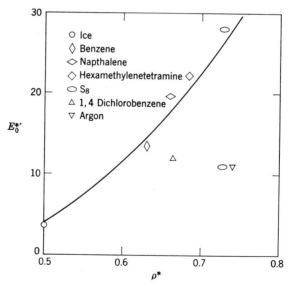

Figure 4.7 Trend of $E_0^{*\prime}$ with the packing density ρ^* at 0.9 T_m or at room temperature [7].

setting $z = 12$ when converting $N_A\epsilon$ in (4.7) and (4.8) to ΔH_s in (4.27) to (4.30). Yet, in contrast to the observations with the bulk moduli of simple compounds, no reasonable change of z appears to improve the correlation.

Although the sharp deviation of the Argon data from the general trend on Figure 4.7 is consistent with its bulk modulus, the wide scatter of the different experimental data for sulfur [45], [46], [54] reflects a strong lack of internal as well as external consistency. Clearly, the definitive elastic constant of this element have yet to be determined.

So few shear-modulus data are available on low-molecular-weight compounds that the derivation of general "rules" is quite impossible. Moreover, appreciable deviations from (4.28) begin at so low a temperature that this temperature function does not represent the data even of argon or of benzene in the temperature range for which data are available. We cannot ascertain the prediction of Ludwig's theory that the temperature coefficient of G is so very much smaller than that for the other two moduli. Yet this evaluation may not be entirely fair because, according to experimental data in Figure 4.6, on all compounds G drops far more rapidly at $T \geq 0.85 T_m$ than the other two moduli. It may be worthwhile to examine why the molecular crystal lattice is so much less resistant to shear than to extension in comparison with predictions from theory.

4.5.2 Flexible Long-Chain Molecules and Polymers

By far the largest amount of E and G data is available for this group of compounds because of the great technological importance of this information for the quality evaluation of paraffin waxes and of semicrystalline polymers. Yet even here the amount of data on pure compounds or—in the case of polymers—extrapolatable to 100% crystalline material, is still quite small.

The anisotropy of the molecules has here a large effect on the properties of the macroscopic crystal, especially in the case of the polymers, which can be oriented along the crystal axis, as in polymer fibers. In the unoriented case, the reduced Young's modulus has the form

$$E^*_{(L)} = E\left\{\frac{V_w}{\Delta H_s}\left[\frac{2}{3}\left(1 + \frac{1}{N_s}\right)\right] + \frac{1}{3E_p}\left(1 - \frac{1}{N_s}\right)\right\} \qquad (4.31)$$

just as in (4.13) for the bulk modulus. For high polymers ($N_s > 10$), it reduces to

$$E^*_{(L)} = E\left(\frac{2}{3}\frac{V_w}{\Delta H_s} + \frac{1}{3E_p}\right). \qquad (4.32)$$

The spectroscopic elastic moduli E_p for various polymeric molecules have been assembled in Table 4.5. Similarly, the average modulus of the unoriented fiber is given by

$$\frac{1}{E} = \frac{2}{3E_\perp} + \frac{1}{3E_p},$$ (4.33)

where $E_\perp$ is the typical modulus of the molecular crystal normal to the long axes of the molecule axis, a direction in which the crystal is held together by van der Waals forces only.

Experimental data for (semi) crystalline polymers at 4°K, taken as practically equal to E_0, have been plotted as E_0^* versus ρ^* in Figure 13.11. Owing to the fact that for these crystals composed of long-chain molecules, E depends on ρ only in two space coordinates, the slope $dE_0^*/d\rho^*$ is substantially smaller than it is for simple solids represented in Figure 4.7.

The indicated relation between E_0^* and ρ^* becomes a useful guide for the preparative chemist only if the temperature dependence of E can also be specified. The strong temperature dependence of the contribution of the intramolecular torsional oscillations to C_v^s, discussed in Section 3.4.3, preclude applicability of the simple relations (4.27) or (4.29) to crystals composed of flexible molecules. A better, although still untried, approach may be to insert the experimental value of C_v^s into b_1 of relations (4.5) and to use the known numerical values of K_1 and θ_D (generally 8 and 120°K, respectively). The appropriate value of C_v^s is probably $C_v - C_{\mathrm{vibr}}$, where C_{vibr} does not include the contributions due to torsional oscillations of skeletal atoms or of rigid groups. If experimental C_v data are unavailable, the relations of Section 3.4.3 plus torsional oscillator contributions should yield C_v^s. In the temperature range of rapid rise of C_v^s with temperature a correspondingly rapid nonlinear drop of the elastic modulus with temperature should be expected for crystals composed of long flexible (polymeric) molecules. Tobolsky's observation [56] that $\ln G$ (and $\ln E$) of crystalline polymers is proportional to (constant $- T$) may thus be accounted for.

The indicated relations are valid only in the absence of first-order phase transitions, and—in dynamic measurements—in the absence of relaxation processes. The shear modulus of normal paraffins has recently been shown by Pechhold et al. [40a] to drop by about two decades at the first-order solid/solid transition point. The magnitude of the drop in elastic modulus at a relaxation process line on the temperature-time scale (frequency) surface depends on the relaxation strength and is therefore notoriously unpredictable for crystalline systems (see Section 5.2.2). At present we can therefore at best estimate an upper limit of the equilibrium elastic moduli of polymer crystals from molecular structure by combining Figure 13.11 with the relations (4.5).

4.5.3   Oriented Polymer Molecules in Crystalline Fibers

Molecular crystals composed of small molecules are ductile only in the temperature range between a strong first-order solid–solid transformation at temperature T_{tr} and T_m. At $T < T_{tr}$ or if there is no such transition, at $T < 0.95T_m$, molecular crystals are invariably brittle, their elongation at break being less than 0.5%. The properties of "plastic" or ductile crystals at $T_{tr} < T < T_m$ are not changed by drawing because their molecules are usually spherical and therefore not orientable, and when they are elongated, as in the case of certain n-paraffins or long-chain esters, they are too mobile on the crystal lattice in the plastic temperature range to permit any permanent orientation.

The large molecules in polymeric crystals are, however, sufficiently immobile on the crystal lattice that they will retain whatever orientation has been mechanically induced at $T < T_m$. Technically, such orientation of molecules in films and fibers is achieved by cold rolling and drawing, that is, by uniaxial or biaxial deformation at $T < T_m$. High degrees of orientation are generally achieved at $(T_m - T) < 0.1T_m$.

The extent of orientation of subunits achieved in the early stages of elongation (drawing) of fibers can be measured as optical birefringence, if the polarizability of the subunit is anisotropic. The appropriate "subunit" is probably the elementary crystallite in the early stages of drawing (to $l/l_0 < 8$) and the repeating unit along the chain molecule in the later stages of drawing (at $l/l_0 > 10$). The anisotropy of polarizability is nearly identical in both assumptions because of the alignment of the polymer chains in the elementary crystallite. According to Ward [61], the average angle of orientation (θ) relative to the stretch axis is related to the observed birefringence (Δn) by

$$\Delta n = n_{\parallel} - n_{\perp} = \Delta n_{max}(1 - \tfrac{3}{2} \overline{\sin^2 \theta}) \tag{4.34}$$

where

$$\Delta n_{max} \approx \frac{2}{3} \pi N_0 \frac{(n_{iso}^2 + 2)^2}{n_{iso}} (p_1 - p_2), \tag{4.35}$$

with p_1, p_2 being the polarizabilities of the subunit parallel and normal to its axis along the chain molecule, n_{iso} = refractive index of the isotropic solid, and N_0 = number of repeating units per cm³ = $N_A/V_{(u)}$.

The effect of orientation on the tensile compliance s'_{33} of the fiber has been estimated by Ward [61] as

$$\overline{s'_{33}} = \overline{\sin^4 \theta}\, s_{11} + \overline{\cos^4 \theta}\, s_{33} + (\overline{\sin^2 \theta \cos^2 \theta})(2s_{13} + s_{44}), \tag{4.36}$$

where the compliances s_{ij} on the right-hand side are those of the fully extended crystal: s_{33} = reciprocal of the extension modulus (E_0) along the draw axis, s_{11} = reciprocal of the modulus (E_{90}) normal to that axis, s_{44} is the reciprocal of the torsional modulus (G) about that axis, and $-s_{13}/s_{33} = \sigma'$ for extension along that axis. Similar equations can be written for the change of each compliance with orientation.

Detailed calculations by Ward [61] have shown that the extensional modulus of the fiber goes through a minimum at low degrees of orientation (low draw ratios) if $s_{44} + 2s_{13} > s_{11}$ or s_{33}. The torsional modulus G, on the other hand, must decrease monotonically, if slowly, with increasing draw ratio. Typical values for $s_{11}{}^{-1}$ and $s_{44}{}^{-1}$ are given in Table 4.7.

Theoretical relations between mechanical (or optical) anisotropy and draw ratio (l/l_0) have been derived by Ward [61], [62] and by Kao and Hsiao [23]. Both theories are in qualitative but not quantitative agreement with experiment. Ward finds that the theoretical draw ratio $(l/l_0)_t$ for obtaining a given anisotropy is related to the experimental draw ratio $(l/l_0)_e$ by a correlation of the shape

$$7 \ln \left(\frac{l}{l_0}\right)_t = \left(\frac{l}{l_0}\right)_e - 1 \qquad (4.37)$$

indicating that, perhaps due to cooperative effects, further orientation depends more on the pre-existing orientation than is predicted by simple (affine deformation) theory. The excellent qualitative correlation between optical and mechanical anisotropy, recently confirmed by Samuels [8] for polypropylene fibers, becomes of little practical use (and probably ceases) at $l/l_0 > 10$ when orientation is so extensive that $\sin^2 \theta$ changes extremely rapidly. For that very interesting regime, another approach is indicated.

Cold drawing beyond $l/l_0 > 10$ appears to lead to partial unfolding of the lamellae in the draw direction. If all the new length of a fiber is derived from the unfolded chain in the draw direction, then at $\varphi_c \approx 1$,

$$\frac{1}{E_{\mathrm{F}}} = \frac{l_0}{l}\left[\left(\frac{l}{l_0} - 1\right)\frac{1}{E_p} + \frac{1}{E_\perp}\right], \qquad (4.38)$$

where E_p is the Young's modulus of the extended molecule calculated from molecular structure and spectroscopic data (see Table 4.5) and $E_\perp$, the modulus normal to the polymer chain, can be taken as equal to $\frac{2}{3}$ of the modulus of the isotropic crystal.

Equation (4.38) will overestimate E_{F} if crystallinity decreases during the drawing process or underestimate it if there is partial orientation in the "amorphous" regions of the fiber. An implicit assumption in (4.38) is that the drawn part of the molecule parallels the fiber axis. Should this extended molecule make an angle θ with the fiber axis, $E_p{}^{-1}$ in (4.38) must be multiplied by $\cos^2 \theta$.

$$\frac{1}{E_{\mathrm{F}}} = \frac{l_0}{l}\left[\left(\frac{l}{l_0} - 1\right)\frac{\cos^2 \theta}{E_p} + \frac{1}{E_\perp}\right]. \qquad (4.39)$$

This expression should also be corrected for the shear at the interface between the elongated regions and adjacent folded-chain crystallites. However, since the shear modulus of the latter is small, that is probably a negligible second-order correction. Far less negligible is the correction for the presence of non-crystalline components of the system.

If we assume that the fully oriented crystalline domains of a fiber form a continuous network with pores of amorphous domains, then in the temperature range where $E_c > 10^2 E_a$, and where $\varphi_c > 0.5$, we might expect

$$E \approx \varphi_c E_c;$$
$$G \approx \varphi_c G_c. \tag{4.40}$$

Combination of (4.38) and (4.40) yields

$$\frac{1}{E_F} = \frac{l_0}{\varphi_c l}\left[\left(\frac{l}{l_0} - 1\right)\frac{1}{E_p} + \frac{1}{E_\perp}\right]. \tag{4.41}$$

The user of (4.41) should keep in mind the excessive conservatism hidden in the assumption $E_c \gg E_a$. Recent NMR and sorption experiments [64] have shown that the mobility and the sorptive capacity of the amorphous component of highly crystalline polyethylene cold drawn to $l/l_0 = 10$ are drastically reduced below those of the undrawn state. The conclusion is inescapable that the amorphous component in the highly elongated sample is also highly elongated and oriented and should have a correspondingly raised elastic modulus. Annealing at elevated temperature returns the properties of the amorphous component to those of the undrawn state, indicating the complete reversibility of the orientation phenomena.

Experimental tests of (4.38) and (4.41) at high draw ratios have been assembled in Table 4.6. In all cases calculation overestimates the modulus of the drawn fiber. The extent of the overestimate is quite instructive, however. When special precautions were taken in the drawing process to filaments of high modulus, the experimental observations closely approach the theoretical prediction. The approach would probably have been even closer had the calculated modulus been corrected for the well-known decrease in crystallinity during high-extension drawing. Conventional drawing techniques, on the other hand, yield polyolefin filaments with moduli far below those of the theoretical prediction. The excellent agreement between calculated and observed moduli of poly (ethylene terephthalate) filaments suggests that achievement of the theoretical maximum modulus is not equally difficult for all kinds of fibers. The very preliminary evaluation of the present primitive theory is sufficiently encouraging to consider its predictions—at least tentatively—as upper limits for the achievable tensile modulus of polymer filaments.

The tensile modulus normal to the draw axis should be dominated by van der Waals interactions to the same extent that the one parallel to the draw axis is dominated by E_p. It should therefore be predictable from the behavior of

Table 4.6   Room Temperature Tensile Modulus of Drawn Filaments [9]

F Filament	Conventional Draw Process			Special Draw Process		
	l/l_0	$E_F(calc)^a$ ($\times 10^{10}$ dyn/cm^2)	$E_F(obs)^b$ ($\times 10^{10}$ dyn/cm^2)	l/l_0	$E_F(calc)^b$ ($\times 10^{10}$ dyn/cm^2)^a	$E_F(obs)^b$ ($\times 10^{10}$ dyn/cm^2)
Polyethylene[b]	10	20	4.4[c]	12	23	16 [d]
				16	64[e]	61 [f]
Polypropylene[b]	12	20	6.4[c]	34	32.6 (18.9)[g]	9.0[h]
				60	38.4	25.6
Poly(ethylene terephthalate)	8	11.3[j]	12.5[k]	—	—	—

[a] Calculated by means of Eqs. (4.38) and (4.41), taking E_p from Table 4.5.
[b] Estimate of $E_\perp$, see Section 4.5.2.
[c] From *Fibre Data Handbook*.
[d] From Higgins and Bryant, *J. Appl. Polymer Sci.* **8**, 2399 (1964); these authors used highest modulus obtained at l/l_0 corresponding to their cold draw ratio.
[e] Calculated from $\varphi_c = 0.80$; $E_F(calc)$ for $\varphi_c = 1.0$ is 70×10^{10} dyn/cm^2.
[f] At 103°K; filament drawn at 1.25 cm/min at 100°C; Data of P. I. Vincent, *Proc. Roy. Soc.* (*London*) A282, 8 (1964).
[g] Value in parentheses is corrected for decrease in φ_c during drawing.
[h] From Sheehan and Cole; (drawn at 135°C), *J. Appl. Polymer Sci.* **8**, 2359 (1964).
[i] Drawn on a special draw bench by G. Lopatin, *Belg. Pat.* 631, 663 (1963).
[j] Calculated with $E_p = 140 \times 10^{10}$ dyn/cm^2; $E_p = 76 \times 10^{10}$ dyn/cm^2 yields $E_F = 10.7 \times 10^{10}$ dyn/cm^2.
[k] Data of Pinnock and Ward [43].

crystals of small molecules. Several measurements indicating the correctness of this conclusion have been assembled in Table 4.7. It is also borne out by the small magnitude of the torsion modulus of drawn filaments obtained by Wakelin et al [59], as compared to the torsion modulus of the unoriented bulk polymer.

4.5.4   Semicrystalline Polymers

In the crystallinity range $\varphi_c > 0.5$, experimental evidence strongly suggests that the crystalline regions form the continuous load-bearing phase, especially at $T \geq T_g$. The elastic moduli of such a diluted structure can be estimated by the method of Hashin and Shtrikman [18] who assume the discontinuous phase to be present as randomly distributed spheres, and obtain for the high-modulus (crystalline) phase as continuous phase:

$$G = G_c + \frac{1 - \varphi_c}{(G_a - G_c)^{-1} + 6\varphi_c(K_c + 2G_c)[5G_c(3K_c + 4G_c)]^{-1}} . \quad (4.42)$$

Transformation of (4.47) into the form

$$\frac{G - C_c}{G_c} = \frac{1 - \varphi_c}{\dfrac{G_c}{G_a - G_c} + \dfrac{6\varphi_c(K_c + 2G_c)}{5(3K_c + 4G_c)}} = \frac{1 - \varphi_c}{\dfrac{G_c}{G_a - G_c} + \varphi_c f(\sigma_c')} \quad (4.43)$$

permits a rapid analysis of the effects of property variables on the change of G with crystallinity (φ_c). The term $f(\sigma_c')$ is actually a very slowly varying function of Poisson's ratio σ_c':

$$\sigma_c': \quad 0.25 \quad\quad 0.33 \quad\quad 0.40 \quad\quad 0.45,$$

$$f(\sigma_c'): \quad 0.49 \quad\quad 0.467 \quad\quad 0.443 \quad\quad 0.425.$$

Hence, aside from φ_c, the fractional difference $(G_c - G_a)/G_c$ has the decisive effect on the mechanical properties of semicrystalline polymers. Numerical illustration is provided in Figure 4.8, which shows not only the shape of the curves of (4.43) for various values of G_a/G_c but also the rather gratifying agreement with the available experimental data. Two facts stand out here. At $T > T_g$, it appears reasonable to set $G_a/G_c \approx 0$, since in fact it is of the order of $<10^{-2}$, which in this calculation is effectively zero. At $T < T_g$, we find G_a/G_c to be significant and increasing with decreasing temperature.

The agreement with experiment strongly suggests that the crystalline component is indeed the continuous, load bearing phase at $\varphi_c > 0.4$, and that the model assuming spherical shape for the amorphous (dispersed) domains may

Table 4.7 Transverse ($E_\perp$) and Torsional (G) Moduli of Highly Oriented (semi) Crystalline Polymers at Room Temperature

Substance	Form	$E_\perp$ (10^{10} dyn/cm^2)	G (10^{10} dyn/cm^2)	$\frac{2}{3}E_c$ (10^{10} dyn/cm^2)
Polyethylene (110)	Film	5.3 ± 0.5[a]		4.4[b]
Poly(vinyl alcohol) (10T)	Film	11 ± 1[a]		
Polyethylene terephthalate	Monofil	0.62[c]	0.74[c]	1.6 to 2.1[d]
Nylon 66	Monofil	0.6[e]		2.6[f]
Polypropylene	Monofil	0.78[e]		1.1[g]

[a] Limiting value for the 100% crystalline component; K. Nakamae et al., *Proc. Intl. Symp. Macromolecules, Tokyo*, 1966, 3.4.01.
[b] Extrapolated to 100% crystallinity, data from [63]; 5MHz.
[c] $E_\perp = S_{11}^{-1}$; $G = S_{44}^{-1}$; at birefringence $\Delta n = 0.187$; P. R. Pinnock et al., *Proc. Roy. Soc. (London)* A291, 267 (1966); static.
[d] From data for $\varphi_c = 0.02$ to 0.41; Kawaguchi et al., *J. Polymer Sci.* 32, 417 (1950).
[e] D. W. Hadley et al., *Proc. Roy. Soc. (London)* A285, 275 (1965); static.
[f] E. Butta and C. Kannucchi, *Chim. Ind.* 45, 323 (1963); 10 kHz.
[g] $\rho = 0.902$ [4].

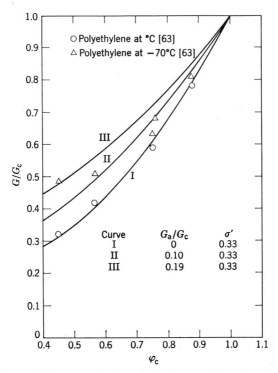

Figure 4.8   Test of (4.8) for prediction of the shear modulus of semicrystalline polymer (at 5 MHz) [8].

not be very far from the truth. Actually this is not too surprising if we remember that the continuum surrounding spherical inclusions resembles an assembly of lathelike shapes. The Young's modulus E of the suspension is obtained by combining the appropriate results of (4.42) and (4.43) with those of Table 4.2 in the form

$$E = \frac{9KG}{3K + G}.$$ (4.44)

The important effect of the magnitude of G_a/G_c on G/G_c implies that T/T_g should be the appropriate temperature scale for semicrystalline polymers, because of the sharp drop of G_a at $T > T_g$ and the rapid rise of G_a at $T < T_g$. The correctness of this deduction is demonstrated by the curves of E^* versus T/T_g in Figure 4.9. The lack of complete coincidence of the curves is, of course, due to the widely differing melting points and dE/dT of the crystalline components.

The agreement with the Hashin–Shtrikman theory has been demonstrated in the high-frequency (5MHz) modulus, and may not be valid to low-frequency moduli. The relation between the low-frequency (shear) modulus and crystallinity has been described in the purely empirical fashion:

$$\ln G(t) = A\rho + B, \qquad (4.45)$$

where ρ is the density of the sample, by Sperati [52] Nielsen [37] and Shibukawa [51]. Aside from the absence of any rationale for this relation, inspection of the data shows that these relations are only of moderate reliability, and do not contain any hint regarding the effect of frequency.

At $\varphi_c < 0.4$, we may consider the amorphous phase as continuous. If that amorphous phase is a simple elastic body, we can again use the applicable Hashin–Shtrikman equation for the low modulus (amorphous) phase as continuous phase:

$$G = G_a + \frac{\varphi_c}{(G_c - G_a)^{-1} + 6(1 - \varphi_c)(K_a + 2G_a)[5G_a(3K_a + 4G_a)]^{-4}}, \qquad (4.46)$$

When the amorphous phase is a liquid, $G_a = 0$, (4.46) yields also $G = 0$. However, in polymeric systems, the amorphous phase is in general not an ordinary liquid but exhibits rubberlike elasticity. Then if we assume the amorphous domains to be the continuous phase, we ascribe all elastic properties to rubberlike (entropic) elasticity and treat the crystalline phase as a filler. The most notable attempt in this direction is that by Nielsen [27] who

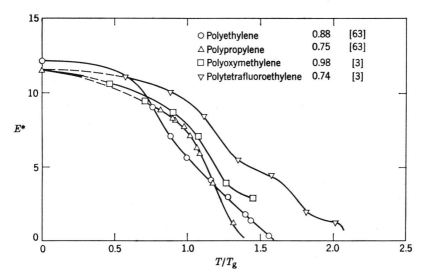

Figure 4.9 Plot of reduced extension modulus of various semicrystalline polymers versus T/T_g [8].

proposed the relations

$$G = \left(\frac{\rho_a RT}{M_c}\right)(1 + 2.5\varphi_c + 14.1\varphi_c^2), \qquad (4.47)$$

where ρ_a = (density of amorphous domains), and the number average molecular weight M_c of chains in amorphous domains connected to two different crystallites is given by

$$M_c = M_A \left[\frac{1 - X_A^{m_0 H}}{X_A^{m_0}(1 - X_A)} - m_0 - \frac{1 - r}{X_A^{m_0}}\right], \qquad (4.48)$$

where M_A = molecular weight of repeat unit in amorphous sequence, X_A = fraction of amorphous sequence in total chain, m_0 = unincorporatable changing sequence lengths ($\sim$15), and $r = M_B/M_A$. Quite plausibly, this relation described the elastic modulus as $f(\varphi_c)$ at least qualitatively quite well at low values of φ_c. But it seriously underestimates the moduli at $\varphi_c > 0.4$, the range of primary interest. The large difference in order of magnitude between the rubber moduli and those of semicrystalline polymers, mentioned earlier, probably precludes success for any theory based on a model which treats the amorphous domains as the continuous phase at $\varphi_c > 0.4$.

4.5.5 Shear and Extension Moduli of Mixed Crystals

The unpredictability of the crystal structure of mixed crystals precludes the predictability of the elastic moduli of mixtures. Even when solid solutions are readily formed, as in mixtures of long-chain paraffins, the shear modulus at $T < T_{tr}$ may be as well above as below that of the mixture components, as is apparent from the data by Pechhold and co-workers [40].

4.6 FINITE DEFORMATION IN EXTENSION AND SHEAR

For molecular crystals the limit of Hookean behavior is generally less than 0.5%, frequently at 0.1% extension [45]. The shape of stress–strain curves of such crystals in the nonlinear region appears to differ from sample to sample. Hence there seems to be little chance of finding a general representation of finite extension (or shear) of the simplicity of (4.16) for finite compression. Moreover, some of the crystals of technical interest, such as the polymer crystals, change morphology on extension so that no law of finite extension is really applicable.

Large deformations of aggregates of molecular crystals involve deformations of superstructures such as lamellae or spherulites which are determined by stress–strain functions that are only indirectly related to the properties of the individual crystallites. Their discussion would go beyond the scope of this book.

Amplitude effects have not yet been examined explicitly with semicrystalline polymers. The notion is common that the low-amplitude dynamic modulus and the high-amplitude static modulus represent the extreme values of such experiments and do not differ sufficiently to make systematic measurements of amplitude worthwhile. Superficially this sounds convincing, but on closer examination, we find that finite deformation at high rates is a sufficiently important phenomenon in strength determinations to deserve more than a guessed datum, especially since the equipment is available and has given rather unexpected results with filled elastomers [39].

4.6.1   Time Effects

Although time and amplitude could—in first approximation—be neglected as variables when dealing with fully crystalline systems, they are significant variables in any mechanical-property measurements on semicrystalline systems. On a macroscopic scale, creep or stress relaxation are the most direct manifestation of time effects. Although time-dependent phenomena are basically outside the scope of the present discussion, it would be pedantic to ignore their existence in this context. The phenomenon is illustrated by the family of shear modulus versus T and ω curves in Figure 4.10. These time effects are commonly described by relaxation-time spectra. But there is as yet no way to correlate such spectra in a quantitative way with molecular-structure information, each sample being a case by itself, especially for semicrystalline polymers, the structure of which depends on their thermal

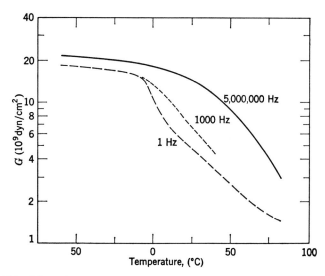

Figure 4.10   Effect of temperature and deformation rate in Hz on the shear modulus of propylene. (From J. Heijboer, private communication.)

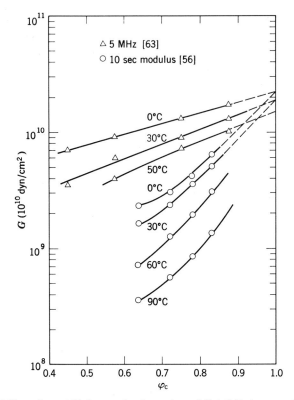

Figure 4.11   Effect of crystallinity on the dynamic and "static" shear modulus of polyethylene.

and mechanical history.[1] With entirely amorphous systems, there is an indication that two dominant relaxation times can be isolated, [57] one of which represents intramolecular (torsional) motions and the other intermolecular displacements (see Section 13.5).

Professor Tobolsky's data [9], [51] on the "static" (10 sec) shear modulus of polyethylene and polypropylene as functions of crystallinity and temperature plotted on the same graph (Figs. 4.11 and 4.12) as the corresponding curves for the high-frequency moduli suggest that the shear modulus at 100% crystallinity ($\varphi_c = 1.0$) is essentially insensitive to time effects. This result is not surprising, since the lack of modulus dispersion at high crystallinities has long been known. It should be noted in passing that the polypropylene data yield meaningful curves only if the x-ray-diffraction-derived crystallinity and not the density-derived information is used.

[1] Fortunately, the real components of elastic moduli are less sensitive to sample preparation than are the loss moduli. See Chapter 5 for specific details.

The location of the 10-sec moduli far below the 5 MHz curves clearly indicates that a factor is operative at longer time deformations which is unimportant in high-frequency deformation. Moreover, a comparison of just the 10-sec modulus with the 5 MHz modulus would be insufficient to establish any definable trend of the sample deflection with time beyond 10 sec and at other temperatures.

An important difference between the well-known time dependence of the modulus of amorphous polymers and that of the modulus of semicrystalline polymers is the modulus range. For amorphous polymers, more than seven decades in shearing frequency would have meant three to four decades in the shear modulus, compared with less than 1 decade for the semicrystalline case. Moreover, in the absence of crystalline material the moduli would be three to four decades lower than observed. Because of this large effect of the crystalline fraction, it is essential to restrict all analyses to a temperature range in which $\varphi_c =$ constant.

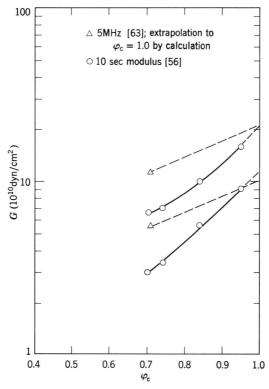

Figure 4.12 Effect of crystallinity on the dynamic and "static" shear modulus of polypropylene.

4.6.2   Creep Compliance

The inverse elastic modulus at finite loading times is generally called "creep compliance." In the following we deal primarily with creep compliance in shear $J(t)$. A fairly representative series of data is available [4], [12], [35], [40]. However, polymers are still insufficiently well defined unless their entire mechanical and thermal history is specified in addition to their molecular weight, molecular-weight distribution, tacticity (when applicable), and crystallinity; and mechanical measuring methods differ enough in (shear) strain, etc., that data obtained by different authors can only rarely be fitted together smoothly.

The largest range of frequencies covered in a single laboratory and on a few identical samples is that obtained by Heijboer [20] and by Waterman [63] especially on a polypropylene sample. In the case of polyethylene only the extreme points 5 MHz and 1 Hz were produced by the same group. A matching set of measurements in the range 0.1 Hz to 36 kHz by Pechhold and co-workers [40] supplies some of the intermediate points, at least at high crystallinities. The 10-sec shear moduli by Tobolsky and co-workers [51], which stimulated this investigation, do not seem to match with the other data on apparently similar polymers, as will be seen in Figure 4.15. This indicates the importance of small differences in composition and sample history.

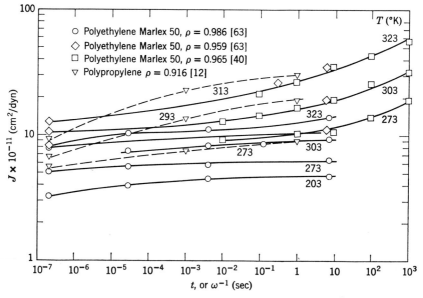

Figure 4.13   Shear compliance of polyethylene (continuous curves) and polypropylene (broken curves) versus time of stress application. All points at $t = 2 \times 10^{-7}$ sec are from [63].

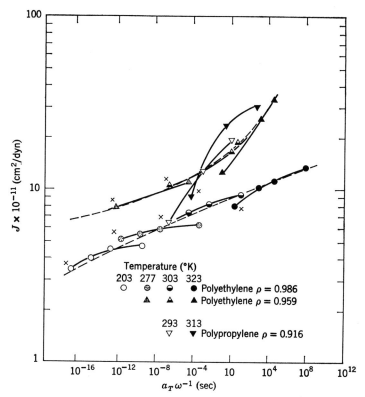

Figure 4.14   Attempt to produce master curves of shear compliance versus reduced time $a_T\omega^{-1}$ ($\times 5$ MHz).

Some of the T.N.O. and the Pechhold data have been assembled in Figure 4.13. They are seen to match smoothly. The comparatively small change of the compliance of the semicrystalline polymers over large ranges of frequency and temperature contrasts sharply with the large changes characteristic of amorphous polymers under similar conditions. A peculiar feature of the compliance versus time curves of high-crystallinity polyethylene and of the (70% crystallinity) polypropylene is the slope reduction at long times, which may well be identified as a form of structure stabilization under stress. Its equivalent in creep tests at constant stress is the continuous reduction in creep rate, known as "strain-hardening." (For "creep" see Section 5.4.)

The shape of these curves seems to preclude simple time–temperature super-position by shifting J-vs-t (or ω) curves along the time axis only (Fig. 4.14). The simultaneous action of several deformation mechanisms such as relative movement of crystallites and lamellar creep within individual crystallites suggests shift along the time as well as the compliance axis [32], [41], or subtraction of a frequency-independent deformation component [35] for the achievement of a form of time–temperature superposition. Such superposition is naturally restricted to the temperature range $T_g < T < T_{tr}$, where T_g is that of the amorphous domains and T_{tr} can be a first- or second-order phase transition of the crystalline phase.

4.7 CONCLUSIONS

Clearly, the attempted correlations of elastic moduli with molecular structure fall short of the goal: prediction from molecular-structure data alone. Part of this failure is due to an inherent problem of organic crystallography: the unpredictability of the packing density, except in a very qualitative way. The melting point is similarly unpredictable, except in a very qualitative way.

Because the elastic properties depend very strongly on the packing density and to some extent on the proximity to the melting point, these two properties must be known before any correlation of elastic moduli can be attempted. When both of these are known the correlation of the bulk modulus has succeeded quite well, whereas those of the extension (Young's) modulus and of the shear modulus are only suggestive, but far from quantitative. It may not be accidental that the quality of the correlation is best where there are the most data (bulk moduli) and poor where paucity of data prevails. Further progress in this field is, therefore, closely tied to an increasing supply of data as well as to greater ingenuity in the development of property correlations.

Achievement of the greatest possible strength has been the primary goal of engineers and chemists in the production of organic crystalline structural materials; hence, the existence of many data on yield strength and on relaxation spectra, as measures of ductility-producing mechanisms. However, now that the design engineer is provided with many polymeric structural materials to choose from, the need for elastic moduli as measures of deflection under load is becoming apparent. More importantly, the engineers' desire for rigidity, that is, high-extension and shear modulus, may become the touchstone for the utility of the materials offered. One of the purposes of the present investigation is, therefore, to guide the preparative chemist towards molecular structures providing for high elastic moduli in all three space coordinates.

The data of Table 4.5 show that almost all macromolecules exhibit a high-extension modulus parallel to their length axis. The magnitude of the moduli normal to the molecule axis, determined by intermolecular forces, is, according to the correlations in Figures 4.3 to 4.9, primarily a function of packing density ρ^*, the parameter $\Delta H_s/V_w$, and the temperatures $fRT/\Delta H_s$,

Table 4.8 Packing Density of Polymer Crystals[a]

Polymer	ρ^*	Polymer	ρ^*
Hydrocarbon Compounds		Oxygen Compounds	
Polyethylene	0.732	Polyoxymethylene, hexagonal	0.672[b]
Polypropylene, isotactic	0.686	Polyoxymethylene, orthorhombic	0.685[b]
Polypropylene, syndiotactic	0.661	Polyethylene oxide	0.662
Poly-1-butene	0.694	Polyethylene terephthalate	0.737[c]
Poly-3-methyl-1-butene	0.68	Polymethyl methacrylate	0.683
Poly-4-methyl-1-pentene	0.606	Polyvinyl alcohol	0.738
Poly-4-methyl-1-hexene	0.614		
1,2-Polybutadiene, isotactic	0.665		
1,2-Polybutadiene, syndiotactic	0.667		
1,4-*trans*-Polybutadiene	0.706		
1,4-*cis*-Polybutadiene	0.699	Halide Compounds	
1,4-*trans*-Polypentadiene	0.687		
1,4-*cis*-Polyisoprene	0.701	Polyvinyl chloride, monoclinic	0.686
Polystyrene	0.676	Polyvinylidene chloride,	
Polyvinylcyclohexane	0.660	monoclinic	0.775
Polyacetylene	0.75	Polymonochlortrifluoroethylene	0.691
Poly-*o*-xylene	0.675	Polytetrafluorethylene, $t < 20°C$	0.737

[a] From x-ray diffraction data at room temperature; from Miller, R. L., and L. E. Nielsen, *J. Polymer Sci.* **55**, 643 (1961).
[b] Carrazolo, G., and M. Mammi, *J. Polymer Sci.* **A1**, 965, 1572 (1963).
[c] Kilian, H. G. et al., *Kolloid-Z.* **172**, 166 (1960).

T/T_m, or T/T_g. A high packing density is achieved by "smoothness" of the molecule surface, and either straight *trans–trans* conformation or tightly wound helix conformation of the backbone chain (Table 4.8).

To the extent of the generality of the reduced modulus correlations given in Figures 4.3 to 4.8, molecular structure determines the absolute magnitude of the elastic moduli through the factor $\Delta H_s/V_w$ (or H_s/V_w per functional group or per repeating unit.) The range covered by this factor is apparent from the data of Table 4.9. Although the total available range spans a factor of 10 (between CH_2 and —OH), among the generally accessible hydrocarbon and functional groups, H_s/V_w varies only by a factor of 3. Diluted by a minimum number of 1 carbon atom per functional group (2 would probably be more realistic) H_s/V_w can hardly rise much above 2×10^{10} dyn/cm². Hence, assuming achievement of $\rho^* = 0.7$ and $T/T_m = 0.6$ in the range of interest by careful molecule design, the highest value of E likely to be achieved in the unoriented state is of the order 20×10^{10} dyn/cm². This is a factor of 10 less than engineers are accustomed to from metallic and metal-oxide structural materials. This discrepancy is not at all unexpected since it represents the difference between the rigidity of van der Waals bonds (holding

CALCULATING PROCEDURES

	Desired Datum	Available Data	Procedure and Equations	Unit	Error %	Section Ref.
4.1	Reducing parameters M' for Rigid nonassociating polar and nonpolar or when *all* intermolecular contacts are hydrogen bonds	Molecular structure	1. Estimate ΔH_s^1 by (15.10). 2. Estimate V_w by (15.1). 3. $M' = 4.18 \times 10^7 \, \Delta H_s^1 / V_w$.	dyn cm^{-2}		4.3.1 4.3.2
4.2	Rigid associating molecules	Molecular structure	1., 2. same as 1., 2. of Procedure 4.1a, b. 3. M' given by (4.11), (4.12).			4.3.2
4.3	Flexible molecules	Molecular structure	1., 2. same as 1., 2. of Procedure 4.1a, b. 3. M' given by (4.13).			4.3.3
4.4	Polymeric crystals	Molecular structure	1. Estimate $H_s(n)$ by (15.10). 2. Estimate $V_w(n)$ by (15.1). 3. M' given by $\left[\dfrac{2}{3} \dfrac{V_w}{H_s} + \dfrac{1}{3} E_p \right]^{-1}$			4.3.3

				Units	±15	
4.5	Zero pressure bulk modulus K_0 for crystals	Density ρ_x at Ref. temperature (room temperature or $0.9T_m$, T_m)	1. Calculate molal weight M. 2. Calculate reducing parameter M' by Procedures 4.1 to 4.4. 3. $K_0 = M'\left(\dfrac{\rho_x V_w}{M}\right)$ $\times \left[31.63 - 23.8\left(\dfrac{T}{T_m} - 0.6\right)\right]$ $-\left[14.20 + 8.80\left(\dfrac{T}{T_m} - 0.6\right)\right]$.	dyn cm^{-2}	±15	4.3.1
4.6	Zero pressure bulk modulus for glasses	Density ρ_x at Ref. temperature or at $0.9T_g$, T_g	1., 2. same as 1., 2. in Procedure 4.5. 3. $K_0 = M'\left\{\dfrac{31.63\,\rho_x V_w}{M}\right.$ $\left. -10.55 - 6.0\left(\dfrac{T}{T_g}\right)\right\}$.	dyn cm^{-1}		13.2.4
4.7	Bulk modulus of crystal or glass at temperature T at pressure P	As for Procedures 4.1 through 4.6	1. Estimate $K_0(T)$ by (4.5) or (4.6). 2. Estimate K_1 by analogy with data in Section 4.4 or assume $K_1 = 8$. 3. $K(P, T) = K_0(T) + K_1 P$.	dyn cm^{-1}		4.4
4.8	Volume of crystal or glass at T, P	As for Procedures 4.1 through 4.6	1., 2. same as 1., 2. of Procedure 4.7. 3. Density ρ at $P = 1$ bar and temperature T. 4. $-\ln (V/V_1) \approx 0.125 \ln \left(1 + \dfrac{8P}{K_0}\right)$ where $V_1 = V$ at $T = T$ and $P = 1$ bar.			4.4

CALCULATING PROCEDURES (*continued*)

Desired Datum	Available Data	Procedure and Equations	Unit	Error %	Section Ref.
4.9 Young's modulus of monomeric crystal	As for Procedures 4.1 through 4.6	1., 2. same as 1., 2. of Procedure 4.5. 3. Estimate number of degrees of freedom by P. 4. $E = M'\left[\dfrac{100\rho_x V_w}{M} - 48.00\right]$ $\times\left(1 - \dfrac{2.34fRT}{\Delta H_s^1}\right)$, valid up to $0.9T_m$ or $0.9T_r$.	dyn cm^{-1}		4.5.1
4.10 Young's modulus (high frequency) for polymeric crystals	As for Procedures 4.1 through 4.6 T_x, T_m, and crystallinity φ_c	1. Calculate molal weight M of repeating unit. 2. Calculate V_w of repeating unit by (15.1). 3. Calculate H_s of repeating unit by (15.10). 4. $E_0 = \dfrac{H_s}{V_w}\left\{41.6\left(\dfrac{\rho V_w}{M}\right)^{1/2} - 22.4\right\}$ (from Figure 13.11). 5. $E(T)$ must be constructed from known T_x, φ_c, T_m, guided by Figure 4.4, etc.			13.3.1 4.5.5 4.5.6

Table 4.9   Reducing Parameter H_s/V_w for Various Functional Groups (All in Units of 10^{10} dyn/cm²)[a]

Group	H_s/V_w	Group	H_s/V_w
Hydrocarbon Groups		**Halide Groups**	
—CH₃	0.75	—CF₂—	0.41
—CH₂—	0.825	—F (aliphatic)	1.77
＼CH／	0.3	—Cl (aliphatic)	1.28
＝CH₂	0.805	—Br (aliphatic)	1.25
＝C＝	1.20	—I (aliphatic)	1.31
＼CH／ (aryl)	0.90		
＼C—／ (aryl)	1.19		
Oxygen Groups		**Nitrogen Groups**	
—O— (aliphatic)	1.75	—C≡N	1.80
—C〈O (aliphatic)	1.20	—NO₂	2.38
		Hydrogen-Bonding Groups	
		—OH	4.9
＼C＝O／—O (aliphatic)	2.28	—NH₂	2.7
＼C＝O／—O (cyclic)	2.88	—C(O)—NH—	2.56
—O—C＝O＼O	2.0	—C(O)—NH—	1.98
—C＝O／O		—C(O)—NH— (cyclic)	2.33
Sulfur Groups			
—S—	1.64		
—S—S—	1.15		
—SH	1.48		
＼S＝O／	2.73		
＼S／ (O, O)	2.5		

a Based on Refs. [6] and [7].

polymer crystals together in two space coordinates) and chemical bonds, which connect all atoms in all directions in metals and metal oxides. The upper rigidity limit that can be accomplished by polymer chemistry can thus at least be guessed from the correlations that have been attempted in this report.

NOMENCLATURE

C_{ij} elastic constants of single crystal (dyn/cm²)
C_p heat capacity at constant pressure (cal/mole°K)
C_v heat capacity at constant volume (cal/mole°K)
E extension, tensile, or Young's modulus (dyn/cm²)
E_F tensile modulus of fibers (dyn/cm²)
E_v Voigt average of Young's modulus (dyn/cm²)
E_0 extension modulus at 0°K (dyn/cm²)
E^* $\equiv EV_w/\Delta H_s =$ dimensionless (reduced) Young's modulus
E_p elastic modulus (spectroscopic) of backbone chain of molecule
F auxiliary magnitude (dyn/cm²)
f number of external degrees of freedom per molecule
G shear or rigidity modulus (dyn/cm²)
G_0 shear modulus at 0°K (dyn/cm²)
G_v Voigt average shear modulus (dyn/cm²)
G^* $\equiv GV_w/\Delta H_s =$ dimensionless shear modulus
ΔH_s heat of sublimation (cal/mole or ergs/mole)
H_s heat of sublimation increment per group (cal/mole or ergs/mole)
K bulk modulus (dyn/cm²)
K_c bulk modulus of crystalline phase (dyn/cm²)
K_v Voigt average bulk modulus (dyn/cm²)
K_o bulk modulus at $p = 0$
$K_0(0)$ bulk modulus at $p = 0$ and $T = 0$
K_1 pressure coefficient of bulk modulus, (4.20)
K^* $\equiv KV_w/\Delta H_s$ (or similar) dimensionless bulk modulus
k Boltzmann constant
l length of specimen (after drawing or elongation)
l_0 length of specimen (before drawing or elongation)
M elastic modulus
N_s number of skeletal atoms per molecule
p pressure (dyn/cm²)
P_i internal pressure (dyn/cm²)
P_s^* reduced pressure, (4.23)
R gas constant (cal/mole °K) (ergs/mole °K)
T temperature (°K)

T_g	glass transition temperature ($^\circ$K)
T_m	melting point ($^\circ$K)
$\tilde{T}$	$\equiv kT/\epsilon$
U	internal energy (ergs/mole)
U_h	internal energy of harmonic oscillator crystal (ergs/mole)
v	volume per molecule (cm^3/molecule)
V	molal volume (cm^3/mole)
V_w	van der Waals volume (cm^3/mole)
z	number of nearest neighbors per molecule
α_s	thermal-expansion coefficient of solid ($^\circ$K^{-1})
β	compressibility (cm^2/dyn)
β_c	compressibility of crystalline phase (cm^2/dyn)
β_L	compressibility of amorphous phase
γ	Grüneisen constant
ϵ	pair potential (ergs/molecule)
ν_{max}	sound frequency of maximum energy absorption (sec^{-1})
ρ	density (g/cm^3)
ρ^*	$\equiv V_w/V =$ reduced density
φ_c	volume fraction crystallinity
σ'	Poisson's ratio

REFERENCES

[1] Alexandrov, U. S. et al., *Soviet Phys.—Cryst.* **8**, 164 (1963).
[2] Anderson, O. L. and G. J. Dienes, *Non-Crystalline Solids*, E. Frechette, ed., Wiley, New York, 1960.
[2a] Anderson, O. L., *Phys. Rev.* **144**, 553 (1966).
[2b] Asahina, M. et al., *J. Polymer Sci.* **59**, 93, 101, 113 (1962).
[3] Baccaredda, M., *Chim. Ind.* (Milan) **44**, 1383 (1962).
[4] Baccaredda, M., and E. Butta, *Chim. Ind.* (Milan) **44**, 1228 (1962).
[5] Barron, T. H. K. and C. Domb, *Phil. Mag.* **45**, 654 (1954).
[5a] Barron, T. H. K. and Klein, M. L., *Proc. Phys. Soc.* (London), **85**, 533 (1965).
[6] Birch, F., *J. Geophys. Rev.* **57**, 227 (1952).
[7] Bondi, A., *J. Phys. Chem. Solids* **28**, 649 (1967).
[8] Bondi, A., *J. Polymer Sci.* A2, 83 (1967).
[9] Bondi, A., *J. Appl. Polymer Sci.* **9**, 3897 (1965).
[10] Bridgman, P. W., *Proc. Am. Acad. Arts Sci.* **76**, 1, 55 (1948); **77**, 115 (1949).
[11] Chakraborty, S. C. and R. K. Sen, *Bull. Natl. Inst. Sci.* (India), No. 14, 20 (1958).
[11a] Chang, Y. A., *J. Phys. Chem. Solids* **28**, 697 (1967).
[12] Faucher, J. A., *Trans. Soc. Rheol.* **3**, 81 (1959).
[13] Frolov, A. et al., *Soviet Phys.—Solid State* **4**, 1178 (1962).
[14] Geil, P., *Polymer Single Crystals*, Wiley, New York, 1963.
[15] Giellessen, J. and J. Koppelmann, *Kolloid-Z.* **172**, 162 (1960).
[16] Hamann, S. D. and H. G. David, *J. Chem. Phys.* **38**, 3037 (1963).
[17] Hansen, D. and H. Rusnock, *J. Appl. Phys.* **36**, 322 (1965).

[18] Hashin, Z. and S. Shtrikman, *J. Mech. Phys. Solids* 11, 127 (1963); see also *Appl. Mech. Rev.* 17, 1 (1964).
[19] Haussühl, S., *Acta Cryst.* 11, 58 (1958).
[20] Heijboer, J., Intl. Conf. Physics of Non-Crystalline Solids, Delft, 1964; *Kolloid-Z.* 148, 36 (1956); 171, 7 (1960), and private communications.
[21] Hellwege, K. H., et al., *Kolloid-Z.* 183, 110 (1962).
[22] Heseltine, J. C. W., et al., *J. Chem. Phys.* 40, 2584 (1964).
[23] Huntingdon, H. B., *Solid State Physics* 7, 214 (1958).
[24] Jona, F. and P. Scherrer, *Helv. Phys. Acta* 25, 35 (1952).
[25] Kao, S. R. and C. C. Hsiao, *J. Appl. Phys.* 35, 3127 (1964).
[26] Kerner, E. H., *Proc. Phys. Soc. (London)* B69, 808 (1956).
[27] Kneer, G., *Phys. Status Solidi* 3, K331 (1963).
[28] Kovacs, A. J., Fortschr. Hochpolym. Forschg. 3, 394 (1964).
[29] Leibfried, G. and W. Ludwig, *Solid State Phys.* 12, 275 (1961).
[30] Ludwig, W., *J. Phys. Chem. Solids* 4, 283 (1958).
[31] Marshall, J. G., et al., *Trans. Faraday Soc.* 52, 19 (1956).
[32] McCrum, N. G. and E. L. Morris, *Proc. Roy. Soc. (London)* A292, 506 (1966).
[33] Moseley, W. W., et al., *J. Appl. Polymer Sci.* 3, 266 (1960).
[34] Murnaghan, F. D., *Finite Deformation of an Elastic Solid*, Wiley, 1951.
[35] Nagamatsu, K., *Kolloid-Z.* 172, 151 (1960).
[36] Nakayasu, H., et al., *Trans. Soc. Rheol.* 5, 261 (1961).
[37] Nielsen, L. E. and F. D. Stockton, *J. Polymer Sci.* A1, 1995 (1963).
[38] Oda, T., et al., *J. Polymer Sci.* A3, 1993 (1965).
[39] Payne, A. R., RAPRA Reports between 1955 and 1964.
[40] Pechhold, W., et al., *Kolloid-Z.* 189, 14 (1963); 196, 27 (1964).
[40a] Pechhold, W., et al., *Acustica* 17, 61 (1966).
[41] Penn, R. W., *J. Polymer Sci.*, A2, 4, 545 (1966).
[42] Peterlin, A., and H. G. Olf, *J. Polymer Sci.* A2, 4, 587 (1966).
[43] Pinnock, P. R. and I. M. Ward, *Proc. Phys. Soc. (London)* 81, 260 (1963).
[44] Pinnock, P. R. and I. M. Ward, *Brit. J. Appl. Phys.* 15, 1559 (1964).
[45] Rao, R. V. G. S., *Proc. Ind. Acad. Sci.* 32A, 275 (1950).
[46] Richards, T. W., et al., *J. Am. Chem. Soc.* 37, 1643 (1915).
[47] Sakurada, I., et al., *Makromol. Chem.*, 75, 1 (1964).
[48] Samuels, R. J., *J. Polymer Sci.* A3, 1741 (1965).
[49] Schuyer, J., *J. Polymer Sci.* 36, 475 (1959).
[50] Sheares, N. H., et al., *SPEJ* 17, 1 (1961).
[51] Shibukawa, T., et al., *Textile Res. J.* 32, 810, 1008 (1962).
[52] Sperati, C. A., et al., *J. Am. Chem. Soc.* 75, 6127 (1953).
[53] Srivastave, R. and S. Chakraburty, *J. Phys. Soc. (Japan)* 17, 1767 (1962).
[54] Sümer, A., *Bull. Turk. Phys. Soc.* 23, (1955).
[55] Tobolsky, A. V., *Properties and Structures of Polymers*, Wiley, New York, 1960.
[56] Tobolsky, A. V., et al., *Textile Res. J.* 32, 810, 1008, 1011 (1962).
[57] Tobolsky, A. V. and J. J. Aklonis, *J. Phys. Chem.* 68, 1970 (1964).
[58] Vincent, P. I., Polymer 1, 7 (1960).
[59] Wakelin, J. H., et al., *J. Appl. Phys.* 26, 786 (1955).
[60] Ward, I. M., *Textile Res. J.* 34, 806 (1964).
[61] Ward, I. M., *Proc. Phys. Soc.* 80, 1176 (1962).
[62] Ward, I. M. and P. R. Pinnock, *Brit. J. Appl. Phys.* 17, 3 (1966).
[63] Waterman, H. A., *Kolloid-Z.* 192, 1, 9 (1963).
[64] Woodward, A. E., *Rheology, Theory and Applications*, Vol. 4, F. R. Eirich, ed., Academic, New York, 1967.

[65] Yum, S. S. and R. T. Beyer, *J. Chem. Phys.* **40**, 2538 (1964).
[66] Ziman, J. M., *Electrons and Phonons*, Oxford University Press, London, 1960.
[67] Zwikker, C., *Properties of Solid Materials* (Pergamon, London, 1954).

GENERAL READING

Kittel, C., *Introduction to Solid State Physics*, Wiley, New York, 1965, 3rd ed.
Nye, J. F., *Physical Properties of Crystals*, Oxford University Press, London, 1957.
Physics of Plastics, P. D. Ritchie, ed., Van Nostrand, Princeton, New Jersey, 1965.
Cottrell, A. H., *The Mechanical Properties of Matter*, Wiley, 1964.

5

Transport Properties of Molecular Crystals

Phonon transport (thermal conductivity) and mass transport (molecular diffusion) are considered. The rate of momentum transport in solids needs no separate treatment, for at the temperatures of practical interest it is determined almost exclusively by the molecular diffusion rate, the movement of dislocations being largely a function of vacancy, hence of molecule movement.

Almost all real crystalline solids are polycrystalline, whereas most theoretical treatments of crystal properties refer to single crystals. Hence theory has been used only as a guide to the rational combination of physical properties and molecular force constants in dimensionless expressions of independent and dependent variables.

Thermal conduction and molecular diffusion along different crystal axes of a single crystal may differ manyfold. The resulting anisotropic transport would be extremely difficult to predict. Restriction of the present treatment to polycrystalline solids introduces the additional simplification of effective isotropy.

5.1 THERMAL CONDUCTIVITY

Detailed consideration of the various transport modes contributing to thermal conductivity λ of single crystals at high temperatures ($T > \theta_D$) led several investigators to the relation

$$\lambda \approx A \frac{mv^{1/3}\theta_D^2}{r^2}\left(\frac{C_p^s}{Dh}\right)^3 \frac{\theta_D}{T},$$ (5.1)

which is clearly dominated by the lattice characteristic, θ_D, the Debye temperature. The constant A is of the order of unity [45], 3.8 in [23]. In either case (5.1) overestimates λ by varying amounts [23].

The thermal conductivity of single crystals at low temperature ($T \ll \theta_D$) should then be given by

$$\lambda \approx A_1 \frac{mv^{1/3}}{r^2}\left(\frac{C_p^s}{Nh}\right)^3 \frac{T^3}{\theta_D} \exp\left(\frac{\theta_D}{\alpha_i T}\right), \qquad (5.2)$$

where the constants $A_1 \approx 2$ and $\alpha_i \approx 1$ [23]. The T^3 term is, of course, the same that characterizes the low-temperature heat capacity between zero and about $0.1\theta_D°K$. A peculiar feature of the low-temperature thermal conductivity of dielectric crystals is the effect of the absolute size of the crystals, for the phonon wavelength is then of the same order as the crystal size. Somewhat surprisingly, even in semicrystalline polymers the mean free phonon path length is of the order of the microscopically observable crystallite dimensions [34].

The thermal conductivity of polycrystalline solids is smaller than that of single crystals because of the phonon scattering at the grain boundaries and, occasionally, because of porosity. These effects are difficult to assess quantitatively, and are most noticeable at low temperatures, where λ can be used as a sensitive measure of such imperfections.

Semiempirical correlations of λ have been proposed, nearly all of which can be related to each other. Owing to the scarcity of reliable thermal-conductivity data for molecular crystals, the range of validity for most of these correlations is difficult to assess.

The thermal conductivity of rare-gas crystals and of other solidified gases at $T > \theta_D$ has been correlated by Keyes [20] within the framework of the usual corresponding-states principle:

$$\tilde{\lambda} = \frac{\lambda\sigma^2}{k}\left(\frac{M}{\epsilon}\right)^{1/2} = \frac{12\epsilon}{kT} = \frac{12}{\tilde{T}}, \qquad (5.3)$$

or

$$\lambda_R = \frac{\lambda T_c M^{1/2} N A^{1/3}}{P_c^{3/2} V_c^{5/6}} = \frac{100}{T_R}, \qquad (5.4)$$

where all constants have their usual meaning (see Nomenclature). The validity of these equations is restricted to crystals composed of small, rigid, nonpolar or weakly polar molecules. In (5.3) the limitation is obvious because the Lennard-Jones force constants σ and ϵ (obtained from gas or crystal properties) are meaningful only for rigid, essentially spherical molecules with 6:12 or closely similar potential field. Such limitations are implicit in the formulation of (5.4), which uses the critical constants as reducing parameters. Figure 5.1, from the paper by Keyes, indicates how well the corresponding-states principle can be used to describe the high-temperature branch of the thermal conductivity of molecular crystals. The low-temperature scatter is indicative of the effects of crystal size, etc., in the low-temperature region.

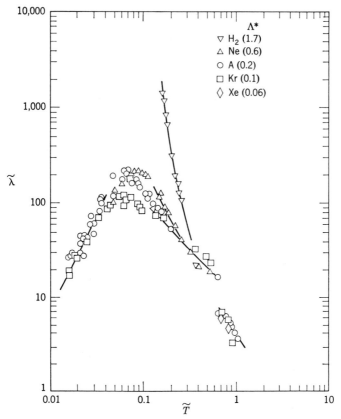

Figure 5.1 Reduced thermal conductivity of simple solids $\tilde{\lambda} = (\lambda\sigma^2/k)(M/N)^{1/2}$ as a function of the reduced temperature $\tilde{T} = (kT/\epsilon)$. The deviations of H_2 and Ne are due to quantum effects [20].

A more general reduced thermal conductivity–temperature relation may be formulated (4) with ΔH_s and V_w as molecular property parameters:

$$\lambda^* = \frac{\lambda V_w^{2/3} N_A^{1/3}}{R}\left(\frac{M}{J\,\Delta H_s}\right)^{1/2} = A_2\frac{\Delta H_s}{fRT}. \tag{5.5}$$

Evaluation of A_2 by means of the rather limited experimental thermal-conductivity data has been carried out from two points of view, namely with the distance parameters $d_w^2 N_A$ and $V_w^{2/3} N_A^{1/3}$. The first implies a thermal-oscillation amplitude $\bar{u}$ proportional to the average diameter of the skeletal atoms of a molecule, and the second assumes this amplitude to be proportional to average diameter of the molecule. For the crystals composed of rigid molecules, the standard deviation from the mean value of A_2 is twice as large for the first assumption as for the second. A striking feature of the A_2 values in Table 5.1 is their uniformity. Aside from the somewhat suspect data for N_2O and HBr, such diverse substances as argon, carbon dioxide, and sulfur yield virtually identical correlations; even ice seems to fit without difficulty. Specific molecular-structure effects appear to be absent in this correlation, at least for rigid molecules.

The seemingly very different relation of λ to the melting point T_m proposed by Keyes [21],

$$\lambda = \frac{(RT_m)^{3/2} \rho^{2/3}}{3\gamma^2 g^3 N_A^{1/3} M_T^{7/6}},$$ (5.6)

can be converted easily to a relation like (5.5) by way of the relations of the expansion coefficient α_s to T_m and ΔH_s presented in Section 3.5. Then $A_2 \approx (5.4/f^{1/3})^{3/2}(3\gamma^2 g^3 N_A^{1/3})$, where f is the number of external degrees of freedom

Table 5.1 Temperature Coefficient A_2 in the Reduced Thermal Conductivity Equation $\lambda^*_{(\text{solid})} = A_2(\Delta H_s^\circ/fRT)$ [4]

Substance	Temperature Range (°K)	f	A_2
Ar	15 to 80	3	1.38
N_2O	90 to 150	5	0.95
HBr	78 to 87[a]	5	1.01
CO_2	130 to 220	5	1.43
Benzene	90 to 273	6	1.67
Naphthalene	293 to 368	6	1.52
Anthracene	293 to 368	6	1.73
p-Dichlorobenzene	293 to 368	6	1.67
p-Diiodobenzene	293 to 368	6	1.54
S_8 (rhombic)	293 to 353	6	1.40
H_2O (ice)[b]	123 to 273	6	1.78
p-Dihydroxybenzene	293 to 368	8	1.93
Diphenyl	293 to 368	7	1.75
Tetraphenyl silicate	273 to 313	10	1.65
			1.81
Polyethylene (100% cryst)	100 to 350	2	(1.94)[c]

[a] Valid only up to 88°K because of phase transitions above this temperature.

[b] E. H. Ratcliffe, *Phil. Mag.* 7, 1197 (1962), mid value. A more accurate equation for ice is:

$$\lambda^*_{(\text{solid})} = 2.09 \frac{(\Delta H_s^\circ)}{fRT} - 1.50.$$

[c] By extrapolation of the data collected by H. Wilski, *Kunstoffe* 53, 363 (1963) [and reduction by Equation (15)].

Table 5.2   Comparison of Thermal Conductivity Calculated by Means
of Equations 5.5 and 5.7 with Experimental Data

Substance	λT (Eq. 5.5)[a] (cal/cm · sec)	λT (Eq. 5.7) (cal/cm · sec)	λT (exp) (cal/cm · sec)	Ref.[b]
Argon	0.077	0.055	0.067	d
Krypton	0.079	0.0522	0.060	d
CO_2	0.24	0.21	0.22	e
H_2O	1.34	0.55	1.47	f
p-Dihydroxybenzene	0.32	0.17	0.385	g
S_8	0.22	0.067[c]	0.199	h

[a] With $A_2 = 1.62$.
[b] References identical with those of Table 5.1.
[c] Use of the atomic weight of sulfur in (5.7) yields $\lambda T = 0.778$ cal/cm. sec.
[d] G. K. White and S. B. Woods, Nature 177, 851 (1956).
[e] A. Eucken and E. Schröder, Ann. Phys. 36, 609 (1939).
[f] Ref. b of Table 5.1.
[g] K. Ueberreiter and H. J. Ortmann, Z. Naturforsch. 5a, 101 (1950).
[h] Gmelin's Handbuch der Anorgan. Chemie 9/3, 637 (1953).

per molecule and g is the fractional vibration amplitude of molecules on the lattice. The correlational form

$$\lambda T = 0.015 \frac{T_m^{3/2} \rho^{2/3}}{M^{7/6}} \text{ (W/cm)}, \tag{5.7}$$

the Keyes relation, appears to give a good first-order estimate of the thermal conductivity of molecular crystals [21], [22]. A comparison of the utility of (5.5) and (5.7) for the calculation of λ is given in Table 5.2. All of the thermal conductivity equations given above assume isotropic solids. Hence they are invalid for those crystals which exhibit mechanical anisotropy. Thermal conduction along different crystals axes can only be estimated if the anisotropy of other properties, such as that of sound velocity (U_s), is known. Then λ in the various directions should vary as U_s.

5.1.1   Comparison with Other Work

Nearly all published thermal conductivity equations for insulating solids can be expressed in a form similar to 5.5:

$$\lambda = \frac{B(\Delta H_s)^{3/2}}{V_w^{2/3} M^{1/2} f T}, \tag{5.8}$$

where B is a universal numerical constant.

For solids composed of rigid molecules disposed in simple cubic lattices we find in Ziman's text [45],

$$\lambda = \frac{AM \, d\theta_D^2}{\gamma^2}\left(\frac{\theta_D}{T}\right),$$ (5.9)

where A is a constant which depends on the units chosen for λ; for example, $A = 5 \times 10^{-8}$ when λ is in W/cm°K. If we call the expression in front of the bracket λ_0, then the reduced thermal conductivity $\lambda/\lambda_0 = (\theta_D/T)$. Since we have seen above that $\nu_D \sim (nm \, \Delta H_s/\nu^{2/3}M)^{1/2}$, obviously

$$\lambda = \frac{Bd(nm \, \Delta H_s)^{3/2}}{\gamma^2 \nu M^{1/2} T},$$ (5.10)

where B is a proportionality constant. It is noteworthy that this formula is almost identical with one recently derived by Kontorova [24]:

$$\lambda = \frac{(mn \, \Delta H_s^\circ)^{3/2}}{(m + n + 3) \, d_w^2 M^{1/2} kT}$$ (5.11)

Likewise Lawson's equation [26],

$$\lambda = \frac{aK^{3/2}}{3\gamma^2 \rho^{1/2} T},$$ (5.12)

is easily transformed to

$$\lambda = \frac{B'' \rho^*(K^* \, \Delta H_s)^{3/2}}{\gamma^2 V_w^{3/2} M^{1/2} T},$$ (5.13)

where the various numerical coefficients have been collected in B''; the generalized bulk modulus K^* will be remembered as being of the order $nm/9$.

Recently [21] Keyes eliminated the bulk modulus from Lawson's equation by means of Lindemann's melting rule and thus obtained (5.6) discussed earlier.

5.1.2 Oriented Polymer Crystals

An extreme case of thermal conductivity anisotropy among molecular crystals can be expected for oriented polymer films and fibers. There is a great temptation to estimate the ratio of the thermal conductivity parallel and normal to the draw direction from the readily available sound-velocity data as

$$\frac{\lambda_{\parallel}}{\lambda_{\perp}} = \frac{u_s(\parallel)}{u_s(\perp)} \approx \left(\frac{E_{\parallel}}{E_{\perp}}\right)^{1/2},$$ (5.14)

where, as is shown later, $u_s(\perp) \approx (\frac{2}{3})^{1/2} u_s$ (unoriented crystal). The tacit assumption underlying this intuitive relation is that the relevant heat capacity C_v and the phonon free path length Λ of the Debye relation

$$\lambda_c = \frac{\frac{1}{3}C_v \rho u_s \Lambda}{M}.$$ (5.15)

are equal in both directions. This may be a reasonable assumption for crystals composed of small rigid molecules, but is not likely to be correct with oriented polymers.

For the latter we might estimate $\lambda_{\parallel}$ as follows: Remembering that for the isotropic polymer crystal

$$\frac{1}{\lambda} = \frac{2}{3\lambda_{\perp}} + \frac{1}{3\lambda_{\parallel}}, \tag{5.16}$$

where the thermal conductivity $\lambda_{\parallel}$ parallel to the oriented molecule is much greater than $\lambda_{\perp}$, the thermal conductivity normal to the oriented molecules, $\lambda_{\perp} \approx \frac{2}{3}$ of the observed isotropic conductivity λ. In principle $\lambda_{\perp}$ should have the value predicted from (5.5) for the repeating unit. The maximum thermal conductivity $\lambda_{\parallel}^{\circ}$ along a fully oriented polymer molecule should be[1] of the order

$$\lambda_{\parallel}^{\circ} = \frac{\sum C_{\mathrm{D}} \rho_w}{M_{\mathrm{osc}}} \left(\frac{E_p}{\rho_w}\right)^{\frac{1}{2}} \Lambda, \tag{5.17}$$

where $\sum C_{\mathrm{D}}$ is the sum of harmonic oscillator (Debye) contributions to heat capacity due to acoustic vibrations of the backbone chain links, M_{osc} is the average molal weight of the oscillators, $\rho_w = M/V_w$ for the repeating unit, E_p is the (spectroscopic) extension modulus of the backbone chain (see Table 4.5) and Λ is the phonon free path length along the chain. The numerical value of Λ can be estimated only if a model is adopted.

Two limiting cases can be recognized. The upper limit is the (wholly improbable) complete elongation of the molecule in the drawn fiber or oriented fiber, when $\Lambda = L$, the number average fully extended length per molecule. A lower limit of Λ is the average height, h, of the folded lamella, assuming the absence of defects inside the crystal. In that case Λ would be of the order 100 to 400 Å, depending on type and thermal history of the crystal. According to the model of Hansen and Rusnock [10], the original folds persist as kinks in the oriented molecule and then $\Lambda \approx h$. The draw model presented in Section 4.5.3, which ascribes cold drawing to unfolding of the folded crystal leads to the drawn-out length $l_d = (l/l_0 - 1)[wL/(h + 20)]$ where l/l_0 is the draw ratio, w is the average fold-to-fold distance in the crystal, usually ≈ 4.5 Å. There is no assurance, however, that this drawn-out length obtains uninterruptedly rather than in small unfolded sections. Here l_d would be the maximum value of Λ.

Whichever value Λ takes on, the effective value of $\lambda_{\parallel}$ for 100% crystalline polymer is related to $\lambda_{\parallel}^{\circ}$ by the series relation

$$\frac{1}{\lambda_{\parallel}} = \frac{\Lambda_c' \cos 2\theta}{\varphi_b \lambda_{\parallel}^{\circ}} + \frac{l_f'}{\lambda_{\perp}}, \tag{5.18}$$

[1] This treatment should be considered as descriptive rather than quantitative.

where θ is the angle which Λ makes with the draw axis, $\Lambda' = \Lambda/(\Lambda + l_f)$ and $l_f' = l_f/(\Lambda + l_f)$, and l_f is the path length of crystal interaction.

In the unlikely case of $\Lambda = L$, $l_f = w_e =$ intermolecular end group distance. On the Hansen and Rusnock model, $l_f =$ projected length of unextended folds, probably of the order of 10 repeating units. On the draw model of Section 3.6, $l_f = w(L \Lambda)/(h + 20)$. Although for polyethylene the backbone conductivity $\lambda_\parallel^\circ$ is the entire conductivity, for polymer molecules with side chains only the fraction φ_b of its total average cross section is occupied by the backbone cross section and thus conducts with $\lambda_\parallel^\circ$. The balance of the molecule cross section conducts in parallel via the regular lattice conduction mechanism.

Similarly, the noncrystalline fraction of oriented films or fibers can be assumed to conduct in parallel with the crystalline-oriented component, so that the over-all conductivity of films or fibers in parallel with the orientation axis can be estimated as

$$\bar{\lambda}_\parallel = \varphi_c \lambda_\parallel + (1 - \varphi_c)\lambda_a, \tag{5.19}$$

where λ_a is the thermal conductivity of the amorphous fraction.

This problem of the thermal conductivity of oriented polymer systems has been dwelt on in detail because it may be of practical importance in the growing number of applications of highly drawn monofilaments such as in polypropylene or nylon ropes. It is also of interest that $\lambda_\parallel^\circ$ has a positive temperature coefficient because of the rise of $\Sigma\, C_D$ with temperature, E_p being independent of temperature. Most experimental data on oriented polymers are for noncrystalline sytems and therefore cannot be compared directly.

5.1.3 Flexible Molecules and Polymers

The thermal conductivity of crystals composed of flexible molecules receives contributions (to heat capacity) from the low-frequency large-amplitude internal degrees of freedom. Some of these are at sufficiently high frequencies that their contribution increases with increasing temperature, thereby reducing the over-all temperature slope of λ below the value given by (5.5) and, more importantly, possibly preventing constancy of λT. A detailed analysis of that contribution to λ is still outstanding.

Thermal-conductivity data for crystals composed of pure flexible-chain compounds could not be found. The technical materials, paraffin wax and low-pressure polyethylene probably exhibit somewhat lower thermal conductivity than 100% crystalline substances would. Here, of course, only d_w^2 is a length dimension of physical meaning. Moreover, as indicated above, a significant portion of the heat conduction path is now contributed by the skeletal chain with its very high elastic modulus E_p and correspondingly high thermal conductivity. The reduced thermal conductivity of long-chain compounds in unoriented polycrystalline systems should therefore be

$$\lambda^* \equiv \frac{\lambda \, d_w{}^2 N_A}{R} \left\{ \left(\frac{M}{J \, \Delta H_s}\right) \left[\frac{2}{3}\left(1 + \frac{1}{N_c}\right)\right] + \frac{\rho_{\text{cryst}}}{3E_p} \left(1 - \frac{1}{N_c}\right) \right\}^{1/2}$$

$$= A_2 \left(\frac{\Delta H_s^\circ}{fRT}\right),$$

(5.20)

which at $N_c \to \infty$ becomes

$$\lambda^* \equiv \frac{\lambda \, d_w{}^2 N_A}{R} \left(\frac{2}{3}\frac{M}{J \, \Delta H_s^\circ} + \frac{\rho_{\text{crys}}}{3E_p}\right)^{1/2} = A_2 \left(\frac{\Delta H_s^\circ}{fRT}\right),$$

(5.21)

where ΔH^s, M, and f are per repeating unit. The number f includes degrees of freedom due to torsional oscillation and bending vibrations, if ν is low enough.

The semicrystalline polymers of commerce have both crystalline and amorphous domains. The elastic moduli at small deformations indicate that in most of these the crystalline phase is continuous. Hence λ can be estimated from the usual mixing rules for porous systems. The exact choice of mixing rule is not very critical because the two thermal conductances are of the same order of magnitude. Because the temperature coefficient of the thermal conductivity of polymer melts is either only slightly negative and may even be positive, as discussed elsewhere, the negative temperature coefficient of the thermal conductivity of semicrystalline polymers decreases as the degree of crystallinity decreases. The thermal conductivity of semicrystalline polymers can be estimated from a knowledge of λ_c and λ_a, the thermal conductivity of crystalline and amorphous polymers, respectively, and φ_c, the volume fraction of crystalline material:

$$\frac{\lambda}{\lambda_c} \approx \frac{2 + \nu - 2\varphi_c(1 - \nu)}{2 + \nu + \varphi_c(1 - \nu)},$$

(5.23)

where $\nu = \lambda_a/\lambda_c$ [13].

5.2 ROTATIONAL DIFFUSION

The transport of ultrahigh-frequency phonons (thermal vibrations) in molecular crystal lattices turned out to be correlated in terms of the variables characterizing the translational vibrations of the lattice points. Phonons of somewhat lower frequency interact with rotational motions of the molecules or of molecule segments located on the crystal lattice points. These rotational motions can be observed directly by dielectric energy absorption if the molecule contains permanent electrical dipoles, or by nuclear magnetic resonance absorption if the molecule contains suitable nuclear magnets (protons, C^{13} atoms, etc.).

Aside from the intrinsic interest of such observations of molecular motion, a strong practical interest is attached to these data because they provide a measure of mechanical-energy absorption and therefore of the crystals' resistance to high-impact loading, that is, its mechanical strength in many important applications. The discussion of the rotational diffusion data is therefore followed by a few examples of related mechanical-energy-absorption phenomena.

The rotational diffusion constant has the dimension (sec^{-1}) and is often referred to as a rotational relaxation frequency (f_m) and its inverse as a rotational relaxation time (τ). Since not all molecules of a sample participate equally in this relaxation process, the system needs two numbers for its characterization: the relaxation frequency and the relaxation intensity, that is, the population of relaxing or rotating molecules.

For the simplest system of hindered rotation of a rigid molecule past an n-fold barrier on its traverse through a full circle, and at constant volume, the frequency of maximum absorption is of the order

$$\nu_m = (2\pi\tau)^{-1}\left[n\left(\frac{V^\circ}{2I}\right)^{\frac{1}{2}}\right]\exp\left(-\frac{V^\circ}{RT}\right) \qquad (5.24)$$

according to Waugh and Fedin,[1] where the expression in square brackets is related to the torsional oscillation frequency ν_r of the molecule in the lattice discussed in Section 3.3. Also appropriate is Eq. (11.3) in Section 11.1.3. There, as here, I is an appropriate, usually the largest, moment of inertia, and V^0, the barrier to external rotation of the molecule in the lattice is—as is shown presently—a fairly uniform fraction of the lattice energy, ΔH_s. Usually $n = 3$, but for symmetrical molecules it can be quite different (e.g., for benzene, $n = 6$). Most measurements are carried out at constant pressure rather than at constant volume, and therefore the exponential temperature factor is designated as the activation energy $\Delta E_{\ddagger}$ rather than V°. So far only one set of (NMR) measurements on crystals has been carried out at constant volume [1]. The results show that $\Delta E_{\ddagger} \approx V^\circ$ when the observed motions are internal rotations or motions of ions, such as NH_4^+ in a crystal lattice. For external rotation on the molecular crystal lattice, $V^\circ < \Delta E_{\ddagger}$ by a factor of 2 to 3. There are too few data to discern more than a qualitative trend of $V^\circ/\Delta H_s'$ with ρ^*, similar to that of Figure 5.2.

Also, the motion across the rotational barrier may involve other degrees of freedom, so that for the balance of this discussion we use the conventional rate-theory equation

$$\nu_m = (2\pi\tau)^{-1} = \nu_r\pi^{-1}\exp\left(\frac{\Delta S_{\ddagger}}{R}\right)\exp\left(\frac{-\Delta E_{\ddagger}}{RT}\right), \qquad (5.25)$$

[1] Reference b of Table 5.3.

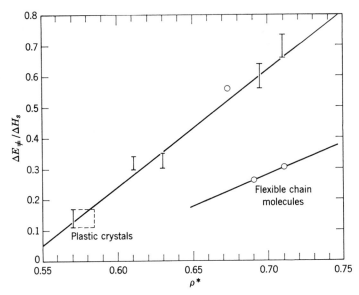

Figure 5.2   Dependence of the reduced activation energy for rotational diffusion of rigid molecules on packing density.

where $\Delta S_{\ddagger}$ is the "entropy of activation," which is small with rigid molecules and is comparatively large with flexible molecules, in which many degrees of freedom may be involved in the passage over the barrier to external rotational motion of a molecule in the crystal lattice.

The population of relaxing molecules is derived from an equilibrium argument and is related to the energy difference ΔE_0 between two equilibrium positions of the rotor on the lattice. The specific form of the relation depends on the physical property under consideration. Whereas the potential barrier to rotation is rather simply related to the lattice energy, the energy difference ΔE_0 is an extremely specific property and is not easily related to any quantifiable property of the crystal. The experimentalist will not be surprised by this conclusion because he knows that even the mechanical preparation of the solid sample affects the height of the relaxation peak, but only rarely its location on the frequency scale.

Many molecular crystals undergo a solid–solid phase transition at temperature T_{tr}. At $T < T_{tr}$ (in its β phase") the crystal is hard and the molecules comparatively immobile, whereas at $T > T_{tr}$ (in its "plastic" or "α phase"), the crystal is soft and the molecules rotate as rapidly as in the liquid phase [3]. Because neither the incidence nor the temperature level of such a phase transition can be predicted with certainty, the incidence of a phase transition (see Chapter 6) must be known before anything can be said about the diffusional rotation rate. (For further details on general principles, consult the very illuminating discussion of the nature of orientational freedom of molecules in crystals by I. Darmon and C. Brot, *Mol. Cryst.* **2**, 301 (1967) et seq.)

5.2.1 Rigid Nonassociating Molecules

Extensive tables of $\Delta S_{\ddagger}$ and $\Delta E_{\ddagger}$ data have been published [28] that have been obtained by evaluating the experimental data in terms of (5.25). The small fraction of data for rigid nonassociating molecules (most are on flexible long-chain compounds) have been assembled in Tables 5.3 and 5.4. Inspection of the tables shows that the energy term $\Delta E_{\ddagger}$ is more readily correlated than is $\Delta S_{\ddagger}$. Expressing $\Delta E_{\ddagger}$ as a fraction of the lattice energy ΔH_s yields a fairly simple picture. The ratio $\Delta E_{\ddagger}/\Delta H_s$ covers a comparatively narrow range in each of the two phases, and—where data are available—follows an intelligible trend paralleling the packing density (Figure 5.2). Even the very small values

Table 5.3 Rotational Reorientation and Diffusion Parameters for Crystals Composed of Rigid Molecules; Hard or Normal Crystal (at $T < T_{tr}$)

Substance	Method[a]	ν_r $(10^{12} sec^{-1})$	$\Delta E_{\ddagger}$, (kcal/mole)	$\dfrac{\Delta E_{\ddagger}}{\Delta H_s}$	$\dfrac{\Delta F_{\ddagger}(293)}{\Delta H_s}$	Ref.
Benzene	NMR	2	3.1	0.30		b
Benzene	NMR		3.7	0.35		c
Benzene			3.5	0.34		d
Hexamethylbenzene	NMR	0.9	5.3	0.33		d
Chloropentamethylbenzene	EDR	200	10.0	0.50		o
Bromopentamethylbenzene	EDR	30	9.2	0.43		o
Chlorodurene	EDR	4000	8.1	0.43		o
1,2,4-Trimethyl-2,5,6-trichlorobenzene	EDR		10.3	0.50	0.326	e
Pentachlorotoluene	EDR		11.6	0.55	0.422	e
Pentachlorobenzenethiol	EDR		11.8	0.49		p
Hexachlorobenzene	NQR		9.9 to 12.6	0.46 to 0.59		f
1,2,3-Trichlorobenzene	NQR		4.6 to 5.7	0.30 to 0.35		f
Ethane	NMR		2.75[i]	0.56		g
Propane	NMR		3.3	0.49		g
1,1,1-Trichloroethane	NMR	9	4.8[i]	0.51		b
Hexafluoroethane	NMR		—	0.57		g
Hexachloroethane	NQR		8 to 9[i]	0.56 to 0.64		h
Thiourea	NMR	75	10.0	−0.7[k]		j
Cyclohexane	NMR		5 to 6	0.45 to 0.54		d
Cyclohexane	NMR	1.0	11.0	1.0		e
Adamantane	NMR	0.9	5.3	0.37		b
Hexamethylene tetramine	NQR	7.6	15.6	0.87		l
H_2S, Phase III	NMR		3.6 ± 0.2	0.57 (at 90 to 104°K)		m
H_2S, Phase III	NMR		5.5 ± 1	0.87 (at 77 to 90°K)		m
H_2S, Phase III	NMR		3.8 ± 0.3	0.60 (at <90°K)		n
H_2Se, Se (Selenium)	NMR		1.4 ± 0.5	0.19		n

[a] Method: EDR = electric dipole relaxation; NMR = nuclear magnet relaxation; NQR = nuclear quadrupole relaxation.
[b] J. S. Waugh and E. I. Fedin, *Soviet Phys.—Solid State* **4.**, 1633 (1963).
[c] E. R. Andrews, *J. Chem. Phys.* **18**, 607 (1950).
[d] T. P. Das, *J. Chem. Phys.* **27**, 763 (1957).
[e] Meakins in *Prog. Dielectrics* **3**, 159 (1961).
[f] I. Tatsuzaki, *J. Phys. Soc. Japan* **14**, 578 (1959).
[g] J. G. Aston, *Discusssions Faraday Soc.* **10**, 73 (1951).
[h] N. E. Ainbinder et al., *J. Struct. Chem.* **2**, 644 (1961).
[i] It is uncertain whether $\Delta E_{\ddagger}$ is the barrier to external or to internal rotation.
[j] D. H. Smith and R. M. Cotts, *J. Chem. Phys.* **41**, 2403 (1964).
[k] A comparatively low value of ΔH_s (14 to 15 kcal/mole) has been estimated because the x-ray diffraction data, G. J. Goldsmith and J. G. White, *J. Chem. Phys.* **31**, 1175 (1959), clearly show the absence of hydrogen bonding in the crystal. Their density, however, yields $\rho^* = 0.710$.
[l] S. Alexander and A. Tzalmona, *Phys. Rev. Letters* **13**, 546 (1964).
[m] D. C. Look et al., *J. Chem. Phys.* **44**, 3441 (1966).
[n] J. S. Waugh et al., *J. Chem. Phys.* **44**, 3912 (1966).
[o] Y. Balcou and J. Meinnel, *J. Chim. Phys.* **63**, 114 (1966).
[p] C. Brot and I. Darmon, *J. Chim. Phys.* **63**, 100 (1966).

Table 5.4 Rotational Diffusion Parameters for Crystals Composed of Rigid Molecules; Plastic Phase (at $T > T_{tr}$)

Substance	Method	$\dfrac{\Delta F_{\ddagger}\,(293)^f}{\Delta H_s}$	$\Delta E_{\ddagger}$, (kcal/mole)	$\dfrac{\Delta E_{\ddagger}}{\Delta H_s}$	Ref.
Furan	EDR	0.35	2.0	0.21	g
Bromodurene	EDR		5.1	0.26	h
Camphene	EDR	0.23	1.6	0.12	a
	EDR	0.21	2.2	0.16	b
d-Camphor	EDR	0.18	2.7	0.16	a
	EDR	0.06 ($\pm$0.05)	1.8 $\pm$ 0.7	0.11 $\pm$ 0.04	b
	NMR		2.8	0.17	c
Bornyl chloride	EDR	0.20	2.5	0.16	b
Isoborneol	EDR	0.18	4.0	0.22	a
	EDR	0.20	5.5	0.30	b
Neopentane	NMR		1.0	0.13	d
2,2-Dichloro-propane	EDR	0.19^e	1.4	0.13	b
	NMR		~3.0	0.28	d
1,1,1-Trichloro-ethane	EDR	0.18^e	(1.1)	(0.10)	b
	NMR		45?		d
t-Nitrobutane	EDR	0.14^e	0.5	0.03	b
2-Chloro-2-nitro-n-propane	EDR	0.19^e	1.3	(0.1)	b
$(CH_3)_3CCl$	NMR		1.5	0.16	d

[a] D. E. Williams and C. P. Smyth, *J. Am. Chem. Soc.* **84**, 1808 (1962).
[b] C. Clemett and M. Davies, *Trans. Faraday Soc.* **58**, 1705, 1718 (1962).
[c] J. E. Anderson and W. P. Slichter, *J. Chem. Phys.* **41**, 1422 (1964).
[d] E. O. Stejskal et al., *J. Chem. Phys.* **31**, 55 (1959).
[e] Reference temp. $= T_m$.
[f] $\Delta F_{\ddagger}$ calc. based on $\nu_r = kT/h$.
[g] F. Fried and B. Lassier, *J. Chim. Phys.* **63**, 75 (1966).
[h] = Ref. o of Table 5.3.

of $\Delta E_{\ddagger}/\Delta H_s$ for the plastic crystal phase of rotating (spherical) molecules fall where they should in the packing-density correlation.

Owing to the definition of $\Delta F_{\ddagger} \equiv RT \ln (D_R/\nu_0)$, in which $\nu_0 =$ (torsional oscillating frequency of molecule on a lattice site) as estimated by the methods in Chapter 3, while some authors take simply $\nu_0 = 10^{12}$ sec^{-1}, the scheme followed in Tables 5.3 and 5.4, except when noted otherwise), a truly reliable correlation of $\Delta F_{\ddagger}$ would be tantamount to predictability of the absolute magnitude of the rotational diffusion constant D_R, whereas the previous correlation of $\Delta E_{\ddagger}$ provides just the temperature coefficient of this diffusion constant.

When a correlation of $\Delta F_{\ddagger}$ cannot be produced, one for $\Delta S_{\ddagger} = R \ln (D_R/\nu_0)$ may be attempted. A well-known relation [25] is

$$\Delta S_{\ddagger} \approx 0.24\alpha_s \, \Delta E_{\ddagger}, \qquad (5.26)$$

which, because of the earlier correlation of $\Delta E_{\ddagger}/\Delta H_s$, can be converted to

$$\Delta S_{\ddagger} \approx A\alpha_s \Delta H_s, \tag{5.27}$$

where A is numerical constant of the order 0.1 and α_s is the thermal expansion coefficient. Because of the correlation (in Section 3.5)

$$\frac{\alpha_s \Delta H_s}{C_v{}^s} = \alpha_s^* \approx 0.44, \tag{5.28}$$

we obtain

$$\Delta S_{\ddagger} = 0.44 A C_v{}^s \tag{5.22}$$

In order to avoid confusion this $\Delta S_{\ddagger}$ should be identified as $\Delta S_{\ddagger}(\alpha)$.

The lattice heat capacity $C_v{}^s$ of rigid molecules at $T > 1.5\theta_D$ is fR, where f, the number of external degrees of freedom can be 3, 5, or 6, depending on the well-known fashion on the structure of the molecule. The generalized expansion coefficient $\alpha^* = 0.44$ is applicable only to the hard phase of solids and not to the plastic crystals. Not enough experimental information is available to arrive at valid generalizations for rigid molecules.

The foregoing discussion of rotational diffusion of the entire molecule dealt with only one source of energy absorption. Crystals of the otherwise "rigid" cyclohexane molecule and its alkyl derivative absorb an appreciable amount of mechanical energy (in shear at 1 Hz) at 140 to 150°K presumably due to chair–chair inversion of the ring [17]. Illers also found that almost all cyclohexyl and cyclopentyl crystals exhibit small energy-loss peaks (in shear at 1 Hz) at <110°K, the origin of which is obscure at present.

5.2.2 Flexible Nonassociating Molecules (Nonpolymeric)

The practical interest in waxes as electrical insulators, moisture barriers, and related applications and as model systems for polymers is largely responsible for the comparative wealth of experimental data. Rotational diffusion data are available from electric-dipole relaxation, nuclear magnetic resonance absorption (magnetic relaxation), and—by inference—from energy absorption in dynamic mechanical testing of these crystalline solids.

Broadly, the following generalizations are suggested by the accumulated data (given in the order of ascending temperature of process[1] location):

1. *The δ (or IV) process.* Detectable by high-frequency (NMR) or >5 kHz dynamic mechanical) measurement at $T < 50°K$ in crystalline or glassy states and ascribed to methyl-group reorientation ($\Delta E_{\ddagger} \approx V° \approx 2.5$ kcal/ mole). The temperature of its incidence, at a given frequency, seems to depend

---

[1] The identifying term process is used for relaxation phenomena throughout this section as well as Chapter 13. The frequently employed term transition should be carefully avoided to prevent confusion with the thermodynamically defined phase transitions.

Table 5.5 Barriers to Rotational Diffusion in n-Paraffins and Related Compounds

Substance	Method	T_c (°K)	$\Delta E_\ddagger$ (kcal/mole)	$\dfrac{\Delta E_\ddagger}{\Delta H_s}$	T_c (°K)	$\Delta E_\ddagger$ (kcal/mole)	$\dfrac{\Delta E_\ddagger}{\Delta H_s}$	T_c (°K)	$\Delta E_\ddagger$ (kcal/mole)	$\dfrac{\Delta E_\ddagger}{\Delta H_s}$
n-C_5H_{12}	NMR[a]	<130	2.75 ± 0.05	0.275	—	—	—	—	—	—
n-C_6H_{14}	NMR[a]	<130	2.95 ± 0.05	0.23	—	—	—	—	—	—
n-$C_{16}H_{34}$ + 10% n-$C_{16}H_{38}$	MEA[b]	190–215	20.0	0.59	—	—	—	—	—	—
n-$C_{20}H_{42}$ + 10% n-$C_{22}H_{46}$	MEA[b]	190–210	17.5	0.41	240	50	1.18	235/75	24	0.57
n-$C_{22}H_{46}$ + 10% n-$C_{24}H_{50}$	MEA[b]	190–210	17.5	0.38	230	45	0.97	260/90	24	0.52
n-$C_{28}H_{58}$ + 10% n-$C_{30}H_{62}$	MEA[b]	—	—	—	—	—	—	290/310	30	0.51
Polyethylene Marlex 50	NMR[c]	~170	1.9	0.94[d]	—	—	—	~270	65	32[d]
Polyethylene Marlex 50	NMR[e]	—	2.25	1.11[d]	—	—	—	—	—	—
Polyethylene Marlex 50 (oxidized)	EDR[b]	160–190	18.0	9	200	8	4	330/400	23	12
	MEA[b]	130–190	7.5	4	200	8	4	—	—	—
Polyethylene Marlex 50	MEA[b]	160–190	18.0	9	300/330	46	23	330/400	32.5	16

[a] F. A. Rushworth, *Proc. Roy. Soc. (London)* **222A**, 526 (1954); this is probably internal rotation.

[b] W. Pechhold et al., *Kolloid-Z.* **196**, 27 (1964).

[c] R. C. Rempel et al., *J. Appl. Phys.* **28**, 1082 (1957).

[d] Based on H_s per repeating unit.

[e] U. Hacherlen et al., *Z. Naturforsch.* **18a**, 689 (1963).

more on intramolecular environment than on molecule size or packing density.

2. *The γ (or* III) *process.* Detectable by 1^+ Hz (dynamic mechanical and NMR) measurements at $> 50°$K in the crystalline as well as in the glassy state. Its incidence is restricted to compounds with an uninterrupted sequence of at least three intramolecularly unimpeded (C—C) bonds including at least two connected methylene groups. Although Illers [16] designates this process broadly as rotational isomerization, that is, formation or disappearance of a non-*trans–trans* conformation, Schatzki [38], and to some extent Pechhold [33], associate it more narrowly with the motion of a chain segment that happens to be in the conformation.

At a given frequency, the temperature and probably also $\Delta E_{\ddagger}$ of the γ process increases slowly but steadily with increasing number of methylene groups (in uninterrupted sequence), as shown by the lower curve of Figure 5.3. The concurrent increase in packing density of the crystal is the most likely cause of this somewhat unexpected trend for an intramolecular motion. In keeping with this sensitivity to packing density Olf and Peterlin [48] deduce from NMR analysis that the population of segments participating in the γ process (in polyethylene) is proportional to the concentration of noncrystalline interlamellar regions, as exemplified by the chain fold regions.

3. *The β (or* II) *process.* This is the common designation of the first relaxation process below T_g occurring in glasses and is therefore discussed in Chapter 13.

4. *The α (or* I) *process.* In glasses this is the glass transition process (at T_g) and that aspect is discussed in Section 13.1. In crystals it is the first relaxation process occurring below a first-order solid–solid phase transition, or in the absence of such, below T_m. It is associated with the rotational or large amplitude torsional oscillation of an entire molecule (in the case of non-polymeric chains) around its long axis within the crystal and is thus truly "rotational diffusion." In the case of nonpolar molecules it is detected by NMR and dynamic-mechanical measurements, and in the case of polar molecules it can also be observed as dielectric loss peak.

At a given frequency, T_α rises fairly steeply with the logarithm of the number of linearly connected methylene groups per moleule, as shown in Figure 5.3. The activation energy for this process seems to be of the order of $0.5 \Delta H_s$ (Table 5.5).

Additional relaxation processes of crystals at $T_\gamma < T < T_\alpha$ have been observed on paraffin wax by Pechhold [33] and in prestrained polyethylene by

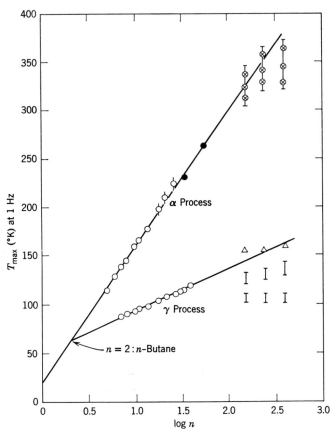

Figure 5.3 Temperature of the high-(α) and low-(γ) temperature relaxation process in crystals composed of *n*-alkanes and alkane derivatives as functions of the number (*n*) of methylene groups per molecule [16].

Moseley [30]. The detailed interpretation of these intermediate processes is complicated by the absence of sufficient data to estimate $\Delta E_{\ddagger}$.

The curves of Figure 5.4 show that some of the fine structure of energy absorption curves of pure *n*-paraffins is lost when a second component is added which forms a solid solution in the original crystal. Multicomponent *n*-paraffin mixtures appear to exhibit just the single peak shown in Figure 5.5. Here molecular rotation and crystal morphology effects are all smeared into one absorption.

Undeterred by the difficulties of obtaining reproducible measurements of relaxation strengths in crystals, Professor Wada's students have begun to develop theoretical relations of relaxation strength in *n*-paraffin crystals to molecular parameters. Because there is at least good qualitative agreement

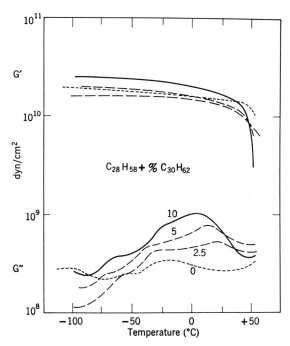

Figure 5.4   Effect of a mixture of a second component on the mechanical energy absorption spectrum of a crystalline *n*-paraffin [33].

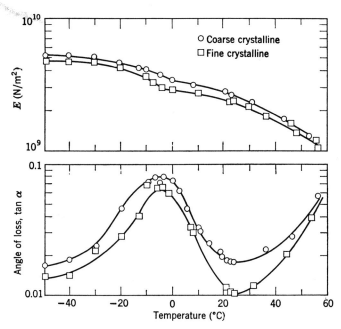

Figure 5.5   Typical mechanical-energy absorption spectrum for a C_{29}–C_{34} *n*-paraffin fraction ex Tandjoeng crude. Melting point, about 68–70°C. (Private communication from C. van der Poel, Koninklijke/Shell Laboritorium, Amsterdam, 1950.)

between theory and experiment, the results are quoted here: The relaxation strength is defined as $\Delta G = G'(0) - G(\infty)$, where $G'(0)$, $G'(\infty)$ are the extrapolated shear storage moduli at zero and infinite frequency, respectively. Then according to Tsuge's modification of Okano's theory [43],

$$\frac{\Delta G}{G'(\infty)} = 1 - \exp\left[-10^{-6}T(0.07N_c{}^3 - 0.28N_c{}^2 + 3.8N_c - 7)\right],$$

where N_c = number of carbon atoms per molecule, indicating that the relaxation strength increases with increasing chain length, as borne out by Tsuge's data. The theory yields for the relaxation time τ_i (i.e., for $\omega_{\max}^{-1}$) at a given temperature

$$\tau_i \approx \left(\frac{\eta}{4}\right)\left(\frac{N_c}{\pi f_i}\right)^4$$

where f is the force constant for the torsional motion ($\sim\Delta H_s$), η is the torsional friction constant, and i is an integer. Since the mode with $i = 2$ makes the dominant contribution, this defines the temperature T as that for which $\omega\tau_2 \approx 1$, that is, for $G''_{\max}$. The friction coefficient is not known in general, but it appears reasonable to assume that it is constant at a given packing density. Comparing data for several n-alkanes at a fixed (packing) density Tsuge finds indeed $\omega_{\max} \sim N_c^{-4}$, a rather surprising result.

In the temperature range between the solid–solid transition and the melting point one finds by NMR measurements that the rotation of the n-paraffin and similar molecules around their long axis is nearly as free as in the liquid state [19]. The soft plastic consistency of the crystals in this temperature range is a mechanical manifestation of this high molecular mobility.

The extensive data on electric-dipole relaxation of polar molecules have been determined in three different environments: solid solutions of polar molecules in paraffin crystals, where the dipoles may be considered—at least in part—as sounding devices for the lattice mobility of the paraffin, crystals of pure polar waxes in the plastic (α) phase, and crystals of pure polar waxes in the hard (β) phase. In the latter two there is appreciable dipole–dipole interaction.

The observations on solid solution have been carried out in the hard (β) phase region. Hence it is not surprising to find (in Table 5.6) $\Delta E_{\ddagger}/\Delta H'_s$ (as well as $\Delta F_{\ddagger}/\Delta H'_s$) for the solid solutions and the pure β-phase crystals to be of similar magnitude. In this connection it is of interest that Chapman and Whittington [5] calculated the repulsion energies of rotating paraffin chains in various crystal modifications from the hydrogen interactions and obtained the following potential energy barriers per CH_2 group: orthorhombic subcell, 0.59 kcal/mole; the two types of triclinic subcells, 0.39 and 0.42 kcal/mole,

Table 5.6 Rotational Diffusion Parameters for Crystals Composed of Flexible Molecules; Hard on Normal Crystal (at $T < T_{tr}$); All by EDR Method[a]

Substance	$\dfrac{\Delta F_{\ddagger}\,(293)}{\Delta H_s}$	$\Delta E_{\ddagger}$ (kcal/mole)	$\dfrac{\Delta E_{\ddagger}}{\Delta H_s}$
Solid Solutions in n-Paraffin Wax[b]			
$(n\text{-}C_8)_2C{=}O$	0.18	11.3	0.318
$(n\text{-}C_9)_2C{=}O$	0.17_5	11.9	0.302
$(n\text{-}C_{10})_2C{=}O$	0.18	14.7	0.338
$(n\text{-}C_{11})_2C{=}O$	0.16_7	15.5	0.327
$(n\text{-}C_{12})_2C{=}O$	0.16_8	17.7	0.345
$(n\text{-}C_{13})_2C{=}O$	0.16_8	18.7	0.337
$(n\text{-}C_{15})_2C{=}O$	0.16	20.5	0.324
$(n\text{-}C_{17})_2C{=}O$	0.15_9	20.7	0.291
$(n\text{-}C_8)_2O$	0.168	10.1	0.297
$(n\text{-}C_{12})_2O$	0.156	15.9	0.319
$(n\text{-}C_{14})_2O$	0.152	17.1	0.295
$(n\text{-}C_{16})_2O$	0.150	17.8	0.270
Ethyl stearate		17.8	0.318
Di-n-octyl nonadioate		14.4	0.260

Pure Compounds $\left(R_1{-}\overset{\displaystyle O}{\overset{\|}{C}}{-}O{-}R_2 \right)$

R_1	R_2			
C_{16}	C_2	0.154	10.0	0.245
C_{18}	C_1	0.147	11	0.257
C_{18}	C_2	0.151	12.9	0.288
C_{12}	C_{10}	0.149	14.9	0.305
C_{22}	C_1	0.151	17.1	0.334
C_{22}	C_2	0.144	17	0.322
C_{14}	C_{12}	0.146	18	0.317
C_{16}	C_{16}	0.136	22	0.321
$(C_{16})_2O$		0.133	20	0.303
$(C_{18})_2O$		0.133	23	0.311

[a] From reference e of Table 5.3, except when noted otherwise.
[b] Assumed $\Delta H_s = [\Delta H_{s(solute)} \cdot \Delta H_{s(paraffin)}]^{1/2}$.

Table 5.7   Effect of Chain Length of Solvent and Solute on Rotational Diffusion in Solid Solutions[a]

Solvent	Solute	$\dfrac{\Delta F_{\ddagger} (253°K)}{\Delta H_s}$	$\Delta E_{\ddagger}$ (kcal/mole)	$\dfrac{\Delta E_{\ddagger}}{\Delta H_{s(\text{solute})}}$
n-Hexadecane	ethyl stearate	0.116 (0.155)[b]	18.5	0.43
Paraffin wax (n-C$_{26}$)	ethyl stearate	0.141 (0.116)[b]	17.8	0.41
n-Hexadecane	cetyl palmitate	0.122 (0.163)[b]	18.4	0.27

[a] Sillars, *Proc. Roy. Soc.* (*London*) **169A**, 66 (1938).
[b] Relative to ΔH_s (solvent).

respectively. In the reduced units of this work they correspond to $V°/\Delta H_s \approx \Delta F_{\ddagger}/\Delta H_s = 0.29, 0.19$, and 0.21, respectively, by order of magnitude in substantial agreement with the data of Table 5.6.

The chain length of the n-paraffin solvent is less important than that of the polar solute as shown by the data of Table 5.7. The large apparent activation energies in the plastic (α) phase shown in Table 5.8 are mostly a measure of the thermal expansion of the nearly liquidlike solid, and probably less than one-half of $\Delta E_{\ddagger}$ is the barrier to rotation, especially since there is NMR evidence for nearly liquidlike rotation of n-paraffin molecules [47] and of the ester molecules around their long axis in this phase [19].

The very slow (almost imperceptible) decrease of $\Delta E_{\ddagger}/\Delta H'_s$ with increasing chain length in both phases implies that throughout the investigated molecular

Table 5.8   Rotational Diffusion Parameters for Crystals Composed of Flexible Molecules; Plastic Phase (at $T > T_{\text{tr}}$)[a]

Substance		$\dfrac{\Delta F_{\ddagger} (293)}{\Delta H_s}$	$\Delta E_{\ddagger}$ (kcal/mole)	$\dfrac{\Delta E_{\ddagger}}{\Delta H_s}$
$(n\text{-C}_{18})_2\text{O}$		0.170	47.4	0.64

$$R_1-\overset{\displaystyle \overset{O}{\|}}{C}-O-R_2$$

R_1	R_2			
C$_{18}$	C$_2$	0.302	43	0.96
C$_{22}$	C$_2$	0.314	48	0.91
C$_2$	C$_{18}$	0.282	32	0.71
C$_2$	C$_{20}$	0.29	36	0.74
C$_2$	C$_{22}$	0.29$_5$	35	0.66
Succinonitrile[b]		0.26		0.15

[a] From Reference e of Table 5.3.
[b] From Reference b of Table 5.4; the value of $\Delta E_{\ddagger}$ applies only to the temperature range near T_m. $\Delta E_{\ddagger}$ increases rapidly as T_{tr} is approached, much like in very viscous liquids.

weight range, both of the observed dipole relaxations involve rotational diffusion (or large-amplitude torsional oscillation), in basic agreement with the observations on NMR and mechanical-energy absorption in the same temperature ranges. The less than linear increase of $\Delta E_{\ddagger}$ with chain length has been accounted for by Fröhlich [10] as a result of chain flexibility, permitting easier passage of the molecule over the rotational barrier such that $\Delta E_{\ddagger}(N_s) = \Delta E_{\ddagger}^1 [n_0 \tanh (N_s/26)]$, where $\Delta E_{\ddagger}^1$ is the barrier to movement of a skeletal segment (CH_2 group), N_s is the number of skeletal atoms per mole molecule, and n_0 is a constant related to the energy required to twist a valence angle. Dipole relaxation in crystals at microwave frequencies involves only the motions of small molecule segments containing permanent electric dipoles [28].

The relaxation strength in long-chain ester crystals has recently been determined systematically (by Dryden and Welsh [9]) as a function of crystal preparation and single-crystal orientation of dodecyl myristate relative to the existing electric field, as well as of mechanical straining, and of time since precipitation and since straining. Here the energy gap, 3.7 kcal/mole, between two alternative orientations in the lattice is comparatively large. Straining by 60% increased the energy absorption more than threefold, but it returned to the starting value by annealing for about 100 h. The absolute level of the dielectric energy absorption was strongly affected by impurities and by their disposition within the solid.

5.2.3 Mixtures of Long-Chain Compounds

The solid solutions of polar compounds in n-paraffin crystals mentioned earlier emphasized only the rotational diffusion of one component, but not the effect of mixing on rotational diffusivity for all molecules on the lattice. The mechanical-energy loss experiments by Pechhold and co-workers [33] in Figure 5.3 show by how much the admixture of comparatively small amounts of a second component only two carbon atoms longer in chain length increases both the temperature and the strength of maximum energy absorption. On a molecular scale this is equivalent to a slight decrease in the population of rotating molecules at low temperature, and a large increase at high temperature. It also appears that increasing admixture of a second component removes much of the fine structure from the mechanical-energy absorption spectrum. The single peak of the multicomponent technical wax in Figure 5.4 is easily visualized as a continuation of the previous figure. The effect of crystallite size shown in Figure 5.4 suggests that the population of rotating molecules in the grain boundaries is not larger than in the bulk. Narrowing the molecular-weight distribution of a paraffin wax (by fractional crystallization) was found by Tsuge [43] to increase the energy absorption.

Because energy absorption is, in principle, a measure of—or at least a necessary condition for—ductile behavior of a solid, the results of Tsuge and of v.d. Poel (Fig. 5.4) run contrary to experience. Narrowing the molecular-weight distribution and coarsening the crystal structure generally increase brittleness. These results emphasize that fracture behavior of crystalline solids often depends more on sample morphology than on energy absorption (molecule mobility).

5.2.4   Associating Molecules

Two kinds of crystals composed of associating molecules are of general interest: (a) the hydrogen bonding compounds with their comparatively

Table 5.9   Rotational Diffusion Parameters in Crystals Composed of Rigid Hydrogen Bonding Substances in Hard (Low-Temperature) Phase[a]

Substance	Method	$\dfrac{\Delta F_{\ddagger}\ (T_{m,n}T_{tr})}{\Delta H_s}$	$\Delta E_{\ddagger}$ (kcal/mole)	$\dfrac{\Delta E_{\ddagger}}{\Delta H_s}$	$\dfrac{\Delta E_{\ddagger}}{H_s\ \text{(H bonding)}^{\text{b}}}$
Ice	EDR	0.84	13.25	1.09	1.09
Ice	MEA[c]	0.90	13.4	1.10	1.10
HCl	EDR	0.50	2.58	0.52	1.08
HBr	EDR	0.62	2.7	0.49	1.2
HI	EDR	0.34	2.2	0.37	1.5
Urea[d]	NMR		9.0	0.43	0.7

[a] From Reference e of Table 5.3 except where noted otherwise.
[b] H_s (H-bonding) $= \Delta H_s(HX) - H_s(X\cdot)_{nonpolar}$ in the case of the hydrogen halides.
[c] P. Schiller, *Z. Physik.* **153**, 1 (1958); $\nu_0 = 530 \times 10^{12}$ sec^{-1}.
[d] J. W. Emsley and J. A. Smith, *Trans. Faraday Soc.* **57**, 1233 (1961); this might be a barrier to motion of the —NH$_2$ group only.

mobile associating group forming linear chains, and (b) metal-oxide derivatives, such as the metal soaps, forming association sheets throughout the crystal by virtue of coordination bonds between the oxygen atom on adjacent soap molecules and the metal ions.

In the case of hydrogen-bonding compounds in the hard crystalline state most molecular measures of rotational diffusion find the independent rotation of the hydrogen-bonding groups rather than that of the entire molecule. With compounds such as water and hydrogen halides, in which the entire molecule is the "hydrogen-bonding group" we find that $\Delta E_{\ddagger}$ is virtually identical with the hydrogen-bond contribution to ΔH_s as shown by the data of Table 5.9. The data for alcohols in [28] suggest that the energies of activation are about integer multiples (1 or 2) of the hydrogen-bond contribution to ΔH_s. In certain cases that can be recognized by inspection of the molecule, only intramolecular resistance to hydroxyl group rotation can be considered; then $\Delta E_{\ddagger}$ is of the order of the appropriate barrier to internal rotation of the hydroxyl group. The free energies of activation of rotational diffusion in alcohol crystals are not easily correlated by any known scheme. Hence the absolute value of the relaxation time is not readily predicted. No data are available on the rotational diffusion in metal soap or similar crystals.

The rotational motions of molecules in "plastic" crystalline alcohols are also largely dominated by the retarding effect of the hydrogen bond. This is evident from the higher temperature level of the γ process, and from the absence of the α process among the n-alkanols with $N_c > 8$ [16]. Particularly striking is the high activation energy for electric-dipole relaxation of cyclopentanol (9.6 kcal/mole) and cyclohexanol (10.4 kcal/mole) in the plastic-crystal phase [7]. To a good approximation, $\Delta E_{\ddagger}$ is the sum of $\Delta E_{\ddagger}$ for over-all rotation in the plastic phase [e.g., $\Delta E_{\ddagger}$ (cyclohexanone) $= 1.64$ kcal/mole [7], and H_s (OH) ≈ 8 kcal/mole]. The mechanical-energy absorption in the hard-crystal phase of cyclopentanol and cyclohexanol (at 1 Hz) at 155 and 197°K, respectively, Illers ascribes to the reorientation of the hydroxyl groups, since no other cyclohexyl derivative exhibits this process.

5.2.5 Rotational Motions in Polymer Crystals

Many of the experiments quoted in the previous paragraphs had been carried out as model experiments to simulate rotational motions of molecule segments in crystalline polymers. However, even if we ignore the contributions of the noncrystalline regions of commercial polymers and consider only the crystalline components, we find one important difference with all of the crystals discussed so far. The chains in polymer crystals cannot rotate freely because the ends are constrained by being part of a long molecule that re-enters the same crystal many times [12]. All rotational motion is, therefore, restricted to the twisting of a chain of finite length. As this length is of the order of 100 to 200 chain links, the rotational amplitude permitted with small energy expenditure in the center is quite appreciable. Hence most of the rotational modes observed in n-paraffin mixtures could also be observed in polyethylene crystals, as shown by the data of Table 5.5.

Although detailed discussions of rotational motions in polymer crystals are beyond the scope of this report and can be found in considerable detail elsewhere [44], it seems appropriate here to direct attention to Illers' observation that the temperatures for the rotational α and γ processes at 1 Hz are located on the curves of Figure 5.3 at the point determined by the fold length of the polyethylene lamellar crystal [16]. The meaning of the indicated fine structure of the energy-absorption maxima is still obscure.

5.3 MASS DIFFUSION

Mass diffusion in and through solids is of direct importance to engineers as a measure of the barrier qualities of solid membranes and when it is necessary to remove small amounts of volatiles held in solid solution in crystalline solids. When macroscopic solids are in mutual contact, the mass diffusion rate often determines whether they will sinter spontaneously to form compacts or "block" when they are supposed to remain easily separable. Diffusion is a prerequisite for the plastic deformation or the flow of solids. Finally, it is an important factor in solid state chemical reactions, such as solid-state polymerization [21].

In spite of the growing interest in these aspects of diffusion in solids only very few meaningful measurements have been carried out on simple molecular crystals. The more extensive experiments on semicrystalline polymers can be excluded from consideration because it has been demonstrated that the diffusing species migrate almost exclusively through crystal defects and/or through amorphous domains of such polymers [18], [29].

Experimentally observed diffusion rates in molecular crystals depend on the method of sample preparation and experimental environment to a degree that is only beginning to be realized. Controlled changes in the crystal growth rate and in subsequent annealing conditions of naphthalene crystals have been shown by Sherwood [46], [49] to produce more than 100-fold variations in the diffusion coefficient, probably because of the attendant differences in crystal defect concentration. The high molecular mobility prevailing in plastic crystals makes the latter somewhat less sensitive to crystal growth and annealing history.

Crystal perfection can also be disturbed locally by chemical conversion of a molecule that will fit less well into the lattice of its neighbors, such as oxidation by ingressed oxygen or by (radiation induced) isomerization. Since *ppm* concentration of such defects can cause large increases in diffusivity, nearly imperceptible chemical changes can seriously falsify the measurements.

A third source of discordant results is the different weight given to grain boundary diffusion, mobility around defects, and "true bulk diffusion" in more perfect domains by the different measuring techniques such as (radioactive) tracer diffusion and NMR, ESR, or NQR measurement. The latter three suffer from the additional disadvantage of having to introduce an often quite arbitrarily chosen molecular distance measure.

The extent of discrepancies among experimental data collected in Tables 5.10 and 5.11 is thus not surprising, but it precludes development of reliable correlations until the experimental variables have gotten under control. Conversely, one may conclude that the diffusion rate in unannealed crystals grown under comparatively uncontrolled conditions will generally be faster than that derived from a correlation based on data obtained with more perfect crystals.

Table 5.10 Molecular Self-Diffusion in "Normal" Molecular Crystals

Crystal	Method	D_0 (cm^2 sec^{-1})	$\Delta E_{\ddagger}$[a] (kcal/mole)	$\dfrac{\Delta E_{\ddagger}}{\Delta H_s}$	$D(T_m)$[b] (10^{10} cm^2 sec^{-1})	Ref.
H$_2$	NMR	1.4×10^{-3}	0.38	1.5	14	c
HD	NMR	0.17	0.60	2.1	13	c
H$_2$ in HD	NMR	10^{-4}	0.40	1.5		c
Ar	Tracer	350 ± 150	4.15	2.2	55	d
Xe	NMR	7.3	7.40	2.0	6.8	e
CH$_4$	NMR		3.2	1.5		f
Naphthalene	Both		39	2.3	0.1	g
Anthracene	Tracer	6.5×10^{10}	42.4	1.8	32	h
Anthracene	Tracer					
lattice diffusion		3.3×10^{-2}	20	0.85	0.47	i
subgrain boundary diffusion		2	13	0.55	3×10^4	i
Phenanthracene in Anthracene	Tracer					
$\perp$ab plane						
lattice diffusion		11	25	1.1	0.7	i
subgrain boundary diffusion		0.011	7	0.3	8×10^4	i
$\perp$ac plane						
lattice diffusion		0.5	22	1.0	0.7	i
subgrain boundary diffusion		0.01	5	0.22	58×10^4	i
Ice (D$_2$O/H$_2$O^{18})	Tracer	—	—	—	1	j
(T$^+$/H$_2$O)	Tracer	—	13.5	1.1	0.4	
Sulfur						
(orthorhombic) (l)	Tracer	8.3×10^{-12}	3.08	0.13		k
(m)	Tracer	1.8×10^{-36}	78.0	3.4	1.0[n]	k

[a] Assuming $D = D_0 \exp(-\Delta E_{\ddagger}/RT)$.

[b] $D(T_m) = D$ extrapolated to $T = T_m$.

[c] M. Bloom, *Physica*, **23**, 767 (1957).

[d] A. Berne et al., *Nuovo Cimento*, **24**, 1179 (1962).

[e] W. M. Yea and R. E. Norberg, *Phys. Rev.*, **131**, 269 (1963).

[f] G. A. deWit and M. Bloom, *Can. J. Phys.*, **43**, 986 (1965).

[g] [46].

[h] J. N. Sherwood and S. J. Thompson, *Trans. Faraday Soc.*, **56**, 1443 (1960).

[i] P. J. Reucroft et al., *J. Chem. Phys.*, **44**, 4416 (1966).

[j] W. Kuhn and M. Thürkauf, *Helv. Chim. Acta*, **41**, 938 (1958).

[k] R. B. Cuddeback and H. G. Drickamer, *J. Chem. Phys.*, **19**, 790 (1951).

[l] D ($\perp$ to c axis) controlling at $T < 340°$K.

[m] D ($\parallel$ to c axis) controlling at $T > 350°$K.

[n] At transition temperature, $369°$K.

Table 5.11 A Molecular Self-Diffusion in Various "Plastic" Molecular Crystals at $T > T_{tr}$

Crystals	Method	D_0[a] $(cm^2 sec^{-1})$	$\Delta E_{\ddagger}$[a] (kcal/mole)	$\dfrac{\Delta E_{\ddagger}}{\Delta H_s}$	$D(T_m)$[b] $(10^{10} cm^2 sec^{-1})$	Ref.
Methane	NMR	7×10^{-6}	1.50	0.75	14.3	c
Neopentane	NMR		6.0	0.76		d
Tetramethylsilane	NMR		6.15 ± 0.44	0.67 ± 0.05		e
Hexamethyldisilane	NMR		10.0	0.77		f
t-butyl chloride	NMR		8.1	0.76		g
Carbon tetrachloride	NMR		6.8	0.66		h
Methyl chloroform	NMR		8.3	0.76		g
Succinonitrile	NMR		10.7	0.64	10^q	h
Trimethylacetic acid	NMR	3.2×10^{-6q}	8.1	0.57	0.6^q	h
Cyclohexane	NMR		8.3	0.79		i
Cyclohexane	tracer	3.6×10^6	16.3	1.46	7000	j
d-Camphor	NMR		14.6	0.89		k
Triethylene diamine	NMR	5×10^{21}	21.7(?)	1.67(?)	5.2^l	h
Triethylene diamine	NMR	8×10^{-21}	16.7	1.28	0.5^l	n
α-White phosphorus	NMR	7.7×10^{-2}	12.1	0.86	3.4	n
α-White phosphorus	tracer	1.07×10^{-3}	9.4^o	0.67		p
		2×10^{46}	80.6^q	5.75		
H_2S (Phase I)	NMR		7.4 ± 0.5	1.17 ± 0.08		r, s
H_2S_e (Phase I)	NMR		6.0 ± 1	0.83 ± 0.15		s

a Reference a of Table 5.10.
b Reference b of Table 10.5.
c E. Waugh, *J. Chem. Phys.* **26**, 966 (1957).
d E. O. Stejskal et al., *J. Chem. Phys.* **31**, 55 (1959).
e G. W. Smith, *J. Chem. Phys.* **42**, 4229 (1965).
f T. Yukitoshi et al., *Proc. Phys. Soc. Japan* **12**, 506 (1957).
g Reference f of Table 10.5.
h H. Suga and S. Seki, Intl. Symp. NMR Spectroscopy, Tokyo, September 1965. A trace of t-buCl was added to the CCl_4.
i E. R. Andrew and R. D. Eades, *Proc. Roy. Soc. (London)* **A216**, 398 (1953).
j G. M. Hood and J. N. Sherwood, *Mol. Cryst.* **1**, 97 (1966).
k J. E. Anderson and W. P. Slichter, *J. Chem. Phys.* **41**, 1922 (1964).
l Assumed $D = \nu/a^2$, where a = lattice parameter; ν = correlation frequency.
m G. W. Smith, *J. Chem. Phys.* **43**, 4325 (1965).
n H. A. Resing, *J. Chem. Phys.* **37**, 2575 (1962).
o Controlling at $T < 303°K$.
p N. H. Nachtrieb et al., *J. Chem. Phys.* **23**, 1187, 1193 (1955).
q Controlling at $T > 303°K$.

Mass diffusion in crystals is commonly represented by the relations

$$D = a^2 \nu_t \exp\left(\frac{\Delta F_{\ddagger}}{RT}\right)$$
$$= a^2 \nu_t \exp\left(\frac{\Delta S_{\ddagger}}{R} - \frac{\Delta H_{\ddagger}}{RT}\right). \tag{5.29}$$

where a is the lattice parameter, and ν_t is the translational vibration frequency of a molecule on the crystal lattice; the activation energy and entropy have the usual meaning. In view of the much larger lattice deformation required for letting an entire molecule pass than for rotation on a lattice site we are not surprised to find $\Delta H_{\ddagger}$ for mass diffusion, in Table 5.11, much larger than for rotational diffusion discussed in the previous section.

Here again we must differentiate between diffusion in the "normal" solid and in the "plastic" phase. The activation enthalpy for diffusion in the normal solid is always larger than the heat of sublimation and seems to be near $2\Delta H_s$ in several instances, suggesting that the rate determining step requires cooperation of several molecules. The activation enthalpy for diffusion in the plastic phase is strikingly uniform at $0.82 \pm 0.05 \Delta H_s$ for widely different compounds.

Correlation of $\Delta S_{\ddagger}$ is far more difficult. Lawson [25] and Keyes [20] proposed the relation (cited earlier)

$$\Delta S_{\ddagger} \approx 4\alpha_s \Delta E_{\ddagger} \tag{5.19}$$

subsequently justified by Rice [35]. In the light of the correlations of α_s in Section 3.5 and of $\Delta H_{\ddagger}$ (in Table 5.10) with ΔH_s, this relation ties $\Delta S_{\ddagger}$ directly to the heat capacity. In view of the fact that $\Delta S_{\ddagger}$ is predicted only to within $\pm 30\%$ by these relations, even for normal solids, there is little point in trying to handle the plastic phase with the means now at hand. Obviously far more work is needed.

The diffusion constant at the melting point of hard crystals covers a tenfold range, if ice is excluded from the comparisons. The differences between individual experimenters on identical substances are nearly as far apart as this entire range. Hence the absence of correlatable order is not surprising. For zeroth-order engineering estimates, this range is, to a fair degree of approximation, $7 \pm 5 \times 10^{-10}$ cm^2 sec^{-1}. Its pressure dependence seems to be related to the concurrent rise in melting point so that, independent of pressure, $-\ln D_s \sim T_m/T$ [35]. In view of the liquidlike rotational diffusion constant of molecules in plastic crystals it is surprising to find their mass diffusion constant at T_m often to be of the same order as in hard crystals.

Whereas the permeation rate of water through n-paraffin crystals (2 to -6×10^{-10} g hr^{-1} cm^{-1} torr^{-1} at room temperature [36]) and of CO_2 through ice (2 to 3×10^{-12} g hr^{-1} cm^{-1} torr^{-1} [40]) have been determined semiquantitatively, the corresponding diffusion coefficients or the diffusion coefficients of any foreign solute through molecular crystals have yet to be determined. If experience with metals is any guide, we will find in general: $D(\text{solute}) > D(\text{self})$.

The diffusion of dyes into crystalline polymer fibers provides the only moderately extensive set of diffusion data for large solute molecules in a "crystalline" matrix. Since the most carefully studied crystals, polyamide fibers, are never 100% crystalline, there would be a finite probability that

Table 5.12   Diffusion of Large Molecules (As Function of Molecule Size) Into a Monofilament of a Semicrystalline Polyamide (6-Nylon) [37]

Penetrant:

R	D (10^{-10} cm^2 sec^{-1})		$\Delta E_\ddagger$ (kcal/mole)	$\dfrac{\Delta E_\ddagger}{\Delta H_s^{1}}$ a	$\dfrac{\Delta S_\ddagger}{R}$
	(60°C)	(80°C)			
CH$_3$	1.1	11	26.8	0.58	18
C$_2$H$_5$	0.26	4.0	31.8	0.63	23
n-C$_4$H$_9$	0.06	0.96	37	0.63	28
H	0.41b				

a ΔH_s^{1} estimated from correlation (Table 14.1).
b Extrapolation of the linear curve ln D_{60} versus $N_c^{1/2}$ would have yielded $D \approx 10 \times 10^{-10}$ cm^2 sec^{-1}. The 25-fold slowdown suggests specific interaction between the sulfamide group and the fiber amide group. This interaction is apparently absent when the penetrant amide group is alkylated.

diffusion proceeded through the amorphous regions. The well-known [37] decrease of the dye-diffusion rate caused by prolonged annealing may mean preferred permeation either through the remaining amorphous regions or along crystallite boundaries and imperfections.

Crystallite (or molecule) alignment by fiber drawing sharply reduces (dye) diffusion parallel and normal to the drawing direction, except that permeation normal to the draw direction increases during the first 100% elongation but sharply falls at higher draw ratios [37]. The activation energy for diffusion increases steeply and monotonically with the draw ratio [37].

The molecular structure of the diffusing solute affects the diffusion rate in a qualitatively easily intelligible way: D decreases and $\Delta E_\ddagger$ increases with increasing molecule size, as shown in Table 5.12. Specific attraction of the solute to the molecules of the fiber results in the expected slowdown of diffusion rate. Permeation of a diffusant that interacts chemically with the fiber substrate must be evaluated with the appropriate kinetics equation in order to extract meaningful diffusion parameters from the experimental data [37].

5.4   CREEP

Creep of molecular crystals has so far been measured only on very few systems and generally in somewhat exploratory fashion. The various relations between creep rate and self-diffusion as well as solute diffusion can, therefore, not be tested quantitatively. The general creep behavior, $\dot{e} = \Sigma A_i t^{-n_i}$, is followed by the above mentioned systems. For most n-paraffins and n-paraffin mixtures, n_i decreases with increasing temperature, starting at $T <$ $0.85 T_m$ or $0.85 T_{tr}$ with $n \approx 0.8$ and tending toward 0.2 at T_{tr}, since it must become ~ 0 (simple viscous flow) at T_m [41]. This means that the creep mechanism changes with temperature between $0.85 T_m$ and T_m. Moreover, molecular crystals are employed as structural materials generally at $T >$ $0.5 T_m$. Hence in the temperature range of interest climbing of dislocations and thus vacancy diffusion will generally control the creep rate, and thus the deformation rate

$$\dot{e} = \frac{CD}{h}\left[\exp\left(n\sigma \frac{b^3}{kT}\right) - 1\right]$$

which for small stresses (meaning $n\sigma b^3 < kT$ and $n \sim \sigma, h \sim \sigma^{-2}$) reduces to

$$\dot{e} = \frac{C'D_s\sigma^4}{kT} = \frac{C''\sigma^4}{kT}\exp\left[-\frac{\Delta E_{\ddagger}(D_s)}{RT}\right],$$

where h = height that dislocation has to climb, n = number of dislocations piled up per obstacle, and b = magnitude of Burgers vector $\approx (V/N_A)^{\frac{1}{3}}$ [39]. Because all constants but $\Delta E_{\ddagger}(D_s)$ have to be obtained from creep experiments, recognition of the importance of self-diffusion for the process enables us to predict only the temperature coefficient of the creep rate (at constant n) if the impurity concentration is low. Otherwise impurity diffusion may determine the creep rate, and no predictions can be made. This may explain the erratic behavior of $\Delta E_{\ddagger}/\Delta H_s$ shown in Table 5.13.

In the light of what has been said about mass diffusion in Section 5.3, the data of Table 5.13 probably represent no more than the state of the art at the time of their publication. The ice data are likely to be superseded by current work at the laboratory of Ref. d of Table 5.13. Since neither sample preparation nor deformation technique was highly refined, it seems dangerous to deduce anything from the odd coincidence that for several crystals $\Delta E_{\ddagger}(\text{creep}) \approx 0.5\Delta E_{\ddagger}(D_s)$ of Table 5.10.

Table 5.13   Creep-Rate Data for Various Molecular Crystals

Substance	$\Delta E_{\ddagger}$ (kcal/mole^{-1})	$\dfrac{\Delta E_{\ddagger}}{\Delta H_s}$	i[a]	Ref.
Ice, low shear stress	31.8	2.6	4.2	b
Ice, high shear stress	28.4	2.33		b
Ice, medium shear stress	14.3	1.17	2.5[c]	d
Ice, very low shear stress, low strain	16.1	1.32	1.6	e
Sebacic acid	17.6	0.46	—	
n-Paraffin wax at $T < T_{tr}$, $T < 0.92\,T_m$	48	0.9	1	
Ammonia, low shear stress	—	—	1	f
Ammonia, high shear stress	5.6	0.8	3 to 4	f
Methane	1.5	0.7	3	g
Krypton	3.2	1.2		g
Argon	2.0	1.1		g

[a] i = exponent on shear stress in $\dot{e} \sim \sigma^i$.

[b] J. W. Clear, *Proc. Roy. Soc.* (*London*) **A228**, 519 (1955).

[c] Exponent decreases to 2.0 when high shear strains (0.25) deform the single crystal.

[d] Readey and Kingery, *Acta Met.* **12**, 171 (1964).

[e] H. H. G. Jellinek and R. Brill, *J. Appl. Phys.* **27**, 1198 (1956).

[f] D. N. Bol'shutkin et al., *Sov. Phys.-Solid State* **7**, 2255 (1966).

[g] D. N. Bol'shutkin et al., *Sov. Phys.-Solid State* **7**, 2110 (1966).

At very low stresses, say 1 % or less of the yield stress, we can treat creep as a form of viscous flow with an effective viscosity η' which, according to Lifshitz [27], is of the order $\eta' \approx kTL^2/D_s v_h$, where L = grain size, v_h = volume of vacancy. For reasonable values of L, v_h, and D_s, we find effective viscosities of the order observed in creep experiments with paraffin crystals [41], shown in Figures 5.6 and 5.7. The steep decrease in viscosity at $T > 0.9T_m$ may well correspond to a sharp increase of the diffusion coefficient. Rather unexpectedly, this effective viscosity is essentially independent of shear stress over nearly a hundredfold range in shear stress until the solid–solid transition temperature is reached. At that point there is a sharp change in magnitude and temperature dependence of η', and the paraffin wax acts between T_{tr} and T_m like a typical non-Newtonian fluid, η' decreasing as the shear stress is increased.

The creep viscosity of polymeric crystals appears to be non-Newtonian at all temperatures ($> T_g$ of the amorphous component); η always decreases with increasing deformation rate. Analysis of the few available long-range creep data of polyethylene by Baker and Hopkins [3] showed that at 25°C its viscosity ranges between 10^{11} and $> 10^{15}$ P, the latter value characteristic of the extremely slow creep rates after very prolonged shear stress relaxation. The limiting unrelaxable shear stress is apparently the rubber elasticity of the amorphous regions, about 10^7 dyn/cm^2.

Representation of the creep of semicrystalline polymers by an "effective viscosity" is rather misleading because the significant decrease in strain rate with time of stress application, the strain-hardening effect, is ignored thereby. So far neither models nor purely empirical equations have successfully described the available creep data. Only qualitative generalizations can be made: that creep rate parallels the initial strain (σ/E), the exponent i in $\dot{e} \sim \sigma^i$ ranging up to 8 (!); that the strain–hardening rate varies inversely as the initial strain; and that at $T > T_g$, the creep rate and the strain-hardening rate decrease rapidly with increasing degree of crystallinity. The great sensitivity of creep and strain hardening rate to thermal and mechanical history of the sample probably precludes development of a more than

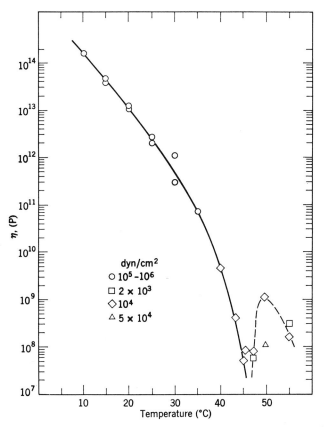

Figure 5.6   Viscosity of macrocrystalline wax 135/40 [30]; 1 poise = 10^{-1} N sec/m^2.

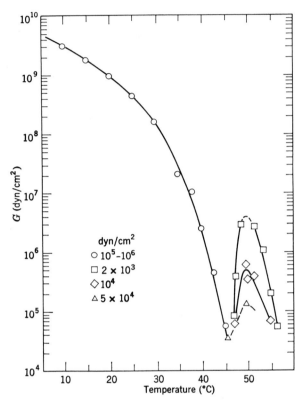

Figure 5.7   Modulus of rigidity of macrocrystalline wax 135/40 after 600-sec loading [30]; 1 dyn/cm² = 10^{-1} N/m².

descriptive theory for some time to come. The data for starting this task are only now beginning to be published [50].

5.5 SINTERING

Metal granules in contact at $T > 0.5T_m$ and certainly at $T > 0.7T_m$ will fuse (sinter) into a single block, especially if pressure is used to maintain good contact over prolonged periods. Molecular crystals will not sinter under similar conditions even over long periods of contact at $0.85T_m$ [11], provided there is no solid–solid transition below the temperature of the experiment. The reason for this difference between metallic and molecular crystals is the much higher diffusion coefficient of metals at comparable values of T/T_m apparent from the graph of D_s versus T_m/T in Figure 5.8.

The low diffusivity of water molecules in ice, at variance with the well-known sintering tendency of ice, suggests an additional property that determines the incidence of sintering. Solids are in initial contact not over their entire geometrical surface area but only with their microscopic protuberances. Hence on a microscopic scale the contact pressures are so much higher than the nominal pressures that the change of melting point with pressure has to be considered. In the case of ice dT_m/dP is well-known to be negative so that T/T_m at the contacts is much higher than for the bulk of the sample, possibly

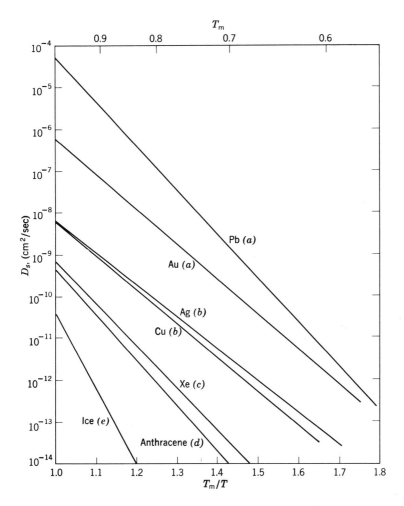

Figure 5.8 Self-diffusion constant D_s of crystalline solids as function of T/T_m. Upper four curves: metals; lower three curves: molecular crystals. (a) R. M. Barrer, *Diffusion In and Through Solids*, Cambridge University Press, Cambridge, England, 1941. (b) O. Kubaschewski, *Trans, Faraday Soc.* **46**, 713 (1950). (c) Reference e, Table 5.10. (d) Reference i, Table 5.10. (e) Reference k, Table 5.10.

even leading to liquefaction at the contact points. In the comparison of molecular with metallic crystals we find $dT_m/dP = \Delta V_m/\Delta S_m$ to cover a similar range of magnitudes. Because of the low yield stress of most molecular crystals, however, only comparatively low pressures are supported by the protuberances before they collapse and thereby reduce the local pressures and thus prevent a significant rise in T_m, at the same time precluding the incidence of pressure welding.

An important driving force to sintering (at $T > 0.8T_m$) of metals, their very high surface free energy, is also missing for most molecular crystals with their comparatively small surface-free energy, as pointed out by Geach and Woolf [11]. The net result of the combined effects is the virtual impossibility to sinter molecular crystals at temperatures below T_{tr}, or at any temperature below T_m if there is no solid–solid transition.

A practical consequence of this behavior is the absence of "blocking" when paraffin-wax[1]-covered surfaces are in contact under pressure at $T < T_{tr}$. The high plasticity at $T > T_{tr}$ causes comparatively rapid flow of the wax crystals in contact into microscopic crevices, so that blocking ensues even if the mass diffusion rate is not particularly high.[2] Semicrystalline polymer of high degrees of crystallinity will behave like other molecular crystals when their surfaces are in contact. Hence they exhibit a rather lower coefficient of friction than prevails between amorphous (glassy) polymers. The latter also sinter and block rather readily because liquidlike mobility of molecule chain segments prevails in the surface even when the bulk is at $T < T_g$.

TENTATIVE CALCULATING PROCEDURES

Procedure 5.1

Desired. Thermal conductivity of polycrystalline solid composed of rigid (monomeric molecules).

Available Data. Molecular structure.

STEP 1: Calculate V_w from molecular structure increments of Table 14.1. Units. cm^3/mole.

STEP 2: Calculate $\Delta H_s'$ from molecular structure increments of Table 14.1. Units. cal/mole.

STEP 3: Fix numbers of external degrees of freedom per molecule.

Type of Molecule	Monatomic	Diatomic or Linear	Polyatomic Nonlinear
f	3	5	6

Add additional degrees of freedom for rotatable groups; for example, for p-dihydroxylbenzene $f = 6 + 2 = 8$.

---

[1] Microcrystalline waxes are excluded from this discussion because of their content in noncrystalline viscous components.

[2] K. Arabian, private communication.

STEP 4: $\lambda \approx \dfrac{1.35 \times 10^{-4} \Delta H_s^{3/2}}{f T M^{1/2} V_w^{2/3}}$ (cal/cm sec°K).

This result should be valid between about $0.5\theta_D$ (Section 3.3 for estimating θ_D) and T_{tr} (if there is a solid–solid transition temperature). Otherwise the upper temperature limit is at T_m. The thermal conductivity of solids between T_{tr} and T_m should be estimated by means of calculating methods for the corresponding liquid.

Procedure 5.2

Desired. Thermal conductivity of polycrystalline solid composed of flexible molecules ($N_s < 50$).

Available Data. Molecular structure.

STEPS 1, 2: Steps 1, 2 of Procedure 5.1.

STEP 3: Number of degrees of freedom $f = 6 + (N_s - 1)$, where N_s is the number of skeletal atoms per molecule.

STEP 4: $\lambda \approx \dfrac{2.70 \times 10^{-24} \Delta H_s}{d_w^2 T(N_s + 5)} \left\{ \left(\dfrac{M}{J\,\Delta H_s} \right) \left[\dfrac{2}{3}\left(1 + \dfrac{1}{N_s} \right) \right] + \dfrac{\rho_s}{3 E_p}\left(1 - \dfrac{1}{N_s} \right) \right\}^{-1/2}$

(cal/cm sec°K)

where E_p is the spectroscopic elastic modulus of the polymer chain and can be found on Table 4.5. This result should be valid between $0.5\,\theta_D$ and T_{tr} (if there is a solid–solid transition temperature) otherwise up to $0.95\ T_m$.

Procedure 5.3

Desired. Estimate of rotational diffusion constant (rotational relaxation time)$^{-1}$ of nonassociating rigid molecules in hard low temperature crystal.

Available Data. Molecular structure, density.

STEPS 1, 2: Steps 1, 2 of Procedure 5.1.

STEP 3: Packing density $\rho^* = \rho V_w/M$.

STEP 4: Activation energy $\Delta E_{\ddagger} \approx \Delta H_s\,(3.75\rho^* - 2.0)$.

STEP 5: For an order of magnitude estimate of the rotational diffusion constant we might use $D_r \approx (\Delta E_{\ddagger}/2\,I)^{1/2} \exp (\Delta E_{\ddagger}/RT)$,[1] where I is the largest moment of inertia of the molecule. This parameter is either available from the literature or can be estimated by several computer programs.[2]

If there is suspicion that the value of D_r so obtained is wrong, one might try to correlate a few published values of $\Delta F_{\ddagger}/\Delta H_s$ versus ρ^*.

When this information is desired to predict mechanical energy absorption, it should be kept in mind that at best the frequency ($\omega_c \sim D_r$)–temperature relation is obtained. The all important intensity of the energy absorption remains unpredictable because the population of rotating molecules is at present unpredictable. It depends critically on the concentration of impurities or intentional second components. Only pure *n*-paraffins may be an exception (see pp. 114 and 116).

---

[1] See Reference a of Table 5.4.

[2] Computer program available from Professors Gwinn and Tolles (University of California) and from Snyder and Schachtschneider (Shell Development Co.).

Procedure **5.4**

> *Desired.* Estimate of rotational diffusion constant (rotational relaxation time)$^{-1}$ of long-chain flexible molecules in hard (low-temperature) crystals.

Available Data. Molecular structure, density.

STEPS 1–3: Steps 1, 2, 3 of Procedure 5.3.

STEP 4: Activation energy $\Delta E_{\ddagger} \approx \Delta H_s (1.75\rho^* - 0.93)$.

STEP 5: For an order of magnitude estimate of the absolute magnitude of the rotational diffusion constant at 20°C we might use

$$D_r \approx \left(\frac{kT}{h}\right) \exp\left(\frac{-0.15\,\Delta H_s}{RT}\right),$$

which at 20°C is

$$D_r \approx 0.61 \times 10^{13} \exp(-2.5 \times 10^{-4}\,\Delta H_s).$$

Then use $\Delta E_{\ddagger}$ from Step 4 to estimate D_r at other temperatures by

$$\ln D_r(T) = \ln D_r(293) + 0.22\,\Delta E_{\ddagger}(3.413 \times 10^{-3} - T^{-1}).$$

Regarding application of this information to mechanical energy absorption, read last paragraph of Step 5 of Procedure 5.2. There is evidence that the mechanical-energy absorption of long-chain compounds represented by the frequency ($\approx D_r$) range of this method is that just below the first-order solid–solid transition, or in the absence of such, just below the melting point. The very low temperature motions (at $T < 200°K$) involve only small parts of the molecule.

Procedure **5.5**

> *Desired.* Rotational diffusion constant of rigid hydrogen-bonded molecules in hard (low-temperature) crystal.

Available Data. Molecular structure.

D_r depends too strongly on details of molecular structure for reliable estimates. See Section 5.2.4.

Procedure **5.6**

> *Desired.* Rotational diffusion constant of rigid nonassociating molecules in plastic crystal.

Available Data. Molecular structure, density, T_m, T_{tr}.

STEPS 1–5: Steps 1 through 5 of Procedure 5.3. If liquid-phase data of D_r (or τ_r^{-1}) are available, or if a method is available to estimate $D_r (= \tau_r^{-1})$ from a correlation for D_r in the liquid phase, just extrapolate to below the melting point but above T_{tr}.

Procedure **5.7**

> *Desired.* Rotational diffusion constant of flexible nonassociating molecules in plastic crystals.

Available Data. Molecular structure, T_{tr}, T_m.

D_r depends too strongly on details of molecular structure for reliable estimates. See text on page 116.

Procedure 5.8

Desired. Mass diffusion of rigid molecules in hard (low-temperature) crystals.
Available Data. Molecular structure.
General
Observations: Currently available data cover only self-diffusion, as does the present correlation. Diffusion of solutes forming solid solutions is likely to be slower—if experience with metallic systems is a valid guide. Hence we may consider the estimates of this Procedure as upper limits when considering the diffusion of foreign (solid) solutes. On the other hand, solutes that are precipitated into the grain boundaries are likely to diffuse rather faster than predicted and in a manner strongly dependent on the thermal and mechanical history of the sample; hence their diffusion rate is basically unpredictable.
STEPS 1, 2: Steps 1, 2 of Procedure 5.1.
  STEP 3: Activation energy $\Delta H_{\ddagger} \approx 2 \Delta H_s$. For large rigid molecules it might only be $\Delta H_{\ddagger} \approx \Delta H_s$ (see Table 10); better data are required to settle the point.
  STEP 4: The absolute magnitude of the mass (self-) diffusion constant D can be estimated only as to order of magnitude since the experimental data are hardly more accurate than that. As a zeroth approximation we might say that at $T_m D \approx 10^{-9}$ cm^2 sec^{-1}. Then at any other temperature T,

$$\ln D(T) \approx -9.0 - 0.44 \Delta H_s \left(\frac{1}{T} - \frac{1}{T_m} \right).$$

Procedure 5.9

Desired. Mass diffusion of rigid molecules in plastic crystals (at $T > T_{tr}$).
Available Data. Molecular structure.
STEPS 1, 2: Steps 1, 2 of Procedure 5.1.
  STEP 3: Activation energy $\Delta E_{\ddagger} \approx 0.8 \Delta H_s$.
  STEP 4: An order-of-magnitude estimate of the mass (self-) diffusion constant D might start from the assumption that at $T_m D \approx 10^{-9}$ cm^2 sec^{-1} (as in Procedure 5.8). Then at temperature $T(> T_{tr})$,

$$\ln D(T) \approx -9.0 - 0.175 \Delta H_s \left(\frac{1}{T} - \frac{1}{T_m} \right).$$

NOMENCLATURE

A_1	proportionality constant in (5.2), dimensionless
A_2	proportionality constant in (5.5), dimensionless
A_b	cross-sectional area of backbone chain (cm^2)
A_c	cross-sectional area of phonon path through backbone chain (cm^2)
A_s	cross-sectional area of side chain (cm^2)
A_w	surface area per mole of molecules (cm^2/mole), Tables 14.1 to 14.16
b	bond length (cm)
C_E	vibrational heat capacity (of backbone chain) (cal/mole °K)
$C_p{}^s$	lattice heat capacity of solid at constant pressure (cal/mole °K)
$C_v{}^s$	lattice heat capacity of solid at constant volume (cal/mole °K)

D_r rotational diffusion constant (sec^{-1})

D_s mass self-diffusion constant (cm^2/sec)

d_w average width of molecule = average sum of van der Waals radii of atoms in nonbonded contacts = average contact distance (cm)

E_p elastic (extension) modulus of polymer molecule (from spectroscopic force constants) (dyn/cm^2)

$E°$ standard energy of vaporization = $\Delta H_v - RT$ at $V/V_w = 1.70$ (cal/mole)

$\Delta E_{\ddagger}$ energy of activation (cal/mole)

$\Delta F_{\ddagger}$ free energy of activation (cal/mole)

f_m relaxation frequency ($= D_r$) (sec^{-1})

f number of external degrees of freedom per molecule including those due to internal rotation

g fractional vibration amplitude of molecules on a crystal lattice = amplitude/lattice parameter

$\Delta H_s'$ heat of sublimation at lowest first order solid–solid transition temperature, often written instead ΔH_s in this report (cal/mole)

h average height of folded lamella (cm)

I principal moment of inertia of a molecule (g cm^2)

J mechanical heat equivalent = 4.18×10^7 (ergs/cal)

k Boltzmann constant

L fully extended length of a molecule (cm)

l length of sample after elongation (cm)

l_0 length of sample before elongation (cm)

M molal weight (g/mole)

M_{osc} molal weight of oscillators on backbone chain

m mass per molecule (g/molecular)

N_A Avogadro's number, 0.602×10^{24} mole^{-1}

N_i number of relaxation peak

n barrier multiplicity

P_c critical pressure

R gas constant (cal/mole °K)

$\Delta S_{\ddagger}$ entropy of activation

T absolute temperature (°K)

T_m absolute melting point (°K)

T_{tr} first-order solid–solid transition temperature (°K)

T_c critical temperature (°K)

T_R T/T_c

u_s sound velocity (cm/sec)

V molal volume (cm^3/mole)

V_w van der Waals volume of mole of molecules (cm^3/mole)

$V°$ potential-energy barrier (cal/mole)

α	valence angle
α_s	cubic expansion coefficient of solid
γ	C_p/C_v
ϵ	molecular pair potential (ergs/molecule)
θ	orientation angle (relative to direction of temperature gradient)
λ	thermal conductivity (cal/cm · sec °K)
$\lambda_\perp$	thermal conductivity normal to oriented molecules
$\lambda_{\parallel}$	thermal conductivity of bulk phase parallel to axis of (oriented) molecules
λ_p	thermal conductivity along polymer backbone chain
λ_s	thermal conductivity of simple liquid
λ_a	thermal conductivity of polymeric amorphous phase
λ_c	thermal conductivity of polymeric crystalline phase
Λ	free phonon path length along polymer molecule in crystalline phase
Λ_p	free phonon path length along polymer molecule in amorphous phase
ν	λ_c/λ_a
ν_m	frequency of maximum (energy) absorption (sec^{-1})
ν_r	frequency of torsional oscillation (sec^{-1})
ρ	density (g/cm^3)
ρ_w	M/V_w (g/cm^3)
ρ_{cryst}	density of crystal (g/cm^3)
ρ^*	$= V_w/V$ (= packing density) (dimensionless)
τ	relaxation time $\approx D_r^{-1}$ (sec)
φ_i	volume fraction of ith component (dimensionless)
φ_c	volume fraction crystallinity
φ_b	cross-sectional area fraction occupied by phonon path through molecule

REFERENCES

[1] Anderson, J. E., and W. P. Slichter, *J. Chem. Phys.* **44**, 1797 (1966).
[2] Aston, J. G., in *Physics and Chemistry of the Organic Solid State*, Wiley, New York, 1963.
[3] Baker, W. O., and I. L. Hopkins, in *Rheology*, F. R. Eirich, ed., Academic Press, New York, 1960, vol. 3, p. 365.
[4] Bondi, A., *J. Appl. Phys.* **37**, 4648 (1966).
[5] Chapman, D., and S. G. Whittington, *Trans. Faraday Soc.* **60**, 1369 (1964).
[6] Clemett, C., and M. Davies, *Trans. Faraday Soc.* **58**, 1705 (1962).
[7] Corfield, G. and M. Davies, *Trans. Faraday Soc.* **60**, 10 (1964).
[8] Das, T. P., *J. Chem. Phys.* **27**, 763 (1957).
[9] Dryden, T. S., and H. K. Welsh, *Trans. Faraday Soc.* **60**, 2135 (1964).

[10] Fröhlich, H., *Theory of Dielectrics*, Oxford University Press, London, 1949.
[11] Geach, G. A., and A. A. Woolf, *International Powder Metallurgy Conference*, 1960, Interscience, New York, 1961, p. 210.
[12] Geil, P. H., *Polymer Single Crystals*, Wiley, New York, 1963.
[13] Gorring, R. L., and S. W. Churchill, *Chem. Eng. Progr.* **57** (7), 53 (1961).
[14] Hansen, D. and H. Rusnock, *J. Appl. Phys.* **36**, 332 (1965).
[15] Hellwege, K. H., et al., *Kolloid-Z.* **188**, 121 (1963).
[16] Illers, K. H., *Rheol. Acta* **3**, 185, 194, 202 (1964).
[17] Illers, K. H., *Proc. Intl. Conf. Phys. Non-Crystalline Solids*, North-Holland, Amsterdam, 1965, p. 320.
[18] Jeschke, D., and H. A. Stuart, *Z. Naturforschg.* **16A**, 37 (1961).
[19] Grant, R. F., and D. L. Williams, *Can. J. Chem.* **41** 378 (1963).
[20] Keyes, R. W., *J. Chem. Phys.* **31**, 452 (1959).
[21] Keyes, R. W., *Phys. Rev.* **115**, 564 (1959).
[22] Keyes, R. W., in *Organic Semiconductors*, Brophy and Buttrey, eds., Macmillan, New York, 1962, p. 123.
[23] Klemens, P. G., in *Solid State Phys.* **7**, 1 (1958).
[24] Kontorova, A. T., *Soviet Phys.—Tech. Phys.* **1**, 1959 (1957).
[25] Lawson, A. W., et al., *J. Chem. Phys.* **32**, 447 (1960).
[26] Lawson, A. W., *J. Phys. Chem, Solids* **3**, 250 (1957).
[27] Lifshitz, I. M., *Soviet Phys.—JETP* **17**, 909 (1963).
[28] Meakins, R. H., *Progr. Dielectrics* **3**, 159 (1961).
[29] Michaels, A. S., and R. B. Parker, *J. Polymer Sci.* **41**, 53 (1959).
[30] Moseley, W. W., *J. Appl. Polymer Sci.* **8**, 2095 (1964).
[31] Mikhailov, I. G. and B. A. Soloreu, *Soviet Phys.—Acoustics* **3**, 67 (1957).
[32] Morawetz, H., in *Physics and Chemistry of the Organic Solid State*, Wiley, New York, 1963.
[33] Pechhold, W., et al., *Kolloid-Z.* **189**, 14 (1963); **196**, 27 (1964).
[34] Reese, W., and T. E. Tucker, *J. Chem. Phys.* **43**, 105 (1965).
[35] Rice, S. A., and N. H. Nachtrieb, *J. Chem. Phys.* **31**, 139 (1959).
[36] Saal, R. N. J., et al., *J. Inst. Petr.* **26**, 29 (1940).
[37] Sand, H., *100 Jahre BASF*, Ludwigshafen a/Rh. **1965**, p. 278.
[38] Schatzki, T. F., private communication.
[39] Schoeck, G., in *Mechanical Behavior of Materials at Elevated Temperatures*, J. E. Dorn, ed., McGraw-Hill, New York, 1961, p. 79 *et seq.*
[40] Scholander, P. F., et al., *J. Cellular Comp. Physiol.* **42**, Suppl. 1 (1953).
[41] Schuringa, A., and Th. W. Niesman, Koninklijke/Shell Laboratorium 1949, private communication.
[42] Takagi, Y., *J. Appl. Polymer Sci.* **9**, 3887 (1965).
[43] Tsuge, K., *Japan. J. Appl. Phys.* **3**, 588 (1964).
[44] Woodward, A. E., and J. A. Sauer in *Physics and Chemistry of the Organic Solid State*; Fox–Labes–Weissberger, eds., Interscience–Wiley, New York, (1965), Vol. II, p. 673.
[45] Ziman, J. M., *Electrons and Phonons*, Oxford University Press, London, 1960.
[46] Hood, G. M., and J. N. Sherwood, *J. Chim. Phys.* 1966, 121.
[47] Odajima, A., J. A. Sauer, and A. E. Woodward, *J. Phys. Chem.* **66**, 718 (1962).
[48] Olf, H. G., and A. Peterlin, *Kolloid-Z.* **215**, 97 (1967).
[49] Sherwood, J. N., *Proc. Intl. Conf. Crystal Growth, Boston*, 1966, Pergamon Press, New York, 1967, p. 839.
[50] Turner, S., *Brit. Plastics*, June 1964 to February 1965, Trans. Plastics Inst. **31**, 60 (1963).

6

Fusion

Although it is intuitively obvious that a crystal lattice becomes unstable as the amplitude of thermal vibration exceeds a critical value (see Section 3.3), no satisfactory theory of fusion has yet been formulated; nor has any theory of dense fluids been able to define the conditions under which a liquid will crystallize. In the absence of guidance from general theory an attempt is being made here to develop some empirical generalizations regarding the change of the following physical properties at the melting point: density, entropy, enthalpy, and heat capacity. This is followed by a discussion of the effect of pressure on the melting point and on the enumerated property changes at the melting point.

Experimental determination of the melting point (T_m) is in general so simple that no effort is made here to develop any detailed correlation of this property with molecular structure. Only the following general guide lines are given. The reduced melting point $kT_m/\epsilon \equiv \tilde{T}_m$ of rare gas solids is a constant, 0.70 [69], suggesting that the absolute magnitude of T_m is a function of the intermolecular forces only. Similarly for other cubic crystals, such as N_2 and CO, $\tilde{T}_m = 0.66$; for O_2, $\tilde{T}_m = 0.47$, however, which shows how rarely we can generalize any statement pertaining to the melting point.

When considering polyatomic molecules, it is useful to remember that $T_m = \Delta H_m/\Delta S_m$. In a given series of compounds one can expect ΔH_m, the heat of fusion, to be roughly proportional to ΔH_s, whereas ΔS_m, the entropy of fusion, is essentially a function of the number of different positions that a molecule can occupy in the liquid as compared with the solid state. Hence, ΔS_m is small for spherical rigid molecules, and large for anisometric flexible molecules, and, at a given molecule size, T_m is high for the former and low for the latter.

6.1 EXPANSION AT THE MELTING POINT (ΔV_{m})

Most molecular crystals expand as they melt (water is the most notable exception), so that the rotation around at least one axis of each molecule be free in the liquid state. Thus the packing density of the liquid at the melting point and the temperature level of the melting point are set by the geometry of the molecule in question. The relation between packing density of most liquids and temperature is given by the curve shown in Figure 6.1. Hence we can often guess the magnitude of T_{m}^{*} within fairly narrow limits.

The packing density of solids, on the other hand, is a highly individualistic function of molecular structure and intermolecular forces [26], [40]. Its magnitude at the melting point ranges from 0.6 for soft, plastic crystals composed of molecules with nearly spherical symmetry to 0.73 for comparatively hard crystals composed of rod or platelike molecules. The data in Table 6.1 show the existence of certain regularities in the relation between packing density at the melting point and molecular structure which can serve as guidelines for an estimate of the expansion at the melting point.

The very small expansions of plastic crystals at their melting point generally result from the fact that a much larger expansion took place at a first-order transition of the crystal at some lower temperature. Only a few such expansions of solids have been determined experimentally, but from the corresponding entropy changes (v.i.) we can guess that the combined expansions of all

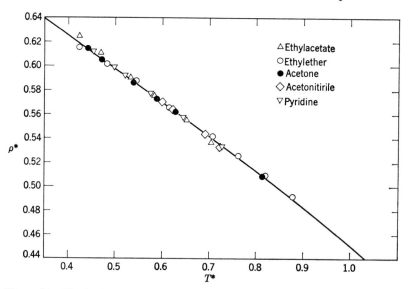

Figure 6.1   Fit of a few typical polar compounds on generalized reduced density ρ^{*} versus reduced temperature T^{*} curve (shown curve).

Table 6.1 Packing Density (ρ_s^*) and Reduced Expansion (ΔV_m^*) at the Melting Point for Various Series of Organic Substances

n-Alkanes

Compound	Methane	Ethane	n-Hexane	n-Octane	n-Dodecane	n-Octadecane	$(CH_2)_\infty$
$\rho_s^*(m)$	0.553	0.673	0.671	0.679	0.682	0.717	0.698
ΔV_m^*	0.158	0.187	0.175	0.217	0.239	0.246	0.310
Ref.	[13]	[13]	[4], [56]	[4], [56]	[43]	[43]	[17]

n-Alkanols

Compound	MeOH	n-prOH	n-C$_5$OH	n-C$_7$OH	n-C$_9$OH	n-C$_{11}$OH	EtOH	n-C$_6$OH	n-C$_8$OH	n-C$_{10}$OH
$\rho_s^*(m)$	0.636	—	0.673	0.659	0.649	0.647	0.678	0.687	0.668	0.670
ΔV_m^*	0.078	0.125	0.125	0.126	0.129	0.144	0.165	0.181	0.174	0.184
Ref.	[56]	[56]	[56]	[56]	[56]	[56]	[56]	[56]	[56]	[56]

Polyaromatics

Compound	φH	φ_2	1,4 $\varphi_2\varphi$	1,2 $\varphi_2\varphi$	φ_2C	φ_2O	Naphthalene	Anthracene	Chrysene	Triphenylene
$\rho_s^*(m)$	0.627	0.677	0.676	0.676	0.677	0.662	0.660	0.649	0.671	0.685
ΔV_m^*	0.202	0.207	0.280	0.141	0.167	0.164	0.255	0.251	0.184	0.211
Ref.	[16]	[3]	[3]	[3]	[60]	[60]	[2]	[2]	[2]	[3]

Table 6.1 (*continued*)

Benzene Derivatives

Substituent	Me	F	Cl	Br	I	NO$_2$
φX, ρ_s^*(m)	0.675	0.665	0.648	0.658	0.662	—
ΔV_m^*	0.147	0.197	0.108	0.125	0.118	0.153
Ref.	a	[60]	[60]	[60]	[60]	[60]
P-φX$_2$, ρ_s^*(m)	0.705	—	0.663	0.682	0.682[a]	
ΔV_m^*	0.314	—	0.306	0.274	0.221[a]	0.206
Ref.	[60]		[55]	[55]	[60]	[60]

Plastic Crystals

Compound	CCl$_4$	Cyclohexane	Succinonitrile	Trimethylacetic acid	O$_2$	F$_2$
ρ_s^*(m)	—	—	0.631	0.593	0.543	0.620
ΔV_m^*	0.079	0.086	0.045	0.113	0.071	0.066
ΔV_{tr}^*	0.194	—	0.128	0.170	0.083	0.079
Ref.	[55]		b	c	d	d

[a] Estimated.
[b] C. A. Wulff and E. F. Westrum, *J. Phys. Chem.* **67**, 2376 (1965).
[c] Y. Namba et al., *Bull. Chem. Soc. Japan* **25**, 225 (1952); **26**, 206 (1953).
[d] J. A. Jahnke, *J. Chem. Phys.* **47**, 336 (1967).

first-order transitions (including melting) will be of the order of 10 to 15% of the volume of the solid at T_m. In processes involving precipitation of the crystal from solutions at $T \leq T_{tr}$ this total contraction will have to be considered.

Certain long-chain compounds (normal paraffins with $13 < N_c < 40$), and the esters of long-chain fatty acids in similar molecular weight ranges also exhibit a solid–solid phase transition and a melting point, but with total

Table 6.2 Effect of Branching and Symmetry of Isoparaffins on the Melting Expansion

Substance	ΔV_m^*	T_m^*	ΔV_{tr}^*	$\Sigma \Delta V_{m,tr}^*$	Ref.
n-Hexane	0.175	0.48	—	0.175	[56]
2,2-Dimethylbutane	~0.02	0.48	>0	>0.02	a
2,3-Dimethylbutane	~0.04	0.40	>0	>0.04	a
n-Octane	0.217	0.514	—	0.217	[56]
Hexamethylethane	0.26	0.8	0.023	0.28	b
2,2,4-Trimethylpentane	0.14	0.406	—	0.14	a
n-Tetracosane	0.162	0.545	0.09	0.252	[43]
Tri-n-octylmethane	0.119		—	0.119	[18]
n-Hexatriacontane	0.27			0.27	[59]
1,1-di-n-Dodecyltetradecane	0.103		—	0.103	[18]

a Estimated from dT_m/dP data given in [20], corrected to atmospheric pressure.
b W. F. Seyer et al., *J. Am. Chem. Soc.* **71**, 3447 (1949), and [54].

expansion about equally divided between the two. In these cases the packing density at the first-order transition equals that at the melting point of the lower members of the series, as is shown on the graphs of Figures 6.2 and 6.3.

The few available data indicate that the more highly branched and the more asymmetrically branched an aliphatic compound is, the lower not only its (reduced) melting point but also its melting expansion (Table 6.2). This is understandable from a study of Figure 6.4, which shows the large difference in slope (i.e., expansion coefficient) of liquid vs solid.

Although the basic relations between ΔV_m and ΔS_m are discussed in Section 6.7, the purposes of estimating ΔV_m from the more easily available ΔS_m might be served by an approximate relation

$$\frac{\Delta S_m}{\Delta V_m} = f(\alpha K_0)_{T_m}, \tag{6.1}$$

which, after substitution of the correlations for α and κ_0 from Sections 8.2

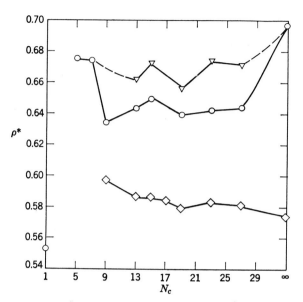

Figure 6.2 Packing density at the melting point [$\diamond = \rho_L^*(m)$, $\bigcirc = \rho_s^*(m)$] and at the first-order solid to solid transition points (∇, $\triangle = \rho_s^*$ (tr) for odd-numbered normal paraffins [4], [17], [43], [56], [59].

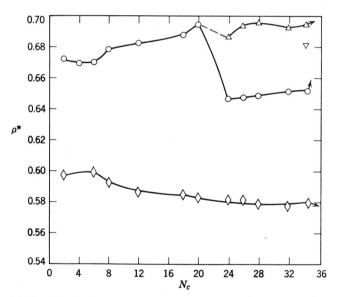

Figure 6.3 Packing density at the melting point [$\diamond = \rho_L^*(m)$, $\bigcirc = \rho_s^*(m)$] and at first-order solid-to-solid transition points ∇, $\triangle = \rho_s^*$(tr) for even-numbered normal paraffins [4], [43], [56], [59].

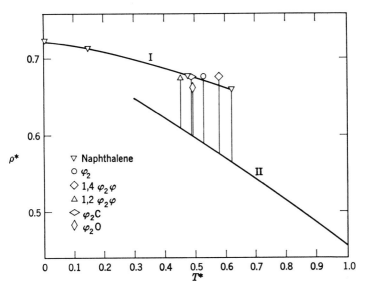

Figure 6.4 Plot of reduced density versus reduced temperature for typical solid (I) and for nonassociating liquids (II).

and 8.3 and rearrangement, yields

$$\Delta V_m^* = \frac{\Delta V_m}{V_w} = f\left[\frac{\Delta S_m \psi(T^*)}{2cR}\right],$$ (6.2)

where

$$\psi(T_m^*) = (1.30 - T_m^*)^{1/3}\left(\frac{2.00}{T_m} - 1.60\right)^{-1}$$

for rigid molecules and

$$\tfrac{2}{3}(1.30 - T_m^*)^{1/3}\left(\frac{2.30}{T_m} - 1.98\right)^{-1}$$

for flexible long-chain molecules. The resulting correlation, shown in Figure 6.5, demonstrates the expected parallelism between $\Delta V_m/V_w$ and ΔS_m. The scatter is indicative of the crude approximations made in the development of the correlation.

Another consequence of the curve form shown in Figure 6.4 is that for a given compound, ΔV_m decreases in a predictable way with decreasing temperature of crystallization, for example, out of a mixture or solution.

Except for the gradualness of the transition on the solid side of the volume–temperature curve, in the melting range, the packing density of crystallizable high polymers does not differ significantly from that of other compounds of

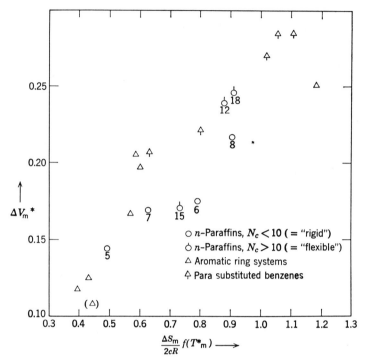

Figure 6.5 Correlation of reduced melting-point expansion ΔV_m^* with reduced fusion entropy function.

related structural geometry, as is shown by the data of Table 6.3. For instance, branch chains reduce the packing density of the solid and thus ΔV_m^*, since the density of polymer melts is unaffected by structural details and is near T_m^*, well represented by the generalized density curve of Figure 6.1.

Specifically, with isotactic and syndiotactic crystalline polymers, the size of side chains affects the openness of the helix conformation forced upon the molecules, and thereby the density of the crystal. The downward trend of the room-temperature packing density of isotactic polymers with increasing side-chain size, shown in Table 6.3, reflects this effect of the helix structure. The most remarkable of these is the poly (4-methylpentene-1) the packing density of which is even smaller than that of the corresponding liquid, that is, the amorphous polymer at the same temperature. Because of the large difference in thermal expansion, however, the crystal is again much denser than the liquid at the melting point (270°C), as shown by the rather normal value for ΔV_m^*.

The estimation of ΔV_m for hydrogen-bonded systems is seriously handi-capped because we have not yet been able to develop a generalized density

Table 6.3   Volume Increase upon Melting and Density of Crystalline Hydrocarbon Polymers (in Reduced Units)

Polymer	ΔV_m^*	$\rho_s^*(m)$	$\rho_L^*(m)$	$\rho_s^*(25°C)^a$	Ref.
Polyethylene	0.310	0.698	0.575	0.742	[17]
Polypropylene	0.234	0.644	0.560	0.686[b]	[17]
Polybutene-1	0.205	0.664	0.584	0.69	[17]
Poly(4-methylpentene-1)	0.160	0.572	0.523	0.606	[52]
Polystyrene	0.183	0.637	0.570	0.677	[17]

[a] Room-temperature density data from [41].
[b] Refers to the isotactic form.

correlation for liquids composed of hydrogen-bonding molecules. A study of Table 6.4 shows that the compounds that form strong continuous hydrogen-bond structures in the crystal, such as water, methanol, and phenol [40], [56], are characterized by low crystal packing densities, hence comparatively small or even negative melting-point expansions. As the size of the hydro-carbon group increases ΔV_m acquires a magnitude quite similar to that of structurally similar nonassociating compounds.

The properties of those compounds that form stable dimers, such as the fatty acids, closely resemble the properties of the structural analogs of the dimers, as is apparent from the data of Table 6.5. As there are more data for fatty acids than for the corresponding hydrocarbons, one might also use this analogy in reverse.

Many metal salts of fatty acids, especially those of alkalis and earth alkalis, exhibit a whole series of solid–solid first-order phase transitions with sub-stantial changes in volume and enthalpy (or entropy) before they reach the melting point. Typical ΔV_{tr}, ΔV_m, ρ^* and ΔS_{tr}, ΔS_m data presented in Table 6.6, indicate the origin of the effect, namely, the strong tendency of the long chains to gain rotational freedom even when their polar ends are fixed in

Table 6.4   Melting Point Expansion ΔV_m^* and Packing Density at the Melting Point ρ_s (m) for Strongly Hydrogen Bonded Crystals

Substance	$\rho_s^*(m)$	ΔV_m^*	Ref.
Water	0.494	−0.167	a
Methanol	0.667	0.078	[56]
Phenol	0.640	0.089	b, [55]

[a] B. P. Nikolski, *Handbuch des Chemikers*, Verlag Technik, Berlin, 1956.
[b] P. Cole, *J. Chem. Eng. Data* **5**, 367 (1960).

tightly bound dipole sheets. When $N_c > 14$, the cohesion of the hydrocarbon tails is so weak after the penultimate transition before the final melting point that a "liquid crystalline" state results. The data in Table 6.6 show that long polar molecules of widely different composition, held together by somewhat weaker dipole interactions than metal carboxylates, form liquid crystals at somewhat lower temperatures and exhibit rather similar sequences of successive volumes and entropies of transition.

Table 6.5   Melting-Point Expansion of Fatty Acids and of the Hydrocarbon Homomorphs of Their Dimers[a]

Fatty acid (homomorph of dimer)	$\Delta V_{\mathrm{m}}^{*}$	ρ_s^{*} (m)
Formic acid	0.245	0.675
(Benzene)	0.202	0.627
Acetic acid	0.299	0.677
(p-Xylene [55])	0.314	0.705
Propionic acid	0.216	0.678
n-Butyric acid	0.164	0.652
n-Pentonoic acid	0.174	
n-Hexanoic acid	0.130	
n-Heptanoic acid	0.184	
n-Octanoic acid	0.183	
n-Nonanoic acid	0.120	
n-Decanoic acid	0.210	
n-Undecanoic acid	0.154	
n-Dodecanoic acid	0.184	
n-Octadecanoic acid	0.199	

[a] From [52] except where noted otherwise.

This phenomenon, like the solid–solid phase transitions of n-alkanes, alkanols, and alkanoic acids, is associated with the possibility of excitation of large-amplitude torsional oscillations of the elongated molecules or molecule segments around their long axis without disrupting the order of the crystal lattice, at least in two dimensions. Apparently a liquid crystal results when the dipole interaction forces are sufficiently strong to retain this two-dimensional order even when the lattice has expanded sufficiently to permit liquidlike nearly free rotation of the long (chain) molecule. The liquidlike packing density (<0.60) is generally acquired after the second solid–solid phase transition. Inhibition of rotational motions, as by attachment of a hydrogen-bonding group in the center of the rotor in 12-hydroxystearates, is reflected in suppression of rotational transitions almost until the melting point has been reached.

Table 6.6 Successive Phase Transitions of Compounds which Pass through Liquid Crystalline States before Finally Melting

Compound	T_{tr}/T_m	$\Delta S_m/R$	$\Delta V/V_s$	ρ^{*a}
Lithium decanoate	0.61		0.036[b]	0.73[b]
$T_m = 511°K$	1.00		0.148	0.57
$V_w \approx 123.5$ cm^3/mole	Σ		0.184	
Lithium hexadecanoate	0.756	4.6[c]	0.036[b]	0.70[b]
$T_m = 496°K$	0.935	4.2	0.072	0.63
$V_w \approx 185$ cm^3/mole	1.00	4.9	0.026	0.60
	Σ	13.7	0.134	
Potassium hexadecanoate	0.545	7.4[c]	0.009[d]	0.70[d]
$T_m = 615°K$	0.657	1.1		
$V_w \approx 204$ cm^3/mole	0.687	1.2	0.013	0.65
	0.728	1.7		
	0.755		0.010	0.61
	0.868	2.4	0.025	
	0.890		0.030	0.57
	1.00			0.53
	Σ	13.8	0.087	
Lithium-12-hydroxystearate	0.895	1.3[e]		
$T_m = 483°K$	0.988	9.7		
	1.00			
		11.0		

Compound	T_{tr}/T_m	$\Delta S_{tr}/R$	$\Delta V/V_w$	ρ^*
4,4′-Dialkoxyazoxybenzenes[f]:				
Dimethylazoxybenzene	0.956	9.1[g]		
	1.000	0.2		
	Σ	9.3		
Di-n-heptylazoxybenzene	0.872	14.2		
	0.925	0.5		
	1.000	0.3(0.6)		
	Σ	15.0(0.3)		
Di-n-dodecylazoxybenzene	0.90	14.3		
	1.00	3.7(4.3)		
	Σ	18.0(0.6)		

[a] V_w of carboxylate and estimated by means of ionic radii of metals.
[b] B. Gallot and A. Skoulios, *Kolloid-Z.* **209**, 169 (1966); density and T_{tr}.
[c] R. D. Vold and M. D. Vold, *J. Phys. Chem.* **49**, 32 (1945).
[d] B. Gallot and A. Skoulois, *Kolloid-Z.* **210**, 143 (1966): density and T_{tr}.
[e] S. T. Abrams and F. H. Stross, *J. Phys. Chem.* **62**, 879 (1958).
[f] Here the temperature usually called "clear point," the transition from liquid crystal to the isotropic liquid, is identified as T_m.
[g] H. Arnold, *Z. Physik. Chem.* **226**, 146 (1964); *Z. Chem.* **4**, 211 (1964); *Mol. Cryst.* **2**, 63 (1966).

6.2 ENTROPY OF FUSION (ΔS_m) [12]

The purpose of the present correlation is to provide the means for the estimation of the heat of fusion from no more information than molecular structure and the melting point. The scope of the method includes all molecular crystals. Owing to the very complicated problems of theory the proposed method is almost entirely empirical.

6.2.1 General Principles

Because the melting point (T_m) of a substance is not easily—if at all—predictable, but is easily determined experimentally, it will be assumed as given. This is an important qualification because calculation of the heat of fusion (ΔH_m) would call for a thorough knowledge of the crystal structure as well as of the expansion at the melting point (ΔV_m), neither of which is often available. However, the entropy of fusion $\Delta S_m = \Delta H_m / T_m$ is related to molecular structure in a manner that permits generalization with very little, if any, extra information.

Several reviews of the relations between the entropy of fusion and molecular structure have appeared in the literature [35], [51], [68], [69]. Several of these also dealt with theoretical problems involved. Their contents will be assumed as known. The insights developed from theoretical analyses will be used in the construction of empirical correlations. An important consideration to keep in mind is the absence, if not impossibility, of an all-inclusive theory because of the large differences in mechanisms of fusion depending on differences in molecular and crystal structure.

As mentioned in Section 6.1, crystals composed of very symmetrical molecules often "melt" in distinct stages, that is, the melting point is preceded by first order solid–solid phase transitions at T_{tr}. The incidence and location of T_{tr} (say, relative to T_m) are rarely predictable. An attempt to estimate the corresponding entropy of transition ΔS_{tr} from molecular and crystal symmetry considerations [49] has been only moderately successful. Hence in the following only the entire melting and transition process are treated, that is, the sum of all entropies of transition and of fusion

$$\sum \Delta S_{m,tr} \equiv \Delta S_m + \Delta S_{tr}(1) + \Delta S_{tr}(2) + \cdots \qquad (6.3)$$

are correlated with molecular structure.

Phenomenologically, the entropy of fusion (and/or transition) consists of two components: that due to the volume increase (ΔV_m), ΔS_m^v, and the entropy of fusion at constant volume ΔS_m^j. The common name "configurational entropy of fusion" for ΔS_m^j should be avoided because of the tacit (popular) implication that it is the part of ΔS_m that is calculated by molecular theories. Now

$$\Delta S_m{}^v = \left(\frac{\partial S}{\partial V}\right)_p \Delta V_m = \alpha K_0 \Delta V_m, \quad \text{and} \quad \Delta S_m{}^j = \Delta S_m - \Delta S_m{}^v, \qquad (6.4)$$

where α, K_0 are the expansion coefficient and zero-pressure bulk modulus. Since at T_m: $(\alpha \cdot K_0)_{\text{liq}} = (\alpha \cdot K_0)_{\text{crystal}}$, the choice of reference phase is immaterial.

Inspection of the $\Delta S_m{}^v$ and $\Delta S_m{}^j$ data in Table 6.7 shows the expected

Table 6.7 Comparison of ΔS_m and $\Delta S_m{}^j$ with Molecular Structure [12]

Simple Molecules	Ar	N_2	O_2	CH_4	
$\Delta S_m{}^v/R$	0.90	0.57	0.36		
$\Delta S_m/R$	1.69	1.36	1.0	1.25	
$\Delta S_m{}^j/R$	0.79	0.79	0.64		
Aryl Halides	φF	φCl	φBr	φI	$p\text{-}\varphi Cl_2$
$\Delta S_m{}^v/R$	2.10	1.42	1.60	1.83	3.16
$\Delta S_m/R$	5.87	5.10	5.26	4.90	6.70
$\Delta S_m{}^j/R$	3.77	3.68	3.69	3.56	3.54
Methylbenzenes	φH	φMe	$p\text{-Xylene}$	$m\text{-Xylene}$	$o\text{-Xylene}$
$\Delta S_m{}^v/R$	1.76	2.0	3.25	2.06	1.63
$\Delta S_m/R$	4.25	4.48	7.20	6.18	6.61
$\Delta S_m{}^j/R$	2.49	2.48	3.95	4.12	4.98

greater regularity among the $\Delta S_m{}^j$ data of a given group of compounds than among their straight entropy of fusion data. This phenomenon is especially striking among the low-molecular-weight substances Ar, N_2, O_2, and among the phenyl halides. Somewhat more surprising is the sequence of $\Delta S_m{}^j$ for benzene, toluene, xylenes, where it should be remembered, however, that ΔV_m (toluene) is only an estimated value. Because the sparsity of ΔV_m data and the absence of any means of predicting ΔV_m preclude the use of $\Delta S_m{}^j$ for engineering calculations, the present work is exclusively concerned with the more difficult task of correlating ΔS_m with molecular structure.

A general molecular model for the melting process by Hirschfelder, Stevenson, and Eyring (HSE) [21] and the similar treatment by Chihara and Shinoda [15a] assume free rotation of the molecules in the liquid and arrive at

$$\Delta S_m = \Delta S_p + \Delta S_m(\text{rot}), \qquad (6.5)$$

where ΔS_p is the entropy contribution due to positional disordering of the crystal,

$$\Delta S_m(\text{rot}) = S_r - S_{\text{tor}}, \tag{6.6}$$

where S_r, the appropriate rotational contribution to gas-phase entropy, is most often given by

$$S_r = R \ln \left[\pi^{1/2} \left(\frac{T}{39.6} \right)^{3/2} 10^{60} \frac{(I_1 \cdot I_2 \cdot I_3)^{1/2}}{\sigma} \right], \tag{6.7a}$$

the entropy contribution of the freely rotating rigid polyatomic nonlinear molecule, and

$$S_{\text{tor}} = \sum_n S_v \tag{6.7b}$$

is the sum of the entropy contributions due to torsional oscillations in the crystal lattice. This term can be quite large. The appropriate libration frequencies are difficult to obtain, but a fair number of such frequencies have been measured [32], and a correlation permitting an estimate from a knowledge of the heat of sublimation and the moments of inertia of a molecule has been prepared (Section 3.3).

According to Lennard-Jones [33] $\Delta S_p = 1.7R$ and according to HSE $\Delta S_p = R$. A hard-sphere model of solid and liquid by Longuet-Higgins and Widom (42) yields $\Delta S_m = 5.8R(V_L - V_s)/V_0 = 1.64R$ and is otherwise in fair accord with the triple point properties of rare gas solids. Globular molecules follow more nearly the HSE prediction (see Table 6.9).

A recent dislocation model of the melting process by Mizushima [42] yields ΔS_p as function of crystal defect characteristics which are well known in metals but generally unknown for molecular crystals. The same author concludes that the change in translational vibration frequency on melting leads to a significant contribution ΔS_{vibr} neglected by Lennard-Jones and by HSE. We can estimate

$$\Delta S_{\text{vibr}} \approx \tfrac{1}{2}(R) \ln \left[\frac{\Delta H_s}{\Delta H_s - \Delta H_m} \right]$$

because $\omega(\text{cryst}) \sim (\Delta H_s/M)^{1/2}$ and $\omega(\text{liq}) \sim (\Delta H_v/M)^{1/2}$.

Since the HSE theory assumes that molecule rotates freely in the liquid state, it should overestimate ΔS_m if the external rotation of molecules is hindered in the liquid state. The effect of hindered rotation in the liquid state on entropy is often expressed as the excess entropy of vaporization $\Delta S_v{}^j$ relative to a freely rotating model liquid at the same vapor volume, that is, at the same value of p/T [10], so that we should expect

$$\Delta S_m(\text{obs}) = \Delta S_m(\text{HSE}) - \Delta S_v{}^j.$$

This supposition has been confirmed for several hydrocarbons [10]. But more work needs to be done on applying this principle to polar compounds.

Table 6.8 Entropy of Fusion Calculated by Means of HSE Theory [12]

Substance	S_r/R	$\Sigma S_{tor}/R$	$\Sigma \Delta S_{m,tr}/R$ (calc)	(exp)
Benzene	8.91	5.40	4.51	4.25
Naphthalene	11.92	6.75	6.17	6.48

A comparison of the various theoretical estimates with experiment is shown in Tables 6.8 and 6.9. Although the agreement with experiment is quite satisfactory, the method is obviously too cumbersome for engineering application. However, the qualitative results of the theoretical analysis provide useful guideposts for the understanding of the data. In order to evade the issue of what dimensions to use for entropy, all data are given in units of R, the universal gas constant (per mole).

6.2.2 Rigid Molecules

The data in Tables 6.10 and 6.11 exhibit on the whole the parallel trend of $\Sigma \Delta S_{m,tr}$ and the moments of inertia of the molecules expected from theory. Notable exceptions are the hydrogen halide crystals and the series CO_2, COS, CS_2. Here the interaction of all variables, T_m, I, and crystal libration frequencies and hindered external rotation in the liquid must be considered

Table 6.9 Entropy of Fusion of Rare Gas Crystals and of Crystals Composed of Globular Molecules[a] [12]

Rare gases	Ne	Ar	Kr	Xe	Lennard-Jones	HSE	LHW
$\Delta S_m/R$:	1.64	1.69	1.70	1.71	1.7	1.0	1.64

Globular Molecules, CX_4: X =	H	F	Cl	Br	Me	SMe	CH_2OH	NO_2
$\Delta S_m/R$:		1.25	0.94	1.2	1.36	1.52	1.44	1.59	1.74

Globular molecules, MH_4: M =	C	Si	Ge
$\Delta S_m/R$:	1.25	0.91	0.94

Globular molecules:	Cyclohexane	Thiacyclohexane	1,4-Dioxane	Camphor
$\Delta S_m/R$:	1.12	1.01	1.04	1.4
Ref.	[44]	[44]	[44]	[44]

[a] All from [32], except when otherwise noted.
[b] See text for references.

Table 6.10　Total Entropy of Fusion and Transition of Various Simple Compounds[a] [12]

Diatomic molecules:	H_2	N_2	NO	CO	O_2	F_2	Cl_2	Br_2	I_2
$\Sigma \Delta S_{m,tr}/R$:	1.04	2.12	2.53	2.72	3.47	3.41	4.47	4.86	4.92

Diatomic molecules: (associating)	HF	HCl	HBr	HI
$\Sigma \Delta S_{m,tr}/R$	2.90	2.97	2.62	2.56

Linear polyatomic molecules:	FCN	HCN	$(CN)_2$	N_2O	CO_2	COS	CS_2
$\Sigma \Delta S_{m,tr}/R$	4.0	3.89	3.98	4.32	4.66	4.24	3.28

Nonlinear polyatomic molecules:	H_2O	H_2S	H_2Se	SO_2	NH_3	PH_3	CH_4	SiH_4	GeH_4
$\Sigma \Delta S_{m,tr}/R$:	2.65	3.30	4.55	4.51	3.48	3.61	1.61	2.13	1.99

Rigid single rings:	Furan	Thiophene	Benzene	Pyridine	β-Sulfolene	Sulfolane
$\Sigma \Delta S_{m,tr}/R$:	4.08	5.01	4.25	4.25	4.86 [36]	4.55 [36]

Rigid condensed double rings	Indene	Indane	Naphthalene	1,4-Dihydro naphthalene	Tetralin	Azulene
$\Sigma \Delta S_{m,tr}/R$	4.52 [49]	4.67 [49]	6.48	4.96	6.33	6.18

Rigid condensed rings:	Acenaphthene	Phenanthrene	Anthracene	Chrysene
$\Sigma \Delta S_{m,tr}/R$:	6.85 [2]	6.02 [2]	7.09 [2]	7.5 [2]

[a] From [32] except when otherwise noted.

in order to understand the data. Strongly hindered rotation in the liquid reduces ΔS_m and must be expected when T_m/T_b is exceptionally small as in the case of CS_2, where $T_m/T_b = 0.50$ compared with the more usual 0.65. On the other hand, ΔS_m can be expected to be higher than "normal" if rotation is entirely free, as would always be the case when $T_m/T_b > 1.0$, keeping in mind that in the present context T_b is the temperature at $P_v = 760$ torr. Among the somewhat larger (organic) molecules one fortunately finds fewer such anomalous series; an example of such a series is that of the halobenzenes shown in Table 6.11. These examples indicate that facile arguments cannot always be used in rationalizing observed entropy of fusion data.

Table 6.11   Comparison of Total Entropy of Fusion and Transition of Geometrically Similar Compounds Composed of Rigid Molecules[a] [12]

Type	$\Sigma \Delta S_{\mathrm{m, tr}}/R$ if X =						
	H	F	Cl	Br	I	Me	NO_2
CHX_3	—	4.0	5.29	4.95	4.97	4.97	—
CX_4	1.61	3.26	3.6	3.72	—	3.74[b]	4.60
C_2X_4	3.42	6.55	5.04	—	—	5.97	—
C_2X_6	3.85	6.19	5.98	—	—	5.01	—
o-di-X-benzene	4.25	—	6.06	—	5.71	6.61	7.05
m-di-X-benzene	4.25	—	6.15	5.96	6.25	6.18	6.76
p-di-X-benzene	4.25	—	6.70	6.70	6.70	7.20	7.59

[a] All from [22], [32], and [66] except when otherwise noted.
[b] For comparison: $\Delta S_{\mathrm{m}}/R$ (Spiropentane) = 4.66. D. W. Scott et al., *J. Am. Chem. Soc.* **72**, 4664 (1950).

Yet very large differences in dipole orientation effects and cohesion forces do not matter if compounds are geometrically similar; nitrobenzene($\Delta S_{\mathrm{m}}/R =$ 5.24), benzoic acid ($\Delta S_{\mathrm{m}}/R = 5.27$), and their homomorph, isopropylbenzene ($\Delta S_{\mathrm{m}}/R = 5.28$), set a good example for this behavior. In the section on hydrogen-bonded substances more is said on this subject.

Table 6.12   Effect of Molecular Symmetry on $\Sigma \Delta S_{\mathrm{m,tr}}/R$[a] [12]

Type						
Asymmetric polymethyl benzenes	1, 2	1, 2, 3	1, 2, 3, 4	1, 3	1, 2, 4	1, 2, 3, 5
$\Sigma S_{\mathrm{m,tr}}/R$	6.61	5.03	4.65	6.18	6.88	5.16
Symmetric polymethyl benzenes	1, 4	1, 2, 4, 5	Hexamethyl[b]			
$\Sigma S_{\mathrm{m,tr}}/R$	7.20	7.18	6.22			
Methyl naphthalene	1	2	2, 3	2, 6[c]		
$\Sigma S_{\mathrm{m,tr}}/R$	5.95	7.10	6.3	7.60		
Reference	(d)	(d)				

[a] From [4] except when otherwise noted.
[b] As the methyl groups are squeezed out of their planar configuration, the molecule has lost the simple geometry of the disk-shaped benzene derivatives.
[c] V. M. Kravchenko and I. S. Pastakhoun, *Nkr. Khim. Zlmni* **19**, 610 (1953).
[d] J. P. McCullough et al., *J. Phys. Chem.* **61**, 1105 (1957).

The effect of symmetry is apparent from the sequence *o-m-p* among the entropy data for the di-substituted benzene compounds of Table 6.11. Further examples are shown in Table 6.12. Another striking example of this symmetry effect is C_2F_6 ($\Delta S_m/R = 6.19$) versus $C_2F_5–Cl$ ($\Delta S_m/R = 5.25$). This symmetry effect originates in part with the high packing density and melting temperature of symmetrical compounds, hence large ΔV_m and ΔS_m^v. The other part derives from the contribution to S_r made by the difference in symmetry number, as the moment of inertia product of *ortho-* and *para-* substituted benzene rings, for instance, is effectively equal.

The fusion entropy of cagelike molecules with nearly spherical symmetry, such as camphor and its many derivatives, is of the order $1.5 \pm 0.5R$ (Table 6.9). The great interest of these substances as solvents for cryoscopy led to their synthesis and to the determination of their heat and entropy of fusion. But their solid–solid transitions have been examined only rarely. Hence only the following few data are available:

Substance:	Camphor	Bicyclo[2, 2, 1]-heptane[c]	Bicyclo[2, 2, 2]-octane	Triethylene-diamine	3Aza Bicyclo[3, 2, 2]-nonane[b]
$\Sigma \Delta S_{m, tr}/R$:	5.2	5.34	5.59[d]	7.05[a]	7.65

[a] J. C. Trowbridge and E. F. Westrum, *J. Phys. Chem.* **67**, 2381 (1963).
[b] E. F. Westrum et al., *J. Phys. Chem.* **67**, 2373 (1963); **68**, 430 (1964).
[c] Low-Temperature Thermodynamics Group, U.S. Bureau of Mines, Bartlesville Petroleum Research Center, Bartlesville, Oklahoma; unpublished work.
[d] I. Darmon and C. Brot, *Mol. Cryst.* **1**, 417 (1966).

A few more data are obviously required to produce a reasonably reliable correlation.

6.2.3 Inorganic Molecular Crystals

There are two classes of inorganic molecular crystal: those composed of covalently bonded molecules, such as SO_2, and those composed of a central metal ion surrounded by monovalent ligands that completely shield the metal ion from interaction with nonbonded ligands. In the latter case a molecular crystal obtains when the shielded fraction A_r of the metal ion surface is larger than 0.8, where $A_r = (N_x/4)(r_1/r_2)^2$ when $l > r_2$ (the most frequent) and $A_r = (N_x/4)(1 - m^2/r_2^2)$ when $l < r_2$, where N_x equals the number of ligand atoms or groups per metal ion, l equals the chemical bond distance between metal and ligand atom, and r_1, r_2 are the van der Waals radii of ligand and metal ion,[1] respectively, $m = (r_2^2 - r_1^2 + l^2)/2l$ [11].

Insufficient shielding ($A_r < 0.8$), often found with fluorides and chlorides when $N_x < 5$, leads to ionic rather than molecular crystals with correspondingly very different entropy of fusion.

[1] To a good approximation $r_2 \approx 0.735R^{1/3}$, where R is the molar refractivity increment of the metal ion in the Eisenlohr system (see Section 14.1.4).

We find that to a first approximation the total entropy of fusion and transition of inorganic molecular crystals can be fitted into the known pattern of inorganic stereochemistry,[1] as is evident from still rather spotty data in Table 6.3.

The first line of Table 6.13 should be composed of the linear molecules of Table 6.4, where the anomalous cases of CS_2 ($T_m/T_b = 0.50$) and CO_2 ($T_m/T_b = 1.1$) have already been discussed. The second line should be V-shaped molecules, such as SO_2 ($\Sigma \Delta S_{m,tr}/R = 4.51$), currently the only datum of that class. The plane triangles BF_3 and SO_3 would be excellent examples of the power of the shape generalization, were it not for the deviant but less symmetrical phosgene. The sequence of the series of trigonal pyramid and of tetrahedral molecules exhibits, perhaps fortuitous, stepwise changes in $\Sigma \Delta S_{m,tr}$ with increasing ligand and/or molecule size. Provided $A_r > 0.8$, the constancy of $\Sigma \Delta S_{m,tr}$ is maintained in the tetrahedral series out to $ThBr_4$ and ThI_4 ($\Sigma \Delta S_{m,tr} \sim 5.0R$), whereas for $ThCl_4$, for which $A_r = 0.73$, a totally different behavior is encountered, the crystal being ionic and $\Delta S_m = 10.4R$.

The constancy of ΔS_m in the tetrahedral series is, in part, associated with the constancy of $T_m/T_b \approx 0.65$. When $T_m/T_b > 1.0$, ΔS_m becomes rather larger than average; SiF_4: $T_m/T_b = 1.05$ and $\Delta S_m = 6.05R$ [14], [35]; and with $ZrCl_4$ $T_m/T_b = 1.18$ and $\Delta S_m \approx 6.35R$ [48]. The effect of moments of inertia on the over-all trend in the tetrahedral series is apparent from the extreme ends, from the low end with $FClO_3$ to the high value of $Ni(CO)_4$ (for which $T_m/T_b = 0.79$, not enough to have much effect).

A striking peculiarity of the MX_3 and MX_4 series is that for them $\Sigma \Delta S_{m,tr}$ is uniformly larger than it is for the corresponding halides of the first-row elements N and C by 1 to $1.5R$. The CX_4 data are given in Table 6.10 and $\Delta S_m(NF_3) = 3.1R$. This difference persists to the series M_2X_6, exemplified by $\Delta S_m(Si_2F_6) = \Delta S_m(C_2F_6) + 1.5R$. The primary difference between the higher metal tetrahalides and the CX_4 series is the occurrence of low-temperature solid–solid phase transitions among all of the carbon compounds, and the absence of such transitions among the other members of the MX_4 series. The origin of the resulting decrement in $\Sigma \Delta S_{m,tr}$ is discussed in Section 6.3.1 on phase transitions.

Regular octahedra YX_6 and MX_6 (line 7) exhibit $\Sigma \Delta S_{m,tr}$ within the range expected from their moments of inertia and their crystal characteristics. However, those of the hexafluoro actinides are so much larger that we strongly suspect their structure to be somewhat elongated bipyramides rather than octahedra as deduced from electron and x-ray diffraction data (71). That X-ray and electron diffraction give unreliable data in this case because of

[1] For an excellent introduction to inorganic stereochemistry see R. J. Gillespie and R. S. Nyholm, *Quart. Rev.* **11**, 339 (1957).

Table 6.13 Total Entropy of Fusion and Transition of Various Types of Inorganic Compounds*a [12]

No.	Shape	Molecule Type	$\Sigma \Delta S_{m,tr}/R$ if X =					Other Molecules of the Same Shape
			H	F	Cl	Br	I	
1	Plane triangle	BX_3		3.5				$O{=}S(O)(O)$: 3.58; $O{=}C(Cl)(Cl)$: 4.76
2	T-Shape	YX_3(Y = Cl, Br)		5.11, 5.12				
3	Trigonal pyramid	MX^3(M = P,c As, Sb)	3.6d	4.7	4.7	4.7		$\ddot{S}(F)(F){=}O$: 5.30; NMe_3: 5.3
4	Tetrahedral	MX_4(M = Si, Gee, Sn, Ti)	2.0 ± 0.1	f	4.75 ± 0.2	5.1 ± 0.1	5.1	$FClO_3$: 3.68g; $O{=}PCl_3$: 5.69 $Ni(CO)_4$: 6.7
5	Square pyramid	YX_5(Y = Br, I)		4.2; 6.4				
6	Regular octahedron	YX_6(Y = S, Te)		4.8				
7	Regular octahedron	MX_6(M = Mo, W)		5.1	≥ 5.5			PtF_6: 5.5
8	Regular octahedron	MX_6(M = U, Np, Pu)h		6.9				
9	Trigonal bipyramid	MX_5(M = P, As, Sb)		7.5 ± 0.4	> 4.4			$Fe(CO)_5$: 6.30i
10	Trigonal bipyramid	MX_5(Nb, Ta)			7.3 ± 1; 8.4 ± 0.8			

* All from [4], [32], and [49] and b except when otherwise noted.
a For various linear and V-shape molecules see Table 6.4.
b Article by D. D. Wagman et al., in *American Institute of Physics Handbook*, 1965.
c The available datum for a P-tri-halide, PCl_3: $\Sigma \Delta S_{m,tr}/R = 3.0$ is probably wrong.
d This is for PH_3; the available information on AsH_3, etc, appears to be incomplete.
e P. Balk and D. Dong. *J. Phys. Chem.* **68**, 960 (1964).
f For SiF_4 $\Delta S_m = 6.05R$ (see text).
g J. K. Koehler and W. F. Giangen, *J. Am. Chem. Soc.* **80**, 2659 (1958).
h [49] the datum for NpF_6 differs slightly (6.44?).
i A. J. Leadbetter and J. E. Spice, *Can. J. Chem.* **37**, 1923 (1959).

excessive scattering by the heavy center atom has been pointed out by Smith[1]; only neutron diffraction can resolve this question.

The best direct evidence for distortion of the actinide hexafluoride octa-hedra into elongated bipyramids by the crystal field comes from NMR spectroscopy [61]. This notion is supported by the data for compounds of elongated bipyramidal structure in lines 9 and 10 of Table 6.13.

The foregoing correlation scheme for inorganic molecular crystals contains just enough systematic features to be useful for extrapolation purposes, and just enough deviations from gross regularities to prevent blindfolded generalizations.

6.2.4 Flexible Molecules

The chain segments of long-chain molecules execute torsional oscillations in the crystal and hindered rotations relative to each other in the liquid. The corresponding gain in entropy yields a rather constant increment for the entropy of fusion per chain link, namely $\approx R \ln 3$ per CH_2-group [6]. The contrast between the resulting rapid rise in ΔS_m with molecular weight for long-chain compounds and the very slow rise with rigid molecules is shown in Figure 6.6.

The equations for the curves of various normal alkyl compounds are presented in Table 6.14. The slopes of these curves fall into two groups, $\Delta S_m/R$ per methylene group $= 1.2 \pm 0.05$ when orthorhombic, and 1.35 ± 0.05 when monoclinic. Less than one-quarter of this amount, $(0.25\ R)$, has been contributed by the volume change [37]. The third term in the equations accounts for the curvature near the parent compound.

A noteworthy aspect of the experimental data is the difference between odd- and even-numbered normal paraffins and their derivatives, which shows the strong effect of crystal structure on the entropy of fusion [37], [41]. In line with this is the identity of the increment per methylene group in poly-ethylene with that for odd-numbered n-paraffins with which it shares the orthorhombic crystal structure [41]. The peculiar nonlinear initial rise of the ΔS_m versus N_c curves of the alkylated ring systems parallels that for the number of external degrees of freedom per molecule for the same compounds in the liquid state and is apparently due to the fact that short—hence internally stiff—alkyl chains rotate so easily on the ring that their motion makes only a small contribution to the change in heat capacity and entropy.

The effect of *cis*- or *trans*-configuration in a hydrocarbon chain is qualita-tively similar to that observed with internal double bonds in low-molecular-weight olefins but is again much more pronounced (if the numbers in Table 6.15 can be believed).

[1] Private communication.

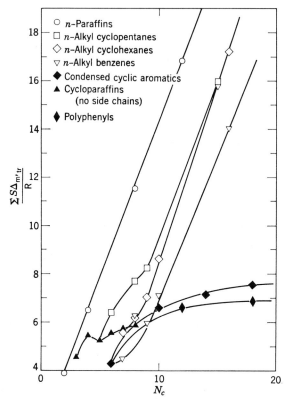

Figure 6.6 Total entropy of fusion and transition versus number of carbon atoms per molecule (N_c) for flexible (open symbols) and rigid (solid symbols) hydrocarbon molecules [12].

Flexible connections between rigid-molecule fragments such as phenyl or other ring systems have about the same effect per link as similar groups in long-chain compounds, as is apparent from the data of Table 6.16. In setting up models for this kind of effect care should be taken to work with rotating groups of the similar size, because, as the data show, very small groups derive no particular benefit from flexible connections.

Hindrance to rotation is a strong function of the nature and size of the central atom around which rotation takes place. This is brought out forcefully by the series of examples in Table 6.17, where the central carbon atom has been replaced successively by atoms of different sizes. The effect of the central atom and of the extent of alkyl substitution is dominated by the effect of these two variables on the mobility of the alkyl group in the liquid state and on the difference in mobility of the alkyl group between the crystalline and the liquid state. The mobility of the alkyl group in the liquid state is largely

Table 6.14 Equations Relating the Total Entropy of Fusion of Long-Chain Compounds to the Number of Carbon Atoms per Molecule[a]

Homologous series[b]	Formula
n-Paraffins (N_c = even)	$\Sigma\,\Delta S_{m,tr}/R = 0.80 + 1.33N_c$
n-Paraffins (N_c = odd)	$\Sigma\,\Delta S_{m,tr}/R = 1.10 + 1.18N_c$
2-Methyl-n-alkanes	$\Sigma\,\Delta S_{m,tr}/R = -1.24 + 1.2N_c + 20/N_c^2$
2,2-Dimethyl-n-alkanes	$\Sigma\,\Delta S_{m,tr}/R = -6.26 + 1.33N_c + 83/N_c^2$
n-Alkyl-cyclopentane	$\Sigma\,\Delta S_{m,tr}/R = -5.1 + 1.30N_c + 131/N_c^2$
n-Alkyl-cyclohexane	$\Sigma\,\Delta S_{m,tr}/R = -6.3 + 1.45N_c + 56/N_c^2$
n-Alkyl-benzene[c]	$\Sigma\,\Delta S_{m,tr}/R = -5.6 + 1.18N_c + 100/N_c^2$
n-Alkane thiols (N_c = even)	$\Sigma\,\Delta S_{m,tr}/R = 3.3 + 1.2N_c$
n-Alkane thiols (N_c = odd)	$\Sigma\,\Delta S_{m,tr}/R = 3.90 + 1.33N_c$
n-Alkyl bromide (N_c = odd)	$\Sigma\,\Delta S_{m,tr}/R = 2.4 + 1.38N_c + 0.54/N_c^2$
n-Alkanoic acid (N_c = even)	$\Sigma\,\Delta S_{m,tr}/R = -2.56 + 1.33N_c + 36/N_c^2$
n-Alkanoic acid (N_c = odd, >5)	$\Sigma\,\Delta S_{m,tr}/R = -2.7 + 1.25N_c$
Na-n-alkanoates (N_c = even)	$\Sigma\,\Delta S_{m,tr}/R = -6.6 + 1.35N_c$

[a] Generally *not valid* for the *first two* members of the series.
[b] The available data for 1-alkenes and 1-alkanols are too irregular (and probably unreliable) for representation.
[c] The datum for ethyl benzene is appreciably higher than predicted by this equation.

determined by the potential energy barrier to internal rotation (see Table 14.29). It would also determine the magnitude of ΔS_m if the alkyl groups were immobile or would perform only small amplitude torsional oscillations in the solid state. NMR linewidth determination easily establishes the alkyl group mobility in the solid state.

In the extreme case of virtually identical mobility of the methyl group in both phases, as in the high-melting neopentane and dimethyl cadmium, internal rotation makes no contribution to $\Sigma\,\Delta S_{m,tr}$. In the other extreme of nearly immobile methyl groups in the solid, as with the low-melting compounds of Table 6.17, it is apparent that in a given series S_{rr}, the contribution of hindered rotation, largely determines the trend of ΔS_m. Here the proximity of $\Sigma\,\Delta S_{m,tr}$ values to each other is far more surprising than their relatively small differences.

Addition of successive methylene groups should raise $\Sigma\,\Delta S_{m,tr}$ by a maximum of $1.2R$ per CH_2 group. In the sequence Et_2CH_2, Et_3CH, Et_4C in Table 6.17 it is apparent that increasing crowding sharply diminishes the increment per methylene group from $1.03R$ to $0.87R$ to $0.50R$, respectively. As expected, the reduced crowding in the sequence et_4C to et_4Si is accompanied by an increase in ΔS_m per CH_2 group from $0.50R$ to $0.92R$. However, there are a few rather unexpected results. The excessively large increment for Et_2S ($1.47R$ per CH_2 group) makes one or both of the ΔS_m values suspect as

Table 6.15 Total Entropy of Fusion and Transition of Model Olefins and Related Compounds[a] [12]

Compounds:	n-butane	butene-1	cis-butene-2	trans-butene-2	butadiene-1,2	butadiene-1,3	1,4-pentadiene[b]	butyne-1	diacetylene[c]
$\Sigma \Delta S_{m,tr}/R$:	6.47	5.27	6.56	7.02	6.12	5.85	5.88	4.89	5.18

Compounds:	n-hexane	hexene-1	cis-hexene-2	trans-hexene-2	cis-hexene-3	trans-hexene-3	cis-3-MeC$_5^=$-2	trans-3-MeC$_5^=$-2
$\Sigma \Delta S_{m,tr}/R$:	8.82	8.43	8.02	7.9	7.32	8.8	5.84	6.75

[a] From Ref. 4.
[b] Bartlesville Petroleum Research Center.
[c] Dannhauser, W. and A. Fluckinger, *J. Chem. Phys.* **38,** 69 (1963).

Table 6.16 Total Entropy of Fusion and Transition of Noncondensed Polycyclic Aromatic Compounds [21] [12]

Compounds:	Diphenyl	Diphenylmethane	Diphenylether	Diphenyl Sulfide
$\Sigma \Delta S_{m,tr}/R$:	6.55	7.44	6.93	
Compounds:	1,1-Diphenylethane	1,2-Diphenylethane	1,2-Diphenylethene (*trans*)	Diphenylethyne
$\Sigma \Delta S_{m,tr}/R$:	8.3	11.36 (?)	9.02	7.76

Table 6.17   Effect of the Central Atom on the Total Entropy of Fusion and Transition of Various Compounds[a] [12]

Compound	Me$_2$CH$_2$	Me$_2$O	Me$_2$S	Me$_2$Cd	Et$_2$CH$_2$	Et$_2$O	Et$_2$S		
$\Sigma \Delta S_{m,tr}/R$	4.95	4.52	5.51	4.31[b]	7.02	5.70	8.46		
Compound	Me$_3$CH	Me$_3$N	Me$_3$In	Et$_3$CH					
$\Sigma \Delta S_{m,tr}/R$	4.82	5.05	5.2[c]	7.42					
Compound[d]	Me$_4$C	Me$_4$Si	Me$_4$Sn	Me$_4$Pb	Et$_4$C	Et$_4$Si	Et$_4$Ge	Et$_4$Sn	Et$_4$Pb
$\Sigma \Delta S_{m,tr}/R$	3.75	4.77	5.22	5.36	5.76	8.26	8.26	7.70	7.40

[a] From [4] and [32] except when otherwise noted.
[b] Li, J. C. M., *J. Am. Chem. Soc.* **78**, 1081 (1956).
[c] [28].
[d] [63].

does the excessively low increment for Et$_2$O(0.59R per CH$_2$ group). In the latter case ΔS_m (Et$_2$O) appears to be far too low in comparison with $\Delta S_m(n$-C$_5$H$_{12}$). Equally unexpected are the very low increments for et$_4$Sn (0.62R per CH$_2$) and Et$_4$Pb (0.51R per CH$_2$) in view of the nearly free rotation around the length of the metal–carbon bonds. These data should either be checked or explained before use for further extrapolation. In all other cases extrapolation of $\Sigma \Delta S_{m,tr}$ for the series of Table 6.17 beyond the ethyl derivative can probably be done quite safely with 1.2R per CH$_2$ group added.

6.2.5   Effects of Strong Dipole Interactions and of Association

The rotational contribution to the entropy of fusion has the magnitude $S_r(g) - S_{tor}(c)$ only if rotation in the liquid state is free. Any interference with free rotation should reduce the entropy of fusion correspondingly. The quantitative correctness of this effect has been demonstrated for long-chain hydrocarbons, where the entropy reduction due to hindered external rotation could be extracted from vapor-pressure data [10]. The same technique is not readily applicable to associating compounds. We shall therefore examine here the possibility of expressing the effect of given types of dipole interaction upon ΔS_m in terms of an additive constant. Theoretical analyses of the observed effects will be left to later efforts, especially in the field of hydrogen bond studies.

A complicating feature in this analysis is the often simultaneous and opposing effect of a given polar group in hindering external and facilitating internal rotation. Aldehyde, carboxyl, and similar groups are typical in this respect. Often the facilitation of internal rotation is most important; then we obtain the enhancement in ΔS_m shown in Table 6.18. With low-molecular-weight

Table 6.18 Increase of ΔS_m by Reducing Hindrance to Internal Rotation* [12]

Compound	$\Sigma \, \Delta S_{m,tr}/R$	Homomorph	$\Sigma \, \Delta S_{m,tr}/R$	δ
Ethylacetate	6.68	2-methylpentane	6.3	0.4
Ethylpropionate	7.61	3-methylhexane	7.4	0.2
Acetaldehyde	5.57	propene	4.10	0.5
n-Butyraldehyde	7.55	pentene-1	6.50	1.0
Methyl cyanide	4.80[a]	propene[h]	4.10	0.7
Ethyl cyanide	4.52[i]	butene-1[h]	4.27	0.25
t-Butyl cyanide	4.90[i]	3,3-dimethyl-1-butene[h]	5.00	−0.10
Vinyl cyanide	4.85[i]	1,3-butadiene[h]	5.85	−1.00
Cyanoacetylene	6.1[c]	1,3-butadiene[h]	5.85	0.25
Trifluoromethyl cyanide	4.64[b]	propene[h]	4.10	0.5
Methylamine	4.12	ethane	3.83	0.3/NH_2
1,2-Diaminoethane	8.26	n-butane	6.48	0.9/NH_2
1,6-Diaminoethane	15.5[d]	n-octane	13.0	1.25/NH_2
1,1-Dimethylhydrazine	5.60	2-methylpropane	4.82	0.8/NH_2
Hydrazine	5.56	ethane	3.83	0.85/NH_2
t-Butylamine	4.11[e]	neopentane	3.75	0.4/NH_2
Aniline	4.75	toluene	4.48	0.3/NH_2
Methanethiol	4.73	ethane	3.85	0.9
Propanethiol	7.48	n-butane	6.5	1.0
n-Butanethiol	7.98	n-pentane	7.02	1.0
n-Pentanethiol	10.70	n-hexane	8.62	2.1
Benzenethiol	5.34	toluene	4.48	0.9
Dimethyl sulfone	6.80[f]	tetramethylmethane	3.75	3.0
Methyl-t-butyl sulfone	8.25[f]	hexamethylethane	5.01	3.2
Diphenyl sulfone	10.9[f]	2,2-diphenylpropane	7.2	3.7
Dimethyl sulfoxide	5.75[g]	2-methyl propene-1	5.38	0.4

* From [4] and [32] except when otherwise noted.

[a] W. E. Putnam et al., *J. Chem. Phys.* **42**, 749 (1965).

[b] E. L. Pace and R. J. Bobka, *J. Chem. Phys.* **35**, 454 (1961).

[c] W. Dannhausev and A. Fluckinger, *J. Chem. Phys.* **38**, 69 (1963).

[d] Efreemova and Serebryakova, *CA* **61**, 90[c].

[e] D. L. Scott et al., API-Project 48, unpublished data.

[f] See [2].

[g] Skulak and Nirkov, *CA* **61**, 2496[d].

[h] The cyanides should be compared with acetylene derivatives for which not enough data could be found. The only exception, diacetylene[c] as homomorph for cyanoacetylene, yields $\delta = 0.9R$.

[i] A. Ribner and E. F. Westrum, *J. Phys. Chem.* **71**, 1208 (1967).

esters we find an almost exact balancing of effects, and rather accurate predictions are made from the readily available data for their hydrocarbon homomorphs.

The expected depression of ΔS_m is found with the various groups assembled in Table 6.19. The decrements are largely self-explanatory.

A plot of $\Sigma \Delta S_{m,tr}$ of the 1-bromo-n-alkanes versus N_c reveals an alteration between odd and even numbers of carbon atoms per molecule for the first

Table 6.19   Reduction of ΔS_m by Dipole Interaction* [12]

Compounds	$\Sigma \Delta S_{m,tr}/R$	Homomorph	$\Sigma \Delta S_{m,tr}/R$	δ
Dimethylether	4.53	propane	4.95	−0.42
Dimethoxymethane	5.97[a]	n-pentane	7.02	−0.52/oxygen
Ethylene oxide	3.90	cyclopropane	4.52	−0.42
Trioxane	3.90[b]	cyclohexane	5.50	−0.53/oxygen
Acetone	3.91	2-methyl propene-1	5.38	−1.5
Methylethylketone	5.50	2-methyl butene-1	7.03	−1.5
Di-methyldisulfide	5.88	trans-butene-2[c]	7.02	−1.2
Di-ethyldisulfide	6.62	trans-hexene-3[c]	8.8	−1.2
β-Sulfolene	4.86[d]	1,1-dimethylcyclopentene-3	(6.7)	(−1.8)
Sulfolane	4.55[e]	1,1-dimethylcyclopentane	5.97	−1.4

* Hindered external rotation in the liquid state.
[a] D. M. McEackern and J. E. Kilpatrick, *J. Chem. Phys.* **41**, 3127 (1964).
[b] J. Rybicky, *C.A.* **62**, 2210[h].
[c] The choice of these homomorphs was determined by the known stiffness of the S–S bond (barrier to rotation ∼9.0 kcal/mole) and the geometry of the C–S–S–C bonds; D. W. Scott et al., *J. Am. Chem. Soc.* **72**, 2424 (1950); **74**, 2478 (1952).
[d] [27].
[e] [15].

four members of the series, whereas the remaining oscillations in the curve appear to be experimental uncertainties rather than real. The opposite trend among the n-paraffins leads to the sharp change in δ with N_c noted on Table 6.20. It is proposed here to accept the usual homomorph basis of calculation only up to n-propyl bromide, and thereafter to set $\Sigma \Delta S_{m,tr}/R = 1.81 + 1.49N_c$ for $N_c > 3$. Too few reliable data are available to develop similar relations for the other halo alkanes. The other seeming generalizations of Table 6.20 should therefore also be used with caution.

The dicyano alkane data on the same table are wholly inconsistent with the monocyano data of Table 6.18, even though consistent with each other. Unfortunately not enough crystal structure data are available on the cyano compounds of the two tables and no heat-of-fusion measurements could be

Table 6.20   Halides and Dicyanoalkanes [12]

Compound	$\Sigma \, \Delta S_{m,tr}/R$	Homomorph	$\Sigma \, \Delta S_{m,tr}/R$	δ
Methyl chloride	4.43	ethane	3.83	+0.60/Cl
Methyl bromide	4.45			+0.62/Br
$C(CH_2F)_4$	8.06[a]			+0.58/F
$C(CH_2Cl)_4$	7.40[a,b]	3,3-diethyl pentane		+0.41/Cl[b]
$C(CH_2Br)_4$	8.27			+0.63/Br
Ethyl chloride	3.95	propane	4.95	−1.0/Cl
Ethyl bromide	4.57			−0.4/Br
1,2-dichloroethane	4.47	n-butane	6.48	−1.0/Cl
1,2-dibromoethane	6.23			−0.13/Br
i-Propyl chloride	4.85	i-butane	4.84	0
i-Propyl bromide	4.76			−0.1
$(CN)_2$	3.98	diacetylene	5.18	−0.6/CN
1,2-dicyano ethane	4.55[c]	1,5-hexadiene	8.4[c]	−1.9/CN
1,3-dicyano propane	6.20[d]	1,6-heptadiene	9.6[e]	−1.7/CN

[a] E. F. Westrum et al., *J. Phys. Chem.* **69**, 1209 (1965).
[b] This datum is questioned by its authors because crystals were poorly developed.
[c] C. A. Wulff and E. F. Westrum, *J. Phys. Chem.* **67**, 2376 (1963).
[d] H. L. Clever and E. F. Westrum, *J. Phys. Chem.* **69**, 1983 (1965).
[e] Estimated by correlation.

found on a series of monocyano alkanes that would yield a hint regarding the relation to molecular structure similar to that available for other alkanes. It is probable that there are two series of cyano increments just as there are two series of halo increments, but the distinguishing criteria have yet to be found.

The most consistent effects are those due to *hydrogen-bond formation*. They have been divided into those due to hydroxyl groups (Tables 6.21 and 6.22) and those involving nitrogen containing groups (Table 6.23). The effect of single aliphatic hydroxyl groups is straightforward, and perhaps remarkable only for its uniformity. Inconsistencies among the higher n-alkanols are most likely due to impurities (they are notoriously difficult to purify).

The behavior of the polyols is particularly interesting. Many of these form continuous networks of hydrogen bonds in the solid crystal. Their liquid-state properties, especially their heat of vaporization, suggest that extensive intramolecular hydrogen bonding takes place in the liquid [11], [47]. If we assume that the vibration frequency of internal and external hydrogen bonds are equal, then the maximum possible change in entropy is $\Delta S_m^v + S_r$. The rotational entropy contributions for the intramolecularly bonded ring systems, shown in Table 6.22, of glycerol, erythrite, pentaerythritol, and mannitol are (in units of R) about 11, 11.5, 13.5 and 14, respectively. Taking as a first approximation for all $\Delta S_m{}^v = 1.3\ R$, the value obtained for glycerol, then the maximum entropy of fusion for these polyols would be (in units of R) 12.3, 12.8, 14.8, and 15.3, respectively. Comparison of these numbers with the observed values in Table 6.22 suggest that (within the framework of our assumptions) intramolecular hydrogen-bond formation in

Table 6.21   Reduction of Entropy of Fusion by Hydrogen Bonding[a] [12]

Compound	$\Sigma\ \Delta S_{m,tr}/R$	Homomorph	$\Sigma\ \Delta S_{m,tr}/R$	δ
Methyl alcohol	2.68	Ethane	3.83	−1.15
Ethyl alcohol	3.84	Propane	4.97	−1.13
n-Propyl alcohol	4.27(?)	n-Butane	6.48	?
i-Propyl alcohol	3.50	i-Butane	4.82	−1.32
n-Butyl alcohol	5.89	n-Pentane	7.04	−1.16
n-Pentyl alcohol	6.06	n-Hexane	8.82	−1.76
2-Methyl butanol-2	3.64	2,2-Dimethylbutane	5.78	−2.14
n-Hexanol-1	8.23	n-Heptane	9.20	−0.97
n-Hexadecanol-1	19.79	n-Heptadecane	(21.0)	−1.21
Cyclohexanol	4.47	Methylcyclohexane	5.54	−1.1
Benzyl alcohol	4.20	Ethylbenzene	6.20[b]	−2.0[b]
Phenol	4.41	Toluene	4.48	−0.1
2-Hydroxy toluene[c]	6.25	o-xylene	6.61	−0.36
3-Hydroxy toluene[c]	4.52	m-xylene	6.18	−1.66
4-Hydroxy toluene[c]	4.96	p-xylene	7.20	−2.24

[a] Hindering external rotation in the liquid with hydroxyl groups. From [4] and [32].
[b] The reported entropy of fusion is out of line on a plot of $\Sigma\ \Delta S_{m,tr}$ versus carbon number for the alkyl benzenes. The interpolated value 5.4 yields the more normal decrement for alcohols $\delta = -1.2$.
[c] R. J. L. Andon et al., *Trans. Farad. Soc.* **63**, 1115 (1967).

the liquid state is far from complete for glycol, but is surprisingly extensive for the three higher polyols. The entropy of fusion of the lower polyols is apparently well represented by that of their homomorphs and the decrement for a single hydroxyl group, the effect of the other groups having been neutralized by some degree of intramolecular hydrogen bonding.

Among the benzene diols, only the *ortho* isomer can and does form intramolecular hydrogen bonds at elevated temperature [11]. However, at the melting point not enough freedom of rotation is gained thereby to raise ΔS_m appreciably. It differs, as the data of Table 6.22 show, only slightly more from the ΔS_m of its homomorph than the entropies of fusion of the other two

Table 6.22 Total Entropy of Fusion and Transition of Various Polyols[a] [12]

Compound	$\Sigma\,\Delta S_{m,tr}/R$	Homomorph	$\Sigma\,\Delta S_{m,tr}/R$	δ
Glycol	5.35	n-Butane	6.48	−1.1
Glycerol	7.63	3 Methyl pentane or Methylcyclo-pentane	(6.55)[b] 6.37	−1.1 −1.3
Erythrit	13.08	2,3-Dimethylhexane		
Penta-erythritol		Tetraethylmethane or Spiro nonane	5.76	
Mannitol	14.70	3,4,5,6-Tetramethyl octane or Perhydro-pyrene	<10 <8	
1,2-Dihydroxy benzene	7.25	o-xylene	6.61	+0.6
1,3-Dihydroxy benzene	6.67	m-xylene	6.18	+0.4
1,4-Dihydroxy benzene	7.36	p-xylene	7.20	+0.2

[a] [4] and [32].
[b] Estimated.

isomers, which are almost certainly hydrogen bonded to their neighbors. The reason for this behavior is not obvious. As the data are quite old the experiments would bear repetition.

Substances that form defined dimers in the liquid state, such as the fatty acids, might be expected to exhibit comparatively simple regularities in the entropy of fusion. However, no clear-cut regularities are discernible with fatty acids with $N_c < 6$. The entropy of fusion of the lower unsaturated and of the aromatic monocarboxylic acids is reasonably predictable from that of their hydrocarbon homomorphs. The datum for orthophthalic acid

Table 6.23 Reduction of the Entropy of Fusion by Hydrogen Bonding with Nitrogen Containing Groups [12]

Compound	$\Sigma \Delta S_{m,tr}/R$	Homomorph	$\Sigma \Delta S_{m,tr}/R$	δ
Formamide	2.90	Propene	4.10	−1.3
Acetamide	4.97	2-Methylpropene	5.38	−0.4/NH$_2$
Urea	4.32	2-Methylpropene	5.38	−0.6/NH$_2$
Formanilide	5.45	n-Propylbenzene	5.90	−0.5
Benzamide	6.18	i-Propylbenzene	5.28	+0.9
Diphenylamine	6.60	Diphenylmethane	7.44	−0.8
α-Naphthylamine	4.98	1-Methylnaphthalene	5.95	−1.0
Pyrrole	3.82	Furan	4.08	−0.3/NH
ε-Caprolactam	5.67[a]	(Methyl) cycloheptane[b]	5.7	0

[a] [39].
[b] In analogy with the pair cyclohexane–methylcyclohexane we assume that there is no change in $\Sigma \Delta S_{m,tr}$ in going from cycloheptane to methylcycloheptane.

suggests nearly free rotation of the intramolecularly hydrogen-bonded species. Extrapolation from this information to a wide variety of carboxylic acids appears hazardous at present.

Hydrogen bonds of amines cause two widely different effects on the entropy of fusion. The small lowering of ΔS_m by the comparatively weak hydrogen bond of primary amines is overcompensated by the fact that the barrier $V°(C—NH_2) < V°(C—CH_3)$, so that—as shown by the data of Table 6.18— δ is positive to the extent of $0.9R$ per primary alkylamine group. Once the rotation of the amino group is hindered, as in Me$_2$NH and α-naphthylamine, $\delta = -0.90\ R$ and $-1.0R$, respectively.

The entropy decrement of amide hydrogen bonds, shown in Table 6.23, appears to be of the order $-0.5R$ per amide NH$_2$. The excessive magnitude of the formamide increment may be due to the hydrogen-bond contribution of the C–H hydrogen. The internal amide NH bond appears to require no decrement, judging by the single example of ε-caprolactam.

6.2.6 High Polymers[1]

The view has been taken that the "configurational" entropy of fusion of polymeric crystals, $\Delta S_\mathrm{m}{}^j \equiv \Delta S_\mathrm{m} - \Delta S_\mathrm{m}{}^v$, is exclusively a function of the difference in the number of conformations accessible to the chain in the liquid as compared to the crystalline state [25], [37], [38]. Correlation of $\Delta S_\mathrm{m}{}^j$ with polymer structure is impeded by the dearth of p-v-T and ΔV_m data for polymers as compared to the fairly large amount of ΔS_m information available [38].

Hence it becomes worthwhile to generalize the few $\Delta S_\mathrm{m}{}^v$ data on polymers for broader applicability. Those summarized by Kirshenbaum [25] can be cast into the empirical relation

$$\frac{\Delta S_\mathrm{m}{}^v}{R} \approx 0.21 n_c + 0.2 n_o + 0.85 n_p - 0.1 n_e, \tag{6.8}$$

where n_c, n_o, n_p, n_e are the numbers of aliphatic carbon atoms, of ether oxygens, of aromatic rings, and of ester carboxyl groups per repeating unit, respectively.

The data in Table 6.24 show that in those cases for which the $\Delta S_\mathrm{m}{}^v$ correlation is suited, the functional-group contributions $\Delta S_c(\mathrm{X}) \equiv [\Delta S_\mathrm{m} - \Delta S_\mathrm{m}{}^v - n_m \Delta S_\mathrm{m}{}^v(\mathrm{CH_2})]$ are somewhat more constant for a given group than are the uncorrected group contributions $\Delta S(\mathrm{X}) \equiv [\Delta S_\mathrm{m} - n_m \Delta S_\mathrm{m}(\mathrm{CH_2})]$ where n_m = number of methylene groups per repeating unit. Nowhere does the correction cause a drastic change in trends. In view of the large experimental uncertainties in ΔS_m, not too much should be made of small differences in these data. Practically all functional groups shown reduce the entropy contribution of conformation changes—accompanying the phase change—below that of the methylene group (per unit volume).

In the case of hydrocarbons and slightly polar groups this drop in ΔS_m is due to rigidity of the backbone structure, whereas with strongly polar groups, this reduction is due to strong association in the melt phase. Conversion of $\Delta S_\mathrm{m}(\mathrm{X})$ to δ by comparison with the appropriate (hydrocarbon) homomorph repeating unit yields the following series of increments:

Functional Group	—O—	F	Cl (iso-tactic)	Cl (syndio-tactic)	Cl (at C²⁻)	—CN	—O—C— $\overset{O}{\diagup\!\!/}$	—N—C— $\overset{O}{\underset{H}{\|}}$
δ (Units of R):	−0.6	−0.2 to −0.5	−1.2	+0.4	−1.5	−1.0	−3.8	−2.4 to −3.5.

[1] In the case of polymers, ΔS_m, $\Delta S_\mathrm{m}{}^v$, $\Delta S_\mathrm{m}{}^j$ are always meant per repeating unit. This is so obvious that the frequently used notation ΔS_u, etc. has not been adopted in the present discussion.

Table 6.24 Entropy of Fusion Per Repeating Unit for Polymers [12]

Polymer	$\frac{\Delta S_m}{R}$	$\frac{\Delta S_m - \Delta S_{mv}}{R}$	Functional Group (X)	$\frac{\Delta S(X)}{R}$	$\frac{\Delta S_c(X)}{R}$	Ref.
Polyethylene	1.18	0.93	—	—	—	a, b
Polypropylene (isotactic)	2.1	1.45	C—Me	0.9	0.5	a, b
Polybutene-1 (isotactic) 1	2.1	1.25	C-et	0.9	0.3	a, b
Polystyrene (isotactic)	2.1	1.0	C—Ø	0.9	0.1	a, b
Polyvinyl fluoride	1.6 to 1.9		C—F	0.4 to 0.7		c
Polyvinyl chloride (isotactic)	0.86		C—Cl	−0.3		d
Polyvinyl chloride (syndiotactic)	2.49		C—Cl	+1.3		i
Polyacrylonitrile	1.07		C—C≡N	−0.1		e
Polyvinyl alcohol	1.65		C—OH	0.47		k
Polybutadiene; 1,4-cis	3.87	3.0	H H C=C	1.5	1.1	f

Polymer			Structure			
Polyisoprene; 1,4-*cis*	1.74	0.85	H, Me on >C=C<	−0.6	−1.0	d
Polyisoprene; 1,4-*trans*	4.40	3.5	Me on >C=C<	2.0	1.6	d
Polychloroprene; 1,4-*trans*	2.86	1.5	Cl on >C=C<	0.5		j
Polyoxymethylene	1.8		—O—	0.6	0.5_7	b
Polyethylene oxide	2.9	2.3_5	—O— (epoxide)	0.5	0.5	b
Alkanedioic glycol esters	—		$-O-\overset{O}{\overset{\|}{C}}-$	−1.7 ± 0.7	−1.2 ± 0.6	b
Terephthalic glycol esters	—		$-\overset{O}{\overset{\|}{C}}-\phi-\overset{O}{\overset{\|}{C}}-O-$	+2.6 ± 0.3	+2.4 ± 0.1	b
Poly *p*-xylene	5.60	4.3	—ϕ—	+3.2	+2.5	g
Nylon 6	5.60		$-\overset{H}{\overset{\|}{N}}-\overset{O}{\overset{\|}{C}}-$	−0.25		b
Nylon 66	10.3		$-\overset{H}{\overset{\|}{N}}-\overset{O}{\overset{\|}{C}}-$	−0.75		b
Nylon 610	13.6		$-\overset{H}{\overset{\|}{N}}-\overset{O}{\overset{\|}{C}}-$	−1.4		b

Table 6.24 (continued)

Polymer	$\dfrac{\Delta S_m}{R}$	$\dfrac{\Delta S_m - \Delta S_m^v}{R}$	Functional Group (X)	$\dfrac{S\Delta(X)}{R}$	$\dfrac{\Delta S_c(X)}{R}$	Ref.
Sebacoyl piperazine	6.9		(piperazine diamide ring structure)	−2.5		d
Polytetrafluoroethylene	0.6		CF_2	(0.6)		h
Polymonochlorotrifluoroethylene	1.25		C with Cl, F	0.65 [relative to (CF_2)]		d

a W. R. Krigbaum and I. Nematsu, *J. Polymer Sci.* **A3**, 767 (1965).
b I. Kirshenbaum, *J. Polymer Sci.* **A3**, 1869 (1965).
c D. I. Sapper, *J. Polymer Sci.* **43**, 383 (1960).
d L. Mandelkern, *Rubber Chem. Tech.* **32**, 1392 (1959).
e W. R. Krigbaum and N. Tokita, *J. Polymer Sci.* **43**, 467 (1960).
f G. Natta and G. Moraglio, *Makromol. Chem.* **66**, 218 (1963).
g T. R. Schaeffgen, *T. Polym. Sci.* **38**, 549 (1959).
h H. W. Starkweather, and R. H. Boyd, *J. Phys. Chem.* **64**, 410 (1960).
i D. Kockett, *Kolloid-Z.* **198**, 17 (1964).
j L. Mandelkern, *Chem. Rev.* **56**, 903 (1956).
k R. K. Tabbs, *J. Polymer Sci.* **A3**, 4181 (1965).
For further data see R. L. Miller, Section III of *Polymer Handbook*, J. Brandrup and E. H. Immergut, eds., Interscience–Wiley, New York, 1966.

Many of these increments are reassuringly similar to those obtained from data on low-molecular-weight compounds in Tables 6.19 and 6.20. The difference between isotactic and syndiotactic polyvinyl chloride is surprisingly similar to that between the two classes of *n*-alkyl halides in Table 6.20. However, the ester group decrement could not have been guessed from data on low-molecular-weight esters, the decrements of which rarely exceed $1.5R$ and are usually close to $0.5R$. The same applies to the amide group. These groups appear to interfere more strongly with the random conformation of the polymer coil than with the external rotation of monomeric molecules in their melts.

The attempt by Kirshenbaum [25] to formalize these relations by setting

$$\Delta S_c(X) = \sum_{j=0}^{j} R \ln N_t$$

[where j = number of bonds other than alkane C–C bonds in the backbone chain (per repeating unit) and N_t = number of stable conformations in that bond relative to the preceding bond] cannot represent the facts in Table 6.24 because $N_t < 1$, required by the several instances where $S_c(X) < 0$ is physically meaningless. Clearly, another approach is needed. The negative values of $\Delta S(X)$ and $\Delta S_c(X)$ more likely mean that the presence of the functional group has also reduced the number of conformations accessible to one or more methylene groups adjacent to the functional group. Conversely, $\Delta S_c(X) > R \ln 3$ per rotatable bond in the functional group suggests that the presence of the functional group has made more conformations freely accessible to the neighboring methylene groups.

6.2.7 Summary of Functional Group Increments δ

For the convenience of the users of this review the functional group decrements obtained in the course of this investigation have been summarized in Table 6.25. The indicated error limits are only moderately meaningful because of the small sample sizes and because of the questionable quality of many of the experimental data from which they had been derived. These increments are to be added to $\Sigma \Delta S_{m,tr}$ of the appropriately chosen hydrocarbon homomorph. The latter can be assumed to be generally available [4, 32], or at least reasonably well estimated from the data and equations given in Tables 6.11, 6.12 and 6.14 and in Figure 6.6.

The corresponding increments for polymers should be taken from column 5 of Table 6.24. Their uncertainty is of the same order as the considerable uncertainty of the experimental data. One of the major problems with several crystalline polymers is the absence of heat-of-transition data for solid–solid first-order transitions known to exist. Their calorimetry is difficult because of the slowness with which transitions proceed to completion.

Table 6.25 Entropy of Fusion Correction δ Due to the Presence of Polar Groups[a,b]

Polar Group	Functional Group	δ[c]
Aliphatic ether	—O—	-0.5[d] ± 0.1
Aliphatic thioether		
(n-alkyl)	—S—	-1.0 ± 0.5[e]
(sec-alkyl) (one)		$+0.85 \pm 0.2$
(both)	—S—	$+1.0$
(t-alkyl)	—S—	-0.3 ± 0.2
Aliphatic and diaromatic ketone	$\backslash$C=O$\diagup$	-1.5 ± 0.1
Quinone	$\backslash$C=O$\diagup$	-0.7 ± 2
Aliphatic aldehyde	—C$\overset{\displaystyle O}{\diagup}\ \underset{\displaystyle H}{\diagdown}$	$+0.8 \pm 0.3$
Aliphatic ester	—O—C$\overset{\displaystyle O}{\diagup}$—	—
Aliphatic alcohol	(One OH-group per molecule)	-1.2 ± 0.2
Aliphatic primary amine	—NH$_2$	$+0.9 \pm 0.3$
Aromatic amine (unhindered)[f]	—NH$_2$	$+0.3$
Aliphatic and aromatic secondary amine	$\backslash$NH$\diagup$	-0.9 ± 0.1
Monocyano alkane	—C≡N	$+0.7 \pm 0.2$
Dicyano alkane	—C≡N	-1.8 ± 0.1
		-0.5 ± 0.1
Alkane amide	—C$\overset{\displaystyle O}{\diagup}$—NH$_2$	
Alkane thiols	—SH (N_c = even)	$+1.0 \pm 0.2$
	(N_c = odd)	$+1.8 \pm 0.1$
Secondary alkane thiols	—SH	$+0.25 \pm 0.15$
Tertiary alkane thiols	—SH	$+1.2 \pm 0.5$
Dialkyl disulfide	—SS—	-1.2
Dialkyl or diaryl sulfone	—SO$_2$—	$+3.3 \pm 0.3$
Heterocyclic sulfone	$\backslash$SO$_2\diagup$	-1.4

a Weighted to emphasize extrapolation toward $N_c > 3$.
b For details on haloalkanes see Table 6.20.
c In units of R.
d This is the most common value; a range trans -1.4 (vinyl and ethyl ether) to $+0.2$ (1,4-dioxane) is found with lesser frequency.
e Very irregular.
f Hindered primary amine $\delta = -0.9$.

6.3 SOLID–SOLID PHASE TRANSITIONS

The correlation of the total entropy of fusion and transition with molecular structure discussed in the previous sections leaves open the question of the incidence and location of first-order solid–solid phase transitions for a given compound. A few general principles can be discussed. Whenever a compound exhibits an anomalously high melting point *and* an entropy of fusion substantially lower than predicted for $\Sigma \, \Delta S_{m,tr}$ from the present correlation, we are likely to find a solid–solid phase transition at the temperature where the melting point "should have been." If only T_m is larger than expected, but ΔS_m is of "about the right" magnitude, as with benzene, then solid–solid phase transition need not be expected. However, under those conditions we may find a loosening of the lattice, evident in NMR linewidth changes or mechanical-energy-loss maximum, in the temperature range where T_m would have occurred for a slightly less symmetrical molecule. With benzene such reorientation phenomena have been noted at 120 to 130°K.

The incidence of frequency-dependent changes in NMR linewidth, elastic storage and loss moduli, dielectric constant, and energy absorption is often also named—quite incorrectly—"transition." The basic difference between such relaxation processes and phase transitions is the frequency dependence of the temperature at which the relaxation processes occur and the temperature invariance of phase transitions (at a given pressure).

Moreover, although (mechanical or electrical) energy absorption in relaxation processes exhibits a maximum at a particular combination of frequency and temperature (as discussed in Section 5.2.2), energy absorption undergoes just a step change at a phase transition.

Obviously there can be no easy method to predict the freakish incidence of phase transitions such as that of n-butane, and the series of complicated multiple transitions among much higher-molecular-weight n-paraffins or among the alkyl naphthalenes. Even if the incidence of such transitions could be fitted into some scheme, the division of the total entropy of fusion and transitions among the transitions would still be left for a separate accounting. Fortunately, however, we usually find that melting-point and transition temperatures of long-chain compounds are so close together that, for the purposes of heat balance calculations, the entire enthalpy change can be estimated for the melting point without great error. If crystallization in the process under design takes place reasonably distant from, say, $\leq 15°C$ below the melting point, it is also safe to estimate the density change as being that due to fusion plus transition. However, the solubility calculated on the assumption of no phase transition may be very much too low if a solid–solid phase transition does, in fact, take place more than a few degrees below the melting point.

The situation is somewhat more predictable for molecules with spherical symmetry. Here the entropy change at the melting point is most often of the order of $1.2 \pm 0.4R$. In some series, such as the carbon tetrahalides, we find—as first pointed out by Trappeniers [67]—the transition temperatures to be approximately constant fractions of the absolute melting point $(\sim 0.87 T_m)$. The fact that for tetramethylmethane $T_{tr}/T_m = 0.55$ shows that we dare not carry analogy very far with crystallization phenomena. Yet, we find that

$$\frac{T_{tr}/T_m(C_2Me_6)}{T_{tr}/T_m(C_2X_6)} = \frac{T_{tr}/T_m(CMe_4)}{T_{tr}/T_m(CX_4)} = 0.63,$$

where for C_2X_6 (X = F, Cl) the lowest transitions are at $T_{tr}/T_m = 0.65 \pm 0.05$. No regularities have as yet been discovered among the alicyclic and heterocyclo aliphatic compounds of related structure. Even the incidence of transitions cannot be related from one cyclic compound to its analog. Hence whenever nearly spherical symmetry or a very low measured entropy of fusion ($<3\,R$) leads us to suspect the incidence of solid–solid transitions we should resort to experimental observation of the transition.

6.3.1 Entropy of Solid–Solid Transitions

In the cases in which $\Delta S_m \approx R$ one would expect from the HSE theory that $\Delta S_{tr} \approx \Delta S_m(rot)$,[1] or in the cases in which $\Delta S_m = R + \Delta S_m(rot)$ (C) that $\Delta S_{tr} = \Delta S_m(rot)^1$ (A, B), where the indicators A, B, C refer to the corresponding principal moments of inertia (in increasing sequence). The second situation is found with many nonspherosymmetric molecules that exhibit solid–solid transitions, such as the monomethyl naphthalenes, tetramethyl ethylene, n-butane, etc. However, the more nearly spherosymmetric molecules CX_4 for which $\Delta S_m \approx R$ exhibit a deficiency $\Delta S_m(rot) - \Delta S_{tr} \approx 1.5R$. Similar deficiencies are found in many cases involving solid–solid phase transitions of crystals composed of highly symmetrical molecules. These are shown in Table 6.26.

This suggests the possibility of somewhat different approach to the calculation of ΔS_{tr}.

For solids, the molecules of which belong to certain restricted symmetry classes, ΔS_{tr} can be estimated if the transition is considered as an order–disorder transition, as has been shown by Guthrie and McCullough [72].

Table 6.26 Comparison of $\Sigma \Delta S_{m,tr}$ of Similar Crystals with and without Solid–Solid Phase Transitions

With Phase Transitions	$\dfrac{\Sigma \Delta S_{m,tr}}{R}$	Without Phase Transitions	$\dfrac{\Delta S_m}{R}$
CCl_4	3.6	$SiCl_4$	4.6
CBr_4	3.7	$SnBr_4$	5.2
PtF_6	5.5	UF_6	6.9
Camphor	5.2	α-d-Bromocamphor	6.8
Furan	4.1	Thiophene	5.0

[1] Where T in $S_r = T_{tr}$.

The basic assumption then is that the molecules in the solid at $T > T_{tr}$ are in a state of definable disorder. Then

$$\frac{\Delta S_{tr}}{R} = \ln\left(\frac{N_2}{N_1}\right), \tag{6.11}$$

where N_1, N_2 are the number of states of disorder statistically occupied in the low- and high-temperature state, respectively.

Table 6.27 Comparison of ΔS_{tr} of Crystals Composed of Tetrahedral Molecules Estimated from Order–Disorder Theory with Experimental Data [12]

Substance	$\dfrac{N_2}{N_1}$ [a]	$\ln\left(\dfrac{N_2}{N_1}\right)$	$\dfrac{n_2}{n_1}$ [b]	$\ln\left(\dfrac{n_2}{n_1}\right)$	$\ln\left(\dfrac{N_2}{N_1}\right) + \ln\left(\dfrac{n_2}{n_1}\right)$	$\dfrac{\Sigma\,\Delta S_{tr}\,(\text{exp})}{R}$	Ref.
CF_4	12	2.48	—	—	2.48	2.32	44
CCl_4	12	2.48	—	—	2.48	2.47	72
CBr_4	12	2.48	—	—	2.48	2.51	72
CMe_4	12	2.48	—	—	2.48	>2.22	72
$CCl_3 \cdot Me$	12	2.48	4	1.38	3.86	4.0	72
t-buCl	12	2.48	9	2.16	4.64	4.4	44
t-buBr	12	2.48	9	2.16	4.64	(>3.8)	44
t-buSH	12	2.48	9	2.16	4.64	4.3	72
$C(SMe)_4$	12	2.48	?		>2.48	2.8	44
$C(NO_2)_4$	12	2.48	?		>2.48	2.9	44
$C(CH_2OH)_4$	12	2.48	>64	>4.2	>6.7	11.5[c]	44

[a] N_1 assumed as 1; N_2 characteristic of crystal structure.
[b] n_2: Number of extra orientations due to the methyl group.
[c] Includes number of internal degrees of freedom gained in transition.

There is at present an element of arbitrariness in the counting of N_1 and N_2, even where the crystal structure of both states is known. The logic is most transparent in the case of molecules with tetrahedral symmetry, the data of which have been assembled in Table 6.27. For molecules of lower symmetry, the assumption is made that the symmetry of the high-temperature state corresponds to that of the molecule's nearest symmetrical homomorph, as indicated by the data of Table 6.28. The minimum value of ΔS_{tr} to be expected in this case is $R \ln \sigma$, where σ is the symmetry number of the symmetrical homomorph of the unsymmetrical compound. Since first-order solid–solid phase transitions occur only with crystals composed of fairly symmetrical molecules, the structural differences between the asymmetrical rotor and its symmetrical analog are usually small. In fact one of the main difficulties here is the a priori predictability of the incidence of a transition. Few would have guessed that the substances in Table 6.28 would even exhibit a first-order solid–solid phase transition.

Table 6.28   Comparison of ΔS_{tr} of Crystals Composed of Slightly Asymmetric Molecules with an Estimate from Order–Disorder Theory [72]

Substance	Symmetrical Analog	$\dfrac{N_2}{N_1}$[a]	$\ln\left(\dfrac{N_2}{N_1}\right)$	$\dfrac{\Sigma \, \Delta S_{tr}}{R}$ (exp)
2,3-Benzothiophene	Naphthalene	4	1.38	1.38
Bicyclo(2,2,1)heptane	Bicyclo(2,2,2)octane	24	3.18	3.82
Cyclopentyl-1-thiaethane	—	2^b	0.69	0.65

[a] N_1 assumed as 1.
[b] N_1 assumed as 2 due to random distribution of molecules at lattice sites in two equivalent conformations.

The entire scheme of accounting for ΔS_{tr} as a definable order–disorder phenomenon breaks down when the external change in order is accompanied by internal motions or when the rotational disorder in the high-temperature phase becomes too great. Examples for the former are the t-butyl halides and the methyl chloroform of Table 6.27, which are still barely manageable and the pentaerythritol derivatives, which involve too many changes in internal and external mobility in the change from low- to high-temperature state for practical accountability. Examples for the excessive external mobility in the high-temperature state are the cycloalkanes in the range cyclobutane to cyclooctane.

We may summarize the present situation by the statement that in the absence of a well-founded theory, the extensive available data provide a basis for guessing whether a solid–solid phase transition is to be expected. In restricted cases, we may also guess how to estimate ΔS_{tr} from crystallographic data and from molecular symmetry. But, in general, existing theoretical insight is—at best—suitable for ex post facto explanation of the observed magnitude of ΔS_{tr} rather than for prediction.

6.4   THE HEAT-CAPACITY DIFFERENCE $\Delta C_p = C_p(\text{liq}) - C_p(\text{crystal})$

The temperature coefficient $(\partial \, \Delta H_m / \partial T)_p = C_p(c) - C_p(\text{liq})$. This difference is generally negative. The magnitude of $\Delta C_p \equiv C_p(\text{liq}) - C_p(c)$ should be estimated from heat-capacity data *only if experimental heat-capacity data are available*. At present, there are no sufficiently reliable methods of estimating the heat capacity of liquids and molecular crystals to obtain a meaningful difference between the resulting uncertain data.

Simple thermodynamic reasoning shows that at the melting point,

$$\Delta C_p = C_v(\text{liq}) - C_v(c) + \left[\left(\frac{\partial V}{\partial T}\right)_p \left(\frac{\partial E}{\partial V}\right)_T\right]_{\text{liq}} - \left[\left(\frac{\partial V}{\partial T}\right)_p \left(\frac{\partial E}{\partial V}\right)_T\right]_c. \quad (6.9)$$

Table 6.29 Heat-Capacity Difference (in C_v) between Solid and Liquid at $T_m{}^a$ [12]

Substance	$[C_v(c) - C_v(liq)]/R$
Argon	0.57
Benzene	0
Naphthalene	0.1
Propane	−0.7
n-Heptane	−1.5
n-Hexadecane	−4.4
n-Paraffins above n-C$_7$	$\dfrac{C_v(liq) - C_v(c)}{R} = 1.5 + 0.29(N_c - 7)$

Because the internal vibration contributions are virtually identical in both phases, one can replace $C_v(liq) - C_v(c)$ by the difference of the now readily calculated "lattice" contributions to $C_v(liq)$ and $C_v(c)$, $C_v{}^\lambda$ and $C_v{}^s$, as given in Sections 9.1 to 9.3, and 3.4. With high-melting crystals comprised of rigid molecules, for which $T_m > 0.25\,\Delta H_s/fR$, where f = number of external degrees of freedom per molecule, we find that at T_m, $C_v(liq) \approx C_v(c)$, as shown in Table 6.29.

If we accept Oriani's suggestion (42)—reasonably well borne out by experiment (Table 6.30)—that at the melting point $(\partial E/\partial V)_{liq} = (\partial E/\partial V)_c$ then

$$\Delta C_p \approx \left(\frac{\partial E}{\partial V}\right)_{T_m}\left[\left(\frac{\partial V}{\partial T}\right)_{liq} - \left(\frac{\partial V}{\partial T}\right)_c\right] + (C_v{}^\lambda - C_v{}^s). \qquad (6.10)$$

The expansion coefficient of liquids, and thus $(\partial V/\partial T)_{liq}$ is generally available (keeping in mind that $d\rho/dT$ is independent of temperature at $T < 0.8T_b$). Should the expansion coefficient of the solid not be known, it can be estimated by methods given in Section 3.4. For nonpolar liquids

Table 6.30 Comparison of $(\partial E/\partial V)_T$ in the Liquid and Crystalline States at the Melting Point

Substance	$\left(\dfrac{\partial E}{\partial V}\right)_{T,liq}$ (cal/cm^3)	$\left(\dfrac{\partial E}{\partial V}\right)_{T,c}$ (cal/cm^3)
Benzene	92	119
Naphthalene	93	103
Glycerol[a]	213	194

[a] [61].

(other than perfluorocarbons) and for nonassociating polar liquids, one can approximate $(\partial E/\partial V)_T$ of the liquid with sufficient accuracy for the present purpose by Hildebrand's rule $(\partial E/\partial V)_T \approx \Delta E_v/V_L$ at the same temperature [1]. Then

$$\Delta C_p = C_v(\text{liq}) - C_v(\text{c}) + \Delta E(\alpha_L - \alpha_c).$$

The energy of vaporization ΔE_v can be estimated by means of the additive increments of ΔE_v (Tables 14.1). For associating liquids $(\partial E/\partial V)_T = T\alpha K_0$ has to be estimated from experimental p–v–T data, extensive collections of which are now available [1].

6.5 COMPARISON WITH PREVIOUS WORK

The oldest generalization is that by Walden [69], who suggested in analogy to Trouton's rule that $\Delta S_m = 6.8R$. This strange finding was, of course, due to the fact that at that time most data had been obtained on coal-tar derivatives, that is, on various substituted benzene and naphthalene derivatives. Aside from the HSE relation discussed earlier, the most elaborate scheme for the prediction of ΔS_m is that by Lüttringhaus and co-workers [35]. They relate $\Sigma \, \Delta S_{m,\text{tr}}$ to the surface area per molecule, as measured on modified Stuart–Briegleb models. Although these areas differ somewhat from those which were calculated from x-ray diffraction data, his results are given here in terms of the latter. Specifically, Lüttringhaus suggests to group molecules into three categories:

  1. Long-chain molecules: $\Sigma \, \Delta S_{m,\text{tr}}/A_w \approx 1.8 \pm 0.1 \times 10^{-9}\,\text{cal cm}^{-2}\,{}^\circ\text{K}^{-1}$;
  2. Disk and ellipsoidally shaped molecules: $\Sigma \, \Delta S_{m,\text{tr}}/A_w \approx 1.3 \pm 0.2 \times 10^{-9}\,\text{cal cm}^{-2}\,{}^\circ\text{K}^{-1}$; and
  3. Tetrahedral and spherically shaped molecules: $\Sigma \, \Delta S_{m,\text{tr}}/A_w \approx 1.0 \pm 0.2 \times 10^{-9}\,\text{cal cm}^{-2}\,{}^\circ\text{K}^{-1}$,

where A_w is the area per mole of molecule in cm^2/mole, as given in Chapters 1 and 14.

A basic difficulty of the Lüttringhaus scheme is the assumption that even for rigid molecules $\Sigma \, \Delta S_{m,\text{tr}} \sim A_w$, which is clearly at variance with the data in Tables 6.10 through 6.13. The method can therefore not be expected to yield reliable results.

The first investigator to notice the strong shape dependence of ΔS_m, Pirsch [51], also observed that within a given family of compounds ΔS_m increases with increasing melting point, but did not recognize the physical origin of this effect. He was primarily interested in the spherically symmetrical molecules with $\Delta S_m \approx R$ because of their utility as cryscopic solvents. For those he found that $\Delta S_m/R = a(1 - b/T_m)$ with typically,

	Tricyclo(2,2,1) Heptanes (Camphors)	Tetracyclic Dicyclopentadiene Derivatives	Pentacyclic Endomethylene Phthalic Anhydride Derivatives
a	4.05	3.85	3.60
b (°K)	260	282	334

These correlations are based entirely on ΔH_m estimated from melting-point depression, and can therefore not be given the same weight as calorimetric measurements.

For tetrahedral molecules, especially substituted methanes, Hood [22] proposed to calculate two limiting values of $\Sigma\,\Delta S_{m,tr}$, using their symmetry number σ. He obtains a lower and an upper limit for $\Sigma\,\Delta S_{m,tr}$, depending on whether the molecule is assumed to rotate freely or to oscillate in the crystal at the melting point. A similar scheme has been proposed by Zeldovich to calculate the changes in melting point, etc., for different isomers of aromatic compounds [73]. As the prediction method of Maslov [39] is restricted to narrowly defined families, it is not discussed here.

6.6 THE EFFECT OF PRESSURE

The change of the absolute melting point T_m with the application of hydrostatic pressure P can be predicted by means of the Clapeyron equation:

$$\frac{dP}{dT_m} = \frac{\Delta S_m}{\Delta V_m} = \frac{\Delta H_m}{T_m\,\Delta V_m}. \tag{6.12}$$

However, this relation is exactly correct only at $P \to 0$. It has to be amended in order to be valid at finite pressure. In spite of much effort there is at present no reliable theory for such a pressure correction. The experimental data could be represented by the series development

$$T_m\frac{dP}{dT_m} = P_0\left[1 + b_1\frac{P}{P_0} + b_2\left(\frac{P}{P_0}\right)^2 + \cdots\right], \tag{6.13}$$

where $P_0 = (\Delta H_m/\Delta V_m)_{p=0}$. Generally $dP/d\ln T_m$ rises linearly with the pressure, so that the first correction term should suffice, leading to the integrated form

$$\ln\left(\frac{T_m}{T_{m,0}}\right) = \frac{1}{b_1}\ln\left(1 + \frac{b_1 P}{P_0}\right), \tag{6.14}$$

where T_m, and $T_{m,0}$ are the melting temperatures at P and at $P = 0$, respectively.

Since ΔV_m is not always known (see discussion in Section 6.1), it seems worthwhile to look for a correlation of P_0 $(= \Delta H_m/\Delta V_m)$ with the readily available physical properties of the liquid. One such path is suggested by a relation proposed by Saupe [58],

$$\frac{\Delta H_m}{\Delta V_m} = \frac{K_0}{2}(1 + 2\alpha T_m),\qquad(6.15)$$

Table 6.31　Correlation of P_0 with the Bulk Modulus $K_0{}^a$ and the Thermal Expansion Coefficient α of the Liquid at T_m

Substance	$P_0{}^b$ $(10^{10}$ dyn cm$^{-2})$	$K_0(T_m)$ $(10^{10}$ dyn cm$^{-2})$	$\dfrac{P_0}{K_0(T_m)}$	$\frac{1}{2} + \alpha T_m{}^c$	$\alpha T_m{}^d$
Ar	0.336	0.49[e]	0.69	0.86[e]	0.36[e]
N$_2$	0.283[f]	0.52[e]	0.55	0.80[e]	0.30[e]
O$_2$	0.464[f]	1.2[e]	0.39	0.69[e]	0.19[e]
Benzene	0.94	1.14[e]	0.82	0.83[e]	0.33[e]
Cyclohexane	0.52	1.0	0.52	0.85	0.35
Methylcyclohexane	2.06	3.1	0.67	0.65	0.15
p-Xylene	0.82	1.23	0.67	0.78	0.28
Nitrobenzene	1.18	2.06	0.57	0.73	0.23
1,4-Dioxane	2.4(?)	1.6	1.5(?)	0.81	0.31
Caproic acid	1.42	1.30	1.09	0.76	0.26
Caprylic acid	1.39	1.39	1.0	0.75	0.25

[a] From sound velocity data in Bergmann, L., *Ultraschall* (S. Hirzel, Leipzig, 1956).
[b] From data collected in Ref. a of Table 6.32, except where noted otherwise.
[c] Upper limit, set by (6.15).
[d] Lower limit.
[e] K_0 and α at T_m from Rowlinson, J. S., *Liquids and Liquid Mixtures*, Academic Press, New York, 1959.
[f] Clusius, K. et al., *Helv. Chim. Acta* **43**, 1290 (1960).

which is obtained under the assumption that the potential energy of the condensed system $\epsilon \sim V^{-2}$, and where K_0 and α refer to the liquid state at T_m. The data in Table 6.31 are in moderately good agreement with this relation. The deviations may well result from the fact that in $\epsilon \sim V^{-n}$; $n \neq 2$. The obvious lower limit $\Delta H_m/\Delta V_m \geq K_0\alpha T_m$ is also shown in Table 6.31. An a priori upper limit cannot yet be formulated.

Regardless of the directness of the connection between P_0 and K_0, the pressure coefficient b_1 should be closely related to the pressure coefficient K_1 of the bulk modulus of liquid and solid (Sections 4.4 and 8.3.3). The fact that the compression is along the melting curve instead of isothermal should not make the correlation unduly complicated because $K_1(\text{liq})$ and $K_1(\text{solid})$ are very nearly independent of temperature. Typical numerical values of b_1 have been assembled in Table 6.32. Since b_1 is in effect the second derivative of the melting curve, a fairly difficult experiment, it would be unrealistic to expect regularity to prevail among these numbers.

Detailed examination of individual experiments reveals rather irregular trends of b_1 with pressure, suggesting occasionally a negative sign for b_2. Only among the straight and branched chain alkanes is $b_2 > 0$ whenever $b_2 \neq 0$. Yet the incidence of $b_2 = 0$ and of $b_2 > 0$ lacks any clear correlation with molecular structure or with bulk properties.

Within these limitations we note the following generalizations. The order of magnitude of b_1 is—perhaps accidentally—very near that of $[K_1(\text{liq}) - K_1(\text{crystal})]$. For substances composed of simple rigid molecules $b_1 \approx 2.3 \pm 0.5$. Downward deviations from this average are generally associated with spherical molecule shape and compact molecular structure. Upward deviations are associated with flexible molecular structure and increase with increasing molecular weight. Hydrogen bonding also causes an increase in b_1, as does the combination of hydrogen bonding with spherical symmetry. Weak hydrogen bonding, as in aniline or phenols, has practically no effect on b_1 relative to the corresponding simple compounds.

The effect of pressure on $dP/d \ln T_{tr}$ is far less generalizable than is that on $dP/d \ln T_m$. In general $b_1(T_{tr}) > b_1(T_m)$. The opposite relation is found only among the n-alkanes.

The melting curve of substances is commonly described by the Simon–Glatzel equation

$$T_m \frac{dP}{dT_m} = ac + cP \rightarrow \ln (T_m/T_{m0}) = \frac{1}{c} \ln \left(1 + \frac{P}{a}\right), \qquad (6.16)$$

where a is P_0/b_1 in our nomenclature and $c = b_1$. In spite of its obvious deficiency of not reducing to the Clapeyron equation as $P \rightarrow 0$, a large amount of effort has been spent on finding theoretical justifications for this equation [14], [19]. The reason for this interest is the ability of the equation to describe data over very wide pressure ranges rather accurately, a matter of great importance, especially for geologists. A new start would probably be more fruitful.

The empirical observation of Kraut and Kennedy [28a] that, for metallic and ionic solids,

$$T_m(P)/T_m(0) = 1 + C \, \Delta V/V$$

where $\Delta V/V$ refers to the compression at a fixed temperature (usually room temperature) may presage a new approach to the problem. Although the inapplicability of the above relation to rare gas crystals suggests a more limited success with molecular crystals, it may still be worthwhile to test the range of its validity here as well. For that purpose it is convenient to replace

Table 6.32 Curvature Coefficient b_1 of the Melting Curve of Various Substances[a]

Substance	b_1	Substance	b_1
Simple Substances			
Ne	1.6	$n\text{-}C_{15}H_{32}$ II	4.2
Ar	1.6	$n\text{-}C_{18}H_{38}$	3.39
Kr	1.62	$n\text{-}C_{24}H_{50}$ I	2.84
Xe	1.59	$n\text{-}C_{24}H_{50}$ II	3.87
H_2	1.79	$(n\text{-}C_8H_{17})_3CH$	3.1[c,d]
N_2	1.79	$(n\text{-}C_{12}H_{25})_3CH$	3.5$_3$[c]
O_2	1.74	Methyloxalate	2.1
P_4	1.92	Ethyl acetate	2.2
CO_2	2.6	Ethyl stearate	3.24
Rigid Sphero Symmetrical Compounds		**Rigid Hydrogen-Bonded Molecules**	
CCl_4	2.12		
$CHCl_3$	1.52	NH_3	4.3
$CHBr_3$	2.08	HCN	3.6
Cyclohexane	1.42	Formic acid	5.2
Methylcyclohexane	2.15	Formamide	2.7
Hexamethylenetetramine	—[b]	Acetic acid I	4.89
Adamantane	—[b]	Acetic acid II	3.45
Rigid Cyclic Compounds		Acetamide I	7.5
		Acetamide II	4.62
Cyclobutanone	2.0	Ethanol	1.61
Thiophene	3.3	Erythritol	11.3
1,4-Dioxane	3.3	**Rigid Spherically Symmetric Hydrogen-Bonded Molecules**	
Benzene	2.60		
Naphthalene	2.49		
p-Xylene	1.76	t-Butyl alcohol	5.6
Chlorobenzene I	2.42	Menthol	4.6
Chlorobenzene II	1.83	**Rigid Cyclic Hydrogen-Bonded Molecules**	
Bromobenzene	2.46		
Nitrobenzene	1.93		
p-Dichlorobenzene	2.8	Phenol I	8.0
p-Dibromobenzene	2.6	Phenol II	2.54
Chlorotoluene	2.48	1-Naphthol	1.98
Bromotoluene	2.50	Guaiacol	3.9
Iodotoluene	2.37	Resorcinol	7.9
p-Nitrotoluene	2.6	o-Cresol I	6.2
o-Nitrotoluene	1.5(?)	o-Cresol II	2.8
Slightly Flexible Cyclic Substances		m-Cresol	1.16
		p-Cresol	1.9
		o-Nitrophenol	1.4
Benzophenone	2.35	m-Nitrophenol	2.0
1,2-Diphenylethane	3.3	p-Nitrophenol	3.0
Diphenylmethane	5.3	Aniline	2.34
Triphenylmethane	3.6	Formanilide	4.9

Table 6.32 (continued)

Substance	b_1	Substance	b_1
Flexible Alkanes		Flexible Hydrogen-Bonded Molecules	
$n\text{-}C_9H_{20}$ I	1.6		
$n\text{-}C_9H_{20}$ II	2.5	Propionic acid	3.4
$n\text{-}C_{12}H_{26}$	3.05	Lauric acid	4.0
$n\text{-}C_{13}H_{28}$ I	4.57	Myristic acid	4.2
$n\text{-}C_{13}H_{28}$ II	2.62	Erucic acid	3.1
$n\text{-}C_{15}H_{32}$ I	3.3	Cetyl alcohol	2.6

[a] $b_1 = c$ of the Simon–Glatzel equation, from compilation by S. E. Babb, Jr., *Rev. Mod. Phys.* **35**, 400 (1963), except as noted otherwise.
[b] C. W. F. T. Pistorius and H. C. Snymas, *Z. Physik Chem.* (*Frankfurt*) **43**, 278 (1964).
[c] W. Webb et al., API-Res. Project 42, private communication.
[d] $b_2 \gg 0$.

$\Delta V/V$ by (4.24) so that the Kennedy-Kraut relation becomes

$$T_m(P)/T_m(0) = 1 + C\left[1 - \left(1 + \frac{K_1 P}{K_0}\right)^{1/K_1}\right]$$

where K_0 and K_1 are defined in equation 4.23. Too few data are available to recognize how the disposable parameter C is related to molecular or to crystal structure.

6.7 MELTING POINT AND PHASE TRANSITION OF MIXTURES[1]

Three cases can be distinguished:

1. The components are completely miscible in the liquid but completely immiscible in the solid state.

2. The components are completely miscible in both phases (form mixed crystals).

3. The components are completely miscible in the liquid state and form addition compounds in the solid state. Moreover, there are, of course, sliding transitions between these three groups of possibilities plus the additional variable of limited miscibility in either phase. For the present purpose, guidance regarding the effect of molecular structure, only the basic cases will be considered.

Case 1a. Here the solubility curve

$$-\ln x_1{}^l \gamma_1{}^l = \frac{\Delta S_{m(1)}}{R}\left(\frac{T_{m(1)}}{T} - 1\right) \tag{6.17}$$

[1] For details see Chapters 22 and 23 of Prigogine, I. and R. Defay, *Chemical Thermodynamics*, Wiley, New York, 1962.

leads to the melting curve on the side of component (1)

$$\frac{T}{T_{m(1)}} = \frac{\Delta S_{m(1)}}{R} \left(\frac{\Delta S_{m(1)}}{R} - \ln x_1^l \gamma_1^l \right)^{-1} \qquad (6.18)$$

(where γ_1^l is the activity coefficient in the liquid phase), and the corresponding equation for component (2). Then the steepness of the gradient dT/dx at the origin is immediately seen to depend on the absolute magnitude of $\Delta S_m/R$, such that at $x_1 \rightarrow 1$

$$\frac{\partial^2 T}{\partial x_1^2} < 0 \quad \text{if} \quad \frac{\Delta S_{m(1)}}{R} > 2,$$

and

$$\frac{\partial^2 T}{\partial x_1^2} > 0 \quad \text{if} \quad \frac{\Delta S_{m(1)}}{R} < 2.$$

The eutectic temperature T_e is estimated by simultaneous solution of the equations

$$-\ln (1 - x_2)_e = \frac{\Delta S_{m(1)}}{R} \left(\frac{T_{m(1)}}{T_e} - 1 \right),$$

$$-\ln (x_2)_e = \frac{\Delta S_{m(2)}}{R} \left(\frac{T_{m(2)}}{T_e} - 1 \right). \qquad (6.19)$$

Less stable crystals, that is, those with lower melting temperatures than predicted by (6.15) to (6.19), are obtained when the two mixture components are members of the same family of strongly polar compounds, but of different chain length. In that case, as was first demonstrated by Oldham and Ubbelohde [68], there is a tendency to form mixed crystals, but the formation of strong dipole sheet in the crystal would lead to the presence of holes in the lattice where molecules of somewhat different length enter the crystal lattice side by side. Preliminary indications are that keto-groups are sufficiently strong dipoles to induce this effect, whereas ester groups are too weak. A systematic study of different types of dipole on the incidence of this effect has yet to be performed.

Case 1b. Two special cases of considerable technological significance are the effects of plasticizers and of comonomers on the melting point of polymer crystals. Plasticizers might not be useful in highly crystalline polymers because of their separation at $T \leq T_m$. However, in semicrystalline polymers they may dissolve in and change the properties of the amorphous regions. Their effect on the melting point of the crystalline domain can be estimated according to Flory [37] through the relation

$$\frac{T_m^\circ}{T_m} - 1 = \frac{R}{\Delta S_{m(u)}} \left[\frac{V_{(u)}}{V_1} \right] (\varphi_1 - \chi_1 \varphi_1^2), \qquad (6.20)$$

where T_m^0, T_m are the melting temperatures of pure and diluted polymer, respectively, $\Delta S_m^{(u)}$ is the entropy of fusion per repeating unit (see Section 6.2.6), $V(u)$, V_1 are the molal volumes per repeat unit and of diluent, φ_1 is the volume fraction of diluent and χ is the diluent-polymer interaction parameter.[1] A special case of plasticizer is the end group, leading to the following effect of polymer molecular weight on T_m:

$$\frac{T_m^{\infty}}{T_m} - 1 = \frac{R}{\Delta S_m(u)\bar{x}}\left(1 + \frac{1}{z}\right), \tag{6.21}$$

where $T_m^{\infty} = T_m$ at $M \to \infty$, and $\bar{x}$ is the number average degree of polymerization of the polymer sample; z is a factor correcting for the excess concentration of molecule ends in the coexisting liquid phase ($z \approx 2$ to 5) [37]. The resulting proportionality $T_m^{-1} \sim M^{-1}$ has been verified for many series of oligomers. The random copolymer case yields to a first approximation [37]

$$\frac{T_m^{(2)}}{T_m^{(1)}} - 1 = \frac{R}{\Delta S_m(u^1)} \ln x_1 \tag{6.22}$$

where x_1 is the mole fraction of comonomer 1 in the mixture. Equation 6.20 is not applicable if the comonomers are of very similar molecular geometry so that solid solution ensues, or if the copolymerization is not random. Special treatises [37] should be consulted for details.

Case 2. Mixed molecular crystals form when the molecules of the mixture component are of very similar geometry and cohesive energy density. Typical examples are n-alkanes or n-alkanoate esters differing by less than five carbon atoms per molecule [23], and mixtures of compounds forming "plastic crystals," as well as binary crystals of aromatic hydrocarbons with heteroaromatics discussed by Kitaigorodskii [25], [28].

The liquidus and solidus curves are defined by the thermodynamic relations

$$x_2 = \frac{\gamma_1^l \gamma_2^s \exp(\lambda_1) - \gamma_2^s \gamma_1^s}{\gamma_1^l \gamma_2^s \exp(\lambda_1) - \gamma_2^l \gamma_1^s \exp(-\lambda_2)}$$

$$x_2^s = \frac{\gamma_1^l \gamma_2^l \exp(\lambda_1) - \gamma_2^l \gamma_1^s}{\gamma_1^l \gamma_2^s \exp(\lambda_1 + \lambda_2) - \gamma_2^l \gamma_1^s}, \tag{6.23}$$

which for ideal solutions in both phases reduce to

$$x_2^l = \frac{\exp(\lambda_1) - 1}{\exp(\lambda_1) - \exp(-\lambda_2)} \quad \text{and} \quad x_2^s = \frac{\exp(\lambda_1) - 1}{\exp(\lambda_1 + \lambda_2) - 1}, \tag{6.24}$$

where

$$\lambda_i = \frac{\Delta S_{m(i)}}{R}\left(\frac{T_{m(i)}}{T} - 1\right);$$

[1] See collection by Sheehan C. J., and A. L. Bisio, *Rubber Chem. Tech.* **39**, 150 (1966).

the $\gamma_i{}^s$ and $\gamma_i{}^l$ are the activity coefficients of the components i in the solid and liquid phase, and $x_2{}^l$ and $x_2{}^s$ are the mole fractions of component 2 along the liquidus and solidus curves, respectively.

The location of solid–solid phase transition temperatures in mixed molecular crystals (at least one component of which exhibits such transition) generally follows eutectoid shape curves with a smoothed minimum. Since almost always $\Delta S_{tr}/R \gg 2$, the gradients dT_{tr}/dx_1 are not very steep at the origin. The number of variables affecting the detailed appearance of phase diagrams of mixed molecular crystals is sufficiently great to make most of what has been said in this section useful as guideline rather than as source of precise prediction.

Case 3. The prediction of molecular compound formation from molecular structure is the subject of a specialized monograph [5] and new types are discovered with increasing frequency. However, a maximum in the T_m versus x diagram can also result if the mixed crystal is more stable than that of either component. Pairs of molecules possessing complementary structures, that fit very closely into a crystal lattice, tend to form such specially stable lattice. Typical examples are racemic mixtures of optical isomers, symmetrical dichloro- + symmetrical tetrachlorohydrocarbons [65] and the somewhat unexpected case cetyl caprate–lauryl myristate [13]. Making the reasonable assumption that the liquid phase is an ideal solution and that the complex is 1:1, the freezing-point curve of such systems is given by

$$\frac{\Delta H_d}{R}\left(\frac{1}{T} - \frac{1}{T_{mc}}\right) = -\ln x_2{}^l(1 - x_2{}^l) + \ln 0.25$$

or

$$\frac{1}{T} = -\frac{R}{\Delta H_d}\ln x_2{}^l(1 - x_2{}^l) + \text{const},$$

where ΔH_d is the heat of fusion = heat of dissociation of the addition compound, and T_{mc} is its melting point. Because at present neither ΔH_d nor T_{mc} can be predicted from molecular structure data, this relation is more useful for interpolation than for predictive purposes.

TENTATIVE CALCULATING PROCEDURE

A truly reliable calculating procedure has to include prediction of the existence and location of solid–solid phase transitions. The ability to do so has eluded us to date. The proposed method of estimating the entropy and heat of fusion therefore includes an estimate of the error that might result if we ignore the occurrence of such phase transitions.

The Heat of Fusion, ΔH_m

In the following procedures the melting point T_m is assumed to be known, so that the prediction of ΔH_m is reduced to the far simpler problem of estimating the entropy of

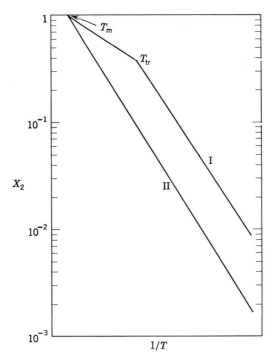

Figure 6.7   Schematic illustration of the effect of disregarding solid/solid phase transitions on solubility calculations [12]. I, correct solubility curve; II, solubility curve calculated without regard for the phase transition at T_{tr}.

fusion, ΔS_m. In order to avoid any confusion of units, the entropy of fusion is given throughout in dimensionless units as $\Delta S_m/R$. Moreover, because of its greater ease of correlation with molecular structure, only the sum of the entropies of fusion and all first-order solid–solid transitions, $\Sigma \, \Delta S_{m,tr}/R$ has been presented.

Errors resulting from the ignorance of first-order solid–solid phase transitions are serious only in two cases: for the heat balance of a crystallization plant that operates at T such that $T_m > T > T_{tr}$; and when ΔH_m is used for the calculation of solubility. Here ignorance of T_{tr} and of the associated subdivision of the total enthalpy change into ΔH_m and the various ΔH_{tr} can lead to a serious underestimate of solubility, as illustrated schematically in Figure 6.7.

The existence of a solid–solid, first-order phase-transition point can be suspected when the melting point of a substance is substantially higher than of most related compounds and when it is either spherically symmetrical or is a completely straight chain compound. In those cases we can guess that the important first-order transition point is at about the temperature when we expect the melting point to be in comparison with members of that particular series of compounds. (Comparison of first-order transition points with melting point of neighboring members within the C_6, C_7, or C_8 series of isoalkanes in the API-44 tables [3] is quite instructive in this respect.)

In the case of globular molecules an approximate breakdown of $\Sigma \, \Delta S_{m,tr}$ is $\Delta S_m \approx R$ and $\Delta S_{tr} \approx \Sigma \, \Delta S_{m,tr} - R$. With long-chain compounds $\Delta S_m \approx \frac{1}{2}\Sigma \, \Delta S_{m,tr}$.

ESTIMATION OF $\Delta H_m + \Delta H_{tr}$

Rigid Molecules

Procedure 6.1

STEP 1: Look up $\Sigma \Delta S_{m,tr}$ for compounds with equal geometry in Table 6.6, 6.8, 6.9, and 6.10 or in the tables of Refs. [3] and [27]. If the compound does not contain the polar group enumerated on Table 6.23, continue with Step 3.

STEP 2: If the molecule contains the polar groups enumerated in Table 6.23, add the increment δ indicated on the table to the $\Sigma \Delta S_{m,tr}/R$ of its hydrocarbon homomorph. For polyols $\Sigma \Delta S_{m,tr}/R$ must be estimated with consideration of the formation of intramolecular hydrogen bonds, as shown in Table 6.19 and as discussed in the text on pp. 166–168.

STEP 3: Now $\Delta H_m + \Sigma \Delta H_{tr} \approx RT_m \Sigma \Delta S_{m,tr}/R$. If we have no reason to suspect the presence of a first-order solid–solid phase transition, $\Sigma \Delta H_{tr} = 0$. If such a transition is expected, we might proceed to guess T_{tr} and the separation of $\Sigma \Delta S_{m,tr}$ into its component part, as mentioned in the introduction to this section.

Procedure 6.2

(Approximate a priori estimate of ΔS_m and ΔH_m for crystals composed of rigid polyatomic molecules.)

STEP 1: If not available from the literature, calculate the moments of inertia of the molecule.

STEP 2: Calculate the rotational entropy contribution

$$S_r = R \ln \left[\pi^{\frac{1}{2}} \left(\frac{T}{39.6} \right)^{\frac{3}{2}} 10^{60} (I_1 \cdot I_2 \cdot I_3)^{\frac{1}{2}} / \sigma \right].$$

STEP 3: Obtain the lattice vibration frequencies due to rotational motions (torsional oscillations) from Section 3.3.

STEP 4: Estimate the harmonic-oscillator contributions to entropy, for the vibration frequencies of Step 3. These can be obtained from tables of Einstein functions for harmonic oscillators. The sum of the three contributions is S_{tor}.

STEP 5: Now $\Sigma S_{m,tr} = R + S_r - S_{tor}$.

STEP 6: $\Delta H_m + \Sigma \Delta H_{tr} \approx T_m \Sigma \Delta S_{m,tr}$, etc. as in Step 3 of Procedure 6.1.

Procedure 6.3

STEP 1: If the substance belongs to any of the homologous series enumerated in Table 6.11, use the equations of that table to estimate $\Sigma \Delta S_{m,tr}/R$. Should the substance belong to a different homologous series, estimate $\Sigma \Delta S_{m,tr}/R$ for the second or third member of the series by a route for rigid molecules (Procedure 6.1 or 6.2 above); then add 1.2 for each additional methylene group.

STEP 2: Then $\Delta H_m + \Sigma \Delta H_{tr} \approx RT_m \Sigma \Delta S_{m,tr}/R$, etc., as in Step 3 of Procedure 6.1 above.

Flexible Molecules $M > 1000$ (High Polymers)

Procedure 6.4

Here the object is the heat of fusion per repeating unit, generally designated as ΔH_m.

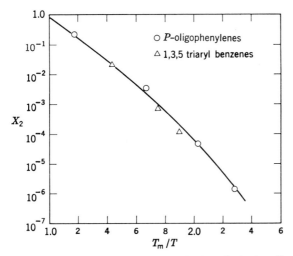

Figure 6.8   Solubility x_2 of p-oligophenylenes and 1,3,5-tripolyphenylbenzenes. From data by H. O. Wirth and W. Kern and E. Schmidt, *Makromol. Chem.* **68,** 69 (1963).

STEP 1: Obtain increments of ΔS_m from Table 6.12. If the required increments are not on that table, a valid estimate of ΔS_m cannot be made at present. A very crude estimate is $\Delta S_m \approx 0.7$ to $1.2R$ per chemical bond in the repeating unit [31].

STEP 2: $\Delta H_m = T_m \, \Delta S_m$.

Procedure 6.5

Estimate. ΔS_m and ΔH_m from solubility determinations.

Available information. Melting point (T_m) and solubility (x_2) in an ideal solvent [judged by the cohesive energy density criterium] at temperature T.

STEP 1: At levels of T_m/T that make

$$[C_p(l) - C_p(s)]\left[\left(\frac{T_m}{T}-\right) - \ln\frac{T_m}{T}\right] \ll \Delta S_m(T_m/T - 1)$$

(which means generally at $T_m/T < 1.5$), one obtains from the solubility in an ideal solution

$$\frac{\Delta S_m}{R} = -\ln x_2 \left(\frac{T_m}{T}-1\right)^{-1}.$$

At $T_m/T > 1.5$, we must use the entire expression

$$\frac{\Delta S_m}{R} = -\left[\ln x_2 + \frac{\Delta C_p}{R}\right]\left(\frac{T_m}{T}-1\right)^{-1} + \frac{\Delta C_p}{R},$$

where $\Delta C_p = C_p(s) - C_p(l)$ is obtained from the calculation in Section 6.4.

STEP 2: $\Delta H_m = T_m \, \Delta S_m$.

STEP 3: For qualitative comparisons of ΔS_m of different compounds (especially those composed of rigid molecules) it is often sufficient to just plot $\ln x_2$ in ideal solvents versus T_m/T for the compounds in question. A typical example is the series of p-oligophenylenes and 1,3,5-triarylbenzene plotted in Figure 6.8, where each point represents the room temperature solubility of a different member of the series. The close proximity of all points to a single curve indicates that the mutual interference of the three rings in the 1,3,5-position does not increase the well-known rigidity of poly-phenylene systems.

REFERENCES

[1] Allen, G., et al., *Polymer* **1**, 456, 467 (1960).
[2] Al-Mahdi, A. A., and A. R. Ubbelohde, *Proc. Roy. Soc. (London)* **A220**, 143 (1953).
[3] Andrews, J. N., and A. R. Ubbelohde, *Proc. Roy. Soc. (London)* **A228**, 435 (1955).
[4] American Petroleum Institute, Research Project 44, "Physical Properties of Selected Hydrocarbons."
[5] Andrews, L. J. and Keefer, *Molecular Complexes in Organic Chemistry*, Holden-Day, New York, 1964.
[6] Aranow, R. H., et al., *J. Phys. Chem.* **62**, 812 (1958).
[7] Aston, J. G., in *Physics and Chemistry of the Organic Solid State*, Wiley, New York, 1963, Vol. 1, p. 571.
[8] Blinc, R., et al., *J. Chem. Phys.* **43**, 3417 (1965); **45**, 1488 (1966).
[9] Babb, S. E., Jr., *J. Chem. Phys.* **38**, 2743 (1963).
[10] Bondi, A., *J. Phys. Chem.* **58**, 929 (1954).
[11] Bondi, A., and D. J. Simkin, *AIChE J* **3**, 473 (1957).
[12] Bondi, A., *Chem. Rev.* **67**, (October 1967).
[13] Bondi, A., and L. B. Scott, *Nature* 167, 485 (1951).
[14] Bradley, R. S., *High Pressure Physics and Chemistry*, Academic, New York, 1963, Chap. 5.3.
[15] Burwell, R. L., and C. H. Langford, *J. Am. Chem. Soc.* **81**, 3799 (1959).
[15a] Chihara, H., and T. Shinoda, *Bull. Chem. Soc. Japan* **37**, 125 (1964).
[16] Clusius, K., and K. Weigand, *Z. physik. Chem.* **46B**, 1 (1940).
[17] Danusso, F., et al., *Chim. Ind.* **41**, 748 (1959).
[18] Dixon, J. A., et al., American Petroleum Institute, Research Project 42, report for period 1 July 1961 to 31 December 1961.
[19] Gilvarry, J. J., *Phys. Rev.* **102**, 325 (1956).
[20] Hamann, S. C., *Physico-Chemical Effects of Pressure*, Academic, New York, 1957, p. 223.
[21] Hirschfelder, J. O., D. P. Stevenson, and H. Eyring, *J. Chem. Phys.* **5**, 896 (1937).
[22] Hood, G. C., *J. Am. Chem. Soc.* **75**, 6315 (1953).
[23] Kieras, J. A., et al., Division of Petroleum Chemistry, ACS Preprints **9**, 257 (1964), where reference to earlier work can be found.
[24] Huffman, H. M., et al., *J. Phys. Chem.* **65**, 495 (1961).
[25] Kirshenbaum, I., *J. Polymer Sci.* **3A**, 1869 (1965).
[26] Kitaigorodskii, A. I., *Organic Chemical Crystallography* (Consultants Bureau, New York, 1961).
[27] Klemm, W. Z., *Elektrochem.* **34**, 526 (1928).
[28] Kostrynkov, V. N., et al., *J. Phys. Chem. USSR* **32**, 1354 (1958).
[28a] Kraut, E. A., and G. C. Kennedy, *Phys. Rev.* **151**, 668 (1966).
[29] Kravchenko, V. M., and I. S. Pastakhova, *Ukr. Khim. Zh.* **19**, 610 (1953).
[30] Laubengayer, A. W., and W. F. Gilliam, *J. Am. Chem. Soc.* **63**, 477 (1941).
[31] Landolt-Börnstein, *Zahlenwerte and Funktionen* I/4, *Kristalle* Springer, Berlin, 1955.

[32] Landolt-Börnstein, *Zahlenwerte and Funktionen*, Springer, Berlin, 1961, Vol. II/4, *Kalorische Zustandsgrössen.*

[33] Lennard-Jones, J. E., and A. F. Devonshire, *Proc. Roy. Soc. (London)* **170**, 464 (1939).

[34] Longuet-Higgins, H. C., and B. Widom, *Mol. Phys.* **8**, 549 (1964).

[35] Lüttringhaus, A., and G. Vierk, *Ber.* **82**, 376 (1949).

[36] Mackle, H., et al., *Trans. Faraday Soc.* **57**, 1058 (1961), and personal communication.

[37] Mandelkern, L., *Rubber Chem. Techn.* **32**, 1392 (1959).

[38] Mandelkern, L., *Crystallisation of Polymers*, McGraw-Hill, New York, 1964.

[39] Maslov, Y. P., *Russ. J. Phys. Chem.* **35**, 478 (1961).

[40] Mendel, H., et al., Koninklijke/Shell Laboratorium Amsterdam, private communication.

[41] Miller, R. L., and L. E. Nielsen, *J. Polymer Sci.* **55**, 643 (1961).

[42] Mizushima, S., *J. Phys. Soc. Japan* **15**, 70 (1960).

[43] Nelson, R. R., et al., *J. Chem. Phys.* **33**, 1756 (1960).

[44] Nitta, Isamu, *Z. Krist.* **112**, 234 (1959).

[45] Ohlberg, S. M., *J. Phys. Chem.* **63**, 248 (1959).

[46] Oriani, R. A., *J. Chem. Phys.* **19**, 93 (1951).

[47] Pace, E. L., and J. S. Mossen, *J. Chem. Phys.* **39**, 154 (1963).

[48] Palko, A. A., et al., *J. Phys. Chem.* **62**, 319 (1958).

[49] Pankov, I., et al., *Proc. Acad. Sci. USSR, Phys. Chem. Section* **126**, 417 (Transl.) (1959).

[50] Pimentel, G. C., and A. L. McLellan, *The Hydrogen Bond*, Freeman, San Francisco, 1960.

[51] Pirsch, J., *Ber.* **70**, 12 (1937); *Mikrochim. Acta* **1956**, 992.

[52] Ranby, B. G., et al., *J. Polymer Sci.* **44**, 369 (1960); **58**, 545 (1962).

[53] Reid, R. C., and T. K. Sherwood, *Properties of Gases and Liquids*, McGraw Hill, New York, 1958, 1966.

[54] Rotariu, G. J., et al., *J. Phys. Chem.* **59**, 187 (1955).

[55] Rozental, D., *Bull. Soc. Chim. Belg.* **45**, 609 (1936).

[56] Sackmann, H., and F. Sauerwald, *Z. Physik Chem.* **A195**, 295 (1950).

[57] Sackmann, H., *Z. Physik Chem.* **208**, 235 (1958).

[58] Saupe, A., private communication.

[59] Schaerer, A. A., et al., *J. Am. Chem. Soc.* **77**, 609 (1956).

[60] Schinke, H., and F. Sauerwald, *Z. Physik Chem.* **216**, 23 (1961).

[61] Schulz, A. R., *J. Chem. Phys.* **51**, 530 (1954).

[62] Smith, A. E., *J. Chem. Phys.* **21**, 2229 (1953).

[63] Staveley, L. A. K., et al., *J. Chem. Soc.* **1954**, 1992.

[64] Stull, D. R., et al., *Pure and Appl. Chem.* **2**, 315 (1961).

[65] Timmermans, J., "*Les solutions concentreés*," Paris, 1936.

[66] Timmermans, J., *Physicochemical Constants of Pure Organic Compounds*, Elsevier, Houston, 1951.

[67] Trappeniers, N., *Changement de phase* Herman et Cie., Paris, 1952, p. 241.

[68] Ubbelohde, A. R., *Quart. Rev.* **4**, 356 (1950); *Adv. Chem. Phys.* **6**, 459 (1964).

[69] Ubbelohde, A. R., *Melting and Crystal Structure*, Oxford University Press, London, 1965.

[70] Von Stackelberg, M., et al., *Z. Elektrochem.* **64**, 381, 386 (1960).

[71] Weinstock, B., *J. Phys. Chem. Solids* **18**, 86 (1961).

[72] Westrum, E. F., and J. P. McCullough, in *Physics and Chemistry of the Organic Solid State*, Wiley, New York, 1965, Vol. I.

[73] Zeldovich, Y. B., *Doklady Akad. Nauk SSSR* **139**, 841 (1961).

[74] Zwikker, C., *Physical Properties of Solid Materials*, Pergamon, London, 1954.

NOMENCLATURE

A_w	surface area per mole of molecules (see Technical Report 140-59)
c	(number of external degrees of freedom per molecule)/3
$C_p(\text{c})$	heat capacity of crystalline solid at constant pressure
$C_v(\text{c})$	heat capacity of crystalline solid at constant volume
$C_p(\text{liq})$	heat capacity of liquid at constant pressure
$C_v(\text{liq})$	heat capacity of liquid at constant volume
E	internal energy (of liquid or solid)
ΔE_v	energy of vaporization
$E°$	standard energy of vaporization (defined in [7] and [8])
ΔH_m	heat of fusion
ΔH_s	heat of sublimation
I_i	moment of inertia of molecule around axis i
K_0	bulk modulus at $P = 0$
K_1	pressure coefficient of bulk modulus
N_c	number of carbon atoms per molecule
N_s	number of skeletal atoms per molecule
R	gas constant
S_r	rotational contribution to entropy (of ideal gas)
S_tor	contribution of torsional oscillations in crystal lattice to entropy of solid
ΔS_m	entropy of fusion
ΔS_tr	entropy of transition
$\Sigma \, \Delta S_\text{m, tr}$	$\Delta S_\text{m} + \Delta S_\text{tr}(1) + \Delta S_\text{tr}(2) + \cdots$
ΔS_m	contribution of volume increase to entropy of fusion
T	absolute temperature
T^*	$5cRT/E° =$ reduced temperature
T_m	melting point
T_m^*	$5cRT_\text{m}/E° =$ reduced melting point
T_tr	temperature of solid–solid transition
V	molal volume
V_w	van der Waals volume per mole (see [10] and [11])
V^*	$V/V_w =$ reduced volume
ΔV_m	molal volume expansion at the melting point
ΔV_m^*	$\Delta V_\text{m}/V_w$
α	cubic thermal expansion coefficient
α_s	cubic thermal expansion coefficient of solid
β	cubic isothermal compressibility
ρ	density
ρ^*	$V_w/V =$ reduced density
$\rho^*(\text{m})$	ρ^* at $T = T_\text{m}$

7

Liquids

In the following sections the physical properties of liquids are described in two broad subgroups: equilibrium properties and transport properties. The equilibrium properties are related to each other by the Maxwell equations of thermodynamics, a fact which serves as a check on the internal consistency of the correlations used. However, the absolute magnitude of the properties can only be obtained from experiment or from a molecular theory, or, in lieu of the latter, from a correlation with molecular structure.

Molecular theories of the physical properties of liquids are far less well established than are those for the corresponding properties of crystalline solids. Nevertheless one finds it rather easier to correlate the physical properties of liquids among each other and with molecular structure than proved to be the case with solids. One reason for this difference is the far greater effort that has been spent on the technologically more important liquids. Another is the ability of the mobile molecules in the liquid state to acquire the highest packing density consistent with the ratio of their kinetic to their potential energy. The substantial absence of steric restriction to close packing removes what proved to be one of the major stumbling blocks to the predictability of the properties of molecular crystals.

A detailed discussion of the theoretical bases for the correlation of the physical properties will soon be found in standard textbooks of physical chemistry. Here only those aspects that are important for an understanding of the point of view adopted are mentioned. For monatomic or similarly simple liquids the Lennard-Jones and Devonshire (LJD) theory with various minor modifications and the Green–Born (GB) molecular theory form the reference background of most modern treatments. Their achievement, especially that of the LJD theory, is the possibility of describing the properties of simple liquids—at least to a zeroth approximation—with molecular parameters derived from observations on crystals or gases, or even from theory. The simple liquids the properties of which are adequately described by these theories (and by the conventional corresponding states principle that can be derived from them) are the major subject of the book by Reid and Sherwood [14]. Here we are concerned primarily with liquids composed of molecules that are too large to be well represented by theories for monatomic liquids.

Before coming to the approach adopted here a reason should be given for the absence of any reference to two important recent theoretical developments: the hard-sphere theory of liquids by Reiss, Frisch, and Lebowitz (RFL) [15] and the significant-structure theory of liquids by Eyring and co-workers [13]. The RFL theory and the correlations of this section both emphasize the packing density as the primary variable determining all other properties of a liquid. Aside from various theoretical shortcomings that severely limit all hard-sphere theories, the RFL theory suffers the serious practical drawback that the reference volume itself exhibits a thermal expansion which is not predictable a priori and the magnitude of which is shown (on pp. 253–256) to be physically meaningless. The significant-structure theory contains one basically unpredictable disposable parameter and one practically unpredictable parameter,[1] so that it is difficult, if not impossible, to construct a more general correlation on the basis of it.

Because most of the larger molecules of interest in the present context can be thought of as composed of several segments, Prigogine's theory of polymeric liquids [12] has been used as the basis of the proposed treatment. However, neither the original theory nor its recent successors, the theories by Simha and co-workers [16], [17] and that by Flory et al. (FV) [4] have been found sufficiently accurate for actual calculations. Even the very carefully developed FV theory exhibits one of the shortcomings of the RFL theory (although to lesser degree)—the thermal expansion of the reference volume, from which the effective packing density is derived. Although substantially smaller than the thermal expansion of the RFL reference volume, it is still far too large to make any physical sense (Section 8.7). Hence in the treatment adopted here theoretical calculations are generally replaced by semiempirical correlations of dimensionless groups suggested by Prigogine's theory.

The order of presentation follows the logic of the parameter requirements for the correlations. First come the vapor pressure and the heat of vaporization. Although rather good relations of the latter to molecular structure have been constructed, only very crude methods could be found to predict either boiling points (at a fixed vapor pressure) or vapor pressures at a fixed temperature.

---

[1] $\Delta V_{m}/V_{s}$ which has been shown in Section 6.1 to be experimentally difficult to determine, as well as quite unpredictable.

The next two items, critical temperature and pressure, are directly related to the energy of vaporization. The interconversion requires an additional parameter, the number of excited external degrees of freedom per molecule (including those due to internal rotation), which is experimentally derivable from the density of the liquid phase, the subject that follows immediately. The closely connected thermal expansion coefficient and bulk modulus make the transition to heat capacity in which their product with temperature, the internal pressure, is an important component of the correlation with molecular structure.

The transport properties lack rigorous relations to equilibrium properties and among each other, with the help of which we can check the internal consistency of proposed correlations. Even though the thermal conductivity even of large molecules appears to be reasonably well correlated with the same molecular properties which determine the equilibrium properties, and is in fact directly relatable to density, the correlation of viscosity and diffusion with molecular structure is in a very unsatisfactory state. The offered treatment is at best a zeroth approximation. Modern transport theoreticians would probably say that a way out of this dilemma will be found only once we have learned to define a "forgetting time" or "forgetting-time distribution" of molecules clearly and to relate it to intramolecular forces, intramolecular mobility, and so on. In the meantime the makeshift correlations of the section on transport properties will have to serve.

7.1 CRITICAL VOLUME, TEMPERATURE, AND PRESSURE

These three constants have long been used as reference properties of liquids, and molecular theory of liquids has shown that they are indeed simple functions of intermolecular force and molecule size [8], [9], [14], at least for small spherical molecules. Experimental determination of T_c, p_c, v_c is inconvenient and frequently impossible. Hence it has long been desirable to express these three properties in terms of more easily determined physical properties, or even replace them altogether. As the main concern of this book is with high-boiling compounds for which the critical temperature is often experimentally inaccessible, the latter course has been adopted, and only enough will be said about the critical properties to permit contact between the long-established property correlations and the newer ones emphasized here.

The *critical volume* of liquids is discussed in Section 8.1.6. The *critical temperature* of liquids composed of small rigid molecules is a direct measure of the intermolecular attractive forces as has been borne out by the uniformity of the ratio kT_c/ϵ in Table 2.1. The internal rotations or oscillations of large flexible molecules contribute to their total kinetic energy which is therefore larger than kT by a factor c, proportional to molecular flexibility (see

Table 7.1 Reduced Critical Temperature

$(T_c^* = 5cRT_c/E°$ for Several Series of Substances[a])

	$N_c = 3$	4	5	6	7	8	9	10	12
n-Alkanes T^*:	1.455	1.42	1.39	1.37	1.355	1.352	1.352	1.356	1.304
i-Alkanes[b]	2m4	2,2m$_2$3	2,4m$_2$5	3e5	2m7	3m7	3e6	3,3m$_2$6	2,2,4m$_3$5
T_c^*:	1.37	1.45	1.36	1.25	1.34	1.30	1.27	1.28	1.335
Cycloalkanes[b] T_c^*:		Cyclopentane 1.365		Methylcyclo C$_5$ 1.38		Cyclohexane 1.31		Methylcyclo C$_6$ 1.30	
Aromatics[c]	φH	φm	1,2m$_2$φ	1,3,5m$_3$φ	φ$_2$	nH	1,mn	2,mn	
T_c^*:	1.29	1.29		1.20	1.18[d]	1.10[e]	1,23[d]	1.25[d]	
Nitrogen compounds	m$_3$N	e$_3$N	pyridine	m-CN	e-CN	φ-CN	m-NO$_2$		
T_c^*:	1.243	1.238	1.240	1.315	1.345	1.253	1.145		
Oxygen compounds	m$_2$O	e$_2$O	φ0m	φ$_2$O	m-OH	e-OH	nprOH	iprOH	n-bu-OH
$T_c^{*\,f}$:	(1.29)	1.29	1.28	1.28	1.38	1.205	1.205	1.202	1.163
Oxygen compounds	m$_2$CO	meCO	m-formate	eOAc					
T_c^*:	1.19	1.21	1.17	1.22					
Halides	mI	1,2eCl$_2$	eBr	nC$_7$F$_{16}$[b]			φ-Cl	φ Br	φI
T_c^*:	1.38	1.27	1.41	1.10			1.31	(1.27)	(1.31)

[a] Data from K. A. Kobe and E. R. Lynn, *Chem. Rev.* **52**, 121 (1953) except when otherwise noted.
[b] Nomenclature: m = methyl, e = ethyl, 2m4 = 2-methylbutane, c5 = cyclopentane, d = *trans* decahydronapthhalene, n = normal.
[c] Nomenclature: φ = phenyl, n = naphthyl.
[d] F. Glaser and H. Rüland, *Chem. Ing. Tech.* **29**, 772 (1957).
[e] D. I. Juravlev, *J. Phys. Chem. USSR* **9**, 875 (1937).
[f] The reducing parameter for the alcohols is $θ_L$ obtained from density measurements of the liquid.

Section 8.1.2). The pair potential ϵ can be evaluated only for small spherical molecules. For large molecules of irregular shape, the average attractive force is most conveniently expressed by the suitably standardized energy of vaporization E° (see Section 15.4.1). Thus we obtain a reduced critical temperature $T^* = ZcRT_c/E^\circ$. As a matter of convenience we took $Z = 10$, so that $T^* \equiv 5cRT_c/E^\circ$. For liquids composed of small rigid molecules, this reduced temperature turns out to be numerically equal to kT_c/ϵ as is apparent

Table 7.2 Reduced Critical Pressures
$[P_c^*(g) = 5V_wP_c/E^\circ$ and $P_c^*(l) = 5V_w(P_c + P_i)/E^\circ$ of various substances[a]]

Substance:	n-Heptane	Benzene	Ethyl Ether	Carbon Tetrachloride
$10^2P_c^*(g)$:	2.70	3.35	2.85	3.35
$10^2P_c^*(l)$	22.5	26.3	21.5	15.5

Substance:	Propane	n-Pentane	n-Octane	n-Hexadecane
$10^2P_c^*(g)$	3.56	3.19	2.44	1.52

Substance:	2,4m$_2$5	2,2m$_2$5	3m3 e · 5	2,3,4m$_3$5	2,2,4m$_3$5
$10^2P_c^*(g)$:	2.89	3.02	3.28	3.17	2.86

Substance:	Cyclopentane	Me-Cyclo C$_5$	Cyclohexane	Me-Cyclo C$_6$
$10^2P_c^*(g)$:	3.8	3.50	3.75	3.44

Substance:	Propene	Propyne	Toluene	Naphthalene
$10^2P_c^*(g)$:	3.59	3.32	3.1	3.49

Substance:	Methyl Formate	Methyl Acetate	n-Propyl Formate	n-Propyl Acetate
$10^2P_c^*(g)$:	3.40	3.19	3.08	2.71

[a] The data for the first line of substances are from [15] and for the balance of substances from the API-44 tables and from K. A. Kobe and R. E. Lynn, *Chem. Rev.* **52**, 121 (1953).

from the common incidence of $T^* \approx 1.3$ in Table 7.1. On the whole, T_c^* is sufficiently uniform to permit an estimate of T_c from E° and c using the correlation equations in Table 14.1. Other more carefully worked out methods to estimate T_c from molecular structure information have been evaluated by Reid and Sherwood [14].

The critical pressure P_c, if treated like the pressure of a gas, is reduced as $P_c^*(g) \equiv 5P_cV_w/E^\circ$. But, if treated like a liquid, the reduced critical pressure should be $P_c^*(l) \equiv 5V_w(P_c + P_i(T_c))/E^\circ$. The data in Table 7.2 show that neither of these two forms of reduced critical pressure is a constant. The variability of these data is too large to be entirely due to experimental difficulties (which are real enough). There may well be a system in the irregularities that—once discovered—should permit an estimate of P_c from P_c^*, preferably from $P_c^*(g)$, because $P_i(T_c)$ is not a commonly available datum. Empirical methods to estimate P_c from molecular structure data can be found in [14].

As mentioned earlier (Section 1.2), molecular anisotropy or anisotropic force fields between molecules must be corrected for when we use the critical constants, or their equivalents in the form of $E°$, V_w and $3c$, in the estimation of liquid properties. Pitzer's acentric factor ω or the closely related Riedel constant α_c, described earlier (Section 2.3 and 2.4) have been designed for this correcting function. It should be noted that $3c$ performs a similar function in the case of long-chain compounds, but not at all for rigid aromatic hydrocarbons, for all of which $3c = 6 \pm 0.5$. The correlation of ω and α_c with molecular structure through the radius of gyration has been mentioned in Section 2.1. When independent information on $E°$, or $H_0°$ and T_c is available, ω (or α_c) can be derived from the relations

$$\omega = \frac{0.0675 H_0°}{RT_c} - 0.419, \tag{7.1}$$

$$\alpha_c = \frac{0.332 H_0°}{RT_c} + 3.75, \tag{7.2}$$

as had first been suggested by Riedel.

7.2 THE HEAT OF VAPORIZATION

The energy of vaporization is the most direct measure of the cohesion of liquids, for which it plays the same role as the lattice energy does for the solid. Three "standard" forms of this magnitude are in common use: $H_0°$, the heat of vaporization extrapolated to $0°K$, $\Delta H_v°$, the heat of vaporization at $25°C$, a convenient standard for thermochemical calculations, and $E°$, the standard energy of vaporization, defined as $\Delta H_v - RT$ at that temperature at which $V/V_w = 1.70$ (see Chapter 14). Only $H_0°$ and $E°$ are at corresponding states. Hence only these two have any hope of simple additivity from molecular structure increments. As a rule $E°$ can be obtained directly from calorimetric or from vapor-pressure data, whereas the numerical value of $H_0°$ depends somewhat on the vapor pressure equation, because

$$H_0° = (F° - H_0°)(\text{liq}) - (F° - H_0°)(\text{g}) - RT \ln p, \tag{7.3}$$

where p is in atmospheres. Appropriate gas imperfection corrections (see below) have to be applied if $p > 0.5$ atm. As sufficient calorimetric information is rarely available, $H_0°$ as used here is that calculated from the Frost–Kalkwarf equation (7.10) using vapor-pressure data between 10 and 2000 torr. A comparison with $H_0°$ calculated from calorimetric and spectroscopic data, in Table 7.3 shows reasonable agreement. Molecular structure increments for $H_0°$ and $E°$ can be found in Tables 14.1 to 14.16.

Just as in the case of ΔH_s, the functional group increments can also be estimated, at least to a rough approximation, from dispersion energy and dipole orientation energy, with intermolecular distances derived from V_w and liquid density. In the absence of any experimental vapor pressure data $E°(X)$ or $H_0°(X)$ could be estimated from $E_L(X)$ and $E_D(X)$, assuming the $E°(R)$ or $H_0°(R)$ are always available from experimental data.

Table 7.3   Comparison of ΔH with ΔH_v at $0°K$[a]

Substance	$\Delta H_0°$ (kcal/mole)	ΔH_v at $0°K$[b] (kcal/mole)
Propane	6.60	6.40
n-Hexane	11.11	10.40
n-Heptane	12.62	12.13

[a] From [3].
[b] Estimated from calorimetric and spectro-scopic data.

The exact value of ΔH_v at any temperature T is

$$\Delta H_v(T) = H_0° - \int_0^T [(C_p(l) - C_p(g)]\, dT - \int_v^\infty \left[p - T\left(\frac{\partial p}{\partial T}\right)_v \right]. \quad (7.4)$$

while $\Delta C_p(\text{lg})$ in the second term on the right is readily available from correlations (see pp. 277–279), the vapor imperfection correction in the third term is estimated easily only when T_c and p_c are also known. However, in that case it is simpler to use the Watson equation for $\Delta H_v(T)$ [14]:

$$\Delta H_v(T) = H_0°(1 - T_R)^{0.38}. \quad (7.5)$$

Specific effects of molecular structure on ΔH_v, not covered by the correlations given so far, are of two kinds. Those due to hydrogen bonding in the liquid state and those due to vapor-phase association (especially dimerization). The effect of hydrogen bonding in the liquid state on ΔH_v differs from that of other functional groups by its peculiar dependence on absolute temperature. Most conveniently we write for hydrogen-bonding liquids:

$$\Delta H_v(T) = E_L(T_R) + \delta_v(X)_T, \quad (7.6)$$

where E_L, the dispersion energy term, is approximated as

$$E_L \approx \Delta H_v^h = \text{heat of vaporization} \quad (7.7)$$

of the hydrocarbon homomorph at the same reduced temperature T_R as the hydrogen-bonding substance. The hydrocarbon homomorph of a compound is that hydrocarbon in which OH or NH groups are simulated by a methyl group. Ethane is thus the homomorph of methanol, or toluene that of phenol.

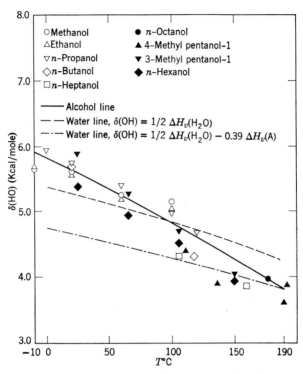

Figure 7.1 Hydrogen-bond increments δ(OH) of primary aliphatic alcohols and water [2].

Table 7.4 Hydrogen Bond Increments $\delta_v(OH)$ (in kcal/mole) of the Heat of Vaporization of Lower Primary n-Aliphatic Alcohols [2]

Alcohol/$t.°C$	0	30	60	90	120	150
Methyl	5.5	5.35	5.2	4.9	4.5	3.85
Ethyl	5.6	5.45	5.2	4.8	4.4	3.85
Propyl	5.9	5.6	5.2	4.9	4.3	3.3

Table 7.5 Hydrogen Bond and Strong Dipole Increments [2]

Functional Group	Increment, δ_v at 100°C (kcal/mole)	$-d\delta_v/dT$ (cal/mole°K)	Number of Compounds Investigated
—OH (aliphatic)	4.6 ± 0.2	10	>10
—NH$_2$ (aliphatic)	1.6 ± 0.2	4.5	5
—NH (aliphatic)	~0	—	3
—C≡N (aliphatic)	2.1 ± 0.4	7.0	10
—NH$_2$ (aromatic)	2.6 ± 0.2	—	3
—C=O (aliphatic) $\overset{\mid}{H}$	1.4 ± 0.2	2.9	9

Table 7.6 Shielding Effects in Aliphatic Alcohols [2]

Group	Compound	$t(°C)$	$\delta(\Delta H_v)$ (kcal/mole)	Δ^a (kcal/mole)
A-1 Secondary alcohols	n-butanol-2 n-hexanol-2 n-octanol-2 n-octanol-4	110 140	3.1–4.0 3.3–3.9	1.0 ± 0.5 0.5 ± 0.3
A-2 Tertiary alcohols	t-butanol 2-methyl pentanol-2 2-methyl heptanol-2	25 70 150	4.3 3.4–4.0 2.1–3.2	1.4 1.4 ± 0.3 1.3 ± 0.5
A-3 "Locked" propyl interaction	3-methyl heptanol-3 2,2 dimethyl butanol-3 2-methyl heptanol-3 3-methyl pentanol-2 2-methyl pentanol-3	25 60 150	4.3–4.7 3.7–4.2 2.2–3.0	1.2 ± 0.2 1.3 ± 0.3 1.4 ± 0.4
B Propyl interaction	n-hexanol-3 n-octanol-3 2-methyl heptanol-5 2-methyl heptanol-1 3-methyl heptanol-2 3-methyl heptanol-4 3-methyl heptanol-5 4-methyl heptanol-3	25 60 150	1.2–2.2 1.1–2.1 1.2–1.9	4.0 ± 0.5 3.6 ± 0.5 2.4 ± 0.3

$^a \Delta = \delta_v(OH)(R - OH - 1) - \delta_v(OH)(R\text{–}OH, \text{isomer})$

Table 7.7 Shielding Effects in Phenols [2]

Compound	T_b, (°C)	ΔH_v, (kcal/mole)	Homomorph	ΔH_v^*, (kcal/mole)	$\delta\Delta H_v$	Decrease in $\delta(OH)$
Phenol	181.7	10.95	Toluene	8.00	2.95	0
o-Cresol	191.0	10.72	o-Xylene	8.80	1.92	1
m-Cresol	202.2	11.32	m-Xylene	8.71	2.61	~0.3
p-Cresol	201.9	11.34	p-Xylene	8.62	2.72	~0.2
2,3-Xylenol	218.0	11.33	Hemimellitene	9.57	1.76	~1.2
3,4-Xylenol	225.0	12.33	Pseudocumene	9.38	2.95	0

Typical values of $\delta_v(OH)$ and $\delta_v(NH)$ are presented as Figure 7.1 and Tables 7.4, 7.5 and 7.6. Special attention should be paid to the effects of temperature and of the steric effects enumerated in Table 7.7. Note that $\delta_v(X)$ is a measure of, but not identical with, hydrogen-bond strength.

When vapor-phase association occurs the calculation of ΔH_v is somewhat more complicated, and can be carried out with any degree of reliability only if independent data on the vapor-phase equilibria and the saturation vapor pressure are available. The appropriate procedure can be found in a series of papers by Gray [7].

7.2.1 Mixture Rules for ΔH_{v}

The mixture rule for the heat of vaporization of liquids is simply

$$\Delta H_{\mathrm{v}} = \sum X_i \, \Delta H_{\mathrm{v}}(i) + \Delta H_{ij}, \tag{7.8}$$

where ΔH_{ij}, the heat of mixing of components i and j, can be estimated from the increasing volume of such data [10], [21]. The group-increment system of Pierotti et al. [11] should be particularly well suited for estimating the heat of mixing of liquids, so that desired data can be derived from systems differing quite widely from that under consideration; excluding, of course, those where specific interactions such as molecular compound or even salt formation have to be expected.

7.3 VAPOR PRESSURE

In principle it is possible to calculate the vapor pressure of a liquid from thermodynamic information alone, just as described in the case of the crystalline solid in Section 3.6; namely,

$$-\ln P_{\mathrm{v}} = \frac{H_0^\circ}{RT} + \left[\frac{(F^\circ - H_0^\circ)(\mathrm{g})}{RT} - \frac{(F^\circ - H_0^\circ)(\mathrm{liq})}{RT} \right] + \frac{B}{v} + \cdots, \tag{7.9}$$

where all constants have their usual meaning. However, this equation can be used only infrequently because experimental data for $(F^\circ - H_0^\circ)(\mathrm{liq})$ are, as a rule, available when the vapor pressure is known anyway, and the prediction of $(F^\circ - H_0^\circ)(\mathrm{liq})$ from molecular structure data is still in a rudimentary state.

The simplest equation for the correlation of vapor pressures with a sound physical basis is the Frost–Kalkwarf [6] equation

$$\ln P_{\mathrm{v}} = A - \frac{H_0^\circ}{RT} - \frac{\Delta \bar{C}_p}{R} \ln T - \frac{aP}{(RT)^2}, \tag{7.10}$$

where the first term contains the rarely known $S_{(\mathrm{liq})}$:

$$-A = \frac{1}{R} [S_{(\mathrm{liq})} - S_{(\mathrm{g})}^\circ - \Delta \bar{C}_p (1 + \ln T)], \tag{7.11}$$

and must therefore be determined by experiment or by correlation. This means that A can be dispensed with if a single vapor-pressure point, for example, the normal boiling point (T_b) is known. Empirical rules for the

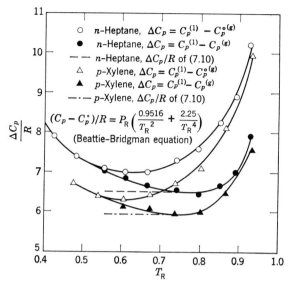

Figure 7.2 $\Delta \bar{C}_p$ as function of temperature [3].

estimation of T_b from molecular structure information have been assembled in a review by Somayajulu et al. [18].

As mentioned earlier, H_0° can be estimated from group increments some of which have been listed in Chapter 14 but most of which have yet to be created from mutually consistent sets of vapor-pressure data, preferably covering a range of 10 to 1500 torr and meeting the quality requirements of the API data collection. If calorimetric heat of vaporization measurements are available, ΔH_0° can be obtained by extrapolation, using the average $\Delta \bar{C}_p$ discussed in the next paragraph, keeping in mind that the H_0° of the vapor-pressure equation is generally close to but not identical with the "true" value of H_0°.

The average heat-capacity difference $(\Delta \bar{C}_p)$ between liquid and vapor occurring in (7.12) cannot be identical with the calorimetric ΔC_p, because the ΔC_p of liquids composed of larger polyatomic molecules is not a constant, as implied by an "average," but varies widely with temperature as shown by the data in Figure 7.2. The $\Delta \bar{C}_p$ of the vapor-pressure equation is, however directly relatable to the "true" average over the temperature range of the vapor-pressure measurement. Moreover, once $\Delta \bar{C}_p$ of the parent compound of a series has been established, the deviations $\delta \Delta C_p$ due to structural modification of that parent molecule are virtually identical with the corresponding $\delta \Delta C_p$, as is illustrated in Table 7.8 for the case of hydrocarbon isomers.

Table 7.8 Effect of Chain Branching on $\Delta \bar{C}_p$

Compound	$\delta(\Delta \bar{C}_p/R)^a$	$\delta(\Delta C_p^\circ/R)^b$
2-Methylhexane	0.26	0.24
3-Ethylpentane	0.39	0.64
2,4-Dimethylpentane	0.28	0.09
3,3-Dimethylpentane	0.66	0.64
2,2,3-Trimethylbutane	0.42	0.40
2,2,4-Trimethylpentane	0.39	0.78[c]

[a] $\Delta \bar{C}_p$ from vapor-pressure data by means of Frost–Kalkwarf equation from [3].

[b] $\Delta C_p^\circ = C_p(l) - C_p^\circ(g)$ at 298°K from calorimetric data, mostly API-Research Project 44, Tables $[C_p^\circ(g)]$ and Landolt-Börnstein, "Zahlenwerte und Funktionen", *Kalorische Zustandsgrössen*, Springer, Berlin, 1961, Vol. II/4.

[c] From somewhat older calorimetric data.

The detailed discussion of the heat capacity of liquids in Chapter 9 will show the dominating effect of $E°$(or H_0°) on ΔC_p. In the present context it suffices that in a given series of compounds $\Delta \bar{C}_p$ can be well approximated as a linear function of H_0°. Typical examples have been assembled in Table 7.9 Although worked out only for hydrocarbons, the same form of relation should also hold for other molecular liquids.

The fourth term, as given, is of the same order of approximation as the second term in a virial expansion in an equation of state. In conventional reduced variables $(D_R = aP_c/(RT_c)^2)$ has the universal value $27/64 = 0.4218$.

Although adequate for the representation of most vapor-pressure data of nonassociating compounds between T_b and T_c, the vapor imperfection correction term can be refined to any desired degree through use of other

Table 7.9 A Method of Estimating Constant C^a [3]

General relation: $C - \sigma = (0.411)(10^{-3} \Delta H_0^\circ)$

For *n*-paraffins and for *iso*-paraffins with unbranched chain of more than four carbon atoms $\sigma = 1.32$

For *iso*-paraffins with two or more side chains one of which is in the 3-position $\sigma = 0.75$.

For alkylcyclohexanes $\sigma = 0.36$

For mono- and dialkylbenzenes (excluding toluene) $\sigma = 0.27$

For tri- and tetraalkylbenzenes $\sigma = 0$

For alkylnaphthalenes (quite uncertain) $C = (0.65)(10^{-3} \Delta H_0^\circ - 5.20)$

[a] $C \equiv \Delta \bar{C}_p/R$.

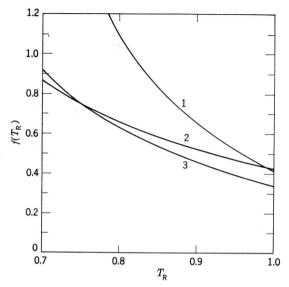

Figure 7.3 Temperature function of the fourth term of (7.10) [3]: 1. Pitzer's function with $\omega = 1$, 2. D_R/T_R^2, $D_R = 0.4218$, 3. Pitzer's function with $\omega = 0$.

equations of state. The effects of such refinement on the magnitude of the fourth term are shown in Figure 7.3. It is seen that the deviations between the simple form given in (7.12) and the more refined correction are large where they matter least, namely at low pressures. The refinements have only a small effect at elevated temperatures.

Once the T_c and p_c of a substance are known or can be estimated (as by methods on pp. 199–201), constant A in (7.10) is determined, and we operate most conveniently with the reduced form of the equation:

$$\ln P_R = A_R - \frac{B_R}{T_R} - \frac{\Delta \bar{C}_p}{R} \ln T_R - \frac{27}{64} \frac{P_R}{T_R^2} \qquad (7.12)$$

where $A_R = B_R - 27/64$, $B_R = H_0^\circ/RT_c$.

Absence of measurements or suitable correlations for T_c is usually indicative of the fact that the substance is chemically stable only in the low vapor-pressure region. The vapor imperfection correction can then be neglected, and (7.10) takes the Rankine form

$$\ln P_v = A - \frac{H_0^\circ}{RT} - \frac{\Delta \bar{C}_p}{R} \ln T, \qquad (7.13)$$

and

$$\ln P_v = \frac{H_0^\circ}{R}\left(\frac{1}{T_x} - \frac{1}{T}\right) - \frac{\Delta \bar{C}_p}{R} \ln (T_x/T) + \ln P_x \qquad (7.14)$$

if A is given in terms of some vapor pressure (P_x) or boiling point (T_x) correlation.

7.3.1 Effects of Molecular Structure

Specific effects of molecular structure on H_0°, ΔC_p, and D beyond those contained in the correlations discussed so far can be found on three levels:

1. Those associated with large molecular anisometry, leading to large and temperature-dependent $\Delta C_p(l, g)$ and by large acentric factors ω also large numerical values of a.

2. Those due to hydrogen bonding in the liquid state, but little if any vapor-phase association.

3. Those due to association in vapor as well as in liquid phase.

Case 1, the *effect of large molecule size*, is manipulated quite easily by the introduction of a temperature-dependent ΔC_p, such as $\Delta C_p = a - b/T$ and the use of an acentric factor correction for the vapor imperfection term, which yields

$$\ln p_V = A - \frac{H_0^\circ}{RT} - \left(a - \frac{b}{T}\right)\ln T$$

$$- P_R\left[\frac{0.1445 + 0.073\omega}{T_R} - \frac{0.330 - 0.46\omega}{T_R{}^2} - \frac{0.1384 + 0.05\omega}{T_R{}^3}\right]. \quad (7.15)$$

The vapor imperfection correction [9] will rarely be important, for few high-molecular-weight substances are stable at temperatures corresponding to $p_V > 0.5$ atm.

Case 2, *hydrogen bonding in the liquid state*, requires a superposition of the hydrogen-bonding equilibrium on the vapor-pressure equation, for most of the vapor pressure will, in general, be exerted by the monomeric components of the system. The most complicated system involving vapor-phase association as well as liquid-phase association is fortunately represented mostly by lower molecular-weight acids and alcohols for which excellent experimental vapor-pressure data are available. With higher molecular-weight acids, bases, and alcohols, vapor-phase association is unimportant, whereas liquid-phase association is so strong that the partial pressure of monomer becomes important only at high temperatures. The requisite equilibrium constants (obtained spectroscopically) will soon be available [19], [20]. Correction for its vapor-pressure contribution will then be straightforward.

CALCULATING PROCEDURES

Procedure 7.1

    Desired Datum. Heat of vaporization $[\Delta H_v(T)]$ of nonassociating compounds.
    Available Information. Molecular structure.

STEP 1: Estimate H_0° by summing H_0° increments of Table 14.1; if none are available, go to Procedure 7.2.
STEP 2: Estimate $\Delta \bar{C}_p$ from H_0° by means of the correlation on Table 7.10.
STEP 3a: If the expected $p_V \le 0.5$ atm, $\Delta H_V(T) = H_0^\circ - \Delta C_p T$.
STEP 3b: If the expected $p_V > 0.5$ atm, estimate T_c by the correlation (15.17) using the Δ_T increments on Tables 14.1, and calculate $T_R = T/T_c$. Then $\Delta H_V(T) = H_0^\circ (1 - T_R)^{0.38}$.

Procedure 7.2

Desired Datum and Available Information. As for Procedure 7.1.
STEP 1: Estimate E° by summing E° increments of 14.1.
STEP 2: Estimate 3c by means of (15.11) or the homologous series equations on Table 14.1. Then $\theta_L = E^\circ/5cR$.
STEP 3: The standardization temperature of E° is $T(1.7) = 0.53\theta_L \,^\circ K$. The reduced desired temperature is $T^* = T/\theta_L$.
STEP 4: If the molecule is rigid, obtain ΔC_p from Figure 9.15 as the average between $T^* = 0.53$ and $T^* = T/\theta_L$. If the molecule is flexible, calculate first ρ^* at T/θ_L from Procedure 8.2, then take average ΔC_p between ρ^* and $\rho^* = 0.588$ from Figure 9.16.
STEP 5: $\Delta H_V(T) = E^\circ + RT(1.7) - \Delta \bar{C}_p[T - T(1.7)]$. (Valid only if $p_V \le 0.5$ atm or at most 1 atm.)

Procedure 7.3

Desired Datum. Heat of vaporization $\Delta H_V(T)$ of nonassociating compounds.
Available Information. Molecular structure and density.
STEP 1: Step 1 of Procedure 7.2.
STEP 2: Estimate M; Estimate V_w by summing V_w increments of Tables 14.1 and 14.2.
STEP 3: Estimate θ_L by Procedure 15.31.
STEP 4 to end: Steps 3 to 5 of Procedure 7.2.
Recommended procedure for estimating the vapor pressure of liquid of various temperatures:

Procedure 7.4

Given. Nonassociating liquid, molecular structure. No physical property is given.
STEP 1: Estimate H_0° by method 15.9.
STEP 2: Estimate $\Delta \bar{C}_p$ by Procedure 9.3 (through Step 5).
STEP 3: Estimate a vapor-pressure point, such as the atmospheric boiling point (T_b) or some other standard point by means of a molecular structure correlation [18] or for high-boiling substances, a relation of the type shown in Table 7.10.
STEP 4: If no molecular structure correlations are available for T_b, an effort should be made to create a correlation on the basis of data for related compounds, since any alternative method to obtain an anchor point for the vapor-pressure curve is likely to be more cumbersome and less reliable.
STEP 5: If the vapor pressure p_V is desired for $T < 0.9T_b$,

$$\ln p_V(T) = \ln p_V(T_b) - \frac{H_0^\circ}{R}\left(\frac{1}{T} - \frac{1}{T_b}\right) - \frac{\Delta \bar{C}_p}{R} \ln\left(\frac{T}{T_b}\right).$$

Table 7.10   Boiling Points (T_x) of Hydrocarbons with 10 to 35 Carbon Atoms per Molecule at 1 torr

---

General correlation: $T_x = 464 \log N_c - \theta$

For normal paraffins: $\theta = 181°K$

For naphthene rings (fused and nonfused, except highly strained ring systems, such as 10,10′ perhydrobianthryl): $\theta = 168°K$

For phenyl and naphthyl rings: $\theta = 142°K$

For phenanthryl and anthryl rings: $\theta = 132°K$

For monoalkyl aromatics: $\theta = 181 - a^3(181 - \theta_a)$, where a = fraction of carbon atoms in aromatic rings, $\theta_a = \theta$ of appropriate aromatics ring type. Generally valid relations for alkylnaphthenes cannot be formulated. In most cases the naphthene effect is prevailing and a relation of the form $\theta = 181 - 13n^{1/2}$ may give some guidance, when n = (fraction of carbon atoms in naphthene rings)

For nonfused naphtheno aromatics: $\theta = 168 - a^3(168 - \theta_a)$

For fused naphtheno aromatics: $\theta = 168 - a^3(168 - \theta_a)$, where θ_a refers to the total ring system, for example, for octahydrophenanthrene, $\theta_a = 132°K$

STEP 6: If $T > 0.9T_b$, estimate T_C and p_C by the methods of Tables 14.1, 15.1 and 7.2 Thus

$$\ln p_R = A_R - \frac{H_0^\circ}{RT} - \frac{\Delta \bar{C}_p}{R} \ln T - \frac{0.4218 p_R}{T_R},$$

where $A_R = H_0^\circ / RT_C - 0.4218$. Because this is an implicit equation it must be solved by trial and error, and is therefore preferably handled on a computer. However, graphical approximation by drawing a straight line of $\ln p_R$ versus T_R^{-1} between the two estimated points for $p_R = 1$ at $T_R = 1$ and $p_R(T_b)$, as T_C/T_b permits a sufficiently close guess to reduce the number of trials to two, or three at the most. The desired vapor pressure then is $p_V = P_R P_C$.

Procedure 7.5

Given. Nonassociating liquid, molecular structure is given and one vapor pressure point. Follow Steps 1, 2, 5, or 6 of Procedure 7.4.

REFERENCES

[1] Black, C., *Ind, Eng. Chem.* **50,** 391 (1958).

[2] Bondi, A., and D. J. Simkin, *AIChE J* **3,** 473 (1957); **4,** 493 (1958).

[3] Bondi, A., and R. B. McConaughy, *Proc. Am. Petr. Inst.* **42,** (III), 40 (1962).

[4] Flory, P. J., et al., *J. Am. Chem. Soc.* **86,** 3507 (1964).

[5] Frisch, H. L., *Adv. Chem. Phys.* **6,** 229 (1964).

[6] Frost, A. A., and D. R. Kalkwarf, *J. Chem. Phys.* **21,** 264 (1953).

[7] Gray, P., *Proc. Roy. Soc.* (*London*) **A264,** 516 (1961); *J. Chem. Soc.* **1963,** 1796, 1807.

[8] Hirschfelder, J. O., R. B. Bird, and C. F. Curtiss, *Molecular Theory of Gases and Liquids*, Wiley, New York, 1954.

[9] Lewis, G. N., and M. Randall, *Thermodynamics*, revised by K. S. Pitzer and Leo Brewer, McGraw-Hill, New York, 1961, 2nd ed.

[10] Lundberg, G. W., *J. Chem. Eng. Data.* **9,** 193 (1964).

[11] Pierotti, G. J., et al., *J. Am. Chem. Soc.* **81,** 2233 (1959); *Ind. Eng. Chem.* **51,** 95 (1959).

[12] Prigogine, I., *The Molecular Theory of Solutions*, Interscience, New York, 1957.

[13] Ree, T. S., T. Ree, and H. Eyring, *Proc. Natl. Acad. Sci.* **48,** 501 (1962).

[14] Reid, R. C., and T. K. Sherwood, *Properties of Gases and Liquids*, McGraw-Hill, New York, 1966, 2nd ed.

[15] Rowlinson, J. S., *Liquids and Liquid Mixtures*, Academic Press, New York, 1959.

[16] Simha, R., and S. T. Hadden, *J. Chem. Phys.* **25,** 702 (1956).

[17] Simha, R., and A. T. Havlik, *J. Am. Chem. Soc.* **86,** 197 (1964).

[18] Somayajulu, G. R., et al., *Ann. Rev. Chem.* **16,** 213 (1965).

[19] Stevenson, D. P., *J. Phys. Chem.* **69,** 2145 (1965).

[20] Stevenson, D. P., private communication.

[21] Van Ness, H. C., *Classical Thermodynamics of Non-electrolyte Solutions*, Pergamon, New York, 1964.

GENERAL READING

"The Structure and Properties of Liquids," *Discussions Faraday Soc.*, No. 43 (1967). See [12] and [15].

8

p-v-T Properties of the Liquid

The purpose of this chapter is the establishment of rational relations between density and molecular structure from two points of view: that of the chemical engineer, namely, to estimate the density–temperature (and possibly pressure) curve(s) from no more information than molecular structure; and that of the chemist, namely, to learn something about internal characteristics, especially internal flexibility of the molecule under consideration, from observed density data.

One of the handicaps for the development of acceptable correlations of the density of liquids has been the very high accuracy (± 2 parts per 10,000) with which this property can be determined in a comparatively simple experiment. Few general correlations can have that kind of accuracy, and the present one is no exception. Another difficulty has been the fact that it is very much easier to determine the density at, or near, room temperature and atmospheric pressure than under any other condition.

Since few substances are at truly comparable (corresponding) conditions at constant absolute temperature, any correlation of such density data must remain completely empirical and therefore of limited utility, especially for obtaining information on molecular characteristics from the data.

The scope of the present effort is set by the desire to produce as general a correlation as is compatible with reasonable accuracy. "Tolerable" accuracy is perhaps ± 2 parts per 1000. This is at the same time at or beyond the maximum accuracy of the auxiliary information required, the nonbonded contact radii, the so-called van der Waals radii of the atoms involved.

The highest degree of structure specificity as well as of experimental precision is usually obtained in the temperature range between the melting point and the atmospheric boiling point. This temperature range is therefore the main object of the present section. In the temperature range between the atmospheric boiling point and the critical temperature the liquid is so expanded that there is little specificity, and the conventional corresponding-states correlations represent the usually only moderately accurate data quite well. In the present context only the upper end of that temperature range is treated, namely, the density at T_c and P_c (the critical density ρ_c).

Lastly, the relations of the expansion coefficient and of the bulk modulus (and of their temperature and pressure dependence) to molecular structure are examined. The resulting overview of the p-v-T relations of liquids in terms of chemical structure effects should convey an understanding for the interrelations of the thermodynamic properties of liquids.

The scope in the coverage of chemical composition is determined by two factors: the specific interests of the writer and the inherent limitations of the

Table 8.1   Comparison of Density ($\rho_4{}^t$) and Packing Density
ρ^* Molecular   Liquids

Substance	V_w (cm^3/mole)	ρ_4^{20a} (g/cm^3)	ρ_4^{*20}	$\dfrac{293}{T_b}$
n-Heptane	78.45	0.685	0.537	0.79
Benzene	48.36	0.879$_5$	0.544	0.83
Tetramethyl tin	72.66	1.314	0.557	0.84
Methyl iodide	32.85	2.279	0.527	0.93
Methylene iodide	48.59	3.325	0.604	0.65

[a] Handbook data.

simple correlation scheme which forms the basis of this work. They are restricted to liquids which require neither quantum corrections nor the consideration of association equilibria. Hence hydrogen-bonding substances and loosely bonded coordination compounds are outside the scope of this work, but the nature of the deviations from normalcy caused by them is described.

8.1   GENERAL PRINCIPLES AND SEMIEMPIRICAL CORRELATION SCHEME FOR DENSITY

A physical understanding of the density of condensed phases is acquired most easily if one expresses it as packing density $\rho^* = \rho V_w/M$, where V_w is the van der Waals volume, calculated from bond distances and van der Waals radii, and M is the molal weight. This procedure brings the density of all liquids into a common magnitude range. Most of the large density differences associated with heavy atoms are thus accounted for. Typical examples are given in Table 8.1.

An a priori range of packing densities of liquids can be given only for spherical molecules. Here the highest possible density at low temperature and atmospheric pressure is the "random close packing" with $\rho^* = 0.64$ [3], [45]. The lower limit might be defined as that obtained in random packing with a coordination number $Z = 3$, since a condensed system with less than three contacts per spherical molecule can hardly be conceived. No calculation has been carried out for this case. Various regular packings yield $\rho^* = 0.2$ to 0.3(3) [32], [51]. This density should correspond to $\rho_c^* = V_w/V_c$, that at critical temperature (T_c) and pressure. However, x-ray diffraction data of argon at the cited temperature and pressure yield $Z = 4$[27]. The upper and

Table 8.2   Calculated Packing Density at Low Coordination
Numbers

System	Z	ρ^* (calc)	Ref.
Regular packing of spheres	4	0.3401	51
Regular packing of spheres	4	0.1235	51
Irregular packing of spheres	3	0.2234	51
Various regular packing of spheres	3	0.056 to 0.172	51
Regular packing of ellipsoids:			*a*
"Cubic," axial ratio $p = 1$	8	0.555	
$p = 3$	8	0.149	
$p = 6$	8	0.042	
"Hexagonal" $p = 1$	6	0.370	
$p = 3$	6	0.070	
$p = 6$	6	0.0185	
Loosest stable $p = 1$	4	0.1235	
$p = 3$	4	0.0181	
$p = 6$	4	0.00467	

[a] R. Kohn, *Kolloid-Z.* **174**, 50, 59 (1961).

lower ends of packing densities of anisometric particles are available only for regular (crystalline) arrays—see Table 8.2—and are therefore of use only for qualitative guidance. In the limit of long cylinders the maximum value of $\rho^* = 0.903$ and the minimum value of $\rho_c^* \sim 0.2/p$, where p is the length/diameter ratio, if we assume that this density corresponds to that just permitting free tumbling rotation of the anisometric molecules.

The generalized plot of ρ^* versus T/T_c would cover the range between these limits conveniently. An example of such a graph is shown in Figure 8.1. The close proximity of the curves to each other permits rough estimate of ρ^* when T_c is known. Substances with appreciable zero point amplitude Λ^* exhibit far lower than average density. Otherwise no systematic deviations are observed.

A basic limitation of that kind of correlation is its dependence on the availability of T_c data. For most liquids T_c is unknown, and although for

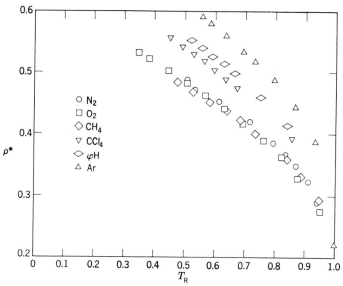

Figure 8.1 Packing density of liquid and gases as a function of T_R. Coincidence of Ar curve with CH_4, N_2, O_2 curve required reduction of r_0 (Ar) by 0.93; conversely, the other radii have to be raised by 1.08 to coincide with Ar.

several organic liquids T_c can be estimated from correlations, for most substances, especially those of higher molecular weight, it is not a meaningful property. Hence another temperature scale has to be adopted, most desirably one that can be related to molecular properties. In connection with the development of a theory of the properties of systems composed of polymeric compounds Prigogine [39] proposed a temperature scale $T^* = ckT/q\epsilon$, where $3c$ is the number of external degrees of freedom per molecule, including those due to to internal rotation, and ϵ is the pair potential between centers of small rigid molecules or between centers of the repeating units of larger flexible molecules. q is defined by $qZ = xZ - Zx + 2$, where x is the number of chain links per molecule, and Z is the number of nearest neighbors per molecule including—in the case of polymeric molecules—the two repeating units on either side of the one under consideration. The pair potential ϵ can be expressed in terms of a "lattice energy" $E° = \frac{1}{2}N_A qZ\epsilon f(V^*)$. Hence, if we define $E°$ as the energy of vaporization for a standard state for which $f(V^*) = 1$, which appears to be the case for $V^* = 1.70$, we have as reduced temperature scale, $cZRT/2E°$. The number Z is in principle obtainable from x-ray diffraction data of liquids. In the two cases for which data are available we find that Z covers a narrow range of values and is a slowly, and nearly universally, varying function of T/T_c. It would be neither practical nor useful to include such a temperature function into the reduced temperature scale, especially if it is essentially universal in character. A convenient starting device is to set $Z = 10$, the value it has for several liquids in the range between T_m and T_b. Only the constant c remains to be considered. For rigid nonlinear polyatomic molecules, $3c = 6$. For completely flexible chain molecules, $3c = 2x + 1$. In the range between these two extremes, c cannot be predicted a priori and must be considered as an empirical (shift) factor. As such it is, however, a quantitative measure of the flexibility of molecules with equal Z. Deviations from the assumed value $Z = 10$ affect only the absolute magnitude of c.

A similar temperature scale has been proposed by Flory et al. [14], [15], but without reference to a lattice model, in which the number of nearest neighbors Z is replaced by the number of contacts s per molecule. This number is proportional to the surface area per molecule A_w and could be set as $s = A_w/A_w(\text{segment})$. Explicit use of s can easily be avoided as follows: Flory's reduced temperature is $\tilde{T} = 2V_0^* c'kT/s\eta$, where V_0, the reference volume (per segment) is the extrapolated liquid volume at $0°K$, $c' = c/x$, x is the number of segments (of volume V_0) per molecule, and $s\eta$ is defined by the intermolecular energy $E° = -xN_A s\eta/2V$, because of the supposition $E° = -(\text{const})/V^m$, where V is the liquid volume per molecule (segment). Since our $E°$ is standardized at $V^* = 1.70$ or at $\tilde{V} = V/V_0 = 1.23$, Flory's generalized temperature in our notation becomes $\tilde{T} = cRT/1.23\, E°$; thus $\tilde{T} = T^*/8.13$.

The simple low-pressure density isobar of Flory's theory,

$$\tilde{\rho} - \tilde{\rho}^{\frac{1}{3}} = \tilde{T} \quad \text{and} \quad \tilde{\rho}^{\frac{1}{3}} = \left[1 + \frac{\alpha T}{3(1 + \alpha T)}\right]^{-1}, \tag{8.1}$$

represents the available density only tolerably well,[1] even if somewhat better than some of the more complicated theories. It shares the difficulty of all hard-core repulsion theories, a variation of the reference volume V_0, and consequently of the reference temperature with temperature. We can always find a "reason" for such variation, but quantitatively these reasons do not stand up.[2] We find that d ln V_0/dT is positive and is of the order of 15 to 30% of the expansion coefficient of the liquid. From the anharmonicity of molecular vibrations one can estimate an effective thermal expansion of the molecule. However, this expansion is only of the order of 5% of the thermal expansion coefficient of the liquid. The Frisch–Reiss–Lebowitz (FRL) hard-sphere theory of liquids [16] yields a reference volume V_0' which decreases with increasing temperature, as did the effective molecular volume in the old kinetic gas theory. Here the "reason" was the increasing interpenetration of

---

[1] Equation 8.1 predicts a larger curvature of the ρ–T curve than is observed experimentally.
[2] See Section 8.7.

the molecules because of their increasing kinetic energy. Rough estimates show that only an insignificant fraction of the change calculated from FRL theory can be accounted for in this manner. We treat the reference volume V_w as temperature invariant and therefore use the theories of Prigogine and of Flory only to define the molecular parameters which should be used in a semi-empirical correlation.

With these general guidelines and the desire to retain an element of continuity between our molecular constants and the frequently used constants ϵ and σ of the Lennard-Jones and Devonshire molecular theory, the present correlation was constructed as follows. The center of many long liquid ranges (T_m to T_b) was found at $V^* = 1.8$, and was chosen as the normalization point for V^*, or its inverse, the packing density ρ^*. The reduced temperature scale was defined by setting θ_L for propane and toluene (the simplest hydrocarbons with long liquid ranges) equal to ϵ/k, as obtained from gas-viscosity measurements. The ρ^*-T^* curves of these two compounds do not coincide, but they cross—at a very oblique angle—at $V^* = 1.8$ and $T^* = 0.652$. The toluene curve turned out to be the locus for the generalized ρ^*-T^* curve of most hydrocarbons above $M \geq 90$ and for most liquids with $M \geq 150$.

The equation of that curve between $0.3 < T^* < 0.9$ is

$$\rho^* = 0.726 - 0.248T^* - 0.019T^{*2} \tag{8.2}$$

and for the range to T_c ($\approx T^* = 1.30$),

$$\ln\left(\frac{\rho^*}{\rho_0^*}\right) = 0.600(1.30 - T^*)^{2/3} - 0.714, \tag{8.3}$$

where $\rho_0^* = 0.726$. Fitting the lower n-paraffins to a generalized curve[1] requires $V_w(CH_3) \geq 1.5 V_w(CH_2)$, whereas x-ray diffraction data of contact radii appear to be compatible only with $V_w(CH_3) = 1.33 V_w(CH_2)$ [4].

The reason for chosing the standardization condition for the energy of vaporization as $V^* = 1.70$ instead of $V^* = 1.80$, the density normalization point, was the desire to have the measured value of ΔE_{vap} in a packing-density range approaching that of practical use of high-molecular-weight substances, and thus at the low end of the liquid range, that is, near T_m for all of the higher n-paraffins. Moreover, with this choice of standard state and the previously announced choice of $Z = 10$, the constant c turned out to have the correct value, 2, for most of the rigid molecules examined. In the light of the wide range of Z covered in x-ray experiments on liquids [27], adjustment of Z to obtain $c = 2$ for rigid molecules, could always be rationalized. So far such adjustment has not been necessary.

The present method allows only for shifts along the temperature coordinate to achieve coincidence with the "general" curve, and the limits of this shift are

---

[1] Prigogine achieved such a general fit by setting $V_w(CH_3) = 2V_w(CH_2)$.

fixed by the requirement that "reasonable" values of c are obtained, since V_w and $E°$ are fixed by independent measurements. The adaptation of Prigogine's theory by Simha and Havlick [45], more definitely restricted to polymers than the present treatment, allows for shifts along both coordinates for coincidence with the theoretical curve, and then obtains the reference volume from the shift along the density coordinate and derives the flexibility measure from a comparison of the shift along the temperature axis with an independent measurement of cohesive energy. A comparison of the information derived from the two methods is given in Table 8.3.

Table 8.3 **Comparison of (Reducing) Parameters of Simha and Havlick [46] with Those of Bondi [6]**

Polymer	$\dfrac{T_0}{\theta_L}$	$\dfrac{N_A v^* s}{n V_w}$	$\dfrac{N_A \epsilon s}{n E°}$	$\dfrac{3c(S + H)}{3c(AB)}$
Polymethylene	7.4	1.54	0.16	1.1
Polytetrafluorethylene	—	1.47	0.16	—
Polystyrene	7.5	0.75	0.81	0.54
Polydimethylsiloxane	8.0	1.0		

In view of the inability of the free-volume theory to represent even the equilibrium properties of liquid rare gases satisfactorily it seems doubtful that Prigogine's theory, which uses the free-volume theory as starting point, should be good enough to yield reliable numerical values for the three disposable constants derived with its help. To the present author it seems preferable to impose the straightjacket of extraneous reference volume and energy parameters and use correlation rather than theory to obtain the single disposable parameter c.

An additional qualification is the tacit assumption of a universal zero-point packing density ($=0.726$) for liquids in the formulation of (8.2) or (8.3). Although this assumption holds for (the extrapolated zero-point packing density of) a surprisingly large number of widely differing liquids, it does not hold universally. Maximum deviation of ± 0.03 have been obtained, but as yet no rationale that would permit prediction of such deviations. More precise prediction of the density of molecular liquids requires therefore more than the knowledge of V_w, $E°$, and c called for in the present approximation.

8.1.1 Structural Specificities at Low Temperatures

One of the advantages of having a generalized correlation is the elimination of all nonspecific interactions. In the present case this means the elimination of molecular geometry to the extent reflected in the "simple" van der Waals volume V_w, and of interaction energy as given by the group additive standard energy of vaporization $E°$. Most specific structural effects are then given by c. However, in some instances only a change in V_w can accomplish fitting of the density curve. Such changes in V_w also affect the magnitude of $E°$ because they change the temperature of the standard state, $V/V_w = 1.70$. They are therefore discussed first.

At this point a basic weakness of the van der Waals volume system should be aired, namely, the assumption that a fixed value of r_w could be associated with a given atom, independent of its chemical environment. The smallness of the electron density at distance r_w from the nucleus makes the comparative constancy of r_w rather surprising. The effect of intramolecular electron density shifts on r_w of light elements has been recognized by examination of crystal x-ray analyses [4]. This appears to be even more pronounced when we deal with electron-deficient compounds, where a "swelling" of all participating atoms, metal, and ligands seems to take place, as shown by the example of $r_w(H)$ in $B_5H_{10} = 1.25$ Å and a similar increase of Cl and Br size in bridge positions. The relation of this apparent weakening of the electron–nucleus interaction to the existing descriptions of electron configuration and energetics of such compounds has yet to be worked out.

Data covering intermolecular interaction effects on the magnitude of r_w are too scanty to permit unequivocal interpretation. In the absence of any evidence to the contrary, only hydrogen-bond formation is considered as a source of intermolecular interaction leading to changes in contact distance.

Intramolecular crowding is a rather more difficult problem. The low electron density appears to permit evasion of crowding pressure by "bulging" of the electron cloud elsewhere around the atom. Escape of volume loss in crowding by bulging should be easiest for monovalent atoms such as the halogens and be progressively more difficult with increasing valence. However, for example, the volume loss of quadrivalent carbon by crowding is bound to be negligible because of the overlap with the other atoms attached to the carbon, as shown for the case of n-paraffins in Figure 8.2.

Hence crowding losses are particularly significant in cycloaliphatic ring systems, where they are a sensitive function of conformation, as shown by the V_w decrements of Table 8.4. With the exception of that for *trans* decalin, these decrements are too large for most derivatives of these ring systems (especially for alkyl derivatives) for which δV_w per ring carbon atom ≈ 0.20 cm³/mole is generally adequate. A detailed study of the peculiar effects of ring conformation has yet to be carried out. Cyclopropane and cyclobutane do not require any correction terms because crowding effects and oversubtraction for carbon atom interpenetration just (accidentally) compensate. This delicate balance ceases when derivatives are formed and a positive volume increment must be expected with derivatives of these, such as spiropentane.

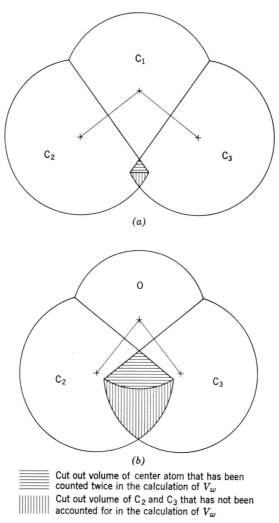

Figure 8.2 Model of _trans chain_—only three skeletal chain atoms are shown: (a) alkyl chain; (b) ether chain.

Adjustment of V_w in order to force a fit to the density curve is not always meaningful, however. A typical case is that of the higher-molecular-weight condensed cyclic naphthenes. Their viscosity data [11] indicate incidence of a glass transition at $T^* \approx 0.3$. The concurrent freezing in of external degrees of freedom begins at $T^* \approx 0.5$ and leads to a progressive increase in the packing density above the generalized curve as T_g is approached (see Section 13.2). This is offered as the tentative explanation for the appearance of the

Table 8.4 Correction Decrements for Cycloparaffins

Cycloparaffins	δ_w[a] (cm³/mole)	δ_w/N_c cm³/C-atom	V_w (cm³/mole)
Cyclopentane	2.0	0.40	49.15
Cyclohexane	2.7	0.45	58.68
Cyclooctane	4.0	0.50	77.8
Cyclodecane	5.3	0.53	97.0
Cyclododecane	3.0	0.25	119.7
trans-Decalin	2.28	0.23	93.12
cis-Decalin	5.0	0.50	90.40

[a] In all cases except *trans*-decalin δ_w is the volume decrement required to make $3c \approx 6$ and fit the density to the generalized curve.

density curve of those compounds, shown in Figure 13.3. It is tentative until high-temperature density data become available. If at $T^* > 0.7$ the ρ^*–T^* data follow the general curve, the explanation will be considered correct; if they fall below the general curve, V_w should be adjusted and a reason found for doing so.

Ether oxygen is so much smaller than the adjacent methylene or phenyl groups that it is "effectively invisible" to other molecules. Its effective diameter is therefore a function of the size of the group to which it is attached. The extent of this effect is shown in Table 8.5. As expected on the basis of its size, no such adjustment is needed for thioether sulfur.

Table 8.5 Van der Waals Volume Increment for Ether Oxygens in Different Compounds (from Fitting of Density Data to ρ^* versus T^* Curve)

Type of Compound	$V_w(>0)$(cm³/mole)
1,4-Dioxane	4.5[a]
Sym-trioxane	3.7
Alkane polyethers	3.7
m-Polyphenylethers	3.2
Alkyl phenylethers	3.0[b]
Polydimethyl siloxans	1.3[c]

[a] Assuming a ring decrement = 1.70 cm³/mole due to crowding of the methylene groups.
[b] From fitting of anisol and phenetol data.
[c] This value obtained by direct calculation from $r_w(0) = 1.50$ Å; the resulting density data fit the ρ^* versus T^* curve without adjustment.

Table 8.6 Effects of Molecular Structure and of Barriers to Internal Rotation (V°) on Molecular Flexibility $(=3c-6)$[a]

Structure Variable	Substance	$3c-6$	V°(kcal/mole)[b] of Linkages
Effect of branch crowding	$n\text{-}C_9H_{20}$	2.1	2.8(8)
	$(C_2H_5)_4\cdot C$	0.3	2.8(4) 4.9(4)
	2,2,4,4-Tetramethylpentane	0.5	4.9(8)
	$n\text{-}C_{14}H_{30}$	4.2	2.8(13)
	2,2,3,3,5,6,6-Heptamethylheptane	0.3	4.9 all
Effect of double bonds	$n\text{-}C_6H_{14}$	0.84	2.8(5)
	n-Hexene-1	0.85	2.8(3) 2.0(1)
	1,5-Hexadiene	1.05	2.8(1) 2.0(2)
	1,3,5-Hexatriene, *cis*	>1.7	1.2(2)
	1,3,5-Hexatriene, *trans*	~1.0	1.2(2)
Rigidity of ring systems	Benzene, naphthalene, etc.	~0	∞
	Cyclopentane, cyclohexane, decalins	~0–0.5	10(1,2)[c]
	Perhydrophenanthrene $(N_c = 14)$	0.5	10(3)[c]
	Perhydrodibenzofluorene $(N_c = 19)$	1.5	10(4)[c]
Mobility of joined rings	Diphenyl, *p*-terphenyl	0.5; 0.9	4.5(1); 4.5(2)
	Dicyclohexyl, 1,3-dicyclohexyl cyclohexane	0.35; 2.1	3.6(1) (3.6(2)[d]
Crowding of rings on alkane axis[d]	1,1- versus 1,2-Diphenylethane	1.0: 1.5	>0(2) 2.8(1); ~0(2) 2.8(1)
	1,1- versus 1,2-didecalylethane	1.2; 2.6	~4 all; 3.5(2) 2.8(1)
	Tricyclopentylmethane	0.95	~5 all
	Tricyclohexylmethane	1.4	~5 all
	Tri(2-cyclohexylethyl)methane	5.1	~3.6(4) 2.8(3)
Effect of monovalent functional groups[e]	1-*n*-Alkyl bromides, iodides	+0.4; +0.9	
	α,ω-Alkane dibromides, iodides	1.3; 1.4	
	1-*n*-Alkyl cyanides	~0	
	α,ω-Alkane dicyanides	~0.3	
	1-*n*-Nitroalkanes	~0	

[a] From density and vapor-pressure data.

[b] The first figure gives V° in kcal/mole and the figure in parentheses is the number of such barriers per molecule.

[c] Cycloparaffins carry out motions which are equivalent to internal rotation. In case of cyclopentane it is called pseudorotation, and in case of cyclohexane and its many derivatives it involves the boat–chain transition for which the barriers are given.

[d] The barriers to rotation around cyclohexyl ring junctions have been taken as equal to those around the diisopropyl bond.

[e] Here the "$3c-6$" column contains the difference $3c$(polar compound) $- 3c$(hydrocarbon homomorph) [$\sim 3c$(hydrocarbon parent molecule) in case of the alkane halides].

8.1.2 Constant c and Molecular Structure

In effect the constant c is the ratio of the standard energy of vaporization of a substance to the temperature at which its packing density has some fixed value. By our convention the fixed value is given as $(\rho^*)^{-1} = 1.80$. Moreover, the assumption is made that the number of nearest neighbors is also a fixed, universal constant. It seems to be impossible to obtain Z and c from density temperature relations only. With this proviso, we shall examine the relation of c, given from here on as $3c$, the number of external degrees of freedom per molecule (including those due to internal rotation) to molecular structure.

8.1.3 Rigid Molecules

The data in Table 8.6 show that for rigid molecules, $3c$ has the expected value 6 ± 0.5. Various structural features make for rigidity. Single and condensed cyclic aromatic rings are rigid, of course. The same is true of single-ring cycloparaffins, and for condensed multiring cycloparaffins up to a certain size. Beyond three condensed naphthene rings, there is apparently enough "breathing" motion in the ring systems to contribute the equivalent of one or more degrees of freedom. Not all ring systems are rigid, however. Internal mobility of the larger cyclophosphazenes appears to be appreciable, in spite of the mounting indications of "aromatic" type delocalization of the π-electrons along the ring skeleton. Suggestive along these lines is the observation that the packing density of the cyclophosphazenes could be fitted to the general curve only when assuming the same dimensions, namely $r_w = 1.77$ Å, as the benzene-ring carbon (or π-electron cloud) dimension, for the P and N atoms of the ring, instead of their accepted van der Waals radii. As is shown later, the siloxane rings also exhibit a great deal of internal mobility. The small rings formed by coordination bonding, such as in

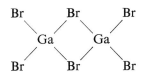

seem to act like rigid systems, although the data are too uncertain at present to exclude addition of one degree of freedom due to low-frequency breathing vibrations.

Another important cause of rigidification shown by the data in Table 8.6 is the close spacing of branches, especially methyl groups along an otherwise flexible saturated carbon–carbon chain. But here the potential energy barrier V° to internal rotation is not infinite, and it is apparent that crowded backbone chains such as in isobutylene polymers with $N_s > 12$ gain one degree of freedom for every five repeat units added to the chain. Chains with

$N_s \leq 12$ are rigid when the number of side branches equals the number of carbon atoms in the chain.

8.1.4   Flexible Molecules

The extreme case of $V° = 0$ makes $3c = 6 + 2n$,[1] if n is the number of chain links per molecule. Among the many substances examined, only polyhenyl ethers approach this condition, if we count $-\varphi-0-$ as one chain link. In all other cases $(3c - 6)/n < 2$, or $(3c - 6)/n < 1$ if there are two rotational isomers, because $V° > 0$, or more importantly because $V°/RT > 0$. Quantitative relations between $(3c - 6)/n$ and $V°/RT$ have not yet been formulated. The expected trend is shown in Figure 8.3. Its comparatively flat slope beyond $RT/V° > 0.2$ is a very important feature that makes it possible to assign a reasonably constant value to c over a wide temperature range. The $(3c - 6)/n$ data used in constructing Figure 8.3 are nearly all from molecules with $N_c > 10$, because small molecules often act as if they were rigid, even when they are composed of flexibly jointed segments, as is apparent from the curves of Figure 8.4. The reason for this behavior is probably that the barrier to external rotation has to be larger than $V°$ before flexibility will be reflected in physical properties, such as density. From electric dipole-relaxation measurements we find that the barrier to external rotation is of the order $0.2E_{ij}°$, where E_{ij} refers to the standard energy of vaporization of molecule i out of solvent j (for pure liquid, $i = j$). An algebraic representation of the molecular-weight dependence of c in a variety of homologous series is given in Table 8.7. The uniformity of behavior is noteworthy, especially when compared with the data for polyethers in Table 8.8.

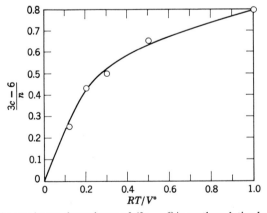

Figure 8.3   Approximate dependence of $(3c - 6)/n$ on the relative barrier height $V°/RT$.

[1] J. Hijmans [8] writes for this case $3c - 6 + (3n - 9)c_m$, where c_m refers to the 4th segment and onward, for which because of the choice between *gauche* and *trans* conformations $0 < c_m < \frac{1}{3}$.

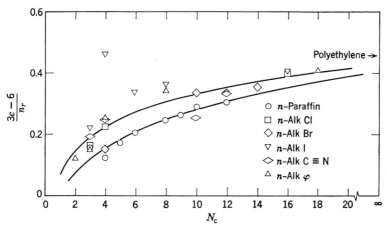

Figure 8.4   Flexibility constant $(3c - 6)/n_r$ versus number of carbon atoms per molecule N_c in various n-alkylhomologous series.

For fairly large groups such as aromatic and other rigid ring systems $0.2\ E° > V°$ at all times. Hence the contribution of their rotation to $3c$ can be determined conveniently. A few examples are given in Table 8.9. Here too, the qualitative sequence is in keeping with expectation from $V°/RT$. The same holds quite well for the $3c$ values per repeating unit in polymers, assembled in Table 8.10, and valid for melts.

There is a size effect that is difficult to account for and actually throws some doubt on the general applicability of $3c$ as a measure of internal flexibility. Inspection of Table 8.9 shows some evidence of inconsistencies caused by a size effect. The ratio of $0.2\ E°/V°$ is identical for 1,2-dibromoethane and for diphenyl, as is $V°/RT_{(1.8)}$ with 4.1 and 4.8, respectively, yet $(3c - 6)/n$ is 0

Table 8.7   Equations to Estimate the Constant c

General Equation: $3c = 6 + a(N_s - 1)\bigg/\left(1 + \dfrac{b}{(N_s - 1)}\right)$

Substance	a	b
n-Paraffins	0.43	5.0
n-Alkyl cyclohexanes	0.44	0
n-Alkylbenzenes	0.43	2.5
n-Alkylcyanides	0.43	5.3
Mono-nitro-n-paraffins	0.43	5
n-Alkyl mononitrates	0.43	5.3
Alkyl polynitrates	0.4	5

Table 8.8 Number of External Degrees of Freedom ($3c$) per Molecule Excited in the Liquid State

Substance	$3c$	$V°$(kcal/mole) (gas phase)
Me—O—(CH$_2$—O)$_n$—Me ($n \geq 3$)	$8.5 + 0.50(N_s - 9)$	$V°$(C—O—C) = 1.6
Me—O—(C$_2$H$_4$—O)—Me ($n \geq 3$)	$9.5 + 0.50(N_s - 12)$	$V°$(C—O—C) = 1.6; $V°$(C—C) = 2.9, 3.7
Et—O—(C$_2$H$_4$)$_2$—Et	9.5	—
$M^{n\ \text{a}}$, φ—O—(φ—O)$_n$—φ ($n \geq 1$)	$7.5 + 1.9n$	$V°$(φ—O—φ) meta = ?
$P^{n\ \text{a}}$, φ—O—(φ—O)$_n$—φ ($n \geq 1$)	$7.5 + 2.0n$ (approx)	$V°$(φ—O—φ) para = ?
Me—Si—O[Si(Me)$_2$—O]$_n$—SiMe$_3$ ($n \geq 1$)	$9.5 + 2.1n$ (approx)	$V°$(Me—Si) = 1.3; $V°$(Si—O—Si) $\approx$ 0 (<1.0)
Me$_3$Si—O—SiMe$_3$	$\sim$10	$V°$(Me—Si) = 1.3; $V°$(Si—O—Si) $\approx$ 0 (<1.0)

[a] M^n stands for : n meta attachments per molecule; P^n stands for : n para attachments per molecule.

Table 8.9 Effect of Segment Size on $3c$ of Bond Joining Rigid Groups

Molecule	$V°$ (kcal/mole)	$0.2\,E°/V°$	$3c - 6/n_{\text{rot}}$
Me—Me	3.0	0.25	0
Cl—C—C—Cl	2.6	0.65	0
Br—C—C—Br	2.6	0.77	0
φ—φ	3.9	0.72	0.47
φ—φ—φ(para)	3.9	1.3	0.45
C=C—Me	2.0	0.5	0.3($\sim$0)
C=C—C—C=C	2.0	0.7	0.6
C=C—C=C	1.2	1.0	0.85
C=C—C=C—C=C(cis)	1.2	1.3	0.85
C=C—C=C—C=C(trans)			0.50
φ—Me	0[a]	∞[a]	0
φ—C≡C—φ	0[a]	∞[a]	0.9
1,3,5-Triphenyl benzene	>3.9	1+	0.83
1,3,5-Trinaphthyl benzene	>3.9	1+	1.2

[a] All the barrier heights $V°$ are for the gaseous state. In this case the liquid-state value may be different from zero.

Table 8.10 Comparison of the Number of External Degrees of Freedom ($3c$) per Molecule Segment with the Barrier to Internal Rotation ($V°$)

Repeating Unit	$3c$	Probable Composition of Degrees of Freedom[a]	$V°$[a] (kcal/mole)
—CH$_2$—	0.44	0.44	2.8

—CH$_2$—CH—
       |
       Me
	1.15	0.43(2), 0.30(1)	2.8(2), 3.9(1)

—CH$_2$—C— / \ Me Me	1.0	0.25(4)	4.9(4)

—CH$_2$—C=C$_H$—CH$_2$(cis-1,4)
       |
       Me
	2.22	0.43(2), 0.68(2)	2.8(2), 2.0(2)

—CH$_2$—CH—
       |
       φ
	2.80	0.43(2), 1.94 (1)	2.9(2), 0(1)

—CH$_2$—O—	1.0	0.5(2)	1.6(2)

—CH$_2$—CH—
       |
       O—C—Me
          ||
          O
	2.46	0.43(3), 0.57(2)	2.8(2), 2.5(2), 0.5(1)

—CH$_2$—C—
    /   \
 Me   C—O—Me
       ||
       O
	1.89	0.43(2), 0.28(1), 0.25(3)	4.3(3), 2.8(2), 0.7(2)

[a] Number in parentheses is the number of bonds of a given kind per repeating unit.

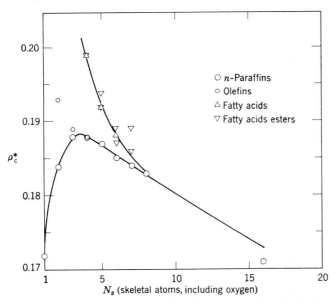

Figure 8.5 Relation between reduced critical density ρ_c^* and molecule size for long-chain components. Based on data from K. A. Kobe and R. E. Lynn, *Chem. Rev.* **52**, 121 (1953).

and 0.5, respectively. Judging by the magnitude of $V°/RT_{(1.8)}(3c-6)/n$ should be smaller than 0.5 for 1,3,5-triphenylbenzene and certainly for 1,3,5-trinaphthylbenzene. Yet, on the contrary, this flexibility constant rises here systematically with the size of the rotating ring substituent. Until this problem has been clarified, the $3c$ per polystyrene repeat unit shown in Table 8.10 and similar cases should not be accepted at full face value.

Table 8.11 Packing Density of Simple
Substances at the Critical Point

Substance	ρ_c^*
Rare Gases	
Ne	0.22
Ar	0.232
Kr	0.225
Xe	0.215
Diatomic Substances	
N_2	0.176
O_2	0.167
$C{=}O$	0.176
Cl_2	0.195
Br_2	0.200
Triatomic Substances	
H_2O	0.211
N_2O	0.196
CO_2	0.21
CS_2	0.184
H_2S	0.186
SO_2	0.175
Polyatomic Substances	
NH_3	0.190
PH_3	0.174
CH_4	0.173
C_2H_2	0.204
C_2H_4	0.193
C_2H_6	0.184
C_6H_6	0.186
CF_4	0.200
CCl_4	0.186
Rigid Molecules of Increasing Anisometry	
Me_4C	0.191
Me_6C_2	0.185
Benzene	0.186
Naphthalene	0.182
φ_2	0.183
$p\text{-}\varphi_3$	0.177

8.1.5   Structural Specificities at the Critical Point

The comparatively large intermolecular distances at T_c are responsible for the absence of substantial specificity effects on the packing density ρ_c^* at T_c. The general downward trend of ρ_c^* with increasing molecule anisometry can be understood in terms of the simple model for rigid molecules discussed in the section on general principles. However, few large anisometric molecules are rigid. For those that are, the trend is well reflected by the ρ_c^* data on Table 8.2. Long flexible molecules, such as the n-paraffins, are known from other measurements to crumple up in the vapor phase [46]. Their configuration is that of open coils. The decrease of ρ_c^* with increasing chain length, shown in Figure 8.5 is therefore smaller than it would be for rigid rods at constant Z (Table 8.2).

Thermal instability precludes the determination of ρ_c^* of larger and more complicated molecules. Hence highly specific effects of molecular structure

Table 8.12   Comparison of the Group Increments of V_c Proposed by Various Authors with V_w

Group	V_c'/V_w	V_c'/V_w (Riedel)[a]	V_c'/V_w (Lyderson)[b]	V_c'/V_w (Vowles)[c]
CH_3-	1.43	5.01	4.03	5.41
$-CH_2-$	1.41	5.66	5.37	5.56
$-CH$	—	—	7.5	5.9
$-C-$	—	—	12.3	6.9
$=CH_2$	—	4.3	3.9	5.33
$\equiv C-H$	—	—	4.5	4.87
$''CH_{cr}$	1.42	—	4.6	4.40
Phenyl—	1.42	—	4.8	4.38
$-O-$	—	5.6	4	5.3
$C{=}O$	—	—	5.1	5.30
$-F$	—	4	3	5.5
$-Cl$	—	4.5	4.1	5.3
$-Br$	—	4.6	4.7	5.6
$-I$	—	—	4.8	5.5

[a] *Chem. Ing. Tech.* **21**, 259 (1954); **35**, 433 (1963), gives a rather accurate method for estimating V_c from V_0', an extrapolated zero point volume.
[b] Based on increments quoted from the book by Reid and Sherwood, because a constant 40 cm³/mole is added to the sum of increments to arrive at V_c, V_c'/V_w ratios of this column are substantially smaller than the experimental average (5.3).
[c] Based on increments quoted from the book by Reid and Sherwood [41].

cannot be observed. The comparative uniformity of ρ_c^*, shown in Table 8.11, is the reason for the existence of the various simple group increment systems for V_c proposed in the literature and compared with V_w in Table 8.12 [41]. If ρ_c^* had a universal magnitude, the group increments should be uniform multiples of their V_w increments, because $V_c = V_w/\rho_c^*$.

8.1.6   Effects of Hydrogen Bonds

Like other chemical bonds, the hydrogen bond forms under loss of van der Waals volume and of external degrees of freedom per molecule. The extent of the loss in V_w is shown in Figure 8.6 as function of hydrogen-bond length. Since the hydrogen bond is comparatively long, the V_w decrement is smaller

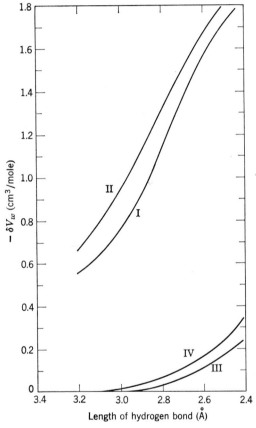

Figure 8.6   Van der Waals volume correction (δV_w) for hydrogen-bond formation [5]. I, linear OH· ·O and NH· · ·O bonds; II, linear NH· · ·N bond; III, angular OH· · ·O bond; IV, angular NH· · ·N bond.

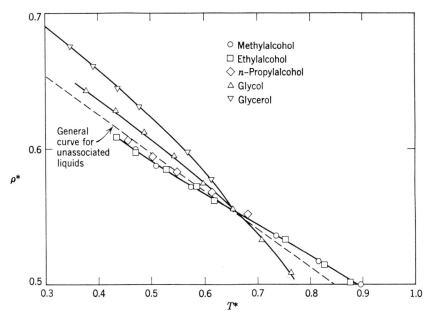

Figure 8.7   Packing density versus temperature curves for alcohols.

than that associated with most chemical bonds. The free energy of hydrogen-bond formation is commonly of an order (1.5 to 3 kcal/mole) that leads to appreciable concentration of both association complex and monomeric compound somewhere in the temperature range of the existence of the liquid phase. As a consequence, the density contribution of this equilibrium is superimposed on the regular density–temperature relation, making the density–temperature curve correspondingly steeper than usual. This is quite apparent from the curves in Figure 8.7.

The ρ^* versus T^* curves of liquid alkanols with more than four carbon atoms per hydroxyl group, of alkanoic acids, and of mono-N-alkaneamids, however, follow the general ρ^* versus T^* curve of "normal" liquids, in spite of their strong hydrogen bonds.

8.2   THE THERMAL EXPANSION COEFFICIENT

The generalized expansion coefficient $\alpha^* = \alpha \theta_L \equiv 1/\rho^*(\partial\rho^*/\partial T^*)$ can be obtained by differentiation of the generalized density/temperature curve over the range for which the latter has been plotted.[1] The data in Figure 8.8 show that, as expected, only the low-temperature region is adequately represented

[1] The Flory theory predicts for the similar reduced expansion coefficient (at $p = 0$) $\alpha T_0 = (3\tilde{V}^{1/3})/[(1 - 3\tilde{V}^{1/3}) - 1]$, that is, a function of $\tilde{V}$, or $\tilde{T}$, only.

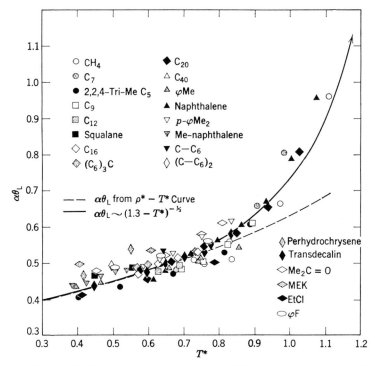

Figure 8.8   Plot of reduced expansion coefficient versus temperature [7].

in this fashion. Representation of the steep increase of α^* as T_c is approached requires inclusion of T_c into the equation. Since for many substances $T_c^* \approx 1.30$, (8.3) could be used as indicated in Figure 8.8.

The meaning of the structure-insensitive generalized expansion coefficient $\alpha^* \equiv \alpha E°/5cR$ is basically that the expansion coefficient is proportional to the ratio of the configurational heat capacity to the "lattice" energy of liquids, a well-known result of the theory of lattice vibrations in cyrstals. For the expansion coefficient of van der Waals liquids composed of rigid molecules Wall and Krigbaum obtained the very similar result that $\alpha \sim R/\Delta H_{\text{vap}}$ [50].

In Figure 8.8, we can discern certain small but systematic deviations from the average behavior. In evaluating these differences, however, we should keep in mind that few density measurements are sufficiently precise to assign significance to differences of 10 % or less in expansion coefficients. The scatter of the data points is of that order of magnitude. Within this scatter, there is a trend for highly branched paraffins to exhibit smaller than average values of α^*, and several polar compounds show not only a slightly higher than average value of α^* but also somewhat smaller than average variations of α^* with temperature. The latter trend, of course, deals with a second derivative of

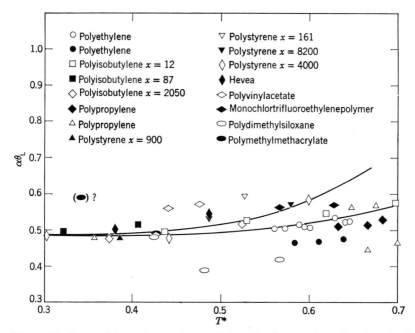

Figure 8.9   Reduced thermal expansion coefficient of polymer melts as function of reduced temperature [7].

density with respect to temperature and all comparisons can note "trends" at best.

The rather good fit of the data of flexible molecules onto the general curve suggests that the parameter c in the reducing temperature $E°/5cR$ accounts adequately for the effect of internal rotation on the thermal expansion coefficient.

In the reduced temperature range $0.3 < T^* < 0.7$ high-polymer melts are very near their glass transition (T_g) temperature. The more rapid change in the number of excited external degrees of freedom over a given temperature interval near T_g is probably responsible for the fact that some polymer melts exhibit a thermal expansion coefficient in excess of expectation from their low-molecular-weight analogs. The characteristic difference between the thermal expansion of amorphous polymers at $T > T_g$ and of simple liquids is apparent from the data of Figure 8.9. In view of the notorious difficulty of dilatometric measurements on polymers we should perhaps not try to rationalize the relations between the data of Figure 8.9 and molecular structure. It is noteworthy that the very accurate data on polyethylene melts by Pals[1] fall very near the curve for simple liquids.

[1] D. T. F. Pals, unpublished information.

Because of the compensating effect of opposing temperature trends, we find that the product $\alpha \cdot \rho = (\partial \rho / \partial T)_p$, *the temperature coefficient of density,* is independent of temperature over the wide range $0.4 < T^* < 0.8$. This very useful fact had been known to petroleum chemists [30], [34], but is not widely appreciated. The incorrect notion that $(\partial v / \partial T)_p$ is constant is rather widespread. Examples of the constancy of $(\partial \rho / \partial T)_p$ and the lack of constancy of $(\partial v / \partial T)_p$ are given in Figure 8.10 for simple liquids as well as polyethylene melts. The data by Murphy et al. [34] show the constancy of $(\partial \rho / \partial T)_p$ for many nonhydrocarbon liquids as well. It should be noted, however, that the above indicated rise in expansion coefficient of polymer melts near T_g leads to $(\partial v / \partial T)_p$ = const as we approach T_g to within about 50°C. Long extrapolation of density or specific volume, as practiced in crystallinity determination, should therefore be carried out with caution.

8.3 BULK MODULUS OF LIQUIDS

The bulk modulus of liquids K_0 (at atmospheric pressure) is far more sensitive to molecular structure than is the thermal expansion coefficient. Yet, as

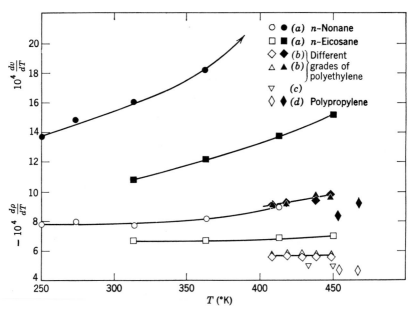

Figure 8.10 Comparison of the temperature coefficients of density (open symbols) with those of specific volume (solid symbols) for *n*-paraffins, polyethylenes, and polypropylene melts [7]. (*a*) API, Research Project 44, tables. (*b*) D. T. F. Pals, unpublished information. (*c*) L. D. Moore, Jr., *J. Polymer Sci.* **36,** 155 (1959). (*d*) F. Danusso et al., *Chim. Ind.* **41,** 748 (1959).

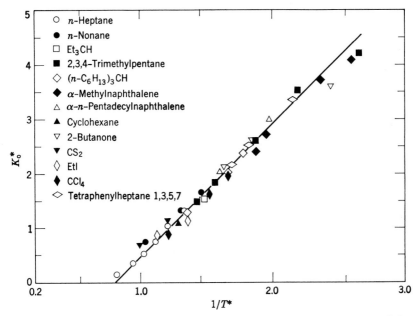

Figure 8.11 Plot of generalized bulk modulus of liquids versus temperature [7].

suggested by Flory's theory[1] and confirmed by the data in Figure 8.11, $K_0^* \equiv K_0 V_w / E^\circ$ is a simple function of ρ^* or T^* for a wide variety of substances, indicating that K_0 is primarily a function of E° and V_w, that is, of the cohesive energy density, besides T^*.

The highly anisometric structure of long-chain compounds and the related anisotropy of "molecular" compressibility requires special consideration. The internal compressibility, E_p^{-1}, of these molecules is nearly 100 times smaller than the compressibility (K_i^{-1}) of the intermolecular space. Hence in the limit of $M \to \infty$ the bulk modulus of the polymer liquid is given by

$$\frac{1}{K_0} = \frac{2}{3K_i} + \frac{1}{3E_p} \approx \frac{2}{3K_i} ; \qquad (8.4)$$

that is, the compression takes place in only two dimensions, normal to the axis of the long molecule. For molecules of finite length we have to consider also the compressibility of intermolecular space between ends of molecules, and the arithmetic becomes a bit more complicated:

$$K_0^*(L) = K_0 \left\{ \frac{Vw}{E^\circ} \left[\frac{2}{3} \left(1 + \frac{1}{N_s} \right) \right] + \frac{1}{3E_p} \left(1 - \frac{1}{N_s} \right) \right\}. \qquad (8.5)$$

[1] According to which at $p = 0$, $\tilde{K}_0 = \dfrac{1 - 3(\tilde{V}^{1/3} - 1)}{3\tilde{V}^2(\tilde{V}^{1/3} - 1)}$.

The general shape of the relation is indicated in Figure 8.12. Typical E_p data have been assembled in Table 4.5 in Section 4.3.3.

Polymers with *cis* configuration in the repeating unit of the backbone chain do not lose van der Waals compressibility parallel to the chain axis. Their bulk modulus in the melt state is therefore correlated as K_0, that is, like that of a monomeric liquid, however, on the polymer correlation curve.

The equations for the two cases shown in Figures 8.11 and 8.12 are quite similar for simple liquids

$$K_0^* = \frac{2.00}{T^*} - 1.60 \qquad (8.6)$$

and for long-chain compounds and polymer melts

$$K_0^*(L) = \frac{2.30}{T^*} - 1.98. \qquad (8.7)$$

Both equations are strictly empirical and are probably valid only in the range $1.0 > T^* > 0.4$. The natural end of the low-temperature scale is T_g, namely, $T^{*-1} \approx 3$ for most substances, and $T^{*-1} \approx 5$ for polyisobutylene, beyond which extrapolation becomes meaningless. At the high temperature end the

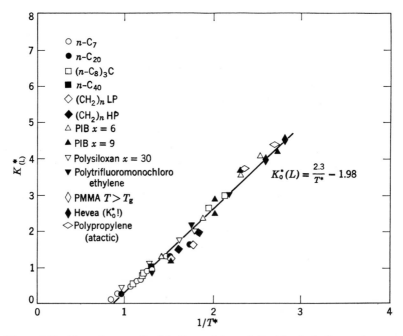

Figure 8.12 Plot of generalized bulk modulus of liquids, including polymer melts, composed of flexible-chain molecules [7].

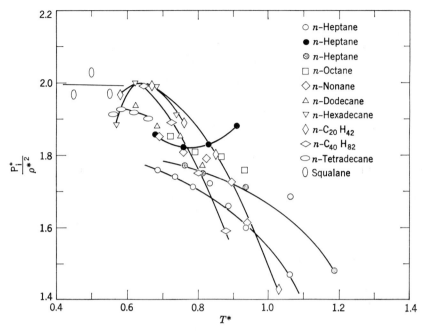

Figure 8.13 Plot of reduced internal pressure function versus reduced temperature for several alkanes [7].

point $K_0^* = 0$ is attained at $T^* = 1.25$, somewhat less than the critical temperature, which as a rule is at $T^* \approx 1.3$. Hence exact expressions for both systems yield S-shaped curves rather than straight lines. Although this deficiency is not a serious problem with most monomeric liquids because they are used largely in the temperature range in which the straight line is a good approximation, it may well become a problem when one is concerned with solutions of polymers at or below their glass transition temperature. The example of polymethylmethacrylate in Figure 8.13 illustrates this point.

Because the thermal pressure coefficient $\gamma (\equiv K_0 \alpha)$ can presumably be measured more accurately than it can be calculated from the independently measured K_0 and α, an attempt has been made to correlate γ directly. Two routes have been tried, as $P_i^* \equiv \gamma T V_w / E^\circ$ and as P_i^* / ρ^{*2} because the latter is often claimed to be temperature independent, at least at low temperatures [1]. A few spot checks of room-temperature measurements yield data in tolerable agreement with each other. However, data taken over an extended temperature range by several well-known investigators are in striking disagreement as shown by the curves of Figure 8.13. The other data on that figure offer little encouragement for the discovery of a universal correlation of P_i^* / ρ^{*2} versus

T^*, since the properties of n-paraffins are generally most amenable to correlation. Convergence of all curves into a single curve is indicated only for the higher-molecular-weight alkanes ($N_c \geq 16$) at low temperatures ($T^* \leq 0.7$). Numerical values of P_i^*/ρ^{*2} have been obtained for various compounds and were found to cover too broad a range even within given chemical series to offer much hope for useful correlation. This lack of simple trends appears to hold even within data series obtained by single and very careful investigators.

Comparison of the reducing parameters V_F^* and T_F^* of Flory's generalized

Table 8.13   Comparison of Flory's Reducing Temperature T_F^* with that of the Present Work (θ_L) and of Flory's Reducing Volume V_F^* with V_0^a [7]

Substance	t (°C)	T_F^*/θ_L	$\rho^* T_F^*/\theta_L$	V_F^*/V_0
CCl$_4$	0	10.9	5.70	0.996
	70	11.5	5.75	1.02
Cyclohexane	0	10.3	5.90	1.01
	70	10.65	5.60	1.03
Methylcyclohexane	65	11.5	6.0	
Benzene	0	10.4	5.77	0.99
	70	11.0	5.61	1.01
Diphenyl	70	9.47	5.60	
n-Hexane	20	12.1	6.31	1.02
n-Heptane	20	11.6	6.20	1.03
n-C$_6$F$_{14}$	20	10.0	5.05	
CF$_3$·Cyclo C$_6$F$_{11}$	65	9.90	5.02	

[a] V_0 = zero-point volume, W. Biltz, *Raumchemie der festen Stoffe*, Leopold Voss, Leipzig, 1934.

equation of state with the corresponding independently determined properties used in the present correlation yields the following results. The volume V_F^* can be compared directly with V_w, and

$$T_F = \frac{s\eta}{2\nu^* cR} = \left(\frac{\tilde{\nu}E_0}{Nrc'R}\right)_F \qquad (8.6)$$

can be compared with $\theta_L = E^\circ/5cR$, where the two energy terms E° and E_0 are not identical by definition, but are likely to be very similar in numerical magnitude. Flory's rc' is only one-half of our c. Hence T_F^*/θ_L should be of the order $10\tilde{\nu}$. This turns out to be the case. Specifically, although the temperature drift of V_F^* prevents a constant ratio, $V_w/V_F^* \approx 0.70 \pm 0.02$, which is of the order of the packing density at $0°K$. Typical comparisons with zero-point volume V_0 are shown in Table 8.13. The same table also shows the ratio T_F^*/θ_L and the almost universal constant factor $\rho^* T^*/\theta_L$, indicating how the two methods of correlation can be interchanged.

8.3.1 Limitations of the Methods

Inspection of Figure 8.9 shows that prediction of the expansion coefficient of monomeric liquids for a generalized curve might be good only to within $\pm 10\%$. This uncertainty can often be reduced to $\pm 3\%$ by starting with a known expansion coefficient of a compound similar to that under consideration; for example, a member of the same homologous series. Its experimental value of $\alpha\theta_L$ versus T^* then locates the curve of

$$\alpha\theta_L \sim (1.30 - T^*)^{-\frac{1}{3}} \qquad (8.7)$$

for the compound under consideration. The thermal expansion coefficient of polymer melts should be estimated from the correlation of Figure 8.9. However, care should be taken not to extrapolate into the immediate neighborhood of or below T_g^* where rather different relations prevail [25], [6].

The average error of the bulk-modulus correlations within the linear range discussed earlier appears to be of the order of $\pm 5\%$, and the maximum error range may be of the order of $\pm 15\%$. Here again the error range can be sharply reduced by sacrificing generality and specializing the correlations for families of compounds.

8.3.2 Sound Velocity

Several extensive collections of liquid-phase sound-velocity data have been published [2], [35], [42]. Data not directly available from the collections should be obtainable by extrapolative use of the various molecular-structure correlations cited in these books. Nozd'rev [35] gives some fairly good corresponding-states correlations of u_s in which T_c is the most important correlating parameter. For the many substances for which T_c is unknown or unknowable, we have to develop another correlation. In the present context the most obvious correlation is $u_s^* = u_s(M/E^\circ)^{\frac{1}{2}}$ versus T^* or versus ρ^*. Since $du_s/dT = \text{const}$ over long temperature ranges (but not over the entire range of T_m to T_b if T_m is very low), the u_s^* versus T^* correlation should also be linear over a long range of T^*. Preliminary trials have shown that such a corresponding states correlation of u_s is not universal, but yields single curves for individual families of compounds, so that it is well suited for extrapolation from known to unknown member of geometrically similar compound families. The adiabatic bulk modulus of a liquid at $p = 0$ is

$$K_0(ad) = \rho u_s^2$$

and its isothermal bulk modulus at $p = 0$ is

$$K_0 = \frac{\rho u_s^2}{1 + M\alpha^2 u_s^2 T/C_p}.$$

In this route one must know u_s, α, ρ, and C_p quite accurately in order to achieve a tolerably reliable datum for K_0.

8.3.3   The Effect of the Time Scale of the Experiment

Liquids composed of simple nonassociating rigid molecules respond to compression with their equilibrium bulk modulus[1] as long as the time scale of the experiment $> \eta/G$, where η is the usual shear viscosity and G is the shear (or rigidity) modulus that we would predict for a solid of the molecular structure and packing density of the liquid, that is by means of the correlations of Section 4.5. To compression or shear waves or pulses of shorter duration, the liquid responds with the bulk and shear moduli of a solid. Such "induced glassiness" is experimentally accessible for relatively viscous liquids with high-frequency mechanical vibrators [31], whereas for liquids of low viscosity it lies in the hypersonic region accessible through the Brillouin shift [10].

Liquids composed of associating rigid molecules, especially alcohols, exhibit glassiness at somewhat lower frequencies than G/η because of a wide distribution of bulk relaxation times [31]. (The criterion G/η assumes the bulk behavior to be governed by a single relaxation time.) Only a beginning has been made with a detailed quantitative correlation of the high-frequency moduli K_∞ and G_∞ and of the corresponding relaxation times with molecular structure [31]. Their representation in reduced coordinates may well fit into the elastic property and relaxation correlations, respectively, for glasses (Chapter 13), but that has not yet been tried.

Liquids composed of flexible (and of dimerizing) molecules often exhibit anomalous dispersion of the bulk modulus at frequencies far below G/η. The cause is the existence of more than one equilibrium conformation of the flexible molecule, and the frequency of the dispersion corresponds to the conversion rate from one conformation to the other. According to Lamb's theory of the phenomenon [29], the temperature dependence of the dispersion maximum yields the activation energy of the conversion ($\approx$ the barrier to internal rotation) and the relaxation strength the energy of rotational isomerization (ΔE_{iso}). However, serious and still-unexplained discrepancies between ΔE_{iso} from mechanical measurements and that derived from infrared spectroscopic have recently been observed [52]. Hence the phenomenon may need some further work. The bulk-modulus dispersion due to reversible dimerization of associating molecules (such as fatty acids) yields the analogous quantities for the dimerization reaction rate and equilibrium [29]. Related phenomena are of considerable practical interest in the so-called secondary relaxation spectra of glassy solids where they are discussed in greater detail (Section 13.5).

---

[1] Isothermal in static compression, and adiabatic in pulsed or oscillatory compression.

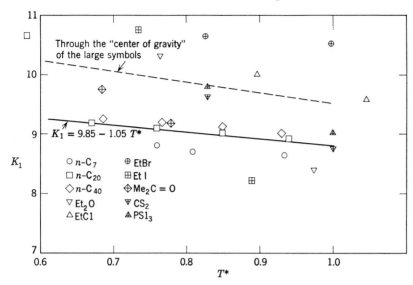

Figure 8.14 Plot of K_1 versus T^* for various liquids. Most symbols are probably uncertain to within $\pm 10\%$.

8.3.4 Compression at High Pressure

The pressure dependence of the generalized bulk modulus is given by Flory's theory as

$$\tilde{K} = \tilde{K}_0 + 3\tilde{P}\left[\frac{1}{3(\tilde{V}^{1/3} - 1)} - 1\right]. \tag{8.8}$$

The expression in square brackets varies only slowly with pressure; hence a good approximation up to quite high pressures is

$$K = K_0 + K_1 P, \tag{8.9}$$

where the dimensionless coefficient K_1 covers a narrow range of numerical values. Since K_1 is a second derivative of pressure with respect to volume, there is some question regarding the accuracy of the results, and much of the scatter of the points in Figure 8.14 may be experimental scatter rather than of physical significance. An average value may therefore be employed as a first approximation.[1] A higher approximation would show a trend with T^* and ρ^*. With K_0 derivable from a K_0^* versus T^*, ρ^* correlation, and K_1 being a nearly universal constant, or available from a simple correlation too, the compression of liquids over a wide range of pressure and temperature is

[1] Recent high-precision data by L. A. Wood and G. M. Martin, *J. Res. Natl. Bur. Std.* **68A**, 259 (1964) yield for unvulcanized polyisoprene $K_1 = 10$. The line for the *n*-paraffins in Figure 8.14 would have predicted $K_1 = 9.4$.

accessible to estimation from simple molecular structure constants ($E°$, V_w, c, E_p, M).

8.4 EQUATIONS OF STATE FOR LIQUIDS

All equations of state for liquids derived from theory in its present state or from models exhibit serious deficiencies in the second derivatives of volume with respect to state variables. Flory's equation of state

$$\frac{\tilde{P}}{\tilde{\rho}^2} = \frac{\tilde{T}}{\tilde{\rho}(1 - \tilde{\rho}^{\frac{1}{3}})} - 1 \qquad (8.10)$$

exhibits perhaps fewer flaws than many. Yet his relation for the change of thermal expansion with T and P

$$(\alpha T_0)^{-1} = \tilde{T}\left[\frac{1}{3(\tilde{V}^{\frac{1}{3}} - 1)} + \frac{2\tilde{P}\tilde{V}^2}{\tilde{P}\tilde{V} + 1} - 1\right] \qquad (8.11)$$

yields the correct sign for $(\partial\alpha/\partial P)_T$, but often the incorrect sign—or at least incorrect magnitude—for $(\partial\alpha/\partial T)_P$, and although (8.11) shows correctly that $(\partial\alpha/\partial T)_P$ decreases as P is raised, it fails to reproduce the change in sign of $(\partial\alpha/\partial T)_P$ at high pressure which Bridgman's experiments have demonstrated to be a characteristic property of liquids. The quantitative representation of experimental *p-v-T* data by Flory's equation of state is not entirely satisfactory also for the reason given earlier, the need to vary the reference volume with temperature. An even larger thermal expansion must be allowed for the reference volume of Simha and Hadden's [46] adaptation of Prigogine's equation of state for polymers in order to fit the experimental data.

Now we are left with the following choices of equations of state, (a) entirely empirical, but accurate algebraic descriptions of the existing data, where the coefficients are valid only for compounds studied but are difficult—if not impossible—to extrapolate to other compounds for which no data are available, or (b) theoretical expressions which are accurate only after "fixing up" the constants in an empirical and therefore only difficultly extrapolatable fashion, or (c) semi-empirical correlations of dimensionless parameters derived from the proposed theories. A beginning has been made with such an approach [9].

8.5 MIXTURE RULES

8.5.1 Density

The packing density of hard spheres (at $0°K$) is increased, in general, when spheres with different radii are mixed [51]. The increase in density is not large when only binary mixtures are considered. However, the random densely packed mixture of spheres with log normal size distribution can reach packing densities of the order 0.80 [51]. Higher packing densities can be achieved when hard spherical and nonspherical particles are mixed. This consideration of forceless mixtures suggests that the mixing of unequally sized molecules at equal reduced temperature should proceed generally with volume contraction ($V^E < 0$). Because forceless systems or mixtures of components at equal reduced temperatures are rarely met with in practice, however, the rather laborious calculations for mixtures of forceless hard spheres is not quoted here.

A more realistic case is the mixture of components with unequal force fields and thus at unequal reduced temperature. It should be said from the outset that the prediction of the excess volume of mixing

$$V_E = V_{\text{mix}} - (x_1 V_1 + x_2 V_2) \tag{8.12}$$

is the severest test of any theory of solutions and mixtures and none has yet met this test [38]. Moreover, the magnitude of $V^E/x_1 x_2 V_{\text{mix}}$ is rarely more than 2%. Hence only the qualitative conclusions of Prigogine's theoretical analysis have been assembled in Table 8.14. The contraction at unequal dispersion forces is predicted by Prigogine's consideration of the effect of mixing liquids which are at unequal reduced temperatures. It should be noted that a geometric mean force law for components of unequal cohesive energy density (at equal reduced temperatures) leads to a prediction of volume expansion on mixing, specifically for regular solutions for which $S^E = 0$. Scatchard's estimate for that case

$$V^E = \bar{\beta}_0 F^E \tag{8.14}$$

has been in only moderate agreement with experiment. Somewhat better agreement has been achieved by Hildebrand and Dymond's [54] improved version

$$\bar{V}_2 - V_2 = \frac{\beta_{01} F^E}{\alpha_1 T} \quad \text{at} \quad x_2 \to 0. \tag{8.14a}$$

Yet better agreement with experiment may be achieved by simultaneous consideration of the effect of differences in T^* and the differences in P_i.

Specific interaction, such as molecular-compound formation leads, of course, to large volume contraction. A typical example is the reaction of tertiary amines with carboxylic acids for which $-V^E \approx 16 \text{ cm}^3/\text{mole}$ [8]. The expansion that results when unequally sized molecules of equal interaction energy are mixed is the result of a subtle entropy effect and is easily overwhelmed by comparatively small differences in interaction energy. Hence it is rarely observed. The expansion predicted for the mixture of polar with nonpolar liquids is the result of the increased disorder (=increased entropy) and is always observed when the dipole-interaction energy μ^2/r^3 of the polar liquid is large. The statements of Table 8.14 suggest that each type of interaction would require a separate correlation.

In view of the technologically insignificant[1] magnitude of V^E, not much research effort in this direction can be expected. Prigogine's school has determined V^E experimentally for a host of systems suitable for the testing of theories.

The only extensive data series for which an elaborate correlation has been developed is that covering mixtures of *n*-alkanes ranging from $n\text{-C}_6\text{H}_{14}$ to

Table 8.14 Excess Volume Relations (according to the Average Potential Model for Mixtures)[a]

Nature of Interaction	$\dfrac{V_1}{V_2^1}$	F^E	ΔH_m	S^E	V^E	$\dfrac{\partial V^E}{\partial P}$
Large dispersion-force difference	~1	>0	>0	<0	<0	>0
Addition compound formation	~1	<0	<0	<0	≪0	>0
Equal dispersion force for both components	≥1	>0	>0	>0	≥0	<0
Dipole orientation energy/dispersion force[b]	~1	<0	<0	<0	<0	<0
Dipole orientation energy/dispersion force[c]	~1	>0	>0	>0	>0	>0

[a] All from Prigogine's book [38].
[b] Dipole contribution to ϵ_{AB} larger than that to ϵ_{BB} (B = polar compound).
[c] Dipole contribution to ϵ_{AB} smaller than that to ϵ_{BB} because of high polarizability of polar component.

$n\text{-C}_{62}\text{H}_{126}$ by Holleman [23], from which Figure 8.15 and the correlation equation have been taken. The correlation is a direct result of the applicability of the principle of congruence, namely, that the properties of a mixture correspond to those of the *n*-alkane with same average number of carbon atoms per molecule ($n = x_1 n_1 + x_2 n_2$) and of the applicability of the corresponding-states principle of Prigogine discussed earlier. A striking feature of this system is the steady increase in $-V^E/x_1 x_2$ with increasing temperature, but even at the highest temperature tried (160°C) $\pm V^E_{max}$ is only about 1% of V_{mix}.

Hence, except in the case of molecular-compound formation, for most practical purposes, that is, within ±1%,

$$V_{mix} \approx \sum x_i V_i, \qquad (8.15)$$

or

$$v_{mix} \approx \sum w_i v_i, \qquad (8.16)$$

where $v = \rho^{-1}$ and w_i is the weight fraction.

[1] A volume change of 1% is technologically significant whenever liquids are sold per unit of volume.

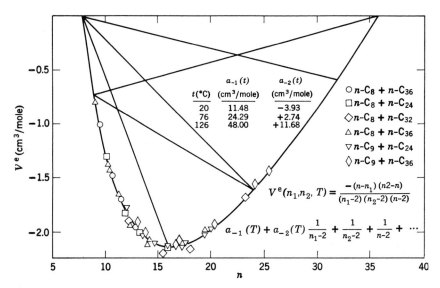

Figure 8.15 Excess volumes of n-paraffin mixtures at 160°C, where n is the (mole fraction) average number of carbon atoms per molecule in the mixture [23]. [See also the somewhat simpler relation proposed by J. Fernandez-Garcia et al., *Helv. Chim. Acta* **49**, 1983 (1966).]

8.5.2 Partial Molal Volumes

This topic is closely related to the previous one and is of particular interest in cases in which density measurements in the liquid state are difficult to do, namely on solutions of sensitive complex chemicals and of gases. The definition and method of determination of the partial molal volume, $\bar{V}_T$, can be found in any physical-chemistry textbook. The quantitative understanding of the magnitude of $\bar{V}_T$, or of the corresponding partial packing density $\bar{\rho}^* = V_w/\bar{V}_T$ is closely tied to the question of what the effective reduced temperature T^* for the solute is. This is probably obtained best by setting up mixing rules for the components of T^*:

$$\langle E^\circ \rangle = x_1^2 E_1^\circ + x_2^2 E_2^\circ + 2x_1 x_2 (E_1^\circ E_2^\circ)^{1/2} \tag{8.17}$$

for T^* of the whole mixture, whereas for the solute molecule at infinite dilution, $E^\circ = (E_1^\circ E_2^\circ)^{1/2}$. Similarly, for the whole solution,

$$\langle c \rangle = x_1 c_1 + x_2 c_2 \tag{8.18}$$

if $M_1 \approx M_2$. However, if $M_2 \gg M_1$, then

$$\langle c \rangle = \phi_1 c_1 + \phi_2 c_2 \tag{8.19}$$

and for the solute (2) at infinite dilution, $c = c_2$. For the often-interesting case of ρ^* at infinite dilution the appropriate T^* is therefore equal to $5c_2 RT/E^\circ$.

Table 8.14 Partial Packing Density (at ~20°C)

Polymer	Solvent	$\bar{\rho}^*$	$\rho^*(l)$	$\rho^*(l)$ (calc.)	$\rho^*(c)$
Polymethylene	Water		0.629[a]	0.624–0.632	0.732
Polyoxymethylene			0.615[a]	(0.635–0.643)	
				L P	
Polyethylene oxide	Water	0.625[b]		0.625–0.633	
Polyvinyl chloride	Cyclohexanone	0.659[b]	(0.613)	0.651	
With Side Chain					
Polyisobutylene	n-octane	0.680[b]	0.666[a]	0.664	
Polyisobutylene	Benzene	0.660[c]			
Polyisobutylene	Chlorobenzene	0.665[a]	0.666[a]		
Polystyrene	Chlorobenzene	0.655[d]	0.652[d]	0.654	0.675[d]
Polystyrene	Bromobenzene	0.6550[d]	0.652[d]	0.654	
Polystyrene	Benzene	0.651[d]			
Polystyrene	Toluene	0.660[b]			
Polystyrene	Chloroform	0.658[c]			
Polystyrene	2-butanone	0.669[c]			
Polydimethylsiloxane	Toluene	0.567[b]	0.567	0.569	
Polyvinyl acetate	Chlorobenzene	0.659[c]	0.655[c]	0.637	
Polyvinyl acetate	Cyclohexanone	0.628[b]			
Polyvinyl methyl ether	n-pentanol-1	0.602[b]			
Polyacrylonitrile	Propylene Carbonate	0.705[e]	0.703[e]	(0.691)	
Polymethyl methacrylate	4-methyl pentane-2	0.686[b]	0.675[a]	0.675	
Polyethyl methacrylate	4-methyl pentane-2	0.673[b]		0.663	
Cellulose triacetate	Symtetrachloro-ethane	0.634[b]			

Hydrogen-Bonded Polymers[f]

				hex	mono	am.
Poly(vinyl alcohol)	Water	0.728[b]				
Nylon 66	99 to 100% Formic Acid	0.695[b]	(0.712)	0.627;	0.736;	0.69 to 0.705
Poly-β-benzyl-L-aspartate	meta-Cresol	0.680[g]			0.695[g]	
Poly-β-benzyl-L-aspartate	N,N-Dimethyl-formamide	0.682[g]				
Poly-γ-benzyl-L-glutamate	N,N-Dimethyl-formamide	0.680[g]				
Poly-γ-benzyl-L-glutamate	N,N-Dimethyl-formamide	0.685[h]	(0.708)		0.687[h]	
Poly-γ-benzyl-L-glutamate	Dichloroacetic acid	0.693[i]				
Poly-DL-phenylalanine	Toluene	0.687[g]				
Poly-L-tyrosine	N,N-Dimethyl-formamide	0.730[g]	(0.714)			
Poly-L-glutamic acid	N,N-Dimethyl-formamide	0.743[g]	(0.722)			
Poly(methacrylic acid)	$\frac{n}{100}$ HCl (aq.)	0.748[b]	(0.730)			

[a] G. C. East, D. Margerison, and E. Pulat, *Trans. Faraday Soc.* **62**, 1301 (1966). (Molal volume extrapolation from liquid oligomer data.)
[b] G. R. Anderson, *Arkiv. Kemi.* **20**, 513 (1963).
[c] A. Horth, et al., *J. Polymer Sci.* **A1**, 2765 (1963).
[d] W Heller, *J. Polymer Sci.* **A-2-4**, 209 (1966).
[e] R. Chiang, *J. Polymer Sci.* **A1**, 2765 (1963).
[f] The appropriate hydrogen-bond decrements were employed in the calculation of V_w.
[g] A. J. Kovacs et al., *Biopolymers* **2**, 43 (1964).
[h] J. H. Bradbury et al., *J. Mol. Biol.* **11**, 137 (1965).
[i] From Ref. (h) random coil in solution.

249

The validity of this approach has been demonstrated by Hildebrand's [21] correlation of $\bar{V}$ for dissolved gases with the energy parameters of solvents and solute.

The available partial molal or partial specific-volume data on more complex solutes cover only narrow ranges of solvents, but indicate a comparatively small solvent–solute interaction effect. The partial specific volume of non-associating polymers in solution (Table 8.14) essentially equals the extrapolated specific volume of the melt, and is considerably smaller than that of the corresponding glass. This result is very convenient for predictive purposes.

Since strongly associating polymers, such as polypeptides, do not exist in the melt stage, their partial specific volume in solution is the only liquid-state density available. Inspection of Table 8.14 shows that here $\bar{v} \approx v_{\text{solid}}$. Nevertheless, insertion of the appropriate values of $E°$, and c into the generalized density equation for polymer melts yields the fairly acceptable prediction shown in Table 8.14.

8.5.3 Thermal Expansion of Mixtures

In general

$$\alpha_{\text{mix}} = \sum \phi_i \alpha_i, \qquad (8.20)$$

where ϕ_i is the volume fraction of component i. For mixtures, such as solutions of gases or solids, in which α_L is not available, we might estimate

$$\alpha_{\text{mix}} = \frac{\alpha^*}{\bar{\theta}_L} \qquad (8.21)$$

Here α^* is obtained from Figure 8.8 and $\bar{\theta}_L = \langle E° \rangle / 5cR$, where $\langle E° \rangle$ and $\bar{c}$ are estimated by the method given in the preceding section.

Neither of these methods is applicable when the mixture is excessively nonideal, as in molecular-compound formation. In the absence of any experimental data we should then assume that the molecular compound is mixed with the component that is in excess (if any) and estimate $E°$ and c as well as possible for the molecular compound.

A question can arise regarding the appropriate expansion coefficient for the polymeric solute at $T < T_{g(\text{polymer})}$. The coefficient for polymeric glasses is nearly independent of molecular structure, $\alpha_g \approx (2.2 \pm 0.1) \times 10^{-4}°\text{K}^{-1}$ [5]. However, the thermal-expansion coefficient of the partial specific volume of polymer solutes at $T < T_g$ (polymer) is within a fairly wide error margin about $0.9\alpha_L$ [43], [44] just as the partial specific volume is more nearly like the extrapolated liquid density than like that of the glass [24]. We may conclude from these observations that the appropriate p–v–T properties assigned to the polymer in the range $T_{g(\text{polymer})} > T > T_{g(\text{solution})}$ are those extrapolated from its melt properties. The properties of polymer solutions at $T < T_{g(\text{solution})}$

are only beginning to be examined [49]. Hence generalizations cannot yet be made.

8.5.4 Bulk Modulus of Mixtures

To a first approximation, that is, in ideal solutions

$$\beta_{mix} = \Sigma \, \phi_i \beta_i. \tag{8.22}$$

However, for nonideal solutions, Hildebrand [19] showed that

$$\beta_{mix} = \beta_0 - \frac{V^E}{V_{mix}} \left[\left(\frac{\partial \ln \beta_0}{\partial P_T} + 2\beta_0 \right) \right] + \cdots, \tag{8.23}$$

where $\beta_0 = \Sigma \, \phi_i \beta_i$, and the pressure coefficient of β_0 can be estimated as $\approx 10\beta_0$ from the nearly universal value of $(\partial K_0 / \partial P)_T \approx 10$. Here again, the above-mentioned mixture rules cannot be expected to apply when molecular compounds are formed. Rough estimates might then be possible if we insert the molecular structure of the molecular compound into the calculations for K_1 as shown in the appropriate calculating procedure.

The bulk modulus of the partial specific volume of polymers (obtained in Ref. b of Table 8.14) in non-aqueous solvents is of the order estimated by correlation (8.7) for pure liquids.

8.6 COMPARISON WITH OTHER WORK

Attempts to relate the density (ρ) of liquids to molecular structure have been made at the very beginning of modern chemistry [26], especially in the form of the molal volume $V \equiv M/\rho$. Whereas many chemists, even now, have succumbed to the temptation to compare densities of molal volumes at constant (room) temperature, Kopp and others realized 80 years ago that valid density comparisons have to be made at a corresponding state. Kopp chose the normal (atmospheric) boiling point. Traube normalized the environment by restricting most comparisons to the partial molal volume of the substance in, usually aqueous, solution.

Another approach has been to compare the molal volume at equal surface tensions, the Parachor, or at equal sound velocity, the Rao number, etc. These two methods are still widely used because of their essential temperature independence and their rather good group increment additivity. Parachor group increments are now available for organic [40] as well as inorganic [33] compounds, and Rao numbers are likewise quite widely used. The main drawback of these methods is that we have to have an additional property datum, surface tension or sound velocity, in order to estimate the density from these numbers. Hence there is still room for a better density–molecular-structure relation.

The most elaborate effort along that line has been made by S. S. Kurtz and his co-workers in more than 20 years of work [28]. For reasons of experimental simplicity, they concentrated on the density at one temperature (25°C). The resulting group increment and other constants are undoubtedly suited for this strictly empirical correlation. However, a consequence of this basically poor choice of standard state is the incidence of, as it were, correction numbers which cannot be connected with any particular group increment. That this correction number has no theoretical significance is apparent from the following argument:

At the constant reduced temperature $T_R = T/T_c = 0.5$, the density of the *n*-paraffin hydrocarbons changes relatively little with molecular weight when $N_c > 7$ and is exactly constant once $N_c > 14$. This constancy is yet more pronounced at higher reduced temperatures since at $T = T_c$ the density is constant at $N_c > 10$. Hence for *n*-paraffins

$$V_L = \frac{1}{\rho(T_R)} (14N_c + 2) \qquad \text{cm}^3 \text{ mole}^{-1}, \qquad (8.24)$$

where $\rho(T_R) = $ density at constant T_R (here $=0.5$). Here the intercept is just the volume contribution of the two extra hydrogen atoms. Hence we find for the alkylcyclohexanes and cyclopentanes essentially zero intercept when plotting V_L versus N_c at $T_R = $ const.

If we adopt as reference temperature Prigogine's $T^* = $ const, which is equivalent to $V^* = V_L/V_w = $ const, when V_w is the van der Waals volume of the molecules, we obtain for the *n*-paraffins,

$$V_L = V^*(10.23N_c + 6.88) \qquad \text{cm}^3\text{mole}^{-1}, \qquad (8.25)$$

when again the intercept represents just the volume contribution of the hydrogen atoms. The slightly different choice of reference temperature scale obviously has a large effect on the magnitude of the intercept. Because 10.23 cm³/mole is the van der Waals volume per methylene group, the (alkyl)naphthenes exhibit no intercept in this scheme.

An exercise in arithmetic shows that the Kurtz intercept is larger than the hydrogen contribution because he makes all comparisons at constant absolute temperature and therefore at continuously varying reduced temperature. The fact that nearly the same value is obtained for his "kinetic impact free volume" for various hydrocarbon and even fluorocarbon series is just the result of the well-known geometrical similarity of the critical temperature versus carbon number curves of these homologous series. Hence, the intercept of a curve V_L versus N_c at $T = $ const can hardly have any physical meaning.

An advantage of the strictly empirical calculating schemes with their basic limitation to certain narrowly restricted groups of compounds is their great accuracy.

The method of this section is far more general in its applicability, being restricted with regard to strongly associating compounds only. Yet this generality had to be purchased at the price of reduced, although usually adequate, accuracy. The primary gain from the use of the present method or the related methods of Simha [46] and Hijmans [18] is that as simple a measurement as density can be made to give quantitative information about one of the most important characteristics of a molecule, its flexibility.

8.7 EFFECT OF TEMPERATURE AND PRESSURE ON V_w

The radii of atoms or molecules calculated from gas imperfections or gas viscosity by means of the classical (hard-sphere) kinetic gas theory decrease appreciably with increasing temperature. The "explanation" for this phenomenon was that the increase of the kinetic energy with temperature causes increasing penetration of the electron clouds during collision. Introduction of a more realistic soft-sphere interaction potential removed these changes of molecule dimensions with temperature, at least in the temperature region (300 to 600°K) of greatest technical interest. Substitution of experimental $p-v-T$ data into the recently proposed hard-sphere kinetic theory of liquids by Frisch–Reiss–Lebowitz [16] and a hard-sphere theory of polymer liquids by Flory and Vrij [14] yield molecule radii which increase with temperature such that the thermal expansion of the molecules contribute an appreciable portion of the total thermal expansion of the liquid. Several less rigorous theories similarly yield molecule radii which increase with temperature and decrease with pressure.

Because in almost every case the authors or their followers argue for the "plausibility" of the observed changes in the molecule dimensions, it appears worthwhile to determine the internal thermal expansion and compressibility of molecules.

The thermal expansion of free molecules has been measured directly by precision electron diffraction [17] of gases over a range of temperatures. Moreover, a recent theoretical analysis [48] permits prediction of the order of magnitude of the thermal expansion of molecules due to anharmonicity of the molecular vibrations and due to centrifugal force. The first of these is the more important one. Typical experimental and calculated results are shown in Table 8.15. There is a rough correlation between these bond expansion coefficients α_b and the appropriate bond-dissociation energies, E, such that $\alpha_b \sim C_E/E$, where C_E is the heat-capacity contribution of the molecular vibration under consideration. Application of a similar argument to the electron cloud shows that even the most loosely held valence electron cannot make a significant contribution to α_m.

Conversion of the linear expansion of the bond distance l to the cubic expansion of V_w can be made exactly only in each individual case. For the present purpose, however, it is sufficient to give an upper limit, which for the range of interest, say 300 to 600°K can be approximated by $V_w(600°K)/V_w(300°K) \leq 1 + 3 \times 300 \times \alpha_b = 1.015$, or a cubic expansion of at most 0.5% per 100°C, usually less than that. Because the cubic thermal expansion coefficient of most organic liquids is of the order of 7 to 10×10^{-4}°C^{-1} and

Table 8.15 (Linear) Thermal Expansion α_b of Covalent Bonds between 300 and 600°K

Substance	Bond	$10^5 \alpha_b$(°K^{-1})	Ref.
Cl_2	Cl—Cl	0.68 (theor)[a]	47
PCl_3	P—Cl	1.4 (exp)	17

[a] Sum of anharmonicity and centrifugal effects.

V_w is generally 0.55 of the total volume, the thermal expansion of V_w can contribute no more than 4% of the observed thermal expansion of the liquid. At $T < 300$°K it will be appreciably less.

The compressibility of molecules is the sum of two components, the compressibility of the bonds β_b and the compressibility of the electron cloud β_e. The calculation of the bond compressibility from the spectroscopic stretching force constants is straightforward. However, the calculation of the compressibility of the electron cloud is a more difficult problem. In principle it could

Table 8.16 Compressibility of Molecules

Substance	Bond	10^{12} K (bond)[a] (dyn/cm^2)	10^{12} K (Molecule) (dyn/cm^2)
n-Paraffins	C—C	3.2	0.15 to 0.30[b]
Aromatic rings	C—C	5	0.2 to 0.32[b]
$CHCl_3$	C—Cl	2.2	0.12 to 0.28[b]

[a] The value for the *n*-paraffin from Table 4.5, the others were obtained by correlation with spectroscopic force constants.
[b] The first value is the bulk modulus at $V = V_0$ and the second is that at $\rho^* \approx 0.9$. All data are from P. W. Bridgman, *Proc. Natl. Acad. Arts Sci.* **77**, 129 (1949).

be estimated from the slopes of the electron density curve $d\psi^2/dr$ at r_w. Yet existing electron-energy calculations are not particularly good in that region, hence, at the moment, we can deduce β_e only as the difference between the compressibility of substances at $\rho^* > \rho_0^*$, where ρ_0^*, the packing density at

$0°K$, is taken as that of the closely packed crystal. This compressibility is generally observed at $p > 15,000$ atm. Typical values for β at these high pressures, β_b, and the deduced β_e are given in Table 8.16. Because the liquid compressibilities in the technically important region of $p < 1000$ atm are generally of the order of $\geq 10^{-10}$ cm²/dyn, the compressibility of V_w obviously contributes only of the order of 1 % of the total compressibility, but, by definition, an increasing fraction of the total compressibility as $\rho^* \rightarrow \rho_0^*$.

One conclusion from the present considerations is that any theory which arrives at thermal-expansion coefficients and compressibilities of molecules larger than a few percent of the total expansion and compressibility coefficients of the liquids under consideration must be suspect.

8.7.1 Inaccessible (or Occupied) Volume and Free Volume

The effective temperature and pressure insensitivity of V_w must be confronted with the—at least qualitatively—successful description of the properties of liquids by means of free-volume models, the inaccessible molecule volume (V_j) of which does vary with temperature and pressure. Since it appears that each author defines these volumes as what he wants them to mean, a clarification of the over-all picture may be useful. The origin of the problem is, of course, the absence of a tractable rigorous molecular theory of liquids. The crude models that have to be used cannot be expected to yield entirely compatible numerical values for the inaccessible volume and/or the free volume in the system. (Even in the highly developed modern kinetic gas theory we find one set of force and occupied-volume constants to describe the equilibrium properties and another set for the transport properties of gases.)

Hence a glossary of definitions of volume terms is offered here to reduce the inevitable confusion somewhat. In an earlier glossary [4] all free-volume terms were based on V_w as the only form of inaccessible (occupied) volume. Since then several additional forms of inaccessible volume have found general use, especially for the correlation of mechanical properties of viscous and viscoelastic fluids.

Aside from comparatively rare inaccessible re-entrant cavities in complicated molecules, the primary cause for $V_j > V_w$ is probably the number density fluctuation of molecules in the liquid such that at any given moment a large fraction is tightly clustered. These clusters then play the role of the "solidlike" molecules in Eyring's significant structure theory. The interior of the cluster is then inaccessible to molecules colliding with the cluster. The smallest, most compact volume for a cluster is V_0, the volume (of the crystal) at $0°K$, usually close to the extrapolated liquid volume at $0°K$, Doolittle's choice for V_j in his viscosity correlation [12]. The earlier discussion showed that $V_j \approx V_0$ in Flory's theory [15] also. Where $V_j \approx V_0$, we may expect that its thermal expansion $\alpha_j \approx \alpha_s$ and its bulk modulus $K_j \approx K_s$.

A more realistic internal density for the cluster is that of a random close-packed system, which is $\rho^* \approx 0.64$ for spheres and about 0.78 for random close-packed (infinitely long) cylinders. Here we may expect $\alpha_s < \alpha_j < \alpha_L$ and $K_s > K_j > K_L$. Needless to say that clusters of this type (for which $V_j \approx V_{rc}$) should also exhibit strongly temperature dependent mechanical properties.

Since clustering of molecules in liquids must at any one moment cover a range of cluster sizes with differing densities, it is not surprising that the amount of inaccessible (or occupied) volume accounted for should depend on the property measured, or perhaps more specifically on the time scale of the experiment [36]. Another consequence is the resulting change in the meaning of "free volume," V_F:

when $V_j = V_w$, we should speak of the empty volume $V_f(T) = V(T) - V_w$;

when $V_j = V_0$, we should speak of the expansion volume $V_E(T) = V(T) - V_0$;

when $V_j = V_{rc}(T, P)$, we should speak of the available volume $V_a(T) = V(T, P) - V_{rc}(T, P)$.

Only the first of these can be related in an approximate way to the volume swept out by the thermal motions of the center of gravity of a molecule, the fluctuation volume $\mho$. This volume, $\mho$, is the characteristic feature of the partition functions of molecules in the liquid state, and therefore the main source of thermodynamic-property calculations by means of free-volume theory. For spherical molecules, Hirschfelder, Stevenson, and Eyring proposed

$$\mho_{(T)} = N_A g^3 \left[v_{(T)}^{1/3} - \left(\frac{V_w}{N_A} \right)^{1/3} \right]^3,$$

where g is a factor of the order 1 to 2, depending on the postulated packing geometry in the liquid. In the general case

$$\mho_{(T)} \approx \frac{4\pi}{3} \left(\frac{V_f}{A_w} \right)^3 N_A,$$

where A_w is the molecule surface area per mole. To a similar crude approximation $\mho_{(T)} \approx V_{(T)} [gRT/\Delta E_v(T)]^3$.

An important consequence of the choice of V_j is the effect on the meaning of property changes along an isochore. If $V_j = V_w$, $V_f = $ const along an isochore. The same is not true, however, for the other choices of V_j. Only the rare case of isochore $\approx$ isobar permits experiments at constant "free volume," namely, experiments near T_g, where volume changes with time are sufficiently slow for property measurements to be carried out during the attainment of equilibrium density. Only one such set of measurements has so far been reported [37].

COMPUTING METHODS

Procedure 8.1

Desired. Density versus temperature curve at atmospheric pressure.

Given. Molecular structure (hence molecular weight M).

STEP 1: Calculate V_w from the group increments in Table 14.1, or, if no increments are available, from the van der Waals radii on Tables 1.2, 14.1–16, and 14.18, covalent bond lengths using the method outlined in Section 14.1.

STEP 2: Calculate $E°$ from the group increment data in Tables 14.1 to 16.

STEP 3: Calculate c from the data given in Tables 14.1 to 16 unless the molecule can be assumed as rigid, in which case $c = 2$.

STEP 4: Now the density ρ can be estimated from the relation

$$\rho = \frac{M}{V_w}\left[0.727 - \frac{1.245cRT}{E°} - 0.475\left(\frac{cRT}{E°}\right)^2\right].$$

This relation is valid only for the saturation curve between the melting point and the atmospheric boiling point. The density may become larger than estimated as the glass transition temperature is approached, that is, when $cRT/E° <$ 0.1. For vinyl polymers, use the second equation in Step 4 of Procedure 8.2.

Procedure 8.2

Desired. Density versus temperature curve at atmospheric pressure.

Given. Molecular structure and the density $\rho(T)$ at one temperature T.

STEP 1: As in Procedure 8.1.

STEP 2: Estimate $\rho^*(T) = V_w \cdot \rho(T)/M$.

STEP 3: Obtain θ_L from Procedure 15.31.

STEP 4: Now for any temperature (for liquids with $150 < M < 2000$):

$$\rho = \frac{M}{V_w}\left[0.727 - 0.249\frac{T}{\theta_L} - 0.019\left(\frac{T}{\theta_L}\right)^2\right],$$

whereas for vinyl–polymer melts at $T > T_g$,

$$\rho = \frac{M(u)}{V_w(u)}\left[0.766 - 0.33\left(\frac{T}{\theta_L}\right)\right].$$

The reasonableness of the result may be checked by estimating $E°$ according to Step 2 of Procedure 8.1. Then $c = E°/5R\theta_L = E°/9.94\theta_L$. Then compare the value of $3c$ with those given in Table 8.7. If it is very different from those expected, or in the case of rigid compound if $3c \neq 6 \pm 0.5$, either the reported experimental density is unreliable or an error was made in the computation of the auxiliary parameters V_w and $E°$.

Procedure 8.3

Desired. The thermal-expansion coefficients of liquids between T_m and T_b at atmospheric pressure.

Given. Molecular structure and one density point at temperature T.

STEPS 1–4: Same as Steps 1–4 of Procedure 8.2.

STEP 5: Read reduced expansion coefficient α^* from Figure 8.8, or calculate from the equation given on that figure, for the desired temperature $T^*(\equiv T/\theta_L)$.[1]

STEP 6: Convert to the unreduced expansion coefficient $\alpha = \alpha^*/\theta_L$. Use the method given at the end of Procedure 8.2 to check the reasonableness of the value of θ_L obtained in Step 4.

Procedure 8.4

Desired. The initial (low-pressure) compressibility of a liquid composed of rigid and of flexible molecules with $N_s < 15$ between T_m and T_b.

Given. Molecular structure (and one density point at temperature T).

STEPS 1–3: Same as Steps 1–3 of Procedure 8.1.

STEP 4: Now the reducing temperature (characteristic temperature of the liquid) $\theta_L = E^\circ/5cR$.

STEP 5: $K_0^* = K_0 V_w/E^\circ = 2.00/T^* - 1.60$.

STEP 6: The desired bulk modulus $K_0 = K_0^* \cdot E^\circ/V_w$. The compressibility $\beta_0 = K_0^{-1}$.

Procedure 8.5

Desired. The high-pressure compressibility of liquids composed of rigid and flexible molecules with $N_s < 15$.

Given. Molecular structure.

STEPS 1–6: Same as Steps 1–6 of Procedure 8.4.

STEP 7: For crude approximation, the pressure coefficient K_1 of the bulk modulus of liquids can be taken as a universal constant $= 11$. Then $K(P, T) \approx K_0(T) + 11P$, where K_0 and P are, or course, in the same units.

STEP 8: A somewhat better approximation is the relation $K_1 = a + b/T^*$, where values for the constants depend somewhat on molecular structure, but have yet to be determined with sufficient accuracy for firm recommendations.

Procedure 8.6

Desired. The initial (low pressure) compressibility of a liquid composed of long flexible molecules ($N_s > 15$).

Given. Molecular structure (one density point at temperature T).

STEPS 1–4: Same as Steps 1–4 of Procedure 8.4 (with E°, c, and V_w in units per repeating unit on the chain, if $N_s > 50$).

STEP 5: Because of the length of the long-chain molecule, an appreciable portion of the compressible environment is replaced by covalently bonded nearest neighbors of a molecule segment. Hence the reduced bulk modulus is

$$K_0^*(L) = K_0\left\{\frac{V_w}{E^\circ}\left[\frac{2}{3}\left(1 + \frac{1}{N_s}\right)\right] + \frac{1}{3E_p}\left(1 - \frac{1}{N_s}\right)\right\},$$

which, for $N_s \to \infty$ and $E_p \gg E^\circ/V_w$, reduces to $K_0^*(L) = K_0 \cdot 2V_w/3E^\circ$, where E_p, the elastic modulus of the molecule along the covalent bonds is calculated from spectroscopic data. Typical examples[2] are (all in units of 10^{10} dynes/cm²): polymethylene chain $E_p = 230$, polypropylene $= 49$ (for other backbones see Table 4.5).

---

[1] For vinyl polymers with $M > 2000$ (at $T > (T_g + 30°C)$): $\alpha = 0.33[\theta_L(0.766 - 0.33T^*)]^{-1}$; $\alpha = 1.65cR[E_{(n)}^\circ(0.766 - 0.33T^*)]^{-1}$.

[2] I. Sakurada et al., *Makromol. Chem.* **75**, 1 (1964).

STEP 6: $K_0^*(L) = 2.30/T^* - 1.95.$

STEP 7: The desired initial bulk modulus

$$K_0 = K_0^*(L)\left\{\frac{V_w}{E^\circ}\left[\frac{2}{3}\left(1 + \frac{1}{N_s}\right)\right] + \frac{1}{3E_p}\left(1 - \frac{1}{N_s}\right)\right\};$$

$N_s \to \infty$ and $E_p \gg E^\circ/V_w$ $K_0 = K_0^*(L) \cdot 3E^\circ/2V_w.$

REFERENCES

[1] Allen, G., et al., *Polymer* 1, 467 (1960).
[2] Bergmann, L., *Der Ultraschall* (S. Hirzel, Leipzig, 1954), 6th ed., Suppl. 1957.
[3] Bernal, J. D., *Nature* 183, 141 (1959); 185, 68 (1960); 188, 910 (1960); *Proc. Roy. Soc. (London)* A280, 299 (1964).
[4] Bondi, A., *J. Phys. Chem.* 58, 929 (1954).
[5] Bondi, A., *J. Phys. Chem.* 68, 441 (1964).
[6] Bondi, A., *J. Polymer Sci.* A2, 3159 (1964).
[7] Bondi, A., *J. Phys. Chem.* 70, 530 (1966).
[8] Bondi, A., and H. L. Parry, *J. Phys. Chem.* 60, 1406 (1956).
[9] Bondi, A., and D. J. Simkin, *AIChE J.* 6, 191 (1960).
[10] Cummins, H. Z., and R. W. Gammon, *J. Chem. Phys.* 44, 2785 (1966).
[11] Deloze, C., P. Saladjan, and A. J. Kovacs, *Biopolymers* 2, 43 (1964).
[12] Doolittle, A. K., *J. Appl. Phys.* 22, 1031, 1471 (1951); 23, 236 (1952).
[13] Doolittle, A. K., et al., *AIChE J.* 6, 150, 157 (1960).
[14] Flory, P. J., et al., *J. Am. Chem. Soc.* 86, 3507 (1964).
[15] Flory, P. J., and A. Abe, *J. Am. Chem. Soc.* 87, 1833, 1838 (1965).
[16] Frisch, H. L., H. Reiss, and J. L. Lebowitz, *J. Chem. Phys.* 31, 369 (1959).
[17] Hedberg, K., and M. Iwasaki, *J. Chem. Phys.* 36, 589 (1962).
[18] Hijmans, J., Physica 27, 433 (1961).
[19] Hildebrand, J. H., and R. L. Scott, *Solubility of Non-Electrolytes*, Reinhold, New York, 1951.
[20] Hildebrand, J. H., Spiers Memorial Lecture, *Faraday Soc. Disc.* 15, 9 (1953).
[21] Hildebrand, J. H., private communication.
[22] Hildebrand, J. H., and J. Dymond, *J. Chem. Phys.* 46, 624 (1967).
[23] Holleman, Th., *Physica* 29, 585 (1963).
[24] Horth, A., et al., *J. Polymer Sci.* 39, 189 (1959).
[25] Kovacs, A. J., *Fortschr. Polymer Forschg.* 3, 394 (1964).
[26] Kremann, R., *Physikalische Eigenschaften und Chemische Konstitution* (Theodor Steinkopff Verlag, Dresden, 1937), p. 14 et seq.
[27] Kruh, R. F., *Chem. Rev.* 62, 319 (1962).
[28] Kurtz, S. S., in *The Chemistry of Petroleum Hydrocarbons*, Reinhold, New York, 1954, Vol. 1, p. 275.
[29] Lamb, J., *Physical Acoustics*, W. P. Mason, ed., Academic Press, New York, 1964, Vol. 2A, p. 203.
[30] Lipkin, M. R., and S. S. Kurtz, *Ind. Eng. Chem., Anal. Ed.* 13, 291 (1941).
[31] Litovitz, T. A., and C. M. Davis, *Physical Acoustics*, W. P. Mason, ed., Academic Press, New York, 1965, Vol. 2A, p. 282.
[32] Manegold, E., *Kolloid-Z.* 96, 186 (1941).
[33] McGowan, J. C., *Rec. Trav. Chim.* 75, 193 (1956).

[34] Murphy, C. M., et al., *Trans. ASME* **71,** 561 (1949).

[35] Nozd'rev, V. F., *Use of Ultrasonics in Molecular Physics*, Pergamon, New York, 1965.

[36] Plazek, D. L., *J. Phys. Chem.* **69,** 3480 (1965).

[37] Plazek, D. L., and J. H. Magill, *J. Chem. Phys.* **45,** 3038 (1966).

[38] Prigogine, I., *The Molecular Theory of Solutions*, Interscience, New York, 1957.

[39] Prigogine, I., A. Bellemans, and C. Naar-Colin, *J. Chem. Phys.* **26,** 741 (1957).

[40] Quayle, O. R., *Chem. Rev.* **53,** 439 (1953).

[41] Reid, R. C., and T. K. Sherwood, *Properties of Gases and Liquids*, McGraw-Hill, New York, 1966, 2nd ed.

[42] Schaafs, W., *Molekularakustik*, Springer, Berlin, 1963.

[43] Schmitt, A., and A. J. Kovacs, *Chem. Rev.* **255,** 677 (1962).

[44] Schulz, G. V., and Hoffmann, M., *Makomol. Chem.* **23,** 220 (1957).

[45] Scott, G. D., *Nature* **188,** 908 (1960).

[46] Simha, R., and A. T. Havlick, *J. Am. Chem. Soc.* **86,** 197 (1964).

[47] Stuart, H. A., *Physik der Hochpolymeren*, Springer, Berlin, 1954, Vol. 1.

[48] Toyama, M., et al., *J. Mol. Spectry.* **13,** 193 (1964).

[49] Ueberreiter, K., and W. Bruns, *Ber. Bunsenges.* **68,** 541 (1964).

[50] Wall, F. T., and W. R. Krigbaum, *J. Chem. Phys.* **17,** 1274 (1949).

[51] Waterman, J. A., Koninklijk/Shell Laboratorium, Amsterdam, private communication.

[52] Wise, M. E., *Philips Res. Repts.* **7,** 321 (1952).

[53] Wyn-Jones, E., and W. J. Orville-Thomas, "Molecular Relaxation Processes," *Chem. Soc. Publ.* **20,** 209 (1966).

9

Heat Capacity of Liquids
and Polymer Melts

9.1 GENERAL PRINCIPLES

The heat capacity of liquids composed of polyatomic molecules can be separated into two parts, the vibrational contribution C_i and the contribution due to the various external degrees of freedom of the molecule. As the internal vibration frequencies ω_i are nearly invariant with change of phase, we assume throughout that C_i is independent of the phase state. The liquid-state contribution to heat capacity, $C_p{}^\lambda$ and $C_v{}^\lambda$ defined by $C_p{}^{(1)} = C_i + C_p{}^\lambda$ and $C_v{}^{(1)} = C_i + C_v{}^\lambda$ is the subject of this section. From here on, C_v is discussed, primarily, because only C_v, the heat capacity at constant volume, is clearly related to molecular mechanics. The difference

$$C_p - C_v = \left(\frac{\partial V}{\partial T}\right)_p \left(\frac{\partial E}{\partial V}\right)_T \tag{9.1}$$

is just the heat-capacity contribution of the work required for the thermal expansion of a liquid at atmospheric pressure. In the absence of data it can be provided from suitable p-v-T correlations.

Intuition suggests the existence of upper and lower limits to C_v by reference to well-known states: $[C_{tr}^{(g)} + C_r^{(g)}] < C_v{}^\lambda < C_v(\text{lattice})$. The data for argon, Figure 9.1, and benzene, Figure 9.2, show that this is not a bad guess in the case of simple substances, at least at $T < 0.9T_c$. The same holds true probably for all compounds with melting points $T_m > 0.5T_c$. However, $C_v^{(l)}$ of very low-melting substances with $T_m < 0.4T_c$ definitely exceeds that of the solid at $T > 0.5T_c$, as shown by the examples of n-heptane and toluene in Figure 9.3.

The heat capacity of monatomic liquids is strictly a function of the ratio $Z\epsilon/kT (= Z/\tilde{T})$, where ϵ is the pair potential at equilibrium separation and Z

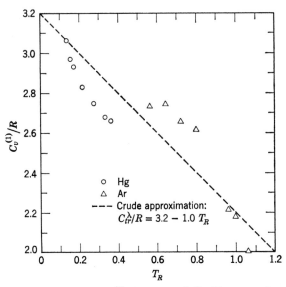

Figure 9.1   Experimental data for $C_v^{(1)}$ of monatomic liquid versus reduced temperature T_R.

is the number of nearest neighbors of a molecule. The Lennard–Jones–Devonshire theory of the liquid state yields the relation between C_v and $\tilde{T}$ shown in Figure 9.4. The mathematical treatment for polyatomic molecules, or for any molecules with nonuniform force fields is quite intractable.

The theories of liquids composed of polyatomic molecules by Prigogine, Simha, and Flory, which served as a basis for p-v-T correlations in Chapter 8 assume that the cell partition function is a function of volume only, and

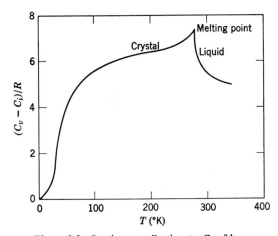

Figure 9.2   Lattice contribution to C_v of benzene.

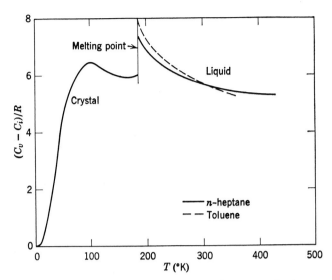

Figure 9.3   Lattice contribution to C_v of n-heptane and toluene.

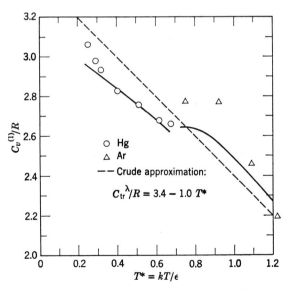

Figure 9.4   Heat capacity C_v of monatomic liquids   (from [7]). Curves I(Hg) and II(Ar) according to LJD theory compared with experimental data [14].

therefore yield $C_v = 0$ [16]. This flaw of their cell partition function was remedied by Renon et al., [16] through the ad hoc introduction of a temperature-dependent term that yields for the heat capacity

$$C_v \approx 0.8cR\tilde{T}^{-2} \sim \frac{cR}{(T^*)^2} \qquad (9.2)$$

in poor-to-moderate agreement with experiment. The data in Figure 9.5 show that the reduced configurational heat capacity $C_v^\lambda/3cR$ of any single liquid or related series of liquids is more nearly linear in $(T^*)^{-1}$. The wide differences between groups of compounds on the same graph also suggest that lumping all degrees of freedom in $3c$ is too blunt a tool for heat-capacity correlations. A theory of liquids (of polyatomic molecules) has yet to be developed which leads to a tolerably good description of the configurational heat capacity.

A simple-minded approach to the analysis of C_v is to break it up into contributions from the various external degrees of freedom of a molecule. This idea is not new, having been proposed previously by Moelwyn–Hughes [12]. The novel aspect of the present work is the attempt to estimate the temperature dependence of the various contributions. The program at hand is

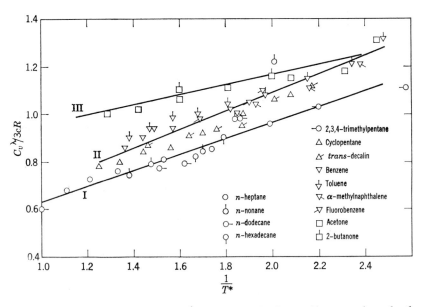

Figure 9.5 Reduced heat capacity $C_v^\lambda/3cR$ of liquid alkanes (I), aromatic and other cyclic compounds (II), and ketones (III), versus reduced temperature T^*.

summarized by the relations

$$C_v^\lambda(T) = C_{tr}^\lambda(T) + C_{hr}(T) + C_b(T) \quad \text{for rigid molecules,} \qquad (9.3)$$

$$C_v^\lambda(T) = C_F^\lambda(T) \qquad\qquad\qquad \text{for flexible molecules,} \qquad (9.4)$$

where C_{tr}^λ is the contribution of translational oscillations, C_{hr} is that due to hindered external rotation of polyatomic molecules, C_b is that due to energy expended in cooperative motions of many molecules (at high packing densities), and C_F^λ is the contribution of mixed hindered internal and external rotation characteristic of flexible molecules. The reason for the split into two different treatments is, of course, the inapplicability of the assumption of separability of the various degrees of freedom—underlying relation (9.2)—to flexible molecules. These four C's are now discussed in the sequence given.

9.2 TRANSLATIONAL OSCILLATIONS

The translational oscillations of a monatomic molecule in the field of force of its neighbors could contribute to C_{tr}^λ a maximum of $3R$ (the Dulong – Petit value for a crystalline solid composed of harmonic oscillators) just above the melting point and a minimum of $\frac{3}{2}R + \delta C_v(P)$ at the critical temperature. Then $\delta C_v(P)$ is the pressure correction to the gas-phase heat capacity, corresponding to P_c at T_c. Calculation of C_{tr}^λ for a monatomic liquid with Lennard–Jones 6:12 potential between neighbors by Prigogine and Raulier [14] yielded the curve shown in Figure 9.1 and found to be in reasonable agreement with the experimental values for argon and mercury.

Since the calculation is somewhat laborious and the Lennard–Jones potential is often a poor approximation to the facts, a simple correlation with the appropriate reduced temperature has been tried. It appears that the linear relation

$$C_{tr}^\lambda R \approx 3.40 - 1.0T^* \qquad (9.5)$$

represents the data quite satisfactorily, if the Hg data are given more weight than the Ar data (see Figure 9.4). The great age of the C_v data of argon and their greater deviation from theory than that for Hg suggests that a redetermination would be in order. At that time, C_v should also be calculated for a fixed volume throughout the liquid range. As there is no reason to believe that C_{tr}^λ for any rigid molecule is likely to differ significantly from C_v of monatomic liquids, (9.5) is used for the estimate of C_{tr}.

9.3 HINDERED EXTERNAL ROTATION [7]

Several qualitative features of the major remaining component of C_v^λ of rigid molecules tempt us to ascribe it to hindered external rotation. These features are: parallel trend for C_{hr} and $E°/T$ (as would be required if $E°$ is taken as the origin of the barrier to external rotation), and a parallelism between the absolute magnitude of C_{hr} and the principal moments of inertia, especially of small molecules, just as we would expect from Pitzer's theory of the heat-capacity contribution of a hindered rotor.

The quantitative evaluation of C_{hr} shows that only a small group of liquids conforms to the simple model of a hindered rotor. Very small and symmetrical molecules such as CH_4 and SiH_4 behave like free rotors with $C_{hr} \lesssim \frac{3}{2}R$ over the entire temperature range. Ethane also acts like a free rotor. Propane is the only lower hydrocarbon, the C_{hr} of which follows the theoretical curve for a Pitzer hindered rotor with barrier height $V° = N_A\epsilon \approx 0.1E°$[1] and the number of barriers per rotation, $n = 5$ to within the experimental accuracy (Fig. 9.6). The C_{hr} curves of the lower alkyl monohalides are qualitatively similar.

The C_{hr} curves of liquids composed of larger rigid molecules are in qualitative disagreement with those of a simple hindered rotor. Whereas for the latter C_{rr} per degree of freedom cannot rise substantially above $C_{rr} = R$, as $V°/RT \to \infty$ corresponding to a torsional oscillator, C_{hr} of the liquids under consideration increases without limit as $E°/RT \to \infty$. Moreover, if we take $10\,RT/E°$ as temperature scale, $\Sigma\,C_{rr} < C_{hr}$ over the entire temperature range (Fig. 9.7). The difference $C_{hr} - \Sigma\,C_{rr}$ might be taken as a measure of a contribution due to the cooperative interaction required for rotation at high

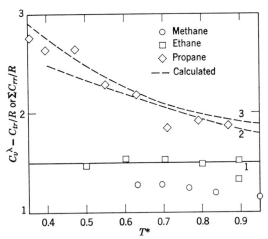

Figure 9.6 Experimental data $C_v^\lambda - C_{tr}$ compared with calculated curves 2 and 3 for hindered external rotation contribution to heat capacity (C_{rr}) of liquids composed of small molecules (from [7]).

[1] The results obtainable with the more realistic temperature-dependent barrier $V° = \Delta E_v(T)$ do not differ sufficiently to make the increased labor worthwhile.

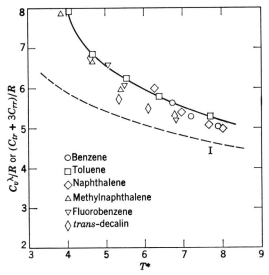

Figure 9.7 Comparison of observed C_v^λ data with universal theoretical curve I for $(C_{tr} + 3C_{rr})$ for liquids composed of rigid molecules ($3c = 6 \pm 0.5$) (from [7]).

packing densities. It turns out that $(C_{hr} - \Sigma\, C_{rr}) = (0.30 \pm 0.08)R(0.1E°/RT)^2$, for the 20 liquids examined. The indicated uncertainty produces significant errors ($\pm 0.5R$) only at very low temperatures where the experimental data for C_v are quite uncertain. In the practically important temperature ranges the uncertainty is of the order $\pm 0.1R$. Hence for liquids composed of rigid molecules with $N_c > 4$, we can write

$$C_{hr} = \sum C_{rr} + 0.30R\left(0.1\,\frac{E°}{RT}\right)^2. \qquad (9.6)$$

Theoretical treatments of cooperative motions of molecules at high packing density do not appear to be sufficiently well developed for the calculation of the heat capacity by any less crudely empirical method.

A yet simpler treatment was tried, namely, to represent C_{hr} as a linear function of $E°/RT$ or of $\Delta E_v(T)/RT$. The basic objection that $E°/RT$ and $\Delta E_v(T)/RT$ tend to 0 as $T \to \infty$ could be removed by inclusion of $\frac{3}{2}R$ as intercept. However, $C_{hr} - \frac{3}{2}R$ is not a simple function of either of the proposed reduced-temperature scales. The extent to which the simple identification $C_{hr}/R = 0.2E°/RT$ and of $C_{hr}/R = 0.216E°(1.3 - T^*)^{1/3}/RT$ represents the data is shown in Figures 9.8 and 9.9. The second form does particularly well at low temperatures, but naturally somewhat poorer at high temperature. When the indicated errors are tolerable, the approximation

$$C_{hr} \approx 0.216\,\frac{E°(1.3 - T^*)^{1/3}}{RT} \qquad (9.7)$$

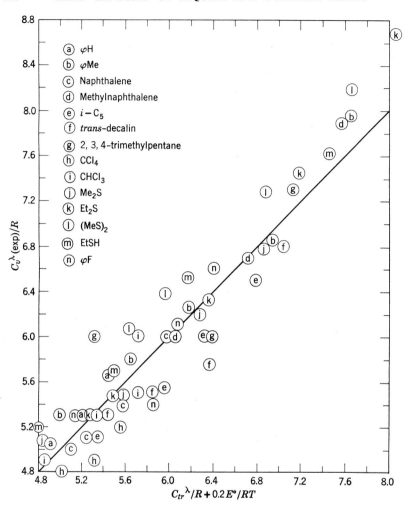

Figure 9.8 Comparison of experimental C_v^λ of rigid molecules with calculation (from [7]). Points on 45° line indicate perfect agreement between calculated and experimental data.

may well be preferable to the somewhat cumbersome method of the previous paragraph.

9.3.1 Very Polar Compounds

The very simple treatment of the previous section contained the tacit assumption that the barrier to external rotation of rigid molecules in liquids is 0.1 $\Delta E_v(T)$, and that the potential-energy barrier is not localized in any part

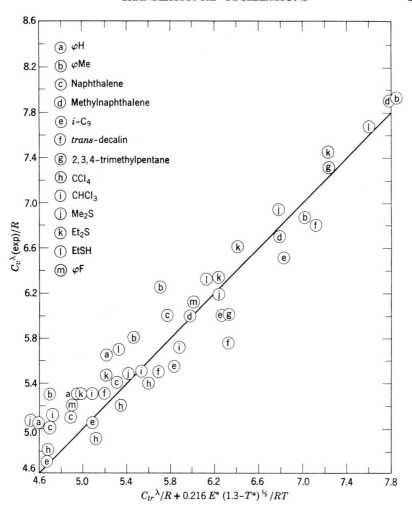

Figure 9.9 Comparison of experimental C_v^λ of rigid molecules with calculation (from [7]). Points on 45° line indicate perfect agreement between calculated and experimental data.

of the molecule. These assumptions cease to be valid when most of the interaction is due to dipole orientation, that is, when

$$E_\mu \approx \frac{2}{3} \frac{N_A \mu^2}{r^3} > 0.2 \, \Delta E_v(T). \tag{9.8}$$

In that case we should take $V^\circ = E_\mu$, and by comparison with experiment, we

Table 9.1 Magnitude of Dipole Orientation Energy E_μ for Frequently Occurring Functional Groups[a]

Functional Group	In Aliphatic Compound (kcal/mole)	In Aromatic Compound (kcal/mole)	In Vinyl Compound (kcal/mole)
F	1.8	1.1	—
Cl	1.5	0.9	0.7
Br	1.3	0.9	0.4
I	1.1	0.7	0.3
Ether —O—	0.4	0.35	0.4
Heterocyclic —O—	1.0	0.13	—
Aldehyde $\diagdown$C=O	2.3	3.0	2.6
Keto $\diagdown$C=O	2.4	2.8	2.8
Carboxylate ester —O—C(=O)—	0.9	1.1	—
Carboxylate ester (heterocyclic) —O—C(=O)	5.0	—	—
Carboxyl anhydride —C(=O)—O—C(=O)—	1.8	—	—
Carboxyl anhydride (heterocyclic) —C(=O)—O—C(=O)—	4.7	—	—
Carbonate ester —O—C(=O)—O—	0.4	—	—
Carbonate ester (heterocyclic) —O—C(=O)—O—	7.0	—	—
Nitro —NO$_2$	4.2	6.0	—
Nitrate —O—NO$_2$	2.7	—	—
Cyano —C≡N	3.2	5.1	—
Thioether —S—	0.35	0.37	0.30
Heterocyclic —S—	—	0.06	—
Disulfide —SS—[b]	0 to −0.4	—	—

[a] $E_\mu = \frac{2}{3}N_A\,\mu^2/d_w^3$, the average orientation value at the closest approach distance $d_w = r_w(1) + r_w(2)$, applicable only in the absence of vicinal effects, that is, with fewer than one permanent dipole per carbon atom in the molecule. The dipole moment chosen is the group moment appropriate for the bond indicated from the collection by Smyth, C.P., *Dipole Moment and Molecular Structure* McGraw-Hill, New York, 1955. See also Tables 1.5 through 1.11 and 14.27.

[b] The dipole interaction of disulfide–carbon bonds ranges from negligible attraction in staggered configuration to repulsion in nonstaggered configuration.

obtain

$$C_{hr} = \sum C_{rr} + 0.2R\left(0.1\ \frac{E^\circ}{RT}\right)^2.$$ (9.9)

The peculiar facet of strong dipole interaction, that C_{hr} decreases more slowly with increasing temperature than we observe with liquids composed of nonpolar molecules, can be associated with the fact that $E_\mu/RT > 3$ over most of the liquid range. Typical values for E_μ are shown in Table 9.1.

In the special case of associating systems we have to consider the additional contribution to C arising from the factor $(dx/dT)\,\Delta H_a$, where x is the mole fraction of association polymer present and ΔH_a is the heat of dissociation.

9.3.2. Molecules with Internal Rotation

A multiple barrier to internal rotation is tantamount to the existence of rotational isomers especially if the barriers differ significantly in height. Differences in depths of successive potential energy wells traversed by the rotor and the energy of isomerization (ΔE_i) between rotational isomers contribute the term $(dx_i/dT)\,\Delta H_i$ to the heat capacity. Details of the calculation have been discussed elsewhere.[1] In the present context the important fact is the frequent large difference in ΔE_i between the gaseous and the liquid state. It often even differs in sign. The peculiar trend of C_v^λ of 1,2-dichloroethane with temperature, shown in Table 9.2 illustrates this effect. As there is no theory to account for this effect, nor enough data for development of a valid correlation, we have to work out the contribution of ΔH_i to C_v^λ, or better to C_p^λ, for each case using whatever data may be at hand.

The change in ΔH_i from gas to liquid phase is closely associated with the accompanying change in barrier height and shape. Only in the case of paraffin hydrocarbons has an attempt been made to estimate the change in barrier height on the basis of the anisotropy of polarizability of the bonds of neighboring molecules and the resulting preferred mutual orientation. [2] In that case the change in barrier height upon immersion of a molecule in a liquid turned out to be representable as a fixed fraction of the heat of vaporization. Similar estimates may be developed for other compounds.

9.4 LONG-CHAIN MOLECULES AND POLYMERS

Flexible long-chain molecules present special problems in more than one respect. The number of rotational isomers is large $[\sim(N_c - 2)]$ and the contribution of $(dx_i/dT)\,\Delta H_i$ is correspondingly important. Superimposed is the effect of the rise in potential barrier to external rotation as the chain length of a molecule is increased. It is, of course, unrealistic to treat n-paraffins or

[1] Lielmesz, J., and A. Bondi, *Chem. Eng. Sci.* **20**, 706 (1965).

HEAT CAPACITY OF LIQUIDS AND POLYMER MELTS

any other chain molecule with $N_s > 5$ as rigid rotors in the sense presented above, because, as Pitzer showed [13], internal and external rotation cannot be separated properly for longer chains; certainly not for $N_s \geq 7$.

In view of the foregoing argument it appeared logical to assume that in long-chain compounds the temperature-dependent term of C_v^λ might be proportional to the total number of external degrees of freedom $(3c)$ (including those due to internal rotation) per molecule. Hence we might try $C_v^\lambda \sim c/T^* \sim E°/5RT$ in Figure 9.10. The long flexible molecules with $N_c > 7$ are

Table 9.2 Heat Capacity of 1,2-Dichloroethane; an Example for the Effect of Rotational Isomerism [4]

T (°K)	23.7	270	307.5
T^*	0.538	0.607	0.692
$C_p^{(l)}/R^a$	15.10	15.14	15.60
$[C_p^{(l)} - C_v^{(1)}]/R^b$	4.82	4.83	4.95
$C_v^{(l)}/R$	10.28	10.31	10.65
C_i/R^c	4.91	5.05	5.22
C_v^λ/R	5.37	5.26	5.43
C_{tr}^λ/R	2.86	2.79	2.71
C_{hr}^λ/R	2.51	2.47	2.72
$\Sigma C_{rr}/R^d$	3.2	3.0	2.8

[a] Pitzer, K. S., *J. Am. Chem. Soc.*, **1939**, 331.
[b] Lagemann, *J. Chem. Phys.* **17**, 369 (1949).
[c] Pitzer, K. S. and Gwinn, *J. Chem. Phys.* **10**, 428 (1942); **16**, 303 (1948); J. Lielmesz and A. Bondi, *Chem. Eng. Sci.* **20**, 706 (1965).
[d] Assume $V° = E_\mu$ (see Table 9.1). It would be incorrect to set $V° = 2E_\mu$, because no single dipole orientation barrier would be higher than E_μ, even if there are two equal dipoles in the molecule.

seen to behave even qualitatively differently from the shorter ones. The lower *n*-paraffins (up to $N_c = 5$) behave essentially like rigid-rod molecules, and the number of external degrees of freedom $3c \approx 6$, and their heat capacity being essentially that of rigid molecules with one axis of rather low moment of inertia. Quantitative explanations are wanting, however, for the rather clearcut beginning of "flexibility" at $n - C_7$.

Within the rather broad scatter of the data (due to inaccuracies in the calculation of $C_p - C_v$), the heat capacity of the C_7^+ *n*-paraffins follows a single curve or at least a narrow band of curves. As $E°$ is easily calculated (from group increments) this is a very convenient correlation. No other heat capacity data of nonpolymeric long-chain compounds being available, the generality of this behavior can only be surmised.

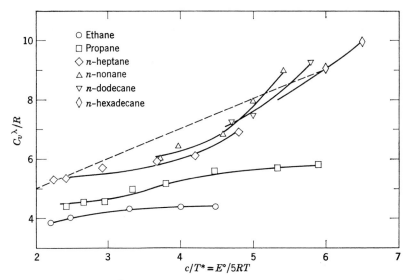

Figure 9.10   Plot of C_v^λ of n-paraffins versus the parameter $0.2\,E^\circ/RT$ (from [7]).

The data are well represented by the relation

$$\frac{C_v^\lambda}{R} = \frac{2.15}{T^*} + \frac{0.2E_u^\circ}{RT}N_c,\qquad (9.10)$$

where E_u° is the energy of vaporization per repeating unit, for example, 1.08 kcal/mole CH_2 groups and $N_c > 7$. This relation cannot be correct at very high temperatures, but there are no data to determine this limiting temperature.

A gratifying confirmation of the generality of (9.10) comes from the observation that its second term has the numerical value of C_v^λ per repeating unit (CH_2) for polyethylene melt at the same reduced temperature (i.e., at the same packing density). This small value of C_v^λ is probably unique for polyethylene and perhaps other all-backbone polymers such as polytetrafluoroethylene. The data in Table 9.3 summarize the very limited available information on polymer melts, and suggest that C_v^λ data of polymers are more difficult to generalize than are the data for simple compounds. In part this may be due to the uncertainty of the vibrational (including internal rotational) contributions that have been derived from calculations for low-molecular-weight compounds. Another uncertainty is caused by the experimental difficulty of obtaining specific heat and p–v–T data on polymer melts, especially at high temperatures.

Within these limitations a few common features can be noted: At $T \gg T_g$, C_v^λ exhibits the normal downward trend with temperature. The most precise

Table 9.3   Heat-Capacity Data for Several High-Polymer Melts [4]

Polymer Melt	T (°K)	T^*	$\dfrac{C_p^{(l)}}{R}$	$\dfrac{C_v^{(l)}}{R}$	$\dfrac{C^i}{R}$	$\dfrac{C_v^{\lambda}}{R}$	$\dfrac{E°}{5RT}$	Ref.
Polyethylene	410	0.583	4.36	3.84	3.56	0.28	0.26	a, b, c, d
	470	0.668	4.59	4.12	3.96	0.16	0.23	
Polypropylene	450		13.73	12.3	11.5	0.8	0.60	b, d, e
	470		14.03	12.6	11.9	0.7	0.58	
cis-1,4-								
Polyisoprene	300	0.39	15.51	13.24	11.83	1.46	1.88	d, f
Polystyrene	373	0.438	22.7 −	20.0 −	18.5[g]	1.5 −	2.1	a, b, d, h
			23.0	20.3		1.8[g]		
	393	0.462	23.8	21.1	19.5[g]	1.6[i]	2.0	
	473	0.557	27.0	23.5	22.8[g]	0.7[i]	1.7	
Polyvinyl chloride	363		12.0	10.0	7.55	2.45[i]	2.1[j]	
	373		12.2	10.3	7.65	2.65[i]	2.0[j]	

[a] Hellwege, K. H. et al., *Kolloid-Z.* **180**, 126 (1962); $C_p^{(l)}$.
[b] Hellwege, K. H., et al., *ibid.* **183**, 110 (1962); K_0.
[c] Pals, D. T. F., and T. N. O. Delft, private communication; α, ρ.
[d] Res. Proj. 44; Tables; Selected Properties of Hydrocarbons"; C_i.
[e] Pessaglia, E., and H. K. Kevorkian, *J. Appl. Phy.* **34**, 90 (1963); $C_p^{(l)}$.
[f] Wood, L. A., and G. M. Martin, *J. Res. Natl. Bur. Std.* **68A**, 259 (1964); $C_p^{(l)}$, K, α, ρ.
[g] Separate investigation showed that these values may be somewhat high, hence C_v^{λ} (polystyrene) data shown here are probably lower limits.
[h] Karasz, F. E., H. E. Bair, and J. M. O'Reilly, *J. Phys. Chem.* **69**, 2657 (1965).
[i] Accuracy of these data is somewhat in doubt because of proximity to T_g.
[j] E_μ/RT.

measurements of this series on polyethylene, *cis*-1,4-polyisoprene (Hevea), and polypropylene show, somewhat unexpectedly, about the same magnitude of C_v^{λ} per carbon atom.

At temperatures just above T_g (about 20 to 100°C above T_g), C_v^{λ} increases with increasing temperature because of the unfreezing of (internal) degrees of freedom. Judging by general experience, this process should be completed at $T^* + 0.2T^*$ which is often of the order of $(T_g + 100)$ °K [5]. Beyond that temperature, C_v^{λ} should again decrease with increasing temperature.

The most surprising result is the agreement between C_v^{λ} and $E°/5RT$ for the hydrocarbon polymers. Simple statistical considerations probably preclude attachment of the adjective "fortuitous" to data on four different polymers. The C_v^{λ} data for polyvinylchloride (PVC) were best represented by the predictor for polar compounds, E_μ/RT. More data on polar polymers are needed before we can accept this result as more than coincidence, especially because of the divergent temperature trend between C_v^{λ} and E_μ/RT in the temperature range of the experiment, just above T_g.

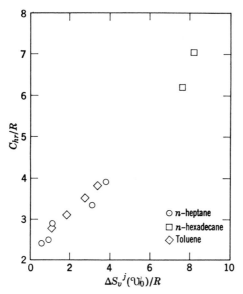

Figure 9.11 Relation between the contribution of hindered external rotation to heat capacity (C_{hr}) and the excess entropy of vaporization calculated from the fluctuation volume ($\mathcal{V}_0$).

9.5 ANOTHER METHOD TO ESTIMATE C_{hr}

In general it is not very helpful to explain one unexplained phenomenon by another. It is interesting, however, to compare two phenomena to which intuition has ascribed the same cause. If one of the two is more easily determined than the other, it may even be useful to calculate one from the other. The couple in point is made up of C_{hr} and $\Delta S_v{}^j$, the excess entropy of vaporization. The latter, defined as

$$\Delta S_v{}^j = \left| \Delta S_v \text{(observed)} - R \ln \left(\frac{RT}{p \cdot \mathcal{V}_0} \right) \right|_T \qquad (9.11)$$

or

$$\Delta S_v{}^j = \left| \Delta S_v \text{(observed)} - \Delta S_v(H_g) \right|_{P/T} \qquad (9.12)$$

has long been recognized as a good measure of the hindrance to free external rotation in the liquid [8], [10], [11]. Some time ago, we showed that $(C_v - \frac{3}{2}R) \sim \Delta S_v{}^j$, which is close to saying that $C_{hr} \sim \Delta S_v{}^j$ [2]. In the light of knowledge increased since then, C_{hr} has been compared with $\Delta S_v{}^j$ for various compounds. The results shown in Figure 9.11 versus $\Delta S_v{}^j(V)$, and in

Figure 9.12 versus ΔS_v^j(Hg) suggest that C_{hr} might indeed be estimated from ΔS_v^j if sufficiently reliable vapor-pressure data were available or could be calculated.

9.6 HEAT CAPACITY AT CONSTANT PRESSURE, C_p

In most engineering applications we deal with systems at constant pressure, hence the thermal properties should be known at constant pressure. The heat capacity at constant pressure, C_p, differs from C_v only by the temperature coefficient of the work done in the thermal expansion of the liquid or

$$C_p - C_v = \left(\frac{\partial V}{\partial T}\right)_p \left(\frac{\partial E}{\partial V}\right)_T = TVK_0\alpha^2. \tag{9.13}$$

In the absence of liquid p–v–T data other than α, we can use Hildebrand's rule $(\partial E/\partial V)_T = n\,\Delta E_v(T)/V(T)$, where n varies for most nonpolar and slightly polar compounds over the narrow range 0.9 to 1.2 [1], [11]. Then at temperature T,

$$C_p - C_v = n \cdot \alpha \,\Delta E_v(\approx 2.16ncR). \tag{9.14}$$

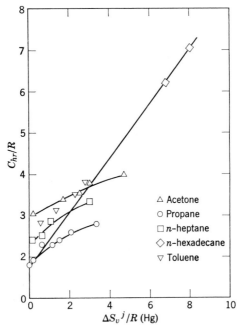

Figure 9.12 Liquid-phase heat-capacity increment due to hindered external rotation C_{hr} as function of the excess entropy of vaporization (relative to mercury).

For nonpolar or slightly polar compounds (and excluding perhalides) it is reasonably safe to assume $n = 1.05$. Then we are not likely to err by more than $\pm 10\%$ in $(C_p - C_v)$, which is usually less than $\pm 3\%$ in C_p.

Another way to the conversion of C_v into C_p is by the classical route, using the sound velocity u_s:

$$\frac{C_p}{C_v} = \frac{1}{2} + \left(\frac{MT\alpha^2 u_s^2}{C_v} + \frac{1}{4}\right)^{\frac{1}{2}}. \tag{9.15}$$

This relation appears somewhat unfamiliar because, to serve our purposes, C_v has to be in the denominator on the right-hand side. We obtain the thermal expansion coefficient α by the route indicated above. The sound velocity can be obtained from the temperature independent Rao parameter $U = u_s^{\frac{1}{3}} M/\rho$, which can be estimated from published group increments. Hence, only the density need be estimated (e.g., by way of our generalized density correlation) to calculate u_s for any temperature. If u_s is known from experiment, du_s/dT can be obtained by Schaafs' method.[1]

Even in the absence of experimental data, we may want to try to calculate K_0 and α from molecular-structure information. Examination of the proposed correlations for α, K_0 suggests that the term

$$K_0 \alpha^2 VT = cRf(T^*), \tag{9.16}$$

where $f(T^*)$ should be a universal, if complicated, function of the reduced temperature T^* only. Hence a plot of the experimental data for $(C_p - C_v)/cR$ versus T^* should lead to a single curve. Wide deviations of data from a single curve, indicate either that there are no general correlations of α and K_0, or that the data are poor. Probably both factors are responsible. It has been shown in Section 8.2 that a very reliable universal correlation of α^* versus T^* could not be produced. Deviations from universality are accentuated by the occurrence of α^2 in (9.16).

9.7 DIRECT ESTIMATE OF $C_p^{(l)} - C_p^{(g)}$

Although even a 10% uncertainty in $(\partial E/\partial V)_T$, hence in $C_p - C_v$, cannot generally introduce an error in excess of about $0.5R$ (because $C_p - C_v$ for most liquids is around $5R$), it becomes worthwhile to examine the possibility of bypassing the lengthy, if interesting, calculation of $C_p^{(l)}$ by the detailed route examined in the previous portions of this section.

In zeroth approximation we can take $\Delta C_p = C_p^{(l)} - C_p^{0(g)}$ as independent of temperature. The required numerical value is then readily available from

---

[1] Schaafs, W. *Acustica* **10**, 160 (1960).

good vapor pressure data because

$$\ln p_v = A - \frac{H_0^\circ}{RT} - \frac{\overline{\Delta C_p}}{R} \ln T - f(p, T), \qquad (9.17)$$

where $f(p, T)$ is a vapor imperfection term which is generally important only at $p > 0.5$ atm. Hence the three-term equation suffices to obtain ΔC_p at low vapor pressures. For low-molecular-weight compounds with $N_c < 6$ (or equal molal volume), ΔC_p is reasonably constant and $\overline{\Delta C_p}$ is not too bad an approximation. However, for larger molecules, ΔC_p varies quite rapidly with temperature, or better, with packing density, and it is advantageous to use calorimetric ΔC_p data as a source of general information.

Most of the direct ΔC_p correlations are restricted to temperatures up to the atmospheric boiling point, that is, up to the minimum in the ΔC_p versus temperature curve. The subsequent rise is almost entirely due to thermal expansion and should be estimated by means of the p–v–T correlation scheme indicated above, or by means of Rowlinson's equation discussed in the last part of this chapter.

9.7.1 Rigid Molecules

Most of the rigid molecules for which heat-capacity data are available are aromatic ring compounds. When their $C_p^{(l)} - C_p^{\,0}(g)$ is plotted against reduced density, one obtains the rather satisfactory correlation shown in Fig. 9.13. However, the density information is rarely available for the entire

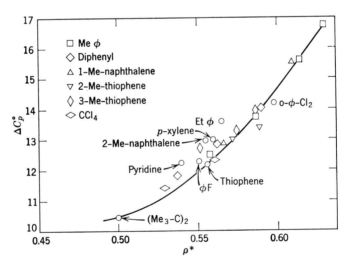

Figure 9.13 Heat-capacity difference ΔC_p between liquid and vapor for aromatic hydrocarbons, aromatic nonhydrocarbons, and other rigid molecules.

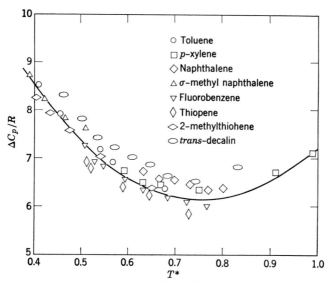

Figure 9.14 Heat-capacity difference $C_p^{(l)} - C_p^{0(g)}$ of rigid molecules as function of reduced temperature T^*.

temperature range of interest, at least without calculation. As most of the compounds in question follow the same reduced density versus temperature relation, the translation to a $C_p^{(l)} - C_p^{0(g)}$ versus reduced-temperature scale was carried out without qualms. The result is shown in Fig. 9.14.

The reason for the existence of these simple correlations is easy to see. For most of the compounds involved, C_v^λ, α^*, V^*, and P_i^* are almost universal functions of the reduced density, ρ^*, or temperature, T^*. Hence it would be odd if the sum of all these properties should not also be a universal function of ρ^* or T^*.

The absence of specific dipole-orientation effects is probably due to the fact that for most of the compounds shown in Figs. 9.12 and 9.13, $E\mu < 0.2E°$. No thermodynamic property data have been found for such highly polar rigid molecules as benzonitrile or ethylene carbonate by which to test the general validity of this correlation.

9.7.2 Flexible Molecules

Just as had been observed in the case of C_v^λ, the heat capacity or ΔC_p of n-paraffins follows two very distinct patterns, one for the group methane to n-hexane and one for all the others from n-heptane onward. Owing to their possession of one axis with very low moment of inertia, they do not fit into the correlation for larger rigid molecules presented in the previous section.

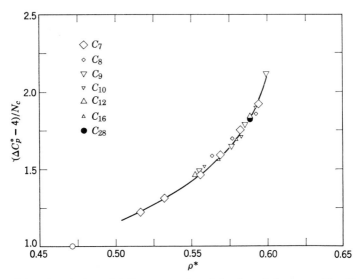

Figure 9.15   Correlation of ΔC_p versus reduced density ρ^* for n-paraffins (from heat-capacity data) (from Ref. [6]). N_c = number of carbon atoms per molecule. For branched-chain compounds, deduct $0.5\,b_1$ (or $0.70\,b_2$) from the calculated value of ΔC_p for the n-paraffin.

The thermal behavior of long-chain molecules from n-heptane onward is largely governed by the contributions of the methylene groups, as was first noted by Pitzer [13]. Their heat-capacity difference is therefore easily correlated as a function of chain length as shown by the curves in Fig. 9.15. The correlating parameter $(\Delta C_p - 4)/N_c$ is based on Pitzer's model for the n-paraffin chain: a flexible chain held fixed by one end. The ΔC_p of that end is taken as $2R$.

9.8   COMPARISON WITH OTHER CALCULATING METHODS

The available methods for the calculation of the heat capacity of liquids can be classed in two groups: rational methods, and strictly empirical methods. The latter are disposed of easily. All [15] are based on the notion that the heat capacity of liquids can be broken down into additive functional group increments just as that of a gas. Most of them yield only $C_p^{(l)}$ at room temperature. Only Riedel's modification of the Duclaux increment method [17] provides a tried method to estimate $C_p^{(l)}$ from -60 to $+140°C$. The basic trouble with the increment method is, of course, that it has no basis in theory and can therefore not be extended beyond the range of compounds for which data happen to be available.

Three rational methods have been proposed in the past. Two assume that $C_p^\circ(g)$ can be calculated from spectroscopic or group increment data, and then proceed to estimate $\Delta C_p = C_{ps}^{(l)} - C_p^\circ(g)$. Watson proposes to use the thermodynamic relation

$$\Delta C_p = -\frac{1}{T_c}\left|\frac{d\Delta H_v}{dT_R}\right. - \left\{\left[\frac{\partial(H^{\circ(g)} - H_s^{(g)})}{\partial T_R}\right]_{P_R}\frac{1}{T_c}\right.$$

$$\left.\left.-\frac{1}{P_c}\left[\frac{\partial(H^{\circ(g)} - H_s^{(g)})}{\partial P_R}\right]_{T_R}\right\}\right|\frac{dP_v}{dT}. \quad (9.18)$$

This relation is useful only if all terms are available from correlations. The first term, which alone need be used at $P_R < 0.02$ ($\leqslant \frac{1}{2}$ atm), could be obtained from Watson's well-known ΔH_v versus T_R equation (7.5) [15]. The two other terms are obtained from a generalized equation of state. This method is probably best at high temperatures and requires a knowledge of T_c, P_c, and the slopes of the vapor pressure and of the ΔH_v versus temperature curves. The latter two could, of course, be supplied from any generalized p–v–T correlation; such as Watson's or Riedel's, etc. The reliability range of the method is therefore restricted to the temperature and molecule type range of validity of the generalized correlations. Their temperature range usually extends from T_c down to the temperature where $P_R > 10^{-3}$. Structure specificity normally precludes the use of this type of corresponding-states correlation at lower temperatures.

The other method to estimate ΔC_p has been proposed by Rowlinson [19]. Although derived in a somewhat obscure fashion—from a molecular theory of liquids composed of molecules with nonuniform force fields—it is in effect a modified corresponding states theorem along similar lines as those by Pitzer [9] and Riedel [18]. The reference substance is liquid argon. The equation for ΔC_p of imperfect liquids is

$$\frac{\Delta C_p}{R} = \frac{\Delta C_{p0}}{R} + \delta\left[-\frac{4u}{RT} + \frac{4C_p}{R} - \frac{2T}{R}\left(\frac{\partial C_p}{\partial T}\right)(1 - T_R)\right]_0 \quad (9.19)$$

where ΔC_{p0} and all terms inside the square bracket refer to liquid argon. The deviation factor, δ, is by definition related to Pitzer's acentric factor as $\delta = 0.42\omega$. However, inspection of Rowlinson's data shows that the heat-capacity data are better represented by 0.4δ. As mentioned earlier, $-u$ is essentially the energy of vaporization of argon at the appropriate reduced temperature T_R.

The argon data as given by Rowlinson can be approximated by the following equations:

$$\frac{\Delta C_{p0}}{R} = 2.56 + \frac{0.436}{1 - T_R} \; ; \quad \frac{C_{p0}}{R} = 4.06 + \frac{0.436}{1 - T_R} \; ; \quad \frac{-u_0}{RT_c} = 6.3(1 - T_R)^{\frac{1}{3}}$$

$$\frac{-u_0}{RT} = \frac{6.3}{T_R}(1 - T_R)^{\frac{1}{3}} ; \quad -\frac{2T}{R}\left(\frac{\partial C_{p0}}{\partial T}\right)_0 (1 - T_R) = +0.872.$$

(9.20)

Hence a working form of Rowlinson's relation is

$$\frac{\Delta C_p}{R} = 2.56 + \frac{0.436}{1 - T_R} + \delta\left[17.11 + \frac{25.2}{T_R}(1 - T_R)^{\frac{1}{3}} + \frac{1.742}{1 - T_R}\right]. \quad (9.21)$$

Inspection of this equation shows that at low values of T_R it is dominated by the second term in the bracket, and ΔC_p decreases as T_R increases, but that the terms in $(1 - T_R)^{-1}$ will take over, and ΔC_p increases, as T_R increases. The location of the minimum in the ΔC_p versus T_R curves shifts to higher reduced temperatures with increasing value of δ. At $\delta = 0.05$, the minimum is at $T_R \sim 0.65$, and when $\delta = 0.1$ at $T_R \sim 0.75$. A quantitative comparison between experiment and calculation is shown in Fig. 9.16 for n-heptane, for which rather good data are available. It is evident that the equation approximates the behavior of this compound quite well. Because n-heptane is one of the substances used in the calibration of the method of Section 9.3, no purpose would be served by calculating the results back for comparison with the experimental data and with Rowlinson's method.

The Rowlinson method does not do quite so well with very polar compounds, where our $C_v^{(l)}$ method does rather better. The Rowlinson method is

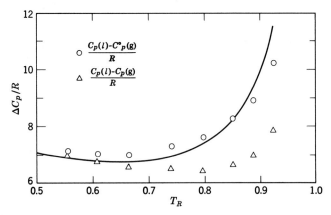

Figure 9.16   Comparison of $\Delta C_p/R$ calculated by means of Rowlinson's theory [9.20], curve I, with experimental data for $n - C_7H_{16}$.

also not likely to be very effective with higher-molecular-weight compounds for which critical temperatures and pressures can be estimated only very crudely, if at all.

An empirical method has been proposed by Sternling and Brown which aims to cover the same range as Rowlinson's equation [11]. It is of the form

$$\frac{C_p^{(l)} - C_p^{\circ(g)}}{R} = a\left[\frac{0.634}{1 - T_R} + 3.67 + 11.4(1 - T_R)^4\right], \quad (9.22)$$

where the constant a depends primarily on Pitzer's acentric factor and can be represented approximately as

$$a = 0.5 + 2.2\omega. \quad (9.23)$$

Comparison with experimental data shows that (9.12) represents the high-temperature data (at $T_R > 0.5$) of most compounds fairly well, and the low-temperature data (at $T_R < 0.5$) of compounds with $\omega > 0.2$. However, ΔC_p of compounds with $\omega < 0.2$ at low temperatures is significantly smaller than predicted by (9.13).

The most ambitious method for the calculation of liquid-state heat capacity, which we have to compare our method with, is that by Sakiadis and Coates [15]. Their basic program was very similar to ours: to separate $C_v^{(l)}$ into the contributions from translational, external rotational, and the various internal degrees of freedom. However, by setting the sum of the contributions of translation and external rotation to liquid heat capacity just as $6R$, independent of temperature, the whole scheme was doomed to failure and rather arbitrary correction factors of various sorts had to be introduced to make the calculations fit the data.

9.9 PROCEDURES TO ESTIMATE THE HEAT CAPACITY OF NONASSOCIATING LIQUIDS

Rational procedures for the calculation of the heat capacity of liquids composed of polyatomic molecules must start with the specification that the heat-capacity contribution C_i from the internal degrees of freedom is known. In practice this means generally that C_i will be derived from ideal gas zero-pressure heat-capacity data, which is equivalent to the assumption that there is no significant change in the frequencies of molecular vibrations upon condensation. In general we find that the frequency changes upon condensation are indeed small enough to be ignored in thermodynamic property calculations.

The requisite ideal-gas heat capacities are available from the following data collections:

Organic Compounds.

1. Westrum, Stull, and Sinke, *Tables of Thermodynamic Properties of 1200 Organic Compounds* (National Bureau of Standards, Washington, D.C., to be published).
2. Landolt-Börnstein, *Zahlenwerte und Funktionen* Springer, Berlin, 1961, vol. II/4, (Kalorische Zustandsgrössen).
3. American Petroleum Institute, Res. Proj. 44, "Selected Physical Properties of Hydrocarbons and Related Compounds," up to date (more or less) through issuance of loose leaves.
4. H. Zeise, *Thermodynamik* S. Hirzel, Leipzig, 1959, vols. III/1 and III/2.

Inorganic Compounds.

5. *JANAF Thermochemical Tables* (Dow Chemical Company), up to date through issuance of loose leaves.
6. Items 2 and 4 above.

The ideal-gas heat capacity of mono-*n*-alkane derivatives of several parent

Table 9.4   Coefficients, a_{ij}, for Equation 9.24[a]

$j =$		1	2	3	Deviation (cal/mole °C)	
$i =$ Identification[b]	0	$\times 10$	$\times 10^4$	$\times 10^8$	(Avg.[c])	(Max.)[d]
0 Carbon number dependence	−0.2183	0.2274	−0.1311	0.2934	—	—
1 *n*-Paraffins	0.7946	(2)	0.04314	−0.3256	0.12	0.35
2 *n*-Monoolefins (1-alkenes)	1.232	−0.1135	0.1111	−0.3484	0.14	0.49
3 *n*-Alkyl cyclopentanes	−10.20	0.1323	−0.0425	(e)	0.24	0.71
4 *n*-Alkyl cyclohexanes	−11.29	0.2278	−0.08822	(e)	0.25	0.83
5 *n*-Alkyl benzenes	−6.597	−0.2335	0.06034	(e)	0.20	0.61

[a] Lundberg, G. W. and A. Bondi, *Proc. Am. Petr. Cont.* **44**, III, 16 (1964).
[b] Excluding the parent compound.
[c] Average deviation, i.e., $\sum_{i=1}^{n} \dfrac{|Y_i - \hat{Y}_i|}{n}$.
[d] Maximum deviation of approximation: Max $|Y - \hat{Y}|$.
[e] Variable made only an insignificant contribution to the fit; it was not entered into the regression equation.

compounds can be calculated by means of the equation

$$C_p^\circ = \sum_{j=0}^{3}(a_0)_j N_c T^j + \sum_{j=0}^{3}(a_i)_j F_i T^j, \quad i = 1, 2, \ldots, 5, \quad (9.24)$$

where the family constants F_i have the range $(0, 1)$, and the coefficients a_{ij} for which have been tabulated in Table 9.4 in units of cal/mole °K. Similar coefficients can undoubtedly be produced for the expansion of other parent compound data into those for their mono-n-alkane derivatives. Then

$$C_i = C_p^{\circ(g)} - 4R. \quad (9.25)$$

If we go about it carefully we can extract C_i increments for specific functional groups from data for simple molecules and then recombine them to the C_i values for other molecules on the basis of simple additivity. Among the precautions to be taken are: maintenance of the heights of barriers to internal rotation during the combination procedures, and consideration of the incidence of rotational isomerism and the associated thermal effects.

An extensive collection of C_i increments in the form of an empirical representation is quoted here as Table 9.5.

Table 9.5   Ideal Gas Heat Capacity Increments[a]

Group	a	$b \times 10^2$	$c \times 10^4$	$d \times 10^6$
Aliphatic Hydrocarbon Groups				
—CH_3	0.6087	2.1433	−0.0852	0.001135
—CH_2	0.3945	2.1363	−0.1197	0.002596
=CH_2	0.5266	1.8357	−0.0954	0.001950
—C—H	−3.5232	3.4158	−0.2316	0.008015
—C— , H	−5.8307	4.4541	−0.4208	0.012630
∖C=CH_2 ∕	0.2773	3.4530	−0.1918	0.004130
∖C=CH_2 ∕	−0.4173	3.8857	−0.2783	0.007364

[a] From Rihani, D. N., and L. K. Doraiswamy, *Ind. Eng. Chem. Fundamentals* **4**, 17 (1965) for the equation

$$C_p{}^0 = \sum a + T \sum b + T^2 \sum c + T^3 \sum d,$$
$$C_i = C_p{}^0 - 4R.$$

Table 9.5 (*continued*)

Group	a	$b \times 10^2$	$c \times 10^4$	$d \times 10^6$
H₂C=CH₂ (H, H / C=C \ H, H)	−3.1210	3.8060	−0.2359	0.005504
H\C=C/ \ /H (trans)	0.9377	2.9904	−0.1749	0.003918
H\ /H C=C (cis)	−1.4714	3.3842	−0.2371	0.006063
\ / C=C / \	0.4736	3.5183	−0.3150	0.009205
H\C=C=CH₂	2.2400	4.2396	−0.2566	0.005903
\C=C=CH₂	2.6308	4.1658	−0.2845	0.007277
H\ /H C=C=C \	−3.1249	6.6843	−0.5766	0.017430
≡CH	2.8443	1.0172	−0.0690	0.001366

Aromatic Hydrocarbon Groups				
—C⟨	−1.4572	1.9147	−0.1233	0.002985
—C⟨	−1.3883	1.5159	−0.1069	0.002659
→C⟨	0.1219	1.2170	−0.0855	0.002122

Contributions Due to Ring Formation				
3-membered ring	−3.5320	−0.0300	0.0747	−0.005614
4-membered ring	−8.6550	1.0780	0.0425	−0.000250
5-membered ring				
(a) Pentane	−12.2850	1.8609	−0.1037	0.002145
(b) Pentene	−6.8813	0.7818	−0.0345	0.000591
6-membered ring				
(a) Hexane	−13.3923	2.1392	−0.0429	−0.001865
(b) Hexene	−8.0238	2.2239	−0.1915	0.005473

Table 9.5 (*continued*)

Group	a	$b \times 10^2$	$c \times 10^4$	$d \times 10^6$
	Oxygen-Containing Groups			
—OH	6.5128	−0.1347	0.0414	−0.001623
—O—	2.8461	−0.0100	0.0454	−0.002728
H | —C=O	3.5184	0.9437	0.0614	−0.006978
\C=O /	1.0016	2.0763	−0.1636	0.004494
O || —C—O—H	1.4055	3.4632	−0.2557	0.006886
O // —C \ O—	2.7350	1.0751	0.0667	−0.009230
O O	−3.7344	1.3727	−0.1265	0.003789
	Nitrogen-Containing Groups			
—C≡N	4.5104	0.5461	0.0269	−0.003790
—N≡C	5.0860	0.3492	0.0259	−0.002436
—NH₂	4.1783	0.7378	0.0679	−0.007310
\NH /	−1.2530	2.1932	−0.1604	0.004237
	Nitrogen-Containing Groups			
\N— /	−3.4677	2.9433	−0.2673	0.004237
N	2.4458	0.3436	0.0171	−0.002719
—NO₂	1.0898	2.6401	−0.1871	0.004750
	Sulfur-Containing Groups			
—SH	2.5597	1.3347	−0.1189	0.003820
—S—	4.2256	0.1127	−0.0026	−0.000072
S	4.0824	−0.0310	0.0731	−0.006081
—SO₃H	6.9218	2.4735	0.1776	−0.022445
	Halogen-Containing Groups			
—F	1.4382	0.3452	−0.0106	−0.000034
—Cl	3.0660	0.2122	−0.0128	0.000276
—Br	2.7605	0.4731	−0.0455	0.001420
—I	3.2651	0.4901	−0.0539	0.001782

Table 9.6 Brock's Rough Heat Capacity Estimate,[a] for Condensed Phases

Assumes $dC_v/dT = 0$; recommends $C_p = C_v$!

$$C_v = R(2b + 3f + 3m + 6n + 5l + 3i)$$

where
n = number of nonlinear groups of atoms in the molecule, e.g.,

$$\text{Me,} \quad -\overset{|}{\underset{|}{C}}-\text{Me,} \quad =N-C, \quad -CH_2-O-.$$

l = number of linear groups of atoms in the molecule, e.g., C = 0.
i = number of simple ions in the molecule, e.g., H+ in acids.

b = number of $\diagdown$CH groups in aromatic rings.

f = number of $\diagdown$C—C$\diagup$ groups in aromatic rings.

m = number of CH$_2$ groups in cyclohexyl rings.

[a] Brock, F. H., *ARSJ*, **31**, 265 (1961).

Table 9.7 Atomic-Group Heat-capacity Contributions at 20°C[a]

	Contribution (cal/g mole °K)
H— (formic acid and formates)	3.55
CH₃—	9.9
—CH₂—	6.3
$-\overset{|}{\underset{|}{C}}-H$	5.4
—COOH	19.1
—COO— (esters)	14.5
$\overset{|}{\underset{|}{C}}=O$	14.7
—CN	13.9
—OH	11.0
—NH₂	15.2
—Cl	8.6
—Br	3.7
—NO₂	15.3
—O— (ethers)	8·4
—S—	10.6
C₆H₅-	30.5

[a] From Johnson, A. I., and C. J. Huang. *Can. J. Technol.* **33**, 421 (1955).

The estimating procedures are arranged in the order of increasing precision, paralleling to some extent the order of increasing availability of other property data. Liquids composed of molecules with $M < 1000$ g/mole are treated first, and are followed by methods for polymer melts.

Procedure 9.1 (Fast Guess 1)

Information Available: Molecular structure.
  Use Brock's method (Table 9.6) for very fast and crude results.
  Use Johnson and Huang's Method (Table 9.7) for more limited results at 25°C only.

Procedure 9.2 (Fast Guess 2)

Information Available: Molecular structure; density.
  Obtain literature data on specific heat (c_p) and density (ρ) of structurally similar compound (II). Then take the heat capacitivity ($c_p \cdot \rho$) of both compounds as equal. Hence

$$c_p(\text{I}) = \rho(\text{I})(c_p \cdot \rho)(\text{II}). \tag{9.26}$$

Moreover, the product $c_p \cdot \rho$ changes only slowly with temperature. Hence, when the density temperature function is known, c_p at other temperatures can also be guessed.

Procedure 9.3 (Medium Quality Estimate for $T < T_b$)

Information Available: Molecular structure, $C_p^{0(g)}$ or C_i.
  STEP 1: Estimate the standard energy of vaporization $E°$ by summing up the appropriate increments of $E°$ taken from Tables 14.1 to 16.
  STEP 2: Estimate the number of external degrees of freedom ($3c$) by means of the equations of Tables 14.1 to 16, unless molecule is rigid when $3c \doteq 6$.
  STEP 3: Now the temperature-reducing parameter $\theta_L = E°/5cR$ in °K.
  STEP 4: Convert the temperature (s) (°K) for which the heat capacity information is desired to the reduced temperature $T^* = T/\theta_L$.
  STEP 5: (a) If the compound is a rigid-ring compound with no, or only, short (methyl or ethyl) side chains or other substituents (or a tightly substituted aliphatic chain compound), obtain ΔC_p^0 from Figure 9.12.
    (b) If the compound is an aliphatic chain compound with a backbone of more than seven chain links (i.e., $N_s < 7$), obtain ΔC_p^0 (paraffin) from Figure 9.14. For each side chain branch point (if any) subtract the decrement indicated on the figure.
    (c) If the long-chain compound has polar groups, estimate the heat-capacity increment $\delta \Delta C_p^0$, from Figure 9.17.
    (d) If the compound is aliphatic with $N_s < 7$, obtain ΔC_p^0 (paraffin) from Figure 9.17. Polar group increments $\delta \Delta_p^0 C$, if any, are obtained from Figure 9.18.
  STEP 6: The liquid phase heat capacity is now:
    (a) For rigid-ring molecules [see Step 5(a)] at temperature T:

$$C_p^{(l)} = C_p^{0(g)} + \Delta C_p^0.$$

    (b) For aliphatic chain molecules [see Steps 5(b)–5(d)] at temperature T:

$$C_p^{(l)} = C_p^{0(g)} + \Delta C_p^0 \text{ (paraffin)} + \delta \Delta C_p^0.$$

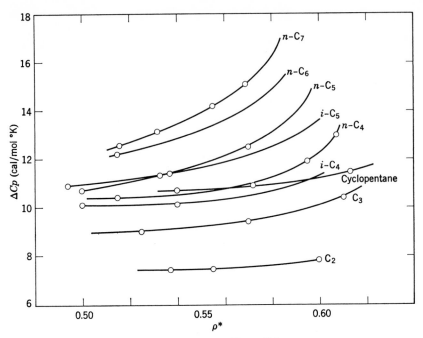

Figure 9.17 Heat-capacity difference $\Delta C_p = C_p^{(l)} - C_p^{0(g)}$ for the lower aliphatic hydrocarbons.

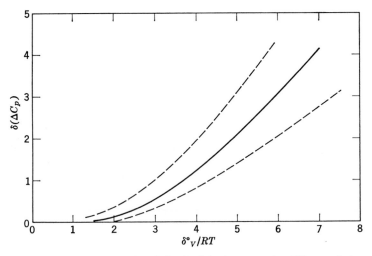

Figure 9.18 "Polarity" correction $\delta(\Delta C_p)$ of the heat-capacity difference between liquid and vapor for aliphatic and cycloaliphatic nonhydrocarbons. The broken lines indicate the scatter in the experimental data.

The method used is valid only up to the reduced temperature limit shown or implied in Figures 9.13 through 9.17 and should *not* be extrapolated beyond that because $\Delta C_p{}^0$ takes a sharp sweep upwards at temperatures above about the atmospheric boiling point, turning toward ∞ at T_c. A procedure to estimate that portion of the curve is given in the next section since more starting information is required. The accuracy of the results obtained in Step 6 is about $\pm 0.5R$ over and above the inaccuracies of the $\Delta C_p^{0(g)}$ data for Figures 9.13 and 9.14. But the increments of Figure 9.18 may be in error by equal amounts, so that for some polar compounds, the uncertainty may be $\pm 1R$.

Procedure 9.4 (Medium Quality Estimate for $T > T_b$)

Information Available: Molecular structure, $C_p^{0(g)}$, liquid density ρ, T_c, P_c (and one vapor pressure point, e.g., the atmospheric boiling point).

STEP 1: Same as Step 1 of Procedure 9.3.
STEP 2: Calculate the van der Waals volume V_w from the increments given in Tables 14.1 to 14.18. Then the van der Waals density is $\rho_w = M/V_w$.
STEP 3: From the experimental density–temperature relation, estimate the temperature T' at which $\rho^* = \rho/\rho_w = 0.555$. Then $\theta_L = T'/0.6518$ (where 0.6518 is the reduced temperature T^* at which in the generalized density correlation, $\rho^* = 0.555$, the normalization point). In order to check the reasonableness of thus estimated—in effect experimental—value of θ_L, calculate $c = E^\circ/5R\theta_L$ and compare with the value that might have been estimated from the equations of Table 14.1 to 16.
STEPS 4–6: Same as Steps 4–6 of Procedure 9.3.
STEP 7: This and the following steps are designed to estimate $C_p^{(l)}$ at $T > T_b$ by Rowlinson's method. Calculate the acentric factor from T_c, p_c and the experimental vapor-pressure p by Pitzer's method. If a vapor pressure is not available, assume $V_c \approx 5.3V_w$ and estimate

$$\omega = \frac{0.802 \cdot RT_c}{P_c \cdot V_c} - 2.67.$$

STEP 8: Convert the temperature (s) T for which $C_p^{(l)}$ is to be determined to $T_R = T/T_c$
STEP 9: Then

$$\Delta \frac{C_p^{\,0}}{R} = 2.5 + \frac{0.436}{1 - T_R} + 0.17\omega \left[17.11 + \frac{25.2}{T_R}(1 - T_R)^{1/3} + \frac{1.742}{1 - T_R} \right].$$

This relation is not very accurate and should therefore not be used for the low-temperature region where the method of Steps 1 to 6 probably gives more reliable results. However, for the high-temperature region there is as yet no other method. One of the temperatures for which the equation of this step is used should be identical with the highest temperature of Step 5 so that the necessary adjustment to the factor in front of ω can be made to obtain a continuous temperature function of $\Delta C_p{}^0$.

STEP 10: Same as Step 6a of Procedure 9.1. The accuracy of the heat capacity estimated in Step 6 ought to be somewhat better than had been obtained by Procedure 9.3 because of the use of experimental rather than estimated reducing parameter θ_L. The accuracy of the result obtained in Step 10 cannot be assessed very well because the constant in front of the acentric factor ω has been determined by comparison with the only two available sets of even moderately reliable data in the high-temperature range.

Procedure 9.5   (*Reasonably Accurate Method for Molecules with* $N \leq 5$)

Information Available: Molecular structure, $C_p^{0(g)}$ or C_i, moments of inertia of the molecules density.

STEPS 1 and 2: Same as Steps 1 and 2 of Procedure 9.3.

STEP 3: Convert the temperatures T for which $C_p^{(l)}$ is desired to $T^* = T/\theta_L$.

STEP 4: Now $C_{tr}^{\lambda}/R = 3.40 - 1.00^*$.

STEP 5: If it is intended to estimate the entropy of the substance at hand, the moments of inertia should be computed by means of a computer program. For the present calculation alone, a much cruder estimate of the moments of inertia of a

Table 9.8   Typical Examples of Moments of Inertia

Molecule	I_A $(10^{-40}$g cm$^2)$	I_B $(10^{-40}$g cm$^2)$	I_C $(10^{-40}$g cm$^2)$	Ref.
MeF	5.49	32.95	$=IB$	a
MeCl	5.49	57.1	$=IB$	a
MeBr	5.51	90	$=IB$	a
MeI	5.51	100	$=IB$	a
Ethane	10.6	41.8	41.8	a
Ethylene	5.75	28.1	33.9	a
EtCl		153	169	
EtBr		220	238	
Propane	29.6	96.8	110.8	a
Benzene	150.8	150.8	301.6	
Toluene	151.5	331.5	477.7	
Chlorobenzene	147	527	674	
p-Dichlorobenzene	150	1234	1384	
Naphthalene	267	667	935	
Diphenyl	292	1470	1762	

[a] Herzberg, G., *Infrared and Raman Spectra of Polyatomic Molecules*, Van Nostrand, Princeton, New Jersey, 1945.

molecule will suffice. From a drawing of the molecular structure and the known bond angles and atomic weights, we find the moments of inertia $I_i = \Sigma \, m \cdot L_i^2$, where L_i = projected distance from center atoms. A few typical guide data are presented in Table 9.8.

STEP 6: For nonpolar and slightly polar molecules set $V^\circ = 0.1E^\circ$, for those polar molecules for which $E_\mu = \frac{2}{3}\mu^2/d_w^3 N_A \geq 0.2E^\circ$ set $V^\circ = E_\mu$. Set $n = 5$, and estimate $Q = 10^{-36}n^2/IV^\circ$, where V° is in cal/mole. For those degrees of freedom for which $Q > 2$, estimate C_{rr} from Table 9.9, and for those with $Q < 2$ use Figure 9.19. Then $C_{hr}^{\lambda} = \Sigma \, C_{rr}$.

STEP 7: If $T^* > 0.6$, no further calculation is required because then $C_v^{(l)} = C_{tr}^{\lambda} + C_{hr}^{\lambda} + C_i$.

STEP 8: The transformation of $C_v^{(l)}$ to $C_p^{(l)}$ can be carried out by different routes, depending on the amount of experimental information available.

(a) No experimental data on α and K_0: Estimate α and K_0 by means of Procedures 8.3 through 8.6.

Table 9.9 C_{rr} as Function of V°/RT and $n^2/IV^{\circ a}$

V°/RT	$10^{-36} n^2/IV$								
	0	1	2	4	8	16	32	64	128
0.0	0.99	0.99	0.99	0.99	0.99	0.99	0.99	0.99	0.99
0.5	1.06	1.06	1.06	1.06	1.06	1.06	1.06	1.05	1.04
1.0	1.22	1.22	1.21	1.21	1.21	1.20	1.19	1.17	1.14
2.0	1.69	1.68	1.68	1.67	1.65	1.61	1.54	1.43	1.22
3.0	2.10	2.08	2.07	2.05	2.01	1.91	1.73	1.47	
4.0	2.29	2.27	2.25	2.21	2.13	1.98	1.73	1.34	
5.0	2.33	2.30	2.27	2.23	2.12	1.89	1.56		
6.0	2.32	2.26	2.22	2.16	2.01	1.70	1.31		
7.0	2.27	2.19	2.12	2.05	1.85	1.52	1.09		
8.0	2.22	2.11	2.04	1.92	1.68	1.34	0.91		
9.0	2.18	2.05	1.94	1.80	1.53	1.19			
10.0	2.15	1.99	1.86	1.68	1.39	1.03			
12.0	2.11	1.89	1.73	1.45	1.15	0.77			
14.0	2.08	1.81	1.61	1.24	0.93	0.55			
16.0	2.06	1.75	1.51	1.06	0.72	0.34			

[a] Reproduced with permission from *A Treatise on Physical Chemistry*, D. Van Nostrand Co., 1942.

(b) Experimental data on α and u_s are available, remembering that u_s is linear in T over wide ranges of temperature.

(c) Experimental data on K_0 are available.

STEP 9: From the data of Step 8 (a) or (c) $C_p^{(l)} - C_v^{(l)} = \alpha^2 K_0 TV$. From the data of Step 8(b), it is more convenient to form the ratio

$$\frac{C_p}{C_v} = \frac{1}{2} + \left(\frac{MT\alpha^2 u_s^2}{C_v} + \frac{1}{4}\right)^{1/2}.$$

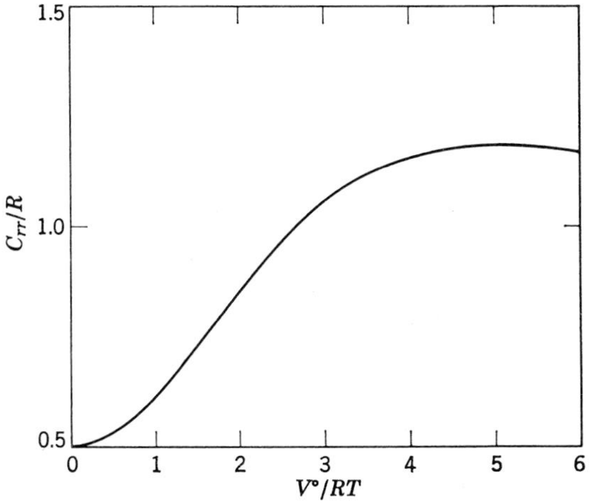

Figure 9.19 Plot of C_{rr}/R versus V°/RT for $Q = 0$.

STEP 10: Finally,

$$C_p^{(l)}(T) = C_v^{(l)}(T) + [C_p^{(l)} - C_v^{(l)}],$$

or

$$C_p^{(l)}(T) = C_v^{(l)}(T) \cdot (C_p/C_v)(T).$$

Procedure 9.6 (Reasonably Accurate Method for Rigid Molecules with $N_s > 5$)

Information Available: Molecular structure, C_i; density.
STEPS 1–3: Same as Steps 1–3 of Procedure 9.5.
STEP 4: (a) Molecule is nonpolar, or, if polar, $E_\mu < 0.2E°$; take $(C_{tr}{}^\lambda + C_{rr}{}^\lambda)/R$ at the value of T^* from the broken curve of Figure 9.6. (b) If molecule is polar, and $E_\mu > 0.2E°$, follow the method implied by Section 9.3.1.

Procedure 9.7 (Reasonably Accurate Method for Flexible Molecules with $N_s > 7$, $3_c > 8$)

Information Available: Molecular structure, $C_p^{0(g)}$ or C_i; density.
STEPS 1–3: Same as Steps 1–3 of Procedure 9.4.
STEP 4: Same as Step 3 of Procedure 9.5.
STEP 5: (a) Molecule is *n*-paraffin of chain length N_c

$$\frac{C_v{}^\lambda}{R} = \frac{2.15}{T^*} + \frac{0.2E_u°}{RT} N_c$$

where $E_u° = 1.08$ kcal/mole.
(b) Molecule is an iso-paraffin with the number of branches $N_b < N_c/2$ and $3c > 8$:

$$\frac{C_v{}^\lambda}{R} = \frac{2.15}{T^*} + \frac{0.2E_u°}{RT} N_c - 0.3N_b.$$

(c) Any other flexible molecule with $3c \geq 8$. The accuracy of this estimate is probably lower than that of (a) and (b):

$$\frac{C_v{}^\lambda}{R} = 3.40 - 1.00T^* + \frac{0.216E°(1.3 - T^*)^{1/3}}{RT}.$$

STEP 6: $C_v^{(l)} = C_v{}^\lambda + C_i$.
STEPS 7–8: Same as Steps 8–10 of Procedure 9.5.

Procedure 9.8 (Polymer Melts, Rough Estimate)

Information Available: Molecular structure. All calculations refer to the properties of the repeating unit and assume $M = \infty$. Estimate C_i from increments of Table 9.5.
STEP 1: Calculate $E_u°$ of the repeating unit from increments in Table 14.1 to 16.
STEP 2: Calculate c from relation in Table 14.1.
STEP 3: Calculate V_w of the repeating unit from increments in Table 14.1.
STEP 4: Now $\theta_L = E_u°/5cR$; convert all temperatures to $T^* = T/\theta_L$.
STEP 5: (a) If the temperature T (for which C_p is wanted) $> (T_g^* + 0.2)$, calculate $\rho = (M/V_w)(0.768 - 0.330T^*)$.
(b) If the temperature $T < (T_g^* + 0.2)$, calculate $V = V_w(1.205 + 0.910T^*)$.
STEP 6: (a) For Case 5(a) estimate $\alpha = 0.33/\theta_L (0.768 - 0.330T^*)$.
(b) For Case 5(b) estimate $\alpha = 0.91/\theta_L (1.205 - 0.910T^*)$.

STEP 7: For polymers other than *cis*-1,4-polyisoprene and *cis*-1,4-polybutadiene: estimate $K_0 = 1.5E^\circ/V_w$ $(2.30/T^* - 1.98)$ dyn cm^{-2}). For the *cis* 1,4-polydiolefins and similar structures, delete the factor 1.5.

STEP 8: For nonpolar polymers, $C_{hr}^\lambda/R = E_u^\circ/RT$. For polar polymers, $C_{hr}^\lambda/R = E_\mu/RT$. Typical values of E_μ are shown in Table 9.1.

STEP 9: Because there is no C_{tr}^λ for polymers, $C_v^{(l)} = c_{hr}^\lambda + C_i$.

STEP 10: Now $C_p^{(l)} = C_v^{(l)} + 2.39 \times 10^{-8}\alpha^2 K_0 TV$. The numerical factor in the second term is J^{-1}.

Procedure 9.9 (Polymer Melt, Fair Estimate)

Information Available: Molecular Structure, melt density.

INTRODUCTION; STEPS 1 and 3: Identical with those of Procedure 9.7.

STEP 4: Estimate the temperature T (1.8) at which $\rho^* = V_w\rho/M = 0.5556$. Then $\theta_L = T(1.8)/0.652$.

STEPS 5–10: Same as Steps 5–10 in Procedure 9.7.

NOMENCLATURE

a_i	coefficients in (9.24)
a, b, c	coefficients in empirical heat-capacity equations
c	one-third of the number of external degrees of freedom per molecule including those due to internal rotation
c_p	specific heat (cal/g °K)
C_{hr}	total contribution of hindered external rotation to $C_v^{(l)}$ (units of R)
C_i	contribution of internal degrees of freedom to C_v or C_p (units of R)
$C_p^{(l)}$	heat capacity of liquid at constant pressure (units of R)
$C_p^{0(g)}$	zero-pressure heat capacity of ideal gas at constant pressure (units of R)
C_{rr}	theoretically derived contribution of hindered external rotation to $C_v^{(l)}$ (units of R)
$C_r^{(g)}$	contribution of free external rotation to heat capacity of gas (units of R)
C_{tr}^λ	contribution of translational degrees of freedom to $C_v^{(l)}$ (units of R)
$C_v^{(l)}$	heat capacity of liquids at constant volume (units of R)
C_v^λ	$C_v^{(l)} - C_i$ (units of R)
C_v'	Rowlinson's configurational C_v of a real liquid (units of R)
C_{v0}'	Rowlinson's configurational C_v of a perfect liquid (units of R)
ΔC_p^0	$C_p^{(l)} - C_p^{0(g)}$

d_w shortest intermolecular distance (cm)

E° standard energy of vaporization, (cal/mole, or units of RT)

E_u° standard energy of vaporization per repeating unit of polymers

$\Delta E_v(T)$ energy of vaporization (at T) $= \Delta H_v(T) - pv(T)$

$E\mu$ dipole orientation energy (cal/mole or units of RT)

E internal energy of liquid (cal/mole or units of RT)

H_a heat of association (cal/mole or units of RT)

ΔH_v heat of vaporization (cal/mole or units of RT)

I_i moment of inertia of a molecule around axis i (g cm²)

K_0 zero-pressure bulk modulus (dyn/cm²)

M molecular weight (mole⁻¹)

n $= (\partial E/\partial V)_T [V(T)/\Delta E_v(T)]$

n number of valleys in sinusoidal potential energy barrier during a 360° rotation

N_c number of carbon atoms per molecule

N_s number of skeletal atoms (or groups) per molecule

P pressure

p vapor pressure (dyn/cm²)

P_i $= (\partial E/\partial V)_T =$ internal pressure (dyn/cm²)

Q $= 10^{-36} n^2/IV^\circ$

R gas constant (cal/mole °K; J/mole °K; Btu/lb mole °F, etc.)

ΔS_v entropy of vaporization (units of R)

ΔS_v^j excess entropy of vaporization (units of R)

T absolute temperature [°K or °R (Rankine)]

T_c critical temperature [°K or °R (Rankine)]

T_g glass transition temperature [°K or °R (Rankine)]

T_R $= T/T_c$

T^* $= 5cRT/E^\circ$

T_g^* $= 5cRT_g/E^\circ$

u_s sound velocity (cm/sec)

$\mathcal{V}_0$ fluctuation volume, see Ref. [2] (cm³/mole)

V molal volume of liquid (cm³/mole)

V_w van der Waals volume, (cm³/mole)

V° height of potential-energy barrier (cal/mole or units of RT)

x concentration in mole fraction

z number of nearest neighbors per molecule

α cubic thermal expansion coefficient (°K⁻¹)

ϵ pair potential (LJD) (ergs/molecule)

θ_L $= E^\circ/5cR$ or $E_u^\circ/5_{cu}R$

REFERENCES

[1] Allen, G. et al., *Polymer* **1**, 467 (1960).

[2] Bondi, A., *J. Phys. Chem.* **58**, 929 (1954).

[3] Bondi, A., *AIChE J.* **8**, 610 (1962).

[4] Bondi, A., *J. Phys. Chem.* **68**, 441 (1964).

[5] Bondi, A., *J. Polymer Sci.* **A2**, 3159 (1964).

[6] Bondi, A., and D. J. Simkin, *AIChE J.* **6**, 191 (1960).

[7] Bondi, A., *Ind. Eng. Chem. Fundamentals* **5**, 442 (1966).

[8] Brown, O. L. I., *J. Am. Chem. Soc.* **74**, 6096 (1952).

[9] Curl, R. C., and K. S. Pitzer, *J. Am. Chem. Soc.* **77**, 3433 (1955).

[10] Halford, R. S., *J. Chem. Phys.* **8**, 496 (1940).

[11] Hildebrand, J. H., and R. L. Scott, *Solubility of Non-Electrolytes*, Reinhold, New York, 1951, 3rd ed.

[12] Moelwyn-Hughes, E. A., *States of Matter*, Interscience, New York 1961.

[13] Pitzer, K. S., *J. Chem. Phys.* **8**, 711 (1940).

[14] Prigogine, I., and Raulier, S., *Physica* **9**, 396 (1942).

[15] Reid, R. C., and T. K. Sherwood, *Physical Properties of liquids and Gases*, McGraw-Hill, New York, 1958; 1965.

[16] Renon, H., C. A. Eckert, and J. M. Prausnitz, *Ind. Eng. Chem. Fundamentals* **7**, 52 (1967).

[17] Riedel, L., in R. Planck, *Handbuch der Kältetechnik*, Springer, Berlin, 1953, Vol. II.

[18] Riedel, L., *Chem. Ing. Tech.* **26**, 83, 259, 679 (1954).

[19] Rowlinson, J. R., *Liquids and Liquid Mixtures*, Academic Press, New York, 1959.

10

Thermal Conductivity
of Non-Associated Liquids

10.1 GENERAL PRINCIPLES

The transport of thermal energy through a dense fluid composed of molecules has resisted satisfactory theoretical treatment, so that barely the qualitative outlines of molecular behavior can be given [11]. All recent molecular theories and their deficiencies have been reviewed by McLaughlin [18]. The prominent molecular properties occurring in current molecular theories of the thermal conductivity (λ) of liquids are the magnitude and shape of the intermolecular force field, the intermolecular separation, and the number density of the fluid. Dimensional analysis of the molecular properties referred to, the pair potential ϵ, molecule diameter σ, molecule mass m, and lattice heat capacity of the monatomic liquid ($3k$), suggest the dimensionless parameters

$$\tilde{\lambda} = \frac{\lambda \sigma^2}{k}\left(\frac{m}{\epsilon}\right)^{1/2} = f_1(\tilde{T}) \quad \text{or} = f_2(\tilde{\rho}), \tag{10.1}$$

where $\tilde{T} = kT/\epsilon$ and $\tilde{\rho} = \sigma^3/v$.

The prediction of the analysis, that at constant $\tilde{T}$ or $\tilde{\rho}$ we should find $\lambda \sim m^{-1/2}$, has been confirmed to within experimental error by comparative measurements on normal and perdeuterated benzene, cyclohexane and water [15]. A successful test of the relation $\tilde{\lambda} = f(\tilde{T})$ has been carried out by Owens and Thodes [12], who found the expected "universal" curve of $\tilde{\lambda}$ versus $\tilde{T}$ for monatomic gases. The inapplicability of the Lennard-Jones and Devonshire theory to molecules with noncentral force interaction precludes successful use of the force constants ϵ and σ, "illegitimately" derived from properties of polyatomic molecules in so sensitive a test as a universal reduced thermal conductivity correlation for liquids. Re-evaluation of the data of simple polyatomic compounds with a self-consistent set of the more appropriate Kihara force constants [8] ought to be more successful.

A more broadly applicable corresponding-states correlation, based on the use of critical constants as reducing parameters, has been developed by Thodos and co-workers [23]. They related the reduced residual thermal conductivity ($\lambda_R - \lambda_R^\circ$) to the reduced density ρ_R, where λ_R° is the reduced thermal conductivity of the gas at low pressure (1 atm) at the same temperature. This term allows for the gas-kinetic collision contribution to thermal conductivity. At typical liquid densities, $\lambda^\circ \ll \lambda$, and can be neglected, so that we should expect a universal relation of λ_R versus ρ_R to hold for liquids at $T < T_b$. A serious disadvantage of this type of correlation is the absence of critical property data for most liquids. Moreover, critical temperature and pressure conditions are experimentally inaccessible for an increasing number of technologically important high-boiling liquids.

10.2 RIGID POLYATOMIC MOLECULES

Formulation of the reducing parameters in terms of experimentally accessible molecular properties offer broad applicability as well as direct insight into the relations between thermal conductivity and molecular structure. The following reducing parameters have been adopted: for intermolecular force, the standard energy of vaporization E°; as unit of length, the average contact distance d_w of the outer atom of neighboring molecules (estimated from their van der Waals radii; for the mass per molecule, the molecular weight M; and for the heat-capacity contribution (in the case of rigid molecules), the gas constant R (the justification for this choice is the structure independence of the translational contribution to the heat capacity of liquids composed of rigid molecules).

The resulting reduced thermal conductivity for liquids composed of rigid molecules is defined as

$$\lambda_s^* = \frac{\lambda \, \overline{d_w}^2 N_A}{R} \left(\frac{M}{JE^\circ} \right)^{1/2}. \tag{10.2}$$

Theory suggests that at atmospheric pressure and at moderate pressures ($P < P_i$), we should obtain a universal function $\lambda_s^* = f_1 (\rho^*)$. The validity of this conjecture is shown in Figure 10.1. For practical purposes, however, it is more desirable to represent λ^* as a function of temperature because density data are not always available at the temperature for which we need to know the thermal conductivity. Since for most liquids $\rho^* = f(T^*)$, where $T^* = 5cRT/E^\circ$, and $f(T^*)$ is a "universal" function [5], we can set $\lambda^* = f_2(T^*)$, with the results shown in Figure 10.2. The scatter shown ($\pm 8\%$) is of the same order as the precision of most experiments. The average straight line connecting the experimental points between $0.4 < T^* < 0.9$ is

$$\lambda_s^* = 3.22 - 1.76T^*. \tag{10.3}$$

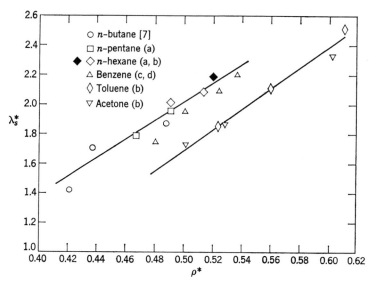

Figure 10.1 Thermal conductivity λ_s^* of various liquids as function of packing density ρ^*. (a) Downey-Smith, J. F., *Trans. ASME*, **58**, 719 (1936); (b) Riedel, L., *Chem. Ing. Tech.*, **13**, 321 (1951); (c) Nederbragt, G. W., and J. W. M. Boelhouwer, *Brit. J. Appl. Phys. Suppl.* **1**, 6 (1951); (d) Scheffy, W. J., and E. F. Johnson, *J. Chem. Eng. Data* **6**, 245 (1961).

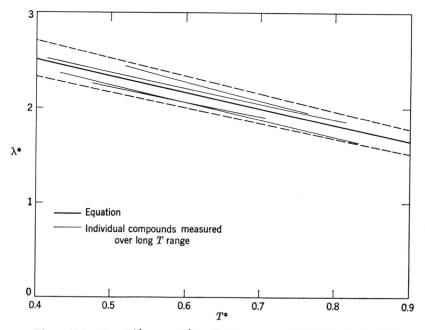

Figure 10.2 Plot of λ^* versus T^* for liquids composed of rigid molecules [3].

This linear relation should not be applied at $T^* > 0.9$ because of the well-known curvature of the thermal conductivity versus temperature curve along the saturation line above T_b and the singularities near T_c.

10.3 TEMPERATURE AND PRESSURE COEFFICIENTS OF λ

The temperature coefficient shown can be compared with McLaughlin's estimates from various theories [18]. All theories show that $(\partial \ln \lambda/dT)_p$ is dominated by the thermal expansion coefficient (α) of the liquid. A quasi-crystalline model of the liquid, for instance, yields

$$-\left(\frac{\partial \ln \lambda}{\partial T}\right) = \frac{\alpha}{3}(1 + 3\gamma), \tag{10.4}$$

where γ is the Grüneisen constant. For the frequent value $\gamma = 2$, we obtain $-(\partial \ln \lambda/\partial T) = 2.3\alpha$, in fair agreement with experiments on many simple liquids. Evaluation of γ by means of various theories of the liquid state produced agreement between calculation and experiment for the curve of $(\partial \ln \lambda/\partial T)_p \alpha^{-1}$ versus $\tilde{v}$ on the harmonic-oscillator model only.

An empirical plot of $-(\partial \ln \lambda/\partial T)_p$ versus α can be reproduced reasonably well by the linear relation

$$-\left(\frac{\partial \ln \lambda}{\partial T}\right)_p = 2.7\alpha - 1.35. \tag{10.5}$$

The curious conclusion from this relation, that $(\partial\lambda/\partial T)_p$ changes sign when $\alpha < 5 \times 10^{-4°}K^{-1}$ is borne out by observations at $T < T_g$ as well as at $P > P_i$. Over the temperature range of validity of (10.3), we find that $-(\partial \ln \lambda^*/\partial T^*) \approx 2\alpha^*$, $(\alpha^* \equiv \alpha E^°/5cR$, in qualitative agreement with the other reported observations.

Similar reasoning produces the other state variables of λ, as shown by McLaughlin [18]:

$$\left(\frac{\partial \ln \lambda}{\partial T}\right)_V \approx 0 \tag{10.6}$$

in qualitative agreement with the few available experimental data, and

$$\left(\frac{\partial \ln \lambda}{\partial p}\right)_T = \beta_T\left(\frac{1}{3} - \gamma\right), \tag{10.7}$$

where β_T is the isothermal compressibility, which is in obvious qualitative disagreement with the experimental relation

$$\left(\frac{\partial \ln \lambda}{\partial p}\right)_T \approx 2.15\beta_T. \tag{10.8}$$

Finally, we must expect

$$\left(\frac{\partial \ln \lambda}{\partial p}\right)_T = -\beta_T \left(\frac{\partial \ln \lambda}{\partial \ln v}\right)_T,$$ (10.9)

a relation that has not yet been tested experimentally.

10.4 LOW-BOILING ALIPHATIC SUBSTANCES

Most of the experimental data used to obtain the relation of Figure 10.2 and (10.3) represent data for liquids composed of rigid molecules and boiling at $t > 100°C$. However, the conductivities of a few low-boiling polar compounds are also well represented. Low-boiling aliphatic compounds were deliberately excluded because their molecules are not entirely rigid and because no modern data from outstandingly careful laboratories were available. The latter point is particularly important with these liquids because their large values for the ratio α/ν, where ν is the kinematic viscosity, easily causes large natural convection errors in thermal-conductivity measurements, unless extreme precautions are taken.

Because the density of these low-boiling compounds does not fit the generalized density–temperature curve that forms the basis of the reduced temperature scale $T^* = 5cRT/E°$, a good fit to the general $\lambda^* - T^*$ curve can hardly be expected. It is not clear, therefore, which cause should be held responsible for the consistent upward deviation of the experimental points for low-boiling paraffins from the standard curve, as shown in Figure 10.3. Crudely all these points fall on a curve

$$\lambda_s^* = 3.92 - 2.17T^*.$$ (10.10)

A few unquestioned data are needed in this area in order to give (10.10) other than provisional character. The recent, presumably very accurate, data by Jobst [16] on n-pentane (-90 to $0°C$) fit (10.10) perfectly, and his data on the lower straight-chain alkanols and alkanones ($N_c < 7$) are also far better represented by (10.10) than by (10.3). However, molecule rigidification by branching leads again toward (10.3) for liquids composed of rigid molecules, as is shown by the data for 2,2,4-trimethylpentane in Figure 10.3.

10.5 MODERATELY LONG FLEXIBLE MOLECULES

Inspection of the reducing parameter for λ shows one molecular property in need of refinement, the translational lattice heat capacity C_v^s. Experimental evidence supports identification $C_v^s = AR$ for liquids composed of rigid molecules, where A is either a universal constant (~ 3) or a universal function

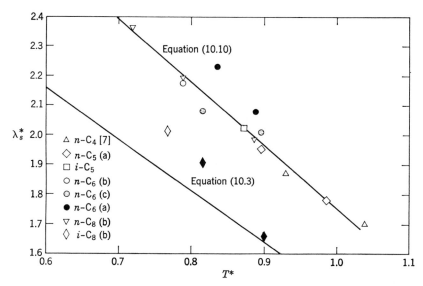

Figure 10.3 Reduced thermal conductivity versus temperature relation for low-boiling alkanes. (a) Downey-Smith, J. F., *Trans. ASME* **58**, 719 (1936); (b) Riedel, L., *Chem. Ing. Tech.* **13**, 321 (1951); (c) Sakiadis, B. C., and J. Coates, *A. I. Ch. E. J.* **1**, 275 (1955).

of T^*. With long flexible molecules, however, translational and internal or external rotational motions cannot be separated, and R must be replaced by a term which is proportional to N_s, the number of skeletal atoms (or rigid units) per molecule. The effective $C_v^c \approx N_s R$ only if all skeletal units are free or nearly free rotors, i.e., if $\omega_R/T < 1$, where ω_R = torsional oscillating frequency in cm^{-1}. If $(\omega_R/T) > 1$, $C_v^c \sim N_s C_E(\omega_R)$, where $C_E(\omega_R)$ is the harmonic-oscillator contribution to heat capacity per degree of freedom at frequency ω_R and temperature T. This correction would exhibit a slightly positive temperature coefficient for typical methylene backbone chain frequencies ($\sim$250 cm^{-1}), and thereby reduce $-(\partial\lambda/\partial T)_p$ somewhat below that for rigid molecules in the same range of T^*.

A second, somewhat simpler alternative is to use the number of external degrees of freedom $(3c)$ estimated from density measurements and set

$$C_v^c \sim \left(\frac{3c - 6}{N_S - 1} + 1\right) N \tag{10.11}$$

as proposed in the earlier treatment of this problem [3]. Since in the usual temperature range of interest $dc/dT \approx 0$, this correction leaves $(\partial\lambda/\partial T)_p$ unaffected. Hence, although the correction is of the right magnitude and has been used successfully for the estimation of λ_F, the thermal conductivity of liquids composed of flexible molecules, by the simple device

$$\lambda_F^* = \lambda_s^* \left(1 + \frac{3c - 6}{N_s - 1}\right), \tag{10.12}$$

it ignores the reduction of $-(\partial\lambda^*/\partial T^*)_p$ with increasing chain length of the flexible molecules shown in Figure 10.4.

This change in slope becomes a real embarrassment with vinyl polymers [13], [25] and with polyphenyl ethers [17] where it leads to a change in sign, and therefore called for design of a new model of heat conduction. This model is discussed in the next section. In the present context it suffices to point out that (10.14) through (10.18) for polymer melts can also be applied to the shorter-chain molecules of this section with two modifications:

1. If $\Lambda_p \geq L$, where L is the total length of a molecule [for n-paraffins $L = 1.27(N_c - 1) + 4.0\,(\text{Å})$], then in all equations Λ_p should be replaced by L;

2. The presence of molecule ends, ignored in the polymer case, must be accounted for. One rather simple route to do this is by way of parallel conduction for the middle-segment interactions (λ_m) and the end interactions (λ_e):

$$\lambda = \frac{N_s/N_\Lambda}{(N_s/N_\Lambda) + N_E}\lambda_m + \frac{N_E}{(N_s/N_\Lambda) + N_E}\lambda_E, \tag{10.13}$$

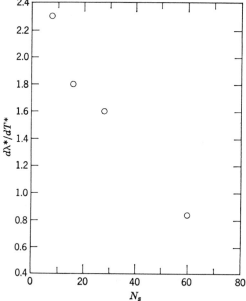

Figure 10.4 Effect of chain length of flexible molecules on the temperature coefficient of thermal conductivity.

where λ_m is the polymer melt conductivity estimated by the method given in the next section, and $\lambda_E = \lambda_s$ calculated for the repeating unit, or for the end unit if it differs substantially from the repeating unit, and $N_\Lambda = \Lambda_p/b \cos(\alpha/2)$. The comparison of calculated and observed thermal conductivity in Table 10.1 suggests that the model represents the trend of chain length effects on λ quite well, but has a tendency to overcorrect the effect of chain length on $d\lambda/dT$.

Table 10.1   Comparison of Calculated with Observed Thermal Conductivity of Liquids Composed of Flexible-Chain Molecules

Substance	T ($^\circ$K)	$10^4\lambda$obs.	$10^4\lambda$calc. (Eq. 10.13)[a]	$10^4\lambda$calc. (Eq. 10.12)
		(All in cal/cm sec $^\circ$C)		
9-n-Octyl heptadecane	300	3.15[b]	5.2 (3.02)[c]	3.62
	410	3.13[b]	4.9 (3.02)[c]	2.68
Olive oil (trioleyl-glyceride)	300	4.0[d]	6.2 (3.6)[c]	3.84
	410	3.87[d]	5.6 (4.6)[c]	3.44
	470	3.78[d]	5.1 (4.3)[c]	3.16

[a] See Ref. (a) of Table 10.2.
[b] W. N. Vanderkooi et al., *J. Chem. Eng. Data* **12**, 377 (1967).
[c] Numbers in parentheses estimated for $\omega = 1000$ cm^{-1}.
[d] From Kaye, L., *Proc. Roy. Soc.* (London) **A117**, 459 (1928).

10.6   POLYMER MELTS

The present model of the thermal conductivity of polymer melts closely resembles that for polymer crystals suggested in Section 5.1.2; namely, the low resistance path due to the high thermal conductivity along the backbone chain

$$\lambda_p = \frac{\sum C_D \rho_w}{M_{osc}} \frac{(E_p)^{1/2}}{\rho_w} 0.5 \varphi_b \Lambda_p \tag{10.14}$$

is in series with a short high resistance path corresponding to the weak van der Waals coupling between molecules (i.e., the usual liquid phase conductivity discussed earlier). All symbols have the same meaning as in (5.17). The largest difference in detail between crystal and liquid is the magnitude of Λ_p. As in the earlier discussion of this model, quantitative representation of the data has not yet been achieved, and it is presented here as a point of departure for further work.

The heat capacity C_D should logically be calculated from the maximum longitudinal backbone vibration frequency, for example, 500 cm^{-1} for polymethylene, several of which have been given by Zbinden (30). These frequencies yield order-of-magnitude agreement with the observed thermal conductivity, as shown on Table 10.2; but the desired compensation of the negative temperature coefficient of the conduction by van der Waals' coupling (λ_s) toward $d\lambda/dT \geq 0$ is achieved only by assigning vibration frequencies of the order 1000 cm^{-1} or higher. These correspond to the optical stretching vibrations of the backbone and are therefore not really appropriate for the present model.

The random orientation of backbone chains corresponds to an average 45° angle (θ) with the direction of the temperature gradient so that $\cos \theta = 0.5$. The fractional crossection φ_b occupied by the unimpeded phonon conductive path along the backbone chain can be estimated from the model of Figure 14.1 as of the order

$$\varphi_b \doteq \frac{\pi N_A a_p \left(r_2{}^2 - \frac{l^2}{4} \right)}{V_u}$$

where a_p is the projected bond length of the repeating unit (1.27 Å for CH$_2$) and V_u is the molal volume of the repeating unit.

The phonon free path along the backbone chain Λ_p is now the length of a polymer molecule segment between direction changes, the so-called persistence length:

$$\Lambda_p = \frac{3.2b}{1 - \cos \alpha} \left(\frac{1 + \eta}{1 - \eta} \right)^{\frac{1}{2}}, \tag{10.15}$$

where b = bond length, α = bond angle, η is a function of $\Delta E_{iso}/RT$ [27], shown in Figure 10.5, and ΔE_{iso} = energy of rotational isomerization along the backbone chain. Typical values of ΔE_{iso} are listed in Table 14.19. The persistence length Λ_p can also be estimated from the properties of solutions of the polymer under consideration in a theta-solvent because we generally ascribe theta-solvent properties to the melt. The relation by Benoit and Doty [2] yields in the limit of large molecular weights

$$\Lambda_p \approx 3\overline{S_0{}^2}/L, \tag{10.16}$$

where $(\overline{S_0{}^2})^{\frac{1}{2}}$ is the unperturbed radius of gyration of the molecule, and L is its fully extended length.

The thermal conductivity of the van der Waals coupling (λ_s) is just the hypothetical conductivity of a liquid composed of the repeating unit,

$$\lambda_s = \frac{R}{N_A \overline{d_w}^2} \left(\frac{JE^\circ}{M} \right)^{\frac{1}{2}} \left(3.22 - \frac{8.8cRT}{E^\circ} \right), \tag{10.17}$$

where $\overline{d_w}$, E°, M, and c now refer to the repeating unit. When the calculation

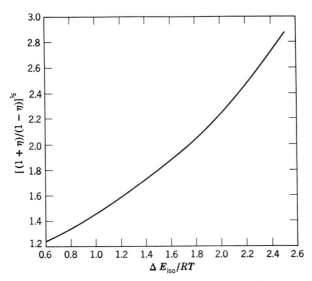

Figure 10.5   Plot of Volkenstein's expansion function.

involves a nonpolymeric long-chain molecule, however, these properties all refer to the entire molecule.

The thermal resistance calculation is then

$$\frac{1}{\lambda} = \frac{\Lambda_p}{\Lambda_p + d}\frac{1}{\lambda_p} + \frac{d}{\Lambda_p + d}\frac{1}{\lambda_s}, \tag{10.18}$$

where $d = d_w + (V_w/A_w)(V^* - 1)$; V_w and A_w are per repeating unit with polymer molecules, otherwise per molecule; and $V^* = M/\rho V_w$. Typical results are shown in Table 10.2.

The thermal conduction contribution of side chains can be taken as a parallel path by van der Waals coupling so that for polymers with many short side chains, such as polypropylene, polystyrene, and so on, we may write

$$\lambda \doteq \frac{q(m)}{q} \lambda_b + \left(1 - \frac{q(m)}{q}\right)\lambda_s$$

where the crossection ratio $q(m)/q = V_u(m)a_p/V_u a_p(m)$, the index (m) referring to the properties of polymethylene, and λ_b is the thermal conductivity λ estimated by means of 10.18. The implicit consequence of this model, that λ decreases and that $d\lambda/dT$ becomes more negative, the larger the side chain contribution is borne out by experiment except for the somewhat uncertain polystyrene data.

A significant aspect of the thermal conductivity of polyvinyl polymer melts is the small negative, or even positive, temperature coefficient, which is due

Table 10.2   Thermal Conductivity of Polymer Melts
(All in cal/cm sec °C)

Polymer	Temp. (°K)	$10^4\lambda_{obs.}$	$10^4\lambda_{calc.}$ (Eq. 10.18)[a]	$10^4\lambda_{calc.}$ (Eq. 10.12)
Polyethylene	410	6.0[b]	7.6 (6.6)[c]	3.7
	470	6.1[b]	6.9 (6.3)[c]	3.5
Polyisobutylene	203[d]	3.2[b]	3.3	3.45
	300	2.93[b]	3.4	3.22
	370	2.97[b]	3.3_5	3.05
Polystyrene	380	3.70[e]	5.0	6.0
	450	3.95[e]	4.5	5.6
	550	4.8(?)[e]	3.9	5.2
Poly(vinyl chloride)	380	3.80[e]	7.7 (5.8)[c]	4.8
	460	4.20[e]	6.6 (5.5)[c]	4.4

[a] E_p from Table 4.5; the effect of branching handled as described in text.
[b] From Ref. (13).
[c] Numbers in parentheses estimated with $\omega = 1000$ cm^{-1}.
[d] $T = T_g$.
[e] From Ref. (25).

to the positive temperature coefficient of C_D and thus of λ_p. This effect is small or nearly absent when λ_p is small, as with siloxane polymers (because E_p is small) or with cis-1, 4-polyisoprene (hevea) because Λ_p and λ_p are small.

The related models for thermal conduction in polymer melts by Eiermann (9) and Lohe (16a) consider conduction along the valence bond chain as infinitely fast, hence cannot account for the large difference in $d\lambda/dT$ between polymers and simple liquids.

10.7   ASSOCIATING LIQUIDS

All of the previously mentioned relations between thermal conductivity and molecular structure are applicable only to non-associating liquids, at least in principle. In associating liquids the transport of the heat of association (ΔH) supplies a parallel—hence additional—conduction path, first formulated by Nernst and given by Haase [12] as of the order

$$\lambda_h = \lambda_0 + \frac{x_2 \bar{D} R}{(\nu x_1 + x_2)^2 \bar{V}} \left(\frac{\Delta H}{RT}\right)^2 \qquad (10.19)$$

where λ_0 is the thermal conductivity in the absence of heat effects; $x_{1.2} = $ concentration of monomers and dimers, respectively, at temperature T; $\nu = n^{-1}$ of the reaction equation $A \rightleftharpoons (1/n)A_n$; $\bar{D} = $ average diffusion coefficient of the reactants; $\Delta H = $ heat of association; $\bar{V} = $ average molal volume of the reactants, C_p = average heat capacity of the reactants. Actual calculation of λ_h for typical cases reveals that λ_h can be significant only when the following rare conditions prevail:

1. The diffusion constant must be $\geq 10^{-4}$ cm/sec. This condition rules out all but hydrogen bonds, where "diffusion" takes place by proton flipping (and exchange), that is, by rotation rather than by mass motion. In most liquids, $D < 10^{-5}$ cm²/sec.

2. The monomer concentration $0.2 < x < 0.8$, so that the second term is large enough to matter.

3. $\Delta H > 2RT$ for the same reason.

Whereas condition 1 determines whether λ_h matters anywhere, conditions 2 and 3 determine the usually quite narrow temperature range over which λ_h can make a significant contribution, or, in the case of water and glycol, produce even a maximum in the λ versus T curve. The first quantitative figures on 2 and 3 have just become available [26], so that the significance of λ_h can finally be tested for liquids. Its significance for reacting and associating vapors had long been established [12].

The restrictiveness of the enumerated conditions has the consequence that the thermal conductivity of many associated substances can be estimated without regard to association. However, before we can use the present correlations, we must find a way to introduce $E°$ since the heat of vaporization, which contains the energy required to break a bond which persists in the liquid state, is obviously not a good measure of intermolecular (i.e., interdimer) attraction. A suitable procedure seems to be to estimate θ_L from density data as usual, assume validity of the appropriate correlation for $3c$ (for the dimer in the case of carboxylic acids). Then take $E° \approx 5cR\theta_L$, and in $E°/M$ use the molecular weight of the dimer if $E°$ is estimated for the dimer. Except for those of acetic acid, Jobst's recent thermal conductivity data [16] of the n-alkanoic acid data are fairly well represented by equations [3] and [12] as applicable. The data in Figure 10.6 illustrate the surprisingly good fit of the ethanol and n-butanol data. Their rather lower than average slope is the only anomaly noted.

10.8 MIXTURES

Mixture rules derived from theory do not appear to offer much more hope for agreement with experiment than had been experienced with pure substances. Moreover, in the most tractable case, calculation requires a knowledge of the various diffusion coefficients as well as of the thermal conductivity of the components. [1] Hence no attempt has been made so far to test the theoretical mixture rules against experiment.

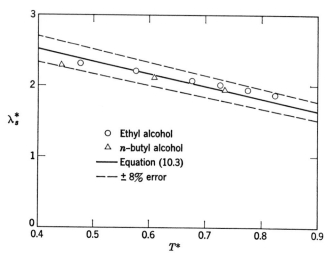

Figure 10.6   Location of the monohydric alcohols; ethyl and n-butyl alcohol data on the plot of λ^* versus T^* of Fig. 10.2. (from Ref. [3]).

A convenient approach to the estimation of mixture properties, especially for computer use, is to estimate the reducing parameters of the mixture from appropriate combination rules and then treat the mixture like any individual compound. Then for mixtures of rigid molecules 1 and 2

$$\lambda_{12} = \frac{R}{N_A \overline{d_w}^2(12)} \left(\frac{J\overline{E^\circ}}{\overline{M}}\right)^{\frac{1}{2}} \left(3.22 - \frac{8.80 \, \bar{c}RT}{\overline{E^\circ}}\right), \qquad (10.20)$$

where $\overline{E^\circ} = x_1^2 E_1^\circ + x_2^2 E_2^\circ + 2x_1 x_2 (E_1^\circ E_2^\circ)^{\frac{1}{2}} - F^E$; F^E is the excess free energy of mixing; $\bar{c} = x_1 c_1 + x_2 c_2$; $\overline{M}_{12} = x_1 M_1 + x_2 M_2$; $\overline{d_w}(12) = x_1 \overline{d_w}(1) + x_2 \overline{d_w}(2)$. Use of the geometric mean energy of vaporization will make λ_{12} somewhat smaller that a linear combination of λ_1 and λ_2. But without the correction of the interaction energy by means of F^E, this might not impart sufficient concavity to the conductivity versus concentration curve to represent the experimental data. If one or both components of the mixture are flexible-chain molecules, the mole fraction (x_i) should be replaced by the volume fraction (φ_i) in the calculations.

A logical mixing rule for any layer thicker than a monolayer might be based on the additivity of thermal resistance so that

$$\frac{1}{\lambda_{12}} = \frac{x_1}{\lambda_1} + \frac{x_2}{\lambda_2} + \psi\left(\frac{F^E}{RT}\right) \qquad (10.21)$$

or

$$\frac{1}{\lambda_{12}} = \frac{\varphi_1}{\lambda_1} + \frac{\varphi_2}{\lambda_2} + \zeta\left(\frac{F^E}{RT}\right), \qquad (10.22)$$

where the form of the function ψ or ζ has yet to be established by comparison with experiment. They are probably just constant factors of the order 0.05 to 0.1 λ^{-1}. Since in many cases of practical interest this correction is small, the simple resistance addition yields quite good approximations, especially when the thermal conductivities of the components differ appreciably. The correction is always important when $\lambda_1 \approx \lambda_2$.

For both kinds of mixture rules we should remember that F^E should not exceed $|2RT|$. With positive sign $F^E > 2RT$ leads to unmixing, and with negative sign $F^E < -2RT$ indicates strong association or molecular-compound formation, so that the transport of the heat of mixing should be taken into consideration, as in other associating systems, before proceeding with the calculation. In the absence of experimental data F^E can be estimated by means of Hildebrand's regular solution approximation [14] with sufficient accuracy for the present purposes.

Two older mixing rules are in use, one by Philippov [20] and one by the writer [3]. The empirical mixture rule by Philippov

$$\lambda_{12} = w_1\lambda_1 + w_2\lambda_2 - 0.7w_1w_2|\lambda_2 - \lambda_1| \tag{10.23}$$

does not represent all data very well because it yields $\lambda_{12} = \lambda_1 (= \lambda_2)$ instead of the experimental $\lambda_{12} < \lambda_1$ even when $\lambda_1 = \lambda_2$.

A more generally satisfactory, if also empirical, mixture rule is

$$\lambda_{12} = x_1\lambda_1 + x_2\lambda_2 - fbx_1x_2, \tag{10.24}$$

where

$$f = \left| \left(\frac{E_1^\circ}{M_1}\right)^{1/2} - \left(\frac{E_2^\circ}{M_2}\right)^{1/2} \right|, \tag{10.25}$$

and $b = 4.5 \times 10^{-5}$ if E° is expressed in cal/mole, or $b = 7.0 \times 10^{-9}$ if E° is expressed in ergs/mole. If one of the mixture components is a high-molecular weight (flexible) chain compound, the mole fraction x_i should be replaced by volume fractions. This rule appears to give reasonable answers even with associating components. However, so few good mixture data are available that surprises cannot be excluded.

10.9 COMPARISON WITH OTHER APPROACHES

Only one other useful calculating method for the low-temperature liquid-state region has been published so far, that by Robbins and Kingrea [24], valid for $0.4 < T_R < 0.9$. It is entirely empirical and has the following form:

$$\lambda = 10^{-5} \frac{(1.81 - 0.101H)}{V^{1/3}} \left(\frac{19.7}{S^*}\right) \left(\frac{0.55}{T_R}\right)^N c_p\rho \;\; (\text{cal/cm sec }^\circ C), \tag{10.26}$$

where $S^* = S_{vb} + R \ln (273/T_b)$, is a modified entropy of vaporization at the normal boiling point, that is 19.7 e.u. for "normal" substances. The empirical constants H and N can take on the values given in Table 10.3. Although the intuitive logic of the treatment is apparent, a clear rationale

Table 10.3   The Robbins–Kingrea Parameters [24]

Functional Group	Number of Groups	H Factor Contribution,[a]
Unbranched hydrocarbons:		
Paraffins	—	0
Olefins	—	0
Rings	—	0
CH₃ branches	1	1
	2	2
	3	3
C₂H₅ branches	1	2
iso-C₃H₇ branches	1	2
C₄H₉ branches	1	2
F substitutions	1	1
	2	2
Cl substitutions	1	1
	2	2
	3 or 4	3
Br substitutions	1	4
	2	6
I substitutions	1	5
OH substitutions	1 (iso-)	1
	1 (normal)	−1
	2	0
	1 (tert-)	5
Oxygen substitutions:		
$\overset{\mid}{-}\overset{\mid}{C}\mathrm{=O}$ (ketones, aldehydes)	—	0
$-\overset{\mathrm{O}}{\overset{\|}{C}}-\mathrm{O}-$ (acids, esters)	—	0
—O— (ethers)	—	2
NH₂ substitutions	1	1

[a] For compounds containing multiple functional groups, the H-factor contributions are additive. For organic liquids with $\rho_4{}^{20} < 1.0$. $N = 1$. For organic liquids with $\rho_4{}^{20} > 1.0$ $N = 0$.

cannot be developed very easily. Yet the excellent agreement with experimental data [6], [22] for those compounds for which the equation is designed should challenge the theoretical analyst.

Conventional corresponding-states correlations of the reduced residual thermal conductivity [(observed thermal conductivity) — (atmospheric-pressure conductivity of the corresponding vapor)] versus the reduced density (ρ/ρ_c) have proven very useful for compressed gases and for liquids in the range $T_b < T < T_c$ [27].[1] The function is extremely steep, however, and therefore less accurate in the liquid region $T < T_b$.

[1] Golubev I. F. and Y. U. Naziev, quoted in the book by Tsederberg.

An excellent summary of most previous work on thermal conductivity of liquids and gases, especially in the Russian literature can be found in the recent monograph *Thermal Conductivity of Gases and Liquids* by N. V. Tsederberg, (MIT Press, Cambridge, Massachusetts, 1965).

REFERENCES

[1] Bearman, R. J., *J. Chem. Phys.* **29**, 1278 (1958).

[2] Benoit, H. and P. Doty, *J. Phys. Chem.* **57**, 958 (1953).

[3] Bondi, A., *AIChE J.* **8**, 610 (1962).

[4] Bondi, A., *J. Phys. Chem.* **68**, 441 (1964).

[5] Bondi, A., and D. J. Simkin, *AIChE J* **6**, 919 (1960).

[6] Braun, W. G., *API—Tech. Data Book-Project;* Pennsylvania State University, private communication.

[7] Carmichael, L. T., and B. H. Sage, *J. Chem. Eng. Data* **9**, 511 (1964).

[8] Danon, F. et al., *J. Chem. Phys.* **36**, 426 (1962); **43**, 762 (1965).

[9] Eiermann, K., Kunststoffe **51**, 512 (1961); Koll. Z **198**, 5 (1964).

[10] Gollins, M. H. et al., *J. Chem. Eng. Data* **7**, 311 (1962).

[11] Green, H. S., *The Molecular Theory of Liquids*, Interscience, New York, 1952.

[12] Haase, R., *Thermodynamik der irreversiblen Prozesse*, Steinkoff, Darmstadt, 1963.

[13] Hennig, J., et al., *Kolloid-Z.* **189**, 114 (1963).

[14] Hildebrand, J. H., and R. L. Scott, *Solubility of Non-electrolytes*, Reinhold, New York, 1953.

[15] Horrocks, J. K. et al., *Trans. Faraday Soc.* **59**, 1 (1963).

[16] Jobst, W., *Int. J. Heat Mass. Transfer*, **7**, 725 (1964).

[16a] Lohe, P., *Koll. Z.*, **205**, 1 (1965).

[17] McCready, D. W., WADC-Technical Report 59-158.

[18] McLaughlin, E., *Chem. Rev.* **64**, 389 (1964).

[19] Owens, E. J., and G. Thodos, *AIChE J.* **3**, 454 (1957).

[20] Phillippov, P., *Proc. Moscow University* **10** (8) 17 (1955).

[21] Powell, R. W., and A. R. Challoner, *Ind. Eng. Chem.* **53**, 581 (1961).

[22] Reid, R. C., private communication.

[23] Reid, R. C., and T. K. Sherwood, *The Properties of Gases and Liquids*, McGraw-Hill, New York, 1958.

[24] Robbins, I. A., and C. L. Kingrea, *Proc. Am. Petr. Inst.* **42**, III, 52 (1962).

[25] Shoulberg, R. H., *J. Appl. Polymer Sci.* **7**, 1597 (1963).

[26] Stevenson, D. P., *J. Phys. Chem.* **69**, 2145 (1965).

[27] Stiel, L., and G. Thodos, *AIChE J*, **10**, 26 (1964).

[28] Volkenstein, N. V., *Configurational Statistics of Polymeric Chains*, Interscience, New York, 1963.

[29] Ziebland, H., and J. E. Patient, *J. Chem. Eng. Data* **7**, 530 (1962).

[30] Zbinden, R., *Infrared Spectra of High Polymers*, Academic Press, New York, 1964.

11

Diffusion of Liquids

The purpose of the present work is to sketch a new approach to the estimation of rotational-diffusion and of mass-diffusion coefficients from molecular-structure information. In the field of rotational diffusion it had long been recognized that the Debye approximation, a special form of the Stokes–Einstein diffusion equation, is inadequate for the correlation of data, especially when the size of the rotating dipole molecule is of the same size or smaller than that of the surrounding medium [21], [22], [26]. The same limitation to the applicability of the Stokes–Einstein diffusion equation has, of course, been noted with mass diffusion [8], [26]. A few engineering correlations have provided quite effective empirical adjustments for these size effects, at least within the limits of molecular weights encountered with liquids in common practice.

However, these adjustments become generally inapplicable when the solvent is a polymeric liquid, that is, either a polymer melt or an elastomer. The present work has been undertaken to handle that particular problem, and has then been applied more broadly to the simpler cases also.

The scope of the work has been set by recognition of the fact that it is less important, at this juncture, to present a fully worked-out method or to continue along well worn, increasingly less remunerative paths than to establish a thought pattern that may be more suitable for the correlation of data, and—hopefully—for the prediction of diffusivities. Hence this section should be taken primarily as a goad to more work.

11.1 ROTATIONAL DIFFUSION

11.1.1 General Principles

The rotation of a molecule in a liquid can be visualized in terms of two widely differing concepts: either as a solid body moving in fluid continuum or as a molecule among other molecules. In the former case we have Debye's expression for the rotational diffusion constant

$$D_r = \frac{1}{\tau_r} = \frac{fkT}{\eta a^3}$$

where a is the effective diameter of the molecule, f is a numerical (geometrical) constant which is unity when the body is a sphere, and depends on the particle geometry for all other cases, and η is the shear viscosity of the surrounding medium. Calculation of f for more complicated geometries is strictly an exercise in fluid mechanics and has been carried out for several cases of practical interest.

Highly anisometric molecules rotate at different speeds around their different axes of rotation. The methods of nuclear magnetic resonance can pick up the different values of D_r if the rotating molecule has at least two differentiable magnetic nuclei [20]. Permanent electric dipoles built into the molecule at a fixed angle to one of its axes of rotation follow the alternating electric field (at resonances) and their actual mode of rotation is the resultant of the (sometimes complicated) interaction of electric and viscous-drag force vectors. In the case of drag-free rotation interaction of electric and inertial force vectors must be considered. Rotor geometry then enters the calculation through the appropriate moments of inertia.

A model of interaction of the rotating molecule with neighboring molecules—instead of a continuum—primarily substitutes the mathematical apparatus of molecular theory for the constant η. This apparatus is cumbersome in its present state of development, and its results are used here only for the formulation of the appropriate dimensionless parameters. Just as in the fluid-mechanical case, three different regions are considered: the friction-free, purely inertial rotation; the rotation—or large amplitude torsional oscillation—of a rigid rotor in the periodic force field of its neighbors; and thirdly, the rotation of rotors with internal as well as external degrees of freedom in an environment with more than one kind of correlation time.

Obviously the first of these is straightforward and requires only the application of well-known but commonly ignored results of kinetic gas theory. The second case is in zeroth approximation manageable by analogy with the similarly well-established mechanics of torsional oscillation of molecules in a crystal lattice. The third case often corresponds to physical reality, but even its simplest model has so far found no rigorous treatment that can supply the needed multiparameter solution. Fortunately a few crude approximations appear to yield useful correlations.

11.1.2   Free Rotors

Kinetic gas theory [13] yields for the average rotation rate of rigid rotors

$$\bar{\omega}_{ri} = 1.47 \left(\frac{kT}{I_i}\right)^{\frac{1}{2}}, \tag{11.2}$$

where I_i is the appropriate principal moment of inertia. In the case of dipole molecules rotating in an alternating electric field "appropriate" means that moment, or the average of those moments, the axis (axes) of which are normal to the electric field that produces maximum coupling with the permanent electric dipole.

Because the rotation rates of the molecules in a given sample are distributed according to a Boltzmann distribution, there is a wide range of rotation rates with the usual spread around the average $\bar{\omega}_{ri}$. Intuition suggests that rotation of molecules in a liquid should be more restricted than in the gas, or that a reduced relaxation time for rotation $\tau_r(kT/I_i)^{\frac{1}{2}}$ should always be larger than 0.68. According to an analysis by Steele [23], intuition is a poor guide; molecular rotation rate in most simple liquids should be determined by inertia.

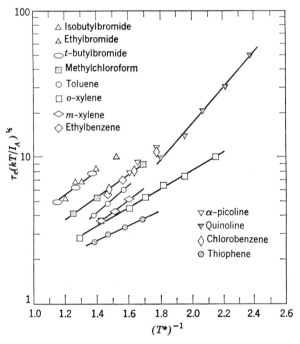

Figure 11.1   Electric-dipole relaxation time of rigid molecules as a measure of hindered external rotation in the liquid phase [4].

The data in Figure 11.1 show that, as usual, there is no single answer. There are few polar molecules which rotate in the liquid nearly as freely as in the gas phase, and those only near (and above) their atmospheric boiling points. This result is in basic disagreement with the common belief of thermodynamicists that rotation in the liquid state is as free as in the gas phase if the entropy of vaporization has its "ideal" value.

A common feature of the few freely rotating polar molecules is not only a comparatively low value of their dipole moment μ, but also a rather "smooth" surface, on which we comment in greater detail in later sections. It should be noted that in all cases $\tau_r(kT/I_i)^{1/2}$ increases, that is, rotation becomes more hindered with decreasing temperature.

A reasonable rule of thumb is that a slowdown by a factor of 5 makes a rotor resemble a torsional oscillator. The observed retardation of dipole relaxation is connected with the reduction of intermolecular distances as $T < T_b$ to the point that the rotating molecule begins to experience a nonuniform force field.

11.1.3 Rigid Hindered Rotors [4]

A theory of the rotation rate of a polar molecule in the periodic force field of its neighbors proposed by Bauer [2] can be used as point of departure. Assuming that the shape of the barrier experienced by the molecule during a rotation on the crystal-like lattice is $W = W_0(1 - \cos \alpha)$, where α is the angle relative to its starting (equilibrium) position, and that the transmission coefficient of the barrier equals unity, Bauer obtains

$$\tau\left(\frac{W_0}{I_i}\right)^{1/2} = A\left(\frac{kT}{W_0}\right)^{1/2} \exp\left(\frac{W_m}{kT}\right),$$ (11.3)

where W_m is the value of W at the angle corresponding to the bottom of the potential energy well, I_i is the appropriate principal moment of inertia of the molecule, and A is a numerical constant that varies between 1.8 and 4.4 depending on the details of the models chosen.

In spite of its attractive simplicity this theory has not been applied to liquids and has remained dormant for 20 years. The appropriate axis of rotation, and therefore I_i, can generally be chosen by inspection. The calculation of moments of inertia is a bit tedious, but many are now available from the literature so that only W_0 and W_m remain to be estimated. With rigid molecules we could obtain W_0 by application of the same periodic-barrier assumption used for the interpretation of the heat capacity of the liquid under consideration (See Chapter 9).

When heat-capacity data are not available we may make the assumption that $W_0 \sim E^\circ$, the standard energy of vaporization. Then we can define a reduced molecular relaxation time for external rotation

$$\tau_i^* = \tau_r \left(\frac{E_m^\circ}{I_i}\right)^{\!1/2}.\tag{11.4}$$

Since numerator and denominator in $(E_m^\circ/I_i)^{1/2}$ generally rise in parallel with increasing molecule size, and variations are damped by the $\frac{1}{2}$ power, this reducing parameter does not vary over a very wide range.[1]

Both ratios kT/W_0 and kT/W_m should then be proportional to the reduced temperature T^* mentioned earlier. They might even be of the same order as T^*. The reasonableness of the theory can be tested by examining the absolute value of τ^* predicted and the linearity of $\ln(\tau^*/T^{*1/2})$ versus $1/T^*$. Taking $kT/W_0 \approx kT/W_m \approx T^*$, we obtain, with $A = 4$ for $T^* = 0.7$ (in the middle

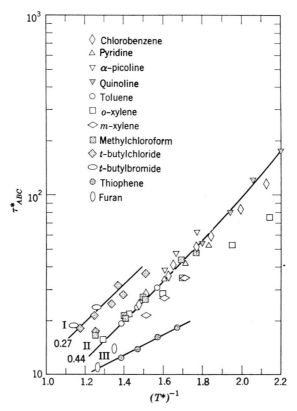

Figure 11.2 Generalized dipole relaxation time of liquids composed of rigid molecules [4]. Random rotation.

[1] $E_m = E^\circ/N_A$, where N_A = Avogadro number.

of the liquid range), $\tau^* \approx 16$, whereas the observed values are $\sim 30 \pm 10$ (at least in the right order of magnitude). Over the usual short temperature ranges, $T^{1/2}$ is unimportant and $\ln \tau \sim 1/T$ is well established.

The possibility of a universal relation $\ln \tau^*$ versus $1/T^*$ hinges upon the universality of the ratios W_m/E°. We can expect these ratios to be constant only within fixed families of compounds, depending upon the relative role played by dipole orientation energies, dispersion energy, and molecular geometry in determining the magnitudes of W_0, W_m, or E°.

The somewhat disappointing spread of curves on the plot of τ_i^* versus $1/T^*$ in Figures 11.2 and 11.3 is therefore not surprising. Uniformity is improved somewhat by the choice of the largest principal moment of inertia of a molecule for the reducing parameter. Close inspection of the curves suggests the existence of three distinct groups of compounds. The least-hindered rotors at the bottom of the graph are the heteroaromatics with smooth molecular surface; the most-hindered rotors, high on the graph, are large (branched) alkyl halides with very bumpy molecule surface, and an intermediate band, composed largely of moderately substituted aromatic-ring

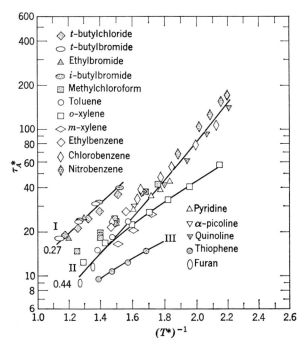

Figure 11.3   Generalized dipole relaxation time of liquids composed of rigid molecules [4]. Rotation around shortest axis. Zone I: bulky aliphatic halides; Zone II: aromatic benzenoid ring systems. Parameter on the curves is the reduced maneuver length d_e^*.

compounds. A suitable measure of molecule smoothness should then serve as third parameter for the characterization of molecular rotation.

11.1.4 Roughness of Molecule Surfaces

The roughness of plane surfaces is conventionally expressed as the rms deviation from the location of a hypothetical "average plane" surface. A second number is required to describe the average width of the roughnesses, unless we assume a regular shape, such as a hemisphere, for the average roughness, which is characterized by a single length.

Characterization of the surface roughness of molecules also starts with the establishment of a hypothetical average surface, the deviation from which is a measure of the average height of the roughness. The total range of van der Waals radii is so small that a second number to characterize the average width of the surface roughness does not seem to be necessary.

The molecular model for making the roughness estimate is identical with that used for estimating the van der Waals volume of molecules. An obvious measure of roughness d_r is

$$d_r = \bar{r} - (r_2{}^2 - m^2)^{\frac{1}{2}}, \tag{11.5}$$

where $\bar{r} = (1/n) \sum_{i=1}^{i=n} r_i$ is the average van der Waals radius of the atoms on the molecule under consideration and

$$m = \frac{r_2{}^2 - r_1{}^2 + l^2}{2l}, \tag{11.6}$$

where r_i are the van der Waals radii of neighboring bonded atoms, taking $r_2 > r_1$; l is the chemical bond length between atoms 1 and 2. The roughness-corrected ("effective") average distance between molecules $d_e = d_s - d_r$. The average distance between molecule surfaces is taken as

$$d_s = \frac{V_w}{A_w} (V^* - 1), \tag{11.7}$$

where V_w and A_w are the volume and surface area, respectively, per mole of molecules. In the molecular-weight range of interest in the present context the reduced volume $V^* \equiv V/V_w$ is essentially a universal function of T^*. A convenient dimensionless form of d_e is

$$d_e^* = V^* - \frac{d_r A_w}{V_w} - 1. \tag{11.8}$$

Typical values of d_e^* for the middle of the liquid range ($V^* = 1.8$) have been entered in Table 11.1 and as third parameter in Figure 11.3. It is apparent that d_e^* serves as ordering parameter for the reduced relaxation time of pure liquids composed of rigid molecules.

Table 11.1 Surface Roughness of Molecules [4]

Type	Bond	d_r (Å)	Typical Compounds	d_r (Å)	d_e^* at $V^* = 1.8$	$d_{\min}^*$
Alkanes	C—C (side)	0.26	n-C$_7$H$_{16}$	0.31	0.37	
	C $\cdots$ C (side	0.57	n-(CH$_2$)$_x$	0.33	0.37	0.11
	C—H	0.27	Neo-pentane	0.36	0.27	−0.04
Perfluoroalkanes	C—F	0.18	n-C$_7$F$_{16}$	0.31	0.32	
	F $\cdots$ F (or CF$_2$)	0.47	n-(CF^2)$_x$	0.32	0.33	0.09
Chloroalkanes	C—Cl	0.30	EtCl	0.31	0.34	0.1
	Cl $\cdots$ Cl	0.75	t-BuCl	0.37	0.27	−0.15
	C $\cdots$ Cl	0.66	MeCCl$_3$	0.47	0.14	−0.17
Bromoalkanes	C—Br	0.29	EtBr	0.31	0.35	−0.04
	Br $\cdots$ Br	0.92	t-BuBr	0.37	0.27	−0.4
	C $\cdots$ Br	0.58				
Aromatic rings	C$_{ar}$—C$_{ar}$	0.14	Benzene	0.34	0.38	0.14
	C$_{ar}$—H	0.53	Chlorobenzene	0.29	0.44	0.15
	C$_{ar}$—N$_{ar}$	0.16	Pyridine	0.30	0.44	0.16
	C$_{ar}$—O$_{ar}$	0.16	Furan	0.28	0.44	0.12
	C$_{ar}$—S$_{ar}$	0.22	Thiophene	0.33		

The foregoing should be regarded primarily as a suggestion for further research. Reasoning from macroscopic mechanics to events on molecular scale is unsafe if not backed up by careful analysis on the basis of first principles. Since an analysis has not yet been carried out, further elaboration of the effect of molecule roughness on rotation in the liquid state would be premature.

11.1.5 Low-Temperature Behavior

The exponential relation $\ln \tau \sim T^{-1}$ predicted by Bauer's simple theory is seen to prevail only at $T^* > 0.6$. At lower temperatures the relaxation time rises rather more steeply, and is well represented by the simple relation

$$\ln \tau^* = \frac{B}{T^* - T_0^*} - A, \qquad (11.9)$$

indicative of the approach to the glass transition temperature T_g to which T_0 is closely related [7]. Various theoretical justifications have been advanced

[6], [19] for the originally empirical equation (11.9), some of which are discussed more fully in Chapter 12. There it is also shown that for liquids composed of small molecules, T_0 is very near, and just below, T_g, whereas for liquids composed of larger molecules, $T_0 \approx 0.8T_g$. More data are needed to ascertain the general (and here tacitly assumed) identity of T_0 obtained from dipole relaxation time with T_0 obtained from viscosity data.

The toluene curve in Figure 11.3 deviates so strikingly from the cluster of curves for the other aromatic compounds because the relaxation-time data shown are unresolved and contain the fast methyl-group rotation (τ_R) as well as that of the entire molecule (τ_1) [5]. These are additive as frequencies, so that

$$\tau^{-1} \approx (1 - G)\tau_1^{-1}, + G\tau_R^{-1}, \tag{11.10}$$

where G is a weighting factor which depends on the theory employed. This relation accounts for the shape of the toluene curve because the unresolved relaxation time τ will be the more strongly influenced by the superposition of the rapid rotation τ_R the larger the absolute magnitude of τ_1.

11.1.6 Evidence for Simultaneous Internal and External Rotation

Substitution of a rotating group for a hydrogen atom on the rigid frame of any of the rigid molecules discussed earlier, especially on cyclic molecules, provides the opportunity for the observation of the simultaneous rotation of the entire molecule and of the side branch if their rotation rates differ by a sufficiently large factor. Such separate rotation can be observed on nonpolar molecules by nmr methods, if the chemical shielding of hydrogen nuclei on the rigid frame (ring) differs substantially from that on the side branch. Typical examples, shown in Figures 11.4 and 11.5, bear out the a priori expectation that methyl or ethyl groups on the ring rotate faster than the entire molecule since the branch rotation rate $\sim (V^0/I_r)^{\frac{1}{2}} \exp{(-V^0/RT)}$.[1]

A permanent electric dipole in the side chain permits determination of the two rotation rates by measuring dipole relaxation over a wide range of frequencies. In some instances separate absorption peaks can actually be observed in the microwave absorption spectrum of the liquid [17]. More frequently one can construct the two peaks from the shouldered shape of the microwave-absorption peak [16]. In the absence of a sufficient number of datum points for the analysis of the shape of the absorption peak many authors resorted to the semi-empirical computational analysis proposed by Budo [5] and others [1], [14], [18], [25] to resolve—albeit very approximately—the relaxation-time spectrum into its two major constituents.

The side-chain rotation of a molecule in a liquid is hindered by two different barriers: that to internal rotation V^0, which would also persist in the gaseous

---

[1] Where V^0 = height of potential-energy barrier to internal rotation, and I_r = reduced moment of inertia of rotor.

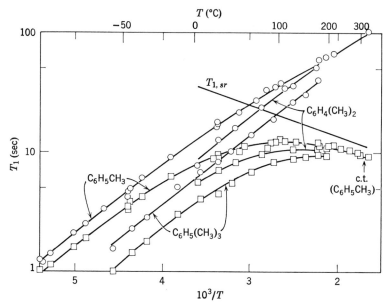

Figure 11.4 Spin-lattice relaxation time for the ring (○ ○) and methyl (□ □) protons in toluene ($C_6H_5CH_3$), p-xylene [$C_6H_4(CH_3)_2$], and mesitylene [$C_6H_3(CH_3)_3$]. $T_{1,sr}$ is a calculated spin-rotation relaxation time for the methyl protons of toluene (from Ref. [9]). The molecular rotational (angular position) relaxation time $\tau_{da} \approx 10^{-10}/(0.76 + 3.05\rho)T_1$.

state, and another one which is proportional to the fraction $A_w(r)/A_w(2)$ of $W_m(2)$. We might expect intuitively that only V^0 matters if $[A_w(r)/A_w(2)]W_m \approx V^0$.

The case of toluene, Figure 11.4, is particularly instructive in this respect because it shows that at $T > 330°K$ ($T^* > 0.7$), the nearest-neighbor force field has become sufficiently smoothed for the methyl group to rotate as freely as in the gas phase, where $V^0 < 0.5RT$. At lower temperatures, however, the barrier to methyl-group rotation is largely determined by the force field of the surrounding molecules. Recent measurement of the methyl dipole relaxation rate of toluene (in cyclohexane) in the region 288 to 330°K [12] yielded a slope in good agreement with that of the NMR measurements in Figure 11.4.

When $[A_w(r)/A_w(2)]W_m$ is sufficiently small, the reduced form of the side-chain relaxation time should obviously be $\tau_r(nV^0/I_{red})^{1/2}$, where V^0 is the barrier to internal rotation of n-fold symmetry and I_{red} is the reduced moment of inertia of the side chain. The corresponding reduced temperature is RT/V^0. The resulting correlation of τ^* versus T^* should in principle be directly comparable with, or even superimposable on, the τ^* versus T^* correlation of the entire molecule. Two factors prevent this ideal situation

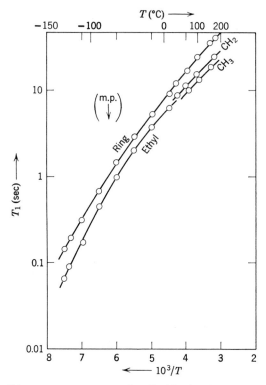

Figure 11.5 T_1's versus temperature for liquid ethyl benzene (from Ref. [20]). The molecular rotational (angular position) relaxation time $\tau_{da} \approx 10^{-10}/(0.76 + 3.05\rho)T_1$.

from being realized. The barrier to external rotation is defined only empirically as $\sim E^\circ$, and the barrier to internal rotation V^0 is generally known only for the isolated molecule in the ideal gas, rather than in the low-temperature liquid of interest.

Inspection of the reduced side-chain relaxation time (in Table 11.2) is far more instructive than that of the absolute values, as is particularly apparent by the large deviation of the case of phenol, undoubtedly due to hydrogen bonding to neighboring molecules.

The absence of similar effects with aniline either confirms the well-known weakness of aniline's hydrogen bonds, or it means that inversion rather than rotation matters in this case [17]. These observations suggest that specific molecular structure effects should be postulated only after the nonspecific effects have been eliminated by the reducing parameter $(V^\circ/I_{\text{red}})^{1/2}$. When $A_w(r)/A_w(2) > 0.2$, V° should be replaced by $\{V^\circ + [A_w(r)/A_w(2)]\Delta E^\circ_{\neq}\}$ in all of the indicated correlations of side-chain motion.

Table 11.2 Relaxation Times of Segmented Molecules (in Benzene Solution)[a]

Solute (all at 293°C)	Whole Molecule Rotating		Smaller Segment Rotating		
	τ(psec)	$\tau \dfrac{*}{ABC}$	Segment	τ_R(psec)	$\tau_R^{*\,b}$
Aniline[c]	7.2	33	$-NH_2$	0.3 to 0.5	9 to 15
Phenol	11.4	54	$-OH$	1.1	42[d]
Anisol	9	36	$-OMe$	0.9	8
2-Methoxynaphthalene	19.7	56	$-OMe$	1.1	10

[a] Data from Klages, G., and P. Knobloch, *Z. Naturforschg.* **20a**, 580 (1965).
[b] $\tau_R^* \equiv \tau_R(V°/I_{red})^{1/2}$, where $V°$ is the appropriate potential energy barrier to internal rotation and I_{red} the appropriate reduced moment of inertia. The magnitude of τ_R^* indicates that the "rotation" is more nearly like a torsional oscillation.
[c] The lower segment relaxation time from Stockhausen, M., *ibid.* **19a**, 1317 (1964). {The short relaxation times obtained by Professor Klages' school have been accepted here as closer to experimental evidence than the longer segment relaxation times reported by other authors [10, 11, 25]. This controversy will probably be settled by scanning through the secondary relaxation region, down to 0.5 mm wavelength or by improved NMR (spin–rotation) relaxation-time measurements on the segment protons of the same compounds.}
[d] This large value suggests appreciable retardation of rotation by hydrogen bonding to neighboring molecules.

The pseudorotation of ring-puckering motions in saturated (five-membered) rings appears to be an additional source of internal motion [24] reducing their measured over-all relaxation time below the magnitude expected from the general correlation for rigid molecules. The order of magnitude of τ_R appears to be predicted correctly by

$$\tau_R^{-1} = \nu_R \exp\left(\frac{-V°}{RT}\right),$$

where ν_R is the equivalent torsional frequency of the pseudorotation.

A third intramolecular high-frequency relaxation process has been widely, albeit still somewhat inconclusively, debated: charge oscillation associated with changes in (hyper) conjugation between rotatable groups during their mutual rotation. The relaxation frequency of such a process would be of the order $[nV°/I_{red}]^{1/2} \exp(-V°/RT)$, where n is the number of charge oscillations per full rotation, making the appropriate reduced relaxation time of the fast process $\tau_2^* = \tau_2(nV°/I_{red})^{1/2}$.

11.1.7 External Rotation of Flexible Molecules [4]

The relaxation-time distribution of long-chain molecules with a permanent electric dipole at one end has been determined sufficiently well to permit at least approximate resolution into two primary relaxation times: that for rotation around the long axis, τ_1, and that for end-over-end tumbling, τ_2 [14]. Owing to the absence of data in the corresponding high-frequency region, τ_1 can be estimated only with limited accuracy, whereas τ_2 is probably quite reliable.

The data in Figure 11.6 reveal a striking difference between the two types of rotation. Rotation relaxation time τ_1 (around the long axis of the molecules) rises only very slowly with decreasing temperature, especially for the series n-propyl to n-hexyl bromide. The data for ethyl bromide cannot be incorporated into this series because the two types of rotation cannot be

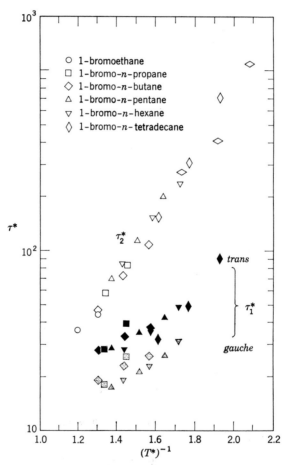

Figure 11.6   Resolved generalized dipole relaxation times of 1-bromo-n-alkanes [4]. τ_2^* refers to tumbling motion of molecules in *gauche* conformation. τ_1^* refers to rotation around long axis.

separated very well. It is doubtful whether the slightly smaller scatter obtained with the moment of inertia of the *gauche* conformation in the reducing parameter for τ_1 has physical significance. The end-over-end tumbling motion τ_2, by contrast, can be correlated on a single curve from ethyl through hexyl bromide only if the *gauche* conformation (at the polar end) is assumed as predominant.

The coincidence of all points on a single curve suggests that *n*-alkanes in the liquid at $T < T_b$ rotate like rigid rods at least up to $N_c = 14$. Their molecular flexibility should become important in rotational motion at $N_c \geq 16$. There should be a chain length beyond which only the terminal segment containing the dipole participates in rotational motions, that is, beyond which τ (at a given value of T^*) becomes essentially independent of chain length. This "critical" chain length, which should be a function of T^*, can only be established by further experiments.

11.1.8 Rotation in Solutions and Mixtures [4]

The rotational relaxation time of polar substances in nonpolar solvents is of greater scientific and technological interest than that in pure liquids because of the elimination of the complication of extensive dipole–dipole interaction and because of the technical importance of dielectric energy losses due to polar substances in insulating liquids and polymers.

At infinite dilution each polar molecule is completely surrounded by solvent molecules. Only if solvent and solute molecule are of equal size is the interaction energy between solvent and solute given by

$$\bar{E}_1^\circ = (E^\circ E_2^\circ)^{1/2} - F^E.$$

In the more general case of different molecule size the averaging should be carried out on the energy per unit surface area (per molecule):

$$\bar{E}^\circ = \left[\frac{E^\circ}{A_w(1)} \frac{E_2^\circ}{A_w(2)} \right]^{1/2} A_w(2) - F^E,$$

where index (2) refers to the solute, and F^E, the excess free energy of mixing (from phase-equilibrium data), is a measure of the specific interaction energy between molecules of solute and solvent.

At finite concentration of solute we must also consider the molecules of solute contained in the "cage" wall surrounding the test molecule. Then

$$\bar{E}^\circ = A_w(2) \left\{ \frac{E_2^\circ}{A_w(2)} \left[x_1^2 \frac{E_1^\circ}{A_w(1)} + x_2^2 \frac{E_2^\circ}{A_w(2)} + 2x_1 x_2 \left(\frac{E_1^\circ}{A_w(1)} \frac{E_2^\circ}{A_w(2)} \right)^{1/2} \right] \right\}^{1/2} - F^E.$$

In either case the reduced relaxation time of the solute is $\tau(\bar{E}^\circ/I_i)^{1/2} \equiv \bar{\tau}^*$.

The appropriate reduced temperature is

$$\bar{T}^* \equiv 5\tilde{c}RT/\bar{E}^\circ,$$

where the property $c =$ one-third of the number of external degrees of freedom; $\bar{c} = \frac{1}{2}(c_1 + c_2)$ in dilute solution and $\bar{c} = \frac{1}{2}[(1 + x_1)c_1 + (1 - x_1)c_2]$ for concentrated solutions. When c_1 is not very different from c_2, it is permissible to form a temperature-reducing parameter for the mixture as

$$\theta_L = [\theta_L(1)\theta_L(2)]^{1/2}$$

because then $(c_1 c_2)^{1/2}$ does not differ much from $\frac{1}{2}(c_1 + c_2)$; $\theta_L \equiv E^\circ/5cR$.

Ideally, a plot of the reduced relaxation time of the solute should be a function of $\bar{T}$ only, independent of the solvent. The most severe test of this approach, the correlation of data points obtained in a nonviscous solvent with those in a very viscous solvent on a single curve has been very well met by the examples shown in Figure 11.7. The close fit of the solution and pure-liquid data for n-tetradecylbromide to a single curve is particularly gratifying.

The sharp reduction of the relaxation-time curve for the methylchloroform solutions below that for the pure liquid, on the other hand, is in rather good

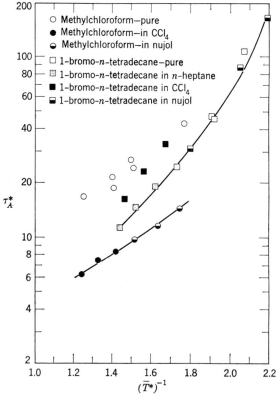

Figure 11.7   Generalized dipole relaxation time of polar molecules in solutions [4].

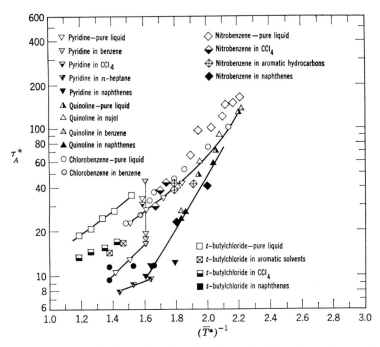

Figure 11.8 Generalized dipole relaxation time of rigid polar molecules in various solvents [4]. Note the lower level of the solution in naphthenic solvents.

agreement with expectation from the "bumpiness" parameter discussed earlier because of the smoothness of the solvent molecules compared with those of the solute. A similar drop below the pure-liquid relaxation curve is observed with solutions of t-butyl chloride, probably for the same reason.

The dearth of extended runs of precision relaxation-time versus temperature on solutions of rigid polar molecules makes it difficult to obtain good evidence for agreement. An indication of the general applicability of the correlation is again obtained from the proximity of the data for quinoline in the viscous Nujol to those of the pure liquid, in Figure 11.8. The scatter of the other solution data on the same figure may be due to the fact that almost every solution point is just a single datum often involving a different author for each point.

11.1.9 An Unsolved Puzzle [4]

The viscosity reduced dipole relaxation time τ/η of solutions of polar molecules in cyclohexane has often been observed as rather lower than in other solvents. Recently Hufnagel and his students [15] demonstrated that this peculiarity of excessively short (τ/η) relaxation times is common to all naphthenes and is the more pronounced the smaller the molecule. This

Calculating Procedures for Estimating the Relaxation Time (τ) of Molecules with Permanent Electric Dipoles in Liquids at $T^* > 0.6$ᵃ

Procedures	System	Available Data	Procedure and Equations	Section
11.1	Pure liquid composed of rigid molecules	Molecular structure	1. Estimate principal moment of inertia I_i of molecule around axis for which rotation is coupled to electric field. 2. Estimate $E°$ from increments of Tables 14 to 14.16 3. Because molecule is rigid, $c = 2$ (unless linear when $c = 5/3$). 4. $\log \tau = \frac{1}{2} \log \left(\frac{I_i}{E°}\right) + \frac{BE°}{5cRT} + A.$ *Molecule Type* *B* *A* Rigid (highly branched) alkyl 1.00 0.10 Rigid aryl 1.25 −0.61 Thiophene and similar 0.59 0.18.	11.1.3
11.2	Pure liquid composed of rigid molecules	Molecular structure and density	1, 2, as in Procedure 11.1. 3. Determine θ_L by means of (15.31). 4. $\log \tau = \frac{1}{2} \log \left(\frac{I_i}{E°}\right) + \frac{B\theta_L}{T} + A.$ A and B from Procedure 11.1.	11.1.3
11.3	Pure liquid compound of flexible alkyl 1-mono-halides or related nonassociating 1-mono-functional alkane	Molecular structure	1. Estimate principal moment of inertia I of prevalent equilibrium conformation. 2. As in Procedure 11.1. 3. Estimate c from equations on Tables 14.1. 4. $\log \tau = \frac{1}{2} \log \left(\frac{I_i}{E°}\right) + \frac{BE°}{5cRT} + A.$ *Rotation* *B* *A* Around short axis 1.51 −0.65 Around long axis 0.62 +0.45	11.1.7

11.4	Molecules, solute, in low concentrations ($X_2 < 0.05$ or $\varphi_2 < 0.05$) in solvent	Molecular structure of solute and solvent	1. Estimate E_1° and E_2°, $A_w(1)$ and $A_w(2)$, C_1 and C_2 from Tables 14.1 and 15.1.	11.1.8
			2. [b] Estimate the average $\overline{E_{12}^\circ} = A_w(2)\left[\dfrac{E_1^\circ}{A_w(1)} \cdot \dfrac{E_2^\circ}{A_w(2)}\right]^{\frac{1}{2}}$.	
			3. Obtain average $\bar{c}_{12}$ from Table 15.2.	
			4. Estimate the applicable moment of inertia of the solute molecule (see Procedure 11.1).	
			5. $T_{12}^* = 5\bar{c}_{12}RT/\overline{E_{12}^\circ}$.	
			6. See subsequent calculations as in Procedure 11.1 or 11.3 (as applicable), Step 4.	
11.5	Solute molecules in low concentrations ($X_2 < 0.05$ or $\varphi_2 < 0.05$) in solvent	Molecular structure of solute and solvent and density of solute and solvent	1, 2. As 1, 2 in Procedure 11.4.	11.1.8
			3. Estimate $\theta_L(1)$ and $\theta_L(2)$ by Procedure 1.5.	
			4. Same as 4 of Procedure 11.4.	
			5. $\theta_L(12) = [\theta_L(1)\,\theta_L(2)]^{\frac{1}{2}}$	
			6. $T_{12}^* = T/\theta_L(12)$.	
			7. All subsequent calculations as in Procedure 11.2, Step 4.	
11.6	Solute molecules at finite concentrations ($X_2 > 0.05$ or $\varphi_2 > 0.05$)	Molecular structure of solute and solvent	1. As in Procedure 11.4.	
			2. Estimate average $\overline{E_{12}^\circ}$ by (15.29). The term F^E need be obtained only if strong nonideality of solution is suspected 3–6 as 3 to 6 of Procedure 11.4.	

[a] τ in seconds; the correlation is too untried to give a meaningful uncertainty estimate.
[b] If strong nonideality of solution is suspected, add $(-F^E)$ to the right-hand side.

331

Calculating Procedures for the Thermal Conductivity of Liquids at $T_m < T < T_b$ or $(T_g + 30°C) < T < T_b$

Procedure	Molecule Type	Available Data	Procedure and Equation[a]	Error (%)	Section
10.1	Rigid molecule other than alkanes, alkenes	Molecular structure	1. Calculate M. 2. Estimate $E°$ by means of (15.8) from increments $E°(X)$ on Tables 15.1 to 16. 3. Estimate d_w by means of (15.3) from r_w data on Tables 14.1 to 16 4. Estimate $3c$ by means of relation 15.11. 5. $\lambda_s = \dfrac{0.646 \times 10^4\, R}{N_A \overline{d_w^2}}\left(\dfrac{E°^{1/2}}{M}\right)\left(3.22 - \dfrac{8.80cRT}{E°}\right)$.	± 8	10.2
10.2	Rigid molecule other than alkanes, alkenes	Molecular structure, density	1, 2, 3 same as 1, 2, 3 of Procedure 10.1. 4. Determine θ_L by means of (15.31). 5. $\lambda_s = \dfrac{0.646 \times 10^4\, R}{N_A \overline{d_w^2}}\left(\dfrac{E°^{1/2}}{M}\right)\left(3.22 - 1.76\dfrac{T}{\theta_L}\right)$.	± 8	10.2
10.3	Straight-chain alkanes, alkenes, alkanals, and alkanones, and $3c < 7$	Molecular structure	1, 2, 3, 4 as in P 10.1. 5. $\lambda_s = \dfrac{0.646 \times 10^4\, R}{N_A \overline{d_w^2}}\left(\dfrac{E°^{1/2}}{M}\right)\left(3.92 - \dfrac{10.85cRT}{E°}\right)$.		
		Molecular structure, density	1, 2, 3, 4 same as 1–4 of Procedure 10.2. 5. $\lambda_s = \dfrac{0.646 \times 10^4 R}{N_A \overline{d_w^2}}\left(\dfrac{E°^{1/2}}{M}\right)\left(3.92 - \dfrac{2.17T}{\theta_L}\right)$.		10.4

10.4	Flexible molecules ($3c < 8$)	Molecular structure	1–5 as in Procedure 10.1 except that $3c$ is estimated from correlations in Tables 14.1 to 16. 6. Approximate relation: $\lambda = \lambda_s \left[\left(\dfrac{3c - 6}{N_s - 1} \right) + 1 \right]$.
10.5	Flexible molecules ($3c > 8$)	Molecular structure, density	1–4 as in Procedure 10.2 5. $c = E^\circ/5 \, R\theta_L$ 6. Same as 6 of Procedure 10.4.
10.6	Polymer melts	Molecular structure	1–5 as in Procedure 10.4 except that all properties are for the repeating unit. 6. Approximate relation: $\lambda = \lambda_s(3c/n_s)$.
10.7	Polymer melts	Molecular structure density	1–5 as in Procedure 10.5 except that all properties are for the repeating unit. 6. Same as 6 of Procedure 10.6.
10.8	Molecular liquids with M < 300 and at at $T < T_b$	Molecular structure, density, normal boiling point (T_b) ΔS_{vb}	1. Equation 10.26 and Table 10.3.

ᵃ Units of λ are (cal cm^{-1} sec^{-1} °K^{-1}].

333

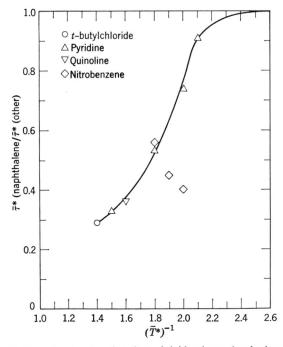

Figure 11.9   Ratio of dipole relaxation time of rigid polar molecules in naphthene solvents to that in other nonpolar solvents as function of reduced temperature [4].

effect could have been ascribed to the somewhat higher viscosity of naphthenes than that of other solvents of the same molal volume. The present correlation, which makes no explicit reference to viscosity, might have been expected to suppress this "naphthene effect." Even cursory inspection of Figure 11.8 reveals, however, that solutions in naphthenes exhibit depressed reduced relaxation times in the present correlation as well.

Expressing the naphthene effect as τ^* (naphthene)/τ^* (pure liquid) we find that the effect is primarily a function of the reduced temperature, regardless of the compound involved. A plot of τ_A^* (naphthene)/τ_A^* (pure liquid) versus T^* in Figure 11.9 shows that the effect decreases with decreasing reduced temperature and seems to vanish at $\bar{T}^* = 0.45$. This relation is, of course, a reflection of the molecule-size effect noted by Hufnagel. A much larger range in absolute temperature needs to be covered in experiments in order to obtain better insight into the possible origins of this effect.

11.2   MASS DIFFUSION

Contemplation of the principles governing mass diffusion in fluids leads to the suggestion that the physically significant property for a molecule is its friction coefficient

$$\zeta = \frac{kT}{D}$$

rather than its mass diffusion coefficient D. The Kirkwood theory of transport in dense fluids then leads to the dimensionless friction coefficient

$$\tilde{\zeta} = \frac{kT\,\sigma}{D(m\epsilon)^{\frac{1}{2}}} = f\left(\frac{\sigma^3}{v}\right), \tag{11.11}$$

where m = mass per molecule, σ = molecule diameter, ϵ = potential energy between two molecules, and v = molecular volume. Converted into technical units relation (11.11) reads

$$\zeta^* = \frac{RT\,d_w}{D(mE^\circ)^{\frac{1}{2}}} = f(\rho^*). \tag{11.12}$$

Preliminary indications are that this combines available data into a fairly narrow band.

NOMENCLATURE

A_w	molecular surface area per mole [cm²/mole]
A	proportionality constant in (11.3)
c	$\frac{1}{3}$ (number of external degrees of freedom per molecule, including those due to internal rotation)
d_e	$= d_s - d_r$ = roughness-corrected average distance between molecules (cm)
d_e^*	dimensionless form of d_e defined by (11.8)
d_{min}^*	minimum value of d_e^* in a particular system
d_r	molecule surface roughness, defined in (11.5) (cm)
d_s	average distance between molecule surfaces, defined in (11.7) (cm)
E°	standard energy of vaporization (cal/mole)
E_m	$2.39 \times 10^{-8} E^\circ/N_A$ (ergs/molecule)
F^E	excess free energy of mixing (cal/mole)
I_i	principal moment of inertia of a molecule around axis i (g cm²)
k	Boltzmann constant (ergs/molecule °K)
l	bond distance (cm)
m	an auxiliary magnitude (cm)
n	number of equivalent positions per complete turn (around bond)
N_c	number of carbon atoms per molecule
R	gas constant (cal/mole °K)
r	van der Waals radius (cm)
T_1	spin–lattice relaxation time (sec)
T	temperature (°K)

T^* $= 5cRT/E°$

T_b atmospheric boiling point (°K)

V^0 height of barrier to internal rotation (cal/°K)

W height of barrier to external rotation (ergs/molecule)

x_i mole fraction of component i

η viscosity (g/cm sec)

$\theta_{\rm L}$ $= E°/5cR$ (°K)

τ electric-dipole relaxation time (sec)

τ_i^* $= \tau(E_m/I_i)^{1/2}$

$\tau_{\rm R}$ electric-dipole relaxation time of internal rotor (sec)

$\tau_{\rm R}^*$ $= \tau_{\rm R}(nV°/I_r)^{1/2}$

REFERENCES

[1] Aihara, A., and M. Davies, *J. Colloid Sci.* **11**, 671 (1956).
[2] Bauer, E., *Cahiers Phys.* **20**, 1 (1944).
[3] Bergmann, K., D. M. Roverti, and C. P. Smyth, *J. Phys. Chem.* **64**, 663 (1960).
[4] Bondi, A., *J. Am. Chem. Soc.* **88**, 2131 (1966).
[5] Budo, A., *Phys. Z.* **39**, 706 (1938); *J. Chem. Phys.* **17**, 686 (1949).
[6] Cohen, M. C., and D. Turnbull, *J. Chem. Phys.* **31**, 1164 (1959).
[7] Davidson, D. W., and R. H. Cole, *J. Chem. Phys.* **19**, 1484 (1951).
[8] Gierer, A., and K. Wirtz, *Z. Naturforschg.* **8a**, 532 (1953).
[9] Green, D. K., and J. G. Powles, *Proc. Phys. Soc.* (*London*) **85**, 87 (1965).
[10] Grubb, E. L. G., and C. P. Smyth, *J. Am. Chem. Soc.* **83**, 4873 (1961).
[11] Hase, H., *Z. Naturforschg.* **8a**, 695 (1953).
[12] Hassel, W. F., and S. Walker, *Trans. Faraday Soc.* **62**, 861 (1966).
[13] Herzfeld, K. F., and H. M. Smallwood, in *Treatise on Physical Chemistry*, H. S. Taylor and S. Glasstone, eds., Van Nostrand, Princeton, New Jersey, 1951, vol. II.
[14] Higasi, K., K. Bergmann, and C. P. Smyth, *J. Phys. Chem.* **64**, 881 (1960).
[15] Hufnagel, F. et al., *Z. Naturforschg.* **18a**, 769 (1963); **20a**, 630 (1965).
[16] Klages, G., and P. Knobloch, *Z. Naturforschg.* **20a**, 580 (1965).
[17] Knobloch, P., *Ber. Bunsenges.* **69**, 296 (1965).
[18] Kramer, H., *Z. Naturforschg.* **15a**, 66 (1960).
[19] Macdonald, J. R., *J. Chem. Phys.* **40**, 1792 (1964).
[20] Powles, J. G., *Ber. Bunsenges.* **67**, 328 (1963).
[21] Riehl, N., and G. Wirths, *Z. Phys. Chem.* **194**, 97 (1944).
[22] Smyth, C. P., *Dielectric Behavior and Molecular Structure*, McGraw-Hill, 1955.
[23] Stockhausen, M., *Z. Naturforschg.* **19a**, 1317 (1964).
[24] Walker, S. et al., *Trans. Faraday Soc.* **62**, 576 (1966).
[25] Walker, S. et al., *J. Chem. Phys.* **44**, 4116 (1966).
[26] Zeidler, M. D., *Ber. Bunsenges.* **69**, 659 (1965).

12

Viscosity

12.1 GENERAL PRINCIPLES

The nature of the viscosity of monatomic liquids is now quite well understood. Molecular theory ascribes the resistance to flow to the deformation of the radial distribution function of the nearest neighbors around a given molecule by the shear stress transmitted through the action of the intermolecular forces [21], [34]. The success of that viewpoint was demonstrated when the viscosity of several monatomic liquids calculated without disposable parameters from the pair distribution function, derived from x-ray diffraction data, came satisfactorily close to the measured value [25]. The application of that theory is restricted to liquids composed of simple (spherical) molecules. For slightly less symmetrical polyatomic molecules we cannot use the theory but we can use dimensionless correlations, employing the molecular parameters that appear in the rigorous theory: the molecule diameter σ, the mass per molecule m, and the pair potential constant ϵ. These can be combined to form the dimensionless variables $\tilde{\eta} = \eta \sigma^2 / (m\epsilon)^{1/2}$, $\tilde{T} = kT/\epsilon$, and $\tilde{p} = p\sigma^3/\epsilon$. The experimental viscosity data of liquid rare gases, expressed in these dimensionless coordinates, are shown in Figure 12.1.

The molecular theory shows that the gaslike collisional interaction between molecules makes a significant, if small, contribution to the viscosity of liquids between T_b and T_c. Using the calculated ideal-gas viscosity η_K as a crude approximation to that kinetic contribution, Thodos and co-workers developed a correlation of the reduced residual molecular force contribution to viscosity $\eta^x_{\text{res}} = \eta^x - \eta_k{}^x$ versus the reduced density $\rho_R = \rho/\rho_c$ [38]. This correlation describes the viscosity of many liquids over the range from T_c down to T_b remarkably well, as can be seen in Figures 12.2 and 12.3. At $T < T_b$, the curve becomes extremely steep and the correlation very inaccurate. {A somewhat more accurate but less easily produced version correlates with the thermal pressure $(\partial P_R/\partial T_R)\rho_R$ in place of the density [13].} An important conclusion is that the viscosity of polar and nonpolar liquids at

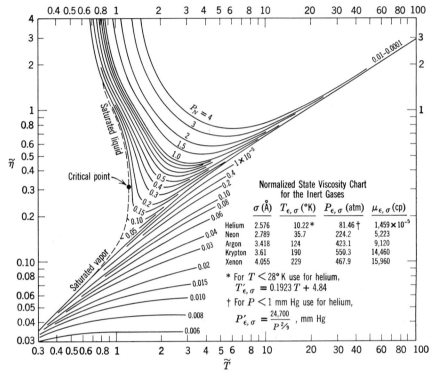

Figure 12.1 Reduced viscosity correlation for the inert gases [from Shimotake, H., and G. Thodos, *A.I.Ch.E. J.* **4**, 261 (1958)].

$T > T_b$ is primarily determined by a geometry factor and the pair potential, with only negligible specific effects of molecular structure. This statement is based on the assumption that Thodos' reducing parameter, the critical constants T_c, ρ_c, and p_c, are (universal) functions of molecule size and pair potential only.

At temperatures below T_b, polyatomic molecules require at least one additional parameter for the description of their equilibrium as well as transport properties (see Chapter 2). Moreover, a scheme that is to encompass substances for which the critical constants cannot be determined must adopt reducing parameters which are accessible to experiment for any liquid. The clearest choices are: in place of T_c (or ϵ) a standard energy of vaporization $E°/z$, where z is the number of nearest neighbors per molecule; in place of σ or ρ_c; the van der Waals volume V_w; and as third parameter, the number of external degrees of freedom ($3c$) including those due to internal rotation.

Based on arguments discussed in Chapters 2, 7, and 8, we obtain the following set of dimensionless parameters: for temperature, $T^* = zcRT/2E°$

(in general we set $z = 10$ for convenience); for density $\rho^* = V_w/V_{(T)}$, the packing density; for the viscosity of rigid molecules $\eta_s^* = \eta \, d_w (A_w/mE°)^{1⁄2}$, where $d_w = (6V_w/\pi N_A)^{1⁄3}$; and for the viscosity of flexible molecules $\eta_F^* = \eta \, d_w{}^2 N_A/(ME°)^{1⁄2}$, where d_w is the average width of the molecule [6].

It is convenient to divide the temperature range below T_b into two regions, a high-temperature region $1.0 > T^* > 0.6$ and a low-temperature (high packing density) region $0.6 > T^* > T_g^*$, where T_g is the glass transition

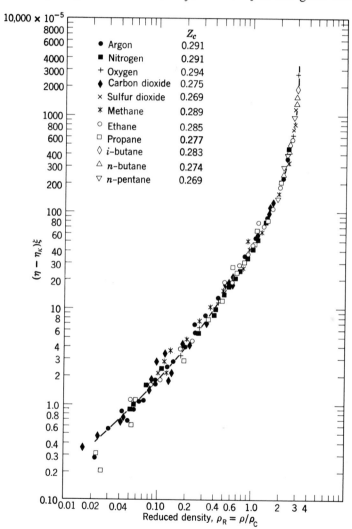

Figure 12.2 Relationship between reduced residual viscosity $(\eta - \eta_\kappa)\xi$ and reduced density ρ_R for nonpolar substances [38].

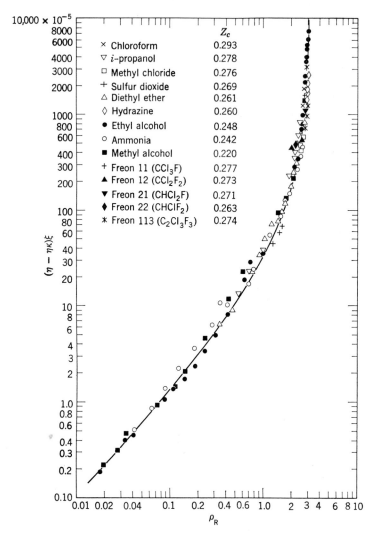

Figure 12.3   Relationship between $(\eta - \eta_\kappa)\xi$ and ρ_R for polar substances [38].

temperature. In the high-temperature region the viscosity is represented by a simple exponential relation $\eta^* \sim \exp(1/T^*)$, whereas the viscosity in the low-temperature region is dominated by the proximity to the glass transition temperature T_g [9].

The recognition of the importance of T_g for the viscosity even at T_g + 100°C for low-molecular-weight liquids is the result of experience gained with high-polymer melts and is of recent origin [7], [14], [37]. Hence the most appropriate mathematical representation of the data, the relation of the coefficients, especially of T_g, to molecular structure and to component properties in mixtures have yet to be developed. The first steps in that direction are presented in the section on low-temperature viscosity. A detailed treatment of the relation of T_g to molecular structure is found in Section 13.1.

Yet even at this early stage of development it is clear that the earlier methods of representation of viscosity–temperature curves of viscous liquids attempted by chemists in the lubricant industry [4] should be turned over to the dustbin of history. Only the facts, but few, if any, of the interpretive treatments of the earlier period will be useful in efforts to arrive at valid generalizations.

One earlier and one more recent simple corresponding states treatment of viscosity should be mentioned here. The frequent parallelism between fluidity and vapor pressure of liquids suggested to Nissan [29a], that $\ln (\eta/\eta_b) = f(T_b/T)$, where the subscript "$b$" refers to the atmospheric boiling point. The validity of this correlation is obviously restricted to the above defined high temperature region. A correlation of $\ln \eta = f(T_m/T)$ recently proposed by Greet and Magill [22a] has been designed primarily for the low temperature regions. The very restrictive conditions discussed in Chapters Three and Six under which T_m is even approximately a corresponding state, and the wide range of values taken by T_m/T_g preclude this method from being very useful in either high or low temperature regions. Cursory inspection of the data for groups of ortho, meta, and para disubstituted benzenes illustrates the point made.

12.2 ESTIMATING METHODS FOR THE HIGH-TEMPERATURE REGIME

12.2.1 Rigid Molecules

In a rough approximation we find the reduced viscosity versus temperature curves of many liquids composed of rigid molecules to fall into one or two narrow bands of η_s^* versus $1/T^*$. However, on closer examination we find that the slope (constant B in $\log \eta_s^* = B/T^* - A$) has a definite upward trend with molecule size as does the constant A. Hence a more accurate description of the viscosity temperature function is

$$\log \eta_s^* = \frac{a + bV_w}{T^*} - (g + dV_w). \tag{12.1}$$

The constants a, b, g, d should ideally be "universal" if viscosity could be described by a simple corresponding-states type of correlation. Actually they vary somewhat among the different families of compounds as shown in Table 12.1.

Table 12.1   Numerical Value of Constants a, b, d, g, for Various Groups of Liquids Composed of Rigid Molecules [9]

Substances	a	b	g	d
Rigid isoalkanes	0.84	0.37×10^{-2}	0.53	0.62×10^{-2}
Rigid nonpolar aromatic ring systems	0.83	0.34×10^{-2}	0.93	0.382×10^{-2}
Rigid nonpolar naphthenic[a] ring systems		$B = 1.18$		$A = 1.12$
Semirigid nonpolar naphthenic[a] ring system	0.65	0.58×10^{-2}	0.496	0.684×10^{-2}
Rigid polar aliphatic compounds	0.84	0.37×10^{-2}	0.80	0.80×10^{-2}
Rigid polar aromatic ring systems	0.79	0.36×10^{-2}	0.70	0.77×10^{-2}
Rigid "per" compounds	0.97	0.73×10^{-2}	0.82	0.77×10^{-2}
Cyclo poly(dimethylsiloxanes)	1.17	0.284×10^{-2}		$A = 1.65$

[a] Exclusive of cyclopentyl derivatives.

The physical meaning of the size dependence of B must be sought in relation to that of the characteristic temperature $\theta_L \equiv E°/5cR$, which determines the effective temperature scale of a compound, at least for equilibrium properties. The temperature coefficients of equilibrium properties such as density, thermal expansion, and bulk modulus are uniquely defined by the temperature scale $5cRT/E°$. Were viscosity a function of volume only, no size dependence of B could be expected. The inference is that the size dependence of B is caused by the existence of an isochoric temperature coefficient of viscosity $(\Delta E_{\pm}{}^j)$ rising with size more rapidly than does $E°$. This strongly size dependent, often major, component of $\Delta E_{\pm}{}^j$ has been identified, at least tentatively, as the barrier to external rotation of molecules in the liquid state [9].

A few aspects of Table 12.1 appear noteworthy. One of these is the absence of any molecule-size dependence of A and B for rigid naphthene ring systems, perhaps due to the comparatively narrow molecular weight range covered, since these are high-temperature data for condensed ring systems in excess of 18 carbon atoms. The name "semirigid" ring systems applies to such molecules as tricyclohexylmethane, 1,1-dicyclohexylethane, etc.

Another peculiar aspect is the steepness of the dependence of A on V_w in the case of polar molecules. These coefficients are based on too few and rather scattered data to be considered more than preliminary figures. A third is the set of comparatively large coefficients for liquids composed of molecules with such tightly spaced permanent electric dipoles [as in CCl_4, $C(NO_2)_4$, perfluorocarbons, etc.] that nearest neighbors experience strong electrostatic

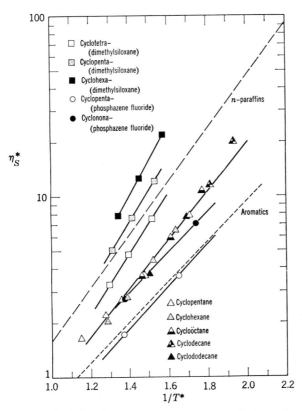

Figure 12.4 Generalized viscosity versus temperature curves for large ring compounds [9].

repulsion. Their coefficients differ from those of other liquids probably because the shape of their potential energy well must be quite different from that of molecules lacking long-range repulsive interaction. The significance of this factor is demonstrated by $CHCl_3$ (which can interact with its nearest neighbors in nonrepulsive configuration)—where B has the normal value 0.80, whereas for CCl_4, $B = 1.35$ (a "normal" value would be 1.04).

Viscosity data for large ring compounds, which range from the classification of "rigid" ($3c < 7$) to that of "flexible" ($3c > 8$), cannot be unified by any of the described dimensionless correlations, since in each series apparently $\eta \sim m^2$ (at constant T^*) as shown in Figure 12.4. No existing theory can account for this observation. Independent measurements such as nuclear magnetic relaxation times and inelastic neutron scattering combined with thermodynamic property data will have to be analyzed in order to provide a picture of the molecular motions in these liquids before a rational analysis of their flow properties can be attempted.

12.2.2 Effect of Pressure

The effect of pressure on viscosity is primarily through its effect on the (packing) density of the liquid. Just as the density and temperature are required to specify the viscosity, so pressure and temperature must be specified together to constitute a meaningful variable for viscosity. The appropriate unit of pressure for liquids is the sum of external pressure P and internal pressure $P_i [\equiv (\partial E/\partial V)_T]$. Hence a reduced pressure is defined as $P^* \equiv 5V_w(P + P_i)/E^\circ$. A "natural" variable for viscosity might then be $P^*/T^* = V_w(P + P_i)/cRT$. The plots of $\ln \eta_s^*$ versus P^* and versus P^*/T^* in Figure 12.5 indicate that this choice of variables permits a fairly good, albeit not very precise, description of viscosity–pressure–temperature relations. In the reduced-temperature range under consideration in this section we find comparatively small molecular structure sensitivity for the slope of these η_s^* versus P^*/T^* curves, which is indicative of the close

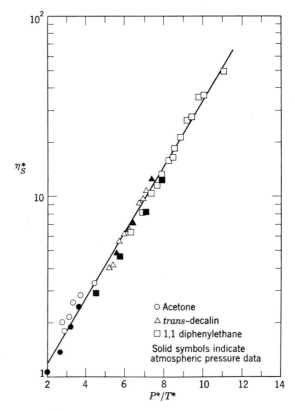

Figure 12.5 Generalized viscosity versus pressure and temperature curve for rigid molecules [6].

relationship between temperature and pressure coefficient of viscosity. Some of the variability in reduced viscosity level may be due to imperfect knowledge of P_i over wide temperature ranges. (For the sake of simplicity, the value of P_i at atmospheric pressure was used throughout.)

These generalized relations obscure somewhat the very large effects of comparatively small differences in molecular structure on the slope of viscosity versus temperature and pressure curves. Specifically, Kuss [26a] finds that at any given level of N_c, $(\partial \ln \eta_a/\partial p)_T$ of iso-alkanes varies exponentially with the very sensitive function $(\bar{R}_n^2/\bar{R}_i^2) - 1$ where $\bar{R}_n^2$, $\bar{R}_i^2$ are the radius of gyration of normal and branched iso-alkanes, respectively.

12.2.3 Flexible Molecules[1]

In the previous graphical representations it appeared that the reduced viscosity of flexible molecules could be represented by a single curve of $\ln \eta_F^* = B_F/T^* - A_F$. Closer examination showed however, that the coefficients here too increase slowly with molecule size. This rise tends toward an asymptotic limit as the chain length rises toward infinity. The data are reasonably well represented by the simplest equation appropriate for such an asymptote

$$B_F^{-1} = a_F + b_F N_s^{-1},$$

where N_s is the number of skeletal atoms in the backbone chain.

The constant A_F can be represented as a function of B_F so that

$$\log \eta_F^* = \frac{(a_F + b_F N_s^{-1})^{-1}}{T^*} + [g_F B_F^{1/2} - d_F]. \qquad (12.2)$$

Numerical values of constants a_F, b_F, g_F, d_F for different series of flexible molecules have been assembled in Table 12.2. The primary barrier to the external rotation of nonpolar flexible molecules in the liquid is the barrier to internal rotation of the chain segments relative to each other. Since the constant "c" [or rather $(c - 6)$] in the characteristic temperature $\theta_L = E°/5cR$ is generally considered as a measure of that chain flexibility, we might have expected B_F to be sensibly constant. The absolute magnitude of B_F and its rise with chain length to an asymptotic limit may be interpreted to mean (a) that B_F is a measure of the ratio of the effective length of a freely rotating chain segment in viscous flow as compared to its effective length in equilibrium properties, and (b) that this effective length reaches an asymptotic limit valid for the equivalent high polymer.

In an earlier discussion [5], [6] the effective freely rotating length L_s of n-paraffins in liquid-state equilibrium properties had been given as 4 to 5

---

[1] The treatment here is restricted to liquids composed of molecules that are *shorter than the entanglement length* [for which consult Porter, R. S., and J. F. Johnson, *Chem. Rev.* **66**, 1 (1966)]; here no reference is made to non-Newtonian behavior.

methylene groups. For the more complete rotation required in shear flow, this length L_c is $B_F L_s$. In infinitely long methylene chains this argument yields $L_c \approx 8$ to 10 methylene groups. This number is somewhat smaller than but of the same order of magnitude as the persistence length L_p defined by Kratky and Porod [31].

The trend of the constants of Table 12.2 with molecular structure is in basic agreement with this picture of their physical meaning. The presence of branches increases B_F beyond the value expected for the given molecule size

Table 12.2   Numerical Values of Constants a_F, b_F, d_F, g_F for Various Groups of Liquids Composed of Flexible Molecules [9]

Substances	a_F	b_F	g_F	d_F
n-Alkanes ($N_c > 8$)	0.565	2.56	3.26	1.70
Flexible iso-alkanes	0.440	2.56[a]	3.17	1.60
Flexible alkyl-aromatics	$\varphi_R B_R + (1 - \varphi_R)B_b$[b]		3.26	1.70
Aliphatic polyethers	$B_p + 0.1$[c]		3.26	1.70
m^n Polyphenylethers	0.450	0.985[d]	5.46	5.20

[a] Add a term $+1.10 \times 10^{-2} S_b$, where S_b = number of carbon atoms per straight chain per branch point; at $S_b \geq 12$ set this condition $= 0$.
[b] φ_R = (volume) fraction of carbon atoms in aromatic rings; B_b is to be calculated in the same manner as B_F for iso-alkanes with "branch point" = ring-alkyl branch point; set equivalent branch length of phenyl group as $N_c = 4$ and equivalent branch length of cyclohexyl group as $N_c = 6$.
[c] $B_p = B_F$ of n-alkanes; calculate for $N_c = N_s$.
[d] Multiplier for b_F is N_φ^{-1}, where N_φ = number of phenylene groups per molecule.

because the increased bulk raises the height of the barrier to external rotation. Likewise, the small constant increment in B_F demanded for the polyethers can be attributed to the increased magnitude of the barrier to external rotation caused by the dipole–dipole orientation interaction between the ether oxygens. The method of counting segments in polyphenyl ethers is so different from that used for polymethylene that a direct comparison is not possible.

One polyether cannot be entered at all: the poly(dimethylsiloxanes). Their oligomers up to the hexamer (the size limit for good equilibrium data) behave reasonably similarly to the corresponding alkanes, as shown by the data in Figure 12.6. However, somewhere between $x = 6$ and $x = 26$, the next set of available data, there is a significant change in properties, as is evident from the fact that B is not constant at $T^* > 0.55$ and the sign of dB/dT is positive in contrast to the behavior of all "normal" liquids for which at $T^* > 0.55$ we find $dB/dT \leq 0$. This peculiar behavior of the high-molecular-weight siloxane polymers may have to do with the often-postulated formation

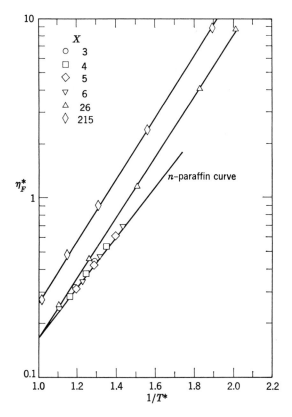

Figure 12.6   Generalized viscosity versus temperature curves of long-chain poly(dimethyl)-siloxanes [9].

of helices at low temperatures. These helices must, of course, disappear at elevated temperature.

Another item of interest is the group of "mixed" compounds in which flexible chains are attached to rigid aromatic or naphthenic ring systems. Here B_F appears to be intermediate between the value for the flexible chain and that for the rigid ring at the same reduced temperature. A linear mixing rule has been developed to estimate B_F from B (ring structures) and B_F (flexible chain). The latter, of course, must be calculated for the entire molecule, which called for the assignment of somewhat arbitrary "equivalent" segment length for the ring systems. As it is well known that there is no significant difference between the viscosity of such a "chemical mixture" and that of the equivalent "physical mixture" [4], [36], the mixture rule found for the components of a single molecule shall also be used to estimate the viscosity of mixtures involving ring structures and flexible chains.

12.2.4 Effect of Pressure on the Viscosity of Flexible Molecules

Here, as before, the effect of pressure is best discussed simultaneously with that of temperature. Inspection of the experimental viscosity versus pressure isotherms of different flexible compounds shows that $\ln \eta \propto p^{1/n}$. Accordingly, a trial plot of $\ln \eta_F^*$ versus $(P^*)^{1/2}/T^*$ has been made and is shown in Figure 12.7 [6]. The representation on this graph is quite good except at low reduced temperature. The physical meaning of the proportionality to a low power of the pressure is obscure.

12.2.5 Viscosity of Mixtures, High-Temperature Range

The viscosity of mixtures is commonly described by the Arrhenius mixture rule

$$\ln \eta = \sum_i x_i \ln \eta_i, \tag{12.3}$$

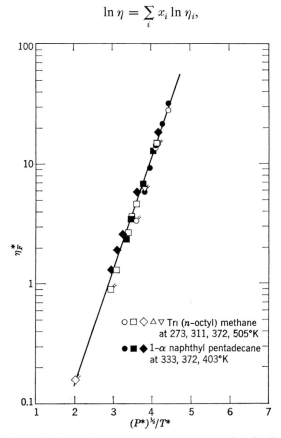

Figure 12.7 Generalized viscosity–pressure–temperature relation for liquid composed of flexible hydrocarbon molecules [6]. The flagged symbols represent experiments at atmospheric pressure.

which can be justified theoretically by assuming linear additivity of the molecular interaction energies. In that case (12.3) represents the ideal solution case, and must be generalized to

$$\ln \eta = \sum_i x_i \ln \eta_i - \frac{wF^E}{RT}, \tag{12.4}$$

in order to be more broadly applicable, where F^E is the excess free energy mixing. This form of viscosity equation had first been proposed by Powell et al. [32], who found that $w = 0.4$.

More recent data by Fort [16], when combined with modern thermodynamic data yield $w = 0.9$. Relations between F^E and molecular structure of the mixture components are beginning to be available from general correlations. If $F^E > 0$, miscibility requirements set the upper limit of F^E at $\frac{1}{2}RT$. If $F^E < 0$, rather stable molecular complexes can be said to make up the entire mixture when $F^E < -2RT$, and the viscosity is more readily expressed in terms of the molecular structure of the complex.

When the component viscosity data are unknown, we should in principle approximate the mixture viscosity as a function of the averaged values $\bar{E}^\circ$, $\bar{c}$, $\bar{m}$, $\bar{A}_w$, $\bar{A}$, and $\bar{B}$ for the mixture as an entity. This procedure has the advantage that it is quite unimportant whether the components are solid, liquid, or gaseous in the pure state. On the other hand, only very limited precision can be expected from the predictions because of the exponential dependence of viscosity on (even small) errors in the mixed correlated parameters.

12.2.6 Mixtures of Liquids Composed of Rigid Molecules

The appropriate parameter mixing rules for this case are found in Table 15.4.2. Here it should just be recalled that the analogy with equation (4) requires

$$\frac{\bar{E}^\circ}{A_w} = x_1^2 \left(\frac{E_1^\circ}{A_w^{(1)}} \right) + x_2^2 \left(\frac{E_2^\circ}{A_w^{(2)}} \right) + 2x_1 x_2 \left(\frac{E_1^\circ}{\Delta_w^{(1)}} \frac{E_2^\circ}{A_w^{(2)}} \right)^{\frac{1}{2}} - \frac{5c\bar{B}_w F^F}{\bar{A}_w} \tag{12.5}$$

All other parameter mixture rules stay unchanged.

12.2.7 Mixtures of Liquids Composed of Flexible Molecules

Here all concentrations are expressed as volume fractions φ_i instead of mole fractions x_i, including an average chain length per molecule

$$\bar{N}_s = \sum_i \varphi_i N_s(i) \tag{12.6}$$

where $N_s(i)$ is the number of skeletal atoms per molecule of species (i). Other factors, such as branch concentration, etc., should be averaged correspondingly.

An important test of the correctness of the adopted mixing rules is their ability to predict the equivalence of physical and chemical mixing at (nearly) equal molecular weight of all components. It would be interesting too if the mixing rules could account for the observed discrepancies between physical and chemical mixing if the molecular weights of the physical mixture components differ substantially, for example, $M_2/M_1 \geq 2$. Actually the magnitude of the reported discrepancies ($\sim$10 to 15%) is, on the whole, within the range of the accuracy of this (or any existing) viscosity correlation.

12.3 LOW-TEMPERATURE–HIGH-PACKING DENSITY REGIME[1]

Shortly after World War I Vogel [39] suggested that the change of the viscosity of liquids, especially of lubricating oils with temperature could be represented by an equation which in present-day notation would be written

$$\log \eta = a + \frac{b}{T - T_0}. \tag{12.7}$$

Many other equally empirical expressions have been used by petroleum technologists since then [4], and Vogel's equation remained unused until its recent rediscovery by Gutmann and Simmons [23].

As an empirical equation with three disposable parameters, Vogel's equation would still be of little interest were it not that two of these parameters have begun to acquire physical meaning. The use of this equation (in a modified form) by Williams, Landel, and Ferry [WLF] [14] to represent the viscosity (and relaxation times) of polymer melts at $T > T_g$ (the glass transition temperature) showed that T_0 is closely related to T_g. Their work also showed that $b \sim \alpha^{-1}$, where α is the cubic expansion coefficient of the liquid. A theoretical justification of such an equation has been derived by Cohen and Turnbull [12] from free-volume theory.

In the reduced coordinates employed in the first section of this chapter the Vogel equation takes on the form

$$\log \eta^* = \frac{\mathcal{B}}{T^* - T_0^*} - \mathcal{A}' \tag{12.8}$$

Moreover, in the reduced coordinates $\log \eta^*$ versus $1/T^*$ appreciable curvature generally commences at $T_1^* \leq 0.7$. Hence at T_1^* the Arrhenius must equal

---

[1] A detailed account of the relations between viscosity and molecular structure in this regime has recently been presented by the writer [9] and is therefore not repeated here. The practical aspects alone, especially the computational ones, are discussed in the present chapter.

the Vogel equation, so that

$$\log \eta^* = B[1 - 1.43T^*]^2 \left\{ \frac{1}{T^* - T_0^*} + \left[\frac{1}{0.70 - T_0^*} - \frac{1.43}{(1 - 1.43T_0^*)^2} \right] \right\} - A$$

$$(12.9)$$

so that the dominant new feature is T_0^*. There is an intuitive relation between T_0 and the glass transition temperature T_g [12] [37]. Neither empirical

Table 12.3 Glass Transition Temperature T_g, Characteristic Temperatures T_0, T_h of the Low-Temperature Viscosity Curves of Simple Liquids (All Made Dimensionless with θ_L) [9]

Substance	T_g^{*a}	$T_0^*(1)$	$T_0^*(2)^b$	T_h^{*b}	θ_L, °K
Aromatic					
Toluene	0.218[c]	0.224[b]			460
	0.246[d]				
Ethyl benzene	0.227	0.206[b]			488
n-Propyl benzene	0.241[e]	0.236[b]	0.218	0.36	
i-Propyl benzene	0.242[e]	0.236[b]	0.184	0.35	508
n-Butyl benzene=	0.243[e]	0.222[b]	0.197	0.36	514
sec-Butyl benzene	0.255[e]	0.252[b]	0.193	0.38	511
1,3,5-Trinaphthyl benzene	0.366[f]	0.36[f]	0.217[f]	0.41[f]	450
Dimethylphthalate	0.279	0.286[b]	0.273	0.40	691
Diethylphthalate	0.266[g]				707
Diisobutylphthalate	0.29	0.310[b]	0.232	0.45?	622?
Di-n-butylphthalate	0.278	0.236[b]			635
Di(2-ethyl hexyl)phthalate	0.294[g]	0.234[b]			643

[a] Except where noted otherwise T_g has been obtained by differential thermal analysis.
[b] Reference [3].
[c] Carpenter, M. R. et al., *J. Chem. Phys.*, **46**, 2451 (1967).
[d] Reference [37].
[e] J. Lamb, private communication.
[f] Plazek, D. J., and J. H. Magill, Presented at Meeting of the Society of Rheology, October 1964; T_g by dilatometry.
[g] Garfield, L. J., and S. E. Petrie, *J. Phys. Chem.* **68**, 1750 (1964).

observation nor theoretical consideration, however, has established a reliable coupling between T_0 and T_g, especially for low molecular weight substances. Only liquids with $N_c > 15$, composed of aliphatic molecules or of cyclic molecules with aliphatic side chains of unbranched chain lengths > 4 carbon atoms per chain, exhibit $T_0 \approx 0.8 \pm 0.05\, T_g$ [37].

In the generalized form $T_0^* = 5cRT_0/E^\circ$ we find no universal numerical value for T_0^* (nor for T_g^*, as is discussed more fully in Section 13.1), but obviously (Table 12.3) the range covered is much smaller than for the absolute value T_0. Because neither 12.7 nor any of its derived functions is an exact representation of the data, the numerical value of T_0 (and of the other constants a, b) depends somewhat on the viscosity range covered. Empirically we observe little change of T_0 (and of a, b) if the lowest viscosity in the range is $\geq 5\text{cP}$, a limit that happens to approximate the limit for unequivocal "Arrhenius" behavior. An upper viscosity limit, characteristic of predominantly cyclic systems, will be discussed later on. T_0 data in the published literature, obtained without that precaution, are not truly comparable and may, therefore, not exhibit any systematic pattern.

An approximate relation of T_0^* to molecular structure is apparent from the curves of Figure 12.8. Our ordering parameter for the different levels of T_0^* at low values of N_c of the homologous series is obviously the degree of hindered external rotation of the end group. The ordering parameter at $N_c \to \infty$ is suggested by the difference between the polymethylene chain and

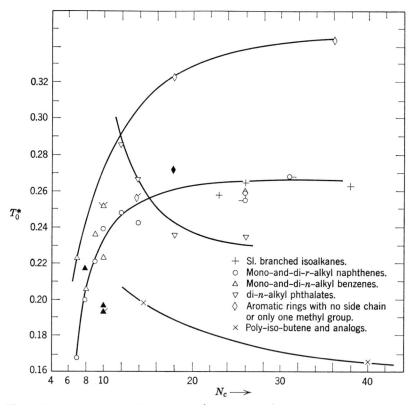

Figure 12.8   Reduced Vogel constant T_0^* ($= 5cRT_0/E^0$) as function of the number of carbon atoms per molecule (N_c). Filled symbols denote constant of "low-temperature equation."

the polyisobutene chain, namely the energy of rotational isomerization ΔE_{iso}, quite similar to what had been observed with T_g^* of high polymers [8, 20].

The disturbing observation has been made by Lamb and co-workers [3] that (12.7) represents the very-low-temperature viscosity data of certain liquids only down to a certain temperature, marked T_h in Table 12.3. Below that temperature the slope steepens and the equation is again applicable, but with a new set of constants. Neither set of constants meets the demands of its free-volume interpretation, that $\alpha B = $ const, where α is the thermal expansion coefficient; nor is there as yet a discernible trend of T_0.

Only two generalizable features emerge from the available data. When expressed as a reduced temperature, T_h^* covers the narrow range 0.3 to 0.4, and is nearly constant at 0.38 ± 0.03 with aromatic substances. Its incidence is restricted to liquids composed of rigid molecules (with $3c < 8$). This is particularly noticeable with the pair di-isobutyl versus di-normal butyl phthalate. These two generalizations also answer the question of why this break has not been observed more often since (as WLF equation) equation 12.7 has not been reported before to fail in the range $T_g < T < (T_g + 100°C)$. For most of the polymers to which the WLF equation has been applied, $T_g^* \approx 0.35 \pm 0.05$; hence the break, had one occurred, would not have been observable. Moreover, their vinyl backbone chain is sufficiently flexible that most polymers would have fallen into the class of the compounds for which (12.7) holds down to T_g.

We may summarize the situation by saying that the incidence of failure of (12.7) with an entire class of liquids has re-emphasized the inadequacy of the free-volume theory of viscosity. However, from a practical point of view, the situation is not as serious because few oils are actually used at $T < T_h$, and those that are used are composed of sufficiently flexible molecules that (12.7) holds down to the glass transition region.

The failure of the simple free-volume-theory equation (12.7) has invited re-examination of the viscosity relation derived by Bueche from a normal coordinate analysis of intermolecular motions [11] and by Arakawa from thermal fluctuation theory [2]

$$\ln \eta = A + B'(v_0/\bar{v}_f)^2 \approx A + \frac{B}{(T - T_j)^2}, \qquad (12.11)$$

where $v_0 = $ "occupied volume", $\bar{v}_f = $ average "free volume," and T_j (like T_0) is a temperature below T_g at which $\eta \to \infty$. This equation seems to represent the low-temperature viscosity data of many, but not all, liquids composed of rigid small molecules more successfully than does (12.7).

Regression analysis of the data of Barlow et al. [3], in terms of equations 12.7 with "high" and "low" temperature constants and with respect to equation 12.11 has shown, however, that for the liquids with the break at T_h only the low-temperature constants of 12.7 yield random values of $\Delta\eta = \eta_{\text{obs}} - \eta_{\text{calc}}$. Qualitatively, equation 12.11 and the high-temperature constants of 12.7 yielded the same systematic trend of $\Delta\eta$ versus T for those liquids composed of comparatively rigid molecules.

A viscosity equation of the form

$$\ln \eta = A' + \frac{B'}{T \ln (T/T_2)} \tag{12.12}$$

has been derived by Adam and Gibbs [1] with the assumption that the configurational entropy S_c approaches at a temperature T_2. No significant gain in precision of data representation is obtained through the use of (12.12), nor is T_2 any more uniformly related to T_g than is T_0. An analysis of the available older data by Greet [22] suggests that for a large number of substances we may get $T_g - T_0 = T_g - T_2 = 55°C$ in contrast to the often assumed relation $T_0 \approx 0.8\,T_g$ [37]. However, the more recent data for low- and medium-molecular-weight substances assembled in Table 12.6 do not encourage any generalization.

The most familiar example of liquids of high packing density composed of flexible molecules is the polymer melt. Because of their non-Newtonian flow character, polymer melts might have been excluded from this book. This strongly non-Newtonian character, however, starts only at the molecule size known as the entanglement length Z_c, so that polymer melts of chain length $Z < Z_c$ clearly belong in this chapter. The entire field of zero shear polymer melt viscosity has recently been reviewed thoroughly by Berry and Fox [3a], and what follows is the result of their evaluation.

The zero shear viscosity of a liquid composed of unentangled chain molecules is, according to theory,

$$\eta = \left(\frac{N_A}{6}\right)\left(\frac{\langle s^2 \rangle_0}{V_a}\right)\zeta, \tag{12.13}$$

where $\langle s^2 \rangle_0$ is the mean square radius of gyration of the molecule, which can be determined directly or from various physical property measurements, V_a is the specific volume per chain atom, and ζ is a (molecular) friction factor. The friction factor is related to temperature by a Vogel equation

$$\zeta = \zeta_0 \exp\left[\frac{B_P}{f_g + \alpha_{\text{L}}(T - T_g)}\right], \tag{12.14}$$

where ζ_0^{-1} is an inherent jump frequency factor that may be slightly temperature-dependent, f_g is the fractional "free volume" at T_g, and B_P is a measure of the void volume required for a segment jump. The factors f_g and B_P become independent of molecular weight at $Z > 80$.

For the general case Fox developed the empirical relation

$$\eta = \frac{N_A}{6} X_c \left(\frac{X}{X_c}\right)^a \zeta_{00} \exp\left(\frac{W}{RT}\right) \exp\left\{\frac{B}{f_g + \alpha_L(T - T_g)}\right\}, \tag{12.15}$$

where

$$X = g\left(\frac{\langle s^2\rangle_0}{M}\right)Z, \quad X_c = X \quad \text{for} \quad Z = Z_c, \quad g = \frac{\langle s_{br}^2\rangle_0}{\langle s_l^2\rangle_0}\bigg|_{M=\text{const.}}$$

and where subscripts br and l refer to branched and linear, respectively, for $X < X_c$, $a = 1$, and $X > X_c$, $a = 3.4$. Typical values for the various parameters can be found in the cited review. For rough estimates, when no information is available, the authors suggest $\log X_c = -14.4$, $\log \zeta_{00} = -10.6$, $(\langle s_l^2\rangle/M)_0 = (20 \times 10^{-18}/m_a)$ for vinyl polymers, m_a = average molal weight per chain atom, $W/RT \approx -1$ for vinyl polymers, slightly more for stiffer chains, less for more flexible chains, $f_g/B \approx 0.025$, $10^{-4}B/\alpha_L$ is between 1.5 and 3, and B is between 1 and 2, increasing with size of side group.

12.3.1 Effect of Pressure

The effect of pressure on viscosity according to free volume theory is clearly associated with the compression of available volume [9], [12], so that

$$\ln \eta = \frac{B''}{\alpha_L(T - T_0) - \Delta V(P)/V_T} - a'', \tag{12.16}$$

where the fractional change in volume caused by pressure P, $\Delta V(P)/V_T$ can be expressed as in Section 8.3.3. A deficiency of this form, however, is the occasional incidence of $\Delta V(P)/V_T > \alpha(T - T_0)$ at pressures far below those at which $\eta \to \infty$. Because, in general, ρ^* at $T_0 \approx 0.68$, whereas for most closely packed solids $\rho_0^* \approx 0.73$, it appears reasonable to provide for $\eta \to \infty$ at higher compression so that an 'effective' $V_f \approx \bar\alpha_L(T - T_0) + 0.05 - [(P/K_0^L + 1)^{1/K_1^L} - 1]$ and

$$\ln \eta = \frac{B''}{\alpha_L(T - T_0) - \left(\frac{P}{K_0^L} + 1\right)^{1/K_1^L} + 1.05} - a''. \tag{12.17}$$

The lack of coincidence of the curves for any given liquid in Figure 12.9 shows that free-volume theory, as expressed in (12.17) does not describe the effect of pressure on viscosity satisfactorily. An apparently successful attempt has been made by Matheson [28a] to salvage the attractively transparent free-volume theory for this case by postulating—in the spirit of Section 8.7.1— that the occupied volume is a dense cluster of molecules with the thermal expansion and the compressibility of the corresponding crystalline solid.

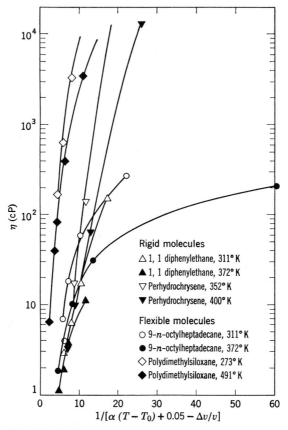

Figure 12.9 Viscosity isotherms versus free-volume parameter for various liquids [9].

Then we obtain

$$\ln \eta = \frac{B'''}{\Delta a(T - T_0) + \left(\frac{P}{K_0^{\,s}} + 1\right)^{1/K_1^{\,s}} - \left(\frac{P}{K_0^{\,L}} + 1\right)^{1/K_1^{\,L}}} - A''', \quad (12.18)$$

where $\Delta a = a_L - a_s$ from the density relation $\rho(T) = \rho_0[1 - a(T - T_0)]$ and the superscripts L and s on the bulk moduli K_0 and their pressure coefficients K_1 refer to liquid and solid, respectively. The latter can be estimated with the help of the correlations in Section 4.3 and 4.4.

In this connection it is noteworthy that in the few instances in which sufficient data are available the extrapolated liquid density at T_0 equals that of the crystalline solid at its melting point. This also means that the low-molecular-weight substances, composed of easily rotatable molecules, for which T_g is within a few degrees of T_0, acquire glassy behavior only at crystal density. Liquids composed of larger or bulkier molecules, by contrast, vitrify at significantly lower than crystal density, and $T_g > T_0$ by 40°C or more.

Relation 12.18 is a significant advance only if a_s and $K_0{}^s$, $K_1{}^s$ are the properties of the solid, with ρ^* corresponding to T_0. Otherwise we have three additional disposable parameters, and an essentially useless equation. The many available data should provide ample opportunity to verify (12.18) experimentally. Assuming that it is valid, the effect of molecular structure on the pressure coefficient of viscosity is easily discerned. Because $K_1{}^L$ and $K_1{}^s$ are of the order of 11 and 8, respectively, the effect of molecular structure on $K_0{}^L$ and $K_0{}^s$ is reduced to insignificance. Hence the magnitude of the pressure dependence of viscosity parallels that of the temperature dependence, an effect that has been known qualitatively for many years as had the other consequence of (12.17) and (12.18) that the curve of $\ln \eta$ versus ρ becomes less steep with increasing temperature.

In reduced coordinates α^*, as well as Δa^*, is an essentially universal constant in the low-temperature regime of interest here, so that temperature- and pressure-dependence are primarily determined by the magnitude of T_0^*, the molecular structure relations of which are illustrated in Figure 12.8. A still unanswered question is which T_0 should be used in (12.17) or (12.18) when we are dealing with liquids composed of rigid molecules, their 'high' or their 'low' temperature value of T_0. Because the packing density at high pressures passes through that at which the low temperature breaks in the Vogel equation parameters occurred, we may have to look for a similar break in the parameters of the pressure equations.

12.4   A MORE COMPLETE FORMULATION FOR VISCOSITY AT HIGH PACKING DENSITIES

The magnitude of the isochoric temperature coefficient of viscosity $\Delta E_{\pm}{}^j$, the potential-energy barrier to motion in the liquid described earlier, suggests an important reason for the failure of the free-volume treatment of viscosity to represent the data at elevated pressures. This failure had been noted by Fox et al. [18], who supplemented the WLF free-volume equation with a term E/RT, where E was defined as the energy required to jump into the hole created by free-volume fluctuations. In a recent paper Fox and Allen [17] give numerical values for E obtained from polymer-melt viscosity data. All of the E values parallel, but are not identical with, the known barriers to internal rotation for the segments under consideration. Macedo and Litovitz [28] suggest the form

$$\ln \eta = A + \frac{H^*}{RT} + \frac{1}{f}, \qquad (12.19)$$

where f is the fractional free volume discussed earlier and $H^* \approx \Delta H_{vap}/5.3$.

Both of these treatments relegate the strong density and temperature dependence of the energy term into the free-volume term. This procedure provides convenient algebra but is probably responsible for the confusion regarding the meaning of the numerical values of f as well as of T_0 in equations expressing f as $\sim \alpha(T - T_0)$. Hence it is proposed to write

$$\ln \eta^* = A - \frac{B_v(\rho^*, T^*)}{T^*} - \frac{L}{\alpha^*(T^* - T_0^*)}, \qquad (12.20)$$

where $B_f = \Delta E_{\pm}{}^j/4.57\theta_L$ and L is a constant not differing much from unity. In the absence of a form for the function $B_v(\rho^*, T^*)$ this equation is just a research program. It should be noted, however, that in the few cases for which data were available the equation yielded values for T_0^* that were quite close to the measured T_g^*. Because T_g^* covers so narrow a range of values, especially for simple compounds, that it can be guessed from molecular structure [9], and the low-temperature limit of α^* is essentially a universal constant, the free-volume term is easily related to molecular structure. There is reason to hope that a way will be found to relate the welter of available $\Delta E_{\pm}{}^j$ data [9] with molecular properties. Then (12.20) can be considered as one further step toward better understanding of the effect of molecular structure on the viscosity of liquids in the high-packing-density regime.

12.5 EFFECTS OF ASSOCIATION (HYDROGEN BONDING) [9]

A corresponding-states treatment of the properties of associating compounds is excluded almost by definition because of the superposition of the highly specific dissociation equilibrium on whatever individual properties the monomers and association polymers have. Techniques to determine association equilibria in pure liquids have been developed very recently and not enough data have been assembled to permit a rational treatment of as complicated a property as viscosity if even the p-v-T properties of alcohols cannot yet be calculated. The relations of viscosity to the molecular structure of hydrogen-bonding substances given in this section are therefore rather crude.

12.5.1 Stable Dimers

The simplest kind of association to handle is that of comparatively stable dimers as those formed by certain carboxylic acids. In the temperature range where association persists to better than 90%, such dimers can be treated as but slightly polar compounds with the molecular structure of the dimer.

Table 12.4   Evidence for the Existence of Fatty Acids
as Double Molecules by Comparison of Viscosity Data
with Those of Hydrocarbons and Esters [9]

	M^a	$\eta(P)$
Propionic acid	(148)	0.011
Propionic anhydride	130	0.011
n-Decane	142	0.0091
Valeric acid	(204)	0.022
n-Tetradecane	198	0.022
n-Heptylic acid	(260)	0.043
n-Octadecane	254	0.045
Oleic acid	(564)	0.318
Oleyl oleate	532	0.330

[a] Data in parentheses are calculated for the double molecule.

The cohering functional group

$$
\begin{array}{c}
\text{O}\cdots\text{H—O} \\
R\text{—C}\diagup\qquad\diagdown\text{C—R} \\
\text{O—H}\cdots\text{O}
\end{array}
$$

can be considered as a planar six-membered ring—like a benzene ring—and all properties calculated accordingly [5]. The viscosity properties of the fatty acids then fall reasonably well into the expected patterns as indicated in Table 12.4.

Broad application of this reasoning must always be preceded by experimental determination of its premise, namely, that stable dimers are indeed formed in the liquid state. Abietic acid is a typical case for the absence of stable dimerization because of steric hindrance. Other acids with very bulky radicals must be treated with corresponding suspicion before an estimate of their viscosity is made. One of the best established methods for determining association equilibria of this type is the sound absorption in liquids [24].

12.5.2 Chain Association

One of the major difficulties with substances in this class is the absence of reliable data on the degree of association prevailing in the pure liquid (in contrast to the rather good data on their association equilibria in dilute solutions). In addition there is no good method of eliminating the nonspecific intermolecular force effects, as the corresponding-states principle permits us to do in the case of the nonassociating substances.

A direct investigation of molecular motions by NMR and dipole-relaxation spectroscopy may serve as a guide to the problem. In the case of

n-octyl alcohol Powles and co-workers [33] found that the rotational motion of the hydrocarbon tail (at 25°C) is about 30 times faster than that of the hydroxyl group.

As a first approximation it appears reasonable, however, to compare the viscosity of associating substances with those of their hydrocarbon homo-morphs[1] at the same packing density $\rho^* \equiv V_w/V$, which means in essence at the same "free volume."[2] This difference $\eta(\text{ass.}) - \eta(\text{hom.})\big|_{\rho^*} \equiv \Delta\eta^h$ may well be considered as a measure of the extra drag due to hydrogen-bond formation over and beyond that caused by the general force field of the neighboring molecules.[3] The curves in Figure 12.10 show the rather interesting result of such a comparison. A downward drift of $\Delta\eta^h$ of the normal primary alcohols with increasing molecular weight renders its asymptotic limit at about C_8, as is evident from the location of $\Delta\eta^h$ for cetyl alcohol. The location of the ethylene glycol data on this graph is rather unexpected, pointing perhaps to water contamination of the glycol sample used in the measurement. If the data are genuine two other possibilities are intramolecular hydrogen bonding,

which should be very weak, and still leave one hydroxyl group for chain formation, or ring formation:

The comparison of the latter case would then be with cyclooctane, which at the same packing density as the glycol, exhibits somewhat higher viscosity, as we might expect because the cyclo-octane ring is more rigid than the association ring. The primary amine data are based on V_w, corrected for the

[1] A hydrocarbon homomorph is a hydrocarbon of the same molecular geometry as the polar compound; for example, toluene is the homomorph of phenol.
[2] Here V_w is corrected for the contraction due to hydrogen-bond formation as discussed in Chapter 8.
[3] This treatment is somewhat similar to that of Thomas, L. H., *J. Chem. Soc.* (*London*) 4906 (1960), who obtains the viscosity increment at constant P_v.

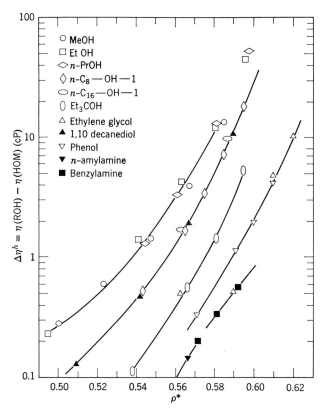

Figure 12.10 Hydrogen-bond contribution to viscosity, $\Delta\eta^h$, versus packing density of hydrogen-bonding substance [9].

formation of two hydrogen bonds. Assumption of only a single bond leads to unreasonably high packing densities and thus to homomorph viscosities higher than those of the amine. As it is, the $\Delta\eta^h$ for amines is almost negligible in magnitude. Although most $\Delta\eta^h$ curves fall in the well-known order of hydrogen-bond strengths, we should not lose sight of the fact that the association equilibrium responsible for $\Delta\eta^h$ depends on the absolute-temperature level [30]. Hence before truly quantitative comparisons can be made, a way will have to be found to compensate for temperature effects. Another way to examine the data is through the ratio $\eta^*(\text{ass.})/\eta^*(\text{hom.})$ at constant ρ^*. According to the definition of the reduced viscosity, this ratio might be taken as $X_a^{1/2}$, where X_a is the number of (alcohol) molecules in an association complex. Such a plot is shown in Figure 12.10. Beyond accentuating the absence of a specific hydrogen-bonding effect with the glycol data, this graph does not teach anything new in comparison with Figure 12.11.

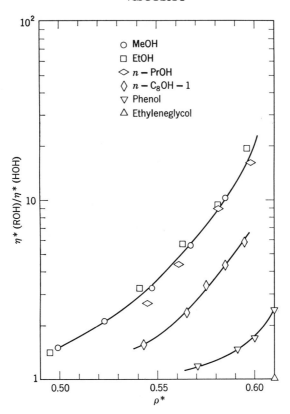

Figure 12.11   Ratio of reduced viscosity of associated compound to that of its hydrocarbon homomorph at fixed packing density ρ^* [9].

The thought of connecting this information with the best established hydrogen-bond characteristic, the excess energy of vaporization [5], is discouraged somewhat by the very small association effect indicated by the viscosity graphs at $\rho^* = 0.50$, which is at or near the atmospheric boiling point. The entropy of vaporization suggests still significant association (or very strongly hindered rotation) at that point.

The specific effects of association on viscosity, other than those due to high packing density (which have been described in this section), are most notable for their comparative constancy within a given group of compounds. This should enable us to make reasonably good estimates of viscosity if we know that of the corresponding homomorph at the appropriate packing density. The choice of the homomorph is quite important here. Whereas for organic compounds the hydrocarbon series generally provide good homomorph data, the homomorphs of inorganic halides should preferably be taken from the corresponding perhalide, known to act "normally."

12.6 VISCOSITY OF MIXTURES, LOW-TEMPERATURE RANGE ($T^* < 0.6$)

When the viscosity of the mixture components is known a rough estimate of the viscosity of the mixture can be obtained by means of (12.3) and (12.4) in Section 12.2.5. If one or more of the components is composed of flexible molecules, or if $V_w(2)/V_w(1) \geq 3$, the mole fractions x_i in these equations should be replaced by volume fractions.

The rather sparse experimental information (only few chemists like to contaminate expensive pure compounds by mixing) shows that the quoted mixture rules are reasonably reliable even at very high-viscosity levels. However, when at least one of the components is a highly branched, for example, 3,3,5-trimethyl . . . , alkane derivative, the mixture viscosity is much higher than estimated from 12.3 and 12.4. In the same instances the observed value of $T_0(12)$ is also larger than expected from any linear combination of the components' $T_0(i)$.

Sophisticated mixture rules for T_0 need be looked for only when dealing with mixtures differing rather widely, say by more than 50°C, in T_0. The mixture rules for T_g, discussed in Section 13.1.1 may well be applicable to T_0. Needless to say that the mixture rules for the reducing parameter θ_L and to components are those of Table 15.2 and of (12.5).

12.6.1 Concentrated Polymer Solutions

A special case of mixtures of flexible molecules at low temperatures is the solution of high polymers. Such a solution is concentrated when the polymer volume fraction

$$\varphi_2 > \tfrac{1}{8}(10^{-4}M)^{-1/2},$$

which means that for $M = 10^5$ any concentration in excess of 4% (v) is concentrated. The effects of a diluent on the individual parameters of the Fox viscosity equation (12.15) have been suggested by Fox to be

$$X = \frac{\langle s^2 \rangle_0 \varphi_2}{v_a} = g\left(\frac{\langle s^2 \rangle_0}{M}\right) \frac{Z\varphi_2}{v_2},$$

which leaves X_c independent of φ_2. The effect of φ_2 on T_g is found in Chapter 13, whereas B and f_g vary only slightly with φ_2 at $\varphi_2 > 0.2$. At $\varphi_2 < 0.1$ only the parameter X remains reliable, but the friction factor of the polymer has become too dilute and should probably be replaced by that of the diluent derived from equations (12.4) and following.

12.6.2 Mixtures of Associating Substances

There are three kinds of mixtures involving associating substances:

1. solutions of associating substances in nonassociating liquids;

2. mixtures of associating substances with each other, and

3. mixtures, the components of which combine into liquid (association) complexes.

The viscosity of none of these mixtures can be treated quantitatively at present. Combination of the very extensive association equilibrium measurements in type 1 solutions with viscosity measurements might yield a basis for predictive calculations, but the problem is not very interesting since only monotonical changes of viscosity with concentration and temperature have been observed (and can be expected).

The best-known example of type 2 is aqueous alcoholic solution. The peculiar maximum in its $\eta-x$ relation is in qualitative agreement with thermodynamic data, but no convincing quantitative analysis of the viscosity data

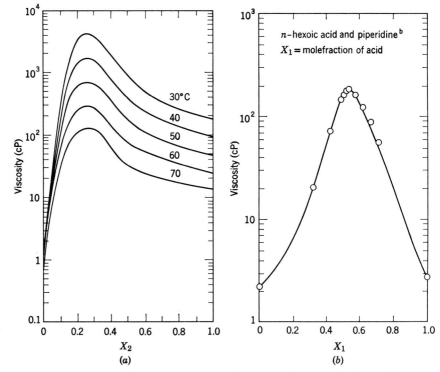

Figure 12.12 Viscosity of mixtures with formation of stable compounds [9]. (a) Acetic acid + 2,4,6 tri(dimethyl-aminomethyl)phenol, X_2 = mole fraction of base. Here the viscosity at the maximum (corresponding to the triacetate) is nearly equal to that of the hydrocarbon homomorph at the same packing density. (b) Estimated viscosity of the hydrocarbon homomorph of piperidine hexoate at the same packing density. The large excess in viscosity is probably due to formation of association polymer.

has been published. Nearly all available data for such systems are well represented by (12.4).

The most interesting systems are those of type 3, where the mixture components enter into more-or-less strong chemical (association) compound formation. In this case F^E is unrelated to viscosity and no attempt need be made to insert it into the mixture equation. The examples of Figure 12.12 show the not-infrequent dramatic maxima in η–x curves of such systems. Although exact quantitative prediction of the maximum viscosity is quite impossible, we can guess the order of magnitude of the expected maximum viscosity from a consideration of the viscosity of known pure liquids the molecules of which have the approximate molecular structure of the association complex. In the absence of model compounds, we can construct the appropriate η^* versus T^* relations described earlier for a compound of the structure of the association complex. The viscosity increase is naturally very large when the association complex is polymeric. Here is an area worthy of further investigation.

12.7 SUSPENSIONS

The viscosity of suspensions can be calculated rigorously only for the case of no particle–particle interaction, namely, $\eta = \eta_0(1 + 2.50\varphi + 14.1\varphi^2)$ for spherical particles, where η_0 is the viscosity of the solvent and φ is the volume fraction of suspensoid. The first-order term is Einstein's exact solution for $\varphi \to 0$, and the second-order term is due to Guth and Eirich [19]. Similar exact equations have been developed for suspensions of anisometric particles [19]. However, none of these relations is useful for most practical applications involving higher concentrations and particle–particle interaction.

A recent development by Landel and co-workers [27] appears to deal rather successfully with concentrated suspensions involving particle interaction. They propose the relation

$$\frac{\eta}{\eta_0} = \left(1 - \frac{\varphi}{\varphi_m}\right)^{-2.5}$$

where φ_m is the maximum possible volumetric loading, that is, the sedimentation volume of the suspensoid in the solvent determined in a sedimentation experiment. This rather simple relation is valid for $10^{-2} < \varphi < 0.95$ and for particle sizes ranging from 0.1 to 200 μ, and over a wide range of materials, shapes and surface conditions.

The sedimentation volume φ_m depends on the particle diameter d and on a parameter β describing the particle–particle interaction energy. The Landel theory describes those interrelationships quantitatively by the surprisingly simple equation

$$\varphi_m = 0.37\left\{1 + \left[1 + 0.424 \exp\left(\frac{\beta}{d}\right)\right]^{-1}\right\}.$$

In the limits this equation predicts $\varphi_m = 0.37$ for small particles and $\varphi_m = 0.63$ for large particles, assuming that β is of an order of magnitude that makes its effect negligible with large particles. The result $\varphi_m = 0.63$, which has been verified experimentally with suspensions of particles covered with a suitable surfactant, corresponds to the random close packing of noninteracting spheres observed by Bernal and Scott [8.3].

The interaction parameter of the particle surfaces appears to be characterizable empirically by means of Krypton adsorption in terms of the BET-theory constant C, namely,

$$\beta \approx \left(\frac{C}{19}\right)^{2.7}.$$

The Landel theory says, of course, nothing about the non-Newtonian flow behavior of the highly interacting or concentrated suspensions, and is valid only for the zero shear viscosity.

NOMENCLATURE

a	empirical constant
a_F	empirical constant
A	dimensionless intercept of η^* versus T^* relation
A_F	dimensionless intercept of η_F^* versus T^* relation
A_w	surface area per mole of molecules
b	empirical constant
b_F	empirical constant
B	dimensionless slope constant of η^* versus T^* relation
B_F	dimensionless slope constant of η_F^* versus T^* relation
B_V	dimensionless slope constant of η^* versus T^* at constant volume
c	$\frac{1}{3}$ of number of external degrees of freedom per molecule
C_V	heat capacity at constant volume
d	empirical constant
d_F	empirical constant
d_w	molecule "thickness"
$\overline{d}_w$	average molecule thickness
E°	standard energy of vaporization $= \Delta H_v - RT$ at temperature at which $\rho^* = 0.588$
ΔE_{iso}	energy of rotational isomerization
$\Delta E_{\ddagger}$	$= R(\partial \ln \eta / \partial T^{-1})_p$

$\Delta E_{\ddagger}^{j}$	$= R(\partial \ln \eta / \partial T^{-1})_v$
f	fractional free volume
F^E	excess free energy of mixing
g	empirical constant
g_F	empirical constant
$g(R)$	radial distribution function
ΔH_v	heat of vaporization
I_i	principal moment of inertia of a molecule around axis i
k	Boltzmann constant
L	length of outstretched molecule
m	mass per molecule
M	molal weight
n	number of skeletal atoms per repeating unit in polymer
N_A	Avogadro number
N_c	number of carbon atoms per molecule
N_s	number of rigid skeletal units per molecule
P	pressure (external)
P_i	$= (\partial E / \partial V)_T =$ internal pressure
P^*	$= 5(P + P_i)V_w / E^\circ =$ reduced pressure
r	intermolecular distance
r_w	van der Waals radius of an atom
R	gas constant
R	intermolecular separation
ΔS_v	entropy of vaporization
$\Delta S_v{}^j$	excess entropy of vaporization
T	temperature
$\tilde{T}$	$= kT/\epsilon$ for simple spherical molecules
T^*	$= 5cRT/E^\circ$ for polyatomic molecules
T_g	glass transition temperature
T_g^*	$= 5cRT_g/E^\circ$
T_0	effective glass transition temperature
T_0^*	$= 5cRT_0/E^\circ$
T_c	critical temperature
T_R	$= T/T_c$
u	energy
V	molal volume at T
V°	barrier to internal rotation
V_w	van der Waals volume
V_0	molal volume at $0°K$
V_f	free volume
V_g	molal volume at $T = T_g$
w	width of a molecule

w_i	weight fraction of component i
x_i	mole fraction of component i
Z_c	entanglement chain length
α	cubic thermal expansion coefficient
α_g	cubic thermal expansion coefficient at $T < T_g$
α_L	cubic thermal expansion coefficient at $T > T_g$
β	compressibility
ϵ	pair potential between two molecules
ρ	density
ρ^*	$= V_w/V$
ρ_0^*	$= V_w/V_0$
ρ_g^*	$= V_w/V_g$
θ_L	$= E^\circ/5cR$
σ	distance between molecules at steepest descent of repulsion branch of potential well
η	viscosity
η^*	$= \eta\sigma^2/(m\epsilon)^{1/2}$
η_s^*	$= \eta d_w(A_w/mE^\circ)^{1/2}$
η_F^*	$= \eta N_A \bar{\alpha}_w^2/(ME^\circ)^{1/2}$
ξ	$= T_c^{1/6}/M^{1/2}P_c^{2/3} =$ viscosity reducing parameter, Ref. [38]

REFERENCES

[1] Adam, G., and J. H. Gibbs, *J. Chem. Phys.* **43,** 139 (1965).

[2] Arakawa, K., *J. Japan Soc. Mat. Sci.* **14,** 245 (1965).

[3] Barlow, A. J., J. Lamb, and A. Matheson, *J. Proc. Roy. Soc.* (*London*) **A292,** 322 (1966).

[3a] Berry, G. C., and T. G. Fox, *Adv. Polym. Sci.*, in press (1967).

[4] Bondi, A., *Physical Chemistry of Lubricating Oils*, Reinhold, New York, 1951, Sections 2.6, 2.7.

[5] Bondi, A. and D. J. Simkin, *AIChE J.* **3,** 473 (1957).

[6] Bondi, A., *Ind. Eng. Chem. Fundamentals* **2,** 95 (1963).

[7] Bondi, A., ACS Division of Petroleum Chemistry, Inc., Preprint **9,** C-33 (1964).

[8] Bondi, A., *J. Polymer Sci.* **A2,** 3159 (1964).

[9] Bondi, A., in *Rheology*, F. Eirich, ed., Academic Press, New York, 1966, vol. 4, p. 1.

[10] Brush, S. G., *Chem. Rev.* **63,** 513 (1963).

[11] Bueche, F., *J. Chem. Phys.* **36,** 2940 (1962); **45,** 4361 (1966).

[12] Cohen, M. H., and D. Turnbull, *J. Chem. Phys.* **31,** 1164 (1959).

[13] Ellington, R. T., private communication.

[14] Ferry, J. D., *Viscoelastic Properties of Polymers*, Wiley, New York, 1961.

[15] Ferry, J. D., and R. A. Stratton, *Kolloid Z.* **171,** 107 (1960).

[16] Fort, R. J., and W. R. Moore, *Trans. Faraday Soc.* **62,** 112 (1966).

[17] Fox, T. G., and V. R. Allen, *J. Chem. Phys.* **41,** 344 (1964).

[18] Fox, T. G., Ref. [9], Vol. 1, p. 484.

[19] Frisch, H. L., and R. Simha in *Rheology Theory and Applications*, F. Eirich ed., Academic Press, New York, 1956, Vol. 1, p. 525.

[20] Gibbs, J. H., and E. A. di Marzio, *J. Chem. Phys.* **28**, 373 (1958).

[21] Green, H. S., *The Molecular Theory of Fluids*, Interscience Publishers, New York, 1952.

[22] Greet, R. J., *J. Chem. Phys.* **45**, 2479 (1966).

[22a] Greet, R. J., and J. H. Magill, *J. Phys. Chem.* **71**, 1746 (1967).

[23] Gutmann, F., and L. R. Simmons, *J. Appl. Phys.* **23**, 977 (1952).

[24] Herzfeld, K. F., and T. A. Litoritz, *Absorption and Dispersion of Ultrasonic Waves*, Academic Press, New York, 1959.

[25] Johnson, M. D. et al., *Proc. Roy. Soc.* (*London*) **A282**, 283 (1964).

[26] Kanig, G., *Kolloid Z.* **190**, 1 (1963).

[26a] Kuss, E., *Ber. Bunsenges*, **70**, 1015 (1966).

[27] Landel, R. F. et al., *Proc. 4th Intl. Congr. Rheology*, Interscience, New York, 1965, Vol. 2, p. 663; *J. Phys. Chem.* **71** (in press).

[28] Macedo, P. B., and A. T. Litovitz, *J. Chem. Phys.* **42**, 245 (1965).

[28a] Matheson, A. J., *J. Chem. Phys.* **44**, 695 (1966).

[29] Miller, A. A., *J. Polymer Sci.* **A1**, 1857, 1865 (1963).

[29a] Nissan, A. H., *Phil. Mag.* **32**, 441 (1941).

[30] Pimentel, G. C., and A. L. McLellan, *The Hydrogen Bond*, Freeman, San Francisco, 1960.

[31] Porod, G., *Mh. Chem.* **80**, 251 (1949).

[32] Powell, R. E., W. E. Rosevaere, and H. Eyring, *Ind. Eng. Chem.* **33**, 430 (1941).

[33] Powles, J. G. and A. Hartland, *Proc. Phys. Soc.* (*London*) **75**, 617 (1960).

[34] Rice, S. A., in *Proceedings of the Symposium on Liquids, Structure, Properties and Solid Interaction*, T. J. Hughel, ed., Elsevier Publishing Company, Inc., Houston, Texas, 1965.

[35] Schiessler, R. W. et al., *Proc. Am. Petr. Inst.* **26**, III, 254 (1946).

[36] Schiessler, R. W., *Ind. Eng. Chem.* **47**, 1660 (1955).

[37] Stearns, R. S. et al., *ACS Div. of Petroleum Chemistry, Inc. Preprints*, Vol. 11, 5 (1966).

[38] Thodos, G. et al., *Ind. Eng. Chem.* **50**, 1095 (1958); *AIChE J.* **8**, 59 (1962); **10**, 275 (1964).

[39] Vogel, H., *Physik. Z.* **22**, 645 (1921).

13

Physical Properties of Molecular Glasses

Numerous review articles on various aspects of organic glasses have appeared in the recent past [16], [53], [39], [100], most of which have focused attention on the very interesting "glass transitions" and related relaxation phenomena, but failed to provide the engineer and the development chemist with a feel for the relations between the other important physical properties of glassy solids and molecular structure.

Included in this section are $p–v–T$ properties, heat capacity, elastic moduli, thermal conductivity, rotational diffusion, mass diffusion, and creep. An attempt has been made to present the data in the form of correlations similar to those used earlier for the generalized description of the properties of molecular crystals. Numerous gaps in knowledge or understanding or both are openly displayed in order to show where more research is needed.

13.1 THE GLASS-TRANSITION TEMPERATURE

Most liquids can be made to solidify in the glassy state if they are cooled through the crystallization temperature range more rapidly than the time required for crystal nuclei to form. This is easy to do if the symmetry of the molecules is of a low order or if the rotational isomerization from the liquid state equilibrium rotamer distribution to that required for crystallization, e.g., to all *trans* in the case of *n*-haloalkanes, is quite slow at $T \leq T_m$ [59a]. In those cases the liquid phase rotamer distribution persists in the glassy state. The most common cause of easy vitrification, however, is a high melt viscosity at or below the melting point.

In the glass-transition-temperature range (it is not a precisely defined temperature *point*) the viscosity of the melt increases very steeply; for example, several orders of magnitude within $10°K$. The viscosity becomes so high that even the volume change with temperature experiences a significant delay [53], [60]. Hence a glass can be considered as fully described only if the cooling rate that prevailed during its preparation is specified. A rapidly cooled liquid

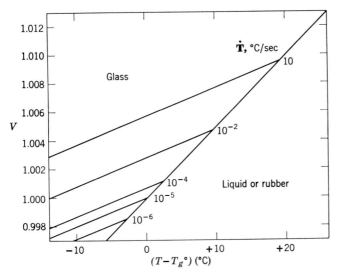

Figure 13.1 Effect of cooling rate $\dot{T}$ on the observed glass-transition temperature and specific volume according to the theory of Saito et al. [79]. The rate 10^{-5} °C/sec was chosen for the standard for which $T_g = T_g^\circ$ and $V_g = 1.000$; dV_g/dT was assumed independent of cooling rate [60].

becomes glassy at higher temperature and is likely to exhibit a lower density than one that has been cooled slowly from the melt state (Figure 13.1). As the density determines nearly all other physical properties of a glass, the cooling rate can have a profound effect on all physical properties of a glass. The finite, and rather low, thermal conductivity of molecular glasses also means that the cooling rate, and therefore the physical properties of a glass, may depend strongly on the geometry that prevails during the cooling process. Worse yet, the properties may differ substantially from the outside to the inside of any massive piece of glass cooled faster than 10^{-5} °C/sec.

An example for the effect of cooling rate on physical properties is shown in Figure 13.2, where we note the far greater creep rate of rapidly chilled as compared with slowly cooled polymethylmethacrylate. This greater weakness of chilled glass is in keeping with its lower density. We should be able to characterize the comparative thermal history of given glasses by their density. The small maximum density difference caused by chilling ($< 1\%$) and the difficulty of measuring the density of solids very accurately militate against the fulfillment of this need. Measurement of refractive index and its conversion to density through use of molar refractivity may be a solution to this problem.[1]

[1] Over the small interval in refractive index (n) usually encountered with a given glass (or liquid), $(n^2 - 1)/(n^2 + 2) \sim (n - 1)$ and therefore $\rho \sim (n - 1)$ with sufficient accuracy.

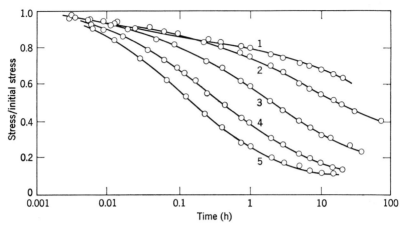

Figure 13.2   Effect of cooling rate on stress relaxation of polymethyl methacrylate at 80°C. Sample cooled from 130°C as follows: (1) 5°C/h; (2) 31°C/h; (3) convection in 25°C; (4) plunged in 25°C oil; (5) plunged in dry-ice–naphtha bath. After J. R. McLoughlin, and A. V. Tobolsky, *J. Polymer Sci.* 7, 658 (1951).

In all elastic modulus and relaxation measurements we must therefore specify the rate and amplitude of deformation as well as the thermal history of the sample and the instantaneous temperature T and thus call for definition of T_g as a discontinuity in a multidimensional coordinate system. The usual "relaxation map" lacks the vitrification rate and the deformation amplitude as coordinates. The amplitude is generally taken as infinitely small.

A conveniently general definition of the glass transition is that temperature at which $N_D = \tau_i/t \geq 1$, where t is the time scale of the experiment and the relaxation times τ_i are defined by $\tau_s = \eta/G_\infty$ for shear stress (flow) experiments, and $\tau_b = \mu/K_\infty$ for dilation or contraction experiments. Here η and μ are shear and bulk viscosity, respectively, whereas G_∞ and K_∞ are the shear and bulk modulus at infinite frequency. Since the magnitude of the glassy state moduli G_∞ and K_∞ can be estimated from the prevailing density and molecular structure by the methods given in Section 13.3, the prevailing T_g can be estimated from the appropriate viscosity data for the time scale under consideration. Calculation of the temperature at which $\eta = 10^{13}$ by extrapolation of the viscosity (12.7) to (12.12) very often—but not always—yields the conventional T_g [especially according to Ref. (a) of Table 13.2]. For those systems T_g in conventional time scale is obviously an isoviscous state.

The extensive work by Litovitz [57] has demonstrated the observability of glass transition at temperatures far above the "static" values of T_g if the time-scale of the deformation is reduced to 10^{-3} sec. In the present context, however, only $t > 10^2$ sec, hence η and $\mu > 10^{12}$ P is considered. Because of the extreme steepness of $(\partial\eta/\partial T)_p$ and $(\partial\mu/\partial T)_p$ near T_g defined by this time scale, a change to $t = 10^6$ sec (11 days) corresponds to a comparatively small change in T_g; but a change from 10^2 sec to geological time scales, corresponding to $\eta \approx 10^{22}$ P, may mean a fairly appreciable change in T_g, as suggested by the estimate in Table 13.7.

Table 13.1 Comparison of the Experimental Glass-Transition Coefficients with Each Other[a]

Substance	dT_g/dP (°C atm^{-1})	$TV\,\Delta\alpha/\Delta C_p$ (°C atm^{-1})	$\Delta\beta/\Delta\alpha$ (°C atm^{-1})
Polystyrene	0.02; 0.02; 0.03; 0.031[b]	0.032[b]	0.045[b]
Polymethyl Methacrylate	0.02; 0.018;[c] 0.023[b]	0.033[b]	0.07;[c] 0.037[b]
Polyvinyl chloride	0.014;[c] 0.016	0.0135; 0.03; 0.02[b]	0.046;[c] 0.02[b]
Polyvinyl acetate	0.022–0.024; 0.02[b]	0.025; 0.023[b]	0.042[b]
Polyisobutylene	0.024	0.024; 0.023[b]	—
Polypropylene (atactic)	0.020 ± 0.004	0.024 ± 0.001	0.021[b]
Natural rubber	0.024	0.020	0.024[b]
Glycerol	0.004	0.0045[b]	0.0036[b]
n-Propanol	0.007	0.005	—
Salicin	0.005	0.005	—
Selenium	0.013	0.017[b]	0.021[b]
B_2O_3	0.020	0.027	—

[a] From data collected by Goldstein [34] except where noted otherwise.
[b] A. J. Kovacs. [41].
[c] P. Heydemann and H. D. Guicking, *Kolloid-Z.* **193**, 16 (1963).
[d] See text regarding the significance of this datum.

Any phenomenological or theoretical discussion of T_g as a material property is therefore meaningful only if the dependence of T_g on t is taken into consideration. Thus the often-discussed Ehrenfest relations

$$\frac{dT_g}{dP} = \frac{\Delta\beta}{\Delta\alpha} = \frac{T_g v_g \,\Delta\alpha}{\Delta C_p} \tag{13.1}$$

can be applied only if all of the physical properties involved have been determined with experiments of the same time scale as the experiments on which the statement dT_g/dP is based. Here $\Delta\alpha = \alpha_L - \alpha_g$; $\Delta\beta = \beta_L - \beta_g$; and $\Delta C_p = C_p^{(l)} - C_p^{(g)}$, where superscript (*l*) refers to liquid and (g) to glass. Several authors [16], [54], [67] have pointed out that $dT_g/dP = \Delta\beta/\Delta\alpha$ *must* be fulfilled if β_g and T_g are defined consistently.

The reality of the many discrepancies between numerical values of the terms of (13.1), assembled in Table 13.1, is thus rather questionable until their internal consistency in terms of "t" has been established. Probably few published data will survive such an analysis for true comparability. However, until such critical data sifting has been carried out, Goldstein's proposal to use the discrepancies in Table 13.1 as means to define glass transition as an isenthalpic, isentropic, or iso-free-volume state [34] cannot be employed. An obvious consequence of the pressure dependence of T_g is that for each temperature $T > T_g$ there is a pressure P_g at which the melt will vitrify. In contrast to the melting curve (Section 6.7), the vitrification curve seems to be linear over most of the range examined to date.

Any theory of glass transition must basically describe the rapid increase of viscosity as a liquid is cooled toward T_g. As mentioned in Chapter 12, the most successful qualitative description ascribes this viscosity increase to the loss of "free volume" (v_f), such that at some temperature T_0 ($<T_g$), $v_f \rightarrow 0$, and $\eta \rightarrow \infty$ [30], [94]. The resulting viscosity equations [(12.4) to (12.8)] account qualitatively rather well for the effect of temperature and pressure on the viscosity in the region $(T - T_g)/T_g < 0.2$. The free-volume concept is also quite useful for the description of the effect of diluent (plasticizers) and comonomers on the magnitude of T_g, as shown later. It appears, however, that thermal expansion alone is insufficient for satisfactory quantitative description of these viscosity functions. The existence of a potential-energy barrier to the redistribution of free volume, that is, to molecular motion must be taken into account explicitly (see discussion in Section 12.4).

The magnitude of v_f at T_g, v_{fg}, required to describe $\eta = f(T)$ correctly is unrelated to any of the known measures of free volume (see Section 8.7.1), suggesting that the effective occupied volume $v_0 = v_T - v_f$ is rather larger than v_w. This might mean that v_0 is really the average specific volume occupied by a molecule aggregate that is more densely packed than the bulk liquid.

A rather different approach to the description of glass transition has been taken by Gibbs and diMarzio [33] and by Gibbs and Adam [3], who assume that at some temperature T_2 ($<T_g$) the configurational entropy $S_{\mathrm{conf}} \rightarrow 0$. The operational definition of this magnitude is

$$S_{\mathrm{conf}} = S - S_c \text{ (at temperature } T\text{)}, \tag{13.2}$$

where S_c is the entropy of the corresponding crystalline solid. From the heat-capacity data presented in Section 13.2.3, we see that this definition of glass transition, although valid for most polymers—for which there is a temperature below which $S_g = S_c$—cannot be valid for glasses composed of simple substances for which $S_g > S_c$ nearly down to 0°K. Prediction of T_g of polymeric solids from molecular structure then obviously depends on the molecular parameters which determine the magnitude of S_{conf}. These are molecule size, the energy of rotational isomerization (ΔE_{iso}), and the potential energy between neighboring nonbonded repeating units E_u (also as a measure of the barrier to motion). The barrier hindering internal rotation should probably also appear in the calculation, but was not considered explicitly by Gibbs et al.

Definition of T_2 as an equilibrium property makes the Gibbs–diMarzio theory a one-parameter theory, as has been pointed out by Staverman [90a]. The correctness of this view was proved experimentally by Eisenberg and Saito [28] when they showed that the presumably independent energy parameters ΔE_{iso} and E_u calculated from the experimental data for many compounds by means of that theory are exactly proportional to each other and that it is therefore equivalent to the free volume theory it was intended to replace. Conversely, there is now little doubt that more than one parameter is required to characterize the transition to the glassy state [18], [90a].

In view of the current state of theory it may be worthwhile to employ the molecular properties suggested by the theoretical conjectures only as reducing parameters for the dimensionless representation of the experimental data of the variables of state. The resulting generalized correlation of the properties of glasses may then give us further hints for the development of theory.

A useful reducing temperature for condensed systems is the ratio of the potential energy between neighboring molecules to the configurational heat capacity per molecule fR, where f is the number of external degrees of freedom per molecule. For all rigid polyatomic molecules $f = 6$; hence only the potential energy need be specified. Cohen and Turnbull chose the heat of vaporization at the normal boiling point (ΔH_{vb}) as a convenient measure of the potential energy, and defined a reduced glass-transition temperature $RT_g/\Delta H_{vb}$, which is indeed sensibly constant as is the even simpler ratio T_g/T_b shown in Table 13.2. Both reducing parameters lose their usefulness, however, when T_b becomes experimentally inaccessible or with substances composed of long flexible molecules or of highly compact ones with (nearly) spherical symmetry. The ratio T_g/T_m, although constant in many homologous series, is otherwise too irregular to be more than a very rough guide.

A reducing temperature of broader applicability is therefore the one discussed earlier, $E°/5cR$, where $3c = f$ is the number of external degrees of freedom per molecule including those due to internal rotation. The standard energy of vaporization is, of course, very similar to ΔH_{vb}, at least in principle. The reduced glass-transition temperature $T_g^* = 5cRT_g/E°$ is also shown in Table 13.2. We see with chagrin, however, that neither form of the reduced glass-transition temperature yields a universal constant, even for comparatively simple compounds. We see a trend toward a limiting value of T_g^* with liquids composed of flexible molecules, but with liquids composed of rigid molecules, T_g^* appears to increase slowly but without limit with increasing molecule size, leading to the possibility of rather high glass transition

Table 13.2 Reduced Glass Transition Temperatures of Monomeric Substances[a]

Substance	$\dfrac{10\,RT_g}{\Delta H_{vp}}$ [b]	T_g^{*} [c]	θ_L (°K) [c]	$\dfrac{T_g}{T_m}$
Aliphatic Substances				
Butene-1[d]	0.229	0.199		0.69
trans-Hexene-2	0.244			0.61
Heptene-1	0.244			0.59(0.67)[j]
cis-Heptene-2	0.250			
cis-Octene-2	0.248			0.60
2-Methylpentane[d]	0.24	0.22		0.67
3-Methylpentane[d]	0.21	0.18		...
3-Methylhexane[d]	0.233	0.214		...
2,3-Dimethylpentane[d]	0.228	0.200		...
3-Methylheptane	0.245	0.232	431	0.65
4-Methylnonane	0.264	0.254		
$(Et)_2C_2H_4(n\text{-}C_{10}H_{21})_2$[e]		0.299		...
Cycloaliphatic Substances				
Methylcyclohexane	0.228	0.194	437	0.58
Ethylcyclohexane	0.238	0.208	470	0.61
i-Propylcyclohexane	0.25	0.212	508	0.59
n-Butylcyclohexane	0.248	0.236	504	0.60
n-Pentylcyclohexane	0.254	0.238	524	0.58
n-Hexylcyclohexane	0.258	0.249		0.58
9-Cyclohexyleicosane	...	0.292	607	...
⬡ S —C—C—C$(nC_8)_2$[e]	...	0.272	613	...
$\left(⬡ S —C—C\right)_2 \cdot C \cdot (nC_8)$[e]	...	0.282	630	...
11-α-Decalylheneicosane[e]	...	0.308	606	...
Aromatic Substances				
Methylbenzene	0.282	0.246	460	0.63_5
Ethylbenzene	0.258	0.227	488	0.62
n-Propylbenzene	0.280	0.242	504	0.70_5
i-Propylbenzene		0.242	508	0.71
n-Butylbenzene		0.242	514	0.68
sec-Butylbenzene		0.246	516	0.67
t-Butylbenzene		0.272	521	0.66
n-Pentylbenzene		0.243	527	0.66
n-Hexylbenzene		0.252	545	0.67
o-Terphenyl[f]		0.340	720	0.71
1,3,5-Trinaphthylbenzene[g]	...	0.366	950	0.72
Distyrene[d]	0.35	0.32		...
Esters				
Di(2-ethylhexyl)sebacate	...	0.270	641	
Dimethylphthalate	...	0.279	691	0.69
Diethylphthalate	...	0.266	707	
Di-*n*-butylphthalate	...	0.278	635	0.74
Di-isobutylphthalate	...	0.29?	622?	
Di(2-ethylhexyl)phthalate	...	0.285	643	

Table 13.2 (*continued*)

Substance	$\dfrac{10\,RT_g{}^{b}}{\Delta H_{vp}}$	T_g^{*c}	$\theta_L{}^{c}$ (°K)	$\dfrac{T_g}{T_m}$
Tritolylphosphate[h]	...	0.301	695	0.82
Phenyl salicylate (Salol)[h]	...	0.322	673	0.69
2-Naphthyl salicylate (Betol)[h]	...	0.326	746	0.66
Miscellaneous Polar Substances[i]				
Isobutyl chloride 0.24	0.224	394	0.62	0.26
n-Butanol-2[k]	0.267	476	0.80	0.34
t-Butanol[k,l]	0.40	450	0.60	0.51
2,2-Dimethylpropanol-1[k,l]			0.51(0.73)	[j]
n-Pentanol-2[k]	0.285	492		0.36
2-Methyl butanol-2[k,l]	0.317	486	0.59	0.41

[a] Except when noted otherwise the glass transition temperatures are from M. R. Carpenter, D. B. Davies, and A. J. Matheson, *J. Chem. Phys.* **46**, 2451 (1967); determined by DTA.
[b] $\Delta H_{vb} = \Delta H_{vap}$ at T_b; hydrocarbon data primarily from "Selected Physical Properties of Principal Hydrocarbons," *Am. Petr. Institute.*
[c] $T_g^* = T_g/\theta_L$, $\theta_L(= E°/5cR)$ determined by density method described in Chapter 8.
[d] From [94].
[e] From [12].
[f] R. J. Greet and D. Turnbull, *J. Chem. Phys.* **46**, 1243 (1967).
[g] D. J. Plazek and J. H. Magill, *J. Chem. Phys.* **45**, 3038 (1966).
[h] E. Jenckel and R. Heusch, *Kolloid-Z.* **130**, 89 (1953).
[i] For additional T_g-data on alkyl halides see Tables 13.13 and 13.14.
[j] The number in parentheses is T_g/T_1, where T_1 is the lowest first-order solid/solid transition temperature.
[k] J. A. Faucher and J. V. Koleske, *Phys. Chem. Glasses* **7**, 202 (1966); T_g determined by torsion pendulum at 1Hz.
[l] Substance does not vitrify easily; T_g determined by extrapolation from T_g of mixtures with other isomers.

temperatures even for nonpolymeric substances. A unifying principle must obviously yet be found for the description of the glass transition of non-polymeric substances.

Paucity of data is perhaps a major reason for the difficulty just mentioned with T_g of monomeric liquids. Far more work has been done on the glass transition of polymers, largely because of the technological importance of this datum. Virtually the same range of reduced glass-transition temperatures $T_g^* = 5cRT/E°$ is covered by polymers as by simple compounds. Here $E°$ and c are per repeating unit. However, there is strong clustering around $T_g^* \approx 0.3$ to 0.35. A trend has been noted for T_g^* to rise with the equilibrium measure of chain expansion, the energy of rotational isomerization, ΔE_{iso}, both in theory [33] as well as in the experimental correlation shown in Table 13.3 [13].

Table 13.3 Limiting Values for T_g^* at $M \to \infty$, Compared with the Energy of Rotational Isomerization (ΔE_{iso})

Polymer	T_g^{*e}	ΔE_{iso} [f] (kcal/mole)
Polyisobutene	0.216	0[a]
cis-1,4-Polyisoprene	0.27	
Polyethylene	0.27	0.5 to 0.6[a]
Poly(dimethylsiloxane)	0.30	0.80[b]
Poly(methyl methacrylate)	0.33	0.8[c]
Poly(n-butyl methacrylate)	0.33	
Polypropylene(isotactic)	0.35	0.6 to 1.5[a]
Poly(monochlorotrifluoroethylene)	0.36	
Poly(vinyl acetate)	0.39	~1.0
Poly(vinyl chloride)	0.42	1.9[d]
Polystyrene	0.435	1.0 to 1.5[a]

[a] T. M. Birshtein and O. B. Ptitsyn, *Conformations of Macromolecules*, Interscience—Wiley, New York, 1966.

[b] P. J. Flory et. al., *J. Am. Chem. Soc.* **86**, 146 (1964).

[c] Quoted as unpublished datum by S. Havriliak from J. Roetling, *Polymer* **6**, 311 (1965); for isotactic PMMA I. Sakurada et al., recommend $\Delta E_{iso} = 1.2$ kcal/mole [*Kolloid-Z.* **186**, 41 (1962)].

[d] H. Germar, *Kolloid-Z.* **193**, 25 (1963); this value is rather high; 1.2 kcal/mole is a more probable magnitude.

[e] For T_g-data on polymers see "Polymer Handbook," Brandrup/Immergut, ed., Wiley, 1966.

[f] For ΔE_{iso}-data see Table 14.29.2.

Comparison of the energy of activation for various types of motion, bulk as well as molecular, around T_g with that for motion at other temperatures suggests that cooperation of 20 to 40 backbone chain links is required near T_g to achieve displacement of one link into a new equilibrium position [2], [3], [16], [80]. High-order transitions at lower temperatures appear to involve only identifiable small molecule groupings along the main chain. The discussion of the many subsidiary transitions is outside the scope of the present work. Their correlation with molecular structure can be found in several recent review articles.

In summary, none of the attempts that have been made to define T_g in terms of free-volume theory—"T_g is an isofree volume state" [29], [89]—or in terms of thermodynamic arguments—"T_g is an isoenthalpic state" [34]—or in terms of mechanical properties—"T_g is an isoviscous state"—has been entirely successful. A general theory of glass transition may not be developed until its phenomenological definition has been clarified. Conversely, we may well find that the sharp rise in viscosity, characteristic of or even the cause of glass transition, cannot be tied consistently to any equilibrium argument. In that case, there will be no clear-cut definition and no general theory.

13.1.1 Mixture Rules for the Glass-Transition Temperature

Mixture rules for the glass-transition temperature are of practical interest in three areas:

1. To estimate the closely related temperature coefficient T_0 of viscosity of mixtures of low-to-medium-molecular-weight liquids in the low-temperature region (Chapter 12).
2. To estimate the reduction in T_g of glassy polymers achieved by plasticizers; a special case here is $T_g = f(M)$.
3. To estimate the glass-transition temperature of copolymers from those of the homopolymers.

Except for linear weight fraction additivity of T_g found by Faucher[1] with mixtures of isomeric alcohols there are almost no experimental data for (1), but a fair amount of information is available for (2) and (3). We may hope that generalizations obtained from (2) and (3) may be applicable to (1). Inspection of the experimental data [for (2) and (3)] reveals that $T_g = f(x_1)$, where x_1 is the concentration of the second component (plasticizer or comonomer), is hardly ever linear. It is not even always monotonic. Minima, and occasionally maxima, have been observed, especially in copolymer systems. The various relations of the form $T_g = T_{g(2)} + b_1 x_1$ reviewed by Shen and Tobolsky [87] can therefore at best yield only the slope at $x_1 \rightarrow 0$. Because none of these relations has a solid basis in theory, coefficient b_1 produces little new physical insight.

The free-volume theory of glass transition permits a fairly successful description of the effect of diluents on T_g. Only the treatments by Kovacs and Braun [15] and by Kanig [49] of the various more-or-less empirical treatments available, incorporate the specific interaction between mixture components that account—at least qualitatively—for the observed deviations from linear-combination rules.

The theory of Kovacs and Braun [15] is particularly simple. The assumption is made that at their respective glass-transition temperatures, the relaxation times $\tau_{g(1)} = \tau_{g(2)} = \tau_{g(12)}$, where subscript (1) refers to diluent, (2) to polymer, and (12) to their mixture. The further assumption of linear volume fraction additivity of v_0 and of $\Delta\alpha$ then leads to

$$\varphi_1 \Delta\alpha_1 [T_{g(12)} - T_{g(1)}] + (1 - \varphi_1) \Delta\alpha_2 [T_{g(12)} - T_{g(2)}] = k\varphi_1 (1 - \varphi_1), \quad (13.3)^2$$

---

[1] Ref. k of Table 13.2.

[2] Together with the Boyer-Simha relation $\Delta\alpha T_g \doteq 0.1$ (discussed in Section 13.2.2); (13.3) leads to the Fox relation $1/T_{g(12)} = \varphi_1/T_{g(1)} + \varphi_2/T_{g(2)} + f(\varphi_1\varphi_2 k)$.

or

$$T_{g(12)} = \frac{\varphi_1 \Delta\alpha_1 T_{g(1)} + \varphi_2 \Delta\alpha_2 T_{g(2)} + k\varphi_1\varphi_2}{\varphi_1 \Delta\alpha_1 + \varphi_2 \Delta\alpha_2},$$

where φ_1 is the volume fraction of diluent, and the factor k contains the interaction contribution of the specific excess volume of mixing v^E to the free volume in the form

$$-k = \frac{(v^E/v_{12})}{\varphi_1\varphi_2}. \qquad (13.4)$$

The dilatometric glass transition data of the few adequately characterized polymer-plasticizer systems [43a], [46b] yield $k = -0.04 \pm 0.01$ and a polystyrene-toluene blend $k = -0.014$. The excess volume derived from the extrapolated melt density of the polymer at or slightly above $T_g(12)$ is of the order required by (13.4). Neither, however, are all the density data sufficiently reliable, nor is the agreement sufficiently extensive for validation of the Kovacs–Braun theory. An unsolved puzzle is why at $T - T_g(12) >$ about $60°C$ v^E is not only far too small for such agreement but occasionally even differs in sign from that demanded by (13.3) and (13.4).

A discontinuity is occasionally observed in the T_g versus φ_1 curve at a temperature T_3 when $T_{g(2)} \gg T_{g(1)}$ [15] and has been ascribed by Kovacs to $v_{f(2)}$ approaching 0 at $T = T_3$. [Approximately, $T_3 = T_{g(2)} - v_{fg(2)}/\Delta\alpha_2$.] Thus T_3 would acquire the meaning of a true equilibrium second-order transition point of the polymer. In the cases studied by Kovacs $T_3 \approx 0.57T_g$, which is still lower than T_2 of Gibbs and diMarzio, which is of the order $0.8T_g$ for most polymers, as mentioned earlier. For mixture glass-transition temperatures $T_{g(12)} < T_3$, (13.3) becomes

$$\varphi_1 \Delta\alpha_1[T_{g(12)} - T_{g(1)}] - (1 - \varphi_1)v_{fg(2)} = k\varphi_1(1 - \varphi_1) \qquad (13.5)$$

or

$$T_{g(12)} = T_{g(1)} + \frac{(\varphi_1^{-1} - 1)v_{fg(2)} + k(1 - \varphi_1)}{\Delta\alpha_1},$$

where $v_{fg(2)}$ is the specific free volume of the polymer at its $T_{g(2)}$. The representation of the available data for such extreme systems as polystyrene-toluene, polystyrene-butanone-2 by (13.4) and (13.5) is surprisingly good [15].

An alternate free volume theory of plasticization by Kanig [49] is somewhat more complicated than that by Kovacs and Braun but has the advantage of referring to the more frequently measured excess free energy of mixing as interaction parameter. The relation is

$$\frac{1}{w_1} - 1 = \frac{1.5a}{R}[2(A_{22} - A_{12}) + 4.18A_{22}b]\frac{1}{T_g(2) - T_g(12)} - a(1 + 4.18b)$$

with   (13.6)

$$a = \frac{v_g(1)\,\Delta\alpha(1)}{v_g(2)\,\Delta\alpha(2)} \quad \text{and} \quad b = \frac{v_g(12)(\Delta\alpha T_g)(12)}{v_g(1)\alpha_L(1)T_g(1)},$$

where the numerical coefficients are "approximately universal" constants observed by Kanig [*loc. cit.*], and the "affinities" A_{ij} can perhaps be set as $0{,}23\, E_{ij}^\circ/5c_{ij}$, so that

$$2(A_{22} - A_{12}) \approx 0.46\left(\frac{E_2^\circ}{5c_2} - \frac{E_{12}^\circ}{5c_{12}} + af^E\right) \quad \text{and} \quad 4.18A_2 \sim \frac{E_2^\circ}{5c_2}, \quad (13.7)$$

where E_{12}° has been estimated by (15.29) and f^E is the thermal component of the free energy of mixing,[1] namely of the order

$$RT[3c_1/2(1 - 0.5V_1^*T_1^*)]\left(1 - \frac{c_2 A_w(2)E_1^\circ}{c_1 A_w(1)E_2^\circ}\right)^2$$

or $V_1\varphi_2^2(\delta_2 - \delta_1)^2$, where δ_1, δ_2 are the solubility parameters of the components [67a].

An important consequence of (13.6) is the straight-line relation between the weight fraction function $[(1/w_1) - 1]$ and the inverse glass transition temperature depression $[T_g(2) - T_g(12)]^{-1}$, which has been verified experimentally. However, the validity of the postulated relation (13.7) has yet to be demonstrated and the numerical value of the empirical coefficient a determined.

The heavy weighting of the component with the larger value of $\Delta\alpha$ (and/or of v_{fg}) in both theories emphasizes the large effect of compounds with low glass-transition temperatures (even at low concentrations), especially if they are composed of flexible molecules. Near immiscibility ($F^E > 0$, $v^E > 0$) reduces $T_{g(12)}$, whereas strong mutual affinity of the mixture components ($F^E < 0$, $v^E < 0$) raises $T_{g(12)}$ beyond expectation from linear mixture rules, just as these same mixture interactions were shown to do in the case of viscosity in Sections 12.2.5 and 12.6.

The addition of an immiscible second phase to a glass-forming liquid has no effect on T_g, regardless of how finely divided it is, nor does the addition of massive amounts of solid fillers change $T_{g(12)}$, even though it raises the elastic moduli appreciable (see Section 13.3.6).

A curve of $v_{(12)}$ versus φ_1 at constant temperature (T) shows a break at that plasticized system for which $T_{g(12)} = T$. The polymer concentration φ_2 at which this break occurs may be called the vitrification concentration $\varphi_g(T)$ for the system at temperature T [96].

13.2 *p-v-T* PROPERTIES

13.2.1 Density

The density of most glass-forming liquids has been determined in the process of ascertaining the location of T_g. It is a rather good measure of the

[1] Or just F^E if the glass to be plasticized is not a polymer.

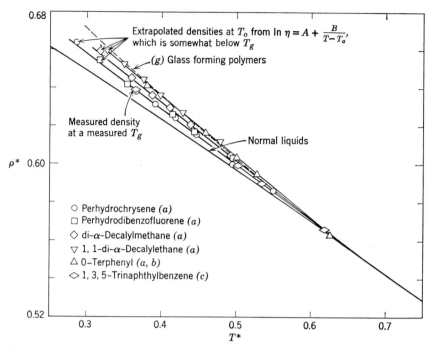

Figure 13.3　Generalized packing density versus temperature plot for glass-forming hydrocarbons. (a) Based on data from API-Project 42; (b) Andrews and Ubbelohde, *Proc. Roy. Soc. (London)* **A228**, 435 (1955); (c) Magill and Ubbelohde, *Trans. Faraday Soc.* **54**, 1811 (1958).

physics of condensed phases when expressed as packing density $\rho^* = \rho V_w/M$. The first indication of a tendency toward glass formation is the rise of the generalized density versus temperature curve (ρ^* versus T^* for ordinary liquids), as shown in Figure 13.3. The cause for this upturn is probably the freezing in of external degrees of freedom $3c$, which effectively reduces the temperature $T^* = 5cRT/E^\circ$ [13]. The shift in T^* required to bring the observed packing-density curve down to the general curve is therefore a measure of the number of degrees of freedom frozen in.

Whereas the melt density of simple glass-forming substances approaches T_g at a slope that is specific for each compound, or perhaps for each type of compound, the melt density of glass-forming vinyl backbone polymers approaches T_g on a common curve, shown in Figure 13.4. The slope of this curve corresponds to a rate of freeze-in of degrees of freedom with decreasing temperature represented by $(c_{\text{monomeric liquids}}/c_{\text{polymer melts}})$ $-1 = 3.7 \times 10^{-3} \exp(1.40/T^*)$ [13], and is thus determined by T^* only. It is plausible that the more flexible *cis*-polyisoprene backbone should freeze in less rapidly than the saturated backbone chain.

The diversity of T_g^* mentioned earlier is seen in Figures 13.3 and 13.4 to correspond to a fairly wide range of ρ_g^*, that is, of packing densities at which vitrification occurs. A more nearly uniform value of density at T_g is V_0/V_g, the density relative to that of the crystal at $0°K$, [13] as shown by the data in Table 13.4. The physical meaning of this observation may well be that—in keeping with an idea proposed by Kanig [48]—the thermal vibration amplitudes of all molecules at T_g are (nearly) identical. As the glass-density data, on which this correlation is based, have not been determined at a standard thermal history, an exact correlation would be fortuitous.

A feel for the relation between the magnitude of ρ_g^* and molecular structure can be acquired from an inspection of Table 13.4. The data support the intuitively plausible notion that the packing density of a glass becomes higher as the molecule becomes more symmetrical. That is particularly apparent with polymers. Too high a degree of symmetry would raise the crystallization tendency and thereby make the glassy state accessible only with difficulty. Polyisobutylene is perhaps the outstanding example of a glass with a high packing density and a very symmetrical molecular structure. Here the high viscosity inhibits crystallization except when the molecules can be oriented by stretching. The very bulky and asymmetrical atactic polystyrene probably vitrifies at the lowest packing density, ρ_g^*, observed so far. It is noteworthy that the apparent lower limit of ρ_g^* is of the same order as the lower limit of packing density for (organic) molecular crystals proposed by Kitaigorodskii, namely, $\rho^* \geq 0.60$.

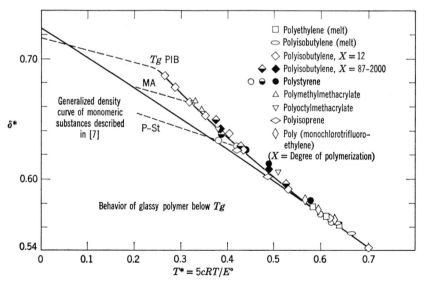

Figure 13.4 Packing density ρ^* of various polymers as function of reduced temperature T^* [13].

Table 13.4 Comparison of Glass Density (at T_g) with Crystal Density at 0°K for Simple Liquids and Polymers [13]

Substance	ρ_g^{*a}	V_g/V_0^b
Butene-1	0.673	1.07
Isopentane	0.678	1.035[c]
2-Methylpentane	0.688	1.025
3-Methylpentane	0.678	1.04
3-Methylhexane	0.678	1.05
4-Methylnonane	0.670	1.08
Ethyl alcohol	0.648	1.072[c]
1,3,5-Trinaphthylbenzene	0.640	1.14
Polystyrene	0.625	1.142[d]
Polyisobutylene	0.680	1.04[e]

[a] For the low-molecular-weight hydrocarbons, the density at the known T_g was estimated by linear extrapolation of the API and other density data below T_m.
[b] V_0 estimated by analogy, except where noted.
[c] W. Biltz, *Raumchemie der Festen Stoffe*. Voss, Leipzig, 1934.
[d] R. B. Scott, *Cryogenic Engineering*, Van Nostrand, Princeton, New Jersey, 1959.
[e] R. F. Robbins et al., *Adv. Cryog. Eng.* **8**, 289 (1963).

Table 13.5 Packing Density of Polymers in Solution.[a] $T < T_g$ (Polymer) All at Room Temperature

Polymer	Solvent	$\bar{\rho}^{*a}$	ρ^*	Ref.
Polystyrene	None	0.653[b]	0.635[b]	c
	o-Dichlorobenzene	0.650		d
	m-Xylene	0.657		d
	Toluene	0.662		e
	2-Butanone	0.666		d
	Chloroform	0.664, 0.658		d, f
Polymethyl methacrylate	None	0.707[b]	0.675,[b] 0.690	g, h
	o-Dichlorobenzene	0.706		d
	m-Xylene	0.712		d
	2-Butanone	0.723		d
	Chloroform	0.727		d

[a] Derived from the partial specific volume; $\bar{\alpha} \approx \alpha_{melt}$ according to (d); See Table 8.14 for additional examples.
[b] Here $\bar{\rho}^*$ refers to the extrapolated liquid density and ρ^* is the packing density of the glassy solid at room temperature.
[c] From data by K. Ueberreiter and G. Kanig, *Z. Naturforsch.* **6a**, 551 (1951).
[d] G. V. Schulz and M. Hoffmann, *Makromol. Chem.* **23**, 220 (1957).
[e] R. S. Spencer and G. D. Gilmore, *J. Appl. Phys.* **20**, 502 (1949).
[f] A. Horth et al., *J. Polymer Sci.* **39**, 189 (1959).
[g] From data by S. S. Rogers and L. Mandelkern, *J. Am. Chem. Soc.* **61**, 985 (1957).
[h] See (c) in Table 13.1.

The partial specific volume of glass-forming substances in ideal mixtures at $T < T_g$ (of the bulk polymer) should be smaller than in the bulk because excessive viscosity should not prevent it from acquiring its equilibrium volume. So far, such measurements have only been carried out with polymers. Typical data are shown in Table 13.5 (expressed as the equivalent packing density) where they are compared with the density extrapolated from the liquid above T_g. The effect of solvent quality is also apparent from the data. Correlation of Δv with the heat of mixing suggested by Horth[1] may serve as a guide for prediction of solution density. Concentrated solutions of glass-forming solutes are themselves glass forming [96]. The characteristic contraction of molecular glasses at low concentrations of diluents or plasticisers is discussed in Section 13.3.4.

13.2.2 Thermal Expansion

The similarity in packing density between glass and crystal suggests that the thermal expansion coefficients of glasses be of the same order as those of the crystal. The data assembled in Table 13.6 bear out this conclusion. Hence the expansion coefficient correlation for crystals, $\alpha_s \Delta H_s / C_v^s = \alpha_s^*$ const, should be applicable, where ΔH_s is the heat of sublimation and C_v^s is the lattice contribution to the heat capacity at constant volume. With rigid polyatomic molecules at $T > \theta_D$, $C_v^s \approx 6R$, and with flexible molecules $C_v^s \approx 6R + (N_s - 1)R$, where N_s is the number of flexibly connected chain links. The few available data (Table 13.6) suggest that no great error is made by setting $C_v^{s(g)} \approx C_v^{s(c)}$, and taking $\alpha_g^* \approx \alpha_s^*$.

Table 13.6 Comparison of Thermal Expansion Coefficients of Crystalline and Glassy Solids

Substance	$10^4\,\alpha_c$	$10^4\,\alpha_g$	Ref.
1,3,5-Trinaphthylbenzene	1.25	1.20	a
Glycerol	1.86	2.4	b, c
Glucose	0.84	0.90	d, c
Polystyrene	~2.8	2.3	e, c
Polyethylene terephthalate	1.71	1.87	f
Polyethylene 1,5-naphthalate	1.85	2.14	f

[a] J. H. Magill and A. R. Ubbelohde, *Trans. Faraday Soc.* **54**, 1811 (1958).
[b] A. K. Schulz, *J. Chim. Phys.* **51**, 530 (1954).
[c] A. J. Kovacs, *Fortschr. Hochpolymer. Forschg.* **3**, 394 (1963).
[d] G. S. Parks et al., *J. Phys. Chem.* **32**, 1366 (1928).
[e] F. Danusso et al., *Chim. Ind.* **41**, 748 (1959).
   H. J. Kolb and E. F. Izard, *J. Appl. Phy.* **20**, 564 (1949).

[1] See (f) in Table 13.5.

Klemm's rule that $\alpha_s T_m = $ const ≈ 0.10 cannot be applied to glasses since T_g cannot be compared with T_m. The equivalent rule for glasses $(\alpha_L - \alpha_g)T_g = $ const ≈ 0.1 [89], would be useful for predictive purposes if it were reliable (which it is not), and if α_L were readily available. The latter can be determined easily for ordinary liquids at convenient temperatures and only with difficulty at elevated temperatures and/or for polymer melts. Estimation methods of fair reliability are available for α_L of ordinary liquids as well as polymer melts (Section 8.2). The constancy of $(\alpha_L - \alpha_g)T_g$ leaves something to be desired, as is evident from the data of Refs. [53] and [51]. Predictions based on this rule must therefore be treated with reserve. Simha and Boyer [16], [89] suggested that the product $(\alpha_L - \alpha_g)T_g$ be considered as a measure of the fraction of the volume available for (thermal) motion of the molecules in the glassy state at T_g. This concept has been rightfully questioned by Kovacs [34], [53]. The ratio $(\alpha_L - \alpha_g)/\alpha_L$, however, which Kanig [49] identifies as the fraction of free volume available in the form of diffusionally accessible vacancies, turns out to be a universal function of T/T_g, being equal to 1.0 at $T = 0°$K, and equal to 0.70 ± 0.07 at $T = T_g$.

Precision dilatometry of a few glassy polymers over a wide temperature range (down to 90°K) by Simha and co-workers [102] shows the expected slow decrease of α_g in the range $0.85T_g \rightarrow 90°$K. A few minor discontinuities in these curves can be associated with second-order transitions or with relaxation processes, but could be ignored in engineering estimates. The expected sharp discontinuity beginning at $\sim 0.9T_g$ is clearly visible even where the amorphous component undergoing the transition is only $\sim 10\%$.

Although the major emphasis so far in this section has been on the thermal expansion of a glass as a typical equilibrium property, we should not lose sight of the fact that glasses do not attain their equilibrium volume instantaneously because of their very-high-volume viscosity. The time required for a typical glass (polystyrene) to contract to its equilibrium volume upon quenching to different temperatures, shown by Jenkel's data in Table 13.7, illustrates this problem rather well.

Extensive and careful measurements of volume creep of 1,3,5-trinaphthyl benzene [69], of polystyrene [91], of several other vinyl polymers [53], and of glassy metal soaps [55] should soon provide enough data for the formulation of at least semiquantitative generalized rate equations. A major complicating factor is, of course, the sensitivity of volume creep rate, just like that of tensile creep rate, to thermal history illustrated in Figure 13.2. Obviously, equilibrium is unattainable at temperatures far below T_g. On the other hand, the data also indicate that a glass can be treated as an ordinary solid at $(T_g - T) > 20°$C. The often-cited characterization of a glass as a subcooled liquid is clearly meaningless even that close to T_g. It is shown in a later section that the creep rate of organic glasses is significantly smaller than

Table 13.7 Time Required for the Density[a] of Polystyrene to Come to within $1/e$ of its Equilibrium Contraction upon Quenching to Various Temperatures

$T - T_g$ (°C)	$t(1/e)$ (sec)	$t(1/e)$ (years)
11	0.01	—
6	1	—
2	40	—
1	120	—
0	300	—
−1	1.1×10^3	—
−2.5	3.6×10^3	—
−4	1.8×10^4	—
−7	1.8×10^5	
−10	5.2×10^6	0.16
−12	3.2×10^7	1
−50	—	10

[a] From [60]; Jenkel used the refractive index n as measure of the density and the items given are those for which the ratio $[n(t) - n(\infty)]/[n(0) - n(\infty)] = e^{-1}$.

that of organic crystals at the same temperature distance from their melting point. In other words a glass at $(T_g - T) > 20°C$, whether at its equilibrium volume or not, is a dimensionally stable solid with repeatable properties, as long as it is not heated to within $(T_g - T) < 20°C$. Detailed discussions of the kinetics of thermal contraction and expansion near T_g can be found in [53] and [60].

13.2.3 Heat Capacity, Enthalpy, and Entropy

The similarity and the difference in packing density between crystal and glass are significant for an understanding of the heat capacity of glasses. The similarity is responsible for the very similar magnitude of the heat capacity of glass and of the corresponding crystal. The smaller packing density of the glass indicates that some volume elements are more loosely packed and should therefore permit molecular oscillation at lower frequency than in the crystal. Hence the lattice contributions to heat capacity and to the entropy of a glass should be, and are in general, slightly higher than they are for a crystal. Some of the very few data demonstrating this point are shown in Figure 13.5.

The near identity of the $[C_p^{(g)} - C_p^{(c)}]$ data of quite different substances at equal value of T/T_g suggests the existence of a yet undefined general principle. The scatter near $T/T_g \approx 1$ is to be expected because of the difficulty of making

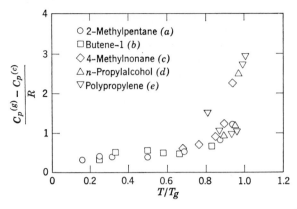

Figure 13.5   Heat capacity difference between glass and crystal for various simple substances. (a) D. R. Douslin, and H. M. Huffmann, *J. Am. Chem. Soc.* **68**, 1704 (1946); (b) J. G. Aston et al., *J. Am. Chem. Soc.* **68**, 1704 (1946); (b) J. G. Aston et al., *J. Am. Chem. Soc.* **68**, 52 (1946); (c) G. S. Parks et al., *J. Am. Chem. Soc.* **63**, 1132 (1941); (d) G. S. Parks et al., *J. Am. Chem. Soc.* **48**, 2790 (1926); (e) [23], adjusted to 0/100% crystallinity; also [66] lower values.

repeatable measurements in that temperature range (v.i.). In contrast to the polypropylene case shown on Figure 13.5, Pessaglia and Kevorkian observe no heat-capacity difference between glass and crystal below $0.9T_g$ [49], an observation that seems to be supported by Dole's earlier measurements on polyethylene [24]. Three sets of precision measurements yield nearly indistinguishable heat capacity for semicrystalline ($\varphi_c \sim 0.4$) and glassy polystyrene from 80°K to $0.9T_g$ [1], [23], [50]. However, recent heat-capacity measurements at 1 to 5°K on polyethylenes differing widely in crystallinity yield $C_p^{(g)} = 300T^3$ erg cm^{-3} °K^{-4} and $C_p^{(c)} = 100T^3$ erg cm^{-3} °K^{-4}, in agreement with expectation from basic principles [71]. Similarly Reese found that at 1 to 5°K the heat capacity of glassy polymethyl methacrylate and polystyrene is 200 to $400T^3$ erg cm^{-3} °K^{-4} larger than estimates from acoustic and modulus measurements [73]. This excess heat capacity of glasses at very low temperature is ascribed to very low vibration frequencies of molecule segments situated near microvoids.

The isochoric heat capacity C_v is generally more instructive because its magnitude can be interpreted directly in terms of molecular mechanics. We obtain C_v from C_p by

$$C_p - C_v = \left(\frac{\partial V}{\partial T}\right)_p \left(\frac{\partial E}{\partial V}\right)_T = K\alpha^2 V T. \tag{13.11}$$

Critical examination of the available data shows, unfortunately, that the uncertainty in K and α of glasses and crystals is often so great ($> \pm 10\%$) that the total uncertainty in $C_p - C_v$ for each phase is of the same order as

$C_v^{(g)} - C_v^{(c)}$. The apparently quite accurate direct measurement of $(\partial E/\partial V)_T$ of polymers, pioneered by Gee and co-workers [6] and also used by Bianchi [10] may improve this situation somewhat, because then only the uncertainty of α (instead of α^2) dominates the uncertainty of the calculation of $C_p - C_v$. The similarity of K and α for glasses and crystals suggests that $(C_p - C_v)_{\text{glass}} \approx (C_p - C_v)_{\text{crystal}}$ and that therefore $[C_p^{(g)} - C_p^{(c)}] \approx [C_v^{(g)} - C_v^{(c)}]$ making perhaps the whole calculation unnecessary. The observed difference $C_p^{(g)} - C_p^{(c)} = R/2$ may therefore have direct physical meaning, which is worth exploring. In very accurate measurements, we should find $C_p^{(g)} - C_p^{(c)} = f(\rho^*)$. However, from an engineering point of view this difference is so small that we can safely use $C_p^{(g)} = C_p^{(c)}$ in engineering calculations until $0.9T_g$, whereas between $0.9T_g$ and T_g we may set $C_p^{(g)} \approx C_p^{(l)}$.

Since theories of the glassy state usually take the liquid state as starting point, a great deal of effort has been spent on the estimation (and the theoretical understanding) of $C_p^{(l)} - C_p^{(g)}$ at $T = T_g$ [3], [9], [33], [101]. Owing to the very uncertain extrapolation of $C_p^{(l)}$ to $T < T_m$, this procedure is of very questionable value for prediction purposes, and the "regularities" found are not recommended for the estimation of $C_p^{(g)}$.

Conversion of the heat-capacity data into enthalpy data by integration,

$$\int_{T_1}^{T_2} C_p \, dT,$$

is straightforward. An easier way would be to sum $H_i + H^s$, where H_i is the internal and H^s the lattice contribution (Section 3.4.4) to the enthalpy.

With many crystalline and glassy polymers we find that the entropy at temperature $T > 2\theta_D$ is $S_T^\circ \approx 1.0 \pm 0.1 C_p(T)$ [23]. There is no theoretical reason for this relation. Hence it should be used with caution.

Time effects are particularly striking in heat-capacity measurements on glasses. The determining factor is the cooling rate through the glass-transition range and the residence time in the temperature range just below T_g. If the sample has been cooled slowly so that its volume V and enthalpy H have approached the equilibrium property (curve B in Figure 13.6a) at T_1, subsequent heating along curve $B \cdots A$ through T_g will produce the indicated enthalpy and heat-capacity curves, the maximum in C_p becoming higher as the heating rate becomes higher (Figure 13.7). The area under all these maxima should be alike and identical with the area enclosed by the broken curve and the up-curve in Figure 13.6b. The origin of these maxima is obviously the system's inability to absorb energy any faster than is consistent with the mobility of the molecules; that is, with the number of degrees of freedom that can be excited and with the rate at which they can be excited at any given temperature. This phenomenon is a reflection of the freezing-in of degrees of freedom as $T \to T_g$ mentioned in the discussion on melt density.

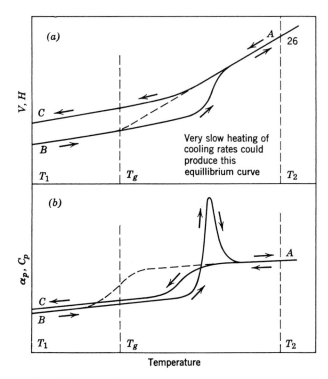

Figure 13.6   Effect of thermal history of thermodynamic response of volume and enthalpy (*a*), and of thermal expansion and heat capacity (*b*), showing maximum in the second-order properties. Sample remained at $<T_g$ long enough to attain the quasi-equilibrium point *B* before beginning of heating cycle [60], [86].

Rapid quenching of the melt through T_g to $(T_g - T_1) > 20°C$ produces the enthalpy and heat-capacity curves shown in Figure 13.8. Curve *B* is not reached by the sample. Heating from T_1 to T_2 along the path $C \cdots A$ now proceeds with the exotherm shown because of the release of frozen-in excess mobility characteristic of the high-temperature state *A* before quenching.

Naturally, whatever has been said about enthalpy and heat capacity applies to the corresponding-pair, volume, and thermal-expansion coefficient, just as indicated schematically on Figures 13.6 and 13.8. Detailed calorimetric observations of these delay phenomena are available for poly (vinyl acetate) and polystyrene [86] from Volkenshtein's laboratory.

13.2.4   Compressibility and Compression

The compressibility of glasses far below T_g is very nearly independent of the time scale of the experiment [43]. At such low temperatures, frequency dependence (anomalous dispersion) of compressibility is observed only in narrow temperature and frequency ranges, and is then associated with the movements of small mobile parts of the molecules in the glass. In the neighborhood of T_g, however, the large volume viscosity mentioned earlier makes compressibility a very sensitive function of the time scale of the compression experiment. Glass transition, as measured by the change from liquidlike to solidlike compressibility, can be observed at temperatures far in excess of the static value of T_g in high-frequency compression measurements [51].

Although this temperature range (around T_g) is of considerable interest for an improved understanding of the nature of the glass transition and for a study of relaxation phenomena, these phenomena are only of minor importance for the user of materials in their glassy state, who is mostly concerned with properties at $T < (T_g - 20°C)$. In that temperature region we cannot ignore the time scale of the compression experiment, but its effects are not large, and they diminish as we make T/T_g smaller.

The sensitivity of glass density, and therefore of its elastic properties, to thermal history makes it unsafe to compare the results obtained by different authors on different samples of a given—usually insufficiently characterized—material. The present evaluation of literature data has therefore more qualitative than quantitative character.

Within these qualifications, the data assembled in Tables 13.8 and 13.9

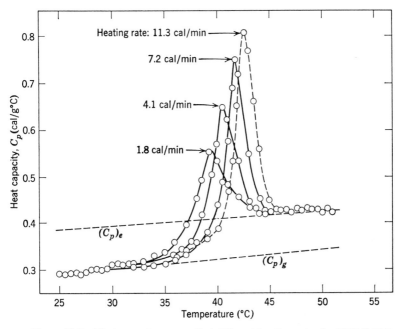

Figure 13.7   Heat capacity versus T at different heating rates for PVAC [86].

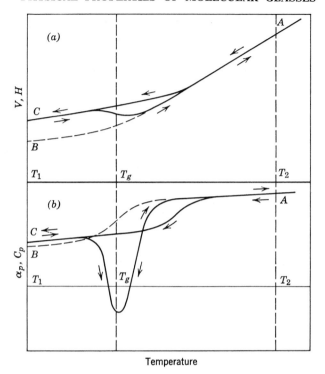

Figure 13.8   Effect of thermal history of thermodynamic response of volume and enthalpy (*a*), and of thermal expansion and heat capacity (*b*), showing maximum in the second-order properties. Heating cycle was started so soon after cooling that sample state was still at *C* instead of *B* as in Figure 13.6 (from [60]).

confirm the intuitive expectation that the elastic properties of glasses are of the same order as those of crystals of the same packing density—at least the fairly good agreement between the observed bulk moduli and those estimated by means of correlations developed for crystals (Section 4.3) encourages further pursuit of such a convenient conclusion. In the use of those correlations the ratio T/T_g was substituted for T/T_m, and the packing density ρ^*, of course, has the same meaning in both solids.

Not enough data are available for glasses of widely varying glass-transition temperature to establish the independent effects of ρ^* and T/T_g. The suggestion by Nanda and Simha [65] that the reduced bulk modulus is primarily a function of the packing density can be considered as confirmed only when one can test it with data for polymers of very different T_g. The close coupling between the temperature coefficient of the bulk modulus and thermal expansion implied by such a relation is inherent in the thermodynamics of solids and is discussed in detail later.

The effect of molecular structure on the bulk modulus of isotropic glasses

Table 13.8 Dynamic Elastic Moduli of Various Polymeric Glasses

Polymeric Glass	(T/T_g)	ρ^*	H_s/V_w $(10^{10}$ dyn/cm$^2)$	K^* (obs)	K^* (calc)[a]	σ'	G^*	E_0^{*}[b]
Polyethyl methacrylate	0.87	0.667	0.842	5.1[c]	5.3	0.353[c]	1.7[c]	9.8
Poly-n-butyl methacrylate	0.91	0.647	0.815	4.0_5[c]	4.5	0.395[c]	0.95[c]	—
Poly-iso-butyl methacrylate		0.635	0.756	5.8[c]		0.395[c]	1.3[c]	9.6
Polyvinyl acetate	0.94	0.638	0.90_5	2.0[d]	4.0		2.0[e]	—
Phenol formaldehyde	(0.90)	0.68	1.15	5.5[f]	5.6	0.28[e]	2.2[e]	5.6_5[e]

[a] (Calc) from (13.13).
[b] From E at 4°K [16] all at $\sim$6 KHz.
[c] R. Kono, *J. Phys. Soc. Japan* **16**, 1501 (1961); all at 2.5 MHz.
[d] From [37] at 50 to 1000 Hz.
[e] Y. Wada et al., *J. Phys. Soc. Japan* **14**, 1067 (1959); all at 33 KHz; here E is at 20°C.
  From [35] at 1 to 10 KHz.

is quite well represented by the reducing parameter $\Delta H_s/V_w$, at least over the comparatively narrow range of available data. This indicates that the bulk modulus (and the other elastic moduli) of isotropic glasses reflects primarily (to within a factor of $\frac{2}{3}$) the van der Waals interaction between molecules. High degrees of crosslinking, such as in phenolic resins, can therefore yield higher bulk moduli than expected from the general correlation.

The anisotropic force distribution around an individual repeating unit on a polymer chain, that is, the strong coupling to its chemically bonded neighbors and the weak van der Waals coupling to its nonbonded neighbors, is observed only indirectly when we deal with an isotropic glass, namely, that a factor of $\frac{3}{2}$ has to be used for normalization in comparison with crystals or glasses from nonpolymeric substances. Orientation of the molecules in a polymeric glass by drawing at $T < T_g$, leads to the expected anisotropy in elastic properties. The bulk modulus parallel to the draw direction $(K_{\parallel})$ is raised above that of the isotropic glass (K_0), and the modulus normal to the draw direction $(K_{\perp})$ is correspondingly reduced to $< K_0$. In general these three moduli are related by

$$\frac{1}{K_0} = \frac{2}{3K_{\perp}} + \frac{1}{3K_{\parallel}}. \qquad (13.12)$$

The compressibility measurements of Hennig [41] on cold-drawn poly-(methyl methacrylate) have confirmed these relations. The magnitude of the drawing effect on $K_{\parallel}$, etc. is closely related to measures of orientation, such as birefringence, but it cannot be predicted from a knowledge of the draw

Table 13.9 Static and Dynamic Elastic Moduli of Various Polymeric Glasses

Polymer	T/T_g	ρ^*	$H_s/V_w\,10^{10}$ (dyn/cm²)	K^* (Static)	K^* (Dynamic)	K^* (Calc)[a]	E^* (Static)	E^* (Dynamic)	E^* (Calc)[a]	G^* (Dynamic)	G^* (Calc)[a]
Polystyrene	0.79	0.633[b]	0.775	4.49[c] 4.67[g] 5.94[h]	5.12[d]	4.7	3.7[e] 4.0	4.83[f] 4.85[d]	(4.7) 3.5	1.75[d]	1.35
	0.90	0.627[b]		3.91[e] 4.02[e]	4.62[d]	4.0		4.40[g] 4.40[d]	(4.0) 3.0	1.07[l] 1.60[d]	1.2
Polymethyl methacrylate	0.77	0.668[b]	0.87	4.40[c] 4.70[g] 6.30[h]	5.2[j] 6.8[l]	6.0	3.5[m]	6.0[k] 6.2[m] 6.8[l,n] 7.2[d]	(6.0) 7.6	2.6[l] 2.56[d]	(2.1)
	0.87	0.661[b]	0.955	3.70[c] 4.0[g]		5.5	2.4[m]	5.4[m]	(5.4) 7.3		(1.8)
Polyvinyl chloride[q]	0.22					0.33	7.9[o]	6.6[p]	6.7		
	0.56			5.55[r]		0.84	3.9[o]		5.4		
	0.66					5.8	2.9[e]		(5.8) 5.0	1.4[d]	(2.0)
	0.83	0.642[b]		4.2[c] 4.4[r] 4.4[g]	6.2[s]	4.8	2.5[e] 2.5[t] 3.7[o]	2.5[t] 3.4[k]	(4.8) 4.3	1.0_5[d] 1.05[l]	(1.6)

[a] K^* calculated by means of (13.13); E^* and G^* calculated from K_0^* (calc) assuming $\sigma' = 0.33$ are put in parentheses; E^* (calc) is calculated by means of (13.9) and (13.12). Both calculations are based on $\rho_{(ref)}^*$ of column 3.

[b] From data of [31].

[c] From [48] calculated by using K_0 from the data of [38], assuming $K_1 = 11$.

[d] (e) of Table 13.8; at 33 KHz.

[e] H. W. Moll and W. J. Lefevre, *Ind. Eng. Chem.* **40**, 2172 (1949).

[f] M. Baccaredda et al., *Chim. Ind.* **28**, 561 (1956); at 30 KHz.

[g] Calculated from data of [38] with no assumption regarding the magnitude of K_1.

[h] P. J. Blatz, GALCIT-Rept. 61-26; calculated from Bridgeman's data by means of (13.8).

[i] A. V. Tobolsky et al., ONR Tech Rept RLT-61, July 1963.

[j] [34] at 1 Hz to 10 KHz.

[k] P. Heydemann and A. Zosel, *Acustica* **12**, 362 (1962) at 1 KHz.

[l] J. Gielesser and J. Koppelmann, *Koll.-Z.* **172**, 162 (1960); at 4 MHz.

[m] J. Koppelmann, *Physics of Noncrystalline Solids*, Wiley, New York, 1965, p. 255; the dynamic data refer to measurements at 10 kc/s, and the data taken at 10^{-4} Hz are here designated as static.

[n] [88].

[o] R. B. Scott, *Cryogenic Engineering* Van Nostrand, Princeton, New Jersey, 1959. Table 10.1.

[p] [16] at 6 KHz.

[q] The rather large differences between different samples of rigid PVC may be due to the plasticizing by unidentified types and amounts of stabilizing agents.

[r] P. Heydemann and H. D. Guicking *Kolloid-Z.* **193**, 16 (1963).

[s] (c) of Table 13.8, at 2.5 MHz.

[t] W. Sommer, *Kolloid-Z.* **167**, 97 (1959); dynamic value at 10 KHz static experiment to 10^5 sec.

ratio because the extent of orientation in glasses is a step function of the drawing rate and of the drawing temperature.

Available experimental evidence suggests that the pressure dependence of the bulk modulus of glasses is linear, to a good approximation, just as in the case of crystals, so that

$$K(P) = K_0 + K_1 P. \qquad (13.13)$$

It will be recalled that for most molecular crystals, $K_1 \approx 8 \pm 1$ (Section 4.4). Nanda and Simha [65] obtained a good representation of Hellwege's compression data by assuming $K_1 = 11$, the value commonly used for high-molecular-weight liquids, including elastomers. Least-squares evaluation of Hellwege's data by the present author yielded K_1 more nearly of the order 7 to 8 and varying with temperature. Similarly, Bridgman's high-pressure data on polystyrene, poly-(methyl methacrylate) and other glassy polymers are best represented with $K_1 \approx 7$ [11]. Needless to say, K_0 obtained by Nanda and Simha [65] differs somewhat from the value obtained without using their assumptions. Moreover, K_0 obtained from Bridgman's high-pressure data is not identical with that from Hellwege's lower-pressure compressions. The lack of characterization data for the samples used by the various authors precludes an assessment of the limits of validity of the linear approximation, (13.13), from these comparisons.

13.3 TENSILE AND SHEAR MODULUS

The similarity in packing density between glass and crystal suggests that not only the bulk modulus but also the other elastic moduli of molecular glasses are of the same order of magnitude as those of molecular crystals and that they should be correlatable by means of the reducing parameter for crystal properties, H_s/V_w, with ρ^* and T/T_g (instead of T/T_m) as the reduced state variables.

In order to avoid the complications caused by relaxation effects we first examine the elastic (tensile) moduli obtained at 4°K (by Sauer and co-workers) [21]. The modulus versus temperature curve of highly crystalline polymers becomes horizontal below 4°K, and thus $dE/dT \to 0$ at $T \to 0$°K, as demanded by the third law of thermodynamics. However, for several, if not most, glassy polymers very clearly $dE/dT < 0$ at 4°K, as shown in Figure 13.9. On the other hand, nothing can relax the requirement that $dE/dT \to 0$ at $T \to 0$°K. The likely continuation of the curve shown in Figure 13.9 is best pictured by using the more appropriate logarithmic temperature scale of Figure 13.10. (That this method of extrapolation of the low-temperature modulus curve is a necessary consequence of the third law of thermodynamics was pointed out to me by Dr. O. L. Anderson of Bell Telephone Laboratories, Murray Hill, New Jersey.)

Although there is a rather good correlation between the experimentally determined reduced modulus E_0^* at $0°K$ and the packing density at room temperature for semicrystalline polymers (with $\varphi_c \geq 0.5$) (Figure 13.11), the corresponding correlation for glasses is rather poor, as shown on the same figure. One cause may be the rather larger differences in thermal expansion among the glasses than among crystals, so that the ordering of the glasses by their density at $0°K$ may differ from their order at room temperature.

The correlation curve that can be drawn through the scatter of points with some justification is very much steeper than the anomalously flat curve linking the points for the semicrystalline polymers. The E_0^* versus ρ_{ref}^* curve

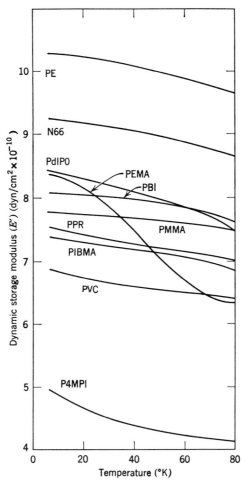

Figure 13.9   Dynamic storage modulus at 6–80°K for various polymers [100].

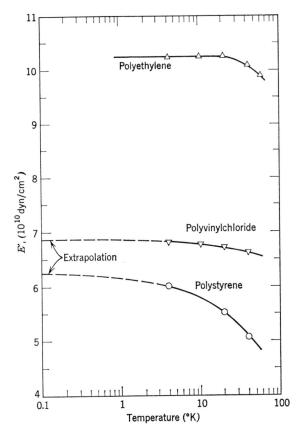

Figure 13.10 Extrapolation of Young's modulus of polymeric glasses polystyrene and polyvinylchloride toward $0°K$. Crystalline polyethylene entered for comparison [100].

of the simple molecular crystals parallels that for the glasses. The correlation curve for the glasses is

$$E_0^* \approx 85.9\rho_{ref}^* - 47.6, \qquad (13.14)$$

where ρ_{ref}^* is the packing density at room temperature or at $0.9T_g$ if $0.9T_g < 298°K$. Since no other elastic moduli have been measured at very low temperatures on these samples, the molecular structure effect on the low-temperature Poisson's ratio, and so on, cannot be assessed at present.

13.3.1 Effect of Temperature on Elastic Moduli

Because the phenomenological or thermodynamic relations between the elastic moduli and the variables of state of isotropic solids apply to glasses as well as to crystals, all of the equations of Section 4.1 are relevant here.

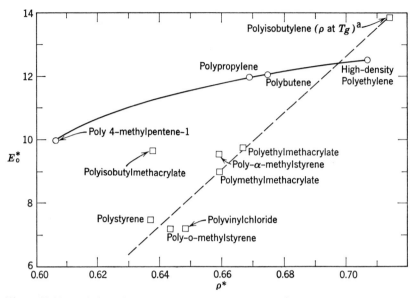

Figure 13.11   Relation of the reduced Young's modulus at 0°K (at 6 kc/sec) to the packing density at room temperature for (semi) crystalline and glassy polymers [4]. (*a*) From E. Butta and P. Sinsti, *Ric. Sci. II*, **2**, 362 (1962).

Specifically we can use (4.4) and (4.5), which relate the temperature co-efficient of the elastic moduli to the nearly universal pressure coefficient K_1 of the bulk modulus. The applicability of this argument and its limitations are illustrated by the experimental data assembled in Table 13.10. There the ratios α_E/α_v, α_K/α_v, and α_G/α_v are about of the expected order (6 to 10) for polystyrene and for polyvinyl acetate when the elastic modulus has been measured at high frequencies. The creep phenomena, which enter in "static" measurements, preclude the applicability of any equilibrium argument. Likewise, incidence of relaxation processes in the temperature (or pressure) and frequency range of interest actually changes the nature of the solid with temperature and thereby invalidates any treatment designed for simple solids. The deviation of PMMA and PVC from simple behavior should be attributed to their well-known relaxation processes near room temperature, as will be discussed later.

Because for most molecular, especially polymeric, glasses θ_D is of the order 120°K, the exponential term in (4.5) changes little in the practically important range $2\theta_D$ to $3\theta_D$, so that (4.5) becomes in that temperature range

$$K(T) \approx K_0(0) - \frac{2.5 C_v^s (K_1 - 1)^2 \cdot T}{V_0},$$

(13.15)

where, in the case of polymers, the lattice heat capacity C_v^s and the zero point volume refer to the repeating unit. The appropriate equation for Young's modulus should have E_0 in place of $K_0(0)$. The estimate of C_v^s is as undeveloped for glassy polymers as it is for crystalline polymers. One reason is the uncertainty of the number of external degrees of freedom (f) (including those due to internal rotation or torsional oscillation) per repeating unit.

Table 13.10 Temperature Coefficients of Elastic Moduli of Polymeric Glasses at $T < T_g$

Property[a]	Frequency	Polystyrene	PMMA	PVC	PVA
$10^4 \, \alpha_v(°K^{-1})$	—	1.9[b]	2.5[b]	2.0[c]	1.9[b]
$10^3 \, \alpha_h(°K^{-1})$	—	3.6[d]	3.1[e]	3.6[f]	—
$-\alpha_E/\alpha_v$	static	25[g]	35[h]	24[g]	—
	33 kHz	9[b]	18[b] (24 at 10 kHz)	30[i] (at 1 kHz)	—
	66 kHz	10.5[b]			
$-\alpha_G/\alpha_v$	33 kHz	8.4[b]	21[b]	—	10.5[b]
	1 MHz	10.5[b]	—	—	
$-\alpha_K/\alpha_v$	static	—	24[c]	24[c]	—
	33 kHz	12.6[b]	—	—	

[a] $\alpha_v \equiv (\partial \ln V/\partial T)_p$; $\alpha_h \equiv (\partial \ln C_p/\partial T)_p$; $\alpha_K \equiv (\partial \ln E/\partial T)_p$; $\alpha_G \equiv (\partial \ln G/\partial T)_p$; $\alpha_K \equiv (\partial \ln K_0/\partial T)_p$.
[b] (e) of Table 13.8.
[c] (c) of Table 13.1.
[d] [20].
[e] J. M. O'Reilly and F. E. Karasz, *Polymer Preprints* **6**, 731 (1965).
[f] S. Alford and M. Dole, *J. Am. Chem. Soc.* **77**, 4774 (1965).
[g] H. W. Moll and W. J. Lefevre, *Ind. Eng. Chem.* **40**, 2172 (1948).
[h] J. Koppelmann, Physics of Noncrystalline Solids, Conf. Delft, 1964, 255; 10^{-4} Hz is here taken as "static."
[i] P. Heydemann and A. Zosel, *Acustica* **12**, 363 (1962).

Hence a relation of the form

$$E^*(T) = E_0^* \left[1 - \psi\left(\frac{fRT}{H_s}\right) \right] \tag{13.16}$$

provides only qualitative guidance, and we would prefer to replace $\psi(fRT/H_s)$ with $\psi'(T/T_g)$. A plot of tensile modulus data (determined at fixed time scale) versus T/T_g (Figure 13.12) suggests that there may be a common function ψ', at least in the practically important range $T < 0.9T_g$.

In that range we find empirically that

$$E^*(T) = E_0^* \left[1 - \frac{b}{E_0^2} \frac{T}{T_g} \right], \tag{13.17}$$

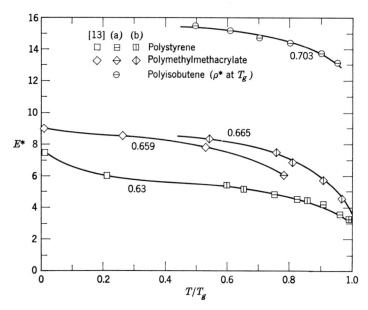

Figure 13.12   Young's modulus (at $\sim$10 kc/sec) of several glasses as a function of T/T_g and of room-temperature packing density (parameter). Note the strong effect of density with the two curves for PMMA (a) From E. Butta and P. Sinsti, *Ric. Sci. II*, **2**, 362 (1962); (b) Y. Wada et al., *J. Phys. Soc. Japan* **14**, 1066 (1959).

where the dimensionless constant $b \approx 30$. Qualitatively, this result is in accord with the expectation from (13.16), but there is no obvious rationale for the E_0^{-2} coefficient.

Because of the extreme sensitivity of E_0^* to packing density, we can expect tolerable prediction of the tensile modulus by this correlation only if the density of the sample is known. This being rarely the case, we must assume a "typical" density for the sample and are likely to make somewhat poor predictions as borne out by the comparisons in Tables 13.8 and 13.9.

The rough correlation of reduced bulk moduli adapted from crystals,

$$K_0^* = 31.63\rho_{\text{ref}}^* - 10.55 - 6.0\left(\frac{T}{T_g}\right), \tag{13.18}$$

contains the temperature coefficient explicitly in the last term, since ρ_{ref}^* is the packing density at room temperature, unless $0.9T_g < 293°\text{K}$, when ρ_{ref}^* is taken from ρ at $0.9T_g$. The examples in Tables 13.8 and 13.9 show that this temperature coefficient is surprisingly correct, remembering that it has been carried over unchanged from crystals except for the basically unjustifiable replacement of T_m by T_g.

A more self-consistent approach is to correlate $d\mathbf{M}/dT$ with a closely related property exhibiting the same time dependence, namely, to follow Heijboer's suggestion[1] to relate this temperature coefficient to the mechanical-energy absorption at the same frequency at which the elastic modulus has been determined. Specifically, he found that in frequency–temperature domains in which no relaxation process is taking place,

$$\frac{d \ln G'(\omega)}{dT} = 1 \times 10^{-3} + 0.1 \,\overline{\tan \delta} \,(^{\circ}\mathrm{K}^{-1}), \qquad (13.19)$$

where $\overline{\tan \delta}$ is the average loss tangent (background loss) in the temperature region of interest at the *frequency* (ω). The physical basis of this relation is quite obvious. At present, $\overline{\tan \delta}$ is also quite well correlated with molecular structure (see Section 13.5) but is not correlated with any other physical property. The implication is, of course, that polymeric glasses containing elements that are mobile at $T \leq T$ (obs) (and at the observation frequency) will exhibit larger temperature coefficients of elastic moduli than those that are very rigid. The relative behavior of the coefficients of (PMMA and PVC) versus (PS and PVA) in Table 13.10 are in excellent agreement with this conclusion. Hence a measurement of the modulus and damping decrement at a single frequency and temperature can provide the temperature coefficient of the modulus as well, provided a relaxation transition has been avoided.

The incidence of relaxation processes at a given frequency and temperature leads to sigmoid-shaped steps in the elastic modulus versus temperature curves. The height of the step is proportional to the height of the corresponding loss (tan δ) peak, and the temperature range over which the drop takes place is determined by the width of the loss peak (on the temperature scale). Once it is possible to predict the height of the secondary loss peaks in glasses (tan $\delta_{\max}$) from the energy of rotational isomerization (see Section 13.5) and/or from other well-defined molecular properties, the trend of the modulus with temperature (at a given frequency) should be predictable from molecular-structure information.

Poisson's ratio (σ') of molecular crystals had been found to exhibit a fairly monotonical trend up with increasing temperature from $0^{\circ}\mathrm{K}$ to T_{m}. In principle, of course, σ' for glasses rises from some low value to $\frac{1}{2}$ at T_g. However, in actual practice we find σ' of glasses to vary very little over long ranges of temperature as shown by the curves in Figure 13.13. It is not obvious at present what determines the magnitude of σ' of various glasses as is evident from an inspection of Table 13.8. There is just an indication that crosslinking depresses σ', but the intuitive expectation of a relation to hardness of the glass at equal T/T_g is not borne out by observation.

[1] Heijboer, *Physics of Non-crystalline Solids*, Wiley, New York, 1965, p. 231.

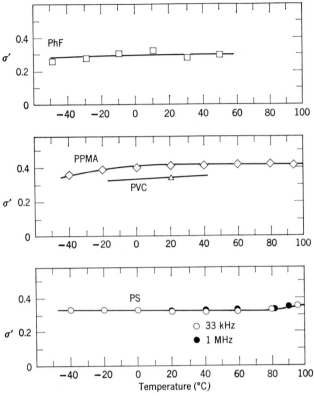

Figure 13.13   Real part of Poisson's ratio calculated from E' and G' at 33 kHz and from K' and G' at 1 MHz. PhF = phenol formaldehyde resin (from Y. Wada et al., *J. Phys. Soc. Japan* **14**, 1066 (1959). PVC from Figure 13.14 and elsewhere).

All of the elastic moduli, including σ', must always be specified in terms of the time scale of the experiment, aside from the obvious definitions of the sample's thermal and mechanical history. Typical trends of moduli with frequency are shown in Figure 13.14.

Little attention is generally devoted to Poisson's ratio, and very little thought given to its intentional modification by chemical or other means. Yet its magnitude determines the quality of stress transfer between embedded filaments in composites. The analysis by Weitsman and Sadowsky [98] has shown that the efficiency of stress transfer between adjacent filaments decreases critically when the Poisson's ratio of the resin matrix increases above 0.3. The meager data available to date show $\sigma' < 0.3$ as having been obtained only with thermoset resin [80]. Intuition confirms that the high rigidity associated with very low values of σ' may be attainable only at very high crosslink density. Poisson's ratio, just like rigidity, of organic glasses, changes with the time of stress application, as has been shown analytically as well as experimentally by Theocaris and Hadjijoseph [93], whose curves of σ' versus t are shown in Figure 13.15. In that case, stress transfer deteriorates with prolonged stress applications to a filament–resin system. Further work is certainly warranted. Care should be taken not to determine σ' on oriented (anisotropic) polymer, because the resulting data can be completely meaningless if not suitably analysed.

The above-mentioned time effect is, of course, directly related to the stress relaxation, the E, G, or V versus time curves, discussed earlier. A theoretical and experimental study by Theocaris [92] demonstrated the existence of a very convenient formal connection between the lateral contraction ratio (Poisson's ratio) at time t, $\sigma'(t)$, and the elastic moduli at time t:

$$K(t) = \xi[\tfrac{1}{2} - \sigma'(t)], \tag{13.20}$$

$$E(t) = 6\xi[\tfrac{1}{2} - \sigma'(t)]^2, \tag{13.21}$$

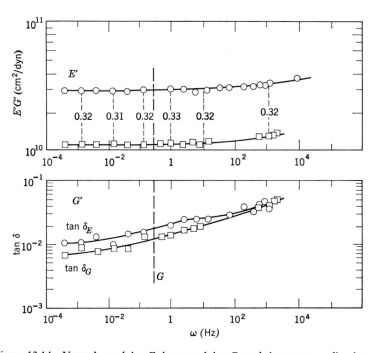

Figure 13.14 Young's modulus E shear modulus G, and the corresponding loss tangents of polyvinylchloride (plasticized with 10% dioctylphthalate) as function of frequency at 20°C. The numbers between lines G' and E' indicate σ' [from J. Koppelmann, *Rheol. Acta* **1**, 20 (1958)].

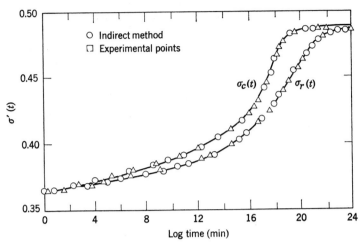

Figure 13.15 Typical master curves for the lateral contraction ratio (Poisson's ratio) σ' at time t (for an epoxy polymer) obtained in creep $[\sigma'_c(t)]$ and in relaxation $[\sigma'_r(t)]$ [93]. Reference temperature: 298°K.

where the proportionality constant ξ is a property of the material and can, at present, only be obtained by experiment. Typical numerical values are for polyisobutylene, 45×10^{10} dyn/cm²; for polymethyl methacrylate, 85.3×10^{10} dyn/cm²; and for a cold set epoxy resin, 11×10^{10} dyn/cm². Having been obtained from time–temperature superposition curves, these constants are independent of temperature by definition.

13.3.2   Effect of Pressure on Elastic Moduli

The effect of temperature on the elastic properties of glasses has received primary attention because of its great practical importance. The effect of pressure on Young's modulus of glassy polystyrene and poly(methyl methacrylate) (PMMA) has just been reported by Holliday and Mann [59]. Thermodynamic reasoning predicts

$$\left(\frac{\partial E}{\partial P}\right)_T = -\left(\frac{V}{K}\right)\left(\frac{\partial E}{\partial V}\right)_T \qquad (13.22)$$

which, for the case of $E \approx K$, makes the right-hand side approximately equal to 2γ, where γ is the Grüneisen constant and thus equal to K_1 (see eq. 4.4). This means that pressure should raise the modulus by an increment that is of the order of magnitude of the applied pressure. Hence a pressure of $0.01E$ should raise Young's modulus of polystyrene at room temperature by about 10%.

The experimental data for polystyrene in Figure 13.16 are too scattered to permit recognition of such a small change in Young's modulus. Particularly noteworthy is the shape of the stress–strain curves in Figure 13.16 because they show that high hydrostatic pressures raise the ductility of this glassy substance appreciably. Moreover, the elongation up to the yield point is reported as fully recoverable within seconds or minutes at most [59]. A more substantial increase in Young's modulus with pressure can be expected when the pressure raises a (relaxational) transition temperature from below (or at) to above the temperature of measurement, as has been observed with PMMA [59]. The magnitude of this rise can in first approximation be taken as equal to the difference in atmospheric pressure modulus below and above the transition temperature.

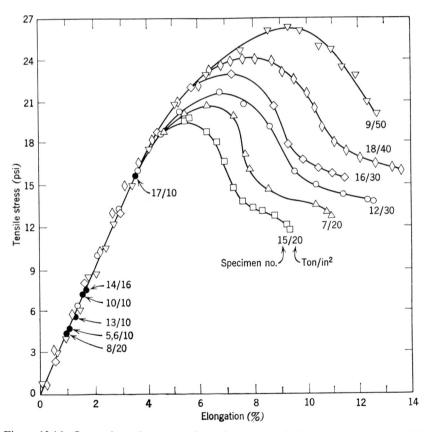

Figure 13.16 Stress–elongation curves for polystyrene under hydrostatic pressure [59].

Table 13.11 Elastic (Tensile) Modulus of Various Unoriented Polymers with Rings in Their Backbone Chain

Repeating Unit	T (°C)	T_g/T	ρ^*	E^*	$H_s/V_w\,10^{10}$ (dyn/cm²)
(aromatic dihydrazide repeating unit)	25		0.736	14	1.39
(aromatic diamide-diamide repeating unit)	25	0.40[b]	0.701	11	1.1
(aromatic amide repeating unit) (all meta)	25	0.44[b]	0.696	10	1.1
(poly-1,3,4-oxadiazole / triazole repeating unit)	25			~10	
(bisphenol A polycarbonate repeating unit)	25	0.75	0.638	2.5	1.0
(polyimide repeating unit)	23 / 200	0.36 / 0.57		2.12 / 1.34	1.27 / 1.27
(poly-p-xylylene repeating unit)	25 / 200	0.845 / 1.34	<.69	2.7 / 0.2	0.87_5

[a] F. T. Wallenberger, *Angew. Chem. Intl. Ed.* **3**, 460 (1964).
[b] T/T_m.
[c] J. Preston, *Polymer Preprints* **6**, 42 (1965).
[d] H. Schnell, *Chemistry and Physics of Polycarbonates*, Interscience, New York, 1964.
[e] W. F. Gorham, *Polymer Preprints* **6**, 73 (1965).

13.3.3 Summary of Relations Between Elastic Moduli and Molecular Structure

The admittedly very approximate correlations of elastic moduli of molecular glasses presented in this section lead to the conclusion that packing density, cohesive energy density (as H_s/V_w), and the glass-transition temperature are (in the order given) the major factors that determine the numerical magnitude of the elastic moduli. All three factors are interrelated. The packing density reflects primarily the simplicity and regularity of the molecular structure, that is, the ease with which neighboring molecules can be fitted side-by-side even under conditions of very low molecular mobility. The steepness of the relation between the tensile modulus and packing density shown in Figure 13.11 is also apparent from the data of the recently developed polymeric glasses with aromatic rings in the backbone chain in Table 13.11. Some of the inconsistencies on this table are probably related to the exploratory nature of the work reported, that is, to the fact that the data often represent the properties of the *only* rather than of the *purest* (best) sample made.

The power of the reducing parameter H_s/V_w is not as much in evidence among the glassy as among the crystalline polymers because the latters' inclusion of polytetrafluoroethylene provides a fourfold range of H_s/V_w, whereas among glasses the range covers only a factor of 2. The dependence of the absolute magnitude of T_g on cohesive energy and molecular flexibility has been discussed earlier.

If the supposition holds that the thermal history of the sample is reflected in its packing density, only two factors have been left out of consideration in the correlation: the effect of relaxation transitions—at each of which the elastic moduli make a step change—and the effect of the time scale of the deformation imposed. These phenomena will always exercise a blurring effect on any correlation attempt, so that the best we can expect from a generalized scheme is rough guidance regarding the manner in which given structural elements may determine the elastic properties of the molecular glass.

All of the above discussion dealt with isotropic glasses. Glasses composed of polymers can be made elastically anisotropic by drawing at $T < T_g$. The change in elastic moduli with extension correlates well with independent measures of orientation, such as birefringence [40], but not with draw ratio, because of the great sensitivity of the final moduli to the applied drawing rate. Moreover, over the investigated range of draw ratios (<8) all the moduli of a drawn glass remain connected by the relations of classical elasticity theory [62], [70]. However, the absence of a simple molecular mechanism for extension of amorphous polymers precluded development of the kind of upper–limit estimate for the modulus of drawn fibers which has been quite successful for (semi) crystalline polymers [15] (Section 4.5.3). See also section for related orientation effects.

13.3.4   Elastic Moduli of Homogeneous Mixtures

The elastic moduli of mixtures of low-molecular-weight glass-forming systems have apparently not been investigated. Most polymers are not miscible with each other. Hence only two kinds of mixtures have been studied, copolymers and plasticizer–polymer blends. The elastic moduli of the copolymers which have been investigated fall in the expected range between that of the homopolymers [4], [83] and are therefore of little interest. However, the elastic properties of several glass-forming homogeneous blends of plasticizers and polymers differ sufficiently from the expected pattern to be worthy of attention.

Since plasticizers reduce T_g, they should also reduce the elastic modulus at a fixed temperature, as indeed generally observed (Figure 13.17). One usually finds a single common curve or narrow band of the (reduced) elastic moduli of plasticized glasses on the generalized temperature scale $T/T_{g(12)}$, where $T_{g(12)}$ is the glass transition temperature of the plasticized glass on the time scale (frequency) of the elastic modulus measurement.

Strong deviations from this simple behavior are noted in Figure 13.18, where the plasticizer is seen to raise the elastic modulus of polystyrene at low temperatures, even though the high-temperature trend is as expected. Shift of the plasticizer concentration level of Figure 13.17 to the range 0 to 10% produces a similar phenomenon in polyvinyl chloride (PVC), except that now the temperature range of the anomalous modulus rise is in the practically important zone near 20°C, as shown in Figure 13.19. The striking variation of the Young's modulus of PVC with plasticizer concentration at a fixed temperature and frequency is shown in Figure 13.20 for three different plasticizers. The bulk modulus of PVC also goes through a maximum at 5 to 10% dioctyl phthalate concentration. However, as seen in Figure 13.20, the maximum is rather more shallow than that of the tensile modulus curves. Hence Poisson's ratio has a sharp minimum at the tensile modulus maximum.

Similar maxima in the Young's modulus versus plasticizer concentration curves have been obtained on various polycarbonates, as shown in Figure 13.20b. On the other hand T_g decreases uniformly with increasing plasticizer concentration in all systems studied so far. The packing density of the polymer is the only equilibrium property which also passes through such a maximum. Unfortunately, this very important property has not been examined in all cases. Yet, it may contain the key to the entire phenomenon of "antiplasticization."

Here it is useful to recollect that the elastic modulus at temperature T is composed of two terms: one is the zero-point modulus, which in reduced form depends primarily on the packing density; the other is the (negative)

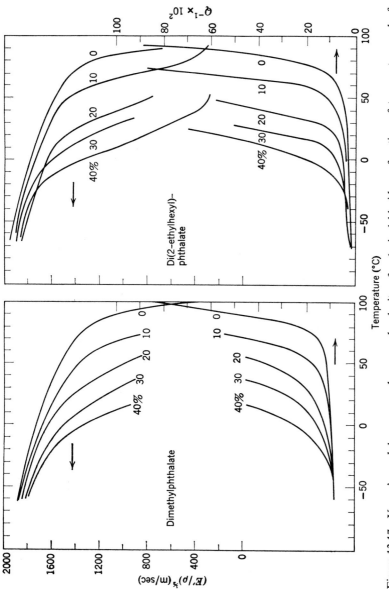

Figure 13.17 Young's modulus expressed as sound velocity of polyvinylchloride as function of temperature and of plasticizer concentration [8].

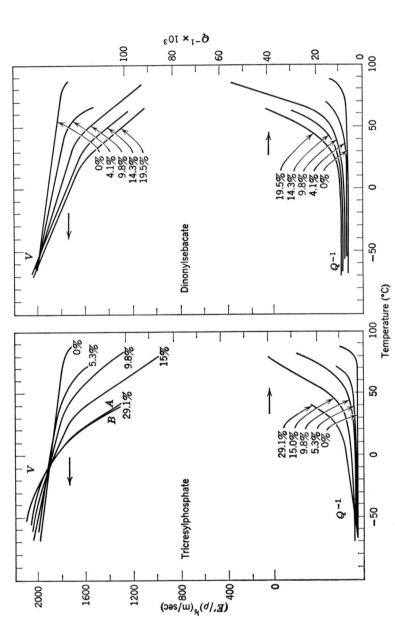

Figure 13.18 Young's modulus expressed as sound velocity of polystyrene as function of temperature and of plasticizer concentration [8].

temperature function, the magnitude of which is largely determined by the contribution of external degrees of freedom, including those due to internal rotation or torsional oscillation, to lattice heat capacity, or—equivalently— to the background mechanical energy absorption, as seen in (13.19).

In the introductory section of this chapter it has been shown that the density of a glass is substantially smaller than that of the equilibrium liquid at the same temperature because the high bulk viscosity prevents attainment of the equilibrium density. Addition of small amounts of plasticizer to the glass loosens the glassy matrix just enough to permit a closer approach to equilibrium density at a given temperature $T < T_g$, provided the system is cooled slowly. Plots of the resulting contraction versus diluent concentration (φ_1) show a maximum, the height and corresponding $\varphi_{1(\max)}$ of which are the larger the higher θ_L. This means that the effect can be maximized by choice of diluents composed of large and stiff molecules. Typical maximum contractions range from 0.5 to 1.5% for the usual aliphatic to aromatic plasticizers in vinyl polymers [10a], [46b], to 2.5% for tetrachloroterphenyl in polycarbonate [46a].

Although in the limit of high dilution (discussed in Sections 8.52 and 13.2.1) the partial specific volume of the polymer equals the melt density (except for a small thermodynamically determined excess volume increment), the above-mentioned contraction of the slightly diluted (plasticized) glass is generally not an equilibrium phenomenon and therefore not directly predictable. From a consideration of Figures 13.3 and 13.4 we can say that maintenance of the highest possible packing density of plasticized resins requires that θ_L of the plasticizer be as high as is consistent with a sufficiently low viscosity, that is, a sufficiently low glass transition temperature. A glance at Table 13.2 shows how this may be accomplished.

The effect of the plasticizer on the temperature coefficient of the elastic moduli through its effect on the mechanical energy absorption background is apparent from the curves marked Q^{-1} in Figures 13.17 and 13.18. The striking suppression of the background value of the equivalent tan δ by the small amounts of plasticizer and the more effective suppression by the stiffer molecule (tricresyl phosphate) than the more flexible dioctyl sebacate is shown in Figures 13.19c,d. The resulting differences in the level and temperature slope of the elastic modulus is shown in Figures 13.19a,b.

When the polymer exhibits a secondary relaxation transition in that temperature range, the rise in packing density generally leads to a decrease in relaxation strength, that is, of mechanical loss tan δ [12]. The connected decrease in the temperature coefficient of the elastic moduli is apparent in Figure 13.19.

Only a systematic experimental and theoretical examination of the effects of plasticizers on packing density and on heat capacity or $\overline{\tan \delta}$ can convert this qualitative discussion to quantitative predictability. Yet the qualitative results suggest that one may be able to handle much or all of the interesting problem of antiplasticization without appeal to specific molecular interactions between polymer and diluent.

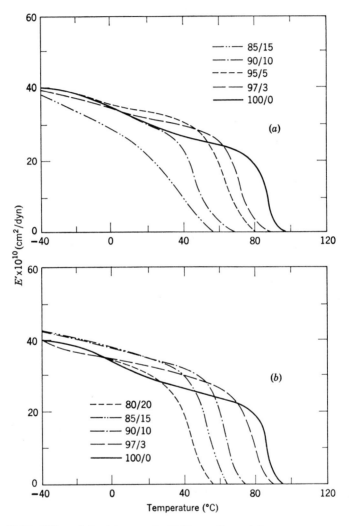

Figure 13.19   Effect of plasticizer on the 10-Hz tensile modulus versus temperature curves of polyvinylchloride [12]. (a) Plasticizer: dioctyl sebacate; (b) plasticizer: tricresylphosphate parameter %PVC/% plasticizer. (c), (d) Effect of plasticizer on the ∼10-Hz mechanical loss d (tan δ) of polyvinylchloride, parameters same as in (a) and (b): (c) tricresylphosphate; (d) dioctyl sebacate.

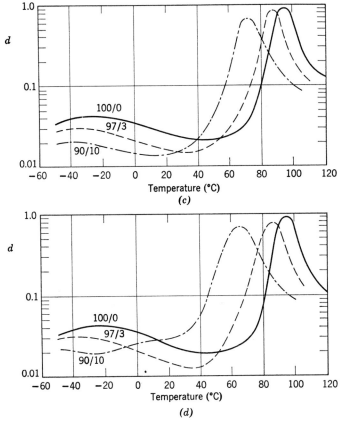

Figure 13.19 (*continued*)

13.3.5 Elastic Moduli of Heterogeneous Mixtures

The nonspecific relations between the concentration of a randomly distributed heterogeneous phase [2] and the elastic moduli of the mixture developed by Hashin and Shtrikman [36] discussed in Section 4.5.5 are applicable to isotropic glassy solids. Two kinds of heterogeneous glassy solids are of technological interest: those for which $G_2/G_1 < 1$ and those for which $G_2/G_1 > 1$. Namely, for G_2/G_1 and $K_2/K_1 < 1$,

$$\frac{G - G_1}{G_1} = \frac{1 - \varphi_1}{(G_2/G_1 - 1) + \varphi_1 f_1(\sigma_1')},\tag{13.23}$$

$$\frac{K - K_1}{K_1} = \frac{1 - \varphi_1}{(K_2/K_1 - 1)^{-1} + \varphi_1 f_2(\sigma_1')},\tag{13.24}$$

where $G - G_1 < 0$, $K - K_1 < 0$, and the functions of Poisson's ratio, σ' of the continuous glassy phase [1] are:

σ_1':	0	0.25	0.33	0.40	0.50
$f_1(\sigma_1')$:	0.534	0.488	0.467	0.443	—
$f_2(\sigma_1')$:	0.333	0.455	0.500	0.540	0.600,

and

$$E = \frac{9KG}{6K + 3G}.$$ (13.25)

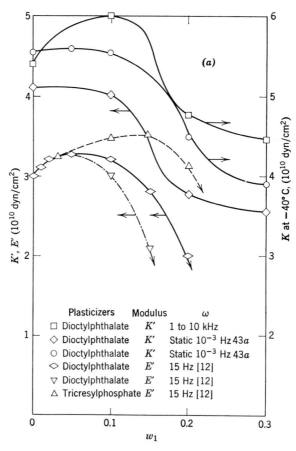

Figure 13.20 (a) Effect of various plasticizers on the tensile and bulk moduli of polyvinyl-chloride, at 20°C; w_1 = weight fraction of plasticizer. (b) Effect of plasticizer composed of rigid cyclic molecules on the tensile modulus of two polycarbonates at 20°C. [from W. J. Jackson and J. R. Caldwell, *Adv. Chem. (ACS)* **48**, 185 (1965)].

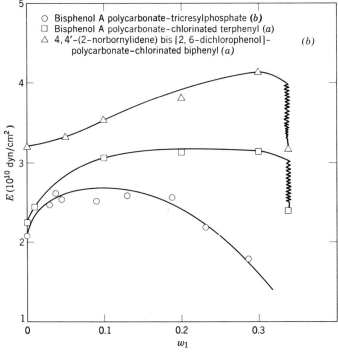

Figure 13.20 (*continued*)

This case is represented by elastomer dispersions in glassy matrices which are commonly employed to achieve high impact resistance at a minimum loss in tensile or shear modulus. Since in that case, $G_2/G_1 < 10^{-3}$, the curve for $G_a/G_c = 0$ on Figure 4.9 should convey a reasonably accurate measure of the drop in modulus to be expected for various volume fractions of dispersed elastomer phase. Quantitative comparisons are somewhat uncertain in the system because the concentration of dispersed phase can be determined only approximately.

Stable dispersions of small liquid droplets in polymer glasses can be produced by rapid quenching of homogeneous solutions of those liquids in the melt which are known to be insoluble in the glass [46]. The elastic properties of the resulting dispersions have been measured only in temperature ranges in which the liquid droplets had been frozen.

The elastic moduli of heterogeneous systems composed of noninteracting isomeric or spherical particles dispersed in (polymeric) glasses with $G_2/G_1 > 1$, are always larger than that of the pure glass because of the fact that most of the deformation takes place in the glass. If $G_2/G_1 > 10^3$, the strain multiplication e_L/e_m from the observed macroscopic strain (e_m) to the local strain (e_L) in the glassy material can be obtained from simple fluid–mechanical considerations as a function of the volume fraction (φ_2) of hard dispersoid

$$e_L/e_m = 1 + 2.5\varphi_2 + 14.1\varphi_2{}^2 + \cdots,$$

or a similar relation [35]. However, when, as more usual in a glassy matrix, $G_2/G_1 < 10^2$, the interaction of shear and compression must be considered, and the Hashin–Shtrikman [36] equations should represent the data quite well. These equations can be put into the convenient form

$$\frac{G - G_1}{G_1} = \frac{\varphi_2}{((G_2/G_1) - 1)^{-1} + (1 - \varphi_2)f_3(\sigma_1')}, \qquad (13.26)$$

$$\frac{K - K}{K} = \frac{\varphi_2}{((K_2/K_1) - 1)^{-1} + (1 - \varphi_2)f_4(\sigma_1')}, \qquad (13.27)$$

$$E_H = \frac{9KG}{6K + 3G}, \qquad (13.28)$$

where $f_3(\sigma_1')$ and $f_4(\sigma_1')$ are functions of Poisson's ratio σ_1':

σ_1':	0.20	0.25	0.33	0.45	0.50
$f_3(\sigma_1')$:	0.515	0.506	0.500	0.486	0.480
$r_4(\sigma_1')$:	0.715	0.757	0.833	0.950	1.00

and, as before, subscripts 1 and 2 represent glassy matrix and hard particle, respectively. That data in Figure 13.21 indicate quite good agreement between observation and calculation for the case of NaCl particles in glass

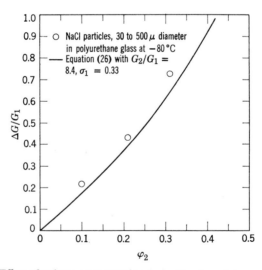

Figure 13.21   Effect of volume concentration (φ_2) of hard particles on the shear modulus of a polymeric glass [F. R. Schwarzl et al., *4th Intl. Congr. Rheol.* **3**, 241 (1963)].

polyurethane prepared from polypropylene ether glycol and toluene diiso-cyanate. The choice of $\sigma_1' = 0.33$ by the authors was quite arbitrary. A some-what higher value of σ' would have yielded yet better agreement. Upward deviations become noticeable at $\varphi_2 \geq 0.4$, possibly due to particle–particle interaction. According to Schwarzl and co-workers [85], [97], the experi-mental data were somewhat more closely reproduced by the rather more complicated theory of van der Poel, which considers the elastic properties of the hard dispersed phase as well.

The elastic properties of the commercially far more important dispersions of stiff fibers in the glassy resin matrix are rather more difficult to estimate. For the case $E_2/E_1 < 10$ and for the trivial, if useful, case of loading parallel to the direction of oriented infinitely long fibers,

$$E_{12} = \varphi_2 E_2 + (1 - \varphi_2)E_1. \tag{13.29}$$

In the more general case, the contribution of fibers to the elastic moduli depends on the strength of the interface bond, on the length/diameter (l/d) ratio of the fibers and on the angle between fiber axis and the stress axis. Assuming strong interfacial bonding and $l/d > 100$ (opinions vary between 10 and 1000), we can estimate the elastic moduli of fiber–glassy resin com-posites by means of the relations given in Table 13.12. For further details the reader is referred to papers by Hashin [37] and to Chapters 2 and 5 of *Com-posite Materials*,[1] L. Holliday, ed., Elsevier Houston, Texas, 1966.

13.4 THERMAL CONDUCTIVITY

The striking dissimilarity between the thermal conductivity versus tem-perature curves of molecular glasses and crystals shown in Figure 13.22 could not have been predicted from their bulk properties. The cause of the difference must be sought in the peculiar effect of a disordered state on phonon transport.

A coherent treatment of the problem has now been presented by Reese [72] based largely on the theoretical work by Klemens [52]. He considers three separate modes of thermal conduction: by longitudinal vibrations of the glassy solid (λ_L), by three-dimensional vibrations of the solid (λ_3), largely governed by the van der Waals coupling of neighboring molecules, and by one-dimensional vibrations along the polymer chain (λ_1). Then in detail

$$\lambda_L = \frac{k^2}{3\pi h} \frac{A}{a} Ty^2 \int_0^\infty \frac{e^x}{(e^x - 1)^2} \frac{x^2}{x^2 + y^2} dx, \tag{13.30}$$

where $A \cdot a$ is the mean free (phonon) path for longitudinal modes, A being a

[1] See (a) in Table 13.12.

Table 13.12 The Relationship of Composite Properties to Fiber Orientation Including the Poisson Effect

	v_c	σ_c	E_c	ω_2	G_c
Reinforcement only, parallel fibers Force ∥ fibers	v_r	$E_r k(\epsilon_x + v_r \epsilon_y) + E_f V_f \epsilon_x$	$E_r(1 - V_f) + E_f V_f$	$1 - V_f + n V_f$	$(1 - V_f)G_r$
Force ⊥ fibers	$\dfrac{kv_r}{k + nV_f}$	$E_r k(\epsilon_x + v_r \epsilon_y)$	$E_r k(1 - v_r v_c)$	$k(1 - v_r v_c)$	$(1 - V_f)G_r$
Two equal groups of parallel fibers parallel and perpendicular to applied force, respectively	$\dfrac{kv_r}{k + \frac12 nV_f}$	$E_r k(\epsilon_x + v_r \epsilon_y) + \frac12 E_f V_f \epsilon_x$	$E_r k(1 - v_r v_c) + \frac12 E_f V_f$	$k + \frac12 nV_f - kv_r v_c$	$(1 - V_f)G_r$
Two equal groups of parallel fibers each forming angles $\phi = \pi/4$ with force	$\dfrac{kv_r + \frac14 nV_f}{k + \frac14 nV_f}$	$E_r k(\epsilon_x + v_r \epsilon_y) + \frac14 E_f V_f(\epsilon_x + \epsilon_y)$	$E_r k(1 - v_r v_c) + \frac14 E_f V_f(1 - v_r)$	$k + \frac14 nV_f - v_c(kv_r + \frac14 nV_f)$	$(1 - V_f)G_r + \frac14 V_f E_f$
Four or more equal groups of fiber, Force ∥ to or at half angle between two adjacent groups Fibers randomly orientated	$\dfrac{kv_r + \frac18 nV_f}{k + \frac38 nV_f}$	$E_r k(\epsilon_x + v_r \epsilon_y) + E_f V_f(\frac38 \epsilon_r + \frac18 \epsilon_y)$	$E_r k(1 - v_r v_c) + E_f V_f(\frac38 - \frac18 v_c)$	$k + \frac38 nV_f - v_c(kv_r + \frac18 nV_f)$	$(1 - V_f)G_r + \frac18 V_f E_f$

[a] Reproduced from *Composite Materials*, L. Holliday, ed. Elsevier, Houston, Texas, 1966. Legend: v = Poisson's ratio; σ = stress; ϵ = strain; E = Young's modulus; G = shear modulus; $n = E_f/E_r$; $\omega_2 = E_c/E_r$; $k = V_f/(1 - v_r^2)$; V_f = volume fraction of fibers; subscripts: f = fiber, r = resin, c = composite, x = stress direction parallels fiber axis, y = stress direction normal to fiber axis.
[b] The relations given should be considered as rough approximations. Because this is an area of rapid development the reader is advised to obtain more quantitative guidance from current issues of the *Journal of Composite Materials*, Technomic Publishing Co, Stamford, Connecticut.

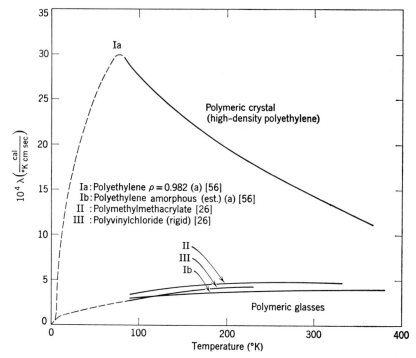

Figure 13.22 Comparison of the thermal conductivity of polymeric glasses (a) K. Eiermann, *Kolloid-Z.* **180**, 163 (1962).

pure number and a the average distance between vibrating units; $x = hv/kT = \theta_x/T$, $v =$ characteristic frequency of longitudinal vibrations (the entire integral being obtainable from the low temperature heat capacity data); $y^2 = (T_0/T)^3$, T_0 is a measure of the coupling between longitudinal and transverse vibrations and seems to be of the same order for most glassy polymers, $7°K$; k, h are the Boltzmann and Planck constants, respectively.

For the three-dimensional vibrations

$$\lambda_2 = \tfrac{1}{3}u_3C_3Ba, \qquad (13.31)$$

and for the one-dimensional vibrations

$$\lambda_1 = f(\alpha)u_1C_1\Lambda_p, \qquad (13.32)$$

where the transverse velocity $u_3 \approx (G/\rho)^{1/2}$ [using the high-frequency value of $G(T)$]. $C_3 =$ heat capacity associated with the low-frequency translational modes of lattice points (neighboring nonbonded molecule segments); $Ba =$ mean free phonon path for transverse modes; $f(\alpha)$ is a pure number that depends on the angle α between the direction of heat flow and the orientation of the polymer chain [for random orientation of the latter $f(\alpha) = \tfrac{1}{3}$]; the velocity of one-dimensional vibration can probably be approximated as $u_1 \approx (E_p/\rho_w)^{\frac{1}{2}}$, where E_p = spectroscopic elastic modulus of polymer molecules, enumerated in Table 4.5, and ρ_w = density of the molecule = M/V_w; C_1 = heat capacity associated with the one-dimensional vibrations frequencies (acoustic modes along the chain); and the phonon mean free path along the polymer backbone Λ_p may be identified with the persistence length defined in Section 10.6 and calculated for $T = T_g$.

The still undetermined constants appear to be of the following order of magnitude: $a \approx [M_{(u)}/N_A \rho l_{(u)}]^{\frac{1}{2}}$, where $M_{(u)}$, $l_{(u)}$ are molal weight and projected chain length per repeat unit; for PMMA or PS, $a \approx 7$ Å. The characteristic temperature θ_3 (corresponding to C_3) might be approximated by $\theta_3 \approx 2 \times 10^{-10} [N_A/V_w(u)]^{\frac{1}{3}} [\Delta H_s(u)/M(u)]^{\frac{1}{2}}$. The frequencies characteristic of the longitudinal acoustic modes are not yet available from independent measurements, but must be established by fitting the low-temperature heat-capacity data of the glass, as outlined by Reese [72].

Finally, combining the three conductivities according to Eiermann's network model [27], we obtain

$$\lambda = \tfrac{1}{3}\lambda_1 + \tfrac{2}{3}(\lambda_L + \lambda_3), \tag{13.33}$$

where the λ_1 term dominates the high-temperature ($\tfrac{1}{3}\theta_1 < T < T_g$) and the other two terms the low-temperature ($T < \theta_3$) region. A typical example, calculated by Reese [72] is shown in Figure 13.23.

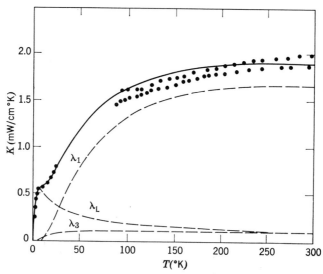

Figure 13.23   Thermal conductivity of polymethyl methacrylate [72]. Points are experimental points from various sources. The dotted lines represent the contributions of the first (λ_1), second (λ_L) and third (λ_3) terms of (13.36), and the heavily drawn curve is their sum.

The indicated temperature dependence of the prevailing conduction mechanisms permits a qualitative prediction of the effect of cold drawing on the thermal conduction parallel to $(\lambda_\parallel)$ and normal to $(\lambda_\perp)$ the drawing direction. Elongation of the molecule in the draw direction increases $f(\alpha) \to 1$, and Λ_p (by a factor that could be estimated from birefringence data) and thus $\lambda_\parallel$ (through $\lambda_\perp$). Hence cold drawing has the following effects on thermal conductivity: at $\theta_1 \le T < T_g$, $\lambda_\parallel > \lambda_0$ and $d\lambda_\parallel/dT > d\lambda_0/dT$, and $\lambda_\perp < \lambda_0$ and $d\lambda_\perp/dT < d\lambda_0/dT$, where λ_0 is the thermal conductivity of the undrawn sample. At very large extension $\lambda_\perp$ could approach $(\lambda_L + \lambda_3)$ and even change the sign of $d\lambda_\perp/dT$. At $T < (\frac{1}{3}\theta_1)$, the effect of drawing should disappear because then $\lambda \to \lambda_L + \lambda_3$, both of which are comparatively insensitive to orientation. All of these predictions are borne out by Hennig's thermal conductivity measurements on drawn glassy polymer sample [41].

The very convenient method of de Sénarmont, recently rediscovered by Müller et al., [64a], yields the ratio $\lambda_\parallel/\lambda_\perp$ of oriented films so readily that quantitative measures of orientation in drawn films should soon be routinely available. A useful by-product, or even the major objective, of such measurements is the corresponding elastic anisotropy, because in solids $\lambda_\parallel/\lambda_\perp \doteq (K_\parallel/K_\perp)^{1/2} \doteq (E_\parallel/E_\perp)^{1/2}$.

13.5 ROTATIONAL DIFFUSION

Experience with macroscopic objects guides our intuitive notion that a tightly packed disordered array of anisometric particles allows far less particle motion than an orderly closely packed array of the same particles. Transfer of this notion to molecular dimension leads to the prediction that rotational motion of molecules in glassy solids should be more restricted than it is in crystals. Comparison of the data in Tables 13.13 and 13.14 with those of the corresponding Tables 5.3 through 5.9 shows that this prediction is borne out rather well by the facts.

The somewhat undefined state of molecular glasses (i.e., the importance of their thermal and mechanical history) is reflected particularly strongly in transport properties because of their strong (exponential) dependence on packing density. Wild excursions of properties from what appear to be well-established regularities should not surprise or dismay, but rather point to some overlooked difference in the experimental technique employed in sample preparation, especially in the cooling procedure. Such otherwise unintelligible discrepancy can be seen from lines 2 and 3 of Table 13.13 for nominally the same compound albeit a technical (isomer) mixture. Further examples are found in the occasional and irregular dips of $\Delta E_{\ne}/\Delta H_s$ among the alkyl halides. More important than the exceptions appears to be how often the activation energy for rotational diffusion of rigid molecules—as measured by

Table 13.13 Rotational Diffusion in Glasses Composed of Simple Nonassociating Substances (from Electric Dipole Relaxation)

	T (°K)	log A[a]	$\Delta S^{\ddagger}$ (e.u.)	$\Delta E^{\ddagger}$ (Kcal/mole)	$\dfrac{\Delta E^{\ddagger}}{\Delta H_s}$	$\dfrac{\Delta F^{\ddagger}(T)}{\Delta H_s}$	Ref.
Rigid Molecules							
Mixed tetrachloro-diphenyls	293	40	126	47	1.55	0.33	b
Mixed pentachloro-diphenyls	293	56	198	66	2.2	0.27	b
Same as above	276		156	55	1.9	0.39	c
Mixed hexachloro diphenyls	293	14	142	54	1.8	0.41	c
Tolyl-xylyl-sulfone	276		137	50	1.3	0.32	c
Dimethyl sulfoxide	178		161	35	2.2	0.34	d
i-Butyl bromide	116	49	167	23	2.2	0.36	b
i-Amyl bromide	128	36	106	18	1.4	0.35	b
n-Butyl bromide	92[f]			23	1.8		e
n-Amyl bromide	109[f]			15	1.0		e
n-Hexyl bromide	115[f]			44	2.7		e
n-Butyl chloride	93[f]			20	1.6		e
n-Hexyl chloride	110[f]			28	1.7_5		e
n-Butyl iodide	105[f]			37	2.6		e
n-Hexyl iodide	118[f]			14	0.8		e
n-Butyl cyanide	110[f]			29	2.0		e
n-Hexyl cyanide	150			37	2.0		e
Ethyl acetate	190			16	1.25		g
Diethyl malonate	153[f]			27	1.2		g
Flexible Molecules							
$(EtO)_3P$	130–140	33.7		18.2	0.79		h
$(n\text{-}BuO)_3P$	140–168	19.8		11.3	0.34		h
	132–157	19.5		10.4	0.31		h
$(i\text{-}C_8O)_3P$	175.5–203	21.9		15.9	0.31		h
	169–192	24.2		17.0	0.33		h
$(n\text{-}C_{10}O)_3P$	189–217.5	21.1		16.1	0.24		h
	–200	21.4		15.7	0.23		h

[a] A in sec^{-1}.

[b] R. Meakins, in *Progress in Dielectrics*, Wiley, New York, 1961, vol 3.

[c] J. W. Winslow et al., *J. Chem. Phys.* **27**, 309 (1957).

[d] M. Freyman et al., *Colloq. Ampere* **11**, 325 (1962).

[e] G. Martin and J. Meinnel, *Colloq. Ampere* **12**, 434 (1963).

[f] G. Martin, *J. Chim. Phys.* **64**, 347 (1967). The temperatures are T_g. In this series $T_g/T_b = 0.27 \pm 0.01$.

[g] M. Jaffrain and C. Marin, *Chem. Rev.* **254**, 2958 (1962).

[h] M. Freyman and G. Mavel, *J. Phys.* **24**, 319 (1963).

Table 13.14 **Rotational Diffusion in Glasses Composed of Simple Hydrogen-Bonding Substances (from Electric-Dipole Relaxation)**

	$T_g{}^{a,i}$ (°K)	T^b (°K)	$\log A^c$	$\Delta S_{\ddagger}$ (e.u.)	$\Delta E_{\ddagger}$ (kcal/mole)	$\dfrac{\Delta E_{\ddagger}}{\Delta H_s}$	$\dfrac{\Delta F_{\ddagger}(T)}{\Delta H_s}$	Ref.
Rigid Molecules								
2,3,4,6-Tetra-		100–200			2.5[d]			e
chlorophenol		200–250			18	0.78		e
Tetrabromo-		149			4.6[d]			e
orthocresol		263			18.4	0.68	0.34	e
Cyclohexanol	161	149	18.0		13.1	0.79	0.31	f
Methanol	108	125	17.7		7.2	0.67	0.40	f
Ethanol	103	119	15.6		5.8	0.46	0.32	f
Allyl alcohol	—	149	18.9		9.5	0.67	0.36	f
Propylene glycol	—	211	23.8		18.0	0.91	0.37	f
Glycerol	186	237	27.9		24.6	0.92	0.31	f
Flexible Molecules								
n-Propanol	108	154	12.7		5.53	0.38	0.36	f
i-Propanol	125	164	12.8		5.76	0.43	0.42	f
n-Butanol	119	166	14.9		7.60	0.47	0.36	f
i-Butanol	116	175	15.1		8.07	0.54	0.40	f
n-Pentanol	120	178	15.2		8.5	0.46	0.33	f
i-Pentanol	125	184	15.3		8.5	0.49	0.37	f
n-Hexanol	125	207	16.1		10.4	0.51	0.35	f
Geraniol	—	208	22.5		15.9	0.62	0.28	f
Acetyl salicylic acid	—	296			38	1.36	0.377	g
Phenyl salicylate (Salol)	217[h]	250			33.5	1.35	0.354	g
2-Naphthol salicylate (Betol)	244[h]	283			34.8	1.11	0.320	g

[a] K. H. Illers, *Rheol. Acta* **3**, 185 (1964); Proc. Intl. Conf. on Physics of Noncrystalline Solids, Delft, 1964, p. 320. T_g is here the glass transition temperature determined by torsion pendulum at 1 Hz.

[b] Temperature of 10^5 Hz absorption maximum, except where ranges are given.

[c] A in $\sec^{-1}$.

[d] Barrier to rotation of the hydroxyl group.

[e] J. Meinnel et al., *Colloq. Ampere* **12**, 429 (1963).

[f] K. Kamiyoshi and T. Fujimura, *J. Phys. Radium* **23**, 311 (1962).

[g] A. V. Komandin et al., *Russ. J. Phys. Chem.* **37**, 399, 702 (1963).

[h] Static values, from Table 13.2.

[i] For the n-alkanols $T_g/T_b = 0.29 \pm 0.01$. See also Table 13.2.

electric-dipole relaxation—is of the order of twice the heat of sublimation. Although a large part of the temperature coefficient of D_r is undoubtedly due to thermal expansion, the magnitude of $\Delta E_{\neq}$ (and $\Delta S_{\neq}$) can safely be taken as evidence for the requirement of more extensive cooperative interaction among neighboring molecules to achieve rotation or large amplitude torsional oscillation of one molecule in a glass than is required in crystals.

Quantitative assessment of the relative magnitude of thermal expansion effects and of the height of the barrier to external rotation of molecules in glasses will be possible once the isochore $(\partial \ln D_r/\partial T)_v$ is determined. Such measurements have so far not been made even for simple liquids. Another avenue closed to correlation is the relation of $\Delta E_{\neq}/\Delta H_s$ versus ρ^* which proved so fruitful in the case of crystals, because the glassy state density has not been measured for any of the compounds represented in Tables 13.13 and 13.14. Moreover, the pre-exponential frequency factor of D_r in glasses cannot be related to the optically active torsional oscillation frequency of the molecule at $0°K$, as proved possible—at least in first approximation—in crystals. There appears to be a possibility of achieving at least order-of-magnitude correlation of D_r at $T = T_g$.

The available data show two common elements with those for crystals. The magnitude of $\Delta F_{\neq}/\Delta H_s$ covers a sufficiently narrow range that approximate predictions of D_r might well be possible. Second, the magnitude of $\Delta E_{\neq}/\Delta H_s$ changes with molecular structure in same direction as for crystals, namely, from high values for rigid molecules to small fractions of unity for flexible molecules, as is shown by the data at the bottom of Table 13.13. Here $\Delta E_{\neq}/\Delta H_s$ is in fact almost identical with that for the structurally similar crystalline esters (Table 5.6). It is perhaps unexpected that the alkyl halides act like rigid molecules even when $N_c = 6$. The reason may be the well-known very unordered weak interaction of the functional group with any part of the neighboring molecule rather than alignment into dipole sheets however unordered.

A few remarkable features among the hydrogen-bonded compounds of Table 13.13 are: (a) the clearly detectable movement of the hydroxyl group of the phenols at very low temperatures, yielding even perfectly intelligible barriers to internal rotation, and (b) the sequence 1.5 kcal/mole with hydrogen atoms in the 2,6 positions; 2.5 kcal/mole with chlorine atoms in the 2,6 positions, and 4.5 kcal/mole with a methyl group in the 2 and a bromine atom in the 6 position appears rather reasonable. The temptation to identify $\Delta E_{\neq}$ at the glass transition with the hydrogen-bond strength would have been irresistible if only data of methanol to propanol, glycols, and glycerol had been available. In the cases of the lower glycols and of glycerol this identification is indeed sensible because all rotational motion requires breakage of the hydrogen bonds and here $\Delta E_{\neq} \approx H_s$ (OH).

However, the steady rise of $\Delta E_{\neq}$ with molecular weight of the mono-alkanols suggests that perhaps the hydroxyl-bond chain is resting while the O–C dipole and its attached alkyl group are rotating in the alternating electric field, at least when $N_c > 2$. Then $\Delta E_{\neq} \approx H_s(R\cdot)$, the ratio $\Delta E_{\neq}/H_s(R\cdot)$ varying from 0.82 to 1.4, centering around 0.92. The very similar magnitude of $\Delta E_{\neq}$ and $\Delta F_{\neq}$, and the resulting smallness of $\Delta S_{\neq}$, for many of the mono-alkanols also argue for a comparatively simple rotational movement. This behavior, as well as that of the alkoxyphosphines of Table 13.13 clearly anticipates the independent side-chain motions, which are so prominent a feature of polymers with side chains (in the glassy solid state).

These electric-dipole relaxation measurements have recently been supplemented by dynamic mechanical measurements on nearly 150 low-molecular-weight substances in a very broad study by Illers [46]. His data were obtained in shear at a single frequency (1 cps), and therefore lack information on the activation energy. On the other hand, mechanical measurements can detect molecular motions at temperatures below T_g (as well as above T_g for the crystal), which seemingly escaped detection in the dielectric measurements. The mechanical-loss measurements permitted the inclusion of hydrocarbons. The glass-transition temperatures, entered in Tables 13.13 and 13.14, are about where we would expect to find them at 1 Hz (as compared to 10^4 Hz in the dielectric measurement).

The additional so-called γ relaxation at low temperatures could, through correlation with molecular structure, be identified with tansitions among rotational isomers. Since the incidence and location of this transition are the same in the glass as in the crystal, it is discussed as part of the rotational diffusion phenomena in crystals (Section 5.2.2).

Rotational diffusion mechanisms in polymeric glasses have been studied very thoroughly [16], [79], [100] because of the great practical importance of the associated relaxation phenomena for the dielectric and the mechanical properties of the polymeric plastic materials. Rotational motions have been examined in several instances by three independent methods: NMR, dielectric loss, and dynamic mechanical-energy absorption. A few typical group motions in polymeric glasses and their characteristic parameters have been assembled in Table 13.15. and in the "relaxation maps," Figures 13.24 and 13.25. These give the location of the maxima in energy absorption (equals average rate of rotational motion) in the frequency-temperature field. Most of the secondary relaxation curves are straight lines, the extrapolation of which cut the ordinate in a narrow range $10^{13} < \nu < 10^{14.5}$ (private communication from J. Heijboer). This is not far from the torsional oscillating frequency of the motions generally associated with these secondary relaxations, which suggests that $\Delta S_{\neq}$ of such secondary relaxation processes is comparatively small. The relaxation strength, on the other hand, is a measure

Table 13.15   Typical Mechanical-Energy Loss Parameters for Secondary Relaxation Peaks of Various Polymeric Glasses[a]

Glass	T (°K)	f (sec^{-1})	tan δ	ΔE_{iso}[b] (kcal/mole)	$\Delta E_{\neq}$ (kcal/mole)	Probable Motion
Polystyrene					9	
Polyisobutylene	120	3×10^2			5.2	Methyl[c]
Polymethyl methacrylate	293	1	0.08	2.0; 3.5	24	Ester group[f]
					5.4	Methyl group
Polyethyl methacrylate	360	10^2	0.25		21	Ester group[f]
	60	5×10^2	0.02		1.6	Methyl group[g]
Poly-n-butyl methacrylate	110	2×10^2	0.05		4.9	Methyl
Polymethyl acrylate	180	3.4×10^2	0.02		9.0	
Bisphenol A polycarbonate	173	1	0.04[d]	0.13	11	?
Polyethylene terephthalate	213	1	0.05[d]	0.9		
Polyvinyl chloride	263	10^2	0.05[e]	1.7	18	

[a] Except where noted otherwise, the data of this table have been taken from a paper by D. W. McCall at the Intl. Polymer Res. Conf., Moretonhampstead, Devon, England, May 1964; $\Delta E_{\neq}$ and ΔH_{iso} have been derived from these data. A more complete collection of such data will be found in the book *Mechanical and Dielectric Relaxation in Polymeric Solids* by N. J. McCrum, G. Williams, and B. E. Read, Wiley, New York, 1967.
[b] By (13.47).
[c] Methyl group on main chain, note that $\Delta E_{\neq} \approx$ barrier in neopentane.
[d] K. H. Illers and H. Breuer, *J. Colloid Sci.* **18**, 1 (1963).
[e] Y. Wada et al., *Rept. Progr. Polymer Phys. Japan* **7**, 189 (1964).
[f] The rotating group is probably

R—O ... O.

[g] Methyl group or methylene group in alkyl side chain.

of the number of moving entities per unit volume and changes with the temperature level (or the density) and the frequency at which relaxation occurs.

If we accept Illers' [46] and McCall's [61] suggestion that the secondary relaxation peaks are caused by rotational isomerism, that is, by transitions of parts of the polymer molecule between two different equilibrium positions, we can relate the height of the dielectric loss peak, that is, its relaxation strength to molecular properties, by

$$\tan \delta_{\max} = \frac{2\pi N_i \mu^2}{(\epsilon_s + n^2)kT} \cdot \frac{4 \exp(-\Delta E_{\mathrm{iso}}/RT)}{[1 + \exp(-E_{\mathrm{iso}}/RT)]^2}, \qquad (13.34)$$

where N_i is the number of permanent electric dipoles per unit volume (cm^3),

μ is the dipole moment of the dipoles, ϵ_s and n are the static dielectric constant and refractive index of the glass, respectively, and ΔE_{iso} is the energy of rotational isomerization or, more generally, the energy difference between two equilibrium positions [31].

The relaxation strength of the secondary relaxation peaks of the bulk modulus should be given by Lamb's formula

$$\tan \delta_{max} = \frac{R(1 - \gamma)}{4C_p} \left(\frac{\Delta H_{iso}}{RT}\right)^2 \frac{\exp\left(\Delta G_{iso}/RT\right)}{[1 + \exp\left(-\Delta G_{iso}/RT\right)]^2}, \quad (13.35)$$

where $\gamma = C_p/C_v$, and ΔH_{iso} and ΔG_{iso} are the enthalpy and free energy of rotational isomerization, respectively. This equation cannot be tested against experiment because of the absence of experimental data for compressional secondary relaxations of glasses. A comparable expression has not yet been developed for the tensile and shear modulus losses. However, although the absolute magnitude of the relaxation strength in shear and in tension cannot yet be predicted, their temperature coefficient can be estimated from the temperature coefficients of $\tan \delta_{max}$ of the elastic moduli.

The magnitude of energy loss in shear or tensile deformation must be obtained from a more specific molecular model for the deformation process. Kastner [47] may have been the first to recognize that a change in over-all chain length due to reorientation of chain segments (as by rotational isomerization) implies activation of such a transition by application of a tensile or shear stress. The relaxation frequency of such a secondary relaxation process is then

$$\omega_{max} = \omega_0 \exp\left(-\frac{\Delta E_{\neq}}{RT}\right)\left[1 + \exp\left(-\frac{\Delta E_{iso}}{RT}\right)\right], \quad (13.36)$$

and its tensile loss compliance (at the loss maximum)

$$D'' = \frac{4N_s V_s}{3RT} \frac{(\Delta V/V)^2 n}{1 + \cos n(\Delta E_{iso}/RT)}, \quad (13.37)$$

where N_s = number of chain segments between entanglement points (or cross links, if any), V_s = molal volume per chain segment, n = number of mobile links per segment (therefore $N_s n$ = number of mobile units between entanglement points), $\Delta V/V$ = fractional volume change accompanying the rotational transition. It should be noted that according to (13.36) D'' rises with increasing temperature to a maximum at $T_{max} = 0.65 \Delta E_{iso}/R$, whence it decreases as $\sim T^{-1}$.

The Kastner theory has two obvious deficiencies: its prediction that ΔE_{iso} rises with the deformation rate (because T_{max} rises with deformation rate) and its incorrect prediction that $D^4 = 0$ for the crankcase type secondary relaxation motion described earlier (Section 5.2.2) for which $\Delta V/V = 0$.

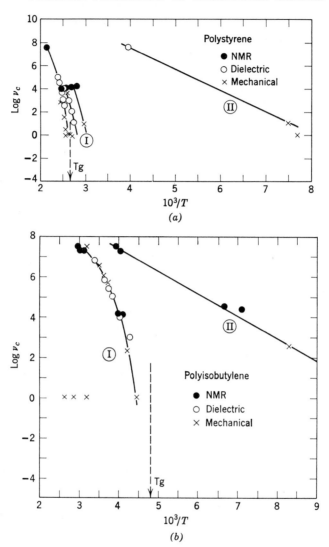

Figure 13.24 Relaxation maps of polymeric glasses. ν_c is the frequency at which $\tan \delta$ reaches its maximum value at a given temperature T [from D. W. McCall, Bell Telephone Laboratories, presented at the International Polymer Research Conference, Moreton-hampstead, England (1964)].

Approximate estimates of ΔE_{iso} have been obtained by various means: For shear and tensile loss moduli McCall [61] suggests

$$\Delta E_{iso} \approx R\left[\frac{d \ln (T \tan \delta_{max})}{d(1/T)}\right] \qquad (13.38)$$

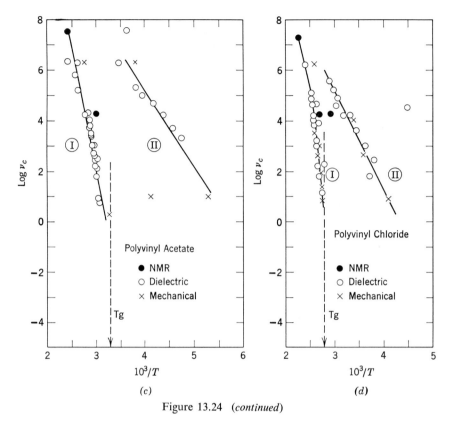

Figure 13.24 (*continued*)

and Schatzki [82] proposes

$$\Delta E_{\text{iso}} = \left[\frac{-2R}{E''(\omega)}\left(\frac{\partial E'}{\partial 1/T}\right)_\omega + \Delta F_{\neq}\right]\left[\frac{\pi}{2}\left(\frac{E'(\omega) - E'(\infty)}{E''(\omega)}\right)\right]^{-1} \quad (13.39)$$

where $E'(\omega)$, $E'(\infty)$ are the storage tensile moduli at frequency ω and ∞, respectively. $E''(\omega)$ is the loss tensile modulus at frequency ω; $\Delta F_{\neq}$ is the free energy of activation for the process.

Even in the present early state of development it is apparent that the secondary relaxations are characterized by two energy parameters. Their frequency–temperature relation is determined by the height of the barrier to rotation, the activation energy $\Delta E_{\neq}$ and their intensity is dominated by the energy of rotational isomerization and by the concentration of relaxing units. Typical values for $\Delta E_{\neq}$ and ΔE_{iso} have been assembled in Table 13.15 and Table 14.29.2. The higher the temperature and the higher the excitation frequency of a secondary relaxation, the greater is the energy absorption. In this context it is important to remember that the fraction of molecules participating in a relaxation transition is very small, and depends on the

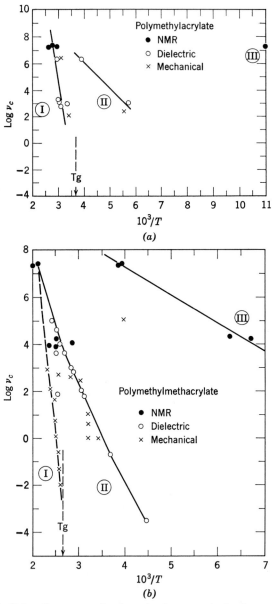

Figure 13.25 Relaxation maps of polymeric glasses. ν_c is the frequency at which tan δ reaches its maximum value at a given temperature T [from D. W. McCall, Bell Telephone Laboratories, presented at the International Polymer Research Conference, Moreton-hampstead, England (1964)].

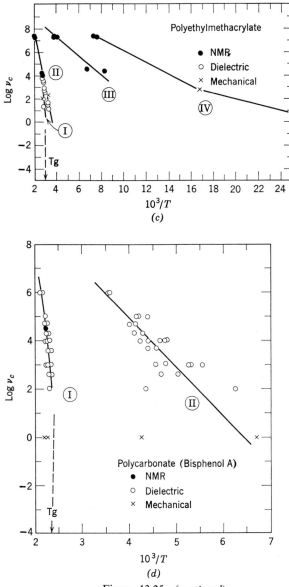

Figure 13.25 (*continued*)

exciting frequency, rather in contrast to thermodynamic solid–solid phase transitions, which involve a large fraction of the sample examined.

The entire area under the energy absorption versus frequency curve is an accurate measure of the population of mobile segments (under the test conditions). This population of mobile molecules or molecule segments, in turn, determines the frequency limit below, or the temperature limit above, which there will be enough relaxing mechanisms available to permit small scale deformation at a particular rate and temperature. Knowledge of the location and area of the loss curve in loss versus ω or loss versus T coordinates permits therefore a reasonable prediction for the possibility of high-speed deformation, or more crudely, of adequate impact strength under various operating conditions.

A curious consequence of the availability of secondary molecular deformation mechanisms is then that a glass is not always brittle. Specifically, polystyrene has only an insignificant relaxation transition at $T < T_g$ (Figure 13.26) and is therefore an especially brittle glass, whereas some glassy polymers exhibit high ductility at $T < T_g$ in conformity with the large areas under their loss curves at $T < T_{(test)}$. It should be noted that the energy-loss spectrum of a given polymer can be modified appreciably by molecule orientation (as by cold drawing). Thus we have more than just chemical degrees of freedom available for polymer design for specific application.[5]

Secondary relaxations can also be modified by admixture of plasticizers or of other polymers. All plasticizers drive the relaxation peaks to lower temperatures. Small amounts of these plasticizers which increase the elastic moduli (see pp. 417–420) also suppress the strength of secondary relaxations [12] and thus embrittle the glass. The rotational motions of the plasticizer molecules in the glassy matrix can be observed by their dielectric loss (if they are polar) and/or by NMR measurements. In view of the valuable information about the mechanisms of plasticizer action that could be obtained by such measurements, the data so far obtained are surprisingly few and fragmentary.

It appears from their comparatively small activation energies for dipole rotation that plasticizer molecules dissolved in glasses, just as the polymer molecules, carry out only segmental motions. The recent NMR measurements by Kosfeld [56] suggest that a certain temperature-dependent fraction of plasticizer is distributed in microcavities in the polymeric glass rather than in molecular dispersion. That fraction becomes smaller with decreasing temperature and the molecules in it have the mobility of the free plasticizer.

Polymers admixed to a given polymeric glass in general form a second phase. Such mixtures therefore exhibit the relaxation loss peaks of the separate bulk components.

[5] A rather complete collection of relaxation spectra will be found in the forthcoming book, *Dielectric and Mechanical Relaxation Spectra*, by McCrum, Read, and Williams, Wiley, New York, 1967.

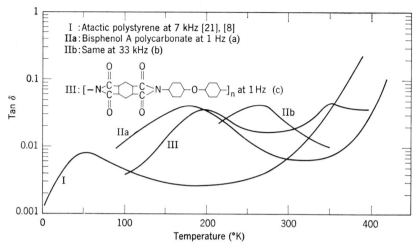

I : Atactic polystyrene at 7 kHz [21], [8]
IIa : Bisphenol A polycarbonate at 1 Hz (a)
IIb : Same at 33 kHz (b)

III : [−N ... −O− ...]n at 1 Hz (c)

Figure 13.26   Mechanical-energy absorption for a brittle (I), a moderately ductile (II), and a ductile polymeric glass. (a) K. H. Illers and H. Breuer, *Kolloid-Z.* **176**, 110 (1961); (b) Y. Wada et al., *Rept. Prog. Polymer Phys. Japan* **7**, 189 (1964); (c) R. M. Ikeda, *Polymer Preprint* **6**, 807 (1965).

13.6   MASS DIFFUSION

Mass transport rate by molecular diffusion in glasses is of the same order of magnitude as that in molecular crystals in spite of the very large differences of rotational diffusion rate between these two types of solids. In glasses as in liquids, D is of the order $D_r d_m^2$ where d_m is the average molecule diameter, whereas in crystals $D_r d_m^2 > 10^4 D$. Comparison of experimental diffusion rates in glasses with those in crystals is not possible at present because no (self) diffusion rates have been measured in glasses formed from monomeric substances. Only diffusion data for polymeric glasses could be found in the literature. The most outstanding review of the field, by Rogers [77], should be consulted for details. The present treatment concentrates on the region $T < T_g$ and on information published since the completion of Rogers' review.

Most of the available gas, moisture, and general vapor permeation data have been obtained in order to determine the suitability of polymers as moisture and vapor barriers. The diffusion rate of dyestuffs is measured when studying the behavior of polymer fibers and films in the dyebath, and the diffusion rate of plasticizers often defines the longevity of plasticized glassy polymers. The last case does not really belong into this chapter because plasticized glasses are rubbers; that is, they are at $T > T_g$ by virtue of plasticization, and plasticizer diffusion is, of course, determined in that temperature range. However, the analysis of the data leads to a correlation of general interest in the present context.

The permeation rate (permeability P) of a membrane is the product of diffusion coefficient (D) and solubility. Hence even if we could estimate D we would not be able to predict P unless we had means to estimate the solubility of the penetrant in the glass.

The solubility of gases (x_2) in polymeric glasses is significantly higher than that expected from melt data (x_2'), probably due to sorption in microcavities [63], [102]. Purely empirically Meares [59] described this effect by the relation

$$x_2 = x_2'/[1 - a(T_g - T)],$$

where $a \approx 0.01 \pm 0.002°\mathrm{K}^{-1}$.

A theoretical model for "dual mode" sorption in glassy polymer proposed by Vieth and co-workers [102], leads to the relation

$$x_2 = x_D + x_H = k_D P + C_H' b \cdot P/(1 + b \cdot P),$$

where x_2 = total sorption of gas (cm³ STP/cm³ polymer), x_D, x_H = solubility in polymer and sorption in microcavities, respectively, P = gas pressure in atm, k_D = Henry's law constant for the system (cm³ STP/cm³ · atm), C_H' = hole saturation constant, and b = "hole affinity" constant (atm⁻¹). The tacit assumption of gas adsorption at the microcavity surfaces underlying the use of the Langmuir equation is supported by the observation that $C_H' \sim A_s$, the area occupied by the sorbate molecules. Moreover, $b \sim \exp(\epsilon/kT)$ and $k_D \sim \exp(-\epsilon/kT)$, where ϵ is the Lennard-Jones force constant of the sorbate gas [94]. The corresponding enthalpy changes are ΔH_D, ΔH_H, the enthalpy of dissolution and cavity filling, respectively. As expected, ΔH_D is nearly like that of the melt and $\Delta H_H < \Delta H_D$. Preliminary observations on polystyrene indicated that orientation decreases primarily x_2, rather in contrast to semicrystalline polymers at $T > T_g$, in which orientation had been shown (Section 4.5.3) to decrease sorption in the bulk amorphous phase.

The same phenomenon of sorption on the walls of microcavities may also account for the noticeable drop in solvent activity (a_1) in polymer/solvent systems at $T < T_g$ observed by Ueberreiter [96]. The enthalpy-change

$$R\left[\frac{\partial \ln a_1(\text{melt})}{\partial 1/T} - \frac{\partial \ln a_1(\text{glass})}{\partial 1/T}\right],$$

which Ueberreiter associates with unrelieved stresses in the glass is more likely ΔH_H, the heat of cavity filling, mentioned earlier. For the case of benzene in polyvinylcarbazole it is of the order 0.8 to 1.4 kcal/mole, increasing with decreasing solvent concentration, quite characteristic of adsorption processes.

The dissolution of any substance causes appreciable local deformation in a glass, and the resulting stresses can often be observed optically [20], [77], so that we can see the advancing "front" of penetrant in many transparent plastics. Glass properties, such as T_g, are therefore changed by the presence of the solute. These property changes are rather minor when poorly soluble penetrants are employed, such as inert gases or incompatibles, for example, methanol in polystyrene. Very soluble penetrants swell the glass into a rubbery mass, which the remaining glass prevents from turning into a liquid. The resulting swelling pressure stresses the remaining glass so severely that it may break [6]. Diffusion into the stressed glass presents peculiar mathematical problems which have been discussed especially by Crank [20]. Needless to say, the diffusion coefficient in such swelling systems is so strongly concentration dependent that the advancing concentration front has very nearly the steepness of a shockwave [6]. The discussion of diffusion in swelling systems clearly falls outside the scope of the present chapter.

Diffusion data of poorly soluble penetrants through various organic glasses have been assembled in Table 13.16. A striking feature of these data is the close association of $\Delta E_{\neq}$ with each penetrant, almost independent of the polymer glass through which it is diffusing. The ratio $\Delta E_{\neq}(\text{glass})/\Delta E_{\neq}$ (melt) is a function of penetrant molecule size and of the polymer and decreases from unity to 0.5 as penetrant molecule size increases. In some polymers, such as ethyl methacrylate, it remains at unity (i.e., T_g has no effect) for the range from H_2 to SF_6 [90], whereas in poly (vinyl acetate) and polyethyleneterephthalate it is <1 over the entire penetrant size range. Empirically we observe often (but not always) that the difference $[\Delta E_{\neq}$ (melt) $- \Delta E_{\neq}(\text{glass})]$ parallels the difference $[\alpha(\text{melt}) - \alpha(\text{glass})]$, which supports the notion that a large fraction of $d \ln D/d(T)^{-1}$ is really due to thermal expansion.

The "dual mode" sorption of gases and poorly soluble penetrants in glasses discussed earlier really calls for a reformulation of the diffusion equation in terms of the appropriate driving force relations

$$D\nabla^2 x_D = \dot{x}_D\left[1 + \frac{C_H' b}{k_D(1 + b \cdot P)^2}\right] \tag{13.40}$$

which yields for low pressures, where $b \cdot P \ll 1$

$$D_{\text{eff}} = \frac{D}{(1 + bC_H'/k_D)}.$$

At high pressures, where $b \cdot P \gg 1$, the usual diffusion equation applies.

The "dual mode" model also accounts for the anomalously low apparent activation energy of diffusion (ΔE_a) often observed with glassy polymers, since the "true" activation energy of diffusion is

$$\Delta E_{\neq} = \Delta E_a + (\Delta H_H - \Delta H_D).$$

Table 13.16 Mass Diffusion Parameters for Various Solutes in Polymers at $T < T_g$

Polymer	Solute	ΔE_a (kcal/mole)	$\log D_0$[a]	T (°K)	$D(T)10^{10}$ (cm² sec⁻¹)	Ref.
Polystyrene	MeOH	9.7	−1.1			
	EtOH	9.8	−2.4			
	CH_2Cl_2	10.0	−2.6			b
	EtBr	12.4	−1.8			
	n-BuOH	34	12	303	0.005	c
Polymethyl methacrylate	H_2O	10.4	−0.2			
	MeOH	12.4	−1.0	290		
	O_2	10.0		298	6	
Polyethyl methacrylate	H_2O	8.7	−0.8			b
	MeOH	9.6	−1.6			
Polybutyl methacrylate	MeOH	9.2	−0.8			
Polyvinyl acetate	Me	4.16				
	H_2	5.17				
	O_2	11.1				d
	Ni	7.36				
	H_2O	6.4	−2.7			b
	MeOH	7.6	−4.0			
Polyvinyl chloride	H_2O	10.0				d
Polyethylene terephthalate (amorphous)	H_2	6.9		338	4,000	e
					180	
	H_2O	10.4	−0.8	298	40	f
	O_2	10.1	−1.4			
Bisphenol A-carbonate (lexan)	H_2	5.0		298	11,000	
	Ar	6.0		298	150	
	H_2O	6.2				g
	O_2	7.7		298	210	
	O_2	7.1	−1.85	298	100	h
	CO_2	9.0		298	48	g
	SF_6	(20.0)		298	0.001	g

[a] D_0 in cm² sec⁻¹.
[b] G. Y. Ryskin, *Zhur. Tekh. Fiz.* **25**, 458 (1955).
[c] K. Kanamaru and M. Sugiura, *Kolloid-Z.* **178**, 1 (1961).
[d] A. T. diBenedetto, *J. Polymer Sci.* **A1**, 3477 (1963).
[e] [25].
[f] H. Yasada and V. Stannett, *J. Polymer Sci.* **57**, 907 (1962).
[g] F. J. Norton, *J. Appl. Polymer Sci.* **7**, 1649 (1963).
[h] R. E. Barker, *J. Polymer Sci.* **58**, 553 (1962).

Needless to say, $\Delta E_{\neq}$ data are truly comparable only at equal values of x_D, since penetrants plasticize the glass somewhat even at very low concentration levels.

Even in the case of poorly soluble penetrants we should expect a finite, if small, plasticizing action on the glass. Hence data obtained at different penetrant concentrations x_2 are not really comparable and $\Delta E_{\neq}$ should be calculated at constant x_2 as

$$\Delta E_a = R \left(\frac{\partial \ln D}{\partial T^{-1}} \right)_{p, x_2}. \tag{13.41}$$

Although perhaps not important with light gases, this consideration may be a serious error source in such systems as polystyrene–n-butanol, where equilibrium sorption at room temperature may be of the order of 1%. One piece of evidence for the modification of the polymer by diffusing species is the incidence of the first break in the diffusion rate versus temperature curve at $T < T_g$, with $(T_g - T)$ generally of the order of 25 to 40°C. All such experiments should be repeated, so that $(\partial \ln D / \partial T^{-1})_x$ can be calculated in place of the common $(\partial \ln D / \partial T^{-1})_p$. In the absence of this kind of information we should accept ΔE_a for diffusion rate of such systems as n-BuOH in polystyrene in Table 13.16 with great reservation.

The apparent activation energy ΔE_a for diffusion through polymeric glasses rises with the size of the penetrant molecule. Taking the molecule diameter σ as determined from gas-phase properties, we observe $\Delta E_a \sim \sigma^n$, where n ranges from 1.6 [poly(ethyl methacrylate)] to 2[poly(vinyl acetate)] and polyethyleneterephthalate [90]. In the melt generally $n \approx 1$. No relation has so far been discovered between σ and the "jump length" d in the activated-state expression for diffusion

$$D = \frac{kT}{h} d^2 \exp \left(- \frac{\Delta E_{\neq}}{RT} \right), \tag{13.42}$$

where $d(\text{glass}) \approx 10$ Å and $d(\text{melt}) \approx 20$ Å. However, (13.42) is probably too primitive to permit assignment of distinct physical meaning to such parameters.

The diffusion of large, poorly soluble molecules such as dyestuffs in glassy polymers has so far been examined for a single system only, polyacrylonitrile [78]. The results for $T < T_g$ are summarized in Table 13.17. For most penetrants in Table 13.17 $\Delta E_{\neq} \approx \Delta H_s$ (penetrant) and $D(T)$ is about where extrapolation from some of the other data would have put it for a given temperature T/T_g. The meaning of such an extremely low diffusion coefficient as 10^{-16} cm^2 sec^{-1} can be appreciated only when translated into time scales via $t = X^2/6D$. Travel over a distance X of the indicated "jump length" (10 Å) would take 17 sec, and a depth of 1μ would be traversed in 1.7×10^7 sec (about $\frac{1}{2}$ year). A diffusion coefficient as low as 10^{-18} cm^2 sec^{-1} was reported for malachite green in an experimental polyacrylonitrile fiber at

Table 13.17   Diffusion of Large Molecules into a Glassy Polymer (Polyacrylonitrile Fiber)[a]

Penetrant	T (°C)	$T_g - T$ (°C)	D (cm²/sec)	ΔE° (kcal/mole)
(Malachite green) in Fiber 1.	27	30	2.4×10^{-18}	a e 37
Same dye in orlon 42	25	45[c]	3.6×10^{-16}	23 ± 7[d]
(Oxazine dye) in Orlon 42	25	45[c]	1.1×10^{-15}	(6)[d]

[a] From aqueous solution into fibers with sulfonate dye sites normal to the fiber draw
direction (draw ratio 8–10). T^g refers to that in aqueous environment, which is 30–35°C
below that for the dry polymers[b].
[b] S. Rosenbaum, J. Appl. Polymer Sci. 9, 2071 (1965).
[c] S. Rosenbaum, private communication.
[d] E is not measured because of examination data scatter.

room temperature [18]. Clearly, dyeing at $T < T_g$ is not a practical operation.
On the other hand, the very slowness of the diffusion process might permit
controlled introduction of extremely thin layers of substances into surface
layers of organic glasses. In conjunction with microscopic observations such
experiments might yield useful information regarding local inhomogeneities.

The diffusion of plasticizers in glassy polymer at $T > T_g$ (of the polymer-
plasticizer combination) has been measured by Luther and Meyer [58]
through the use of a microinfrared absorption method. Here the diffusion coefficient is, of course, strongly concentration dependent, and at
the concentration level x_g at which the plasticizer–polymer system is a glass
at the operating temperature, the plasticizer is effectively nonparticipating in
the diffusion flux. Hence Luther and Meyer obtained a more uniform diffusion
coefficient when they used $x - x_g$ rather than x as the driving force. Since
loss of plasticizer is generally by evaporation, the surface layer attains x_g
first and becomes a glass before the bulk concentration decreases to the glass
level.

The dependence of the permeability on solubility as well as on the diffusivity of the penetrant makes prediction of this technically important property "by intuition" extremely difficult. A typical example is provided by the long list of oxygen and moisture permeability data for a wide range of poly (hydroxy ethers) [74], where only the extreme cases are "obvious." All others would have to be calculated in detail. A yet more difficult, not to say puzzling, picture is presented by the permeability of glassy polymer films to odoriferous substances, such as camphor, eugenol, eucalyptol, etc. [44]. The puzzling aspect is the tendency of certain substances to block the glassy [poly (vinyl chloride) and polyethylene terephthalate] films to further permeation after a rapid initial flux of penetrant. This phenomenon does not seem to have been observed on the often more permeable (for aromatic substances) semicrystalline membranes. Another puzzling aspect is the absence of 1:1 correlation between permeability for these comparatively high-molecular-weight penetrants and the time required for their odor to appear.[6] As these phenomena affect the utility of polymer foils in a very large market, they clearly deserve more attention than they seem to have received to date.

13.7 CREEP

The relation between high-temperature creep and mass (self) diffusion is intuitively obvious and experimentally well established for crystals. A similarly convincing relation of high-temperature creep to molecular events has yet to be developed for molecular glasses. (All molecular glasses are used at "high" temperature, i.e., at $T > 0.5T_g$.) Creep of glasses composed of small molecules, such as colophony, glassy glucose, etc., under the influence of steady shear or tensile stress is viscous and its rate is probably determined by the mass (self) diffusion rate of the individual molecules of the glass. Short periods of stressing make the deformation due to creep of similar order as those due to elastic deformation, and each glass has at a given temperature and pressure a characteristic time of stress application, the relaxation time, below which most of the deformation is elastic. The response of polymeric glasses to slow stress oscillations exhibits far less viscous character than does that of low-molecular-weight glasses. The very different character of the two types of glass is shown by the internal friction versus stress frequency curves in Figure 13.27.

The observation of anelasticity, that is, of full recovery of even large deformations of glassy polymethyl methacrylate by Sherby and Dorn [88]

---

[6] These peculiar phenomena might also be artifacts caused by selective migration of radioactively tagged low-molecular-weight impurities; the permeability measurement of [44] having been carried out with tagged material. The difficulties associated with the synthesis of pure correctly tagged substances are only now beginning to be realized.

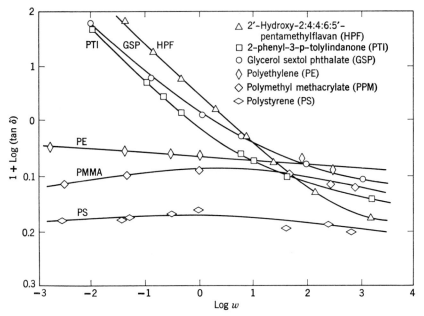

Figure 13.27   Internal friction against frequency curves for organic glasses and polymers [J. J. Benbow and D. J. C. Wood, *Trans. Faraday Soc.* **54**, 1581 (1958)].

suggests that mass diffusion of molecules is either absent or very unimportant in the creep of polymeric glass. Hence, the creep rate of polymeric glasses should depend primarily on the rotational motions of molecule segments, especially side chains. Thus we come to the curious conclusion that rotational diffusion of the kind measured in dielectric-loss experiments and in mechanical-relaxation experiments may play the same role in the creep of polymeric glasses that is played by mass diffusion in the high-temperature creep of crystals. A formal relation of this kind has been proposed by Schwarzl [84] who set for the permanent length change e due to the tensile stress σ during the time t:

$$e = \sigma \int_0^\infty J(\tau_r)[1 - e^{-t/\tau_r}] \, d \ln \tau_r, \qquad (13.43)$$

where $J(\tau_r)$ is the applicable retardation-time spectrum of the substance, and the retardation time τ_r can be transformed to the more common relaxation-time spectrum by use of a suitable model. The relaxation-time spectrum, in turn, is produced during the preparation of the previously mentioned rotational diffusion constants. One of the earliest tests of the correctness of this view has been the observation by Sato et al. [80] that the activation energy of the creep rate of a sample is identical with that obtained in dynamical tests for the appropriate relaxation process.

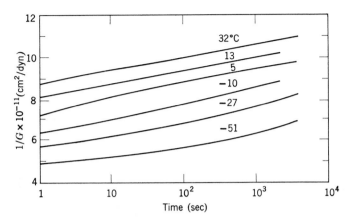

Figure 13.28 Experimental creep curves (compliance as functions of time) at various temperatures [80].

When the sample under consideration undergoes only one relaxation process or only one dominant relaxation process in the temperature range of practical interest, we can (or should be able to) use the simple time–temperature superposition principle for the conversion of isothermal creep curves into generalized master curves. A typical example is poly(methyl methacrylate) in the temperature range −51 to +32°C where Sato et al., converted the individual creep curves of Figure 13.28 by simple shift along the ln t axis into the single master creep curve of shear compliance versus reduced time shown in Figure 13.29. The activation energy characterizing

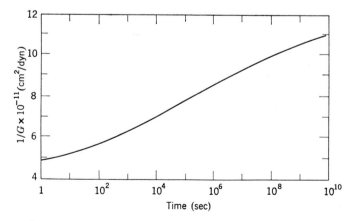

Figure 13.29 The master creep curve at −51°C for polymethyl methacrylate [80]; $\Delta E_{\neq} = 30$ kcal/mole.

such a curve refers to $(\partial \ln t_d / \partial T^{-1})_e$, that is, the time t_d for a fixed deformation e. How safe it is to extrapolate such a curve to creep over three years (10^8 sec) at 25°C when the experimental data at about that temperature go only to 10^4 sec is an as-yet-unanswered question. It is noteworthy that at -51°C a given stress applied over three years produces only twice the extension obtained when the same stress is applied only for 1 sec, a truly powerful demonstration of the rigidity of a glass. Attempts to produce creep master curves from recent creep data on polyvinyl chloride[7] and polystyrene[8] glasses have not been successful because no single shift factor would join the various curve segments smoothly to each other.

All of the creep data referred to so far were obtained with application of very small stresses ($\leq 10^{-4}$ E or G) or corresponding small strains. Creep of polymeric glass to larger strains under the influence of stresses of up to 0.02 E or G differ sufficiently from that at very small stresses that we may suspect different deformation mechanisms to be operative. The thorough study of the creep of polymethyl methacrylate between 263 and 320°K, tensile stresses of up to 0.01 E, and true strains up to 0.04 conducted by Sherby and Dorn [88] provide an excellent overview of the peculiar anelastic creep of polymeric glasses. The general term seems to be applicable, since several of their findings on poly(methyl methacrylate) have been confirmed on polystyrene by R. B. Shaw (private communication).

Over the temperature range from 263 to 320°K they found that the tensile creep rate $\dot{e}$ of glassy polymethy methacrylate can be described by the Kauzmann–Eyring type relation

$$\dot{e} = A \sinh \left(-\frac{(\Delta H_{\neq} - B\sigma)}{RT} \right) \approx A \exp \left\{ -\frac{(\Delta H_{\neq} - B\sigma)}{RT} \right\}, \quad (13.44)$$

which is based on the concept that passage over the potential-energy barrier is biased by the application of a stress σ, and where the constant A is a decreasing function of the creep strain e. Hence, the creep rate at any strain level is an exponential function of the applied stress, and the decrease of A with increasing strain means that the material strain hardens. The strain hardening, however, is not accompanied by a rise of the activation enthalpy $\Delta H_{\neq}$.

The activation enthalpy $\Delta H_{\neq}$ is with 48 kcal/mole (and $B = 1.5$ l/mole), very much larger than the 30 kcal/mole of the low-stress-level experiments mentioned earlier. Strong stress-level effects would have prevented the use of the time–temperature superposition noted earlier, because widely different stress levels had been employed in some of the creep experiments. The magnitude of the activation-energy difference is great enough to preclude any

[7] W. Sommer, Kolloid-Z. **167**, 97 (1959); W. Retting, Kolloid-Z. **203**, 108 (1965).
[8] M. Takanashi et al., ONR Technical Report RLT-61 (1963).

similarity in the rate-determining process. In the case of polystyrene ($\Delta H_{\neq} = 65$ kcal/mole, $B = 6.2$ l/mole) visual evidence suggests that the decisive deformation rate process is microcrack nucleation [R. B. Shaw, *loc. cit.*]. Similar behavior has not been observed with the polymethyl methacrylate. Yet something other than the chain rotation, for which $\Delta H_{\neq} = 30$ kcal/mole, must determine its creep rate. A light-scattering measurement on the deformed bar of the clear resin should help to answer this question.

The form of the stress dependence of creep rate (as bias for the activation energy) is, of course, independent of the detailed mechanism. It could be as valid for a nucleation rate process as for the passage over any other potential-energy barrier. There is, however, a striking difference between various experimental data. In an earlier creep experiment on polystyrene Sauer [81] found not only a direct connection between the creep rate and the energy absorption (ΔW) in oscillation equipment, namely $\dot{e} \sim (\Delta W)^2$, but also $\dot{e} \sim \sigma^{4.5}$. Sauer's coefficient is equivalent to $B \approx 1.8$ l/mole, hence more nearly like that found by Sherby and Dorn for PMMA. Sauer also carefully avoided the deformation regime accompanied by visible craze crack formation.

An alternative interpretation of the parameter B is contained in the recent theory of plastic flow of molecular polymeric glasses by Robertson [76]. His model of the polymeric glass assumes flexing of backbone bonds under the influence of an applied (shear) stress from the equilibrium distribution toward higher concentration of *gauche* conformations. The region in which this flexing takes place becomes in effect less viscous that the average glass. According to Robertson $B \approx \mathcal{V}_u/2\chi$, where $\mathcal{V}_u$ is the volume of a repeating unit (per mole) and χ, the number of flexed bonds along the backbone chain per unit volume, is given by

$$\chi^{-1} \approx 1 + \exp\left(\frac{\Delta E_{iso}}{RT}\right),$$

where ΔE_{iso} is the energy of rotational isomerization along the backbone chain. Experimental and analytical verification of this theory would not only reduce the number of disposable parameters in the mechanical equations of state of solid polymers, it would also provide the conceptual connecting link with the relaxation phenomena discussed in Section 13.5. So far no theory has contributed to an even qualitative understanding of strain hardening, a phenomenon buried in the pre-exponential factor A of (13.44).

A drastic, virtually discontinuous, change in creep rate and its temperature and stress dependence takes place as the β-transition temperature of polymethacrylate near $320°$K is exceeded. The factor B rises by a factor of 3 over a range of $20°$C, and $\Delta H_{\neq}$ takes on the well-known upward swing toward 100 kcal/mole at T_g is approached. The "high-temperature" behavior is therefore in keeping with general observations.

CALCULATING PROCEDURES

Procedure 13.1

Estimate.   The thermal-expansion coefficient of a glass.
Available Data: Molecular structure, density (ρg).

STEP 1: Estimate H_s from molecular structure increments of Tables 14.1 to 16.

STEP 2a: Glass is formed from rigid monomeric molecules: $\alpha = 0.44\rho_c C_v{}^s/\Delta H_s \rho_g$, where ρ_c is the density of the corresponding crystal. If ρ_c is not known, set $\rho_c/\rho_g \approx 1.05$. The lattice heat capacity $C_v{}^s$ can be approximated as $6R$.

STEP 2b: Glass is formed from flexible monomeric molecules: $\alpha = 0.31\rho_c(5 + N_s)R/\rho_g\Delta H_s$, where N_s is the number of chain links per molecule.

STEP 2c: Glass is formed from long-chain polymer molecules: $\alpha = 0.3\rho_c nR/\Delta H_s(n)\rho_g$, where n is the number of mobile segments per repeating unit, $\Delta H_s(n)$ is the heat of sublimation per repeating unit.

Procedure 13.2

Estimate.   The heat capacity of a glass.
Available Data: Molecular structure, T_g.

STEP 1: Estimate the heat capacity of the corresponding crystal by the appropriate method of Section 3.4.4.

STEP 2a: $T \leq 0.85\,T_g$: C_p (glass) = C_p (crystal) + $0.5R$.

STEP 2b: $T > 0.85\,T_g$: C_p (glass) = C_p (crystal) + increment read in Figure 13.7.

Procedure 13.3

Estimate.   An elastic modulus (bulk modulus, shear modulus, or Young's modulus) of a glass.
Available Data: Molecular structure, density T_g.

STEP 1: Step 1 of Procedure 13.1.

STEP 2: Estimate V_w form group increments of Tables 14.1.

STEP 3: The reference packing density ρ^*(ref) at room temperature or at $0.9T_g$ if $0.9T_g < 298°K$: ρ^*(ref) = $\rho V_w/M$, where V_w and M refer to the repeating unit if we are concerned with a polymeric glass.

STEP 4a: The zero-pressure bulk modulus (dependent on time scale at $T < 0.9T_g$,:

$$K_0 \approx \frac{H_s}{V_w}\left[31.63\rho^*(\text{ref}) - 10.55 - 6.0(T/T_g)\right].$$

STEP 4b: The approximate high-frequency Young's modulus (storage modulus) at $T < 0.9T_g$:

$$E \approx \frac{H_s}{V_w}\left[E_0^*\left(1 - \frac{30}{(E_0^*)^2}\frac{T}{T_g}\right)\right],$$

where $E_0^* \approx 85.9\rho^*(\text{ref}) - 47.6$.

NOMENCLATURE

A	pre-exponential factor in Arrhenius equation
A_w	area per mole of molecules calculated from van der Waals dimensions, Tables 14.1 to 14.18 (cm^2 mole^{-1})
a	coefficient in empirical equations
b	bond distance, cm
c	concentration
c	number of external degrees of freedom per molecule including those due to internal rotation
C_E	contribution of vibrational degrees of freedom to the heat capacity (cal mole^{-1} °K^{-1})
C_p	heat capacity at constant pressure (cal mole^{-1} °K^{-1})
ΔC_p	$= C_p(l) - C_p(g)$ at $T = T_g$
$C_p(l)$	$=$ heat capacity of liquid
$C_p(g)$	$=$ heat capacity of glass
C_v^s	lattice contribution to the heat capacity of a crystal at constant volume
D	diffusion coefficient (cm^2 sec^{-1})
D_r	rotational diffusion constant (sec^{-1})
d	distance between molecule centers (cm)
E	internal energy (cal mole^{-1})
E	Young's modulus (dynes cm^{-2})
E_0	Young's modulus at $T = 0°$K (dynes cm^{-2})
E^*	$= EV_w/\Delta H_s$ or EV_w/H_s
E_p	$=$ Young's modulus of a long chain molecule (dynes cm^{-2})
$E°$	$=$ standard energy of vaporization $= \Delta H_v - RT$ at $\rho^* = 0.588$ (cal mole^{-1})
ΔE_{iso}	$=$ energy of rotational isomerization (cal mole^{-1})
$\Delta E_{\ddagger}(X)$	$=$ energy of activation for rate process (X) (cal mole^{-1})
$\Delta F_{\ddagger}(X)$	$=$ free energy of activation for rate process (X) (cal mole^{-1})
G	shear (rigidity) modulus (dyn/cm$_2$)
G^*	$= GV_w/\Delta H_s$ or GV_w/H_s
G'	$=$ storage (real) component of shear modulus (dyn/cm^2)
G''	loss (imaginary) component of shear modulus (dyn/cm^2)
H_e	configurational enthalpy at $T = T_g$ (see [24])
H_i	contribution of internal degrees of freedom to enthalpy (cal/mole)
H^s	lattice contribution to enthalpy (cal/mole)
h	Planck's constant (erg mole^{-1} sec)
J	compliance (cm^2/dyn)

K	bulk modulus (dyn/cm²)
K_0	bulk modulus at $p = 0$ (dynes cm^{-2})
k	Boltzmann constant (erg moles^{-1} °K^{-1})
M	molecular weight
M_u	reduced mass of oscillators along a backbone chain
n	refractive index
N_A	Avogadro number
N_D	$= \tau_i/t =$ Deborah number
N	number of mobile segments per molecule
P	permeability
P	pressure (dyn/cm²) or (atm)
R	gas constant (cal/mole °K)
S_e	configurational entropy contribution at $T = T_g$ (see [24])
s	solubility
t	time
t_d	time required for a given deformation
T	temperature (°K)
T_b	atmospheric boiling point (°K)
T_g	glass-transition temperature (°K)
V	molal volume (cm³/mole)
V_w	van der Waals volume (cm³ mole^{-1}), see reference 11
V_e	free volume at $T = T_g$ (see [34])
v_g	specific volume at T_g
X	length, distance (cm)
x	mole fraction
α	half of the bond angle
α	cubic expansion coefficient (°K^{-1})
α_c	cubic expansion coefficient of crystalline solid (°K^{-1})
α_g	cubic expansion coefficient of glassy solid (°K^{-1})
α_L	cubic expansion coefficient of liquid (°K^{-1})
β	compressibility (dyne^{-1} cm²)
β_g	compressibility of glassy solid (dyne^{-1} cm²)
β_l	compressibility of liquid (dyne^{-1} cm²)
γ	$= C_p/C_v$
γ	Grueneisen constant
δ	loss angle
ϵ	dielectric constant
ϵ_s	static dielectric constant
θ	angle between direction of temperature gradient and molecule axis
θ_D	Debye temperature of solid (°K)
Λ_p	phonon path length taken as persistence length (13.35)

λ	thermal conductivity (cal/cm sec °K)
λ_0	thermal conductivity of isotropic solid
$\lambda_{\parallel}$	thermal conductivity parallel to direction of orientation
$\lambda_{\perp}$	thermal conductivity normal to direction of orientation
μ	dipole moment, e.s.u.
ξ	material property in (13.20) and (13.21) (dyn/cm²)
ρ	density
ρ^*	$= V_w/V$
ρ_c	density of crystalline solid
ρ_g	density of glassy solid
ρ_w	$= M/V_w$
$\bar{\rho}$	inverse of partial specific volume
σ	stress (dyn/cm²)
$\sigma_i{}'$	lateral contraction ratio (Poisson's Ratio) (of component i)
τ	relaxation time (sec)
τ_r	retardation time (sec)
φ_i	volume fraction of component i
ω	frequency (sec⁻¹)

REFERENCES

[1] Abu-Isa, I., and M. Dole, *J. Phys. Chem.* **69**, 2668 (1965).

[2] Adam, G., *Kolloid-Z.* **180**, 11 (1962); **195**, 1 (1964).

[3] Adam, G., and J. H. Gibbs, *J. Chem. Phys.* **43**, 139 (1965).

[4] Albert, W., *Kunststoffe* **53**, 86 (1963).

[5] Alfrey, T., et al., *J. Appl. Phys.* **14**, 700 (1943).

[6] Alfrey, T., et al., *J. Polymer Sci.* **C12**, 249 (1966).

[7] Allen, G., et al., *Polymer* **1**, 467 (1960); **2**, 375 (1961).

[8] Baccaredda, M., et al., *Chim. Ind.* **40**, 356 (1958).

[9] Bestul, A. B., and S. S. Chang, *J. Chem. Phys.* **40**, 3731 (1964).

[10] Bianchi, U., and C. Rossi, *Chim. Ind.* **44**, 1362 (1962).

[10a] Birnthaler, W., *Kunststoffe* **38**, 11 (1948).

[11] Blatz, P. J., *GALCIT* Rept 61–26.

[12] Bohn, L., *Kunststoffe* **53**, 826 (1963).

[13] Bondi, A., *J. Polymer Sci.* **A2**, 3159 (1964).

[14] Bondi, A., *Phys. Chem. Solids* **28**, 649 (1967).

[15] Bondi, A., *J. Appl. Polymer Sci.* **9**, 3897 (1965).

[16] Boyer, R. F., *Rubber Chem. Technol.* **36**, 1303 (1963).

[17] Braun, G., and A. J. Kovacs, in *Physics of Non-Crystalline Solids*, North-Holland, Amsterdam, 1965, p. 303.

[18] Breuer, A., and G. Rehage, *Kolloid-Z.* **216**, 159 (1967); *Ber. Bunsenges* **71** (1967).

[19] Conix, A., and L. Jeurissen, *Advan. Chem. Ser.* **48**, 172 (1965).

[20] Crank, J., *Mathematics of Diffusion*, Oxford University Press, London 1956 (see also [59]).

[21] Crissman, J. M., et al., *J. Polymer Sci.* **A2**, 5075 (1964); **A3**, 2693 (1965).

[22] Cunningham, R. E., *J. Polymer Sci.* **42**, 571 (1960).

[23] Dainton, F. S., et al., *Polymer* **3**, 263–321 (1962).
[24] Dok, M., *Fortschr. Hochpolymer, Forschg.* **2**, 221 (1960).
[25] Draisbach, H. C., et al., *Z. Naturforsch.* **17a**, 447 (1962).
[26] Eiermann, K., *Kunststoffe* **51**, 512 (1961).
[27] Eiermann, K., *Kolloid-Z.* **198**, 5 (1964).
[28] Eisenberg, A., and S. Saito, *J. Chem. Phys.* **45**, 1673 (1966).
[29] Ferry, J. D., and R. A. Stratton, *Kolloid-Z.* **171**, 107 (1960).
[30] Ferry, J. D., *Viscoelastic Properties of Polymers*, Wiley, New York, 1962.
[31] Fröhlich, H., *Theory of Dielectrics*, Oxford University Press, London, 1949.
[32] Gee, G., Report to Mich. Foundation for Adv. Res., 1965.
[33] Gibbs, J. H., and E. A. diMarzio, *J. Chem. Phys.* **28**, 373, 805 (1958).
[34] Goldstein, M. J., *Chem. Phys.* **39**, 3369 (1963).
[35] Guth, E., *J. Appl. Phys.* **16**, 20 (1945).
[36] Hashin, Z., and S. Shtrikman, *J. Mech. Phys. Solids* **11**, 127 (1963).
[37] Hashin, Z., and B. W. Rosen, *Trans. Am. Soc. Mech. Engrs., Ser. E.* **31**, 223 (1964).
[38] Hellwege, K. H., et al., *Kolloid-Z.* **180**, 126 (1962).
[39] Hellwege, K. H., et al., *Kolloid-Z.* **183**, 110 (1962).
[40] Hellwege, K. H., et al., *Kolloid-Z.* **188**, 121 (1963).
[41] Hennig, J., *Kolloid-Z.* **200**, 46 (1964); **202**, 127 (1965).
[42] Hennig, J., *Kolloid-Z.* **196**, 136 (1964).
[43] Heydemann, P., *Acustica* **9**, 446 (1959).
[43a] Heydemann, P., and H. D. Guicking, *Kolloid-Z.* **193**, 16 (1963).
[44] Hoffmann, W., et al., *Chem. Ingr. Tech.* **37**, 34 (1965).
[45] Horsley, R. A., *Plastics Progress* 1957, Philosophical Library, London, 1958, p. 77.
[46] Illers, K. H., *Rheol. Acta* **3**, 185, 194. 202 (1964).
[46a] Jackson, W. J., Jr., and J. R. Caldwell, *Advan. Chem. Sci.* **48**, 185 (1966); *J. Appl. Polymer Sci.* **11**, 211, 227 (1967).
[46b] Jenckel, E., and R. Heusch, *Kolloid-Z.* **130**, 89 (1953).
[47] Kastner, S., *Kolloid-Z.* **206**, 29 (1965).
[48] Kanig, G., *Kolloid-Z.* **190**, 1 (1963).
[49] Kanig, G., *Kolloid-Z.* **203**, 161 (1965).
[50] Karasz, F. E., et al., *J. Phys. Chem.* **69**, 2657 (1965).
[51] Krause, S., et al., *J. Polymer Sci.* **3**, 3575 (1965).
[52] Klemens, P. G., *Non-Crystalline Solids*, V. D. Frechette, ed., Wiley, New York, 1960.
[53] Kovacs, A. J., *Fortschr. Hochpolymer. Forschg.* **3**, 394 (1963).
[54] Kovacs, A. J., *Rheol. Acta* **5**, 262 (1966).
[55] Kovacs, A. J., unpublished measurements.
[56] Kosfeld, R., *Advan. Chem. Ser.* **48**, 49 (1965).
[57] Litovitz, T. A., and C. M. Davis, *Physical Acoustics*, W. P. Mason, ed., Academic Press, New York, vol. 2A, 1965.
[58] Luther, H., and H. Meyer, *Z. Elektrochem.* **64**, 681 (1960).
[59] Mann, J., and L. Holliday, private communication.
[59a] Martin, G., *J. Chim. Phys.* **64**, 347 (1967).
[60] Marvin, R. S., and J. E. McKinney, *Physical Acoustics*, W. P. Mason, ed., Academic Press, New York, vol. 2B, 1965.
[61] McCall, D. W., *J. Phys. Chem.* **70**, (1966).
[62] McLaughlin, E., *Chem. Rev.* **64**, 389 (1964).
[63] Meares, P., *Trans. Faraday Soc.* **54**, 40 (1958).
[64] Meares, P., *J. Am. Chem. Soc.* **76**, 3415 (1954).
[64a] Müller, F. H., W. Hellmut, and H. G. Killian, *Kolloid-Z.* **218**, 10 (1967).

[65] Nanda, V. S., and R. Simha, *J. Chem. Phys.* **41**, 3870 (1964).
[66] Passaglia, E., and H. K. Kevorkian, *J. Appl. Phys.* **34**, 90 (1963).
[67] Passaglia, E., and G. M. Martin, *J. Res. Natl. Bur. St.* **68A**, 273 (1964).
[67a] Patterson, D., *Rubber Chem. Technol.* **40**, 1 (1967).
[68] Pinnock, P. R., and I. M. Ward, *Proc. Phys. Soc.* (London) **81**, 260 (1963).
[69] Plazek, D. J., and J. H. Magill, *J. Chem. Phys.* **45**, 3038 (1966).
[70] Raumann, G., *Brit. J. Appl. Phys.* **14**, 795 (1963).
[71] Reese, W., and J. E. Tucker, *J. Chem. Phys.* **43**, 105 (1965).
[72] Reese, W., *J. Appl. Phys.* **37**, 3227 (1966).
[73] Reese, W., *J. Appl. Phys.* **37**, 3959 (1966).
[74] Reinking, N. H., et al., *J. Appl. Polymer Sci.* **7**, 2135, 2145, 2153 (1963).
[75] Robertson, R. E., *J. Phys. Chem.* **69**, 1575 (1965).
[76] Robertson, R. E., *J. Chem. Phys.* **44**, 3950 (1966).
[77] Rogers, C. E., *Physics and Chemistry of the Organic Solid State*, Fox, Labes, and Weissberger, eds., Wiley, New York, vol. 2, 1965, p. 510.
[78] Rosenbaum, S., *J. Polymer Sci.* **A3**, 1949 (1965).
[79] Saito, N., et al., *Solid State Phys.* **14**, 344 (1963).
[80] Sato, K., et al., *J. Phys. Soc. Japan* **9**, 413 (1954).
[81] Sauer, J. A., et al., *J. Appl. Phys.* **20**, 507 (1949).
[82] Schatzki, T. F., private communication.
[83] Schreyer, G., *Rheol. Acta* **3**, 218 (1964).
[84] Schwarzl, N., *Kolloid-Z.* **165**, 88, 94 (1959).
[85] Schwarzl, F. R., et al., *TNO Nieuws* **21**, 74 (1966).
[86] Sharonov, Y. A., and M. V. Volkenshtein, *Soviet Phys.-Solid State* **5**, 429 (1963); *Vysokomolekulyarnye Soedineniya* **4**, 917 (1962).
[87] Shen, M. C., and A. V. Tobolsky, *Advan. Chem. Ser.* **48**, 27 (1965).
[88] Sherby, D. N., and J. E. Dorn, *J. Mech. Phys. Solids* **6**, 158 (1958).
[89] Simha, R., and R. F. Boyer, *J. Chem. Phys.* **37**, 1003 (1962).
[90] Stannett, V., and J. L. Williams, *J. Polymer Sci.* **C10**, 45 (1965).
[90a] Staverman, A. J., *Rheol. Acta* **5**, 283 (1966); *Kolloid-Z.* **216**, 81 (1967).
[91] Struik, L. C. E., *Rheol. Acta* **5**, 303 (1966).
[92] Theocaris, P. S., *Rheol. Acta* **3**, 299 (1964).
[93] Theocaris, P. S., and C. Hadjijoseph, *Kolloid-Z.* **202**, 133 (1965).
[94] Turnbull, D., and M. H. Cohen, *Modern Aspects of the Vitreous State*, J. D. Mackenzie, ed., Butterworths, London, 1960.
[95] Turnbull, D., and M. H. Cohen, *J. Chem. Phys.* **34**, 120 (1961).
[96] Ueberreiter, K., and W. Bruns, *Ber. Bunsenges.* **68**, 541 (1964); **70**, 17 (1967).
[97] Waterman, H. A., *Rheol. Acta* **5**, 140 (1966).
[98] Weitsman, Y., and M. A. Sadowsky, *Int. J. Mech. Sci.* **6**, 241 (1964).
[99] Wilkinsen, R. W., and M. Dole, *J. Polymer Sci.* **58**, 1089 (1962).
[100] Woodward, A. E., and J. A. Sauer, *Physics and Chemistry of the Organic Solid State*, Fox, Labes, and Weissberger, eds., Wiley, New York, vol. 2, 1965, p. 637.
[101] Wunderlich, B., *J. Phys. Chem.* **64**, 1052 (1960).
[102] Vieth, W. R., et al., *J. Coll. Sci.* **20**, 9 (1965); **22**, 454 (1966).

GENERAL READING

Die Physik der Hochpolymeren, H. A. Stuart, ed., Springer, Berlin, Vol. 4, 1956, Chapters 6, 8, 9.

"Glass Transitions in Polymers," M. C. Shen and A. Eisenberg, in *Progress in Solid State Chemistry*, Vol. 3, Pergamon Press, 1966.

14

Catalog of
Molecular Properties

Most of the correlations of this book are based on the use of experimentally accessible molecular properties as correlating parameters, the van der Waals (contact) dimensions and volumes, a standard energy of vaporization (for liquids), and a standard heat of sublimation (for solids). The group increments for all of these and for several related (molecular) properties have been assembled in the tabulated array, Table 14.1 to 16. Supplementary information is collected in the individual subsections of this Chapter.

14.1 VAN DER WAALS VOLUMES AND RADII

The central position of the packing density $\rho^* \equiv \rho V_w / M$ in the present scheme of property correlations for solids and liquids demands the availability of reliable information for calculating the van der Waals volume V_w. V_w is calculated from experimental data, namely, from bond distances l and the nonbonded contact radii, the so-called van der Waals radii r_w, by means of the purely geometrical method shown in Figure 14.1.

The underlying assumptions are that the appropriate values of l and r_w are known and that the geometry of Figure 14.1 represents the facts. The appropriate value of l is known very accurately from the extensive collections of x-ray diffraction and microwave data that are generally available [4] [9]. Moreover, bond-radii are commonly transferable and corrections due to specific effects have also been well established. The van der Waals radii (r_w), by contrast, are only moderately well established, and the rules for their transferability are only beginning to be worked out [2]. Considering the weakness of the cohesive forces in molecular crystals, we may marvel at the degree of transferability of r_w data actually observed.

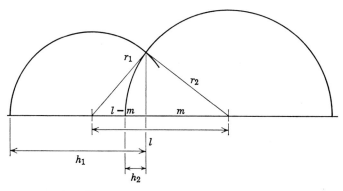

r_1, r_2 = van der Waals radii,
   l = covalent bond distance,
  m = auxiliary parameter,
h_1, h_2 = height of sphere segments,

$$m = \frac{r_2^2 - r_1^2 + l^2}{21} \; ; h_1 = r_1 + 1 - m; h_2 = r_2 - m,$$

$$V_1^1 = \pi h_1^2 \left(r_1 - \frac{h_1}{3}\right); \Delta V_{2-1} = \pi h_2^2 \left(V_2 - \frac{h_2}{3}\right); V_2 = \frac{4\pi}{3} r_2^3.$$

Example. van der Waals volume of diatomic molecule:

$$V_w = N_A(V_1^1 + V_2 - \Delta V_{2-1}) \times 10^{-24} \text{ cm}^3/\text{mole},$$

where $N_A = 6.02 \times 10^{23}$ molecules/mole and r's are given in Angstrom units.

Volume of center atom = total volume of atom.

Surface area = $2\pi rh$; $A_w = 2\pi N_A(r_1 h_1 + 2r_2^2 - r_2 h_2)$.

Figure 14.1   Methods of calculation of van der Waals volumes.

Two aspects of atom shapes are not considered in the model of Figure 14.1: (a) The increasing evidence for true anisometry of bonded atoms parallel and normal to their covalent bonds in specific bonding states, and (b) the pear shape which has been deduced from the absence of thermochemical and spectral evidence of strain, where the nominal van der Waals radii should have caused appreciable repulsion within a given molecule. Neither of these deviations from the assumption of sphericity has as yet been established in sufficient detail for rigorous calculation of V_w. Hence deviations from sphericity must be handled by empirical correction of V_w to meet the requirement that the observed density and energy of vaporization of a given compound lead to the correct number of external degrees of freedom per molecule (Chapter 8).

The rarity of the need for empirical corrections in very crowded molecules can be understood by inspection of Figure 8.2. The small amount of overlap of neighboring atoms in nonbonded positions is generally just compensated by the volume of intersection of cut-out sphere segments on the central atom, which had been ignored in the calculation and thus subtracted unnecessarily. This compensation is insufficient if

$$l < 0.9 r_w(L) \qquad \text{as well as} \qquad r_w(C) < r_w(L),$$

where C and L refer to central and ligand atoms, respectively. This comparatively rare case is exemplified by the ethers discussed earlier, and has been incorporated in the catalog of V_w increments, Tables 14.1 through 14.16.

Currently recommended van der Waals radii have been cataloged in Tables 14.1 through 14.16 and 14.18. Deviations from earlier values are based on more recent x-ray diffraction data. The currently recommended V_w increments have been cataloged in Tables 14.1 through 17.

Most of the changes from the earlier compilation are toward somewhat lower numerical values as the quality of x-ray diffraction data improves. This trend also makes the resulting volume increments more consistent with the p-v-T data of liquids, although a few exceptions can be noted.

We may conclude from a recent discussion [2] that the V_w increment of metals in nonionic metal–organic compounds should be taken as identical with their refractivity in the Batsanov Table 14.19. Although no significant deviation from this guideline has so far been found, it should be treated with caution. The identity may not be applicable in highly associated alkali-metal alkyls or in systems involving strongly electron-deficient binding as in the aluminum alkyls. Its applicability is most unlikely whenever the metal atom is bound to noncarbon atoms, or when its binding state differs substantially from that in metal alkyls, as it does in the ferrocene-type compounds. The appropriate values of $[R]_\infty$ must then be determined experimentally before insertion into the V_w calculation.

14.2 ENERGY OF VAPORIZATION, E°

The standard energy of vaporization, as defined for the purposes of liquid-phase property correlations is given by

$$E^\circ = \Delta H_v - RT$$

at that temperature T at which

$$V^* = M/\rho V_w = 1.70.$$

This standard state corresponds to the temperature near the melting point of most low-melting organic compounds and had been chosen in order to relate most closely to the packing density prevailing in high-molecular-weight liquids and polymer melts in the temperature range of technical interest. A fixed packing density as standard state implies the dependence of the physical properties on a central force field, and can therefore lead only to approximate property correlations.

Table 14.1 General Catalog of Group Increments* for Molecular Properties. Alkyl Groups

No.	Property	Units	—Me	—Et	—n-pr	—i-pr	—t-bu	Me Me >C<	>CH₂	>CH	>C<
1	V_w	cm³/mole	13.67	23.90	34.13	34.12	44.34	30.67	10.23	6.78	3.33
2	A_w	10^9cm²/mole	2.12	3.47	4.82	4.81	6.36	4.24	1.35	0.57	0
3	r_w	10^{-8} cm	2.0	2.0	2.0				2.0		
4	$d_w (=1.47\, V_w^{1/3})$	10^{-8} cm	3.5	4.2	4.8	4.8	5.2	5.1^d	4.2^d	3.7^d	
5											
6	$E°$	cal/mole	2000	3130	4200	3900	4610		1070		
7	$H_0°$	cal/mole	2520			4975	5650	2920	1515		
8	H_s^1	cal/mole	2450^a	4280	6100	4950	5600		2000		
9	$3c^b$	—	b = 5.0								
10	f^b	—	$(N_s - 1)$	2.0	3.0	3.0	4.0	3.0	1.0	1.0	
11	[P]	—	55.5	95.5	135.5	133.3	170.4	115	40.0*		
12	[R]$_D$	cm³/mole	5.718						4.618	3.518	2.418
13	V_0(Riedel)	cm³/mole									
14	V_0(Biltz)^c	cm³/mole	20.2 even 21.2 odd						13.4^e	8.5	3.4
15	Δ_T(Riedel)	(see eq. 15.17)	0.16						0.16	0.013	0.003

* For additivity relations see Table 15.1.

^{a} For n-alkanes $H_s(-\text{Me})$ even = 2,140 cal/mole; $H_s(-\text{Me})$ odd = 1,910 cal/mole.

^{b} For homologous series, for which

$$3c = 6.0 + a(N_s - 1)\left(1 + \frac{b}{(N_s - 1)}\right);$$

^{c} Developed from Biltz' original data. These are not Biltz' increments.

^{d} For these enchained groups $d_w = (2.12\, V_w/l_p)^{1/2}$ in 10^{-8}cm, where l_p = projected length of the group.

^{e} This is the generally valid datum; in alkyl aromatics and in dioic acids $V_0(CH_2) = 14.0$ cm³.

N_s = number of skeletal atoms or groups per molecule; a = 0.43 unless noted otherwise.

453

Table 14.2 General Catalog of Group Increments for Molecular Properties. Cycloalkane Derivatives

No.	Property	Units	Cyclopropyl-	Cyclobutyl-	Cyclopentyl-	Cyclohexyl-	Decalyl-
1	V_w	cm^3/mole			46.5	56.8	
2	A_w	10^9cm^2/mole					
3	r_w	10^{-8} cm					
4	$\overline{d_w}(=1.47\,V_w^{\frac{1}{3}})$	10^{-8} cm			5.3	5.7	
5							
6	$E°$	cal/mole			$6100 - 200\Sigma$[f]	$6850 - 200\Sigma$[f]	
7	$H_0°$	cal/mole			8060	$9123 - 150\Sigma$	9120
8	H_s^1	cal/mole			9000	$8500 + \dfrac{700}{N_B}$	13,100
9	$3c^b$	—	1.0			$6 + 0.44(N_c - 6)$	
10	f^b	—		1.0	1.0	1.0	1.0
11	$[P]$	—			188.0	225	
12	$[R]_D$(Riedel)	cm^3/mole					
13	V_0(Biltz)[c]	cm^3/mole					
14	V_0(Biltz)[c]	cm^3/mole			13.8/CH$_2$	13.8/CH$_2$	
15	Δ_T(Riedel)	(see eq. 15.17)					

f $\sum = \sum\limits_{2}^{N_B} \dfrac{1}{N_B - 1}$, where N_B = number of carbon atoms in alkyl branch chain.

Table 14.3 General Catalog of Group Increments for Molecular Properties. Alkene Derivatives

No.	Property	Units	=CH₂	=CH—	>C<	Allene =C=	H—C≡	≡C—	—C≡ (Diacetylene)
1	V_w	cm³/mole	11.94	8.47	5.01	6.96	11.55	8.05	7.82
2	A_w	10⁹cm²/mole	1.86	1.08	0.61		1.74	0.98	0.96
3	r_w	10⁻⁸ cm					1.78	1.78	1.78
4	$d_w(=1.47\,V_w^{1/3})$	10⁻⁸ cm	3.3	3.9ᵈ	3.0ᵈ	3.3ᵈ	3.3	3.5ᵈ	3.5ᵈ
5									
6	$E°$	cal/mole	3150				3650		
7	$H_0°$	cal/mole							
8	H_s^1	cal/mole	2140	2000	1500	(2300)	3400	2180	
9	$3c^b$	—							
10	f^b	—	0.5	0.5	0.5		0.5	0.5	0.5
11	$[P]$		59	41.5	26		65	49.6	
12	$[R]_D$	cm³/mole	5.485	4.385	3.285	4.151	5.916	4.816	
13	V_0(Riedel)	cm³/mole	17.0	(10.7)					
14	V_0(Biltz)ᶜ	cm³/mole							
15	Δ_T(Riedel)	(see eq. 15.17)	0.015	0.015	0.003	0.003			

Table 14.4 General Catalog of Group Increments for Molecular Properties. Aromatic Groups

No.	Property	Units	$=$CH ar	C ar cond	$=$C—R al ar	Phenyl[g]	Phenylene[g]	Naphthyl[g]
1	V_w	cm³/mole	8.06	4.74	5.54	45.84	43.32	71.45
2	A_w	10^9cm²/mole	1.00	0.21	0.30	5.33	4.65	7.76
3	r_w	10^{-8} cm	1.77	1.77	1.77	3.73/2	3.73/2	
4	$\overline{d_w}(=1.47\,V_w^{1/3})$	10^{-8} cm				5.3	4.4[d]	6.1
5								
6	$E°$	cal/mole	1.41	0.6		$7270 - 300\Sigma$	$6070 - 300\Sigma$	10,520
7	$H_0°$	cal/mole				$9800 - 440\Sigma$	$8580 - 300\Sigma$	15,230
8	H_s^1	cal/mole	1.73	1.35		$8400 + \dfrac{1600}{N_B}$	$7000 + \dfrac{4800^h}{N_B}$	15,000
9	$3c^b$	—				b = 2.5		
10	f^b	—				1.0	1.0	1.0
11	$[P]$					188.5		
12	$[R]_D$	cm³/mole				24.42	22.74	38.63
13	V_0(Riedel)	cm³/mole						
14	V_0(Biltz)[c]	cm³/mole	11.55	5.1	5.7	63.4	57.5	96.5
15	Δ_T(Riedel)[d]	cm³/mole						

g Items 6, 7, 8, 9 for alkyl derivatives.
h For 1,4 1,3 1,2 position
  Subtract 0 0.9 2.4 kcal/mole

Table 14.5 General Catalog of Group Increments for Molecular Properties. Nitrogen Groups

No.	Property	Units	$-NH_2$ al	$-NH_2$ ar	$>NH$ al	$>NH$ ar	$>NH$ hetero–al	$>NH$ hetero–ar
1	V_w	cm³/mole	$10.54 - \delta V_w$	$10.54 - \delta V_w$	$8.08 - \delta V_w$	(8.08)		
2	A_w	10⁹ cm²/mole	$1.74 - \delta A_w$	$1.74 - \delta A_w$	$0.99 - \delta V_w$	(0.99)		
3	r_w	10⁻⁸ cm	1.7_5	1.7_5	1.6_5	1.6_5		
4	$\overline{d_w}(=1.47\,V_w^{1/3})$	10⁻⁸ cm	3.2	3.2	3.8^d	3.8^d		
5								
6	$E°$	cal/mole	4330	4240	3260		2900	3200
7	$H_0°$	cal/mole						
8	H_s^1	cal/mole	6350	6500	4500		4880	7300
9	$3c^b$	—						
10	f^b	—	1.0	1.0	1.0	1.0	1.0	1.0
11	$[P]$		44.0	41.0	29.3	25.0		
12	$[R]_D$	cm³/mole	4.522		3.602			
13	V_0(Riedel)	cm³/mole						
14	V_0(Biltz)ᵉ	cm³/mole						
15	Δ_T(Riedel)	cm³/mole	0.027	0.027	0.027			

Table 14.6 General Catalog of Group Increments for Molecular Properties. Nitrogen Groups (continued)

No.	Property	Units	⟩N— al	⟩=N— hetero-ar	⟩N (ring) ar	—N=N— ar	—C≡N al	—C≡N al per	—C≡N ar
1	V_w	cm³/mole	4.33	5.2	43.0		14.7	(14.7)	14.7
2	A_w	10^9 cm²/mole	0.23				2.19	(2.19)	2.19
3	r_w	10^{-8} cm	1.5_5	1.6		1.60	1.78	1.78	1.78
4	$d_w(=1.47\,V_w^{1/3})$	10^{-8} cm			5.1		3.6	3.6	3.6
5									
6	$E°$	cal/mole	(400)	2300	8030		$5350 + \dfrac{1000}{N_c}$		(5000)
7	$H_0°$	cal/mole							
8	H_s^1	cal/mole	0	4150	12,500	4700	$6180 + \dfrac{2240}{N_c}$	3900	
9	$3c^b$	—							
10	f^b	—			1.0	1.0 $\binom{45\ \text{al}}{53\ \text{ar}}$	1.0	1.0	1.0
11	$[P]$		10.5				66		69
12	$[R]_D$	cm³/mole	2.840		22.78		5.536		
13	V_0(Riedel)	cm³/mole							
14	V_0(Biltz)^c	cm³/mole							
15	Δ_T(Riedel)	cm³/mole	0.012				0.053		0.053

Table 14.7 General Catalog of Group Increments for Molecular Properties. Nitrogen Groups (continued)

No.	Property	Units	—NO₂ mono, al	—NO₂ per, al	—NO₂ mono, ar	—NO₂ di, tri, ar	—O—NO₂ al, mono	—O—NO₂ al, di, tri
1	V_w	cm³/mole	16.8					
2	A_w	10^9 cm²/mole	2.55					
3	r_w	10^{-8} cm						
4	$\dfrac{r_w}{d_w}(=1.47\,V_w^{1/3})$	10^{-8} cm	3.8					
5								
6	$E°$	cal/mole	$5600 + \dfrac{1600}{N_c}$		4870		$5200 + \dfrac{1400}{N_c}$	
7	$H_0°$	cal/mole						
8	H_s^1	cal/mole	9600	3260	6800	5500	9600	9200
9	$3c^b$	—						
10	f^b	—	1.0	1.0	1.0	1.0	1.0	1.0
11	[P]		73		75		95	
12	$[R]_D$	cm³/mole	6.71				7.24	7.24
13	V_0(Riedel)	cm³/mole						
14	V_0(Biltz)ᶜ	cm³/mole						
15	Δ_T(Riedel)	cm³/mole						

Table 14.8 General Catalog of Group Increments for Molecular Properties. Phosphorous Groups

No.	Property	Units	—PH₂ al, mono	>PH al	$\overset{\|}{\underset{al}{-P-}}$	$\overset{\|}{\underset{ar}{-P-}}$	(—O)₃P=O al	(—O)₃P=O ar
1	V_w	cm³/mole	16.6	13.5₃	10.44	10.44	25.8	25.8
2	A_w	10⁹ cm²/mole						
3	r_w.	10⁻⁸ cm			1.80	1.80		
4	$\overline{d_w}(=1.47 V_w^{1/3})$	10⁻⁸ cm	3.7	3.6ᵈ	3.2ᵈ	3.2ᵈ	(4.3)ᵈ	(4.3)ᵈ
5								
6	$E°$	cal/mole					$2100 + \dfrac{13{,}600}{N_c}$	
7	$H_0°$	cal/mole						
8	H_s^1	cal/mole	4750	4600	2930		9000	
9	$3c^b$							
10	f^b		1.0	1.0			1.0	1.0
11	$[P]$							
12	$[R]_D$		11.34	10.24	9.14	10.2	10.89	(10.9)
13	V_0(Riedel)	cm³/mole						
14	V_0(Biltz)ᶜ	cm³/mole			14.4			
15	Δ_T(Riedel)							

Table 14.9 General Catalog of Group Increments for Molecular Properties. Oxygen Groups

No.	Property	Units	—O— al	—O— ar	—O— hetero, al	—O— hetero, ar	—OH al	—OH ar
1	V_w	cm³/mole	3.7	3.2			$8.04 - \delta V_w$	$8.04 - \delta V_w$
2	A_w	10^9 cm²/mole	0.60	0.54			$1.46 - \delta A_w$	$1.46 - \delta A_w$
3	r_w	10^{-8} cm	1.45	1.45				
4	$\overline{d_w}(=1.47\,V_w^{1/3})$	10^{-8} cm	2.6^d	2.7^d	—	—	2.9^d	2.9^d
5								
6	$E°$	cal/mole	$1600 + \dfrac{400}{N_c}$			1750		
7	$H_0°$	cal/mole						
8	H_s^1	cal/mole	$1550 + \dfrac{2360}{N_c}$ $b = 5.0^i$	1000	$1060 + \dfrac{8800}{N_c}$	1600	8200	6800
9	$3c^b$							
10	f^b	—					1.0	1.0
11	$[P]$	—	20	22	21	23	30*	34
12	$[R]_D$	cm³/mole	1.643				2.625	4.629
13	V_0(Riedel)	cm³/mole						
14	V_0(Biltz)^c	cm³/mole	7.0				12	14.8
15	Δ_T(Riedel)	cm³/mole	0.020				0.070	0.029

^{i} Extra term: $+0.06\,N(C—O)$ where $N(C—O)$ = number of C—O bonds per molecule.

461

Table 14.10 General Catalog of Group Increments for Molecular Properties. Carbonyl and Aldehyde Groups

No.	Property	Units	$>C=O$ al	$>C=O$ ar	$C=O$ hetero, ar	$O=C-OH$	$H-C=O$ al	$H-C=O$ ar
1	V_w	cm³/mole	11.70				15.14	15.14
2	A_w	10^9 cm²/mole	1.60				2.37	2.37
3	r_w	10^{-8} cm					1.65	1.65
4	$d_w\,(=1.47\,V_w^{1/3})$	10^{-8} cm	4.4^d		—		3.64	3.64
5								
6	$E°$	cal/mole	$2400 + \dfrac{3800}{N_c}$	3500			5200	5000
7	$H_0°$	cal/mole						
8	H_s^1	cal/mole	5600	3600	6000		6400	
9	$3c^b$	—						
10	f^b	—	1.0	1.0	1.0	2.0	1.0	1.0
11	$[P]$	—						
12	$[R]_D$	cm³/mole	4.629				5.728	5.729
13	V_0(Riedel)	cm³/mole						
14	V_0(Blitz)^c	cm³/mole	14.8			24.5	19.0	19.0
15	Δ_T(Riedel)	cm³/mole	0.046					

Table 14.11 General Catalog of Group Increments for Molecular Properties. Carboxyl Ester and Carbonate Ester Groups

No.	Property	Units	O=C−O− al	O=C−O− hetero, al	O=C−O− ar	−O−C=O al	−O−C=O hetero, al	−C−O−C=O al	O=C−O−C−O=C hetero, al
1	V_w	cm³/mole	15.2		15.2				
2	A_w	10⁹ cm²/mole	2.20		2.20				
3	r_w	10⁻⁸ cm							
4	$d_w(=1.47\,V_w^{1/3})$	10⁻⁸ cm	3.65d		3.65d				
5									
6	E°	cal/mole	$3430+\dfrac{200}{N_c}$	8750	3300	4700	11,500	5600	11,200
7	H_0°	cal/mole							
8	H_s^1	cal/mole	$4400+\dfrac{5100}{N_c}$	10,500			13,100		14,500
9	$3c^b$	—	1.0						
10	f^b	—		1.0	1.0	1.0			
11	$[P]$								
12	$[R]_D$	cm³/mole	6.272						
13	$V_0(\text{Riedel})$	cm³/mole							
14	$V_0(\text{Biltz})^c$	cm³/mole							
15	$\Delta_T(\text{Riedel})$	cm³/mole	0.039						

Table 14.12 General Catalog of Group Increments for Molecular Properties. Sulfur Groups

No.	Property	Units	—S— al	—S— Heterocyclo aliphatic	—S— ar	—S— hetero, ar	Thio-phenyl-	—S—S— al	S=C(S)(S) (heterocyclic)
1	V_w	cm³/mole	10.8	10.8		11.10	41.74	22.7	
2	A_w	10^9 cm²/mole	1.30	1.30		1.35		1.80	
3	r_w	10^{-8} cm	1.80	1.80		1.82		1.80	
4	$\bar{d}_w (=1.47\,V_w^{1/3})$	10^{-8} cm	3.9[d]	—		—	5.1	3.1[d]	
5									
6	$E°$	cal/mole	$2500 + \dfrac{2000}{N_c}$	$2500 + \dfrac{2000}{N_c}$		2900	7100	$4400 + \dfrac{1900}{N_c}$	13,600
7	$H_0°$	cal/mole							
8	H_s^1	cal/mole	$4280 + \dfrac{1600}{N_c}$	$3530 + \dfrac{6000}{N_c}$		3900	10,500	$5600 + \dfrac{4800}{N_c}$	15,500
9	$3c^b$						1.0	1.0	
10	f^b	—							
11	$[P]$	—	49.1		10.4	7.26		15.84	
12	$[R]_D$	cm³/mole	8.00						
13	V_0(Riedel)	cm³/mole							
14	V_0(Biltz)[e]	cm³/mole							
15	Δ_T(Riedel)	(see eq. 15.17)	0.012						

Table 14.13 General Catalog of Group Increments for Molecular Properties. Sulfur and Selenium Groups

No.	Property	Units	—SH al	—SH ar	$\diagdown$S=O al	$\diagdown$SO$_2$ al	$\diagdown$SO$_2$ hetero, al	$-O-SO_2-O-$ al	—Se—
1	V_w	cm³/mole	14.81	14.81	15.54	20.3		35.1	
2	A_w	10⁹ cm²/mole			1.94	2.60		3.4	
3	r_w	10⁻⁸ cm							1.90
4	$\overline{d_w}(=1.47\,V_w^{1/3})$	10⁻⁸ cm	3.5$_8$	3.53	4.7ᵈ	5.4ᵈ	—		
5									
6	$E°$	cal/mole	$3360+\dfrac{50}{N_c}$						
7	$H_0°$	cal/mole		3500					
8	H_s^1	cal/mole	$5260+\dfrac{1050}{N_c}$	5100	10,900	$7250+\dfrac{13,900}{N_c}$		9100	5600
9	$3c^b$								
10	f^b		1.0	1.0	1.0	1.0		1.0	
11	$[P]$								
12	$[R]_D$	cm³/mole	8.91	9.66	9.07	8.87		11.18	63
13	V_0(Riedel)	cm³/mole							10.78
14	V_0(Biltz)ᶜ	cm³/mole							
15	Δ_T(Riedel)	cm³/mole	0.12						

Table 14.14 General Catalog of Group Increments for Molecular Properties. Halide Groups: F, CF$_3$

No.	Property	Units	$-$F 1-n-, al	$-$F ar, mono	$-$F ar, di, tri	$-$CF$_3$ al	CF$_3$ ar	$-$F per, al	$-$F per, cyclo-al
1	V_w	cm^3/mole	5.72	5.80	5.80	21.33	21.33	6.00	6.00
2	A_w	10^9 cm^2/mole	1.10	1.10	1.10	3.45	3.45	1.15	1.15
3	r_w	10^{-8} cm	1.40	1.47	1.47	2.5	2.5	1.47	1.47
4	$d_w(=1.47\,V_w^{1/3})$	10^{-8} cm	2.6$_4$	2.65	2.65	4.1	4.1	2.7	2.7
5									
6	$E°$	cal/mole	2450	1400	1300	3300	2200	$510 + \dfrac{1250}{N_F^j}$	$520 + \dfrac{1250}{N_F}$
7	$H_0°$	cal/mole							
8	H_s^1	cal/mole	$2430 + \dfrac{600}{N_c}$	1900	1550	4400	3200	$740 + \dfrac{1700}{N_F^j}$	890
9	$3c^b$		$6 = 3.8$						
10	f^b	—				1.0	1.0		
11	$[P]$	—							
12	$[R]_D$	cm^3/mole				6.14		1.24	1.24
13	V_0(Riedel)	cm^3/mole	0.997						
14	V_0(Biltz)^c	cm^3/mole		8.3	7.9 to 9.3^k p m				
15	Δ_T(Riedel)^d		0.015						

^{j} N_{Cl} = number of chlorine atoms per molecule. N_F = number of fluorine atoms per molecule.
^{k} p, m, in para- and metaposition, respectively.

Table 14.15 General Catalog of Group Increments for Molecular Properties. Halide Groups: Cl

No.	Property	Units	—Cl 1-n-al	—CHCl$_2$ 1,1 n-al	—CCl$_3$ al	—Cl al, per	—Cl ar, mono, di	—Cl ar, tri	—Cl ar, per
1	V_w	cm^3/mole	11.62	31.26		12.24	12.00	12.00	12.24
2	A_w	10^9 cm^2/mole	1.80	4.21		1.82	1.81	1.81	1.82
3	r_w	10^{-8} cm	1.73	(3.00)		1.77	1.77	1.77	1.77
4	$\overline{d_w}(=1.47\,V_w^{1/3})$	10^{-8} cm	3.30	5.1					
5									
6	$E°$	cal/mole	$3400 + \dfrac{390}{N_c}$	6000	6450	2080	2960	2360	2000
7	$H_0°$	cal/mole							
8	H_s^1	cal/mole	$3550 + \dfrac{1370}{N_c}$	8400	8500	$1870 + \dfrac{2900}{N_{Cl}^j}$	3500	2800	2820
9	$3c^b$		$b = 4.5$						
10	f^b			1.0	1.0				
11	[P]								
12	[R]$_D$	cm^3/mole	5.97						
13	V_0(Biltz)	cm^3/mole					16		
14	V_0(Riedel)^c	cm^3/mole	$14.3 + 0.87 N_{Cl}^1$						
15	Δ_T(Riedel)^d		0.013						

[1] N_{Cl} = number of chlorine atoms attached to a single carbon atom. N_{Br} = number of bromine atoms attached to a single carbon atom.

Table 14.16 General Catalog of Group Increments for Molecular Properties. Halide Groups: Br, I

No.	Property	Units	—Br 1-n-al	—Br al, per	—Br ar, mono	—I 1-n-al	—I al, t, sec	—I ar
1	V_w	cm³/mole	14.40	14.60	15.12	19.18	20.35	19.64
2	A_w	10⁹ cm²/mole	2.08	2.09	2.13	2.48	2.54	2.51
3	r_w	10⁻⁸ cm	1.84	1.85	2.01	2.01	2.06	2.06
4	$\overline{d_w}(=1.47\,V_w^{1/3})$	10⁻⁸ cm						
5								
6	$E°$	cal/mole	$4000 + \dfrac{440}{N_c}$	2800	3350	$5150 + \dfrac{500}{N_c}$	3300	4100
7	$H_0°$	cal/mole						
8	H_s^1	cal/mole	$4120 + \dfrac{1620}{N_c}$	3340	4280	$5860 + \dfrac{1320}{N_c}$	4600	5030
9	$3c^b$		$b = 4.3$			$b = 2.7$		
10	f^b	—						
11	$[P]$	—						
12	$[R]_D$	cm³/mole	8.86			13.80		
13	V_0(Riedel)^c	cm³/mole			19			
14	V_0(Biltz)^c	cm³/mole	$19.0 + 0.53\,N_{Br}^1$			26.2		24.5
15	Δ_T(Riedel)^d		0.010			(0.01)		

Table 14.17 Corrections to V_w and A_w Necessitated by Intramolecular Effects

Source of Corrections	δV_w $(cm^3\,mole^{-1})$	δA_w $(10^9\,cm^2\,mole^{-1})$
Decrement per single bond between conjugated double bonds	−0.25	
Decrement per single bond adjacent to carboxyl or amide groups	−0.22	
Decrements due to hydrogen-bond formation	—[a]	
Increment per cyclopropyl ring in single-bond attachment[b]	+1.8	
Decrement per cyclopentyl[b] ring and per cyclohexyl ring singly bonded or in condensed cyclic naphthene in *trans* conformation	−1.14	−0.57
Decrement per ring in condensed cyclic naphthene in *cis* conformation	−2.5	−1.2
Decrement per methylene ring condensed to aromatic ring (system), as in tetralin and indane	−1.66	−0.7
Decrement per dioxane ring	−1.70	−0.7

[a] Obtain decrement from Figure 8.7.
[b] Decrements for unbranched single rings are found in Table 8.4.

Standardization at equal Kihara interaction distances would probably be a better choice, leading to higher degrees of approximation in the resulting correlations. However, at the present state of experience with and development of the Kihara potential as correlating tool, that would not have led to easily workable correlations. Further work in this area should be carried out with the Kihara or similar potentials as a point of departure.

The above-defined standard energy of vaporization $E°$ of a given compound is the sum of functional-group contributions, which are nearly independent of the molecular environment. The increment form $E°(X) = a + b/N_c$ expresses the reduction in high-energy $X \cdots X$ contacts by the increase in $X \cdots CH_2$ contacts as the number of carbon atoms (N_c) in the alkyl radical is increased. The relation of $E°(X)$ to the dipole orientation energy and to dispersion energy has been discussed in Chapter 1.

Table 14.18 Recommended van der Waals Dimensions for Multiply Bonded Atoms (Å)

Atom	r_w(head-on)	r_w(lateral)	r_w(average)
C=		1.74 ± 0.02	1.74
C≡		1.78	1.78
N=		1.47 (aromatic)	1.55
N≡	1.40 ± 0.02	1.70	1.60
O=	1.40 ± 0.05	1.60 ± 0.05	1.50

Table 14.19 System of Atomic Refractions [1][a]

Group / Period	1a	2a	3a	4a	5a	6a	7a	8a	1b	2b	3b	4b	5b	6b	7b	8b
I															H 1.02	He 0.50
II	Li 12.6	Be 4.8									B 3.5	C 2.08	N 2.20	O 1.99	F 1.60	Ne 0.95
III	Na 22.8	Mg 13.8									Al 9.9	Si 9.06	P 8.6	S 7.6	Cl 5.71	A 4.00
IV	K 43.4	Ca 25.6	Sc 15	Ti 10.7	V 8.2	Cr 7.2	Mn 7.3	Fe 7.0_5 / Co 6.6 / Ni 6.5_5	Cu 7.0_5	Zn 8.9	Ga 11.6	Ge 11.08	As 10.3	Se 10.8	Br 8.09	Kr 6.04
V	Rb 53.1	Sr 33.2	Y 20.2	Zr 13.9	Nb 10.8_5	Mo 9.4	Tc (8.4)	Ru 8.1 / Rh 8.2 / Pd 8.8	Ag 10.1	Cd 12.7	In 15.3	Sn 16.0	Sb 18.1	Te 14.4	I 14.08	Xe 9.90
VI	Cs 65.9	Ba 37.3	La 22.1	Hf 13.4	Ta 10.8_5	W 9.5	Re 8.8	Os 8.4 / Ir 8.5 / Pt 9.0	Au 10.1	Hg 13.8	Tl 16.9	Pb 17.9	Bi 21.0	Po —	At —	Rn —

Lanthanides

Ce 20.6	Pr 20.7	Nd 20.6	Pm —	Sm 21.7	Eu 29.0	Gd 19.7	Tb 19.1	Dy 19.0	Ho 18.8	Er 18.2	Tm 18.1	Yb 24.7	Cp 17.9

Actinides

Th 19.8	Pa 15.0	U 12.5	Np 11.6	Pu —	Am 20.8

[a] In cm³/g atom.

Caution should be exercised when assembling $E°(X)$ increments of several nonhydrocarbon functional groups in a single molecule, especially when the groups have fewer than one unsubstituted methylene group between them. Closer proximity leads to appreciable reduction in the $E°(X)$ increment. The appropriate corrections should be obtained from data for analogous compounds. Per-substitution is an extreme case where most intermolecular contacts of the dipoles are in an electrostatically repulsive orientation. The consequences for $E°(X)$ are illustrated by the data of Table 1.5.

The few $E°(X)$ data given for hydrogen-bonding groups should be taken as illustrative only. They should be used only for the types of compounds indicated (alcohols, amines, etc.) because hydrogen-bond interaction with other functional groups such as ethers, ketones, sulfones, etc., are often very specific and should be the subject of a special investigation. In the present context the lack of this information will rarely be felt because the physical properties of hydrogen-bonding compounds can in general not be correlated by the methods developed for non-associating liquids and solids. The association equilibrium data required for the development of such correlations are becoming available just now [7].

New group increments should be obtained by estimating ΔH_v (from calorimetric and/or vapor-pressure data) of the parent (or any) compound of a series at the temperature at which $V^* = 1.70$, and subtracting from this number $E°$ of the appropriate alkyl group shown in Table 14.1.

14.3 HEAT OF VAPORIZATION AT $0°K$, $H_0°$

Evaluation of vapor-pressure data by means of correctly formulated vapor-pressure equations leads to the extrapolated heat of vaporization at $0°K$, $\Delta H_0°$, as a parameter. When using this number we should always remember that it is not an experimentally accessible physical property, but only an extrapolation. Its numerical value is therefore a function of the degree of approximation achieved by vapor-pressure equations of the approximate nature of practical equations, such as the Frost–Kalkwarf equation; values of $H_0°$ of different compounds are comparable only if they have been obtained by means of the same equation for the same vapor-pressure range. Specifically, the $H_0°$ data given in Table 14.1 to 16 have been obtained over the range 10 to 2000 torr. They should be supplemented therefore by vapor-pressure data of other compounds covering the same, or nearly the same, vapor-pressure range. (See Section 7.3 for details.)

14.4 STANDARD HEAT OF SUBLIMATION

The standard heat of sublimation ΔH_s^1 is defined as the heat of sublimation at the lowest first-order phase transition of the solid [3]. Only this heat of sublimation can be decomposed consistently into additive group contributions. The reason is, of course, that solids above first-order phase transitions often exhibit sharply reduced lattice energy and are unrepresentative of the "typical" solid.

We note in Table 14.1 through 16 that many group contributions $H_s(X)$ of polar functional groups are of the form $H_s(X) = a + b/N_c$ even though the polar groups are generally located in dipole sheets that stretch throughout the entire crystal. The argument of "diluted" contact energy is therefore inapplicable. Polar-group interactions in crystals can be—and often are—weakened by alkyl groups because the accommodation of a large alkyl group in the crystal lattice leads to larger than minimum contact distances in the dipole–dipole interaction region. We could have made the assumption that the polar-group increment $H_s(X)$ is constant, and that the hydrocarbon radical increment $H(R)$ should be considered variable. Aside from being physically unrealistic, this assumption would have led to the very awkward situation of widely varying increments $H(R)$ for a given (R) depending on the chemical composition of the crystal. Hence here, as well as in the case of $E°$ and $H_0°$, all increment calculations are based on the assumption that the interaction energy of alkyl groups is identical with that in the alkanes. A practical advantage of this position is the availability of outstandingly precise calorimetric data for most of the basic members of the alkane series.

The combining rules for $H_s(X)$ are the same as described for $E°(X)$. The same precautions should also be observed when combining functional group increments of several groups in a single molecule, etc.

It is obviously incorrect to add polar-group increments to each other to produce the increment of a new polar group. Examples for such injudicious use of this information are presented in Table 14.20. The effects of steric shielding and of mutual interference of several polar groups in a single molecule must also be considered.

Yet, in spite of the stated difficulties, sufficient regularity seems to prevail in crystal structure patterns, to permit the extraction of fairly orderly additivity patterns from the available data. Typical examples of additivity and nonadditivity are presented in Table 14.21.

Table 14.20   Examples Showing How Not to Estimate Functional Group Increments

Wrong Method of Estimation	Observed Increment
$H_S(\cdot NO_2) + H_S(\cdot O\cdot) \rightarrow H_S(\cdot ONO_2) = 11.7$ to 12.2 kcal/mole	$H_S(\cdot ONO_2) = 9.6$ kcal/mole
$H_S(:C{=}O) + H_S(\cdot O\cdot) \rightarrow H_S(\cdot OC{=}O) = 7.7$ to 8.2 kcal/mole	$H_S(\cdot OC{=}O) = 4{-}6$ kcal/mole

Table 14.21 Additivity of Increments[a]

Combination	Calc, kcal/mole	Observed, kcal/mole	Ref.
H_s(i-propenyl) + H_s(carboxylate) + H_s(methyl) = ΔH_s(methyl methacrylate)	14.7	14.2[b]	
$H_s(\cdot C \overset{O}{\underset{}{\parallel}} \cdot)_{ar}$ + H_s(phenylene) + $H_s(\cdot O \cdot)$ + $2H_s$(methyl) = ΔH_s(p-acetyl anisole)	19.5	18.6[c]	
$2[2H_s(CH_2) + H_s$(primary)(Cl)] + H_s(S) = $\Delta H_s^{\circ}(ClC_2H_4)_2S$	20.4	20.2	d, e
H_s(naphthyl·) + H_s(Br^{ar}) = ΔH_s°(1-bromonaphthalene)	19.3	18.9	f, g
$4[H_s$(Br) + $2H_s(CH_2)] = \Delta H_s^{\circ}(BrC_2H_4)_4C$	21.6[h]	20.1	f
$H_s(\cdot CCl_3) + 2H_s$(Cl) + $2H_s$(phenylene) + H_s(CH) = ΔH_s°1,1-bis(4-chlorophenyl)-2,2,2-trichloroethane (DDT)	33.3[i] 30.1[j]	28.2 28.2	d d

[a] All examples are compounds that have not been used in the preparation of the correlation.
[b] From Landolt-Börnstein, *Tabellen*, 6th ed., Springer, Berlin, 1951, vol. II/2.
[c] A. Aihara, *Bull. Chem. Soc. Japan* **32**, 1242 (1959).
[d] E. W. Balson et al., *Trans. Faraday Soc.* **43**, 42–60 (1947); ΔH_v, (ΔH_s).
[e] Estimated $\Delta H_m = \Delta T_m[\Delta S_m(Et_2S) + \Delta S_m(1,2\text{-EtCl}_2) - \Delta S_m(\text{ethane})]$.
[f] Landolt-Bornstein Tables 1951; ΔH_v. The density correlation suggests that E°(Br-naphthalene) is low and should be 13.7 kcal/mole.
[g] Assumed $\Delta S_m = 13.5$ e.u. (typical for aromatic molecules of this type).
[h] H_s(neo-pentyl quadruple radical) = 4.30 kcal/mole; not tabulated elsewhere.
[i] Estimated ignoring all shielding effects.
[j] Estimated taking shielding effects into consideration.

14.4.1 Method of Data Generation for Enlarging the Correlation

When the necessary data are available, the heat of sublimation of a solid is calculated from the vapor pressure of the crystal by means of the Clausius–Clapeyron equations. However, in most instances the data are obtained by the scheme

$$\Delta H_s^{\circ} = \Delta H_V(\text{liq}, T_a) + \int_{T_a}^{T_m} \Delta C_p^{\,l} \, dT + \Delta H_m + (T_m - T_i)\Delta C_p^{\,s} + \Delta H_{tr},$$

where $\Delta H_V(\text{liq}, T_a)$ is, if possible, a calorimetric measurement or derived from good vapor pressure. The heat-capacity difference $\Delta C_p^{\,l}$ and its temperature dependence are obtained either directly or from a previously established correlation (Chapter 9).

The heat of fusion ΔH_m and transition ΔH_{tr} are, whenever possible, taken from calorimetric measurements. In the absence of good calorimetric data, ΔH_m is obtained by the procedures at the end of Chapter 6.

Since the hydrocarbon-group increments form the backbone structure of the entire correlation scheme and must be readily available for the generation of new functional-group increments from an organic substance for which data happen to be available, the hydrocarbon base data are included in this section.

14.4.2 Globular Molecules [3]

The series CH_4, $(CH_3)_2$, $(CH_3)_4C$, $[(CH_3)_3 \cdot C]$, etc. is of special interest because intermolecular contacts are restricted to those of primary hydrogen atoms. The data of Table 14.22 indicate that the contribution per primary

Table 14.22   Heat of Sublimation and Energy of Vaporization of Globular Molecules [3]

Compound	ΔH_s	ΔH_s/H-atom
CH_4	2.20	0.55
C_2H_6	4.90	0.82
$(CH_3)_4 \cdot C$	7.93	0.66
$[(CH_3)_3 \cdot C]_2$	11.74	0.65
$[(CH_3)_3 \cdot C]_2 \cdot CH_2$	12.87	0.645
$Et_4 \cdot C$	14.09	0.70
$[(CH_3)_3 \cdot Si]_2$	12.39	0.69
$(CH_2)_n$	2.0	1.0
$(CH_3)_4 \cdot Si$	9.22	0.77

hydrogen atom $H_s^\circ (\cdot H_p)$ is quite uniformly 0.65 kcal/mole, ethane being the only significant exception, probably because of the possibility of (somewhat attenuated) C—C/C—C interaction.

The magnitude of $H^\circ (\cdot H_p)$ is, of course, significantly larger than $\frac{1}{2}\Delta H_s^\circ$ (H_2) because the internuclear distance H $\cdots$ H in hydrocarbon crystals is much shorter than it is in the hydrogen crystal (2.35 Å at $0°K$ for the paraffins [8] compared with 3.76 Å in the H_2(crystal), and more important, because the interaction is really between C–H bonds.

14.4.3 Normal Paraffins

This is the best-measured series of chemical compounds. The data calculated from vapor pressures could therefore be checked frequently against good calorimetric measurements. Whenever necessary, the calorimetric heats of vaporization were extrapolated to the melting point and transition points by means of the readily available ΔC_p data. All available data have been assembled in Table 14.23.

Inspection of this table shows the expected uniformity of increase of ΔH_s° with chainlength after the first two members of the series, provided the comparisons are made within the series of odd- and even-numbered n-paraffins, respectively.

14.4.4 Branched-Chain Paraffins [3]

The primary effect of a branch in the paraffin backbone chain of a molecule is the conversion of a readily accessible C–H bond into an almost inaccessible

Table 14.23 Heat of Sublimation of n-Paraffins at Their Lowest First-Order Transition Temperature [3]

N	$T_1(^{\circ}K)$	$\Sigma\Delta H_{tr,m}$	$\Delta H_v(T)$	ΔH_s	ρ_s^*
1	90	—	—	2.20	0.553
2	90	0.68	4.22	4.90	0.673
3	86	0.84	5.97	6.81	—
4	107	1.61	6.84	8.57	0.670
5	143	2.01	8.02	10.03	0.676
6	178	3.11	9.04	12.15	0.671
7	183	3.37	10.46	13.83	0.675
8	216	4.96	11.31	16.27	0.679
9	219	5.20	12.62	17.82	—
10	243	6.86	13.40	20.26	—
11	236.6	6.94	14.88	21.82	—
12	263	8.80	15.50	24.30	—
16	291	12.75	19.59	32.24	—

C–C bond. Hence the heat of sublimation decrement Δ/b per branch point should be of the order

$$\left(\frac{\Delta}{b}\right) \approx -\frac{3}{2} H_s(CH_2) + 3H_s(H_p) \approx -1.1 \frac{\text{kcal}}{\text{mole}}$$

in fair agreement with experimental observation as shown by the data in Table 14.24. The tendency of Δ/b for gem-branch points to be somewhat larger is, of course, related to the increased shielding effect. However, too few data are available to make a detailed examination of this aspect worthwhile at present.

14.4.5 Cycloparaffins (Ring Structure Only)

The heat of sublimation of the first three members of this series is, as the data of Table 14.25 shows, slightly higher than are estimated for the methylene-group increments of the normal paraffins. All three have planar, or

Table 14.24   Heat of Sublimation of Isoparaffins [3]

Compound	T	ΔH_v	$\Sigma \Delta H_{m,tr}$	ΔH_s	$-\Delta/b$
2-Methyl propane				7.71	0.86
2-Methyl butane	113	8.43	1.23	9.66	0.75
2,2-Dimethyl propane	160	5.73	1.39	7.93	1.05
		(at 256.8)			
2-Methyl hexane	155	10.08	2.20	12.28	1.31
3-Ethyl pentane	154	10.16	2.28	12.44	1.15
2,4-Dimethyl pentane	155	9.61	1.64	11.25	1.17
2,2-Dimethyl pentane	150	9.52	1.39	10.91	1.34
3,3-Dimethyl pentane	138	9.69	1.69	11.38	1.11
2-Methyl heptane	165	11.75	2.83	14.60	1.70
2,5-Dimethyl hexane	181	10.58	3.07	13.65	1.15
2-Methyl-3-ethyl pentane	158	10.95	2.71	13.66	1.15
2,3,4-Trimethyl pentane	163	11.20	2.22	13.42	0.95
Hexamethyl ethane	152	—	—	11.74	1.05
3,3-Diethyl pentane	240	11.74	2.35	14.09	1.68
2,2,4,4-Tetramethyl pentane	206	10.55	2.32	12.87	1.24

Table 14.25   Heat of Sublimation of Cycloparaffins [3]

Compound	$T(^\circ K)$	ΔH_v (kcal/mole)	$\Sigma \Delta H_{m,tr}$ (kcal/mole)	ΔH_s^1 (kcal/mole)
Cyclopropane	145	5.69	1.30	6.99
Cyclobutane	145	7.04	1.67	8.71
Cyclopentane	122	8.80	1.39	10.19
Cyclohexane	186	8.91	2.22	11.13
Cycloheptane	134	10.97	1.81	12.78
Cyclooctane	166	11.87	2.18	14.05
Cyclotetradecane	320	—	—	32.0[a]
trans-Decahydronaphthalene	241	12.37	3.44	15.82
cis-Decahydronaphthalene	230	13.21	2.34	15.48
trans-syn-trans- Perhydroanthracene	—	—	—	21.0[a]

[a] Heat of sublimation from vapor pressure of crystal.

nearly planar, molecules allowing close approach of nearest neighbors in the crystal lattice. The higher cycloalkanes, with their well-known puckered configuration, pack so poorly that their lattice energy is distinctly lower than predicted from $H_s(CH_2)$. This effect is yet more pronounced for the condensed cyclic naphthenes.

14.4.6 Cage Molecules

In spite of their increasing importance in synthetic organic chemistry, surprisingly few data have been obtained on cage molecules. In fact most available heat-of-sublimation data for cage molecules are on polar compounds. The heat-of-sublimation increments for hydrocarbon components of these cage molecules, presented in Table 14.26 have been estimated from the

Table 14.26 Estimate of the Standard Heat-of-Sublimation Increment of Cage Molecules [3]

Substance	ΔH_s (kcal/mole)	Increments
1,4-Ethylene piperidine	12.20	$\overline{H}_s(CH_2 \text{ or } CH) = 1.45$ kcal/mole
Triethylenediamine	13.00	$\overline{H}_s(N \vdots) \qquad = 2.25$ kcal/mole
Hexaethylenetetramine	18.00	

heat of sublimation of the polar compounds. They should therefore be regarded as only approximate.

14.4.7 Aromatic Ring Systems (without Side Chains) [3]

In the series benzene, diphenyl, 1,4-diphenyl benzene we observe remarkable regularity, and that, rather exactly,

$$\Delta H_s^\circ = 1.73 N_{CH} + 0.90 N_{ct} \text{ kcal/mole}$$

when N_{ct} = number of tertiary carbon atoms on the ring. Substitution of two phenyl rings in the 1,3-position of a benzene ring does not reduce the packing density of the crystal significantly, but the heat of sublimation is reduced by virtue of a strong shielding effect, such that now

$$\Delta H_s^\circ = 1.73 N_{CH} + 0.30 N_{ct} - 0.9 N_{cm}$$

when N_{cm} = number of ring carbon atoms in meta substitution. The relation holds rather well for 1,3-diphenyl benzene and 1,3,5-triphenyl benzene and should therefore be of general validity. No data could be found for the heat of sublimation of 1,2-diphenyl benzene. The mutual shielding of the crowded, out-of-plane phenyl rings should cause appreciable reduction in ΔH_s°. From the heat-of-vaporization data we might guess that the corresponding increment $N_{ct} \approx -2$ kcal/mole yielding a guessed value of ΔH_s° (1,2-diphenyl benzene) ≈ 19.8 kcal/mole.

The standard heat of sublimation of the condensed cyclic aromatics also follows rather simple trends, which are, of course, related to the simple planar shape of these molecules and their easy parallel alignment in the crystal. A reasonably reliable relation for the kata-condensed series benzene, naphthalene, anthracene, etc., is

$$\Delta H_s^\circ = 1.73 N_{CH} + 1.35 N_{ct}.$$

For peri-condensed compounds, such as phenanthrene, chrysene, etc., a shielding correction has to be made for the crowded ring carbon atoms (N_p) 1 and 8 etc., such that

$$\Delta H_s^\circ = 1.73 N_{CH} + 1.35 N_{ct} - 0.40 N_p.$$

14.4.8 Alkyl and Aryl Aromatics [3]

A peculiar feature of the standard heat of sublimation of various alkylated aromatic hydrocarbons is the decrease in the magnitude of the ring increment with increasing length of the alkyl chain. One of the reasons for this trend is probably the difficulty of accommodating a large alkyl chain and an aromatic ring in the same crystal structure. Once the alkyl chain reaches a certain size ($\sim C_5$) the ring has to accommodate itself to the arrangement of the chains in the crystal lattice. The change of $H_s^\circ(R\cdot)$ with alkyl chain length is not as smooth as we might like to see, probably because of discontinuous changes of crystal structure and packing density.

The decreasing effect of chain branching and of multiple branches on the heat of sublimation increment of the ring system is somewhat smaller than we might have expected. It appears that only few substituents prevent close packing or close-range interaction of neighboring aromatic rings.

A somewhat unexpected feature is the peculiar shape of the $H_s(R)$ versus number of alkyl chain relation. An algebraic representation of the observations of moderate accuracy is

$$\Delta H_s^\circ = A - bD - \frac{bC}{N_B} + H_s(\cdot B),$$

where b is the number of branches per ring, N_B is the number of carbon atoms per branch; B denotes the branch radical (see Table 14.27), and A, C, D, are empirical constants.

14.4.9 Shielding Effects

The heat-of-sublimation increment of the phenyl group in t-butyl benzene, and of the phenylene group in di-t-butyl benzene is somewhat larger (0.25 and 0.5 kcal/mole, respectively) than expected. The bulky t-butyl groups apparently pack well, with the phenyl rings.

In most other cases one finds strongly interacting portions of a molecule shielded by t-butyl and other bulky organic groups the more effectively the stronger the interaction forces that have been blocked. The effect will be encountered with polar molecules of many kinds and is particularly striking when the coordination valences of heavy metal atoms are made inoperative by bulky organic groups.

Although the incidence of shielding can be predicted from simple geometrical considerations, its quantitative effect is difficult to predict. A minimum value of the heat of sublimation can, of course, always be estimated, namely, the sum of the group increments of the bulky groups. A maximum

Table 14.27 Standard Heat of Sublimation Increments for Aromatic Rings [3]

Type	Fragment (X)	$H_s(X)$, kcal/mole
Monoalkyl benzenes	$\phi\cdot$	$8.40 + 1.60/N_B$[a]
Dialkyl benzenes[b]	$\phi:$	$7.0 + 4.80/\Sigma N_B$[a]
Trialkyl benzenes[b]	$\cdot\phi:$	8.1
Tetraalkyl benzenes[b]	$:\phi:$	6.8[c]
Hexaalkyl benzenes	$:\phi:$	4.6[c]
Monoaryl benzene	$\phi\cdot$	9.6
p-Diaryl benzene	$\phi:$	8.6
1,3,5-Triaryl benzene	$\cdot\phi:$	5.0
Monoalkyl naphthalene	naphthyl·	15.0[c]
1,2-Dialkyl naphthalene	1,2-naphthylene	14.2

[a] N_B = number of carbon atoms in alkyl chain; ΣN_B = total number of carbon atoms in alkyl chains.
[b] Averaged over position isomers, except for 1,3,5-trialkyl chains for which ΔH_s is 0.8 kcal lower than for the other isomers, and were therefore omitted in the averaging.
[c] Derived from data on methyl derivatives only.

value can be estimated only if association is known to be absent. The maximum value is simply the minimum plus the full polar-group increment.

14.5 DIPOLE MOMENTS

The self-explanatory tabulation of (group) dipole moments in Table 14.28 has been included in order to permit estimates of functional-group contributions to the heat of sublimation and the energy of vaporization as outlined in Sections 1.2, 1.4, and 14.2 to 14.4. Owing to the close proximity of molecule interaction in condensed phases, the individual group moments in polyfunctional molecules rather than their vector sums should be used for these calculations. Heterocyclic compounds, such as ethylene carbonate, are the only apparent exception to this rule because their dipole moments are uniquely associated with the peculiar conformation of their polar groups.

Table 14.28 **Dipole Moments of Common Functional Groups**[a,b] **in Debye Units (10^{-18} e.s.u.)**

Functional Group:	Attached to:						
	ethynyl	ethenyl	phenyl	methyl	ethyl	t-butyl	cyclohexyl
—Me			0.37	0	0		
—C=CH$_2$			<0.2	0.35	0.37		
—C≡CH			0.7	0.74	0.80		
—C≡N		3.88	4.39	3.4	3.57	(3.7)(s) 4.3(g)	3.71(s)
(Me)$_2$N—			1.61	0.64	0.8		
MeNH—				1.02			
—NH$_2$			1.48	1.23	1.2	1.29(s)	1.32(s)
—NO$_2$			4.21	3.50 =	3.68		
—O—NO$_2$				2.85(s)	2.91(s)		
—OMe	1.98	1.2	1.35	1.30	1.22		1.29
—C(=O)H		3.04	3.1(2.76)(s)	2.72	2.73		
—C(=O)Me	3.2(s)	3.0(s)	3.00	2.84	2.78	2.8	
—O—C(=O)Me				1.83(s)	1.67	1.76	1.91(s)
—SMe		1.20	1.27(s)	1.40(s)			
—S—C≡N				3.6(s)	3.6(s)		
—N=C=S				3.2(s)	3.3(s)		
—SH			1.3(s)	1.26	1.56		
F			1.59(1.46)(s)	1.81	1.92	2.05	
Cl	0.44	1.44	1.70(1.58)(s)	1.87	2.05	2.13	(2.2)(s)
Br	0	1.41	1.73(1.54)(s)	1.80	2.01		(2.2)(s)
I		1.26	1.7 (1.30)(s)	1.64	1.87		(2.0)(s)
Me	0.74	0.36	0.37	0	0	0	0

[a] Taken from C. P. Smyth, *Dipolemoment and Molecular Structure,* McGraw-Hill, New York, 1955.

[b] Except when marked [(s) for solution], these are all gas-phase values.

Table 14.29.1 Barriers to Internal Rotation ($V°$) and Energies of Rotational Isomerization (ΔE_{iso})[a] (All in kcal/mole)

Rotor	Frame	—CH₃	—CH₂F	—CH₂Cl	—CH₂Br	—CH₂I	—CHF₂	—CHCl₂	—CHBr₂	—CF₃	—CCl₃	—CH=CH₂	—C(F)=O
CH₃—[b]	$V°$	2.88	3.96	3.56	3.57	3.22	3.2	3.55		3.1	2.95	1.98	1.04[v]
et—[b,c]	$V°$	3.30	2.69	3.61	3.68	4.07							
	ΔE_{iso}		0.47	(0.3)° 0.68	(0.44)° 0.97	1.17							
	$V°(\mathrm{CH_3})$		2.32	2.78	2.36	2.47							
CH₂X[e]	$V°$			5.1[z]	0.77(1.8)[g]			(7.2)[z] 5.8[d]	6.4[d]	4.2[d]	12.4[d]		1.2[v]
	ΔE_{iso}							0.2	0.5				0.9[v]
—CX₃[e]	$V°$	1.98		10.0[z]			5.3[p]	14.2[z]		3.92	17.5[z]		1.4[v]
—C(H)=CH₂	$V°$	1.14									3.1	4.9	
	ΔE_{iso}											2.3	
—C(H)=O	$V°$	1.15								5.4	2.3	5.0[u]	
	ΔE_{iso}											2.1[u]	

Rotor	Frame	—C(=O)F	—C(=O)Cl	—C(=O)Br	—C(=O)CH₃	—C(=O)OH	—C(CH₃)=CH₂	—C(F)=CH₂	—C(F)(H)=CH	—CH=C=CH₂	—CH=C=O
CH₃—[b]	$V°$	1.04	1.30	1.31	0.76	0.48	2.12	2.42	2.15	1.59	1.20

l

Rotor	Frame	—OCH₃	—O—C(=O)H	—O—NO₂	—S—CH₃	—S—S—CH₃	—NH₂	—NHCH₃	—N(CH₃)₂	—NO₂	—PH₂	—P(CH₃)₂
CH₃—[b]	$V°$	2.72	1.19	1.96	1.50	1.50	1.5	2.11	3.23	6.03	1.23	2.60

Rotor	Frame	Me	Et	i-pr	t-bu	—C≡CH	—C(CH₃)=CH₂	—C≡CH	Phenyl	—N(Me)₂
Me	$V°$	2.88	3.30	3.9	4.3	~0	1.98	4.3	<0.5	4.41
—OH[b,r]	$V°$	1.07	0.80	0.80	(1.36)				1.1	—
—SH[b,s]	$V°$	1.65[x]	(1.64)	1.42					0.28[x]	2.2[t]
—C(=O)H[q]	$V°$	1.17		1.19						

Rotor	Frame	—SiH₃	—SiH₂CH₃	—Si(CH₃)₃	—SiH₂F	—SiF₃	—GeH₃
CH₃—[b]	$V°$	1.70	1.65	1.30	1.56	1.20	1.24

14.6 BARRIERS TO INTERNAL ROTATION AND ENERGIES OF ROTATIONAL ISOMERIZATION

The importance of molecular flexibility for many of the physical properties discussed in earlier sections suggests that quantitative measures of such flexibility be available as the reasonably complete collection of Table 14.29.

Table 14.29.2 Barrier to Internal Rotation ($V°$) and Energy of Rotational Isomerization (ΔE_{iso})[a] in Larger Aliphatic Molecules and Polymer Chains

	$V°$ (kcal/mole)	ΔE_{iso} (kcal/mole)
1,1,2,2-Tetrabromoethane[f]		0.9
2-Chlorobutane[f]		0.37
2-Bromobutane[f]	4.7	0.26
2-Methylbutane[f]		0.
2,3-Dimethylbutane[f]		0.1
1,2-Dichloro-2-methylpropane[f]		0.
1,2-Dibromo-2-methylpropane[f]	5.5	0.74
Polyethylene[g]	3.0	0.7
Polyisobutylene[g]	4.9	~0
Poly(vinyl chloride)[h]		1.2
Poly(methylmethacrylate)[i]		0.8 (1.2 for isotactic)
Poly(dimethyl siloxane)[j]	~1	0.8
Polyoxyethylene[y]		1.0

Table 14.29.3 Barrier to Internal Rotation ($V°$) and Energy of Rotational Isomerization (ΔE_{iso})[a] in Cyclic Compounds

	$V°$ (kcal/mole)	ΔE_{iso} (kcal/mole)
Diphenyl[k]	3.9	7.0[l]
2,2'-Difluorodiphenyl[k]	6.0	
2,2'-Dimethyl diphenyl	15.1	
Cycloalkanes[m]		
1,3-Dioxanes and 1,3-dithianes[n]		

[a] $V°$ are mostly from gas-phase microwave studies, whereas ΔE_{iso} has generally been chosen from liquid-phase data, except where noted as (g).

[b] W. Maier, *Ber. Bunsenges.* **67**, 539 (1963).

[c] K. Radcliffe and J. L. Wood, *Trans. Faraday Soc.* **62**, 1678 (1966).

[d] H. G. Silver and J. L. Wood, *Trans. Faraday Soc.* **59**, 588 (1963).

[e] X = halide of the "frame."

[f] E. Wynne-Jones and W. J. Orville-Thomas, *Chem. Soc. Publ.* **20**, 214 (1966).

[g] Generally accepted values.

h For ΔE_{iso}, H. Germar, *Kolloid-Z.* **193**, 25 (1963) gives 1.9 kcal/mole; the above quoted value is considered more likely.
i Atactic: S. Havriliak quoted in *Polymer* **6**, 311 (1965); isotactic: Sakarada, I. et al., *Kolloid-Z.* **186**, 41 (1962).
j P. J. Flory et al., *J. Am. Chem. Soc.* **86**, 146 (1964) (rotation of entire repeating unit).
k K. E. Howlett, *J. Chem. Soc.* **1960**, 1055.
l Stabilization energy of the planar state.
m Extensive data collection presented in *Conformational Analysis* by E. L. Eliel et al., Wiley, New York, 1965.
n H. Friebolin et al., *Tetrahedron Letters* **1962**, 683.
o Y. A. Pentin et al., *CA* **55**, 21, 797 (1961).
p CF_3—CF_2Cl; J. G. Aston and T. P. Folki, *J. Am. Chem. Soc.* **77**, 804 (1955).
q A. M. Roun and R. C. Woods, *J. Chem. Phys.* **45**, 3831 (1966).
r J. H. S. Green, *Trans. Faraday Soc.* **59**, 1559 (1963).
s H. L. Finke et al., *J. Am. Chem. Soc.* **74**, 2804 (1952).
t F. Conti and W. von Philipsborn, *Helv. Chim. Acta* **50**, 603 (1967).
u Data obtained by sound absorption in the liquid phase, J. Lamb in *Physical Acoustics*, W. P. Mason, ed., Academic, New York, 1965, vol. 2A; see (f) for inherent uncertainties of this measurement of ΔE_{iso}.
v E. Saegebarth and E. B. Wilson, jr., *J. Chem. Phys.* **46**, 3088 (1967).
x K. O. Simpson, and E. T. Beynon, *J. Phys. Chem.* **71**, 2796 (1967).
y J. E. Mark, and P. J. Flory, *J. Am. Chem. Soc.* **87**, 1415 (1965).
z G. Allen et al., *Trans. Farad. Soc.* **63**, 824 (1967).

REFERENCES

[1] Batsanov, S. S., *Refractometry and Chemical Structure* Consultants Bureau, New York, 1961.
[2] Bondi, A., *J. Phys. Chem.* **68**, 441 (1964); **70**, 3006 (1966).
[3] Bondi, A., *J. Chem. Eng. Data* **8**, 371 (1963).
[4] Pauling, L., *Nature of the Chemical Bond* Cornell University Press, Ithaca, New York, 1960, 3rd ed.
[5] Prout, C. K. et al., *J. Chem. Soc.* **1965**, 4838, 4851, 4867.
[6] Schmidt, G. M. J. et al., *J. Chem. Soc.* **1964**, 1996, 2000, 2014, 2030, 2068.
[7] Stevenson, D. P. (See [19] and [20] in Chapter 7.)
[8] Strel'tsova, I. N., and Y. T. Struchkov, *J. Struct. Chem.* **2**, 296 (1961).
[9] Sutton, L. E., ed., *Tables of Interatomic Distances and Configurations in Molecules and Ions*, The Chemical Society, London, 1958.

15

Computing Schemes

The purpose of this chapter might have been to collect calculating methods for physical properties in a form convenient for translation into computer programs. A master program for route selection through the maze of such property correlations has been prepared under the auspices of the American Institute of Chemical Engineers [1]. Its special feature is the route selection for minimum error propagation. Realization of this feature requires the determination of the uncertainty range of each calculating method for any given class of chemical compounds.

Few authors of correlations present uncertainty evaluations of their methods, and their own evaluations would not be very meaningful because they would only reflect the goodness of fit to the data that they used in generating the correlation. A first attempt at an independent evaluation of many correlations was made by Reid and Sherwood [11] who covered a wide range of methods with a wide range of chemical compounds, but only few members of each class of those compounds. A detailed evaluation of many physical property correlations with respect to their ability to represent the property data of four important classes of hydrocarbons has been undertaken by M. R. Fenske and co-workers [4] under the auspices of the American Petroleum Institute Subcommittee for the preparation of the *API Technical Data Book* [3]. It will be apparent that a great deal more work needs to be done in this area. No independent error estimates are as yet available for the solid-state properties.

The scope of the correlations of this book must be seen in the framework of needs versus means. The known number of organic compounds and of inorganic compounds forming molecular crystals, liquids, or glasses is of the order of 4×10^6. Reliable measurements of all or most physical properties (covered by this book) have been carried out on less than one thousandth of that number. A thousandfold increase in the volume of precision property data is neither feasible nor sensible. Instead we have two options.

One option is to create the mathematical apparatus with the help of which we can expand the precision property data obtained on a parent compound of a given series to a large volume of high-precision physical-property data for all members of that series. We could create by procedures similar to those employed by Research Projects 44 and 51 of the American Petroleum Institute for the creation of their exemplary physical-property data for several families of hydrocarbons. This would be a fairly costly but highly rewarding effort, which will undoubtedly be undertaken within the present generation.

The other option is to forego precision (that is, $a \pm 2\%$ uncertainty) and be satisfied with correlations which produce physical property estimates to within $\pm 20\%$ uncertainty. Such correlations would in general be based on the principle of corresponding states, and use the entire array of available data plus guidance from theory to estimate physical properties of other compounds. The methods collected at the end of each chapter are almost exclusively such corresponding-states correlations, and their property predictions are therefore of the limited precision (and accuracy) that this qualification implies.

The main reason for the low accuracy and precision of such correlations is the fact that substances of practical interest are usually composed of molecules which are too complex to meet the basic requirements of the theory of corresponding-states correlations. A way out of this impasse is to specialize numerical coefficients of a correlation in any given case for the family of chemical compounds under consideration. Uncertainty reductions by as much as a factor of 10 have thus been achieved.

15.1 CHOICE OF METHOD

The physical properties of simple liquids with $M \leq 150$ to 200 are probably more easily estimated by the conventional corresponding-states correlations (based on critical constants) collected in the book by Reid and Sherwood [11] than by the methods of this book. For the reader's convenience there is a small amount of method overlap between the two books.

The physical properties of liquids with $M > 150$ or of liquids whose critical constants can neither be measured nor estimated are more appropriately estimated by the methods of this book. This includes especially the properties of plasticizers and of polymer melts (except the flow properties at above the entanglement point).

The physical properties of molecular crystals and glasses can at present probably not be estimated by methods other than those presented in this book.

We might have hoped for an easy interconvertibility of the reducing parameters based on molecular force and geometry constants into those based on

Table 15.1 Estimation of Reducing Parameters

Equation No.	Equation	Units	Uncertainty (%)	Chapter	Table
A. Parameters Requiring Molecular Structure Information but *No* Physical Property Data					
(15.1)	$V_w = \sum V_w(X)$	cm³ mole⁻¹		8,14,15	14.1 to 14.18
(15.2)	$A_w = \sum A_w(X)$	cm² mole⁻¹		14,15	14.1 to 14.18
(15.3)	$\bar{d}_w = \dfrac{2}{n}\sum_0^n r_w(X)$	cm		14,15	14.1 to 14.18
(15.4)	$d_w^s = 1.47(V_w)^{1/3}$	cm		12,15	14.1 to 14.18
(15.5)	$d_w^s(X) = 1.47[V_w(X)]^{1/3}$	cm		12,15	14.1 to 14.18
(15.6)	$V_c \approx 5.3\,V_w$	cm³ mole⁻¹	±10	8.1.6	—
(15.7)	$V_c = \sum V_c(X)$ Riedel	cm³ mole⁻¹		8.1.6	8.12
(15.8)	$E° = \sum E°(X)$	cal mole⁻¹		14,15	14.1 to 14.16
(15.9)	$\Delta H_0° = \sum H_0°(X)$	cal mole⁻¹		7,14,15	14.1 to 14.16
(15.10)	$\Delta H_s^1 = \sum H_s^1(X)$	cal mole⁻¹		1,2,3,14	14.1 to 14.16

(15.11)	3c: monatomic linear di- rigid
	             or polyatomic polyatomic
	      3 5 6				

(15.12)	3c: for flexible molecules ($3c \geq 8$)		—	8	8.6 to 8.8, 14.1 to 14.16
(15.13)	$f = 3c$ for all but flexible molecules		—		
(15.14)	f for flexible molecules: $f = N_s - 1$, where N_s = number of skeletal atoms or rigid segments per molecule		—	3.4.3; 3.5.4	
(15.15)	$\theta_L = E°/5cR$				
(15.16)	T_b = from methods of Ref.18 in Chapter 7	°K	—ᵃ		

(15.17) $T_c = T_b/[0.574 + \sum \Delta_T$ (Riedel)] usable only when correlation 15.16 applies, otherwise T_b must be available from experiment   °K   14.1 to 14.16

(15.18) $[P] = \sum [P](X)$

(15.18a)   surface tension $\gamma = ([P]\rho/M)^4$

(15.19) $[R]_\omega = \sum [R]_\omega(X)$

B. Parameters Requiring Molecular Structure *and* Physical Property Data

(15.31) θ_L (experimental): requires at least $\rho(T)$ and preferably $A = d\rho/dT$ at $T < 0.8T_b$. If A is not available, it can be estimated as $A \approx 1.21\ cRM/E°V_w$; V_w from (15.1)   8.1

$$\theta_L = 1.535 \left[T + \frac{\rho(T) - 0.596\ M/V_w}{A} \right]$$

(15.32) c (experimental) $= E°/5R\theta_L$ (experimental) [$E°$ from (15.8)]   °K   8.1

     —   8.1.2

(15.33) T_c: requires experimental T_b; $T_c = T_b/(0.574 + \sum \Delta_T)$ (Riedel)   °K

(15.34) $E_\mu = N_A \mu^2/d_w^3$ requires (group) dipole moment μ, usually from experimental data or from Table 14.28.

---

a ±3% for flexible molecules; ±8% for rigid molecules.

487

critical properties, so that we need to carry only one kind of reducing parameter in the easy-access computer memory. It is perhaps not too surprising to find that interconvertibility by means of "universal functions" is limited to comparatively simple compounds. Hence the choice of method involves also an economic decision in terms of optimum computer usage.

15.2 PROPERTIES OF MIXTURES

Physical properties of crystalline solids composed of more than one chemical compound in the form of mixed crystals are in principle not predictable from the component properties. Similarly, the complicated phase diagrams of systems forming solid solutions suggest that property predictions for these systems are likely to be hazardous. Only the properties of two-phase mixtures of (crystalline) solids can be estimated from the component properties and concentrations. The extreme specificity of molecular packing in crystals is the primary reason for the indicated difficulties.

This packing problem is absent in liquids and glasses, the packing density of which depends almost entirely on the ratio of the potential to the kinetic energy of the individual molecules (or their segments in the case of polymer melts). Hence the bulk properties of liquid or glass mixtures can, with few exceptions, be estimated from component properties and concentrations.

There are basically two different ways of estimating the properties of mixtures:

(a) To estimate the property G of the mixture from the properties G_i and concentrations x_i of the mixture components (i).

(b) To estimate the appropriate reducing parameters of the mixture and then calculate the properties from the usual correlations, treating the mixture as a pure compound.

Method (a) might be called the "classical method" and is the best choice when the component properties are available as experimental data. It is also the only usable method for most phase-equilibrium calculations, as well as for estimates—if at all possible—of interfacial tensions. It offers no particular advantages for the calculation of the bulk properties of mixtures when no experimental data are available. Method (b) undoubtedly offers the fastest path to estimates of the bulk properties of mixtures and is particularly well suited for the estimation of the entire array of physical properties for a given mixture, so often required in engineering calculations.

15.3 ESTIMATION OF REDUCING PARAMETERS FOR PURE COMPOUNDS AND FOR MIXTURES

The mode of addition of the group increments on Tables 14.1 through 14.17 is probably obvious. Nevertheless it seemed useful to summarize all the addition rules in Table 15.1. That table has two sections. Section A is for the case in which all reducing parameters are to be built up from group increments. That path will in general be taken only in the complete absence of reliable experimental data because of the inherent uncertainty in such a

Table 15.2 Reducing Parameters for Mixtures

Equation No.	Equation	Units
(15.20)	If $V_w^{(2)}/V_w^{(1)} \leq 3$: $\bar{V}_w = \Sigma\, x_i V_w(i)$	cm^3 mole^{-1}
(15.21)	If $V_w^{(2)}/V_w^{(1)} > 3$: $\bar{V}_w = \left(\Sigma\, w_i \dfrac{V_w(i)}{M(i)}\right) \bar{M}_j$[a]	cm^3 mole^{-1}
	$\bar{V}_w^{-1}(n) = \Sigma\, \dfrac{\varphi_i}{V_w(i)}$	cm^3 mole^{-1}
(15.22)	If $V_w^{(2)}/V_w^{(1)} \leq 3$: $\bar{A}_w = \Sigma\, x_i A_w(i)$	cm^2 mole^{-1}
(15.23)	If $V_w^{(2)}/V_w^{(1)} > 3$: $\bar{A}_w(w) = \Sigma\, \varphi_i A_w(i)$	cm^2 mole^{-1}
	$A_w^{-1}(n) = \Sigma\, \dfrac{\varphi_i}{A_w(i)}$	cm^2 mole^{-1}
(15.24)	If $V_w^{(2)}/V_w^{(1)} \leq 3$: $\bar{d}_w = \Sigma\, x_i d_w(i)$	cm
(15.25)	If $V_w^{(2)}/V_w^{(1)} > 3$: $\bar{d}_w = \Sigma\, \varphi_i d_w(i)$	cm
(15.26)	If $V_w^{(2)}/V_w^{(1)} \leq 3$: $\bar{c} = \Sigma\, x_i c_i$	—
(15.27)	If $V_w^{(2)}/V_w^{(1)} > 3$: $\bar{c} = \Sigma\, \varphi_i c_i$ or $(\bar{c}_2(n))^{-1} = \dfrac{w_i}{c_i}$	—
(15.28)	If $V_w^{(2)}/V_w^{(1)} \leq 1.5$: $\bar{E}^\circ = x_1^2 E_2^\circ + x_2^2 E_2^\circ + 2x_1 x_2 (E_1^\circ E_2^\circ)^{1/2} - F^E$	cal mole^{-1}
(15.29)[b]	If $V_w^{(2)}/V_w^{(1)} > 1.5$: $\bar{E}^\circ = \bar{A}_w\left[\varphi_1^2 \dfrac{E_1^\circ}{A_w^{(1)}} + \varphi_2^2 \dfrac{E_2^\circ}{A_w^{(2)}}\right.$	cal mole^{-1} g mole^{-1}
	$\left. + 2\varphi_1\varphi_2 \left(\dfrac{E_1^\circ}{A_w^{(1)}}\dfrac{E_2^\circ}{A_w^{(2)}}\right)^{1/2}\right] - F^E$	
(15.30)	$\bar{M}_j = \Sigma\, w_i M_i$; $\bar{M}_n^{-1} = \Sigma\, \dfrac{w_i}{M_i}$	

[a] Where $\bar{M}_j$ is the appropriately averaged molal weight (see equation 15.30); if V_w is wanted for packing density determination, there is no need for $\bar{M}$, because the desired packing density of the mixture is $\bar{\rho}^* = \bar{\rho}\, \Sigma\, w_i\, V_w^{(i)}(i)$ where $\bar{\rho}$ is the experimental density of the mixture.

[b] Delete F^E when using this relation for (13.7).

system. Especially θ_L should, if possible, be obtained from experimental density data, because it is central to many physical property calculations of liquids and glasses. Section B of Table 15.1 describes the few reducing parameters that benefit particularly from the use of experimental data.

The reducing parameter collection for mixtures on Table 15.2 contains a rather arbitrary dividing line, the component molecule size ratio of 3, below which mole-fraction additivity is assumed, and above which volume-fraction additivity is decreed. This dividing line was suggested by experience with polymer/solvent—oligomer/solvent—systems. A ratio of 10 may be a better dividing line, especially with very rigid molecules. The smaller dividing line with $E°$, (15.28/9) is because molecule interaction in condensed phase is at such close range that a smaller molecule "sees" only that portion of a larger neighbor that is of its own size.

15.4 EXAMINATION OF EXPERIMENTAL DATA FOR INTERNAL AND EXTERNAL CONSISTENCY

Experimental data from uncritical data collections or that have not been examined critically in their original publication should always be tested for internal and for external consistency. Rigorous internal consistency tests exist only for equilibrium properties and will be illustrated further on. External consistency is defined as the fit of the new data points into correlations of the type discussed in this book or in that by Reid and Sherwood (*loc. cit.*) or, more generally, as agreement with existing information. Substantial deviation of a property datum for a nonassociating substance from any of the correlations given should make the datum immediately suspect, as erroneous, or as being a new discovery. Hardly any of the correlations are sufficiently accurate to permit rejection on the basis of minor deviations.

Test Plan (for all but Thermochemical Properties)

A typical plan to check the probable correctness of a datum proposed for publication might proceed by the following route:

1. Screening by comparison with results from general property estimation or from upper and lower limit estimates. If the comparison is satisfactory and no high degree of accuracy is claimed by the author the test is completed, but if high accuracy is claimed by the author the next tests should be applied.

2. Fit into multiple regression of the family of compounds of which the compound under consideration is a member. This fit will generally supply a measure of the accuracy of the proposed datum.

3. Internal consistency tests of thermodynamics should then be applied, if the datum under consideration is an equilibrium (thermodynamic) property.

Comparison with General Property Estimation

If the property and the compound under consideration are of a kind for which insufficient data are available to use any of the tests under 2 and 3, the questioned datum should be produced by a physical properties computer program such as the A.I.Ch.E. program (APPES) [1] or the thermodynamic network generator program by Reid [8], if applicable.

This program calculates the physical properties described in Table 15.3

Table 15.3 Physical Properties Calculated by A.I.Ch.E. Physical Properties Computer Program

	Gas Phase	Liquid Phase
Critical constants	X	X
Density	X	X
p-v-T relations, equations of state	X	...
Vapor pressure, ΔH_{vap}	...	X
Heat capacity	X	X
Surface tension	...	X
Viscosity	X	X
Thermal conductivity	X	X
Diffusion coefficient	X	X

from molecular structure and the atmospheric boiling point as data input, and gives an estimate of the expected error limit of its own calculation, the combined error of the correlation schemes used in the calculation. The accuracy of the questioned datum should be declared doubtful if it falls outside the error limits of the computer estimate.

The indicated use of APPES presupposes a high degree of reliability of the correlation selection system appropriate for given types of compounds built into that computer program. Such a degree of reliability is achievable in principle for many types of compound. Properties of compounds outside the scope the correlations built into the program may be checked by means of a limit system outlined in the following section.

Limit System

A lower limit can be set for the numerical value of physical properties of compounds for which the previously described checking scheme cannot be used. The scheme is based on the supposition that the physical property of the hydrocarbon homomorph of any polar organic compound at the same reduced temperature is the lower limit to the numerical value of that property of the compound under consideration.

The reduced temperature is ideally the ratio T/T_c, so that the scheme pre-supposes existence of a method to estimate T_c for the compound in question (unless its T_c is known). If that is not the case the ratio T/T_b could be used as reduced temperature. If T_b is neither known nor estimable by means of any boiling-point estimating method, recourse can be had to another corre-sponding-states method: comparison at the same packing density, $\rho V_w/M$. This supposes that the density, ρ, of the compound under consideration is available for the temperature at which the property is to be checked. The van der Waals volume, V_w, can be calculated for both the compound under consideration and for its hydrocarbon homomorph from increments (Tables 14.1 to 14.17).

The hydrocarbon homomorph property under consideration is then taken from the American Petroleum Institute Research Project 44 Tables, "Selected Physical Properties of Hydrocarbons" [2], for the reduced-state value of the compound under consideration. The result should be considered as lower limit for the numerical value of that property.

Automation of this scheme is feasible only when a structure code is available that can translate any molecular structure of a polar compound into the structure of its hydrocarbon homomorph. The method cannot be used for nonpolar nonhydrocarbons such as perhalides, percyano compounds and the like.

Multiple Regression

The *availability of extensive information* on the property under consideration for several members of the chemical family of the compound under consideration permits the construction of a very powerful filter, the multiple regression. In that type of regression we represent a given property not only as a function of a state variable (T, p) but also as a function of chemical composition [9]. This presupposes guidance from theory or experience regarding the most useful functional relation between coefficients and the important elements of molecular structure.

"Family of compounds" in the present context can mean any regular progression of structure changes, such as in homologous series, or the successive substitution of hydrogen atoms by a given functional group, as in mono-, di-, tri-, and so on, halobenzene, -ethane (taking due account of molecular geometry) or the series monofluoro-, -chloro-, -bromo-, or -iodobenzene, or a series of isomers of a given compound, and so on.

Degree of fit or misfit of a set of data under scrutiny into such a regression is easily established. On the other hand, sight should not be lost of the cumbersome procedure of setting up the original regression, an effort that can only be justified by frequent use of such a program.

Internal Consistency Tests (Other Than Thermodynamic)

Whenever data of two or more different physical properties are submitted for a given compound or composition and these data are entered into the APPES the program output will state whether the input data were mutually consistent in terms of the correlations contained in the system. One case not contained in APPES, refractivity, illustrates this principle rather well. If the refractive index and the density (and molal weight) of a compound are given, these can be combined in the Lorentz-Lorenz molar refractivity and compared with the refractivity calculated for that particular molecular structure from one of the well-established refractivity-structure correlations [15]. Deviation of the experimental from the calculated refractivity by more than the very narrow error limits of the correlation makes density and refractive index suspect. Because the latter is more easily determined with high accuracy the major doubt will fall on the density datum.

Internal Consistency Tests for Thermodynamic Properties

1. The internal consistency tests of vapor p-v-T data can be obtained from textbooks of thermodynamics[1] and will therefore not be recounted here except to say that not many experimental data yield smooth first derivatives and hardly any survive the requisite direct second differentiations with respect to the state variables. Hence it is generally more realistic to fit the data to an appropriate equation of state and to test their quality and internal consistency by observing the error pattern in the least-square fitting to that equation of state. This procedure permits the simultaneous application of external consistency tests by comparing the coefficients of the equation of state with well-established patterns, especially in terms of reduction with the critical constants.

2. An internal consistency test for vapor pressure data of individual compounds is the set of inequalities at $\theta_D < T < T_b$;

$$\frac{d}{dT}\left(R\frac{d\ln p_v}{d(1/T)}\right)\bigg|_{\text{sat. liq.}} = C_s(g) - C_s(l) < 0 \quad \text{because of} \quad C_p(l) > C_p(g)$$

and

$$\frac{d}{dT}\left(R\frac{d\ln p_v}{d(1/T)}\right)\bigg|_{\text{sat. solid}} = C_s(g) - C_s(s) < 0 \quad \text{because of} \quad C_p(s) > C_p(g);$$

at $T < \theta_D$:

$$\frac{d}{dT}\left(R\frac{d\ln p_v}{d(1/T)}\right)\bigg|_{\text{sat. solid}} > 0 \quad \text{because} \quad C_s(s) \to \; <C_s(g)$$

$$\text{since} \quad C_p(s) \to 0 \quad \text{as} \quad T \to 0°\text{K}.$$

If either measured or reliably estimated values of $C_s(l)$ and $C_s(g)$ or of $C_s(l) - C_s(g)$ are available (produced by the program), the consistency test can be made more precise by testing

$$\frac{d}{dT}\left(R\frac{d\ln p_v}{d(1/T)}\right)$$

against the values of $C_s(g) - C_s(l)$. In the range $T_b < T < T_c$, $d^2\ln p_v/d(1/T)^2$ may change sign due to vapor imperfections. The location of this inflection

[1] For example, B. F. Dodge, *Chemical Engineering Thermodynamics*, McGraw-Hill, New York, 1944.

and the absolute value of $d^2 \ln p_v/d(1/T)^2$ in that region can be checked by combining the heat capacity with the equation of state data.

When calorimetric or reliably estimated data are available for the heat of vaporization, ΔH_v, or for the heat of sublimation, we can test at $T < T_b$

$$R \frac{d \ln p_v}{d(1/T)}\bigg|_{\text{sat. liq.}} - \Delta H_v = 0; \quad \text{and} \quad R \frac{d \ln p_v}{d(1/T)}\bigg|_{\text{sat. solid}} - \Delta H_s = 0.$$

At higher temperatures the test involves also the equation of state because then

$$R \frac{d \ln p_v}{d(1/T)}\bigg|_{\text{sat. liq.}} = \frac{\Delta H_v}{\Delta Z}.$$

3. Critical constants. The correctness of determined or estimated T_c and p_c can be assessed by testing their consistency with known or estimated values of ΔH_v (at $T = T_b$) and of T_b, as suggested by Edwards [7].

Properties that Cannot be Checked by Calculation

Computational check of the accuracy of a reported datum requires either the availability of structural additivity relations for the property under consideration or that the property can in some way be related to other experimentally available properties or to other additive properties. A typical set of properties for which no such relation applies is the melting point (T_m), the first-order solid/solid transition temperatures (T_{tr}), the heat of fusion (ΔH_m) if T_m is unknown, and the heat of transition if T_{tr} is unknown. The sum of the entropy of fusion and of the entropy of transition is well correlated with molecular structure (Chapter 6). Fortunately, T_m is also obtainable without very great effort. Hence the inability to check the accuracy of a reported melting point is not a great handicap. The transition points, T_{tr}, are more difficult to determine and, with few exceptions, even more difficulty to rationalize. Hence there is at present no way to check a reported value of T_{tr}.

Equilibrium Properties of Mixtures

To a first approximation linear additivity prevails in the volume functions of liquids (v, α, β) so that these mixture properties are checked easily. High-precision checking is unattainable because the excess volume, V^E, cannot be predicted. Volume functions of solutions of gases or solids in liquids are more difficult to check, unless the liquid state properties of the substances are known. Similarly, the specific heat of liquids is to a first-approximation linearly additive in weight fractions. Higher approximations are inaccessible to check by calculation because the heat capacity change on mixing cannot be predicted at present.

In general only an upper-limit check (linear volume fraction additivity) can be given for the surface tension of liquid mixtures. More accurate estimates [10] generally falter over the difficulty of defining the surface area per molecule required in the calculation.

Transport Properties of Mixtures

An upper-limit check of the thermal conductivity of liquid mixtures is the weight-fraction linear combination of the component conductivities. The downward deviation from this average is generally small and can be estimated only by means of empirical correlations (Section 10.8).

There is no safe check for the viscosity of liquid mixtures. Approximate mixture rules are contained in the A.I.Ch.E. computer program, but their utility for checking purposes is very limited.

Basically Unpredictable Properties of Mixtures

Although the melting point of mixtures can often be estimated from the component melting points by means of the solubility relation quoted earlier, the upward and downward deviations due to specific effects are too frequent to consider any quantitative relation as safe for checking of proposed data. The same applies to first-order solid/solid transition temperatures of mixtures.

Testing Program for Mixture Properties

The most convenient first check of the properties of mixtures, as of pure compound properties other than phase equilibra, is by way of APPES [1].

REFERENCES

[1] A.I.Ch.E. Physical Properties Computation Program, 1965.
[2] American Petroleum Institute, *Res. Proj.* 44: Tables, "Selected Values of Properties of Hydrocarbons and Related Compounds" (available in punched-card form).
[3] American Petroleum Institute, *Technical Data Book*, 1965.
[4] American Petroleum Institute, *Documentation Reports*, Division of Refining, New York, N.Y., 10020.
[5] Batsanov, S. S., "Refractometry and Chemical Structure," Consultants Bureau, 1961.
[6] Bondi, A., *J. Chem. Doc.* **6**, 137 (1966).
[7] Edwards, D. G., UCRL-7167 Rev. I (1964) and UCRL-7843 Rev. (1966).
[8] Gruber, G., C. M. Mohr, and R. C. Reid, *Proc. Am. Petrol. Inst.*, **45**, III (1965).
[9] Lundberg, G. W., and A. Bondi, *Proc. Am. Petrol. Inst.* **44**, III, 16 (1964).
[10] Prausnitz, J. M., C. A. Eckert, *A.I.Ch.E. Journal*, **11**, (1965).
[11] Reid, R. C., and T. K. Sherwood, *Properties of Gases and Liquids*, McGraw-Hill, New York, 1958, 1966.

Index

The detailed ans systematic organization of the Contents, especially with regard to the sequence of chemical types discussed in each chapter, has made it unnecessary to name chemical entities in the index except when they appear in unexpected places.